C A L I F O R N I A
COASTAL RESOURCE
G U I D E

C A L I F O R N I A
COASTAL RESOURCE
G U I D E

STATE OF CALIFORNIA
George Deukmejian, *Governor*

CALIFORNIA COASTAL COMMISSION

Peter M. Douglas, *Executive Director*   James W. Burns, *Chief Deputy Director*

Pat Stebbins, *Coastal Resource Program Manager*

Editors

Madge Caughman, *Designer and Cartographer*   Joanne S. Ginsberg, *Writing and Research*

Staff

Cartographers

Ruth A. Askevold
Mark S. Safran

Principal Illustrator

Judith Feins

Writers

Trevor Kenner Cralle
Trish Mihalek
S. Briggs Nisbet
Mary Travis

Additional Staff

Illustrators

Pieter Folkens
Jane Heaphy
Karen Jacobsen
Valerie Kells
Anna V. Kondolf
Kendal Morris
Gianmaria Mussio

Writers

Merle Betz
Heather Baird Donovan
Linda Goff Evans
Christopher Kroll
Jeanine Olsen-Stojkovich
Steve Scholl
Sharon Selvaggio
Sharon J. Tracey

Susan M. Hansch, *Consulting Editor*

UNIVERSITY OF CALIFORNIA PRESS
Berkeley   Los Angeles   London

Printed in the United States of America.

Cover Photograph: *Dune, Oceano, California, 1963*, by Ansel Adams.
    Courtesy of the Trustees of the Ansel Adams Publishing Rights
    Trust. All Rights Reserved.

Library of Congress Cataloging-in-Publication Data

California Coastal Commission.
    California coastal resource guide.

    Bibliography: p. 374
    Includes index.
    1. Pacific Coast (Calif.)—Guide-Books.   2. Natural
areas—California—Pacific Coast—Guide-books.
3. California—Description and travel—1981-   —Guide-
books.   I. Caughman, Madge.   II. Ginsberg, Joanne S.
III. Title
F859.3.C263   1987   917.94′0453′09146   87-13946
ISBN 0-520-06185-3
ISBN 0-520-06186-1 (pbk.)

        4   5   6   7   8   9

CONTENTS

DEDICATION

INTRODUCTION

COASTAL GEOGRAPHY

LIVING RESOURCES

CULTURAL RESOURCES

COASTAL COUNTIES

FEATURES

Ansel Adams, February, 1984

Thank You For Shopping At The
Monterey Bay Aquarium
Receipt required for Returns

124 LINDSEY

CHK 1494 JAN10'05 1:55PM

RETAIL

9280
1 CALIFORNIA COAST   22.50
17911
1 PVC MBA DOLPHIN   6.95
10.00 %
   MEMBER DISCOUNT   2.95-
XXXXXXXXXXXX1982   11/06
DISCOVER   28.42

   SUBTOTAL   26.50
   TAX   1.92
   TOTAL PAID   28 . 42

DEDICATION

WE TAKE GREAT PLEASURE in dedicating this book to photographer Ansel Adams, who lent his support and enthusiasm to the California Coastal Commission, and, throughout his life, to the environmental movement. He was a dedicated conservationist, believing strongly in the protection of our natural resources, and his vision is reflected in his work.

In 1916, at the age of fourteen, Ansel Adams first visited Yosemite National Park with his family and began to photograph there, using his box Brownie camera. The beauty and grandeur of Yosemite inspired in him a love and respect for nature that provided a foundation for the ideals and convictions that would guide his life. Ansel Adams became involved with the Sierra Club in 1919, and was elected to the Board of Directors in 1934. Through the years he used the Club as a forum to speak about his environmental concerns. A founding member of the Big Sur Foundation in 1979, he became vice president of the Board of Trustees. He was a leader of the conservationist movement, lobbying tirelessly for environmental protection, writing scores of letters to newspapers, and lecturing throughout the country, never hesitating to speak his mind about his beliefs.

In 1980 he was presented the Presidential Medal of Freedom, the nation's highest civilian honor, by President Jimmy Carter. The citation reads:

At one with the power of the American landscape, and renowned for the patient skill and timeless beauty of his work, photographer Ansel Adams has been visionary in his efforts to preserve this country's wild and scenic areas, both on film and on Earth. Drawn to the beauty of nature's monuments, he is regarded by environmentalists as a monument himself, and by photographers as a national institution. It is through his foresight and fortitude that so much of America has been saved for future Americans.

By the time of his death in 1984, Ansel Adams had become a hero of the environmental cause, and a symbol of the land he loved. He was an artist without peer, as well as an accomplished musician, writer, and teacher.

Ansel Adams's photograph *Dune, Oceano, California, 1963* graces the cover of this book. Our thanks to the Trustees of the Ansel Adams Publishing Rights Trust for allowing us to feature his work.

DEL NORTE

HUMBOLDT

MENDOCINO

SONOMA

MARIN

SAN FRANCISCO

SAN MATEO

SANTA CRUZ

MONTEREY

SAN LUIS OBISPO

SANTA BARBARA

VENTURA

LOS ANGELES

ORANGE

SAN DIEGO

N

0   150
    Miles

INTRODUCTION

THE CALIFORNIA COAST is a region of unsurpassed beauty and natural splendor, blessed with an abundance of rich and varied resources. The coast supports a diversity of plant communities and tens of thousands of species of insects and other invertebrates, amphibians, reptiles, fish, birds, and mammals, including numerous rare and endangered species. From the lush redwood forests and rocky shores of the north to the wide, sandy beaches of the south, California's 1,100-mile-long coast contains a number of distinct habitats.

California's first inhabitants, the native Indians who lived along the coast as early as 10,000 B.C., fished the coastal streams, estuaries, and nearshore waters, collected shellfish, gathered acorns from the oak trees, and hunted land mammals and marine mammals, little affecting the natural balance of their environment. Since the arrival of the Spanish in the late 1700s, settlers have exploited California's coastal resources, logging hundreds of thousands of acres of redwood forest for timber, decimating seal and sea otter populations for fur and whales for oil, damming streams for irrigation and hydroelectric power, and diking, dredging, and filling wetlands for agricultural and urban development—destroying the habitats of plants, birds, fish, and other organisms.

Since the 1850s, 90 per cent of the state's highly productive coastal wetlands have been destroyed, and almost every major coastal river has been dammed, depriving coastal estuaries of their sources of fresh water and beaches of their supply of sediments and sand. Along portions of the densely populated Southern California coast, intensive urban development has resulted in a nearly continuous wall of private homes, preventing public access to state tidelands, as well as obliterating the view. A number of species unique to the California coast, including the California clapper rail, the Santa Cruz long-toed salamander, and the Smith's blue butterfly, are now endangered and threatened with extinction because their habitats have been polluted or eliminated.

In November 1972, the people of California passed Proposition 20, the Coastal Initiative, which set up a commission to regulate coastal development. Proposition 20 led to the enactment of the California Coastal Act of 1976, and the creation of a permanent California Coastal Commission, which is charged with the duties of conserving and managing the resources of the coast.

In 1982 legislation introduced by State Senator Jim Ellis declared that the coastal zone "is one of (California's) most precious natural resources, rich in diversity of living and nonliving resources and in the wide range of opportunities it provides for the use and conservation by the people of this state and nation." The bill directed the Coastal Commission to prepare a guide that would include an inventory of natural and manmade resources of environmental, social, cultural, historic, economic, and educational importance to the public, to increase public understanding and appreciation of the value of California's coastal resources.

The California Coastal Commission has therefore prepared the *California Coastal Resource Guide*, which describes the geography and natural habitats of the coast, including mountains, beaches, and wetlands; the flora and fauna; and the cultural resources such as history, recreation, and economic development. The book also includes detailed maps and site-by-site descriptions of beaches, parks, wetlands, coastal towns and cities, missions, and museums, with information on each site's habitats, wildlife, and history. The guide features a list of selected species of interest for each county, with brief descriptions of characteristic, endangered, or unique plants and animals.

The *California Coastal Resource Guide* is a companion to the *California Coastal Access Guide*, first published in 1981 following legislation initiated by State Senator Barry Keene that directed the Commission to prepare a guide identifying public accessways to the coast and explaining the rights and responsibilities regarding public use of coastal resources.

The California brown pelican is an apt symbol for the *California Coastal Resource Guide*, and we have chosen it for our logo. Once on the brink of extinction, these magnificent seabirds, which breed only on the Channel Islands, have been making a remarkable recovery since the pesticide DDT was banned in 1972. The pelicans are living proof that the protection of our natural environment is a worthwhile endeavor. We hope that an increased awareness of the natural and cultural endowments of California's coast will ensure that a balance is maintained between the need for development and the need for enjoyment of these finite resources. This can be accomplished only by the wise management and continuous protection of our spectacular but fragile coast.

COASTAL MOUNTAINS

MARINE TERRACES

ROCKY INTERTIDAL

BLUFFS AND HEADLANDS

BEACHES

COASTAL SAND DUNES

COASTAL GEOGRAPHY

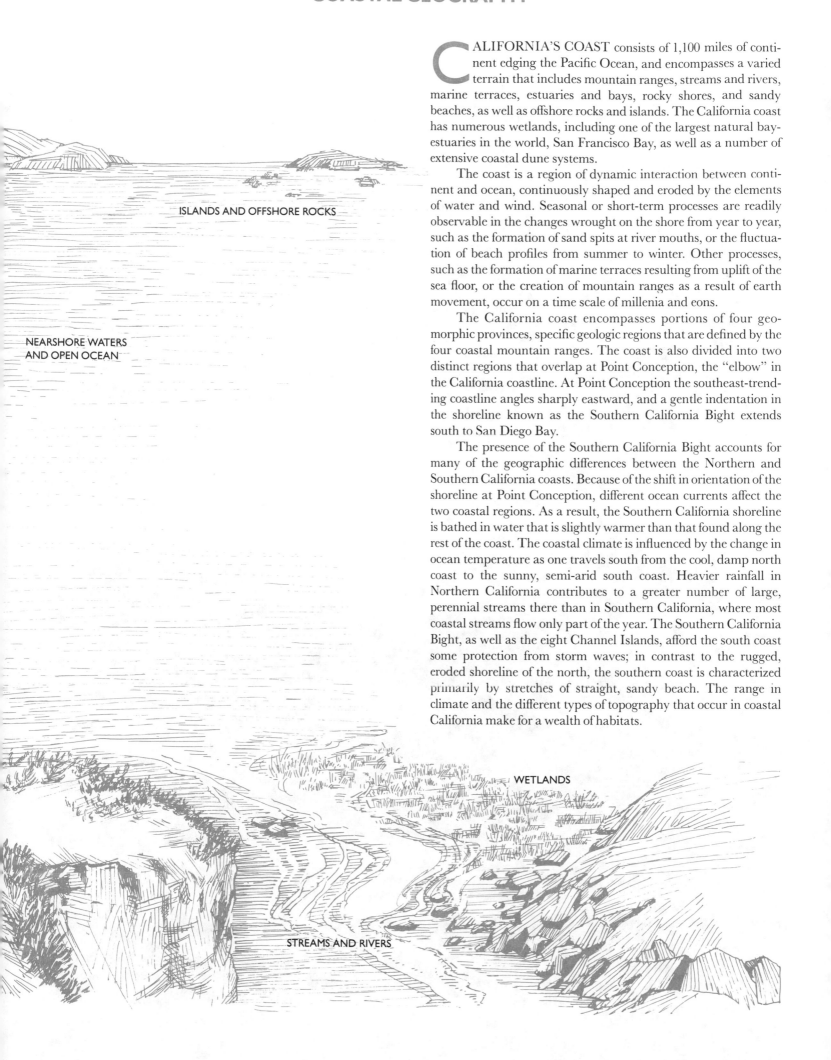

ISLANDS AND OFFSHORE ROCKS

NEARSHORE WATERS
AND OPEN OCEAN

WETLANDS

STREAMS AND RIVERS

CALIFORNIA'S COAST consists of 1,100 miles of continent edging the Pacific Ocean, and encompasses a varied terrain that includes mountain ranges, streams and rivers, marine terraces, estuaries and bays, rocky shores, and sandy beaches, as well as offshore rocks and islands. The California coast has numerous wetlands, including one of the largest natural bay-estuaries in the world, San Francisco Bay, as well as a number of extensive coastal dune systems.

The coast is a region of dynamic interaction between continent and ocean, continuously shaped and eroded by the elements of water and wind. Seasonal or short-term processes are readily observable in the changes wrought on the shore from year to year, such as the formation of sand spits at river mouths, or the fluctuation of beach profiles from summer to winter. Other processes, such as the formation of marine terraces resulting from uplift of the sea floor, or the creation of mountain ranges as a result of earth movement, occur on a time scale of millenia and eons.

The California coast encompasses portions of four geomorphic provinces, specific geologic regions that are defined by the four coastal mountain ranges. The coast is also divided into two distinct regions that overlap at Point Conception, the "elbow" in the California coastline. At Point Conception the southeast-trending coastline angles sharply eastward, and a gentle indentation in the shoreline known as the Southern California Bight extends south to San Diego Bay.

The presence of the Southern California Bight accounts for many of the geographic differences between the Northern and Southern California coasts. Because of the shift in orientation of the shoreline at Point Conception, different ocean currents affect the two coastal regions. As a result, the Southern California shoreline is bathed in water that is slightly warmer than that found along the rest of the coast. The coastal climate is influenced by the change in ocean temperature as one travels south from the cool, damp north coast to the sunny, semi-arid south coast. Heavier rainfall in Northern California contributes to a greater number of large, perennial streams there than in Southern California, where most coastal streams flow only part of the year. The Southern California Bight, as well as the eight Channel Islands, afford the south coast some protection from storm waves; in contrast to the rugged, eroded shoreline of the north, the southern coast is characterized primarily by stretches of straight, sandy beach. The range in climate and the different types of topography that occur in coastal California make for a wealth of habitats.

Coastal Mountains

CALIFORNIA'S coastal mountains trace a sinuous 800-mile course from the northwest corner of Del Norte County south to the Mexican border. Except for a break in the chain at the Golden Gate, they form a continuous series of ranges and valleys, separating the coast from the Great Central Valley and the deserts of the interior. This mountainous barrier has a dramatic effect on California's climate: storms originating over the Pacific Ocean bring rain to the western slopes, while the eastern slopes remain relatively dry. Many of California's industries flourish in the climatic conditions created by the coastal mountains—the evergreen trees that support the north coast timber industry thrive on the increased rainfall and frequent fog of the region; coastal fog cools hot inland valleys just east of the coast mountains where wine grapes are cultivated; and fruit and nut trees and cool weather vegetables are grown in coastal areas from San Mateo County to San Diego.

The geologic history of California's coastal mountains begins several hundred million years ago when, according to current geologic theory, movement of the earth's crust set in motion the processes that created the coastal ranges. The geologic theory of plate tectonics describes the system of loosely interlocking plates, floating upon an underlying mantle of less solid material, that cover the earth's surface. The North American Plate supports the continent of North America, and the Pacific Plate lies beneath the Pacific Ocean. About 250 million years ago these two plates, which had been gradually moving towards each other, collided; the sea floor crust of the Pacific Plate slipped beneath the continent, heating and melting as it reached the earth's interior. Between 150 and 140 million years ago this molten rock, or magma, began to push upward, forming the Klamath and Peninsular ranges.

About 30 million years ago the relative movements of the North American Plate and the Pacific Plate changed from a head-on contact to a lateral slipping against each other. This zone of slippage, extending nearly the length of the state, is called the San Andreas Fault. Along this zone, folding of the sea floor along the margin of the North American Plate resulted in the creation of the Coast and Transverse ranges, which are composed of the crushed, crumpled, and folded sea floor sediments.

Geomorphic Provinces

Santa Lucia Mountains, Big Sur Coast

The coastal mountains constitute four geomorphic provinces or geologic regions within California. The northernmost is the Klamath Mountains province, which lies near the coast in northwestern Del Norte County and extends north into Oregon. The northwest-trending Coast Ranges, the largest of the state's geomorphic provinces, rise abruptly from the shore in northern Humboldt County and extend 400 miles south to the Santa Ynez River in Santa Barbara County. The Transverse Ranges lie along an east-west axis, from the Santa Barbara coast to the Mojave Desert, creating a natural barrier between Central and Southern California. The massive Peninsular Ranges complete the coastal mountain system, extending south from the Los Angeles Basin to the tip of the Baja Peninsula.

In Northern California, the Klamath Mountains are composed of metamorphic and granitic rock—formed as a result of extreme changes in temperature, pressure, and chemical composition that occurred when molten material from below the earth's crust was pushed to the surface. South of the Klamath Mountains, the Coast Ranges lie close to the continent's edge, from Humboldt County to San Francisco Bay, forming a series of low mountains paralleling the coast. South of the bay, which separates the Coast Ranges into northern and southern ranges, are the Diablo, Gabilan, Santa Cruz, and Santa Lucia mountains, the highest of which reach to 4,000 feet. The sea floor sediments—sandstones and shales—that make up the Coast Ranges were crumpled so completely that it is difficult to discern individual layers of sedimentation. Visible in the sea cliffs along the Northern California coast are massive and steeply dipping rock layers, called the Franciscan Formation; a spectacular example of this geology can be seen along the cliffs at Devil's Slide in San Mateo County.

The Transverse Ranges include the Santa Monica Mountains, which extend offshore to form the Northern Channel Islands of Santa Cruz, Santa Rosa, and San Miguel off the coast of Santa Barbara County. Three hundred miles east, the Transverse Ranges terminate abruptly in the San Gabriel and San Bernardino mountains, dropping off into the Mojave and Colorado deserts. Severely folded, twisted, and uplifted, these mountains exhibit extreme differences in geologic age. Sedimentary rocks are most common on the western slopes such as in the Santa Ynez and Santa Monica mountains, which hug the coast from Santa Barbara County south to Los Angeles County; in the rugged eastern mountains, granitic and metamorphic rocks dominate.

To the south, the Peninsular Ranges—steep, narrow, and northwest trending—include in the southeast the rugged San Jacinto, Santa Rosa, Agua Tibia, and Laguna mountains that plunge into the Coachella and Imperial valleys. To the west, the rolling slopes of the Santa Ana Mountains gradually descend onto broad marine terraces that front the ocean; these mountains submerge westward, forming the Southern Channel Islands of Santa Barbara, San Nicolas, and San Clemente. The highest of the coastal mountain ranges, the Transverse and Peninsular Ranges both contain peaks of over 10,000 feet.

Dramatic changes in elevation and a variety of climatic zones contribute to a diversity of plant life in California's coastal mountains. Conifers—redwood and Douglas-fir—cloak the windward slopes of the Klamath Mountains and the northern Coast Ranges. Heavy winter rainfall, summer fog, and moderate temperatures have produced redwood groves where 2,000-year-old trees tower more than 300 feet above the forest floor. South of San Francisco Bay, the slopes of the Santa Cruz Mountains are covered with stands of redwood, while the drier regions of the southern Coast Ranges are vegetated with oaks, pines, and chaparral. As precipitation decreases southward, in the central and southern Coast Ranges, stands of hardwoods including tanbark oak, coast live oak, big-leaf maple, and madrone begin to outnumber conifers. On steeper slopes and exposed ridges where thin soils lose moisture rapidly, drought-resistant chaparral species such as chamise, manzanita, sage, and scrub oak take hold.

In the semi-arid Transverse and Peninsular ranges, chaparral is abundant on windward and southwest-facing slopes, whereas mixed-coniferous forest—ponderosa pine, sugar pine, and white fir—grows in isolated stands in protected areas. Hardy, drought-resistant digger and knobcone pines grow on the dry, rocky slopes.

Franciscan Formation along Highway 1 near Devil's Slide, San Mateo County

ON THEIR WAY to the ocean, California's coastal streams and rivers flow through the canyons and valleys of coastal mountains, linking forest, chaparral, scrubland, grassland, and marsh. Riparian woodlands develop along stream banks and floodplains, and coastal wetlands and estuaries form where the rivers enter the sea. Rivers transport nutrients, sediments, and oxygen through the watershed, and life flourishes in their path.

Streams and the surrounding riparian woodlands support numerous animal species, including frogs, salamanders, snakes, muskrats, beavers, and river otters. Spruces, maples, cottonwoods, alders, and willows grow along the stream banks, and attract large numbers of resident and migratory birds. An entangling understory of shrubs, flowering plants, and vines provides sites for nesting, shelter, and shade for many animals. Algae and mosses proliferate in the water and on rocks. Leaves swept into the current decompose, adding nutrients and organic matter. Insects thrive here and in turn provide an abundant food source for invertebrates, fish, and birds. Anadromous fish such as salmon and steelhead migrate from the sea to fresh water to spawn, and depend on well-oxygenated streams and gravelly streambeds as spawning sites.

The largest coastal rivers are found in Northern California, where sixty per cent of California's annual rainfall occurs. The Klamath River, whose watershed drains 12,000 square miles, is the second largest river in the state, after the Sacramento River. Flowing through the northern redwood and fir-forested mountains to the coast, the Klamath, Trinity, Salmon, Smith, Eel, and Van Duzen rivers are protected by the Wild and Scenic Rivers Act of 1972. The Act preserves the free-flowing natural state of rivers by prohibiting dam construction and diversion structures.

River runoff, the amount of water discharged through surface streams, is determined by a combination of factors, including local geology, topography, drainage area, and rainfall patterns. As rainfall and moisture diminish southward along the California coast, runoff decreases, and rivers are accordingly smaller in size. In Southern California, rivers and streams only maintain year-round flows near their headwaters. At river mouths, groundwater and agricultural runoff may provide the only source of water flow in summer.

As they flow down from their headwaters toward the coast, rivers carve steep, narrow canyons through the mountains. As they approach the coast they lose speed, depositing sediment to build broad floodplains with rich, deep soils. Large river floodplains, such as the Eel River Delta, the Salinas River floodplain, and the Oxnard Plain, tend to be productive agricultural regions, and are often centers of urban and industrial development. The Los Angeles Basin, formed by the Los Angeles, San Gabriel, and Santa Ana rivers, contains California's largest urban population. Because river lowlands are subject to periodic flooding, streams in populous regions are often contained within levees or concrete channels to limit their potential destructive force.

Coastal rivers play a crucial role in replenishing sand lost from beaches. In Northern California, the larger, perennial rivers carry sediments eroded from their upper watersheds to coastal beaches throughout the year. But in Southern California, where rivers run intermittently, stream sediments reach the beaches only during large storms and floods. Dam construction and urban development along these rivers have reduced their natural sediment loads, resulting in serious sand supply and erosion problems on south coast beaches.

Dam construction, channelization, water diversion projects for agricultural irrigation, and the increased water demands of growing urban areas have dramatically diminished the size of many California rivers and reduced the diversity of species associated with riparian habitat. By decreasing water flows, a dam can transform a perennial stream into an intermittent one, block the path of migrating fish, damage fish spawning gravels, deprive estuaries of needed fresh water, and reduce sediment nourishment of beaches.

Rivers of California

16

Marine Terraces

FROM CAPE VIZCAÍNO in Mendocino County south to San Diego, the California coast comprises a discontinuous series of narrow, flat-lying marine terraces, or wave-cut benches, located between the sea cliffs and coastal mountain foothills. These terraces are characteristic of exposed, windward coasts where waves pound against the shore, cutting a vertical cliff face over time. The surging ocean then planes smooth the sea floor at the base of the cliff, forming the flat step of the submerged terrace. The existence of several terrace levels at one coastal site is evidence of the long-term geologic processes affecting the California coast. Between one and two million years ago the oldest and highest terraces were uplifted by the same mountain-building process that created the Coast Ranges. In addition to the incremental rise of the coast, the subsequent advance and retreat of Ice Age glaciers caused sea level to alternately drop and rise, and sequences of terraces were cut by waves and currents in the intervening periods of sea level stability.

The most extensive marine terraces along the California coast are exposed along the sides of the Palos Verdes Hills in Los Angeles County, where a series of thirteen terraces rises to 1,300 feet above sea level. More than twenty stepped terraces are visible along the coast of San Clemente Island. Well-developed terraces along the Men-docino coast near Jug Handle Creek feature five wave-cut platforms—the highest, at 600 feet, is 500,000 years old, and the youngest terrace, presently 100 feet above sea level, emerged 100,000 years ago. Other terraces are visible at Fort Bragg in Mendocino County, at Duxbury Reef in Marin County, along the Santa Cruz coast, at Point Buchon in San Luis Obispo County, and at Dana Point in Orange County. Submerged terraces to depths of 500 feet lie just offshore of the coast from Santa Barbara to San Diego. Less than 25,000 years old, these terraces are in the process of forming.

Terrace soils are generally thin, commonly composed of rock debris, marine fossil fragments, and shells that were deposited on the once-submerged terrace. These marine sediments are often buried under thick alluvial deposits of sand and gravel from streams and rivers crossing the terraces after they emerged from the sea. Grasses grow on many terraces. In Northern California the terraces are covered by redwood and pine forests. On the Mendocino coast, a unique forest of pygmy cypress and pine trees has adapted to the sandy, nutrient-deficient soils on the upper marine terraces.

Abalone Cove, Palos Verdes Peninsula, Los Angeles County

Westport-Union Landing State Beach, Mendocino County

Bluffs and Headlands

THE PRECIPITOUS CLIFFS, steep-walled bluffs, and rocky headlands that characterize much of California's coastline are evidence of the ongoing geologic processes that shaped the western margin of the North American continent. Unlike the Atlantic and Gulf coasts of North America, whose gently sloping seashores are the result of gradual submergence of the continent's edge, the sheer walls and elevated terraces of the California coast were created by abrupt faulting and uplift. Bluffs and sea cliffs are a testament to the erosive power of waves, winter rainstorms, and wind, while headlands remain where coastal rock has withstood weathering by these elements.

Coastal bluffs are actually the seaward edges of marine terraces, shaped by ocean waves and currents, and uplifted from the ocean floor. Characteristic of the California coast from Mendocino County to San Di-

ego, coastal bluffs are less evident along the Northern California coast where the coastal mountains plunge abruptly into the ocean. Rocky headlands are more prevalent along the Northern and Central California coast but may occur anywhere erosion-resistant rocks are found along the shore.

Coastal bluffs are composed mainly of sedimentary rocks such as sandstones and shales that are particularly prone to erosion. Grains of quartz, feldspar, and mica compressed into layers of sandstone crumble easily; when wet, shales and siltstones disintegrate, and clays and mudstones soften and liquify. Lying on top of the sedimentary deposits of many bluffs is alluvial soil, loosely consolidated sand and gravel deposited by ancient rivers and streams. Examples of sedimentary coastal bluffs are the sandstone bluffs of Santa Cruz, the alluvial cliffs at La Jolla, and the shale cliffs of Point Loma in San Diego County.

Rocky headlands are composed of igneous rocks—granites and basalts—that are resistant to wave erosion. Granitic formations include the Point Reyes Headlands in Marin County. Morro Rock in San Luis Obispo County, Point Dume in Los Angeles County, and Point Sur in Monterey County are outcroppings of basaltic lava.

Sea caves, sea stacks, and arches are created by erosion of less resistant components of coastal landforms. Sea caves are formed by wave erosion where fractures occur in the bluff face. Sea stacks and arches, numerous along the wave-battered Mendocino coast, mark the last stand of more resistant rocks. Erosion of the sandstone cliffs at Natural Bridges State Beach in Santa Cruz created a number of arches; today only one remains, and eventually it too will collapse into the surf.

Landslides and cliff retreat are part of the natural process of coastal erosion along the California shore. Waves that undercut bluffs often initiate landslides. During winter storms heavy surf drags sand offshore, denuding many beaches and exposing the cliff base to direct wave attack. Most cliff retreat occurs at this time; powerful breakers crash into the cliffs, splintering the softer rocks into fragments that fall into the retreating surf. Incessant winter rains beating down on coastal bluffs slowly penetrate rock fractures, lubricating the joints between the rock layers. Fractured shales, sandstones, and siltstones are most likely to slip and cause landslides, especially at locations where the land slants toward the beach. A coastal landslide of mud and rock can scrape a clean path, sweeping away roads and structures as it plunges seaward. Areas well known for landslides are Devil's Slide in San Mateo County and Pacific Palisades in Los Angeles County.

Development of coastal sites has increased the rate of coastal erosion by the introduction of drain pipes and septic tanks that saturate soils with runoff; the irrigation of lawns and gardens can cause even the most stable sedimentary bluffs to collapse and slide into the sea.

Though California's coastal cliffs are inhospitable environments for much plant and animal life—windy and dry, with shallow, salty soils—a specialized community of plants and animals has adapted to them. Ledges, gullies, slopes, and cracks provide spaces where soil can collect and seeds germinate. Sea figs, ice plants, and coyote brush grow on steep bluffs. Wildflowers such as poppies, irises, and lupines bloom in colorful profusion on the bluffs in spring; introduced annual grasses and native fescues produce a carpet of bright green after winter rains, turning honey-colored in the dry season. Buffered from the driving wind on protected ledges, seabirds such as common murres rest and build nests.

Garrapata State Park, Monterey County

Coastal Sand Dunes

SHAPED BY WIND into curving ridges, coastal sand dunes are among the most dynamic and fragile natural formations. Their contours shift over time until hardy dune pioneer plants take hold in the drifting sand and create a stable landform. Even then, dunes can change form rapidly under the stress of storm waves and wind, or the traffic of human activity.

Offshore sandbars and sediment deposited at the mouths of rivers are the most important sources of material for dune building; sediment is carried by longshore currents until a projecting landform traps the particles and they are deposited on the beach by wave action. Dune formation begins when wind blows dry sand particles landward from the beach. Drifts accumulate around objects, such as plants and logs, that interrupt the wind flow. With steady winds, the sand drift acts as a barrier to moving sand, and the drift gradually grows into a sizeable mound. Until a dune is completely veiled and stabilized by plant cover, sand may be borne away by winds.

Coastal dune fields form characteristic patterns. A common pattern along the Northern California coast is a series of parallel ridges perpendicular to the prevailing winds, called "transverse ridges." The parabola-type dune field is a series of U-shaped dunes with the concave side facing the prevailing wind direction; this dune type is found at Pismo Beach in Central California. All dune fields consist of two or three sets of parallel dunes, with the most recently formed foredunes nearest the beach, and the older, usually vegetated and stabilized dunes farthest inland; the inland dunes may be as much as 18,000 years old.

Deep-rooted succulent, matted plants such as beach strawberry, silver beach-weed, and yellow sand verbena grow on the foredunes along with various dune grasses. The aggressive European beach grass, planted on California dunes in the 1930s, rapidly extends new shoots when half buried by sand drifts. The new shoots snag more sand, building and stabilizing the dune, and crowding out native species. The globose dune beetle, which cannot survive under European beach grass, is restricted to areas where native dune plants persist.

Protected by the foredunes from salt spray and wind, wild buckwheat, yellow bush lupine, and purple-flowered beach lupine grow on the richer soils of the backdunes. At least three rare insect species, the San Francisco tree lupine moth, the Pheres blue butterfly, and the Morro blue butterfly, lay eggs on the lupines. Wild buckwheat is a favorite food of the endangered Smith's blue butterfly larvae.

Deer mice, California voles, and black legless lizards burrow into the sand dunes, seeking cover from predators such as the northern harrier. This white-rumped hawk hovers a few feet above land; concave disks on the sides of its head funnel sound into the ears, enabling the hawk to detect the slightest movement of its prey. Gray foxes and striped skunks eat insects and dune plants. Mule deer wander over the dunes, browsing on shrubs.

Dunes shield low lying inland areas from violent storm waves. Sand eroded from dunes and beaches during winter storms usually forms a sandbar a short distance offshore. This sand is gradually returned to the beach during the calm summer season. A stable dune system can undergo some wave erosion without permanent damage.

California's dunes were formed over thousands of years, yet today, dune erosion is outstripping sand deposition. Dams trap river sediments, depleting the sand supply, and coastal protective structures, such as seawalls, disrupt the natural recycling of sand from sandbar to beach. Coastal development has disturbed dunes at many points along the coast. Off-road vehicles, foot traffic, and horses can damage dune plants, loosening the sands and leaving the dunes vulnerable to wind erosion and blowouts.

Of the 27 dune fields in coastal California, the largest are the Monterey Bay dunes, covering about 40 square miles, and the 18-square-mile Nipomo Dune complex, north and south of the Santa Maria River. Other major dune fields are located at Humboldt Bay and San Diego Bay.

Año Nuevo State Reserve, San Mateo County

BEACHES ARE DYNAMIC landforms altered by wind and waves in a continual process of creation and erosion. Seasonal cycles of sand deposition and loss dramatically affect the appearance of beaches from summer to winter. Wide and gently sloping in summer, they become steep-fronted and narrow in winter, and can vanish overnight, stripped of sand by violent storm waves. Most of the sand removed from winter beaches is deposited in offshore sandbars and is returned to the beach during the mild summer months by gentle swells that push the sand to the exposed shore. River sediments are the source of 80 to 90 per cent of beach sand; some beaches are built to great widths by sediments washed to the sea by episodic floods, gradually eroding until the next major flood replenishes the sand.

Beach formation begins as eroded continental material—sand, gravel, and cobble fragments—is washed to sea by streams and rivers. Two separate processes result in the deposit of this sand and sediment on the shore. Most sediment is suspended in sea water and transported along the coast by the longshore current, a stream of water flowing parallel to the beach that is created by the action of waves breaking at an angle to shore. Longshore transport can deliver up to a million cubic yards of sediment annually to a single beach. In the second process, sand deposited onshore by the longshore current is then oscillated by waves breaking onto and receding from the beach. This continual onshore-offshore

movement of the waves gradually pushes the sand along the beach edge. Both the longshore transport of sediment along the coast and the movement of sand by waves along the foreshore are part of the process called littoral drift.

The California coastline has been divided into geographic segments, called littoral cells, that incorporate a complete cycle of beach sediment supply, sand transport by the longshore current, and eventual permanent loss of sand from the littoral cell. The five types of littoral cells along the California coast are each characterized by a different littoral process determined by the geographic features unique to the cell type. One type of cell is defined by a long stretch of coastline that begins at a headland and terminates in a submarine canyon, such as at Mugu Canyon in Ventura County, and La Jolla Canyon in San Diego County; another cell type consists of a large river delta bounded on either side by rocky headlands, such as at Humboldt Bay; a third type of littoral cell is defined by a crescent-shaped bay downcoast of a promontory, like Half Moon Bay in San Mateo County; and a fourth type of cell consists of a rocky headland downcoast of a beach where waves break in a line parallel to the shore, as at Ten Mile Beach in Mendocino County. Finally, lagoons and closed bays with restricted tidal flow create a fifth type of littoral cell, such as Bolinas Bay in Marin.

Apart from littoral cell type, there are characteristic differences between Northern and Southern California beaches, depend-

San Mateo coast south of Mori Point

Dunes Beach, Half Moon Bay, San Mateo County

ing upon the direction of prevailing winds and upon local coastal geology. Along California's north coast, cove or pocket beaches are common where the granitic and basaltic rock that composes the sea cliffs has been sculpted by prevailing northwesterly winds and battered by high energy waves over millions of years. In Southern California, beaches often consist of long ribbons of sand interrupted by widely separated rocky points. The bluffs of easily eroded shales and sandstones that edge the coast here continuously crumble away, creating an even coastline over time.

Some beach types are found along both Northern and Southern California coasts. Narrow cove beaches like those at Laguna Beach in Orange County form where the coast is composed of conglomerate rock and hard sandstone; even when exposed to direct wave attack this rock type is highly resistant to erosion. The narrow beaches formed within these coves often lose all their sand during winter storms, exposing the underlying cobbles, as at Boomer Beach, south of Point La Jolla in San Diego County. Barrier beaches and sand spits are also present along the coast at river mouths, bays, and lagoons; examples are Silver Strand Beach in San Diego, Zuma Beach in Malibu, and beaches at the Smith, Salinas, Pajaro, and Santa Maria River mouths.

Beaches vary in color according to the mineral content of the sand, which is also a clue to the origin of the eroded sediments that make up the sand supply. Eroded shale cliffs create the charcoal gray beach sand at Shelter Cove in Humboldt County. North of Humboldt Bay, the coarse sands of Agate Beach are multi-colored agates that have been ground and polished by the surf. Ground quartz and feldspar minerals make up the stark white beaches of Carmel, while

a few miles to the north in Sand City, amber-colored sand indicates the presence of iron minerals. Close inspection reveals that white sand beaches are a mosaic of pale quartz grains, pink, green, or white feldspar, and flecks of black mica.

Beaches are inhabited by a variety of invertebrates and insects. In the surf zone, bivalve mollusks, crustaceans, and tube-building worms adapt to their environment of tide cycles and buffeting waves by burrowing to protect themselves from wave impact, temperature fluctuations, desiccation, and predation. The smooth shells of clams and other bivalve burrowers reduce friction when they tunnel through the fine sandy beaches of their preferred habitat. At low tide, water retained between the sand particles is filled with millions of microscopic diatoms and zooplankton upon which the buried bivalves feed, using long siphons that reach to the sand surface. Fine screens within the siphons filter out sand particles but allow the passage of water and suspended organic material that provide an abundant food supply for the filter-feeding bivalves. Razor clams, surf clams, and coquina clams are common burrowers along California beaches. Pismo clams occupy a special niche in the surf zone of Central California beaches, well-adapted to the crashing surf by nature of their large, heavy shells, which act as anchors. These giant clams are dependent upon the high-oxygen content of the roiling surf to survive.

Inland from the surf zone, sand crabs scavenge in the sun-dried kelp and bury in the sand, using their antennae to rake food particles to their mouths. Kelp flies, wrack flies, rove beetles, tiger beetles, and dune beetles roam the beach foreshore. The dry upper beach is inhabited by air-breathing pill bugs and beach hoppers. Numerous

beetle species inhabit the dunes, some burrowing in the sand during the day to escape predators and heat.

The natural process of beach building and erosion has been altered by extensive development of the California coast. Prior to development, natural loss of sand from beaches, largely to dunes and submarine canyons, and natural sand supply, mostly from rivers and streams, were in rough balance. The damming of rivers alone has reduced half of the natural sand supply to beaches from Santa Barbara to Mexico. The natural balance of beach sand supply and loss has been altered by the construction of offshore breakwaters, groins, and jetties, which may divert sand from one location to another and change beach slope. In a few locations large-scale beach nourishment projects have created wide beaches that may last several decades or more before eroding away, but not all coastal areas are suitable sites for such projects; even where these projects have been successful, this solution to the problem of beach erosion is costly and impermanent.

Santa Monica Beach, Los Angeles County

Western grebes, Tijuana River National Estuarine Research Reserve

Wetlands that are less common along the coast are freshwater marshes, riparian wetlands, bogs, and vernal pools. Freshwater marshes occur in ponds and slow-moving streams. Like salt marshes, they are vegetated mostly with herbaceous plants, predominantly cattails, *Typha* spp., and species of sedges, *Carex* spp., and rushes, *Juncus* spp. Freshwater marshes have mineral soils that are less fertile than those of salt marshes, and exhibit a greater variety of plant species than do salt marshes. Riparian wetlands, which occur on the banks of streams, rivers, and lakes, commonly feature woody vegetation such as red alder, *Alnus oregona*; wax myrtle, *Myrica californica*; and willow, *Salix* spp. Bogs, unlike marshes and streams, have detrital soils composed of peat, and are vegetated mostly with mosses. Vernal pools occur in small depressions underlain by dense, impermeable claypan soils that allow water to accumulate in winter and spring. The pools support small, usually annual plants, which flower as the water in the pools begins to evaporate.

Vegetation in estuarine wetlands varies with the extent of tidal exposure and salinity. Subtidal mudflats are often vegetated with extensive meadows of eelgrass, *Zostera marina*; intertidal mudflats may support seaweeds or microscopic diatoms. Salt marshes border the mudflat community. In the lowest zone of the salt marsh, inundated by the tides twice a day, stands of tall cordgrass, *Spartina foliosa*, typically predominate. The middle marsh, which experiences less tidal inundation, is characterized by low-growing pickleweed, *Salicornia* spp.; in the upper marsh, where conditions are more terrestrial, stiff, wiry saltgrass, *Distichlis spicata*, predominates.

Northern and Southern California salt marshes differ somewhat in plant species composition. This is partly due to the lower salinity of marsh soils in the north, which are diluted by rain and river runoff. In Southern California, lower annual rainfall and high rates of evaporation from higher temperatures result in marsh soils that are hypersaline. Salt marsh plants are halophytic—able to tolerate varying levels of salt, either in the soil or by tidal inundation. Plant distribution reflects individual species' tolerance to levels of salt and duration of tidal inundation.

The wetlands of the Humboldt and Mendocino County coasts are generally estuarine with regular freshwater inflow. Humboldt Bay, which contains California's second largest salt marsh, is typical of this type. On the subtidal mudflats are extensive beds of eelgrass that afford habitat for numerous fish and invertebrates, and food for waterfowl such as the brant, a small goose that feeds exclusively on eelgrass. A species of cordgrass introduced from Chile, *Spartina densiflora*, is dominant in the low

C OASTAL WETLANDS include a number of natural communities that share the unique combination of aquatic, semi-aquatic, and terrestrial habitats resulting from periodic inundation by tidal waters, rainfall, or runoff. Wetlands provide habitat for a vast array of organisms, including many endangered species. During peak annual migration periods, hundreds of thousands of birds migrating along the Pacific Flyway descend upon these coastal wetlands in search of refuge and food. Coastal wetlands form a vital link between land and sea, exporting nutrients and organic material to ocean waters, and harboring juveniles of numerous aquatic species including many fish. Water flow in these highly productive communities circulates food, nutrients, and waste products throughout the wetland system. Wetlands buffer the effects of storms, thereby reducing shoreline erosion, and improve water quality by filtering and assimilating many pollutants from sewage outfalls and agricultural runoff. In addition, wetlands provide an opportunity for nature study.

Most of California's coastal wetlands are estuarine salt marshes with associated tidal channels and mudflats. Estuaries are formed where freshwater streams meet the sea, and contain variably brackish water. Salt marshes develop along the shores of protected estuarine bays and river mouths, as well as in more marine-dominated bays and lagoons. Unlike the Atlantic coast, with its wide continental shelf and extensive salt marshes, the Pacific coast is rugged and precipitous, with few areas suitable for wetland vegetation to develop. The San Francisco Bay estuary is the largest wetland complex in California, accounting for nearly 90 per cent of all California's salt marsh acreage. About 25 smaller salt marsh systems between the Oregon and Mexico borders make up the remaining 10 per cent.

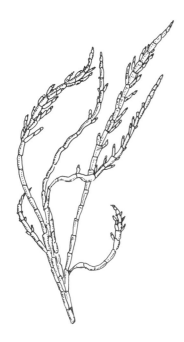

pickleweed (*Salicornia virginica*)
8 to 25 inches high

intertidal zone, and grows in clumps interspersed with broad patches of pickleweed. In the high intertidal areas saltgrass; jaumea, *Jaumea carnosa*; and arrowgrass, *Triglochin maritima*, are common, along with occasional clumps of stringlike, parasitic orange dodder, *Cuscuta salina*. Humboldt Bay supports endangered plants including the Point Reyes Bird's beak, *Cordylanthus maritimus palustris*, and the Humboldt Bay owl's clover, *Orthocarpus castillejoides humboldtiensis*.

Wetlands along the Sonoma and Marin coasts, such as Bodega Bay and Bolinas Lagoon, have salinities approaching marine waters. Little fresh water flows into these wetlands, although seasonal rains temporarily increase the streamflow. Mudflats are prevalent in the relatively undisturbed tidelands of these wetlands, and are important habitats for burrowing and surface-dwelling invertebrates, as well as feeding grounds for birds. Rodeo Lagoon, in Marin County, is a respite for snowy egrets and endangered California brown pelicans.

Because of its great size, San Francisco Bay and estuary contains many different wetland habitats ranging from entirely freshwater upstream to strictly marine toward the mouth. The bay marshland is home to two endangered mammal species, the salt marsh harvest mouse and the Suisun shrew. The endangered California clapper rail and the threatened California black rail also inhabit the bay's salt marshes.

Along the central California coast, from San Francisco to Santa Barbara counties, the largest wetlands are Elkhorn Slough, Morro Bay, and Pescadero Marsh. Pickleweed predominates in these mostly saltwater wetlands, and cordgrass is conspicuously absent. Elkhorn Slough, a tidal embayment that extends inland for over seven miles, includes freshwater and brackish water marsh, salt marsh, and mudflats, and provides important habitat for fish, invertebrates, and many species of migratory birds. Eelgrass grows extensively in Morro Bay, providing essential forage for thousands of migrating waterfowl.

Southern California wetlands have suffered the most from human disturbance. Between Point Conception in Santa Barbara County and the Mexico border, only about 25 per cent of the original wetland acreage remains. Mugu Lagoon and Anaheim Bay are the largest Southern California wetlands. Cordgrass occurs where tidal flushing is dependable, but is usually absent in wetlands that are seasonally or permanently cut off from the ocean. Saltwort, *Batis maritima*, and an annual species of pickleweed, *Salicornia bigelovii*, both absent in the north, are particularly well adapted to the hypersaline soils of these wetlands. Southern California marshes are the habitat of the light-footed clapper rail and Belding's savannah sparrow, both endangered, and the threatened California black rail. Populations of these species have declined due to urban encroachment and to increased human activity in the wetlands.

Wetlands are unique among biologic communities in that they are characterized by both aquatic and terrestrial features.

saltgrass (*Distichlis spicata*)
8 to 12 inches high

Plants and animals that inhabit wetlands have successfully evolved morphological and physiological adaptations to the presence of high levels of salt and periodic inundation and desiccation, as well as to low concentrations of dissolved oxygen in the water-logged soils and exposure to alternating fresh and salt water. Many wetland inhabitants, including salt marsh plants such as cordgrass and saltgrass, and water birds such as mallards and godwits, are able to excrete the excessive amounts of salt that are absorbed or ingested.

Ecologists have estimated that a healthy salt marsh produces from five to ten times as much oxygen and corresponding carbohy-

great egret (*Casmerodius albus*)
3¼ feet long

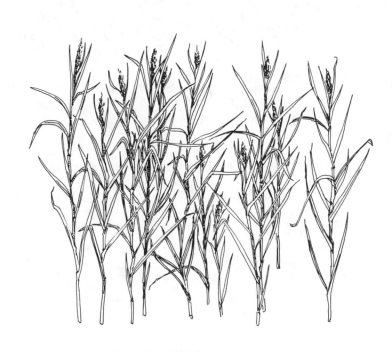

cordgrass (*Spartina foliosa*)
1 to 4 feet high

bulrush (*Scirpus robustus*)
1½ to 4½ feet high

drate biomass per acre as a wheat field. Marsh plants capture the energy of sunlight and, through the process of photosynthesis, convert it to carbohydrates that provide food for herbivores. Omnivorous and carnivorous animals, in turn, eat other plants and animals. A key part of each food chain in the marsh begins with the breakdown of plant matter into detritus, which is then consumed by filter feeders, deposit feeders, and other omnivores and scavengers. This assemblage of producers and consumers creates a large food web, with fish, birds, and humans as ultimate links.

Decomposers, such as bacteria and fungi, also break down plant and animal matter and recycle the nutrients. Excrement from birds, fish, and invertebrates further enhances marsh soils and waters with nitrogen-rich compounds, which are taken up by algae and vascular plants. These materials are transported and mixed by streamflows,

tidal circulation, and even the activities of burrowing clams and shrimp. As a result, the mudflats become rich in inorganic nutrients and organic foods. This "mixing bowl" helps to support the many links of the marsh's food chains. Salt marsh food webs are among the most complex in nature.

Coastal wetlands are home to a variety of animals. Numerous fish species, including California killifish, bay goby, striped bass, topsmelt, and starry flounder, are residents of wetlands, or depend upon them for reproduction. Subtidal eelgrass beds shelter larval and juvenile fish, as well as hydroids, bryozoans, nudibranchs, crabs, and shrimp. Mudflats are inhabited by an abundance of invertebrates, including polychaete worms, moon snails, horn snails, clams, fiddler crabs, and ghost shrimp. A unique mudflat inhabitant is the fat innkeeper, a burrower that shares its tunnel with other mud-dwellers. This large worm pumps water through its U-shaped, tubular burrow by contractions of its body. It spins a mucous net at one end of the tube that traps detritus and food particles suspended in the water. When the net is full, the worm eats it and spins a new one. Discarded food particles are scavenged by pea crabs, scale worms, and gobies, which live in and around the fat innkeeper's burrow.

Salt marshes are home to insects such as the salt marsh water boatman, wandering skipper, and numerous species of beetles and flies, which graze on leaves and seeds, help to pollinate the wetland flowers, and prey upon a variety of small animals. Clapper rails build platform nests in the low marsh, whereas Belding's savannah sparrows nest in and feed on the pickleweed of the higher marsh. Salt marsh mammals include shrews, harvest mice, and other rodents; harbor seals haul out on pickleweed and saltgrass in south San Francisco Bay.

Although relatively few bird species are year-round residents of coastal wetlands, many species temporarily inhabit salt marshes during their annual migrations. Coastal California is part of the Pacific Flyway, one of the four principal bird migration routes in North America. During the spring and fall months, coastal wetlands support flocks of waterfowl such as brant, pintails, mallards, and canvasbacks, and shorebirds such as sandpipers, curlews, willets, and godwits, which stop here to rest, feed, and, in some cases, overwinter.

Since the 1850s 90 per cent of California's original coastal wetland acreage has disappeared, and many of the remaining wetlands are in danger of being further degraded or destroyed due to landfill, diking, dredging, pollution, and other human disturbances. However, a growing awareness of the importance of this habitat has led to efforts to protect existing wetlands, and to restore those that have been degraded.

Upper Newport Bay Ecological Reserve

BETWEEN THE HIGH and low tide marks lies a strip of shoreline that is regularly covered and uncovered by the advance and retreat of the tides. This meeting ground between land and sea is called the intertidal. The plants and animals inhabiting this region are hardy and adaptable, able to withstand periodic exposure to air and the force of the pounding surf. Intertidal communities occur on sandy beaches, in bays and estuaries, and on wharf pilings, but the communities of rocky shorelines are perhaps the most diverse and the most densely populated. Rock faces, crevices, undersides of rocks, and tidepools each support an array of species.

The plants and animals of the intertidal are subject to a range of conditions not encountered in the relative stability of the deep ocean. Three factors—substrate, wave shock, and exposure to drying—are important in determining the types of organisms found in a given intertidal community. Soft substrates, such as sandy beaches and mudflats, support an abundance of burrowing animals, whereas sessile, or attached, organisms are more typical of rocky shores. The surf has the potential to batter or dislodge plants and animals. Some areas of the coast, particularly rocky headlands and exposed outer coasts, experience tremendous wave action; here only the most tenacious organisms survive. Sheltered embayments, and coastal areas protected by offshore rocks, reefs, or islands, receive considerably less wave shock, and support a variety of more delicate forms. However, the ability to withstand desiccation and overheating while exposed to air by low tides may be the most important factor in determining where marine organisms occur in the intertidal. The extent to which an organism is exposed to air is largely determined by its vertical position in the intertidal region, and the pattern of the tides.

The tides are generated by the gravitational forces of the moon, and, to a lesser extent, of the sun. Because these astronomical motions are very regular, tides are highly predictable. Gravitational forces attract the earth and moon to each other, whereas centrifugal forces keep them separate. On the side of the earth closest to the moon, the moon's gravitational pull is stronger than the centrifugal force, and causes the earth's waters on this side to bulge out. On the opposite side of the earth, centrifugal forces override the moon's gravitational force, and result in a second, equal bulge of water. Between the two bulges are corresponding areas of low water. In this idealized picture of the earth as a completely water-covered globe, these two high tide and two low tide zones remain more or less aligned with respect to the moon as the earth essentially rotates beneath them. With each rotation of the earth, a given location passes once through each of the two high tide and two low tide zones. The earth completes this tidal cycle every 24 hours and 50 minutes—the time it takes the earth to revolve relative to the moon. The continental land masses disrupt this ideal picture somewhat and result in the tidal pattern peculiar to each coastal location.

Because of the sun's greater distance from the earth, its influence on the tides is only about half that of the moon. Twice a month, the sun and moon are in a line with the earth, and their combined gravitational forces produce tides that are of greater magnitude than average; these tides, called spring tides, occur at new and full moon. At first- and third-quarter moon, when the sun and moon are at right angles to each other with respect to the earth, the sun's effect on the tides partially cancels the effect of the moon; the magnitude of the resulting tides, called neap tides, is less than average.

In some coastal areas the two daily high tides and low tides are of nearly equal magnitude. On the California coast, the pairs of high and low tides differ in magnitude, so that there is a higher high tide, followed by a lower low tide, a lower high tide, and a higher low tide each day. These mixed tides are caused by the moon and sun's changing position with respect to the earth's equator. If the moon and sun were always directly over the equator, the two daily high tides experienced at any one place would be equal in magnitude. But because the earth is tipped on its axis, as the moon orbits around the earth it moves higher and lower in the sky relative to the equator twice each month, thus shifting the position of the tidal bulges. Similarly, as the earth orbits around the sun, the sun moves higher and lower in the sky twice each year.

Tides of maximum range, called tropic tides, occur twice a month when the moon is over the Tropic of Cancer or the Tropic of Capricorn. Tropic tides are particularly large in summer and winter when the sun is respectively highest and lowest in the sky. Tides of minimum range, or equatorial tides, occur twice a month when the moon is over the equator. Tides are the largest single factor contributing to sea level changes in California. Other influences such as storms, warming of ocean water, and El Niño conditions raise the sea temporarily, and so far are not predictable.

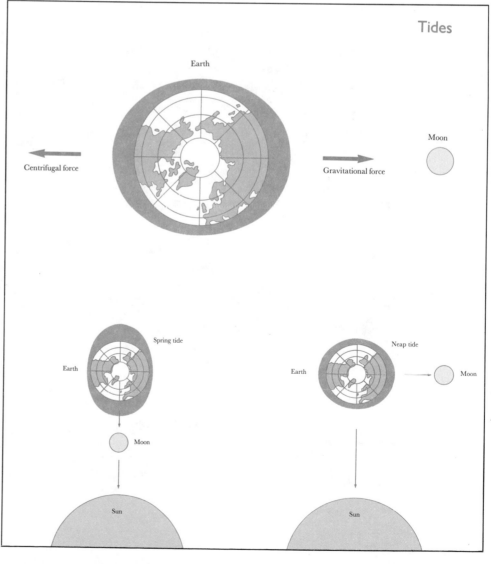

Intertidal plants and animals tend to occur in distinct bands, or zones, along the shore. Where organisms occur in the intertidal depends upon their varying responses to exposure to air, heat, and sunlight, predation or grazing, and competition for space. The intertidal can be divided into four zones, according to the extent of tidal exposure: the uppermost horizon, and the high, middle, and low intertidal zones. The exact tidal level at which these zones occur on a given shore varies; wave action tends to widen the zones, whereas in areas of quiet water, the zones are narrow.

The uppermost horizon, or splash zone, is the area above the mean high tide level that receives spray from waves. Almost always exposed to air, the splash zone is sparsely vegetated, and inhabited by relatively few animals. The rock louse, *Ligia occidentalis*, an isopod often seen scurrying over rocks, is an air-breather; it obtains moisture merely by dipping its tail end into tidepools, and would drown if submerged. The eroded periwinkle, *Littorina keenae*, a tiny snail that grazes on algal films, can survive out of water for two months. The snail retains moisture by closing its shell with a horny membrane called an operculum. At low tide the ribbed limpet, *Collisella digitalis*, clings tightly to rock to avoid desiccation.

Below the splash zone and extending to the mean higher low tide level is the high intertidal. Less harsh than the splash zone, this zone is home to a larger diversity and number of plants and animals. Large algae, mostly absent from the splash zone, occur here, providing shelter for small animals and a food source for herbivores. The red alga *Endocladia muricata*, which grows in low, crinkly tufts, is abundant on surf-exposed rocks. The rockweeds *Pelvetia fastigiata* and *Fucus distichus*, brown algae with slippery, greenish-brown blades, are also common. Filter-feeding acorn barnacles, *Balanus glandula*, form a distinct band in this zone; also abundant is the herbivorous black turban snail, *Tegula funebralis*, which clusters in tidepools and crevices, and the rough limpet, *Collisella scabra*, which spends high tide in a specific "home site" on the rocks. Scavengers of the high intertidal include the lined shore crab, *Pachygrapsus crassipes*, which is dark green or red and square-shelled, and the hermit crab *Pagurus samuelis*, which occupies old turban snail shells.

The middle intertidal extends to the mean level of the lower low tide—the zero, or tidal datum, of the tide tables (tidal datum is not the same as average sea level,

Intertidal Zonation

Splash Zone: approximately 7' to 5'
Highest high tide to mean high tide

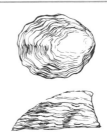

rock louse *(Ligia occidentalis)*
2.5 cm long

eroded periwinkle *(Littorina keenae)*
shell to 1.8 cm long

ribbed limpet *(Collisella digitalis)*
shell 1.5-3 cm long

High Intertidal Zone: approximately 5' to 2.7'
Mean high tide to mean higher low tide

red alga *(Endocladia muricata)*
4-8 cm high (section 1-2 cm)

rockweed *(Pelvetia fastigiata)*
to 90 cm long (section 20 cm)

rockweed *(Fucus distichus)*
10-25 cm long (section 8 cm)

acorn barnacles *(Balanus glandula)*
shell to 2.2 cm in diameter

Middle Intertidal Zone: approximately 2.7' to 0'
Mean higher low tide to mean lower low tide

goose barnacles *(Pollicipes polymerus)*
to 8 cm long

California mussels *(Mytilus californianus)*
shell to 13 cm long

aggregating anemone *(Anthopleura elegantissima)*
to 8 cm across tentacular crown

rock snail *(Nucella emarginata)*
shell 3 cm high

Low Intertidal Zone: approximately 0' to −1.6'
Mean lower low tide to lowest low tide

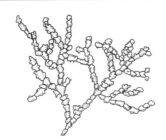

California dorid *(Hypselodoris californiensis)*
to 6.7 cm long

coralline alga *(Calliarthron tuberculosum)*
to 20 cm high (section 10 cm)

purple sea urchin *(Strongylocentrotus purpuratus)*
body 5 cm in diameter, spines 1.3 cm

which is at a tidal level of three feet). This zone, teeming with life, is covered and uncovered by the tides twice a day. In areas of heavy surf, the middle intertidal is characterized by a band of California mussels, *Mytilus californianus*, and goose barnacles, *Pollicipes polymerus*, both of which are well adapted to heavy surf. The mussel beds shelter algae, worms, and crustaceans.

Other prominent animals of this zone include the aggregating anemone, *Anthopleura elegantissima*; rock snail, *Nucella emarginata*; purple shore crab, *Hemigrapsus nudus*; and ochre star, *Pisaster ochraceus*. The aggregating anemone has an adhesive body surface that collects sand, thereby reducing water loss. Among the many algae are the sea palm, *Postelsia palmaeformis*; the bumpy, reddish-black Turkish towel, *Mastocarpus papillatus*; the ruffled, bright green sea lettuce, *Ulva taeniata*; and feather boa kelp, *Egregia menziesii*. To resist wave shock, the sea palm anchors itself with a tough, gnarled holdfast, and has a supple, resilient stalk.

From tidal datum to the level of the lowest low tide is the low intertidal, by far the richest and most densely populated zone. Many of the plants and animals of this zone, which is uncovered only at "minus" tides, also occur subtidally. The low intertidal's lush vegetation includes the brown sea cabbage, *Hedophyllum sessile*; the kelp *Laminaria farlowii*; the purplish, iridescent *Iridaea cordata*; several species of coralline algae; and a flowering plant, the emerald green surfgrass, *Phyllospadix scouleri*. Sessile, soft-bodied animals such as sponges, hydroids, bryozoans, and tunicates cover the rocks; sponges are eaten by nudibranchs such as the blue and gold California dorid, *Hypselodoris californiensis*. Sea stars are abundant, as well as brittle stars; purple sea urchins, *Strongylocentrotus purpuratus*; kelp crabs, *Pugettia producta*; black chitons, *Katherina tunicata*; and giant green anemones, *Anthopleura xanthogrammica*.

Many species would thrive lower in the intertidal than they are normally found, but are confined to higher levels by competitors, predators, or herbivores. For example, the acorn barnacles *Balanus glandula* and *Chthamalus dalli* are capable of living over a wide vertical range, but in the middle intertidal, the predatory rock snail, *Nucella emarginata*, eats juvenile barnacles that settle there. In the high intertidal, where the rock snail cannot survive, the barnacles flourish. In addition, *Chthamalus* is kept higher still by *Balanus*, because *Balanus* outcompetes it for space, and *Chthamalus* can tolerate greater exposure to air and heat than *Balanus*. Farther down in the intertidal, the predatory ochre star regulates the distribution of its prey, the California mussel: in the middle intertidal, mussels displace other organisms, eventually forming huge beds; however, in the lower part of this zone, ochre stars prey on mussels, thereby limiting the lower extent of the mussel beds. In addition, by removing mussels, the sea stars clear space for other species, thus increasing the diversity in a given area.

Rocky intertidal areas can be found all along the California coast; they are best observed at the lowest tides. Some good places to observe intertidal life include Trinidad State Beach in Humboldt County, Shell Beach in Sonoma County, Fitzgerald Marine Reserve in San Mateo County, Point Piños in Monterey County, Crystal Cove State Park in Orange County, and Children's Pool Beach in San Diego.

High Intertidal Zone

black turban snail (*Tegula funebralis*)
3 cm in diameter

rough limpet (*Collisella scabra*)
shell to 3 cm long

lined shore crab (*Pachygrapsus crassipes*)
carapace to 4.7 cm wide

hermit crab (*Pagurus samuelis*)
carapace to 1.9 cm long

Middle Intertidal Zone

purple shore crab (*Hemigrapsus nudus*)
carapace to 5.6 cm wide

feather boa kelp (*Egregia menziesii*)
5-15 m long (section 30 cm)

sea palm (*Postelsia palmaeformis*)
to 60 cm high

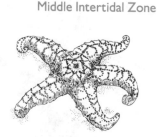
ochre star (*Pisaster ochraceus*)
arm radius 14 cm

Low Intertidal Zone

brittle star (*Opionereis annulata*)
disc 1.2 cm, arms to 10 cm

giant green anemone (*Anthopleura xanthogrammica*)
to 25 cm across tentacular crown

kelp crab (*Pugettia producta*)
carapace to 9 cm wide

black chiton (*Katherina tunicata*)
12 cm long

THE ISLANDS, ROCKS, and sea stacks offshore of California's coast are unique habitats that provide protected breeding sites for thousands of resident and migrating seabirds and marine mammals. Though their isolation from the mainland and their relative inaccessibility make islands and offshore rocks prime sanctuaries for birds and marine mammals, they have historically been sites of plunder and slaughter of wildlife for profit. The 19th-century trade in seal skins and seabird eggs resulted in the virtual elimination of northern elephant seals, northern fur seals, common murres, Cassin's auklets, and tufted puffins from the California coast. California's islands, in particular the Channel Islands, harbor many rare, endemic species that have evolved or survived as a consequence of their isolation from the mainland, and the characteristics of their specialized island habitats. Today, Año Nuevo Island is a state reserve, and national marine sanctuaries protect the Farallon Islands and five of the eight Channel Islands.

More than half the California population of resident and migratory seabirds nests on the Farallon Islands, a group of seven sparsely vegetated granite outcroppings located offshore of the Golden Gate channel. The rest breed mostly on the small islands and offshore rocks between the Oregon border and Cape Mendocino in Humboldt County. Only seven acres in area, Castle Rock, offshore of the Del Norte County coast, is California's second largest seabird rookery after 65-acre Southeast Farallon Island; Castle Rock is also a Steller sea lion haul-out and a harbor seal nursery.

The breeding season of many seabird species that nest on California's islands and offshore rocks coincides with annual upwelling and the resulting increase in biological productivity of ocean waters along the California coast. Beginning in spring, a layer of deep, cold, nutrient-rich water rises, initiating surface blooms of phytoplankton; these microscopic marine plants are then grazed by zooplankton such as krill, a shrimplike animal that is important in the

Fisherman's Bay, Southeast Farallon Island

diet of breeding seabirds such as Cassin's auklets and common murres.

San Miguel Island, one of eight Channel Islands, is the only place in the world where five pinniped species—California sea lions, Steller sea lions, harbor seals, northern fur seals, and northern elephant seals—congregate and breed. Año Nuevo Island, in San Mateo County, has the largest Steller sea lion rookery in California, and also supports a large population of breeding northern elephant seals.

The Channel Islands and the Farallon Islands were created as a result of an extended period of geologic activity millions of years ago. The Farallones are composed of 89-million-year-old granite that emerged as molten rock from below the sea floor; uplifting of the Pacific Plate during the mid-Pleistocene completed the island-making process. The four northern Channel Islands are actually the western terminus of the Santa Monica Mountains, separated from the mainland by the waters of the Santa Barbara Channel. Twenty thousand years ago, when worldwide sea level was 300 feet lower than at present, the four islands formed one large island. The four southern Channel Islands are thought to have once been connected to the mountains of the Peninsular Ranges, but faulting in the San Pedro Channel 30 million years ago cut them off from the mainland.

Offshore rocks and sea stacks are of more recent origin than California's islands. North of Point Conception, where most offshore rocks are found, storm waves generated in the North Pacific buffet the shore and whittle away the coastal cliffs, leaving isolated stands of the most resistant rock. Fewer rocks lie offshore of the Southern California coast, where the buffering effect of the Channel Islands and the Southern California Bight—an indentation and southeasterly shift in the coastline south of Point Conception—reduces the impact of storm waves on coastal cliffs.

Island endemics, species that are found only on islands, are the result of divergent genetic evolution from mainland species. The island fox, found on six of the eight Channel Islands, has no predators and is considerably smaller than its mainland ancestor, the gray fox. The Santa Cruz Island scrub jay, another Channel Island endemic, is noticeably larger than its mainland relatives. Endemic island plant species may be climatic relicts, like the island ironwood tree that grows on four of the Channel Islands. The wet, cool island climate is similar to the climate of the Pleistocene, when these trees were widespread in western North America. The island populations were able to survive the post-Pleistocene climatic changes that resulted in the demise of ironwood forests on the mainland.

California sea lions and northern elephant seals at Point Bennett, San Miguel Island

ALIFORNIA'S NEARSHORE waters provide a rich and varied habitat for a diversity of marine life; vast numbers of algae, invertebrates, fish, seabirds, and mammals inhabit these shallow waters, which overlie a gently sloping region called the continental shelf. Where the shelf drops off to the deep sea floor, the open ocean begins; in contrast to the especially rich nearshore waters, the open ocean is much less fertile, gradually becoming less productive farther from shore. The fertility of nearshore waters depends upon patterns of oceanic circulation that supply the nutrients necessary to support life.

Beneath the waters of the Pacific Ocean lies a topography as varied as that found on the continents. Along some shorelines, such as the Atlantic coast, the continental shelf is broad, but on the geologically active California coast, the shelf is very narrow, often no more than four or five miles wide. The shelf is widest outside the Golden Gate, where it spreads to about 30 miles wide and is composed of a broad bank of sandy and silty sediments punctuated by the rocky peaks of the Farallon Islands. South of Point Conception, the nearshore area is rugged and complex, with basins, deep troughs, shallow reefs, steep escarpments, canyons, and the high peaks of the Channel Islands. This area, formed by relatively recent faulting, is referred to as the California Continental Borderland.

At an average depth of 600 to 650 feet, California's continental shelf ends abruptly and the continental slope begins. The edge of the continental shelf throughout most of the world's oceans occurs at a fairly uniform depth, averaging about 400 feet. Scientists believe that this shelf break might have been formed 20,000 years ago when sea level was at its lowest during the Pleistocene Ice Ages, and that the shoreline at that time was at the seaward edge of the present-day continental shelf. The continental slope descends steeply to the deep sea floor; at the base of the slope, at depths of 6,000 feet and more, is the abyssal region, which comprises flat, sediment-coated abyssal plains, broad abyssal hills, and isolated volcanic peaks called seamounts.

All along the California coast, the continental shelf and slope are etched by submarine canyons. Created by a series of complex processes, submarine canyons continue to be carved by sporadic turbidity currents—waterfalls of sand, gravel, and muddy sediments. Longshore transport along the shoreline carries beach sand and sediments into the submarine canyons, where they are swept to the deep sea floor.

The oceans are in constant motion due to wind-driven ocean currents. The difference in air temperature between the equator and the poles creates strong winds that sweep across the ocean surface; because of the effects of the earth's rotation, these winds

drive large circular currents, or gyres, in the oceans. The gyres flow clockwise in the Northern Hemisphere, and counterclockwise in the Southern Hemisphere. Once the North Pacific Gyre reaches the west coast of North America and turns south, it is termed the California Current.

The California Current, carrying water cooled by its passage through northern latitudes, flows southward along the shore from the Washington-Oregon border to Southern California. At Point Conception, the coastline turns sharply eastward, and the California Current no longer flows close to shore; this allows for a northward, warm-water flow, called the Southern California Countercurrent, in the Santa Barbara Channel. The meeting of cold-water and warm-water currents at Point Conception creates a transition zone between marine organisms characteristic of northern waters and those of southern waters. A subsurface, northward-flowing countercurrent, called the California Undercurrent, also flows along the coast inshore of and beneath the California Current.

This basic current pattern is modified by seasonal variations in wind direction that give California's nearshore region its three more or less distinct "oceanic seasons." Beginning in about March, prevailing northwesterly winds, combined with the effects of the earth's rotation, drive surface waters offshore. These waters are replaced by deep,

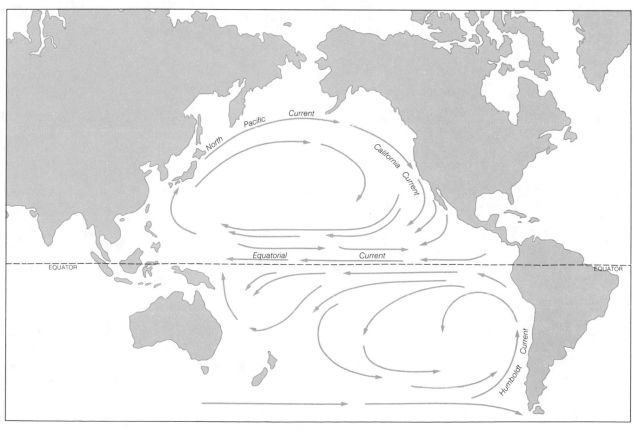

Pacific Ocean Currents

phytoplankton: *microscopic, not to scale*

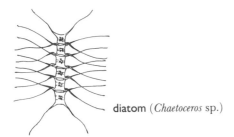

diatom (*Chaetoceros* sp.)

dinoflagellate (*Ceratium* sp.)

diatom (*Thalassiosira* sp.)

zooplankton: *microscopic, not to scale*

echinopluteus (*Echinocardium cordatum*) larval form of sea urchin

auricularia (*Labidoplax digitata*) larval form of sea cucumber

bipinnaria (*Asterias rubens*) larval form of sea star

zooplankton:

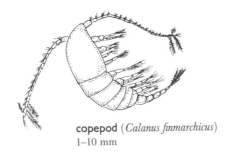

copepod (*Calanus finmarchicus*)
1–10 mm

krill (*Thysanoessa* sp.)
5–10 cm

cold water that flows up over the continental shelf to the surface, carrying with it dissolved nutrients from the decay of organic material that had sunk to the ocean floor. This process, known as upwelling, is restricted mainly to west coasts of continents, and is responsible for the high productivity of California's nearshore waters: abundant nutrients in the well-lighted surface waters, or photic zone, stimulate a proliferation of tiny, single-celled algae called phytoplankton, which in turn support other forms of marine life. The upwelling period continues until about September, when northwesterly winds die down, and the cold upwelling water begins to sink. This period, characterized by relatively high surface temperatures, is known as the oceanic period, and lasts through about October.

In winter, changes in atmospheric conditions over the Pacific Ocean bring southwesterly winds to the California coast. In response to these winds, a northward surface current begins north of Point Conception and flows along the coast inshore of the California Current. This current, called the Davidson Current, is believed to be the surface manifestation of the California Countercurrent. The Davidson Current period generally lasts through February, when the prevailing winds shift again. Several other factors affect local circulation in nearshore waters, including shoreline topography, waves, tidal motion, and freshwater discharge from rivers.

The exact timing of California's oceanic seasons varies from year to year, but every few years the pattern is disrupted by a phenomenon called El Niño. When a periodic change in atmospheric pressure in the Southern Hemisphere causes the westward-blowing trade winds above and below the equator to abate, warm water normally piled up by these winds on the coastlines of the West Pacific floods eastward to South America. The water then flows north and south from the equator, floating over cold, and therefore heavier, water and forcing it deeper. Nearshore areas are then bathed in unusually warm, nutrient-poor water, affecting food webs—phytoplankton production drops, fisheries decline, seabirds starve, and marine mammals fail to breed. El Niño, named by Peruvian fishermen for the Christ child because it often occurs around Christmas in Peru, is associated with large-scale changes in global weather patterns; in California, El Niño's effects may bring violent storms and exceptionally heavy rains.

In normal years, spring and summer upwelling supplies surface waters with nutrients that are used by phytoplankton. These drifting, microscopic plants are restricted to the photic zone by their dependence on sunlight for photosynthesis. Phytoplankton are extremely varied in shape, and have elaborate projections and indentations in their cell walls that may prevent them from sinking out of the photic zone. The most abundant groups of phytoplankton in California's coastal waters are the diatoms, which have siliceous cell walls that form two closely fitting halves, and the dinoflagellates, which can propel themselves with whip-like flagella. Certain dinoflagellate species are responsible for the phenomenon known as red tide; their populations occasionally reach such high densities that they color the water red. Some dinoflagellates that are abundant in summer produce toxins that may accumulate in the tissues of mussels and other filter-feeding mollusks, making them poisonous to humans.

In spring, storms and winds along the coast that mix the water column decrease, and a stable water layer forms at the surface, enabling phytoplankton to remain near the lighted surface waters. The increased sunlight of longer days warms the water surface, and phytoplankton populations begin to "bloom" in nearshore waters. The abundance of plant material results in blooms of both herbivorous and carnivorous zooplankton—animals that, like phytoplankton, drift with ocean currents. Zooplankton communities contain representatives of most animal groups; some of the more common members include protozoans, jellyfish, copepods—which are among the most numerous animals on earth —and shrimplike krill, as well as the larvae of mollusks, arthropods, echinoderms, and fish. The zooplankton provides food for fish, which in turn are eaten by birds and mammals. Phytoplankton production declines in summer, in part because of grazing by zooplankton, and then increases again in early fall; there may be a continual bloom if upwelling persists. Later in fall, day length shortens and upwelling ends, and the phytoplankton and zooplankton populations drop to their winter levels.

In addition to phytoplankton communities, a lush growth of large algae flourishes in nearshore waters. The kelp forest is a diverse and complex community that occurs along much of the California coast. Kelp forests are composed of dense stands of large brown algae, predominantly giant kelp, *Macrocystis pyrifera*, with an understory of several species of red and brown algae. Giant kelp is one of the fastest growing plants known, growing an average of over ten inches a day in spring; it may reach a length of 250 feet. Giant kelp usually grows on rocky bottoms, attaching with its strong holdfast, and occurs at depths of 20-200 feet. The fronds grow up toward the water surface, buoyed by their gas-filled floats.

Kelp forests are extremely variable, but typically consist of several layers of vegetation, comparable to the vertical structure of terrestrial forests. The dominant plants are the perennial giant kelp, which grows all along the California coast, and bull kelp, *Nereocystis luetkeana*, an annual that occurs in northern and central California. Feather boa kelp, *Egregia menziesii*, and *Cystoseira osmundacea* form beds inshore of giant kelp and bull kelp, and may also intermingle with the two larger species. The floating kelp fronds form a thick canopy at the water surface, below which may be an understory of shorter kelps such as *Laminaria* spp. and *Pterygophora californica*. Closer to the bottom is a layer composed of various low-growing species of red and brown algae. A fourth layer, which may cover the surface of exposed rock, consists of encrusting red algae.

Kelp forests provide food and shelter for an array of organisms. The kelp blades and holdfasts are home to invertebrates such as hydroids, bryozoans, worms, snails, crabs, amphipods, and brittle stars. Anemones, abalones, sea stars, urchins, and sea cucumbers live on the rocky bottom. Some animals graze directly on the living plants, whereas others feed on plant material that has been broken off by storms and has drifted down to the sea floor. Kelp beds are inhabited by fish such as blacksmith, kelp bass, señorita, and several species of rockfish and surfperch. Sea otters live in the canopy, feeding on abalone, sea urchins, and other invertebrates they catch on the bottom, and harbor seals enter the kelp beds to forage for fish.

The upwelling process that makes California's nearshore waters so fertile does not occur in the open ocean (except along the equator), and nutrients that have been utilized by phytoplankton, or that have sunk to deep water, are not quickly replenished. As a result, the vast open ocean is relatively unproductive. Because food is less abundant here, pelagic fish must be able to travel great distances to find prey. Plankton-feeding fish that range from nearshore waters into the open ocean include Pacific herring and northern anchovy; predators include species of marlin, tuna, mackerel, and salmon, as well as squid. Many whales and porpoises also feed in the open ocean.

Kelp Forest

CALIFORNIA has one of the most diverse floras on earth. A wealth of distinct habitats, varied soils, and microclimates, in combination with millions of years of semi-isolation by the Pacific Ocean to the west and the rugged mountains and deserts to the east, have produced a terrestrial vascular flora estimated to contain more than 5,000 native species and 1,000 introduced species. In addition, nutrient-rich ocean currents along the coast support a diverse marine flora of about 670 species.

Thirty per cent of the state's native plant species are found only in California. These are called endemics. Common endemic plants include many species of manzanita, *Arctostaphylos*, and monkeyflower, *Mimulus*. A striking feature of the California flora is the mix of evolutionarily "young" and "old" species. Tree species such as coast redwood, *Sequoia sempervirens*, which date back millions of years, provide a glimpse into the primordial past, whereas species of tarweed, *Madia* spp., are of recent origin, perhaps only a few thousand years old.

Botanists divide the plant kingdom into several major morphological groups. Flowering plants are the largest of these, in terms of the total number of species they contribute to the plant kingdom, but other, smaller groups are equally important. These include conifers; ferns and their allies; mosses; and algae. All of these groups are distinguished on the basis of three general characteristics: type of vascular tissue differentiation—presence or absence of special vascular cells called xylem and phloem that are essential for transport of water and nutrients within the plant; their overall morphological organization—presence or absence of roots, stems, and leaves; and their reproductive organs—presence or absence of cones, flowers, or other structures.

Plants are also classified by where they grow. The number and kinds of species found in a particular place are the result of complex interactions between different species, and between the plants and the physical environment. Such ecological assemblages of species are called plant communities. Some communities, such as the coastal strand, are relatively simple, consisting of a few plants adapted to a highly specialized environment. In contrast, grasslands and forests are extremely complex; hundreds of species coexist through a dynamic ecological balance. Ecologists recognize as many as 80 different plant communities constituting what is known as the California Floristic Province. Eleven of these communities, of which five are tree communities, are represented along the California coast.

Marine algae, or seaweeds, are the oldest members of the plant kingdom, extending back many hundreds of millions of years. They have little tissue differentiation, no true vascular tissue, no roots, stems, or leaves, and no flowers. Algae range in size from microscopic individual cells to huge plants more than 100 feet long. Although the flora is continuous along the coast, an abrupt change in overall species composition occurs at Point Conception, where nutrient-rich northern currents meet warmer southern ones.

Zonation patterns within algal assemblages are dictated by tidal exposure and wave impact, as well as by species interactions such as grazing by invertebrates, and by competition for space and light. The sea palm, *Postelsia palmaeformis*, for example, finds refuge on wave-pounded rocks where predators, such as sea urchins, are unable to follow. The sea palm's tough, cartilaginous stipe and holdfast (analogous to a stem and root in vascular plants) absorb wave shock, and the thick, slippery cell walls reduce desiccation. In contrast, calmer waters support more delicate membranous and leaf-like seaweeds such as *Botryoglossum*, *Porphyra*, and *Plocamium* species.

turkish towel
(*Mastocarpus papillatus*)
to 6 inches long

sea lettuce
(*Ulva angusta*)
to 3¼ feet long

bull kelp
(*Nereocystis luetkeana*)
to 125 feet long

giant kelp
(*Macrocystis pyrifera*)
to 250 feet long

sea palm (*Postelsia palmaeformis*)
to 2 feet high

Common algae of the high intertidal include Turkish towel, *Mastocarpus papillatus*, and rockweed, *Fucus distichus*. Common in the middle and lower intertidal are sea lettuce, *Ulva* spp.; feather boa kelp, *Egregia menziesii*; dead man's fingers, *Codium fragile*; and the iridescent, rubbery *Iridaea* species.

Kelp forests, found in subtidal waters as deep as 100-200 feet, are a unique ecosystem largely restricted to the west coast of the Americas, and best represented in California's coastal waters. Giant kelp, *Macrocystis pyrifera*, and bull kelp, *Nereocystis luetkeana*, are the largest non-vascular plants known. Their blades are harvested for industrially valuable gels, called alginates. The multilayered canopy of kelp fronds provides a complex aquatic habitat for thousands of fish and invertebrates.

In addition to seaweeds, marine flowering plants called seagrasses are also present in some intertidal assemblages. These plants can dominate mudflats and exposed rocks, in some cases virtually excluding the algae. Eelgrass, *Zostera marina*, is common in quiet waters with a sandy or muddy substrate, whereas surfgrass, *Phyllospadix* spp., is common along exposed rocky shores, often in high-energy surf zones.

The harsh environment of the coastal strand community is characterized by wave-pounded beaches, shifting sands, relentless winds, and saline soils. Here species diversity is low in comparison to most other plant communities. Strand plants have evolved numerous adaptations for survival. Low, sprawling shoots and hardy root systems are common, as are thick leathery or hairy leaves that help minimize water loss. Many strand plants have also developed physiological mechanisms that have enabled them to adapt to high-salt and low-nutrient soils. For example, saltbush, *Atriplex* spp., has evolved special cells for salt excretion on its stems and leaves. Sea rocket, *Cakile maritima*, and the non-native, curly-leaved European beach grass, *Ammophila arenaria*, are among the hardiest species and earliest colonizers of open sands. In more stabilized areas, beach pea, *Lathyrus* spp.; yellow bush lupine, *Lupinus arboreus*; pink and yellow sand verbena, *Abronia* spp.; beach morning-glory, *Convolvulus soldanella*; and gray-green silver beachweed, *Ambrosia chamissonis*, are common. The tough, rubbery Hottentot fig, *Carpobrotus edulis*, and the sea fig, *C. chilense*, are important non-native species. These succulents have thick, triangular stems and showy, pink or yellow flowers.

Each spring a flush of green grasses covers the rolling hills and bluffs above the sea, and within a few weeks thousands of wildflowers burst forth in brilliant colors. By midsummer the grasses set seed and the hills change back to their green and golden slumber. This is the coastal prairie community, which extends intermittently south from Eureka to Point Reyes and between San Francisco and Monterey.

surfgrass (*Phyllospadix torreyi*)
to 16 inches long

eelgrass (*Zostera marina*)
to 1 foot long

saltbush (*Atriplex patula* var. *hastata*)
12 to 40 inches high

sea rocket (*Cakile maritima*)
to 2 feet high

yellow sand verbena (*Abronia latifolia*)
to 1 foot high

beach pea (*Lathyrus littoralis*)
4 to 24 inches high

sea fig (*Carpobrotus chilense*)
3 feet long

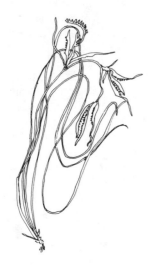

bush lupine (*Lupinus arboreus*)
3 to 6 feet high

Until late in the last century the coastal prairie was almost entirely composed of native perennial grasses. These relatively slow-growing grasses have deep root systems and creeping stems that help to ensure their long-term survival; some individual plants are known to be more than 100 years old. Early European settlers found the naturally treeless coastal grasslands ideal for agriculture and ranching. As grazing operations expanded, fast-growing, non-native annual grasses were gradually introduced and these began to outcompete the slow-growing, native perennials. Some introductions were accidental and others intentional. Annual grasses live only a single growing season but good seed dispersal en-

sures their return year after year. As a result, few intact native grassland communities remain today.

Representative native grasses include species of bentgrass, *Agrostis*; hairgrass, *Deschampsia*; reedgrass, *Calamagrostis*; and oatgrass, *Danthonia*. At least four species of bentgrass are endemic, whereas others are introductions from Australia or Europe. Hairgrass provides excellent forage and can withstand close grazing without destruction of its delicate root system, whereas reedgrass is important in the prevention of erosion. Commonly encountered non-native grasses include wild oat, *Avena* spp., and bromegrass, *Bromus* spp.

Bracken fern, *Pteridium aquilinum*, and numerous wildflowers abound, especially in spring. Ecologists believe that the presence of annual grasses has actually increased the number of wildflower species able to survive in this community. Blue and white Douglas iris, *Iris douglasiana*; California buttercup, *Ranunculus californicus*; and the brilliant orange California poppy, *Eschscholzia californica*, are common inhabitants of the grassland community.

Coastal scrub communities are characterized by low shrubs and an absence of trees. Types of shrubs include either pure stands, or mixtures of low, thick-leaved evergreens and coarse, deciduous species that drop their leaves in response to periodic drought conditions. Three representative scrub assemblages (not strictly limited to the coast) are the northern coastal scrub, southern coastal sage scrub or soft-chaparral, and arid hard-chaparral.

Low shrubby overstory and lush herbaceous undergrowth often characterize the

northern coastal scrub community, which may grade into adjacent coastal prairie. Many northern scrub species retain their leaves throughout the year. Native coyote brush, *Baccharis pilularis*, is the most abundant plant in this community and is easily identified by its white fall flowers. California blackberry, *Rubus ursinus*, and poison oak, *Toxicodendron diversilobum*, are other common shrubs. The predominantly gray-green northern scrub landscape is accented by colorful monkeyflowers, *Mimulus* spp., and tall cow parsnip, *Heracleum lanatum*, with its characteristic yellow-green foliage and flat, silvery-white flower clusters.

In contrast, the more arid and gravelly soils along the southern coast support mostly drought-adapted shrubs with few or no understory species. This is the southern coastal sage scrub, or soft-chaparral, community named for the ubiquitous black, purple, and white sages, *Salvia* spp. Sage scrub communities are easily identified by their characteristic fragrance and long flowering season, which may extend over half the year. Ecological adaptations include the production of two sets of leaves. In sages, the larger leaves fall off during the dry summer season, reducing evaporative water loss, while the smaller ones remain intact. Other species, such as deerweed, *Lotus scoparius*, drop their leaves completely. Sage ensures its success as a dominant community member by releasing chemical compounds into the soil that prevent other plants from establishing themselves. This is called allelopathy. Additional inhabitants of this community include California sagebrush, *Artemisia californica;* lemonadeberry, *Rhus integrifolia;* and poison oak.

California poppy (*Eschscholzia californica*)
8 to 24 inches high

bentgrass (*Agrostis longiligula*)
2 to 2½ feet high

coyote brush (*Baccharis pilularis*)
2 to 5 feet high

Douglas iris (*Iris douglasiana*)
to 3 feet high

black sage (*Salvia mellifera*)
3 to 6 feet high

Hard-chaparral is a scrub community unique to California and southwestern Oregon. It occurs in drier regions characterized by mild, wet winters and very hot summers. In the northern part of the state this community occurs inland, but in the southern Coast Ranges it is contiguous with the sage scrub community. Hard-chaparral shrubs can form dense, impenetrable stands of a few species, or diverse species assemblages. More than 900 plant species have been found in association with different chaparral communities. Common inhabitants include chamise, *Adenostoma* spp.; California lilac, *Ceanothus* spp.; and manzanita, *Arctostaphylos* spp. Fire is an important ecological factor in maintaining hard-chaparral communities because, among other things, it helps to cleanse the soil of allelopathic compounds and clear space for new and different plant species.

Coastal salt marshes develop along the intertidal shores of bays and estuaries. Estuaries occur where a river meets the sea, and the water is somewhat brackish. In general, salt marshes along the Northern California coast have a relatively low salinity because of substantial river runoff, whereas those along the southern coast, where there are fewer rivers and less runoff, are of higher salinity. San Francisco Bay contains the largest and one of the most complex salt marsh systems in the state.

Salt marsh plants are adapted to a harsh, semi-aquatic environment and saline soils. Species diversity is low. Stout stems, small leaves, and physiological adaptations for salt excretion and gas exchange characterize the inhabitants of the salt marsh, which are mostly grasses and low perennial herbs. The tangle of marsh plant roots and stems helps to stabilize the muddy bottom, as well as to trap debris and dissolved nutrients with each tidal cycle. Bacteria convert this oasis of detritus into food resources for microscopic algae, invertebrate larvae, and larger animals. Salt marshes are about twice as photosynthetically productive as corn fields and provide critical nursery grounds for numerous organisms.

Species composition and zonation in the salt marsh are governed by salinity gradients in combination with the amount of intertidal exposure. Eelgrass, *Zostera marina*, for example, occupies the lowest or most marine zone. It cannot tolerate a freshwater environment or intertidal conditions that would expose its roots to air. Cordgrass, *Spartina foliosa*, occurs in the marine-to-terrestrial transition zone, characterized by lower salinity and periodic exposure to the air. Shoreward, where conditions are even drier, pickleweed species belonging to the genus *Salicornia* are common. On higher ground, where tidal intrusions are rare, the wiry, prickly-leaved succulent jaumea, *Jaumea carnosa*, is common, as are the bushy shoregrass, *Monanthochloe littoralis*; tall and slender sea arrowgrass, *Triglochin maritima*; and endangered salt marsh bird's beak, *Cordylanthus maritimus*. The green, wiry-leaved saltgrass, *Distichlis spicata*, is widespread, occurring from the middle to high marsh, as well as in dunes and on salt flats. An unusual saltmarsh plant is the orange, parasitic dodder, *Cuscuta salina*. Its tiny, scale-like leaves and thread-like stems frequently invade and cover large areas of vegetation.

Coastal freshwater marshes are sometimes found in association with salt marshes, especially along the northern coast where there are more rivers, and ponds are fairly numerous. Freshwater marsh plants have adapted to their aquatic environment in several ways. Most species have developed air tubes to their roots, buoyant leaves, or porous leaf coverings that enhance gas exchange. In contrast to salt marshes, freshwater marshes have little if any water movement.

Typical freshwater marsh plants include numerous species of sedges; these grass-like plants often exceed five feet in height. Slough sedge, *Carex obnupta*, is one of the most common. Familiar cigar-shaped cattails, *Typha latifolia*, form thick stands and are so proliferous that a single plant can rapidly fill in a small pond. Bushy, needle-leaved rushes, *Juncus phaeocephalus*, are also common. Aquatically adapted wildflowers such as yellow pond-lily, *Nuphar polysepalum*, with broad oval leaves up to 16 inches in diameter; water buttercup, *Ranunculus orthorhynchus*; and succulent water parsley, *Oenanthe sarmentosa*, are also typical freshwater marsh inhabitants.

sea arrowgrass (*Triglochin maritima*)
1 to 2 feet high

saltgrass (*Distichlis spicata*)
8 to 12 inches high

pickleweed (*Salicornia virginica*)
8 to 25 inches high

cordgrass (*Spartina foliosa*)
1 to 4 feet high

ECOLOGISTS recognize at least 13 major tree communities within California. Five of these are associated with the coastal regions. There are approximately 129 species of native trees in California, 63 of which are endemic. It is estimated that another 1,000 have been introduced from all over the world, but most of these are limited to private gardens. Nevertheless, about 30-50 introduced species have become naturalized, including the ubiquitous blue gum, *Eucalyptus globulus*.

California's north coastal forests are divided into separate communities that intergrade with one another. The largest and most important of these communities are the coastal redwood, Douglas-fir, and mixed-evergreen forests. From the coast inland, species composition is dictated by moisture gradients. These gradients are determined by rainfall and the ability of soils to retain water. In the wettest coastal areas, where fog alone can account for up to ten inches of added yearly precipitation, coast redwood, *Sequoia sempervirens*; Sitka spruce, *Picea sitchensis*; western hemlock, *Tsuga heterophylla*; and canoe cedar, *Thuja plicata*, are dominant. In moderately moist areas, farther inland, Douglas-fir, *Pseudotsuga menziesii*, takes over. Mixed-evergreen forests occur in warmer areas and are highly variable in their species composition.

Coast redwood forests are probably the best-known forest community in California. Coast redwood forests were once widespread but are now relicts, restricted to a narrow belt from southern Oregon to Monterey County. Rising from massive trunks, they are the tallest trees in the world, some more than 300 feet tall. Coast redwoods have thick, reddish bark and two types of needle-like leaves. Those leaves found on the outermost twigs are of unequal length, occurring in two rows, whereas those of the central portion of the branch are short and scale-like. Despite their size, redwoods have an unusually shallow root system that makes them vulnerable to toppling over if the soil becomes overly wet for long periods.

Redwoods are remarkably fire-tolerant and long-lived; 500 years is an average life span, but some are more than 2,000 years old. An unusual adaptation is the ability of redwoods to produce new shoots from roots, especially after fire damage. Root sprouting is common, and, in some cases, a perfect ring of clone trees may coalesce to form a natural enclosure around the parent tree. In this way, a single tree can be perpetuated more or less indefinitely.

Relatively few understory species are able to flourish in a mature redwood forest because of the extreme shade, wet soil, deep leaf litter, and redwood root competition. Trees such as California bay laurel, *Umbellularia californica*, and Douglas-fir are successful short-term competitors where shade is not too severe, as is tanbark oak, *Lithocarpus densiflorus*, whose acorns provide food for many animals. Sword fern, *Polystichum munitum*, and five-finger fern, *Adiantum pedatum*, grow well in this environment and add to the primordial grandeur of the community. The shady redwood forest is brightened by clover-leaved, white- and pink-flowered redwood sorrel, *Oxalis oregana*; inside-out flower, *Vancouveria parviflora*; and brilliant rhododendrons, *Rhododendron macrophyllum*, in several shades of pink.

Douglas-fir forests intergrade with and eventually replace coast redwood forests inland, where fog and rainfall are more moderate. Douglas-fir is one of the most important commercial timber species in California. It is easily identified by flattened needles spirally arranged around twigs in double rows. At maturity the branches have a characteristic droop; young trees, however, form almost perfect conical shapes.

Mixed-evergreen forests occur throughout coastal California, as well as inland, where the climate is generally drier and warmer. These communities consist of mixed species assemblages including conifers and hardwoods that form associations with neighboring plant communities such as coast redwood and Douglas-fir forests, coastal prairie, or even chaparral. Typical inhabitants of mixed-evergreen forests include many species of maple (*Acer*) and oak (*Quercus*), as well as bay (*Umbellularia*). Red- and green-barked madrone, *Arbutus menziesii*, and giant chinquapin, *Castanopsis chrysophylla*, with its burr-covered nuts, are also commonly found growing with the coniferous forest species.

Closed-cone coniferous forests are another unique California community occurring in patches along the coast from Humboldt to Santa Barbara County. The name of this community derives from the fact that the seed-bearing cones remain

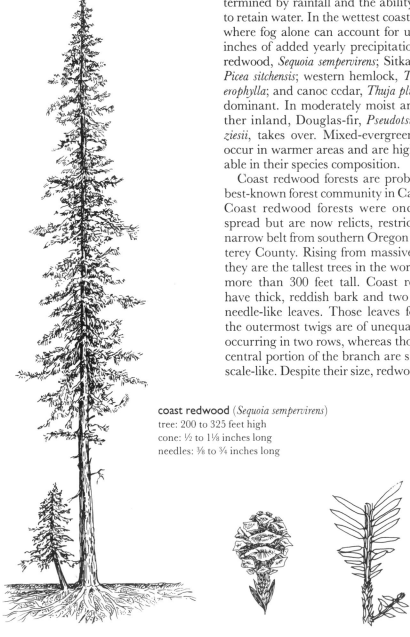

coast redwood (*Sequoia sempervirens*)
tree: 200 to 325 feet high
cone: ½ to 1⅛ inches long
needles: ⅜ to ¾ inches long

closed for several years, a reproductive adaptation that ensures survival. Only age, excessive hot weather, or fire opens them. The fossil record indicates that closed-cone forests were once widespread but are now remnants on their way to natural extinction. Gnarled and slanted stands of pine and cypress form natural windbreaks along fog-shrouded headlands. Some of the most eerily beautiful of these stands are found along the Monterey Peninsula. In more protected areas, trees of these same species are more symmetrical, forming conical or umbrella-like shapes. Bishop pine, *Pinus muricata;* beach pine, *P. contorta;* and Monterey pine, *P. radiata,* are easily identified by the characteristic number of needles per sheath: one, two, and three respectively. Gowen cypress, *Cupressus goveniana,* and Monterey cypress, *C. macrocarpa,* are distinguished by their distinctive scale-like leaves and fragrant foliage.

Miniature closed-cone forests, called pygmy forests, occur in Mendocino County. Extremely hard, acidic soils have stunted the growth of mature trees, some of which are only one to two feet tall. Dwarfed endemic species are the Mendocino or pygmy cypress, *Cupressus pygmaea,* and the Bolander pine, *Pinus contorta bolanderi.*

Riparian woodlands occur in ribbon-like bands along stream beds where rich soils and high humidity produce a natural greenhouse effect. Although this unique community accounts for less than one per cent of California's total forest acreage, it supports one of the most diverse ecological communities of plants and animals. Tall deciduous trees such as big-leaf maple, *Acer macrophyllum,* and the evergreen California bay laurel tower above a lush understory of ferns and delicate wildflowers. Unfortunately, many riparian woodlands have been destroyed over the last century because the fertile soils along rivers are among the most sought after for agricultural lands, and because numerous rivers have been channelized for flood control projects.

Where rainfall is heavy, as along the north coast, riparian woodlands mingle with adjacent forests. The predominantly deciduous trees, with their bright green leaves, contrast sharply with their dark green coniferous neighbors. Along the south coast, where drier conditions prevail, the contrast between the lush, green riparian community and the drier, brown surroundings may be even more striking.

Common to practically all riparian communities are big-leaf maple and California bay laurel. Red alder, *Alnus oregona,* and black cottonwood, *Populus trichocarpa,* are typical of northern and central coastal regions, whereas Fremont cottonwood, *Populus fremontii,* and western sycamore, *Platanus racemosa,* are common riparian trees in central and southern coastal regions.

Below the canopy of trees, rich riparian soils support many species of ferns and willows such as the coarse and wiry bracken fern, *Pteridium aquilinum;* tall, graceful lady fern, *Athyrium filix-femina;* and sandbar willow, *Salix hindsiana.* Velvety-leaved canyon gooseberry, *Ribes menziesii;* California blackberry, *Rubus vitifolius;* and twinberry, *Lonicera involucrata,* are frequently encountered shrubs in riparian communities.

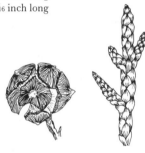

Monterey cypress (*Cupressus macrocarpa*)
tree: 60 to 80 feet high
cone: 1 to 1⅜ inches long
leaves: over 1/16 inch long

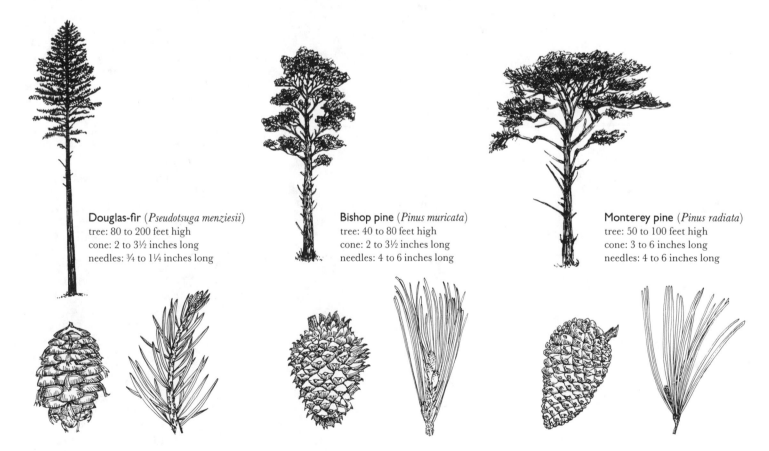

Douglas-fir (*Pseudotsuga menziesii*)
tree: 80 to 200 feet high
cone: 2 to 3½ inches long
needles: ¾ to 1¼ inches long

Bishop pine (*Pinus muricata*)
tree: 40 to 80 feet high
cone: 2 to 3½ inches long
needles: 4 to 6 inches long

Monterey pine (*Pinus radiata*)
tree: 50 to 100 feet high
cone: 3 to 6 inches long
needles: 4 to 6 inches long

INSECTS, which constitute over half of the world's animal species, inhabit almost every type of ecological niche. The diversity and biological success of insects can be attributed to a number of factors—a fast reproductive cycle that dramatically speeds up the evolutionary process, enabling generations to rapidly adapt to environmental change; an enormous reproductive capacity; the ability to disperse effectively and widely; specialization in their habitat use, reducing competition for resources; and a small body size that demands little food or water for survival.

Insects are characterized by three pairs of legs, three body segments, a rigid exoskeleton, and, in most species, wings during the adult stage. Some insects undergo simple metamorphosis, in which the eggs hatch into nymphs that look like tiny, wingless adults. Most insects undergo complete metamorphosis, which enables the adults to exploit a different habitat from that of the young, and reduces resource competition within a species. Complete metamorphosis entails four distinct stages of development— the egg; the larva, or feeding and growth stage; the pupa, or resting and transformation stage, and the adult stage. To grow, insect larvae must molt, replacing the exoskeleton with a new, larger one. Larvae— for example, caterpillars, grubs, and maggots—eat voraciously and may cause severe crop damage. Adult insects do not grow; many adults are short-lived, surviving only several days or weeks in order to reproduce.

One of the best-known insects of the California coast is the Monarch butterfly, *Danaus plexippus*. Every fall hundreds of thousands of Monarchs gather from all over the western United States and migrate to coastal wintering grounds. Although not all butterflies survive the entire migration, some individuals make flights of up to 2,000 miles. Monarchs can be seen from October to February at several locations along the coast, including Natural Bridges State Beach in Santa Cruz County and Pacific Grove in Monterey County.

Coastal wetlands teem with insects. Tiny brine flies, *Ephydra riparia*, comb the mud surface for microorganisms and feed in saline pools. Salt marsh water boatmen, *Trichocorixa reticulata*, propel themselves through the marsh with their oarlike hind legs, feeding on algal mats and protozoa. Southern salt marsh mosquitoes, *Aedes taeniorhynchus*, breed in brackish marsh waters. Predatory beetles burrow into sand and mudflats, aerating the soil. The wandering skipper, *Panoquina errans*, depends on salt grass as food for its larvae.

Sand dunes are home to numerous beetles, which constitute the largest insect group. Globose dune beetles, *Coelus globosus*, live in dunes around the decaying leaf litter of coastal scrub plants. Snout beetles, *Trigonoscuta spp.*, burrow into sand dunes during the day to escape predators and heat; at night they move out onto the dunes to feed on strand vegetation.

Kelp washed up on the beach provides habitat for the larvae of several species of flies, including the flat-backed kelp fly, *Coelopa vanduzeei*, and wrack flies *Fucellia costalis* and *F. rufitibia*. The decomposing kelp also supports predatory insects such as the black rove beetle, *Hadrotes crassus*, which probably feeds on the fly larvae. Among other predators on the beach are the pictured rove beetle, *Thinopinus pictus*, which preys on amphipods, and the quick and rapacious tiger beetles (of the family *Cicindelidae*). Tiger beetle larvae construct burrows where they await passing prey; adults stalk their prey on the sand.

One factor in the biological success of insects—habitat specialization—also makes them vulnerable to extinction. The destruction of coastal habitat has led to the extinction or near extinction of several butterflies whose larvae are plant-specific feeders. The Xerces blue, *Glaucopsyche xerces*, fed on lupines in the San Francisco sand dunes; with the destruction of the dunes, the species became extinct in 1942. Endangered and near extinction are the San Bruno elfin, *Callophrys mossii bayensis*, which feeds on stonecrop; the Mission blue, *Icaricia icarioides missionensis*, which feeds on lupine; and the El Segundo blue, *Euphilotes battoides allynii*, and Smith's blue, *Euphilotes enoptes smithi*, both of which eat wild buckwheat. The San Francisco tree lupine moth, *Grapholita edwardsiana*, is another uncommon resident of the sand dune community.

Xerces blue butterfly (*Glaucopsyche xerces*)
1⅛- to 1¼-inch wingspan (29 to 32 mm)

pictured rove beetle (*Thinopinus pictus*)
½ to 9⁄10 inch long (12 to 22 mm)

salt marsh water boatman (*Trichocorixa reticulata*)
1⁄10 to 2⁄10 inch long (2.8 to 5.4 mm)

southern salt marsh mosquito (*Aedes taeniorhynchus*)
1⁄10 to 13⁄100 inch long (2.8 to 3.2 mm)

Monarch butterfly (*Danaus plexippus*)
3¼- to 4-inch wingspan (83 to 101mm)

INVERTEBRATES are animals without backbones. Encompassing 95 per cent of all animals—everything but fish, amphibians, reptiles, birds, and mammals—they range in complexity from the simple sponges to the intricate and highly specialized arthropods. Major groups of marine invertebrates include sponges, cnidarians (also known as coelenterates), bryozoans, mollusks, annelid worms, arthropods, echinoderms, and tunicates. Representatives of these groups may be seen in rocky intertidal areas, in mudflats, or on sandy beaches.

Sponges, the simplest invertebrates, lack well-formed organs; their bodies are supported by a calcareous, siliceous, or fibrous framework. Sponges are colonial, sessile filter-feeders. Water, which carries both food and oxygen, enters the sponge through small surface pores and circulates through a network of canals, flushing out through large pores, or oscula. Dozens of species, varying in shape and color, occur in the low intertidal on California's rocky shores. The cream-colored urn sponge, *Leucilla nuttingi*, is vase-shaped with a single osculum at the top, and grows in upright clusters to five centimeters long.

Cnidarians, which include hydroids, jellyfish, and sea anemones, possess a nerve net, a muscular system, a digestive cavity, and a mouth encircled by tentacles. Cnidarians occur in two body types—a cylindrical polyp, which is usually sessile, and a bell-shaped medusa, which is free-swimming. Some species pass through both stages during their life cycles, whereas others exist only as one type or the other. The carnivorous cnidarians have specialized stinging structures called nematocysts that contain poisons to stun their prey.

Hydroids typically occur as delicately branched, upright stalks, and have both a polyp and a medusa stage. One unusual hydroid is the pelagic by-the-wind-sailor, *Velella velella*, which has a transparent sail set diagonally on its blue, seven-cm-long body. By-the-wind-sailors frequently drift into nearshore waters and are washed up on shore in great numbers.

In jellyfish, the solitary, free-swimming medusa is the dominant type, and the polyp stage is reduced or absent. Jellyfish swim by rhythmic pulsations of the muscular bell; as the bell contracts, water is expelled from the central cavity. The purple banded jellyfish, *Pelagia colorata*, has a dome-shaped bell that is pale silver with purple bands.

Sea anemones and the closely related corals and sea pens lack a medusa stage. Sea anemones are solitary polyps with stout, muscular bodies, and a mouth surrounded by flower-like tentacles. Though usually sessile, attaching to rocks or burrowing in sand or mud, anemones can glide slowly on their pedal disks, and some can swim or roll. The aggregating anemone, *Anthopleura elegantissima*, reproduces asexually by fission to create genetically identical clones. When members of different clones come into contact, they sting each other with special knob-like protuberances packed with nematocysts. The anemones then draw away from each other, leaving a bare zone between clones.

Bryozoans are sessile, colonial organisms that grow on rocks, shells, algae, and wharf pilings. Bryozoan colonies begin with one sexually produced individual, and grow by budding. Each individual feeds by means of a crown of ciliated tentacles that sweeps water into its mouth. Some bryozoans are encrusting; others form erect tubes, bushy branches, or flattened blades. *Membranipora tuberculata* appears as a white, honeycomb-like crust on giant kelp and other algae.

Mollusks are a large and diverse group, and display great variation of a general form. They typically possess a head with a hard, tongue-like rasping organ called a radula, a muscular foot, a soft body protected by a hard shell, a fleshy mantle that secretes the shell, and well-developed organ systems. Some mollusks are hermaphroditic, but in most the sexes are separate. The largest and most familiar classes of mollusks are the chitons, gastropods, bivalves, and cephalopods.

Chitons, most commonly found in the rocky intertidal, are flat and oval-shaped, with shells composed of eight overlapping calcareous plates partly or fully embedded in a muscular girdle. Most chitons are herbivorous, using their radulae to scrape algae off rocks. The world's largest chiton is the gumboot chiton, *Cryptochiton stelleri*, which grows to 33 cm in length. A tough, brick-red girdle completely covers its shell; its hard, white, butterfly-shaped plates are often found washed up on the beach.

Gastropods, comprising over 80 per cent of the mollusks, include abalones, limpets, snails, sea hares, and nudibranchs. Gas-

urn sponge (*Leucilla nuttingi*)
2 inches high

lined chiton (*Tonicella lineata*)
to 2 inches long

banded jellyfish (*Pelagia colorata*)
bell to 30 inches in diameter

feather duster worm (*Sabella crassicornis*)
2 inches long

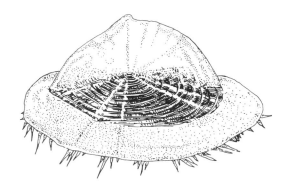

by-the-wind-sailor (*Velella velella*)
2¾ to 3 inches long

Lewis's moon snail (*Polinices lewisii*)
shell to 5 inches in diameter

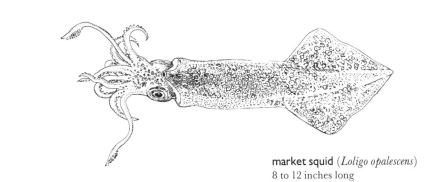

market squid (*Loligo opalescens*)
8 to 12 inches long

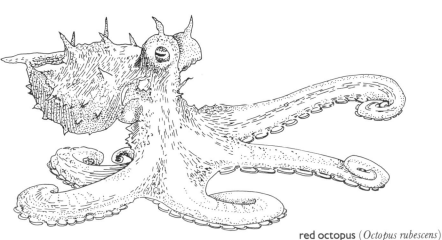

red octopus (*Octopus rubescens*)
6 inches long, including tentacles
dorsal mantle 2 to 4 inches long

tropods are an extremely diverse group, differing greatly in appearance and behavior. In limpets, the one-piece shell is cap-shaped; in most snails, it is coiled; in abalones, it is also flattened. Sea hares have only a small internal shell, and the colorful nudibranchs, or sea slugs, lack a shell completely. The flat foot may be used for creeping, clinging to rocks, grasping prey, burrowing, or swimming. In abalones, limpets, many snails, and sea hares, the radula is used to graze on algae; predators such as the rock snail, *Nucella emarginata*, use it to drill into their prey. Reproductive behavior is also variable. Abalones and limpets release eggs and sperm into the sea water, where fertilization occurs. In other gastro-

pods, fertilization is internal. After mating, female Lewis's moon snails, *Polinices lewisii*, produce a collar-shaped egg case formed of sand and mucus. The hermaphroditic California brown sea hare, *Aplysia californica*, may form mating chains, in which each animal both gives and receives sperm.

Bivalves, comprising mussels, oysters, scallops, and clams, are usually sedentary filter-feeders possessing a two-piece hinged shell and a bladelike foot. All bivalves lack a radula. When submerged, bivalves relax their shells slightly, and cilia drive water through the gills, which filter suspended organic material. Mussels attach to firm substrates by secreting strong byssal threads; oysters secrete a cement to adhere to rocks, shells, and pilings. Scallops swim by clapping their shells together. Clams burrow in sand or mud, or bore into rock or wood, and feed by means of long siphons they extend to the water above.

Cephalopods, which include squids, octopuses, cuttlefish, and nautiluses, possess complex eyes, keen vision, the largest brain of any invertebrate, and sucker-bearing arms that surround the head. In males, one arm is modified for transferring sperm packets into the bodies of females. Cephalopods swim by jet propulsion by forcing water out of the mantle cavity. They can change color for camouflage or for communication; when threatened, they release a cloud of ink. Most cephalopods are deep-water species, and are uncommon near shore. The market squid, *Loligo opalescens*, comes inshore to mate, spawn, and die. The red octopus, *Octopus rubescens*, which lives in subtidal reefs and kelp beds, is occasionally found in the low intertidal.

Annelids comprise earthworms, leeches, and the mostly marine polychaetes. Annelids have soft, segmented bodies; paired fleshy appendages bear tiny bristles that help the worms anchor themselves. Polychaetes occur in all marine habitats. Many are free-moving, burrowing in sand or mud, or seeking shelter under rocks, in mats of algae, or among mussels; some inhabit the open ocean. Others are sedentary, spending their lives in tubes made of mucus, sand, or calcium carbonate. *Sabella crassicornis* lives in a sand-encrusted tube in the rocky intertidal, and captures food particles with a plume of feathery red gills.

Arthropods constitute the largest, most widespread, and most diverse animal group. Like annelids, their bodies are segmented, but the segments are generally developed into distinctive body regions, such as a head, thorax, and abdomen. They have chitinous exoskeletons, and jointed appendages modified into antennae, mouthparts, pinchers, and legs for swimming, walking, or digging. Crustaceans, a mostly marine class of arthropods, comprise by far the largest number of animals in the ocean. They include the minute copepods, which occur in vast numbers in plankton of the open ocean; barnacles; isopods, such as the rock louse, *Ligia occidentalis*; amphipods, such as the beach hopper, *Orchestoidea californiana*; and decapods, which include shrimps, crabs, and lobsters.

Barnacles are sessile as adults, attaching as larvae by their heads to hard surfaces or to other organisms. They are protected by shells formed of calcareous plates. To feed, they extend their feathery legs and sweep food from the water into their mouths. A common species is the volcano-shaped acorn barnacle, *Balanus glandula*, which crowds on rock faces in the splash zone.

Decapods have five pairs of legs and a hard covering called a carapace. The first pair of legs is often enlarged and modified to form pinchers. Some decapods, such as the Franciscan bay shrimp, *Crangon franciscorum*, are streamlined swimmers, with slender legs and compressed bodies. Others, such as the lined shore crab, *Pachygrapsus crassipes*, are adapted for crawling, and have heavier legs. Decapods inhabit tidepools, sandy beaches, mudflats, and offshore waters.

Echinoderms include sea stars, brittle stars, sea urchins, sand dollars, and sea cucumbers. They have a spiny endoskeleton composed of calcareous plates, and a unique water-vascular system that enables them to move, capture food, and adhere to surfaces. Their bodies are rounded, cylindrical, or star-shaped, without a head or brain. Echinoderms inhabit the ocean floor at all depths.

Sea stars have flattened bodies consisting of a central disk and five or more tapering arms. Their top surface is often rough and spiny; the mouth is on the underside of the disk, and the arms are equipped with sucker-tipped tube feet operated by the water-vascular system. The ochre star, *Pisaster ochraceous*, which lives in the rocky intertidal and subtidal, uses its tube feet to pry open mussels and other prey. The star wraps itself around the mussel, adheres with its feet, and pulls, then extrudes its stomach into the mussel's shell, where digestive enzymes dissolve the flesh.

Brittle stars occur from the intertidal to the abyssal sea floor. They have long, thin, flexible arms set off from a circular disk. The grayish *Amphiodia occidentalis* is sometimes found under rocks or in algal holdfasts in tidepools. It often burrows in sand, and feeds by extending its arms above the surface, collecting food particles on its tube feet, and passing the material to its mouth.

In sea urchins, the internal calcareous plates form a solid shell, or test; bleached tests of dead urchins are often found washed up on shore. Urchins lack arms, and move by means of their tube feet and long, flexible spines. The red sea urchin, *Strongylocentrotus franciscanus*, is a subtidal species that feeds on giant kelp and other algae. The sand dollar, *Dendraster excentricus*, is a flattened urchin; it occurs subtidally in sand, and filters detritus from the water.

The sluggish, cylindrical sea cucumbers live on the sea floor, or burrow in sand or mud. Some are filter feeders, catching food in the sticky tentacles that surround their mouths; others eat mud and digest the food particles in it. Many species, such as *Parastichopus californicus*, which inhabits rocky shores, have a unique defense strategy: when threatened or irritated, the cucumber may spew out its internal organs through its anus to distract its attacker; the body wall then crawls off, and eventually regenerates new organs.

Of all invertebrates, tunicates, or sea squirts, are the most closely related to vertebrates; like vertebrates, they are chordates, and in their larval stage, they possess the common chordate features, such as a hollow, dorsal nerve cord, and a skeletal supporting rod, called a notochord. However, as adults, tunicates lose many of these features, becoming modified to sessile, filter-feeding organisms. The adult tunicate is protected by a tough "tunic" that surrounds its body; two siphons allow water to circulate through the body. When disturbed, it may contract its body and expel water from its siphons. Some tunicate species occur as stalked, solitary forms; others are encrusting colonies, forming gelatinous sheets on rocks and wharf pilings. *Styela montereyensis* is a solitary tunicate common on rocks and pilings in the low intertidal. This species has a long, cylindrical body on a thin stalk, and usually reaches up to 15 cm; its leathery, ridged tunic is yellowish or dark reddish-brown.

red sea urchin (*Strongylocentrotus franciscanus*)
body to 4 inches in diameter
spines to 2 inches long

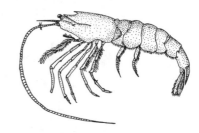

Franciscan bay shrimp (*Crangon franciscorum*)
2 inches long

sand dollar (*Dendraster excentricus*)
to 3 inches in diameter

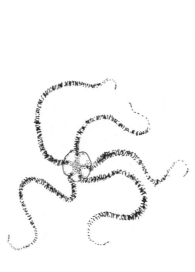

lined shore crab (*Pachygrapsus crassipes*)
1½ to 2 inches wide

brittle star (*Amphiodia occidentalis*)
disc to ½ inch in diameter
arms to 4 inches long

stalked tunicate (*Styela montereyensis*)
3 to 6 inches long

AMPHIBIANS and reptiles are collectively referred to as herpetofauna, from the Greek *herpeton* ("creeping thing"). Although often studied together, amphibians—which in California include salamanders, frogs, and toads—and reptiles—represented here by turtles, lizards, and snakes—are similar only in that they are ectothermic terrestrial vertebrates. Modern amphibians are the descendents of the first vertebrates to colonize land; they occur only where water or humidity is sufficient to allow for breathing and breeding. Amphibians possess simple, inefficient lungs, and a porous, moist skin that they use as an accessory breathing organ; gelatinous eggs are laid in water or in moist places, generally hatching into aquatic, gilled larvae. Reptiles, on the other hand, can survive in arid habitats because of their well-developed lungs, a fat layer in the skin that retards water loss, and shelled eggs that contain food and protective membranes to support embryonic development on dry land.

Amphibians probably evolved from the lobe-finned fish, which had lungs for breathing air, and strong fins with which they could move about on land. Amphibians are carnivorous, and eat anything from insects to small mammals. Many possess poison glands that make them distasteful to potential predators. Present-day amphibians that perhaps most resemble their ancestors are the salamanders, which typically have four legs and a long tail. Many species, such as the familiar brown and orange California newt, *Taricha torosa*, spend the summer under rocks or in logs, and migrate during fall and winter rains to aquatic breeding sites. Fertilization is internal: the male deposits a sperm packet that the female crawls over to enable the sperm to enter her body. In water-breeding salamanders, the eggs hatch into gilled juveniles that resemble the adults in form. The lungless plethodontid salamanders, which include the clouded salamander, *Aneides ferreus*, breed on land and lay eggs that hatch into fully formed young.

Frogs and toads are characterized by a broad head and short trunk, strong hind legs modified for jumping, and no tail. Toads are distinguished from frogs by their shorter legs, stouter bodies, and warty skins. Frogs and toads catch prey with their long, sticky tongues. During the breeding season, males croak to attract females; in mating, males embrace the females to stimulate egg laying. Fertilization is usually external; eggs hatch into legless tadpoles with gills and long, finned tails. Common frogs of the California coast include the Pacific treefrog, *Hyla regilla*, found beside marshes and ponds, and the red-legged frog, *Rana aurora*, which inhabits ponds and streams in humid forests and grasslands.

Reptiles, which evolved from amphibians, owe their success on land to a desiccation-resistant fat layer in their scaly skins and to their shelled eggs, internally fertilized via copulation. Some species, such as northern alligator lizards, *Gerrhonotus coeruleus*, and garter snakes, *Thamnophis* spp., bear live young. Most reptiles are carnivorous; to assist in capturing prey, they have clawed toes, strong jaws, and well-developed sense organs. Like amphibians, reptiles are ectothermic: they derive energy from solar heat to raise their body temperatures above ambient air temperature. Turtles, an ancient reptile group, are encased in horny shells into which they are able to withdraw their head, limbs, and tail. The olive to dark brown western pond turtle, *Clemmys marmorata*, is found in ponds and along streams with pools, rocks, and logs.

Quick and agile lizards are commonly seen scampering over rocks in dry, brushy areas. The long tails of many lizards break off easily, which serves to distract attackers; the bright blue tails of young western skinks, *Eumeces skiltonianus*, may divert predators to this expendable body part. Some male lizards defend territories with threats and displays; the blue-bellied western fence lizard, *Sceloporus occidentalis*, bobs its head and does "pushups" as both a warning and a courtship ritual. The four legs typical of most lizards are absent in the California legless lizard, *Anniella pulchra*, distinguishable from snakes by its movable eyelids.

Snakes possess elongated, legless bodies, and unjointed lower jaws that allow them to swallow very large prey. Although they can detect low frequency vibrations, snakes cannot hear airborne sound, and many have poor vision. Their sense of smell is well developed: forked tongues pick up scent particles and convey them to the Jacobson's organ, an olfactory organ on the roof of the mouth. Western rattlesnakes, *Crotalus viridis*, have heat-sensitive pits on the sides of their heads that aid in detecting prey. Rattlesnakes, which inject a tissue-destructive venom into victims through hollow fangs, are the only dangerously venomous snakes along the California coast; most snakes are harmless to humans. Many species such as the gopher snake, *Pituophis melanoleucus*, and common kingsnake, *Lampropeltis getulis*, kill their prey by constriction.

western rattlesnake (*Crotalus viridis*)
1 to 5 feet long

western pond turtle (*Clemmys marmorata*)
3½ to 7 inches long

red-legged frog (*Rana aurora*)
1¾ to 5¼ inches long

Pacific treefrog (*Hyla regilla*)
¾ to 2 inches long

FISH are the oldest and largest group of vertebrates; they are the evolutionary predecessors of all amphibians, reptiles, birds, and mammals. Both in numbers of species and in individual living members, fish outnumber all other vertebrates combined, with 25,000 species identified, perhaps as many as an additional 20,000 species still unidentified, and new species continuing to evolve. California coastal waters are home to at least 525 species of fish.

Most fish can visually distinguish predator, prey, companion, and their surroundings. Some deepwater fish are blind, but the rest see movement, color, and shading variations better than they see shapes. In addition to using sight, many fish also sense their immediate environment with a grouping of pressure-sensitive organs called a lateral line, which runs horizontally from the head along both sides of the body. The lateral line registers changes in water currents and vibrations as water passes around fixed or moving objects; a fish uses its lateral line to sense other animals in the water, and to perceive objects such as rocks and kelp. Some species may use the lateral line to navigate during long migrations, as it enables them to perceive the direction of major ocean currents. Fish also smell and taste chemical changes in the water with receptors embedded in the skin and mouth.

Fish spend the greater part of their lives feeding or searching for food. Fish swallow their prey whole; they cannot chew as mammals do, because to do so would prevent water from flowing over their gills, depriving them of oxygen. Carnivorous fish eat other animals including zooplankton, invertebrates, other fish, or, in the case of sharks, marine mammals. They usually have teeth developed to catch and hold their prey, or to pry or pluck their quarry off rocks. Plankton feeders, the most abundant of all fish, strain phytoplankton and zooplankton from the water with specially developed sieve-like gill rakers. Plankton foragers are usually pelagic, roaming surface waters of the open sea, and often traveling in schools; the smaller fish are a primary food source for larger predatory fish, marine mammals, and seabirds. Omnivorous fish eat plants and animals. Parasitic fish suck flesh and body fluids from other fish.

Reproductive patterns in fish vary with respect to how different species fertilize and care for the eggs. Fertilization can be either external or internal. External fertilization involves simultaneous release of eggs and milt (male seminal secretion) outside the body of the female. In some pelagic species, such as Pacific barracuda, *Sphyraena argentea*, or northern anchovy, *Engraulis mordax*, the males and females swim together and release extraordinary quantities of eggs and milt. In territorial species, such as garibaldi, *Hypsypops rubicundus*, the male or female prepares a nest by rearranging bottom debris or by cleaning a small cave, and then attracts a member of the opposite sex to release milt or eggs. Some fish, such as cabezon, *Scorpaenichthys marmoratus*, guard their nests until the eggs hatch; others, such as king (chinook) salmon, *Oncorhynchus tshawytscha*, entrust the eggs to environmental conditions. Internal fertilization occurs in fish with modified fins or appendages that allow the male to clasp the female and transmit milt directly into her oviduct. Some female fish release the eggs following fertilization; others, such as sharks or surfperch, incubate the eggs internally until they hatch and the young are born live.

Fish coloration often blends well with habitat to aid in concealment from predators. Colorful contrasting patterns, stripes, or spots tend to match varied patterns of algae and invertebrates on underwater rocks; they also serve to camouflage the true outline of the fish's body. Fish in kelp forests have mottled brown and green coloration. The tops of flatfish appear sandy or gravelly to match varied substrates. Surface feeders are often dark topside and light underneath, so that a predator looking down toward the marine bottom has trouble spotting its prey's dark back, and one looking up toward the light sees, at best, a light underside. In many species an involuntary response triggered by light hitting specialized skin cells allows fish to change their coloring to match their surroundings.

Many fish travel in schools, or large groups. Schooling fish may appear to predators as one large animal, creating a larger shape in passing, or producing stronger water vibrations, than each fish would individually. Close packing of fish within a school ensures proximity of simultaneously

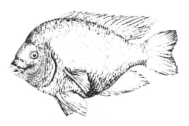

garibaldi (*Hypsypops rubicundus*)
to 14 inches long

northern anchovy (*Engraulis mord*
to 9 inches long

cabezon (*Scorpaenichthys marmoratus*)
to 3¼ feet long

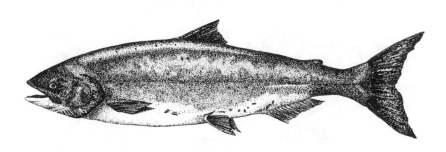

king salmon (*Oncorhynchus tshawytscha*)
to 5 feet long

released eggs and milt; fish may also school to forage together. Different species of fish, such as mackerel and anchovy, can sometimes be seen schooling together.

Fish shapes have evolved to promote individual species' success in different habitats. Many pelagic species have spindle- or torpedo-shaped bodies that allow them to cover distances quickly and overtake prey. Fish inhabiting rocky areas are often laterally compressed for quick turns around rocks and in and out of reefs. Flatfish are horizontally flattened for camouflage on the ocean bottom. Schooling fish tend to have smaller pectoral fins that reduce drag and allow rapid travel in tight aggregations.

Taxonomically, fish are divided into two superclasses: jawless fish, and those with jaws. Fish without jaws, such as the Pacific lamprey, *Lampetra tridentata*, are the closest living relatives of the earliest vertebrates. Jawless fish are largely parasitic and are found in rivers, estuaries, and deep seas.

Jawed fish are subdivided into two more classes: those with a cartilaginous skeletal frame, including sharks and rays, and those with a true bony skeleton—all other fish.

California's nearshore waters offer fish great diversity in prey and habitat. Nearshore schooling fish include Pacific barracuda and Pacific bonito, *Sarda chiliensis*. Pacific barracuda occur in Southern California and grow to four feet in length. They follow warmwater currents, north in summer, south in fall; the young also enter bays. The Pacific bonito belongs to the tuna and mackerel family, characterized by pointed snouts and rapid, long-distance schooling. The white shark, *Carcharodon carcharias*, notorious for its voracious feeding on fish and marine mammals, is found in nearshore waters, especially near islands and coastal areas that shelter seal and sea lion rookeries. It can grow to 20 feet long, and is also found in shallow bays and farther offshore. The striped bass, *Morone saxatilis*, swims along

beaches beyond the breaking surf in spring and summer. It is anadromous—migrating from the sea to fresh water to reproduce. In fall, the striped bass returns from the ocean to bays and deltas for wintering and for spring spawning.

Rocky areas, reefs, and kelp beds are habitats for the greatest number and variety of fish. Along the California coast, members of the rockfish family, sometimes incorrectly referred to as rock cod, are some of the most abundant and diverse fish, with at least 65 known species. They have slightly venomous spines on their heads and fins, and may attain lengths of one to two feet. Fertilization occurs internally, and the young are born live. Rockfish occur in a wide spectrum of colors that distinguish one species from another. The blue rockfish, *Sebastes mystinus*, dark blue with light blue mottling, is one of the few schooling rockfish, and is widely distributed. The kelp rockfish, *S. atrovirens*, often found singly or in large aggregations in kelp beds or reef areas, has a mottled gray and olive coloring that blends well with its habitat. The bocaccio, *S. paucispinis*, a huge rockfish that grows to three feet long and can live to at least 30 years of age, is most often found over rocky reefs or in deep water to 1,050 feet.

The garibaldi is a bright orange fish common in many Southern California reef areas. During nesting, male garibaldi fiercely defend and will not leave their nests, which shelter fertilized eggs. Garibaldi are protected by legislation, and it is illegal to spear or keep one if accidentally caught. Also found in rocky areas are California sheephead, *Semicossyphus pulcher*. Male sheephead have black, humped foreheads, red midsections, and black tails. Sheephead mature sexually as females: at seven or eight years of age their ovaries become testes and they are male for the rest of their lives. The barred sand bass, *Paralabrax nebulifer*, with faint to dark vertical bars on its sides, inhabits sandy bottoms in rocky areas. It resembles the kelp bass, *P. clathratus*, found in or near kelp beds.

Kelp canopies are a favored shelter for the señorita, *Oxyjulis californica*, a yellow, cigar-shaped cleaning fish that nibbles ectoparasites off other fish. The opaleye, *Girella nigricans*, with distinctive blue-green eyes, feeds mostly on seaweed and in spring is found in dense schools in kelp beds. Just outside of kelp beds, especially along submarine canyon drop-offs, the giant sea bass, *Stereolepis gigas*, can be sighted. It can grow to seven feet long, weigh more than 500 pounds, and live to 70 years old.

Sandy bottoms just beyond the breaking surf are favored habitats for flatfish. Flatfish are distinctive for the manner in which the young mature: when they hatch they are laterally compressed like most other fish,

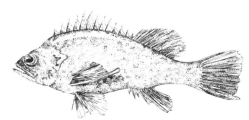

kelp rockfish (*Sebastes atrovirens*)
to 1⅓ feet long

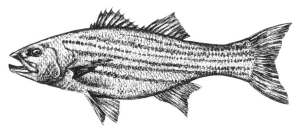

striped bass (*Morone saxatilis*)
to 4 feet long

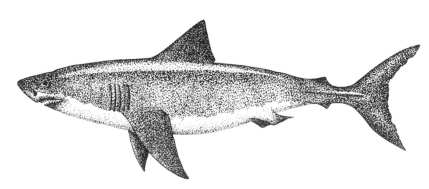

white shark (*Carcharodon carcharias*)
to 20 feet long

with opposing fins and one eye on each side of the head. During maturation, one eye moves to the other side as that side becomes the dominant, colored topside, and the side without an eye becomes the lighter underside. Starry flounder, *Platichthys stellatus*, and California halibut, *Paralichthys californicus*, are common California flatfish. The starry flounder, distinguished by white knobby tubercles scattered across its brown-black topside, may also be found on mud bottoms of estuaries because it can tolerate low salinity. The California halibut is an important sport and commercial fish. It most often moves in summer from deep to shallow waters, where it can be found buried beneath a thin layer of sand. The diamond-shaped bat ray, *Myliobatis californica*, grows to six feet wide, and is found along sandy or mud bottoms near shore, in bays, and under kelp forests. It has a powerful jaw that it uses to pry mollusks off rocks, and a whip-like tail with venomous spines.

California grunion, *Leuresthes tenuis*, were reportedly described by California Indians as "fish that dance on the beach at the full moon." Grunion spawn on the beach at night during peak high tides, during and just after the full and new moons. The female rides the surf to the highest point on the sand, then digs in tail first to deposit eggs, while as many as eight males surround her, releasing milt. The eggs, safely buried and free from the wash of normal tides, incubate during the time between peak high tides, about two weeks. With the next extreme high tide, the eggs hatch, and the young ride the receding surf to sea.

California's offshore waters have less varied habitats and food sources for fish than do nearshore waters. To compensate, offshore fish are able to travel long distances to feed. The yellowfin tuna, *Thunnus albacares*, and the albacore, *T. alalunga*, are large, carnivorous, highly prized game fish caught offshore. The albacore, also an important commercial fish, migrates west in winter, sometimes as far as Japan, and returns to the California coast in summer. The abundant northern anchovy is an offshore schooling plankton feeder also found near shore and in bays.

King salmon and steelhead trout, *Salmo gairdnerii*, both popular sport fish, are found offshore except during spawning, when they can be seen in Northern and Central California estuaries. They are anadromous, and noted for their spawning migration, during which they travel far upstream from hundreds of miles at sea to lay and fertilize eggs in the same area of the gravelly stream where they hatched, which they locate in large part by smell. Salmon can weigh as much as 100 pounds. They make their migration once at four or five years of age, fasting for the entire trip. They die upstream shortly after spawning.

California grunion (*Leuresthes tenuis*)
to 7½ inches long .

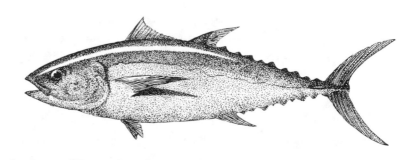

yellowfin tuna (*Thunnus albacares*)
to 6 feet long

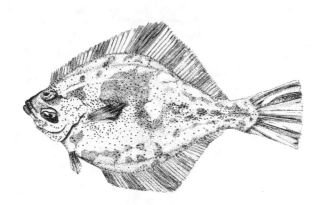

starry flounder (*Platichthys stellatus*)
to 3 feet long

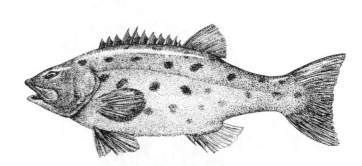

giant sea bass (*Stereolepis gigas*)
to 7½ feet long

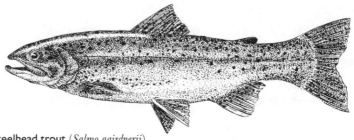

steelhead trout (*Salmo gairdnerii*)
to 3¾ feet long

MILLIONS OF WATER birds and land birds inhabit the California coast. Many are permanent residents, and many more birds visit here while migrating to and from their breeding grounds in other parts of the country or the world. Commonly sighted water birds can be divided into groups that include seabirds, shorebirds, marsh-associated birds, wading birds, and waterfowl. Common land birds along the coast include birds of prey, perching birds, quail, pigeons and doves, woodpeckers, and hummingbirds.

Every aspect of avian anatomy and physiology has evolved to facilitate flight. Feathers, which are unique to birds and enable them to fly, are derived from the scales of their reptilian ancestors. Like mammals, birds are endothermic—able to maintain high body temperatures irrespective of their surroundings; endothermy assures a continued high metabolic rate that gives birds sustained energy for flight. Birds are lightweight and aerodynamically shaped to enhance flight—their bones are laced with air cavities, making their skeletons light, and their weight is concentrated in the midsection. Through evolution, their forelimbs have been modified into wings. Birds' heads have no weighty eye muscles; their field of vision is extended by their extraordinary neck mobility. Also lacking developed jaw muscles, they are able to swallow their food whole; food is ground up in the grit-filled

sanderling (*Calidris alba*)
8 to 9 inches long

tufted puffin (*Fratercula cirrhata*)
14 to 16 inches long

gizzard, which is part of the stomach. Birds' gonads are atrophied to near-weightlessness through most of the year, and engorge only during breeding season. Because birds cannot carry the added weight of unborn offspring, avian reproduction involves external laying and incubating of eggs.

Birds migrate in larger numbers and for greater distances than any other animal group. Migration allows birds to inhabit amenable climates year-round, and to breed in areas that have both abundant food and relative freedom from land predators. Most North American birds migrate north in spring, south in winter. Birds have been found to use landmarks, ocean currents, the sun, stars, or the earth's magnetic fields for orientation during migration. California's coast is the western edge of the Pacific Flyway—one of four major avian migration routes in North America.

Avian breeding behavior may be unique for the exceptional amount of care parents exhibit preparing for and protecting the egg. In most species, males initiate courtship by selecting a nest site and then attempting to attract females with displays of their breeding colors, with ritualized movements, and/or with song. After mate selection, many birds may reinforce pair bonds by joining in ritual dances, feeding each other, or offering each other twigs or other objects. Copulation and joint nest-building follow. In many species, parents take turns incubating the eggs and bringing food to the nest; in some species, only one parent guards and incubates the eggs. Most birds lose their bright colorings after breeding so nests are less conspicuous.

The various groups of birds have special adaptations that enable them to live in their particular habitat. Birds in marine environments have salt glands over each eye that remove the excess salt from their blood that results from ingesting ocean fish and seawater. Most birds have a feather-protecting oil stored in a gland near the tail; this oil, which keeps feathers waterproof and supple, is distributed to the feathers by preening with the bill. In waterbirds, the oil gland is more developed. Most water birds also have webbed feet for paddling or for underwater propulsion. Many shorebirds have spindly legs with slender, splayed toes to facilitate wading. Perching birds have tendons that enable them to lock their toes around twigs, even while they sleep. Birds' bills also vary in shape and function, being pointed for fishing, blunt for hammering or cracking seeds, needle-like for gleaning insects, or sharp and hooked for tearing meat.

Seabirds inhabit the open ocean and nearshore waters. The pelagic species eat, sleep, and sometimes even copulate at sea, landing on islands and offshore rocks only to lay and incubate eggs. These seabirds are rarely seen from the mainland, but can often be observed from ocean-going boats. In late summer, hundreds of thousands of pelagic sooty shearwaters, *Puffinus griseus*, migrate along California's offshore waters to their breeding grounds off Cape Horn and New Zealand. Common murres, *Uria aalge*, and tufted puffins, *Fratercula cirrhata*, roam the sea throughout the year, but appear in spring along the coast from Alaska south to California's islands and offshore rocks, where they breed and nest. Ashy storm-petrels, *Oceanodroma homochroa*, endemic to coastal California, nest in spring in island rock crevices, but then migrate in fall to an undetermined location.

Seabirds inhabiting nearshore waters also breed and nest primarily on islands and offshore rocks, but, unlike more pelagic species, do not remain on the open sea for months at a time. California brown pelicans, *Pelecanus occidentalis californicus*, breed and build their stickpile nests only on the Channel Islands. These pelicans are endangered as a result of eggshell thinning and subsequent low reproduction rates caused by accumulated pesticides in their fish diet. Since 1974, they have appeared to be slowly increasing in numbers after the use of DDT was banned. Another subspecies, the Mexican brown pelican, forages in large numbers along the California coast between June and October. Brandt's cormorants, *Phalacrocorax penicillatus*, are plentiful along the California coast and in coastal bays. Cormorants are often seen perched with their wings outstretched to dry, because, unlike that of most water birds, their plumage takes on water to reduce buoyancy when diving.

Gulls and terns are common along the California coast. Although a number of gull species winter along the coast, the western gull, *Larus occidentalis*, is the only species that breeds here. Terns feed on the wing, or plunge head-first into the water after their prey, whereas gulls scavenge food on land, or fish by alighting feet-first on the water. The majority of elegant terns, *Sterna elegans*, nest in Mexico and South America, but many forage on the California coast in fall and winter. California least terns, *S. antillarum browni*, smallest of the terns, migrate north from Mexico and Central America in spring to nest on beaches and salt-pond dikes along the California coast. They have become an endangered species, their numbers declining due to loss or disturbance of their nesting sites as a result of human activity in their preferred beach habitat.

In winter, shorebirds are found in abundance on tidal flats and ponds, and sandy and rocky shores. Many shorebird species breed on Alaskan tundra, or on the prairies of the U.S. and Canada. Shorebirds often feed in large flocks composed of several species. The greatest variety is found on tidal mudflats; here whimbrels, *Numenius phaeopus*, and long-billed dowitchers, *Limnodromus scolopaceus*, probe deeply for food with their long bills in the mud and sand exposed at low tide. Long-billed curlews, *Numenius americanus*, usually forage in homogeneous flocks, whereas marbled godwits, *Limosa fedoa*, are often seen in the company of willets, *Catoptrophorus semipalmatus*. Western sandpipers, *Calidris mauri*, feed in small flocks, startling into flight and wheeling in unison when disturbed. Strikingly patterned black and white American avocets, *Recurvirostra americana*, sweep the shallows with their upcurved bills.

Shorebirds that forage primarily in rocky intertidal areas include American black oystercatchers, *Haematopus bachmani*, and small congregations of black turnstones, *Arenaria melanocephala*. Flocks of diminutive sanderlings, *Calidris alba*, run after receding waves to forage in the wet sand. Higher up on the beach, snowy plovers, *Charadrius alexandrinus*, chase insects on the dry sand. They are one of the few shorebird species that nests in California, laying camouflaged eggs in depressions in the sand lined with bits of shell. Like least terns, snowy plovers' fragile existence in California is threatened by human impact on beaches.

Salt and freshwater marshes provide more vegetative cover than do tidal flats. California clapper rails, *Rallus longirostris obsoletus*, and California black rails, *Laterallus jamaicensis coturniculus*, are secretive marsh dwellers. Because they are weak flyers, they rely on the pickleweed and cordgrass of the salt marsh for concealment from predators. Both species face a decline in numbers because of habitat loss from marsh landfill and development projects, and from industrial pollution. Wading birds, such as great blue herons, *Ardea herodias*, and great egrets, *Casmerodius albus*, hunt by standing motionless in shallow marsh waters, waiting to take their prey with a quick lunge of their long necks. Snowy egrets, *Egretta thula*, are more aggressive hunters, pursuing their prey in shallow water.

Waterfowl—ducks, geese, and swans—frequent tidal estuaries, marshes, bays, nearshore waters, and inland lakes. A few species inhabit the California coast year-

American avocet (*Recurvirostra americana*)
16 to 20 inches long

snowy egret (*Egretta thula*)
20 to 27 inches long

osprey (*Pandion haliaetus*)
20 to 27 inches long, 4½- to 6-foot wingspan

round; others are migrants, descending by the thousands in fall and winter during their migrations between northern breeding grounds and inland habitats. Mallards, *Anas platyrhynchos*; northern pintails, *A. acuta*; and American wigeons, *A. americana*, common in coastal bays and estuaries, are known as dabbling ducks, because they tip forward to feed just below the surface of the water. Canvasbacks, *Aythya valisineria*; buffleheads, *Bucephala albeola*; and lesser scaups, *Aythya affinis*, are diving ducks that feed along the bottoms of coastal bays and tidal flats, and in calm nearshore waters. Surf scoters, *Melanitta perspicillata*, often dive in breakers near the beach. Brant, *Branta bernicla*, are geese that prefer saltwater habitats and migrate almost exclusively along the coast. Nearly the entire population of endangered Aleutian Canada geese, *B. canadensis leucopareia*, gathers on California's small islands along the north coast during migration between Alaska and the Central Valley. These geese seek shelter offshore, but come inland daily to feed in grain fields.

Coots, loons, and grebes are water birds that are sometimes mistaken for ducks because of their similar shape and diving behavior. American coots, *Fulica americana*, are abundant in marshes, lakes, and mudflats. Long-necked western grebes, *Aechmophorus occidentalis*, and red-throated loons, *Gavia stellata*, frequent nearshore waters and coastal bays in flocks during the winter.

Many species of land birds can be seen along the coast. Vultures, hawks, eagles, and falcons are raptors, or birds of prey, that hunt during the day, relying on their exceptionally keen vision, strong hooked bills, and powerful, gripping talons. Turkey vultures, *Cathartes aura*—large, black birds with reddish, featherless heads—are often seen soaring over coastal canyons and open hillsides. Broad-winged red-tailed hawks, *Buteo jamaicencis*, soar at great heights, whereas northern harriers, *Circus cyaneus*, fly a few feet above meadows and marshes in search of prey. Ospreys, *Pandion haliaetus*, are exceptional divers, catching fish in bays and calm nearshore waters. American kestrels, *Falco sparverius*, are small falcons often seen perching on roadside fence posts and telephone wires. Owls are nocturnal hunters with soft, fluffy plumage that allows silent flight. Burrowing owls, *Athene cunicularia*, nest in abandoned squirrel tunnels on dry hillsides. Short-eared owls, *Asio flammeus*, hunt small animals in marshes, dunes, and grasslands. Two birds of prey now endangered and rarely seen on the coast—the bald eagle, *Haliaeetus leucocephalus*, and the American peregrine falcon, *Falco peregrinus anatum*—have suffered population declines because of pesticide poisoning, habitat destruction, and other human disturbances.

More than half of all known bird species are of the type known as perching birds. Perching birds resemble each other in shape and plumage, and many of them are known for their distinctive songs. Larks, swallows, jays, crows, chickadees, nuthatches, wrens, thrushes, bluebirds, vireos, warblers, blackbirds, finches, and sparrows are some of the perching birds commonly seen along the California coast. Other land birds that are found throughout the coast in chaparral, woodlands, forests, grasslands, and riparian habitats include California quail, *Callipepla californica*, and mourning doves, *Zenaida macroura*, as well as band-tailed pigeons, *Columba fasciata*; Nuttall's woodpeckers, *Picoides nuttallii*; and tiny Anna's hummingbirds, *Calypte anna*.

northern pintail (*Anas acuta*)
20 to 26 inches long

mallards (*Anas platyrhynchos*)
21 to 28 inches long

CALIFORNIA's varied coastal habitats, ranging from coniferous forests to chaparral, oak woodlands, grasslands, marshes, and sandy beaches, support seven orders of land mammals; 19 mammalian orders exist worldwide. Mammals are most easily distinguished from other animals by having hair or fur, and mammary, or milk-secreting, glands. Coastal land mammals include opossums, shrews and moles, bats, rabbits and hares, rodents, carnivores, and hoofed mammals.

Eating, and foraging or hunting for food, constitute the greater part of mammalian lives. The evolutionary development of differentiated teeth, and the ability to hold food in their mouths while breathing, allow mammals to exploit a greater variety of food sources than other animal groups. Herbivorous (plant-eating) mammals such as the California vole, *Microtus californicus*, have incisors for gnawing and/or molars for grinding. Carnivorous (meat-eating) mammals, such as the long-tailed weasel, *Mustela frenata*, have canine teeth and cheek teeth for piercing and slicing.

Like birds, mammals are endothermic—physiologically able to maintain a constant high body temperature without depending exclusively on heat from their environment. Hair, or fur, enhances mammals' ability to stay warm. Some mammals in cold regions hibernate to survive cold seasons; true hibernators, including some California ground squirrels, *Spermophilus beecheyi*, lower their body temperatures to nearly that of their surroundings, concurrently slowing their body processes for weeks at a time. Many squirrels found along the coast do not hibernate because of relatively warm temperatures during winter. Simulating hibernators, such as the black bear, *Ursus americanus*, and the Virginia opossum, *Didelphis virginiana*, sleep for long periods of time in winter, but their body temperatures only fall slightly below normal, and they remain alert and can be easily awakened.

The physiology of mammalian reproduction contributes to mammals' presumed superior intelligence and advanced levels of social development. Placental nourishment of the embryo and subsequent feeding of the young from the mothers' mammary glands eliminates competition among young for survival, and results in mammals spending more time caring for their offspring than do other animals. Because mammalian young do not have to immediately fend for themselves, they have a longer time to learn behavior from their parents, and their brains are able to grow proportionately larger than those of other animals.

The nocturnal and solitary Virginia opossum, easy to identify with its long,

furless tail, pink-tipped ears, and pointed nose, is the only marsupial, or pouched mammal, in the United States. It is ubiquitous in coastal wooded and urban areas. Opossum gestation lasts about two weeks; the young are born in an undeveloped state and climb into the mother's fur-lined pouch, where they attach to a nipple for two months. The opossum was introduced to California from Arkansas in the early 1900s.

Shrews and moles are insectivores. They feed continuously, foraging mostly by their sense of smell, and they spend much of their lives underground. Some shrew species are the smallest known mammals. The Trowbridge shrew, *Sorex trowbridgei*, found in canyon bottoms and on chaparral slopes, grows to two and a half inches long. The broad-footed mole, *Scapanus latimanus*, remains underground most of its life. Its feeding tunnels are often visible in porous soils, appearing as a line of turned-up soil.

Bats, such as the Townsend's big-eared bat, *Plecotus townsendii*, are the only mammals that truly fly. They are nocturnal, supplementing their vision with a process known as echolocation, in which they emit ultrasonic sounds that reverberate back to their highly sensitive ears. Echolocation assists them in perceiving their immediate surroundings. Many bats along the coast are hibernators; they migrate in winter in search of cooler environments. Many bats also have a unique reproductive capability: copulation occurs in the fall or early winter, but females store sperm in the uterus while hibernating, and do not ovulate and become pregnant until early spring, just before they cease hibernating.

Rabbits and hares, known for their long ears and long hind legs, are abundant along the coast. The black-tailed jack rabbit, *Lepus californicus*, is found in meadows, often concealed in tall grass. Its lean, pronounced

black-tailed jack rabbit (*Lepus californicus*)
18 to 24 inches long

black-tailed deer (*Odocoileus hemionus columbianus*)
height at shoulder: 3 to 3½ feet
length, nose to tail: 3¾ to 6½ feet

black bear (*Ursus americanus*)
height at shoulder: 3 to 3½ feet
length, nose to tail: 4½ to 6¼ feet

haunches and exceptionally large hind feet allow it to leap suddenly, and to hop up to 20 feet at a time to escape from predators, at speeds of up to 35 miles an hour.

Rodents, the most numerous of all mammals, are known as gnawing mammals because of the manner in which they use their sharp incisors for feeding and for building shelters. The dusky-footed woodrat, *Neotoma fuscipes*, or pack rat, builds stick lodges in wooded areas. The western gray squirrel,

salt marsh harvest mouse
(*Reithrodontomys raviventris* ssp.)
head & body: 2½ to 3 inches long
tail: 2 to 3½ inches long

Sciurus griseus, and the Sonoma chipmunk, *Tamias sonomae*, can be seen in oak and pine forests, chaparral, and riparian areas, foraging for acorns and seeds. The California ground squirrel is common in grasslands and open areas. It often stands upright on its hind legs on fence posts, or next to its own entrance to a communal burrow. Botta's pocket gophers, *Thomomys bottae*, also dig extensive burrows, depositing fan-shaped mounds of earth at their burrow entrances on the surface. Several coastal rodents, including the salt marsh harvest mouse, *Reithrodontomys raviventris*, and the Morro Bay kangaroo rat, *Dipodomys heermanni morroensis*, have become endangered because of habitat destruction. The salt marsh harvest mouse, one of the very few mammal species known to be able to drink salt water, is endemic to the upper edges of salt marshes around San Francisco Bay, which have been considerably reduced by landfill, salt recovery operations, and building construction. The Morro Bay kangaroo rat's habitat has been greatly reduced in size by residential development.

Carnivores all have teeth adapted for tearing flesh, although some carnivores also eat fruit, plants, and insects. Raccoons, *Procyon lotor*, are common in cities and in wildlands near wooded streams, where they leave human hand-like prints in the mud while foraging for fish, amphibians, reptiles, fruit, insects, and small mammals. The raccoon appears to wash its food before eating

raccoon (*Procyon lotor*)
head & body: 18 to 28 inches
tail: 8 to 12 inches

it, but this is actually a method of heightening sensitivity on its paws, so that while kneading the food the raccoon can discern which parts are edible. The coyote, *Canis latrans*, is most often found in range land, whereas the smaller gray fox, *Urocyon cinereoargenteus*, is more restricted to chaparral areas. Coyotes howl in chorus to keep track of group members after nights of solitary hunting for small mammals and carrion. The gray fox can climb trees in pursuit of the small rodents that are often its prey.

One of the largest carnivores, the grizzly bear, *Ursus horribilis* (the official state mammal), once roamed the Coast Ranges, but is now extinct in California because of excessive hunting. Ranchers in the 1800s offered bounties for grizzlies that were killing livestock, and the bears were also hunted by gold rush miners. The black bear, *Ursus americanus*, inhabits forests in the northern and southern Coast Ranges, foraging nocturnally in a territory of 10 to 15 square miles for grasses, berries, insects, carrion, and fish. The black bear's fur can be black or cinnamon colored. Females breed once every two or three years; in the interim they care for cubs that remain with them for at least two and a half years. The mountain lion, *Felis concolor*, also known as the cougar or puma, preys primarily on deer and elk. It stalks areas as large as 50 square miles in coniferous forests and chaparral-covered foothills in the coastal mountains. The mountain lion is secretive and generally solitary. Females den and give birth in spring in caves or crevices in rocky areas.

Hoofed mammals are mostly herbivorous. They include wild swine, deer, and elk, and many domestic animals, such as horses, cattle, and sheep. The wild pig, *Sus scrofa*, which in California can grow to 350 pounds, inhabits brushy areas and swamps, foraging for acorns, tubers, and small animals. Black-tailed deer, *Odocoileus hemionus columbianus*, are common in the Coast Ranges. The Roosevelt elk, *Cervus elaphus roosevelti*, and the tule elk, *C. e. nannodes*, both members of the deer family, were once plentiful in woodlands and grassy valleys along the coast. Many were hunted by gold rush settlers, and their populations were further reduced when their habitats were altered by cultivation and fencing. A few herds of Roosevelt elk still roam the coastal forests and mountains of Del Norte and Humboldt counties. Several tule elk were reintroduced at the Point Reyes Peninsula, where thousands once roamed, and now a small herd appears to be thriving there. Male deer and elk have antlers, with which they fight other males during the rutting season by interlocking antlers and wrestling to contest harem domination. The mating call of the male elk—a bellow followed by a loud whistle and a series of grunts—is unmistakable.

ABOUT THIRTY-FIVE species of marine mammals occur along the California coast. These species are distributed among three orders: Cetacea, which includes whales, dolphins, and porpoises; Pinnipedia, which includes sea lions, fur seals, and true seals; and Carnivora, with one representative, the sea otter. Like other mammals, marine mammals have mammary glands and a four-chambered heart, bear live young, and have hair in at least some stage of development. The mammalian ancestors of marine mammals were once terrestrial, but tens of millions of years ago they began to adapt to life in the sea. Whale fossils date from 60 million years ago, whereas the earliest known seal fossils are from about 20 million years ago. Sea otters are the most recently evolved marine mammals; their fossils date from about five million years ago. All marine mammals are protected under the Marine Mammal Protection Act; many, including the sea otter and several whale species, are endangered or threatened, and are additionally protected under the Endangered Species Act.

Among marine mammals, cetaceans are the most highly adapted to an aquatic existence. Their bodies are streamlined with few projecting parts; most have no external ears, and genitalia are tucked into protective slits. Normal swimming speeds are about 4-8 knots for whales and 18-20 knots

for dolphins and porpoises. Cetaceans are well-insulated, having a thick fat layer called blubber that ranges from an inch to more than two feet thick. For some cetaceans, blubber also serves to sustain them during prolonged migration periods that may last many months. Cetaceans generally have a poor sense of smell, but they have good vision and superb hearing.

Cetaceans have made numerous physiological adaptations to their marine environment. Sperm whales, *Physeter macrocephalus*, for example, are able to hold air in their lungs for up to an hour, while diving to depths as great as 3,000 feet. This is possible because whales are able to renew up to 90 per cent of the air in their lungs with each breath, as compared to only 10-20 per cent renewal in terrestrial mammals. Cetaceans also have an increased concentration of oxygen-carrying hemoglobin and myoglobin molecules in their blood and their muscle tissue. In addition, they are able to reduce their heart rate while diving.

The order Cetacea is divided into two suborders: the Mysticeti, or baleen whales, and Odontoceti, or toothed whales. Baleen whales feed by filtering large volumes of water into their mouths using brush-like strainers called baleen, often referred to as whalebone. Some baleen whales prey on small fish, whereas those with finer, more closely packed baleen feed on shrimplike krill and other zooplankton. An important group of baleen whales is the finback

whales, or rorquals, which are well represented off the California coast. Blue whales, *Balaenoptera musculus*, are the largest living animals, reaching lengths of 100 feet. They are blue-gray in color, long and sleek, and have a small dorsal fin. Blue whales feed almost exclusively on krill, consuming several tons of these tiny crustaceans each day. Fin whales, *B. physalus*, are similar in body shape but reach a maximum length of only 75 feet. Their coloration is distinctive, with the white of the underside reaching higher up the right side than the left.

Humpback whales, *Megaptera novaeangliae*, are smaller yet, reaching a maximum length of 50 feet. They are black or gray with some white on the throat and belly. The flippers of the humpback are exceptionally long, up to one third of the total body length. Along the California coast, humpbacks range as far south as Southern California in summer; in winter they migrate to warmer waters off Baja and central Mexico. Humpbacks are known for their unique songs and their dramatic breaches from the water. They may be observed in California offshore waters from boats, particularly near the Farallon Islands.

Another important baleen whale is the gray whale, *Eschrichtius robustus*. Gray whales are 35-50 feet long, and do not have a dorsal fin; instead they have a prominent midline ridge extending from the head along the length of the back, culminating in a series of bumps near the tail. They feed

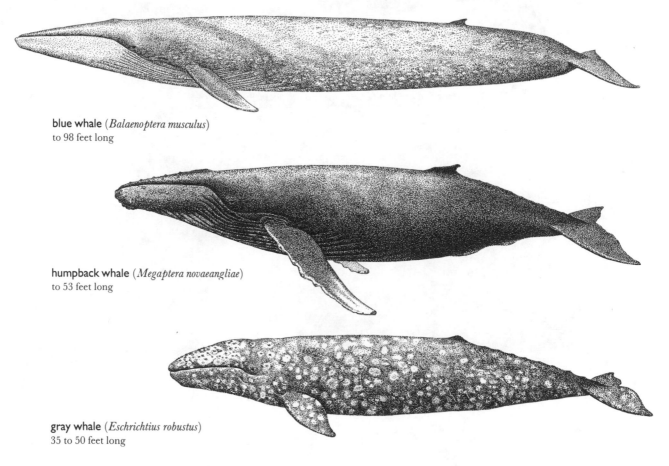

blue whale (*Balaenoptera musculus*)
to 98 feet long

humpback whale (*Megaptera novaeangliae*)
to 53 feet long

gray whale (*Eschrichtius robustus*)
35 to 50 feet long

primarily on benthic amphipods they obtain by stirring up the muddy bottom. In winter, gray whales migrate 6,000 miles from the Arctic to the warmer waters of Mexico and Central America to deliver their calves. Calving takes place in lagoons on the west coast of Baja California. Baby whales are born underwater, tail first, and must swim to the surface for their first breath. Midwife whales may be nearby to assist the newborns, who are up to 25 feet long. Calves nurse for several months on the richest milk produced by any mammal. The milk is 40 per cent fat and nearly 40 per cent protein, with relatively little sugar.

Gray whales often travel only a few hundred yards offshore, and can be observed during their migration (November through early May) along the California coast. Point Reyes in Marin County, Davenport Landing near Santa Cruz, Dana Point in Orange County, and Point Loma in San Diego are prime whale-watching promontories.

The suborder Odontoceti, or toothed whales, includes sperm whales, beaked whales, dolphins, and porpoises. Toothed whales prey on squid, octopus, and fish. The sperm whale, which reaches 60 feet in length, is easily identified by its massive, squared-off head and rounded dorsal fin;

sperm whales can be seen near the Farallon Islands. These whales have been widely exploited for their ambergris (a waxy substance taken from the lower intestine that is used mostly in fine perfumes), their high quality oil, and their bone. Another noteworthy species is the Baird's beaked whale, *Berardius bairdii*, which grows to 35 feet long, with a pointed, dolphin-like beak. Baird's beaked whales, which feed on squid, octopus, and fish, are common along the Central California coast from June to October.

Dolphins and porpoises are the smaller members of the Odontoceti. Those with long beaks are usually called dolphins, whereas short-beaked species are generally referred to as porpoises. The common dolphin, *Delphinus delphis*, and the Pacific white-sided dolphin, *Lagenorhynchus obliquidens*, are the most frequently sighted dolphins along the California coast, especially from August to January. They often run with ships.

Bottle-nosed dolphins, *Tursiops truncatus*, have shorter beaks and stouter bodies than many other dolphin species. They are common in Southern California, especially around the Channel Islands, although they are occasionally seen as far north as San Francisco. Bottle-nosed dolphins are intelligent, and friendly toward humans. Their

large brains and range of auditory communication are thought to be the most sophisticated among all cetaceans.

The killer whale or orca, *Orcinus orca*, is the largest member of the dolphin family. Adults grow to 25 feet in length; their striking black and white coloration, rounded flippers, and large, sharply triangular dorsal fin make them easily recognizable. Killer whales often hunt cooperatively in groups, and may prey on seals, other dolphins, and even occasional blue whales. They have gained a reputation for being ruthless killers, but cetacean biologists have found that they are no more aggressive than other mammalian predators.

The order Pinnipedia (meaning feather feet) includes eared seals—fur seals and sea lions—and earless, or true seals—harbor seals and elephant seals. Pinnipeds are insulated from the cold by fur, a thick hide, and a fat layer; their limbs have been modified as flippers for swimming. Pinnipeds are carnivorous, and feed primarily on fish and squid. Sea lions and fur seals have small external ears, and their hind flippers can turn forward; this is useful on land where they are able to move about quite efficiently. Under water, the foreflippers provide the main propulsion, whereas the hind flippers are used for steering. Fur seals have two layers of fur—a dense undercoat and a coarse topcoat. Sea lions have only a single coarse coat of fur that has never been considered to be of commercial value.

Sea lions and fur seals maintain rookeries on offshore islands and on some isolated stretches of coast where they return generation after generation. Males battle for territory and control harems of as many as 50

Pacific white-sided dolphin (*Lagenorhynchus obliquidens*)
7 to 7½ feet long

Steller sea lion (*Eumetopias jubatus*)
7 to 12 feet long

California sea lion (*Zalophus californianus*)
5 to 8 feet long

54

females. Younger males do not mate until they can successfully defend a territory against other males. The northern fur seal, *Callorhinus ursinus*, is occasionally seen in California waters. Its luxuriant fur is dark brown except for a light patch on the chest. Males may be seven to eight feet long and weigh up to 700 pounds. In California, northern fur seals breed on San Miguel Island in the Channel Islands.

Sea lions are the most frequently encountered marine mammals along the California coast. Steller sea lions, *Eumetopias jubatus*, which are the largest of the eared seals, are found along the entire California coast, but mostly north of Point Conception. Large populations are found at Año Nuevo, the Farallon Islands, and Seal Rocks, offshore of the Cliff House in San Francisco. Steller sea lions are tawny yellowish-brown, up to 13 feet long, and weigh as much as 2,000 pounds. California sea lions, *Zalophus californianus*, are the "seals" seen in captivity at circuses. They are up to seven feet long and may weigh between 500 and 750 pounds. Although California sea lions are seen as far north as San Francisco, their principal California rookeries are on the Channel Islands and at Point Piedras Blancas in San Luis Obispo County. They are most easily distinguished from Steller sea lions by their incessant barking and their smaller size. Males are characterized by a midline ridge on the skull called a saggital crest.

The true seals lack external ears; they cannot turn their hind flippers forward, and are therefore less mobile on land, able only to wriggle on their bellies. Unlike sea lions and fur seals, true seals float in the water vertically, with only their heads sticking out. When ready to submerge, they sink straight down, tail first, rather than diving forward. Harbor seals, *Phoca vitulina*, can reach six feet in length and weigh up to 300 pounds. They have a chunky build and large eyes, and their coats are silvery-gray with black spots. Harbor seals are not as numerous as sea lions, but are common in most bays. Social structure is loose in comparison to other marine mammals; there are no organized rookeries and mating is promiscuous. Northern elephant seals, *Mirounga angustirostris*, are the largest of the true seals, reaching 16 feet in length and weighing 5,000 pounds. Males have large, bulbous, inflatable snouts and rough, dry-looking skin. Elephant seal social structure is male-dominant like that of sea lions; however, rather than defending territories, elephant seal males establish a dominance hierarchy among themselves, and the top-ranking male mates with most females. Elephant seals breed from December to March. Principal rookeries are on the Channel Islands, at Año Nuevo in San Mateo County, and on Southeast Farallon Island.

The order Carnivora has one marine representative along the California coast, the sea otter, *Enhydra lutris*. Sea otters are about four feet long, weigh up to 90 pounds, and have beautiful reddish-brown to black fur, often with silvery or white faces. Because they have no fat layer, sea otters rely exclusively on their thick coats for warmth. They spend considerable time grooming, as their fur loses its insulating properties if soiled; because of this, otters are especially vulnerable to death from oil spills. Their hind feet are webbed, and they have a well-developed tail. Their stout forepaws and blunt fingers are used to capture and hold food. Tool use is well-documented for sea otters, as in higher primates. A small rock is often used as a hammer to open clams and to crack crabs. Sea otters float on their backs and from this position they swim, eat, and nap. Kelp beds are their favored habitat; the waters off the Monterey Peninsula are one of the best natural viewing areas. Sea otters have a high food requirement and must consume one fourth or more of their body weight per day; they eat a varied diet of sea urchins, abalones, crabs, and other invertebrates. Sea otters may live for 20 years, reproducing about every second year between February and June. Birthing usually occurs in water.

harbor seal (*Phoca vitulina*)
4 to 6 feet long

northern elephant seal (*Mirounga angustirostris*)
9 to 21 feet long

Red-headed woodpecker dance, Yurok Indians near Klamath, Del Norte County, ca. 1900

THE PEOPLE OF CALIFORNIA represent many ethnicities, cultures, and languages. Historically, explorers and missionaries, merchant seamen and gold seekers, as well as a steady stream of immigrants from around the world, have disembarked along the California coast. But even before Cabrillo set foot on the shore of the legendary "island of California," it was inhabited by the ancestors of people who had migrated from the Pacific Northwest and the western plains and southwestern deserts of North America thousands of years earlier.

The native people of California, who numbered over 300,000 individuals before the coming of the first Spanish colonists in the 18th century, descended from six linguistic families, or tribes. These tribes comprised many splinter-groups, or tribelets, who had, over centuries, developed distinctive dialects and cultural traditions, and dispersed over a wide territory. The California native groups lived in remarkably peaceful coexistence. Intertribal conflict was rare, perhaps because the land provided more than enough food for everyone's needs. Agriculture, though not unknown, was not developed; in general, the abundance of acorns, roots, bulbs, seeds, herds of deer, flocks of waterfowl, and, in the bays and estuaries and along the coast, congregations of sea mammals and a variety of fish, shellfish, and aquatic plants was more than sufficient to sustain a gradually increasing population. Only after missionization, when they were cut off from their traditional livelihoods and forced to rely on often inadequate mission food supplies, did the native people suffer from hunger or poor diet.

Today the cultural legacy of the California Indians is often obscured by the state's history of immigration since the gold rush. But what we know of the complex cultural and ethnic mosaic that was their civilization shows us a people who, with all their dissimilarities, practiced in common a stewardship of the land that was founded on a belief in the indivisibility of the human and non-human community.

Since 1769, when Portolá landed in San Diego Bay, the 200-year history of immigration to California has been the common thread linking most of its residents, resulting in a population with a complex ethnic and cultural mix of people from most of the nations of the world. By 1900, just a partial list of the nationalities entering California's coastal ports would have included Italians, Portuguese, Greeks, Slavs, and Armenians; Chileans and Peruvians; and Hawaiians, Japanese, and Chinese.

Since the immigrants from China's Kwangtung Province came to seek the riches of Gum Shan, the "Golden Mountain" of the California Mother Lode, immigrants to the state have brought new cultural influences, exploited new resources, and contributed important innovations. Chinese fishermen dried and exported the native shrimp of San Francisco Bay, and introduced culinary arts that are now integral to California cuisine; Japanese immigrants gathered seaweeds and dried abalone. In 1898, the first abalone cannery was established at Point Lobos in Monterey County by Gennocuke Kodani, a Japanese immigrant who developed a specialized diving suit for abalone fishing—a precursor to the modern wet suit. Portuguese sailors from the Azores who first came to California aboard whaling ships in the early 1800s brought with them the islands' native sweet potato; today sweet potatoes are an important commercial crop. From the British Isles and Europe came many of the men and women who figure prominently in California's history. Refugees from Central Europe in the mid-1880s who entered America at the port of New York City often kept going west until they reached the Pacific coast. Adolph Sutro, a Prussian-born Jew who immigrated to Baltimore in 1860, came west during the Comstock bonanza, made his fortune in the mines, and settled in San Francisco to become that city's populist mayor in 1894. A group of Polish and Russian Jews who immigrated to San Francisco in the late 1880s formed a socialist agricultural community in nearby Petaluma that was the first commercial chicken and egg farming operation in California.

During World War I, many Filipinos entered California, as did large numbers of Mexicans. When national immigration quotas ended in 1965, increasing numbers of Japanese and Filipinos entered California's port cities. Since the Vietnam War, a steady influx of refugees from Vietnam, Cambodia, and Laos have entered the country via California, where the majority of immigrants settle at least temporarily. Political refugees from Central America constitute large communities within the ethnic enclaves of California's coastal cities.

Not all immigrants came from abroad; many 19th century Americans left homes and farms in the east and midwest, attracted by the promise of new, richer land in California, or by the lure of its gold mines. Phoebe Apperson Hearst came from her native Illinois to be with her husband, Comstock millionaire George Hearst. A former schoolteacher, Phoebe was an early advocate of higher education for women, and a generous benefactor of the fledgling University of California. In this century, the Depression forced farmers to emigrate from the eroded farmlands and dust-shrouded plains of Arkansas, Oklahoma, and Texas to the more prosperous valley farm towns and coastal cities of California. During World War II, laborers needed to work in California's shipyards, steel mills, and in the aircraft industry were recruited from the southern states, resulting in mass immigration of blacks to the San Francisco Bay Area. American immigrants to California also include Native Americans of many tribes, who now constitute half the ethnic native population; the remainder are the descendents of the six tribes of California.

Coastal Timeline

10,000 B.C.- 19th Century Native Americans

Native Americans inhabit the California coast, subsisting on the natural resources of the land and sea.

Chumash tomol, or plank boat, used for transportation between the mainland and the Channel Islands.

Pomo necklace made of clam shell beads and pieces of abalone shell.

1542-1821 European Exploration and Spanish Settlement

1542 Juan Rodríguez Cabrillo sails into what is now San Diego Bay, which he names "San Miguel Bay."

1579 Francis Drake enters "a convenient and fit harborough" near the latitude of San Francisco; claims "Nova Albion" for Queen Elizabeth I of England.

1602 Sebastián Vizcaíno charts the coast, sailing into San Miguel Bay; renames it San Diego; sails north to anchor in Monterey Bay.

1769 Gaspar de Portolá undertakes overland expedition from Baja California to San Diego; continues north and seeks but bypasses Monterey Bay; sights San Francisco Bay.

Father Junípero Serra, who accompanies Portolá, establishes Mission San Diego de Alcalá, the first Alta California Mission; Presidio of San Diego is founded.

1770 New Portolá expeditions, by land and sea, locate Monterey and establish the Presidio of Monterey; San Carlos Borromeo de Monterey, the second mission, is also established.

1775 Juan Manuel de Ayala, in the ship *San Carlos*, becomes the first European to enter and explore San Francisco Bay.

First rebellion against the mission system by Native Americans occurs at Mission San Diego.

1542, Cabrillo's San Salvador   *1579, Drake's* Golden Hinde   *1602, Vizcaíno's* San Diego

1776 Presidio of San Francisco is founded; Mission San Francisco de Asís established.

1777 Monterey becomes Spanish capital of Alta California.

San José de Guadalupe, first Spanish pueblo in Alta California, is founded.

1781 El Pueblo Nuestra Señora la Reina de Los Angeles de Porciúncula, later called simply Los Angeles, is established.

1782 Spanish presidio is established at Santa Barbara.

1797 Pueblo of Branciforte is established on the site of the present Santa Cruz.

1812 Russians build a trading post, now called Fort Ross, on the Sonoma County coast.

American whalers come from East Coast to hunt whales in Pacific waters.

Flag of the Spanish Empire of 1785

Mission San Francisco de Asís

1821-1847 Mexican Rule

1821 California becomes a province of Mexico when Mexico's independence from Spain is declared.

Cattle hide and tallow trade begins.

1834 Missions secularized between 1834 and 1837. Land ownership is transferred to Mexican "Californios"; cattle ranching is prominent.

1835 Richard Henry Dana sails along the coast; later recounts his adventures in *Two Years Before the Mast*.

1841 First overland immigration to California by U.S. citizens.

Flag of the Mexican Republic of 1823

1846-1848 Yankee Takeover

1846 War between U.S. and Mexico is declared.

Bear Flag is raised at village of Sonoma.

Californian, first California newspaper, is published in Monterey.

1848 Treaty of Guadalupe Hidalgo, ending war with Mexico, is signed; United States formally acquires California.

Gold is discovered by James W. Marshall at John Sutter's sawmill on the South Fork of the American River.

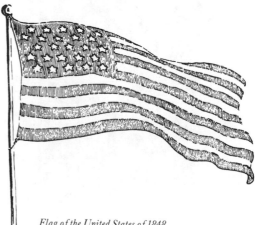

The Bear Flag of 1846

Flag of the United States of 1848

Official flag of the State of California, adopted by the legislature in 1911.

1849   Gold Rush passengers arrive in San Francisco on steamer *California*, which sailed from New York.

State Constitution is adopted at Monterey, which designated San Jose as the first capital of the new state.

1850   California is admitted as the 31st state of the Union.

1851   Capital is moved to Vallejo.

Shore whaling is started in Monterey by Captain John P. Davenport.

First tannery begins operation in the town of Bodega, Sonoma County.

1853   Capital is moved to Benicia.

1854   Capital is moved to Sacramento.

First Pacific Coast lighthouse is built on Alcatraz Island, San Francisco Bay.

1856   Eucalyptus trees are imported from Australia for ornamental use and timber potential.

1861   First oil well in California is drilled at Petrolia, Humboldt County; the well proved unsuccessful.

First oil company, Los Angeles Brea Co., is founded.

Central Pacific Railroad Co. of California is incorporated.

1868   University of California is chartered.

1869   First transcontinental railroad system, the Central Pacific and Union Pacific, is completed at Promontory Point, Utah.

1879   New State Constitution is adopted including provision ". . . that access to the navigable waters of this state shall always be attainable for the people thereof."

1880–1900   The Railroad Era

1880s   Railroads promote California in books, posters, articles, and brochures; property sales boom.

1880   Hotel Del Monte is built as seaside resort in Monterey.

University of Southern California is founded in Los Angeles.

1886   First trainload of California-grown oranges is sent from Los Angeles to the East Coast.

1887   Santa Fe Railway reaches Los Angeles and begins rate war with Southern Pacific; thirty to forty thousand people a month come to Southern California by rail.

1888   Hotel Del Coronado opens as seaside resort in Coronado, San Diego County.

1892   Hopkins Marine Laboratory, Pacific Grove, is founded.

        Doheney and Canfield discover oil in Los Angeles and develop Los Angeles City Field.

1894   California Midwinter International Exposition opens in San Francisco.

1899   Construction on the Port of Los Angeles begins at San Pedro, Wilmington, and Terminal Island.

California-grown oranges

1900-1920   Early Twentieth Century

1900   Mail service to Catalina Island starts via carrier pigeons.

1901   Pacific Electric Railway company incorporated, later becoming the interurban transportation system for the entire Los Angeles Basin.

1902   Big Basin Redwoods are acquired, becoming the first redwood park of California State Park System.

1903   Scripps Institution of Oceanography, then called Marine Biological Association of San Diego, is founded in Coronado.

1904   Venice of the West created on tidal flats west of Los Angeles.

1906   Earthquake and Great Fire, San Francisco.

1907   Surfing is introduced to California at Redondo Beach; demonstrations given by George Freeth.

1911   First studio in Hollywood for motion picture production; Southern California locales were used in movies as early as 1906.

1913   Los Angeles/Owens River Aqueduct is completed.

Pacific Electric Railway

Motion picture production

1914   Panama Canal opens; coastal harbors expand facilities.

       San Diego dredges harbor.
       Long Beach enlarges port.
       Los Angeles builds new facilities at San Pedro.
       San Francisco expands dock facilities.
       Oakland begins additional port development.

1915   Panama-Pacific International Exposition opens, San Francisco. Panama-California Exposition opens, San Diego.

1919   William Randolph Hearst begins construction of his estate at San Simeon on the San Luis Obispo County coast.

       The University of California expands to include a Los Angeles campus.

1920-1930   The Twenties

1920   Population of Southern California surpasses Northern California in decade from 1910 to 1920.

       Aviation industry is established in Southern California between 1915 and 1930.

1921   Oil is discovered at Signal Hill near Long Beach.

1923   Seven U.S. destroyers run aground in the fog 60 miles northwest of Santa Barbara.

1924   Los Angeles Planning Department approves as many as forty new subdivisions a week.

1925   Earthquake causes heavy damage in Santa Barbara.

1927   State Legislature establishes Department of Natural Resources including the Division of Fish and Game and the Division of Beaches and Parks.

1928   Saint Francis Dam, northeast of Ventura, collapses; 400 killed by massive flood through Santa Clara River Valley to the sea.

1929   Pacific Coast Highway, through Malibu, opens.

Curtiss aircraft of the 1920s

Oil derrick

1930-1940   The Thirties

1931   Los Angeles leads the nation in failed businesses.

1932   Tenth Olympic games open in Los Angeles.

1934   1,250,000 people out of work in California.

       Prison on Alcatraz Island is converted to high-security federal penitentiary.

1936   San Francisco-Oakland Bay Bridge opens.

1937   Golden Gate Bridge opens.

       Highway 1, Carmel to San Simeon, opens.

1939   Treasure Island is created in San Francisco Bay for Golden Gate International Exposition.

1940-1950   The Forties

1940   California's first freeway, the Arroyo Seco Parkway in Pasadena, opens to traffic.

1941   Japanese attack Pearl Harbor; United States declares war.

1942   Japanese-Americans are ordered into "relocation" camps.

1943-1945   Wartime production adds workers to aircraft and shipbuilding industries.

Petroleum industry increases production by 50%.

Hundreds of thousands of troops are stationed at coastal training camps and defense bases.

Mitchell Bomber of 1942

1945   United Nations is founded in San Francisco.

1947   California's first regular commercial television station, KTLA, is established in Los Angeles.

Hollywood Ten refuse to testify before Congressional Committee on Un-American Activities.

1949   All employees of University of California are required to sign a loyalty oath.

United Nations

1950-1960   The Fifties

1945-1955   Subdivisions of mass-produced houses constructed as state's population doubles.

1950   California becomes West Coast center of jazz movement; abstract expressionist painting flourishes; beatniks reside in San Francisco.

1951   First scientific diving in the U.S. takes place near Scripps Institution of Oceanography in La Jolla.

1952   Wetsuits for divers and surfers developed in San Francisco by Jack O'Neill.

1953   Congress passes law granting tidelands oil deposits to states.

Disneyland

1954   Independent, noncommercial public television station KQED is founded in San Francisco.

1955   Disneyland opens in Anaheim.

1957   San Francisco and Los Angeles Stock Exchanges consolidate as Pacific Coast Stock Exchange.

1958   Vandenberg Air Force Base is created on Santa Barbara County coast; used for missile testing and satellite launching.

1950-1960   Growing defense industries obtain government contracts for missiles and jet planes; scientists and engineers are employed in new technology centers.

1960-1970   The Sixties

1961   The Beach Boys rock group is formed, making the "California sound" popular.

1962   California surpasses New York as the nation's most populous state.

Congress begins to acquire land for Point Reyes National Seashore.

1963   First nuclear power plant in California opens at Humboldt Bay; it has been closed since 1976 for seismic modification.

1964   Twelve-foot-high waves generated by Alaskan earthquake destroy Crescent City's central business district.

1965   San Francisco Bay Conservation and Development Commission is established by State Legislature.

1965-1970   Vietnam War troops move through coastal defense centers.

1967   "Summer of Love" in Haight-Ashbury district of San Francisco.

1968   Congress creates Redwood National Park in Del Norte and Humboldt Counties.

San Onofre Nuclear Generating Station begins operation, San Diego County.

1969   Santa Barbara Channel oil spill; more than thirty miles of beaches contaminated with oil.

Photos of earth from space are widely circulated; awareness grows concerning finite resources of the planet.

1970-1980   The Seventies

1970   California Environmental Quality Act is passed by State Legislature.

California's economic output exceeds all but five world nations.

1971   San Fernando Valley earthquake.

1972	Proposition 20, the Coastal Initiative, passes, authorizing a commission to regulate and manage coastal development.
	Congress creates Golden Gate National Recreation Area in Marin and San Francisco counties.
1973-1974	Energy crisis; oil prices quadruple.
1975	California's first computer store opens in Santa Monica.
1975-1977	Drought years in California.
1976	State Legislature adopts California Coastal Act of 1976, creating a permanent Coastal Commission; State Coastal Conservancy is created.
	California Conservation Corps is established to accomplish public service environmental work.
1978	Congress creates Santa Monica Mountains National Recreation Area in Los Angeles and Ventura Counties.
	Taxes are cut by state constitutional amendment (Prop. 13); massive reduction in government revenues.

1980-1990   The Eighties

1980	More than 23 million people live in California, about 10.5 per cent of the nation's population.
	Congress creates Channel Islands National Park.
1981	Point Reyes-Farallon Islands National Marine Sanctuary is established.
	U.S. Interior Secretary James Watt proposes opening four basins off the Northern California coast to oil drilling.
1982	Unemployment exceeds 10% in California.
1983	El Niño, a warm ocean current, brings northward migration of southern species of marine life.
1984	Twenty-third Olympic games held in Los Angeles; brings hundreds of thousands of visitors to California's coast.
	Monterey Bay Aquarium opens on Cannery Row.
1986	Diablo Canyon Nuclear Power Plant starts operation on the San Luis Obispo County coast.
	California becomes major center of trade, commerce, and cultural exchange for nations of the Pacific Rim.
1987	California's population reaches 27 million.

Sea otter, Monterey Bay Aquarium

Economic Resources

The economic resources of California's coast are those elements of nature—the climate, water, soil, topography, flora, and fauna—that can be transformed into marketable commodities. This transformation is accomplished by a process as relatively simple as netting ocean fish, or as complex as extracting and refining crude oil from offshore deposits. The amenities of the California coast such as its beneficent climate and scenic beauty are valuable economic resources in a highly mobile culture where the peregrinations of the tourist and traveler are the basis of a major industry. Increasingly, coastal land near the large metropolitan regions is valued as urban real estate; burgeoning populations in these highly urbanized places are contributing to the spread of new residential development along the coast, resulting in urban sprawl surrounding many metropolitan areas.

The industries of California's coast are important in the state's economy. Agriculture and oil are two of California's top industries that are of major importance on the coast; timber, shipping and ship building, and commercial fishing are coastal-dependent industries that grew out of the gold rush economy, and were the basis for the expansion of California's port cities. Military and defense operations on the coast reflect the importance of coastal sites for naval activities and missile launches.

Lumber schooner Bobolink, *Mendocino County coast, 1898*

Tourism and travel-related services are among the biggest revenue-producers in the state, and most of this revenue is generated in the coastal counties. More than half of California's population is concentrated on the coast, mostly in the Los Angeles, San Francisco, and San Diego metropolitan areas, which are the destinations of most visitors.

The first links of a maritime trade between colonial California and New England were established in the late 18th century with the ventures of Yankee fur traders to the Pacific coast. American, British, and Russian ships plied Pacific coast waters in search of valuable otter and seal pelts. When the War of 1812 disrupted whaling in the North Atlantic, the New England industry relocated to the Pacific, and whaling stations were established on the California coast. By 1822, the fur trade was in decline due to overhunting, but the link forged by fur traders and whalers between New England and colonial California enabled development of the highly profitable hide and tallow trade in the mid-19th century. As New England became a center of factory production, Boston merchants saw an opportunity to market their manufactured goods in exchange for California cattle hides and tallow—the raw materials needed for the leather, soap, and candle industries. Between 1822 and 1848, an estimated 1.4 million hides from California ranchos were shipped to New England ports.

To facilitate commerce between merchant ships and the scattered coastal ranchos, a resident-merchant system was established by English and American middlemen in the hide and tallow trade, who centralized the import and export of goods in port settlements such as Monterey and San Diego. These businessmen were the first California bankers, advancing credit to the rancheros who had land and cattle but little capital. The subsequent expansion of ports at Monterey, Los Angeles, and San Diego, and the creation of a commercial port in 1834 in San Francisco Bay at the height of the hide and tallow trade, focused economic development in these ports from the 1848 gold rush to the present day.

In the 50 years following the discovery of gold in California, demands for building materials, food, and transportation were met by exploiting resources such as coast redwood timber and ocean fish, and by development of a shipping industry. Lumber for mine construction and to build and rebuild towns (San Francisco burned five times in the two years after the gold rush began) was supplied by harvesting coast redwood trees from forests that covered an almost continuous 450-

Redwood logging, Mendocino County, ca. 1890

mile-long strip, from the Oregon border to Monterey County. By 1860, easily accessible redwood groves on the east shore of San Francisco Bay and in San Mateo and Santa Cruz counties had been logged, and in the redwood country north of San Francisco there were 300 sawmills.

Making lumber out of the world's tallest living things required an extraordinary amount of labor. Before the innovation of the crosscut saw in the 1880s, a chopper with a long-handled ax might work a 12-hour day to fell an eight-foot-diameter redwood tree. Early lumbering was also inefficient; after a tree was felled, a few logs were cut from the lower, branchless portion of the tree, and the rest was left on the ground and burned. Primitive logging methods in the first 40 years of the industry removed only about 15 per cent of the virgin redwood forest. However, steam engines, drag lines, and bigger saws came into use by 1900, and tractors and portable chainsaws opened up the most remote regions to logging in the 1940s. By 1950 only 10 per cent of the original two million acres of redwood forest remained. Today, Douglas-fir accounts for most of the timber cut in the state; redwood timber constitutes only 19 per cent, but contributes a third of the total value.

The challenge of maneuvering a wooden-hulled sailing ship along the rocky coast of Northern California's redwood country encouraged the invention of a unique hybrid vessel—the steam-schooner. About 1880, the installation of coal-fired steam engines aboard windjammers engaged in the lumber trade greatly improved the maneuverability of the little ships in the often treacherous seas of the Humboldt and Mendocino County

coasts. Steam-schooners plied the coastal waters until the 1920s, carrying lumber to Central and Southern California ports and returning with cargoes of agricultural goods from coastal ranches and farmlands; rail lines connecting the remote Northern and Central California coasts with the state's major metropolises were not completed until the early 1900s.

Until completion of the transcontinental railway in 1869, ocean transport provided the only practical way to move people and goods between the East Coast and California. Ships from New England and Europe had to negotiate the long sea journey around Cape Horn, or passengers and goods had to be transferred to trains for the Panama Isthmus crossing, and then reloaded on the Pacific Ocean side. It typically took six to eight months for the voyage around the Horn, and five to eight weeks via the Panama sea-and-land route, whereas the overland trip from New England took 60 to 90 days on horseback, or three to five months by wagon.

California's early coastal shipping trade extended into the Pacific Northwest and Alaska as well as to New England and Britain. Even after completion of the transcontinental railway, most bulk goods were carried by ships, which continued to be a cheaper mode of transport. In 1868, 20 million bushels of California-grown wheat were shipped from San Francisco Bay ports; wheat continued to be exported to world markets until the 1890s. Ships carrying wheat to Australia and England returned with coal and iron to fuel expanding industries in San Francisco.

Hailed as the "Queen City of the Pacific Slope," San Francisco dominated maritime trade between 1850 and 1900, until it

began to be rivaled by the ports of Oakland, Seattle, and Los Angeles, especially after the opening of the Panama Canal in 1914. As centers of maritime finance, insurance, and warehousing, California's port cities provided the commercial foundation upon which great industrial complexes were built. The ports of Long Beach and Los Angeles are today among the world's busiest, with Long Beach claiming the title of general cargo tonnage leader; together these two ports constitute one of the largest container shipping complexes in the United States, and, along with Port Hueneme (in Ventura County), account for most of the country's foreign auto imports, as well as the import and export of a host of raw materials and finished products. San Francisco Bay has major oil tanker facilities and container ports, whereas fish and forest products constitute the major exports from Humboldt Bay.

Shipbuilding was integral to California's early coastal and transpacific trade; in 1854 Mare Island in San Francisco Bay was chosen as the site of the first Pacific Coast naval shipyard, in recognition of the strategic importance of the deepwater bay to national defense. Wartime ship production in the 1940s spurred industrial activity and was the cause of a population boom in the San Francisco Bay area; military operations in San Diego and Los Angeles during both world wars have contributed to the growth of defense-related industries such as aerospace and electronics. Today the value of federal defense contracts to California industries is twice that of any other state. Coastal military installations occupy over 75 miles, or 7 per cent, of California's shoreline, and include

Port of Long Beach, Los Angeles County

major bases in San Diego, Orange, Ventura, and San Francisco counties.

Commercial fishing in California developed in the first decade after the discovery of gold in 1848, as a growing population created a demand for sources of protein. In the 1850s, most fish from California's coastal waters were line-caught, and herring were seined from the beaches. In 1876, the introduction to San Francisco Bay of the Mediterranean trawl net, or paranzella, greatly increased the potential catch for fishermen. Later innovations in commercial fishing were the use of single-boat trawling and gasoline-powered boats. Perhaps most important to the development of the industry was the introduction of fish canning, which led to expansion of consumer markets worldwide.

In 1864 the first cannery on the Pacific Coast began operation on the Sacramento River, then the largest salmon spawning run in the state. The use of gill nets to catch the salmon eventually resulted in overfishing, and after 1919 the practice was banned on most Northern California rivers. Sardine canning began in San Francisco in 1889, and the introduction of the purse seine a few years later enabled large numbers of schooling fish such as sardine and mackerel to be taken. At its height in the 1930s and early 1940s, the West Coast sardine fishery, centered in Monterey Bay, accounted for nearly 25 per cent of all fish caught in the United States. However, within 20 years the sardines had virtually disappeared from California waters—whether from overfishing or natural causes no one is sure.

The volume of fish caught off California's shores peaked in 1936 at 1.76 billion pounds, but by 1984 had declined to 460 million pounds. Today, tuna and salmon are the main commercial species. The ocean salmon catch is highly variable from year to year, but since the peak landings of over 13 million pounds recorded in the mid-1940s there has been a gradual decline, and only about 2.9 million pounds were caught in 1984. The sportfishing industry relies on such species as kelp bass, sand bass, yellowtail, and Pacific barracuda; party boat rentals for sport fishing are important in local economies, particularly along the north coast.

The first commercial oyster cultivation began in San Francisco Bay in the early 1850s with a species introduced from Japan. The industry in San Francisco Bay reached a peak at the turn of the century, but began declining rapidly due to increasingly poor water quality, and was finally abandoned in 1939. The oyster industry today utilizes Elkhorn Slough and Humboldt, Tomales, Drakes, and Morro bays; seed oysters are set in nursery areas and then are transferred to tideland beds, where they mature in two to four years. Cultivation of salmon, scallops, mussels, lobster, shrimp, and abalones has been less successful than oyster cultivation, although abalone farms now produce a small quantity of the marine snails for commercial sale.

Agriculture in California developed along the coast in the late 1700s. The first crops of wheat, barley, oats, cotton, grapes, oranges, olives, and English walnuts were grown at Franciscan mission settlements. Mission food production was just adequate to sustain the small colonial population, and it was not until the mid-19th century, when the gold rush precipitated a sudden increase in population,

that the coastal terraces and fertile inland valleys were plowed and irrigated.

Although many early settlers came in search of gold, it might be said that California's riches lay not so much in the gold found in the earth as in the soil itself. Commercial agriculture developed first in the San Francisco Bay and Delta regions, then spread along the railroad lines into the interior, where most crops are grown today. Citrus farming was introduced in Southern California in the mid-1800s, and since then a variety of fruits and vegetables has been grown in California's central and southern coastal areas. Today the annual value of the state's agricultural commodities is far greater than the value of all the gold mined in California between 1848 and the Civil War.

California is the world's biggest producer of fruits and vegetables. Agriculture in the coastal counties is characterized by crops such as lemons and Valencia oranges, artichokes, broccoli, cauliflower, celery, and Brussels sprouts, which thrive in the moderate temperatures and rich soils of coastal farmlands. California supplies most of the country's lettuce, and half of the state's lettuce crop is grown in the Monterey Bay area. Most of the state's strawberry, broccoli, celery, and cauliflower crops are grown in Monterey, Santa Barbara, Ventura, and Orange counties. The coastal counties from Del Norte to Santa Barbara are important for livestock and dairy production; Santa Barbara County is one of the world's biggest commercial producers of cut flowers and house plants.

The origins of California's tourist industry can be traced to the 1880s, when the state established a reputation as a land of

Crescent City Harbor, Del Norte County

exotic attractions with the Southern California cultivation of such novelties as oranges, a rare delicacy in 19th century America. The association of the subtropical fruit with California was a boon to the early resort hotel entrepreneurs. Touted as the "Italy of America" by 19th century travel writers, California's southern coast was favorably compared with famous European spas of the day, and by the late 1880s health seekers were flocking to the grand, new resort hotels in San Diego, Santa Barbara, and Monterey. The first direct rail link between Los Angeles and the east, completed in the mid-1880s, generated a real estate boom in the newly accessible region. Immigrants to California were lured by unscrupulous land hawkers and, briefly, by a preposterously low one-dollar rail fare to Los Angeles from St. Louis—a result of the fierce competition between the Santa Fe and Southern Pacific railroad companies.

The first oil well in California was drilled along the coast in 1861 in the tiny town of Petrolia in Humboldt County, but the first oil boom began in Southern California. In 1892, over 300,000 barrels of crude oil were pumped out of the ground in Los Angeles. In 1896, the first productive offshore oil wells were drilled from piers in the town of Summerland on the Santa Barbara Channel. The first tidelands leasing act was passed in 1921, requiring drillers to lease offshore oil tracts from the state, and construction of the first permanent offshore oil platform began in 1958 in the Santa Barbara Channel, several years after state jurisdiction over federal submerged lands was clarified. Offshore wells today supply about a fourth of the state's energy needs; port facilities,

onshore refineries, and petrochemical plants are located all along the coast, but particularly in Long Beach, San Pedro, and El Segundo, along the Santa Barbara County coast, and in San Francisco Bay.

Coastal power plants are a major source of electrical energy for California. Of the 25 major plants on the coast, two are nuclear-fueled, and the rest are powered by oil and gas. Water is used both as a source of steam to drive electricity-generating turbines and as a coolant; water is also used in nuclear-fueled power plants to cool the reactor.

Salt extraction and kelp harvesting are examples of coastal-dependent industries. Salt extraction operations are located in

San Francisco and San Diego bays, where average high temperatures and low humidity results in a high evaporation rate. For each six gallons of sea water, a pound of crude salt is produced from salt ponds over a five year period. In San Francisco Bay, 40 square miles of salt ponds produce more than a million tons of salt annually. The fast-growing giant kelp, a marine alga, is harvested from Southern California's coastal waters and then processed to produce algin, used as a medicinal additive and as a thickener and stabilizing agent in cosmetics and food. The industry, centered in San Diego Bay, processes over 200 million wet tons of kelp a year.

Platform Harvest, offshore of Point Conception, Santa Barbara County

North of Smith River, Del Norte County

Native American
ca. 10,000 B.C.-19th Century

Spanish Adobe
ca. 1770-1850

Hispanic Tradition
ca. 1770-1850

Greek Revival
ca. 1850s-1860s

Gothic Revival
ca. 1860s-1880s

Italianate
ca. 1860s-1880s

Stick-Eastlake
ca. 1870s-1890

Queen Anne
ca. 1880s-1890s

Romanesque Revival
ca. 1890-1900

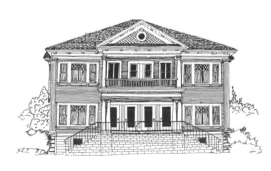

Colonial Revival
ca. 1880s-1920

Mission Revival
ca. 1890s-1915

ARCHITECTURAL STYLE is found in the everyday building, as well as in the monument. In coastal California, for every grand edifice such as Hearst Castle, there are thousands of ordinary buildings that express style in a humbler way. Every town is representative of some period in the state's history, even if it is the easily overlooked recent past. Happily, most of the state's architectural history can still be observed in coastal communities. The variety of building types, often all mixed together in one neighborhood or even in one building, makes the viewing interesting.

The coast has been a focus for new development since the first European colonists established missions at San Diego, Monterey, and Santa Barbara. A visually eclectic community such as Santa Cruz exhibits fine examples of grand Victorian homes, amusement park architecture, resort motels, and modern government buildings. Santa Barbara has a more uniform Mediterranean appearance, but even there variations are evident, from early Spanish adobes to the robust Spanish Colonial Courthouse to the more modern Spanish themes of new commercial buildings.

The first buildings on the coast made use of locally abundant materials and the simplest of designs. Indian dwellings were impermanent structures, built perhaps only of sticks and grasses. The Spanish settlers introduced more durable structures of adobe, another readily available material. Adobe houses consisted of one or more rooms in a row with only minimal window and door openings due to the remoteness of the new settlements from glass and hardware manufacturers. The architecture of the missions recalled in a modest way the more elaborate churches of colonial Mexico. Typical elements include rectilinear building form, round arched openings, and tiered bell towers. Today, many of the mission churches exhibit later, more elaborate additions that mask their original simplicity.

As coastal towns prospered, new settlers undertook more ambitious building designs. Yankee settlers brought sawmill technology, along with their own familiar building styles, such as the Greek Revival. In California, this style was applied to many a wood frame farmhouse. Characteristic features include symmetrical window arrangement and rectangular shape, with a low-pitched roof forming a triangular pediment over the entrance. The Gothic Revival is best known for its use in churches where its vertical emphasis, pointed arch windows, and assymetrical façade recall European cathedrals.

The Italianate style is characterized by ornament with classical references, such as half-columns with elaborate capitals flanking tall windows, and rows of brackets beneath the eaves. Like the Italianate, the later Stick-Eastlake emphasizes the vertical dimension and the picturesque, but differs in its use of thin, jigsawn ornament, exposure of roof braces, and contrasting patterns of wood siding. The Queen Anne style emphasizes elaborate and irregular roof shapes, often with a corner tower topped with a witch's cap, and shingled siding in varied patterns. The Italianate, Stick-Eastlake, and Queen Anne styles, which appeared during the reign of England's great nineteenth century monarch, are referred to as Victorians.

The Romanesque Revival is associated primarily with public buildings or churches, which often are made of stone and use broad, round arches and heavy columns with medieval capitals. The Colonial Revival features careful proportions, symmetrical façade, low-angled hipped or gabled roof, and a one- or two-story porch supported by classical columns.

The turn of the century brought a wave of interest in California's Spanish heritage. The Mission Revival looks backward in a fanciful way through use of white stucco

Covarrubias Adobe, Santa Barbara

Spanish Colonial Revival
ca. 1915-1930s

walls, scalloped parapets with quatrefoil windows, low-pitched tiled shed roofs over window openings, and somewhat ponderous proportions. The Spanish Colonial Revival is more graceful and has come to be the emblem of many California coastal communities. Typical are thick walls pierced by irregularly placed windows, tile roofs, towers with Mediterranean or Islamic motifs, and decorative ironwork. The Craftsman esthetic is best reflected in the California bungalow, a low, one-story house with broad overhanging roof, prominent porch, and ground-hugging landscaping. The Beach Cottage features a simple shape, unadorned façade, and frequently amateur design and construction.

In contrast to the period revival styles, the Moderne is self-consciously up-to-date, within the idiom of the 1930s and 1940s.

The streamlined esthetic includes smooth surfaces, curved walls, and nautical imagery such as porthole windows. The International Style rejects added-on ornament and emphasizes articulation of structural members, horizontal planes, and extensive use of glass, especially in ribbon windows.

Roadside Vernacular style buildings in the shape of giant animals or oranges were once common along California's highways. More examples remain of Drive-In architecture, which features flamboyant roof shapes and bright colors. Also dating from the 1950s are boxy stucco apartments. Typical two-story Stucco Boxes with carports on the ground level make vague references to the International Style through ubiquitous strip aluminum windows and flat roofs, but add abstract ornament to the street façade and perhaps an evocative name incorporating the words "tropical" or "dunes."

The California Ranch House is one of the most durable images of suburban housing developments. Distinguishing features include long, low form, a low-pitched roof of wood shakes, and prominent garage which overshadows the rather inconspicuous entry. The Cut-Out Vertical Box, first used at the Sea Ranch in Sonoma County, emphasizes simple geometric shapes, shed roofs, and wood siding which is often unpainted, evoking utilitarian ranch buildings.

As in previous periods, current building styles reflect elements of the past, often juxtaposed in new ways, along with fresh ideas. High-tech, Post-Modern structures incorporate elements of Streamline Moderne such as ship railings and glass blocks with hard-edged form and square factory windows. A new Spanish Revival is found in shopping centers and condominiums, although its references to the past are often limited to stucco walls and tile roofs or trim.

Tours of architectural and historical points of interest are available in many coastal communities. An excellent walking tour which includes early adobe buildings from the Spanish colonial period is the Path of History in Monterey. Call (408) 372-2608 for details. In San Francisco, walking tours are conducted by the City Guides Program of the public library. Call (415) 358-3981 for information. In San Juan Capistrano, Sunday walking tours begin at the Mission; call (714) 493-8444. Tours which pass grand mansions and the landmark Hotel Del Coronado are available in the town of Coronado; call (619) 435-5993.

Other communities of historical architectural interest include Eureka, Ferndale, Mendocino, Capitola, Carmel, Santa Barbara, Long Beach, and San Diego. Call the local Chamber of Commerce or Historical Society for information.

Craftsman (Bungalow)
ca. 1900-1920

Beach Cottage
ca. 1910-1930s

Streamlined Moderne
ca. 1930s-1940s

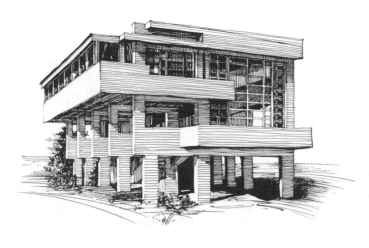

International Style
ca. 1930s-1940s

Stucco Box
ca. 1950s-1960s

California Ranch House
ca. 1940s-1960s

Drive-In Vernacular
ca. 1930s-1950s

Cut-Out Vertical Box
ca. 1960s-1970s

High-tech Post-Modern
ca. 1970s-1980s

Lighthouses

Pigeon Point Lighthouse

THE NAME PACIFIC, meaning "peaceful," belies the harsh reality of California's coastal waters. During the 16th to the 19th centuries, Spanish, English, and Russian sailors learned the fury of this rugged coast when many of their voyages were ended by shipwreck. In spite of the hazards, mariners continued to travel along the unmarked coast.

The King of Spain ordered the California coast to be charted for safe harbors in 1594. The Spanish galleon *San Augustin*, homeward bound from a trip to the Orient, attempted to survey and chart the Northern California coast. Filled with silk, porcelain, and gold, the ship laid anchor near Point Reyes. While most of the crew was ashore, a storm struck, smashing the ship and its rich cargo onto the rocks.

Unfortunately, history was to repeat itself on numerous occasions. It was not until the discovery of gold in California, when shipping activity and shipwrecks increased in frequency, that any attention was given to establishing navigational aids. Once California entered the Union in 1850, shipping interests demanded protection from natural hazards along the Pacific coast. Congress responded by appropriating funds for eight lighthouses, and on June 1, 1854, Alcatraz Island Lighthouse became California's first lighthouse. Its architectural design, a cylindrical tower emerging from a Cape Cod style house, reflected an East Coast influence. Located in San Francisco Bay, Alcatraz Island is more commonly noted for the federal prison that later overshadowed the original lighthouse. Today, the island and prison are open to the public as a national park.

The U.S. Lighthouse Service established its first Pacific Coast headquarters in San Francisco in 1852. Three of the original eight West Coast lighthouses were constructed in the San Francisco Bay area—at Alcatraz Island, Fort Point, and Southeast Farallon Island. The remaining five lighthouses were located at strategic points ranging from Cape Disappointment in Washington to Point Loma at the entrance to San Diego Bay.

In time, California was to have 48 lighthouses beaming from her shores; 33 are still standing. The locations and architectural styles were largely determined by the topography, the lens specifications, and the local availability of materials. A few were built in the Victorian style, popular during the late 1800s. Good examples of these are East Brother Lighthouse in San Francisco Bay and Point Fermin Lighthouse near the San Pedro/Long Beach Harbor. Pigeon Point Lighthouse, on the San Mateo County coast, displays the classic 1870s design of a towering brick spire guarding the edge of the continent.

The northernmost California lighthouse, at Saint George Reef, was also the most expensive to construct. Completed in 1891, it took ten years to build, at a cost of $704,633. The hazardous environment—a dangerous sea-swept rock—coupled with exorbitant maintenance costs resulted in the Coast Guard's decision to abandon this lighthouse in 1975.

California's first lighthouses were constructed during a time of transition in lighthouse development. The lighting was being changed from the older, and less efficient, Argand lamps to the more modern biconvex Fresnel lenses. This new optic consisted of a single light source, refracted, reflected, and magnified through glass prisms into a brilliant, concentrated beam of light. The Fresnel lens resembles a giant beehive of glass and brass.

Early lighthouses required constant attention from the "wickies," as keepers were

Point Bonita Lighthouse, Marin County

called. The brass and glass needed frequent cleaning; the wicks had to be trimmed; the fuel had to be replenished; and the cannons, the fog bells, and the flashing mechanisms at the light stations needed to be serviced. Provisions were furnished by supply ships that visited the remote sentinels quarterly.

Technological advances changed the form and function of lighthouses and their resident keepers' duties. The U.S. Coast Guard took over the U.S. Lighthouse Service in 1939, and began automating the lighthouses and radio beacons in the 1960s. Consequently, many of the civil service lighthouse keepers retired soon after the Lighthouse Automation and Modernization Program (LAMP) was instituted. In 1949, the Coast Guard built a "robot light," the first totally automated unit, equipped with a light, foghorn, and radio beacon all in a rectangular tower. Henceforth, the look

of lighthouses changed dramatically from a solid shaft topped with a multi-faceted lantern, to a skeletal tower or steel pole with a rotating aero beacon.

Most of the original lighthouses have been abandoned or even razed. Even though many are considered historical landmarks, increasing maintenance costs jeopardize their future; the Coast Guard has been working with public agencies and non-profit organizations to lease and restore abandoned lighthouses. Maritime museums now occupy several former lighthouses, and Pigeon Point, Point Montara, and Point Arena Lighthouses now have overnight visitor accommodations. A nationwide association, the United States Lighthouse Society in San Francisco, hopes to generate widespread interest in restoring lighthouses; call: (415) 585-1303.

Point Fermin Lighthouse

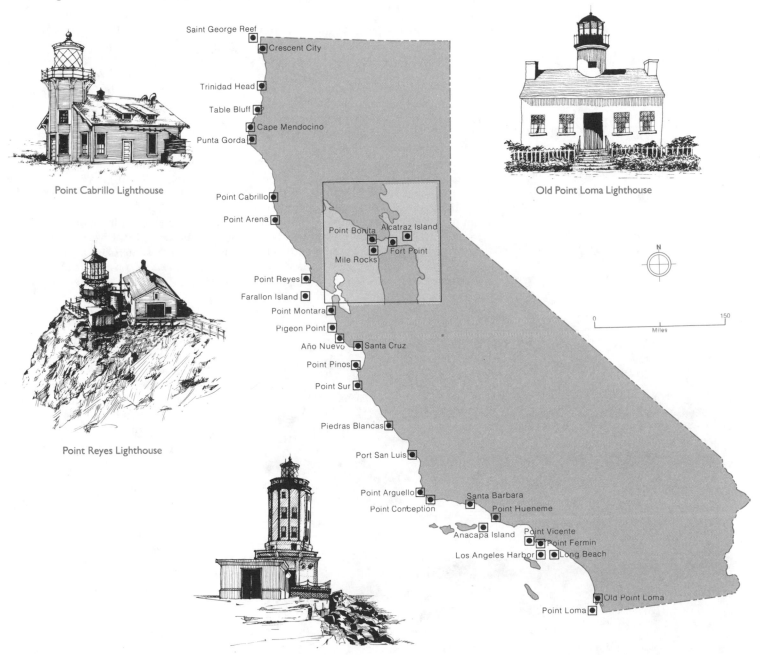

Point Cabrillo Lighthouse

Point Reyes Lighthouse

Old Point Loma Lighthouse

Los Angeles Harbor Lighthouse

Saint George Reef
Crescent City
Trinidad Head
Table Bluff
Cape Mendocino
Punta Gorda
Point Cabrillo
Point Arena
Point Bonita
Alcatraz Island
Fort Point
Mile Rocks
Point Reyes
Farallon Island
Point Montara
Pigeon Point
Año Nuevo
Santa Cruz
Point Pinos
Point Sur
Piedras Blancas
Port San Luis
Point Arguello
Santa Barbara
Point Conception
Point Hueneme
Anacapa Island
Point Vicente
Point Fermin
Los Angeles Harbor
Long Beach
Old Point Loma
Point Loma

N

0   150
Miles

Following a horseback tour of the California coast in 1913, author J. Smeaton Chase wrote of Point Lobos:

Point Lobos State Reserve, Monterey County

Pines grew here along the cliff, outlining with tawny stem and dark magnificence of foliage the most exquisite of vistas. The coast was broken by little bays full of brown seaweed that rose and fell indolently with the slow breathing of the sea. Islets were scattered along as if they had been dropped like pebbles out of a full hand. I do not think there can be anywhere on our shores a more enchanting piece of coast than this and the next ten miles to the north. It is the acme of what is generally named the romantic in sea scenery, and is calculated, I should think, to throw an artist into a frenzy in which he would paint one final and conscious masterpiece, then close color-box, camp-stool, and umbrella, and hurl them all over the cliff together.

California Coast Trails—
A Horseback Ride from Mexico to Oregon

EARLY CHRONICLERS of California's golden shore often spent all their grand prose describing the view, as if no other enjoyment of the coast were possible. Nowadays people find a multitude of recreation opportunities on the coast, from capturing with paint box or camera the ever-popular views to more athletic pursuits like surfing or hang gliding. At its most basic, coastal recreation requires little more than a picnic basket or a beach blanket. But recreation may also encompass learning about early settlers or inspecting the inhabitants of tidepools. California's State Park system has the triple goals of preserving the state's cultural heritage, protecting natural resources, and providing pure recreation.

Many state parks include campgrounds, but overnight opportunities are not limited to conventional family campgrounds. Some state parks include environmental campsites developed with minimal landscape disturbance, while certain especially popular parks include enroute camping areas for one-night-only occupancy by recreational vehicles. Equestrian camping facilities are available at several coastal parks, including Topanga State Park near Los Angeles. Wheelchair-accessible facilities are found at most units of the state park system.

Fort Ross State Historic Park offers a unique view of a one-time Russian settlement on California's shore. Wildlife can be seen close-up at Año Nuevo State Reserve where visitors share the sand dunes with wintering elephant seals, or at Torrey Pines State Reserve where dolphins and porpoises swim below the cliffs. Clamming is popular at Pismo Beach State Park. Several state parks include undersea areas, such as the Point Lobos State Reserve near Carmel which includes 775 acres of offshore marine wilderness, part of which is available to scuba divers for exploration and underwater photography. Bird watchers have plenty to do most anyplace along the coast, but especially near coastal streams and wetlands and during peak winter migrations. For information on California State Parks, call: (916) 445-6477; for reservations, call: 1-(800)-446-7275. For information on environmental camping, disabled veterans camping, and Steep Ravine Cabins, call: (916) 323-2988.

Federally operated coastal recreation areas provide a wide spectrum of recreational opportunities. The Golden Gate National Recreation Area includes the headlands of San Francisco Bay and shoreline units in three counties. The National Maritime Museum at Aquatic Park in San Francisco features nautical exhibits and a chance to tour several historic ships moored nearby. Adventurous souls may enjoy hang gliding on the updrafts at the Fort Funston bluffs, while those who prefer to keep their feet on the ground may hike the network of trails overlooking both sides of the Golden Gate. Together, the units of the GGNRA serve over 16 million visitors annually, more than any other in the 336-unit National Park Service system.

Visitors seeking respite from urban delights need not look far; the Point Reyes

Cabrillo Beach, Los Angeles County

Off Dockweiler State Beach, Los Angeles County

National Seashore in Marin County offers many miles of remote beaches for exploring. Part of Point Reyes is a designated wilderness. Visitors to the National Seashore may learn lessons about the earth's changing surface in the rift valley of the San Andreas Fault near Olema, where the great 1906 earthquake was centered.

The Santa Monica Mountains National Recreation Area is a haven of open space for the Los Angeles metropolitan area. Surfing and sunning on the Malibu beaches are world famous; less well known are the miles of hiking and equestrian trails through the canyons and ridges of the adjoining Santa Monica Mountains. Scenic Mulholland Drive winds along the spine of the mountains from central Los Angeles west to the Ventura County line; an unpaved portion west of the San Diego Freeway seems pleasantly at odds with its metropolitan setting.

Other federal coastal parks include Redwood National Park, with over 100,000 acres of forests and streams in Humboldt and Del Norte counties, the Channel Islands National Park and Marine Sanctuary off the state's south coast, and Cabrillo National Monument at Point Loma in San Diego. An important federal holding outside the National Park Service system is the 60,000-acre King Range along the coast of southern Humboldt and northern Mendocino counties. Designated as a National Conservation Area by the Bureau of Land Management, the King Range encompasses the largest roadless area on the California coast. Hiking, fishing, and the search for solitude on a wild and natural shoreline are prime pursuits here.

Fishing is an important element of the coastal recreation scene. Those on shore can fish for surfperch or catch grunion. Party boats depart from many coastal ports in search of salmon, rockfish, bonita, or mackerel. Ocean piers provide an easy introduction to ocean fishing: no license is required on public piers. Boating is popular everywhere. Launching facilities and boating supplies are found along most stretches of the California coast, with a concentration along the more gentle waters from Point Conception to the Mexican border.

Development of a California Coastal Trail along the entire coast is a priority of the Coastal Commission, the Coastal Conservancy, and the Department of Parks and Recreation. Some segments of the trail through public recreation areas or along beaches are already available; other links await land acquisition or development. The Pacific Coast Bicentennial Bike Route, established in 1976 and designated by signposts, stretches the length of the coast.

Overnight lodgings along the coast include luxury hotels with world-class golf courses as well as simple inns in historic homes. Eighteen hostels from Arcata to Imperial Beach provide low-cost accommodations to both old and young. Additional hostels are planned so that any one facility will be no more than 20 to 30 miles from the next, encouraging use by travelers without motorized vehicles. Shopping and dining facilities are available on most parts of the coast, especially at old fishing ports and along urban waterfronts. The Monterey Bay Aquarium and Sea World in San Diego provide outstanding exhibits of marine resources in spectacular settings.

IN THE LATE NINETEENTH century, amusement parks and pleasure piers provided visitors a way to enjoy California's scenic coastline and temperate climate. Simple amusements such as saltwater plunges and boardwalks for strolling were followed in the early twentieth century by games with kewpie doll prizes and rides meant to frighten the customer into having a good time. Since World War II the number of shoreline amusement parks has dwindled, and today only Santa Cruz's historic oceanfront amusement park remains.

Santa Cruz was a resort destination long before its beachfront amusement park began to take form. As early as 1868, the beach adjacent to the mouth of the San Lorenzo River was the setting for a bathhouse, swimming tank, and entertainment house. By 1903, the present Boardwalk began to emerge. After the 1904 Casino burned, a second, grander edifice replaced it, this one in wildly eclectic Mission Revival style adorned with domes and obelisks. John Philip Sousa and his band performed at the opening. Other amusements appeared, including the pleasure ship, the *Balboa*, moored offshore in 1907 and reputedly available for illicit delights.

The first small railway ride at Santa Cruz designed purely for amusement was built in 1884 and reached the dizzying height of 24 feet above the ground. In 1908 a new, 1,050-foot-long "scenic railway" appeared, said at the time to be the longest in the United States. Today's great wooden seaside roller coaster dates from 1923-24 and is still in use. The Giant Dipper reaches a height of 70 feet above ground and provides a delightfully terrifying ride just under two minutes long.

The carousel at Santa Cruz, created in 1911, features 62 horses hand-carved by Charles Looff, creator of classic carousels. The Boardwalk also features some 22 other rides including a Ferris wheel, logchute, bumper cars, and games of skill and chance. The amusements are open daily from mid-May to mid-September and on weekends and holidays the rest of the year (400 Beach Street, Santa Cruz, 408-426-7433).

San Francisco's Playland-at-the-Beach originated in 1928 as Whitneys-at-the-Beach. The park featured inventions of owner George Whitney such as the Photo-While-You-Wait booth and cartoon cutouts for snapshot poses. At its peak, the park covered most of five city blocks at Ocean Beach between the Cliff House and Golden Gate Park. Features included a carousel of Charles Looff design, the Big Dipper roller coaster, and the Fun House, where visitors were greeted with relentless hilarity by mechanical Laughing Sal. The park was torn down in 1972.

Although all traces of San Francisco's Playland are gone from the site, the carousel has taken on new life at Shoreline Village in Long Beach, an area of shops and restaurants adjacent to the Long Beach Downtown Marina. The carousel was created about 1906 and spent seven years at Luna Park in Seattle, as well as some 44 years in San Francisco, before reopening in Long Beach in 1982. There are 50 horses with real horsehair tails, four each of camels, giraffes, and rams, and four chariots, all handsomely restored in jewel-bright colors.

At one time, Santa Monica Bay in Los Angeles County featured three major amusement parks located seaward of the surf on piers. Ocean Park Pier at the south edge of Santa Monica featured a "scenic railway" and other attractions as early as 1905. South of Ocean Park, developer Abbott Kinney built Venice, a theme community based on canal-side living. By 1905, Kinney, who had been responsible for the earlier development at Ocean Park, had built the Venice Pier with a pavilion, auditorium, and ship-hotel. Kinney strove for a refined, sober atmosphere with cultural amenities such as classical sculpture, grand opera, and an aquarium.

As time went on, amusement parks became gaudier, and perhaps more entertaining. After a 1920 fire, the Venice Pier was rebuilt as a full-scale amusement park with rides and games. At Santa Monica, the area's third major amusement park pier was built after World War I, featuring a roller coaster, ballroom, and vibrantly colorful hand-carved carousel.

The introduction of roller skates in 1871 started a craze in Los Angeles that peaked in the 1880s with newspaper editorial concern for pedestrian safety on downtown sidewalks. However, skating was not a specially popular pastime at the beach, as it is today, nor was bicycling, which came into vogue in the 1880s. When the early beach

The Giant Dipper at Santa Cruz Boardwalk

resorts were being built, swimming and tanning were not the major reasons for going to the beach; surfing was introduced to California from Hawaii in 1907, but attracted a limited following until lightweight fiberglass boards were developed in the 1950s. The amusement piers provided something to do at the beach in an era when standards of modesty required people to remain more or less fully dressed when in public.

As tastes in recreation changed, so did the amusement parks. The Venice Pier disappeared in the late 1940s, and the Ocean Park Pier had one last gasp as Pacific Ocean Park in the late 1950s before it too vanished. Today, of the three amusement park piers, only the Santa Monica Pier remains. The Blue Streak Roller Coaster is long gone, but a few rides remain, along with a game arcade, restaurants, and seafood sales. The great carousel has been restored, and the city plans future improvements to the pier.

Redondo Beach was promoted as a resort destination as early as the 1880s. A branch railroad line brought cargo to the shipping wharves and visitors to the Redondo Hotel, Carnation Gardens, and the shoreline. Later improvements included a music pavilion, a concrete U-shaped "Endless Pier," and, in the 1920s, a roller coaster perched on the sandy beach. Today near the foot of Torrance Boulevard are a series of piers and the International Boardwalk featuring the Fun Factory, a small-scale amusement center with several rides and many games.

Nearby are the Redondo Beach Marina and other attractions.

The Pike, an amusement park in Long Beach, appeared in the 1880s. Rides and carnival attractions were added until eventually the Pike became so typical of the species that it was used regularly by Hollywood for location shots. The Cyclone Racer roller coaster was a major attraction until 1968. Soon after, most of the park was demolished. The few remnants off Ocean Boulevard near downtown include the building in which Charles Looff created his

Venice Pier, ca. 1905

classic amusements after he moved to Long Beach in 1910.

The Fun Zone on Balboa Peninsula in Orange County is a small amusement area created in the 1930s at Bay Front Walk near the Balboa Ferry landing. The Fun Zone features a Ferris wheel, carousel, and other attractions.

San Diego's oceanfront amusement park was the Belmont Amusement Center on Mission Beach. The centerpiece of the park was the 1925 woodframe Giant Dipper roller coaster which rises 75 feet above the ground. Although out of commission since 1976, the coaster still stands, having survived at least two fires and years of neglect. The coaster is now on the National Register of Historic Places, and local preservationists are seeking to save it from destruction, perhaps in conjunction with a roller coaster museum.

Redondo Beach, ca. 1924

Del Norte County
Selected Species of Interest

Plants: Sand dune phacelia (*Phacelia argentea*), endangered; grows in dunes near Lakes Earl and Talawa. **Redwood sorrel** (*Oxalis oregona*), found in redwood and Douglas-fir forests; has glossy, clover-like leaves.

Trees: Coast redwood (*Sequoia sempervirens*), restricted to a narrow strip along the Northern California coast in moist, foggy areas. **Sitka spruce** (*Picea sitchensis*), conifer found on coastal bluffs and in redwood forests.

Insects: Carolina grasshopper (*Dissosteira pictipennis*), very large, has black hind wings with yellow edges; found in open fields and pastures. **Great tiger moth** (*Arctea caja*), largest tiger moth; inhabits forested areas.

Invertebrates: Rocky coast snail (*Monadenia fidelis pronotis*), uncommon snail found on marine terraces near Point St. George. **Sun star** (*Pycnopodia helianthoides*), ten-armed sea star, inhabits low intertidal at Enderts Beach.

Amphibians and Reptiles: Del Norte salamander (*Plethodon elongatus*), inhabits damp coastal forests. **California slender salamander** (*Batrachoseps attenuatus*), short-limbed and slim; found under logs and in leaf-litter.

Fish: Steelhead trout (*Salmo gairdnerii*), anadromous; spawns in Smith and Klamath rivers. **Eulachon** (*Thaleichthys pacificus*), anadromous sport fish; also called candlefish; Indians used dried fish as torches.

Birds: Common murre (*Uria aalge*); large breeding colonies on False Klamath and Castle rocks. **Aleutian Canada goose** (*Branta canadensis leucopareia*), endangered; gathers at Castle Rock to rest and feed during migration.

Land Mammals: Mountain beaver (*Aplodontia rufa*), rodent found in Del Norte Coast Redwoods State Park. **Ringtail** (*Bassariscus astutus*), nocturnal, squirrel-sized carnivore that inhabits brush and woodlands near streams.

Marine Mammals: Steller sea lion (*Eumetopias jubatus*), common in ocean waters near Smith River mouth. **Northern elephant seal** (*Mirounga angustirostris*), largest seal species; has been sighted near Castle Rock.

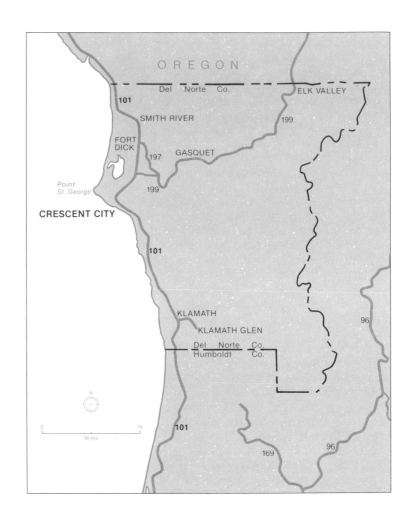

Del Norte County

DEL NORTE COUNTY lies in the extreme northwest corner of California. The county's 42-mile-long coastline begins at the Oregon border, and is characterized in the north by narrow sandy beaches and low-lying terraces, which widen into a coastal plain that contains the floodplain of the Smith River and the scenic Lakes Earl and Talawa. Northwest-trending dunes fringe the western edge of the coastal plain as far south as the windswept Point St. George. Crescent City, sheltered by the curve of Crescent Bay, is situated on a wide coastal terrace that extends south to the rugged, rocky shore near Enderts Beach. Farther south, the coastline is typified by high, eroded cliffs that stretch to the mouth of the Klamath River. The county's south coast is dominated by the dense redwood and Douglas-fir forests of Del Norte Coast Redwoods State Park and Redwood National Park.

Del Norte's first inhabitants were the Tolowa and Yurok Indians, who occupied the area for 2,000 years before being driven out by white settlers in the late 1800s. The Tolowa lived in the Smith River area, whereas the Yurok lived in villages along the banks of the Klamath and on the coast near lagoons and at the mouths of streams. Both groups were hunter-gatherers who subsisted on mollusks, acorns, fish, and water birds, and hunted marine mammals from redwood dugout canoes.

During his 1828 expedition, trapper-explorer Jedediah Smith became the first white man to enter what is now Del Norte County, but it was not until the discovery of gold on the Trinity River in 1850 that settlers began to flock to California's north coast. Many were drawn to the area by tales of the "lost cabin," which supposedly contained gold hidden by a legendary prospector. In 1851, a schooner arrived at the mouth of the Klamath River, and settlers established a community called Klamath City. The town grew rapidly, attracting prospectors and traders in search of gold on the Klamath, but its prominence was short-lived, and the town was deserted by 1852. The need for a north coast seaport led to the establishment of Crescent City, which was laid out in 1853 and soon became chief port of entry and supply center for the area. As the population grew, the demand for farm products increased, and the Smith River floodplain was exploited for agricultural development; in 1853 the town of Smith River was established. By 1857 ferries were operating on the Smith and Klamath rivers, and a road was later built between Smith River and Crescent City.

Hostilities between the Indians and white settlers began as early as 1853; numerous injustices and atrocities were committed against the Indians. In 1855 the Klamath River Reservation was formed to contain the Indians, and in 1862 a new reservation was established at the mouth of the Smith River. The Indians were removed to the Hoopa Valley Reservation inland in 1870.

During and after the Civil War the county experienced a brief flurry of mining activity, which died down by the 1870s. In 1869 a lumber company was formed in Crescent City to exploit the area's extensive forests, and a mill was established soon afterwards on Lake Earl. Trees at first were floated to the mills or moved by oxen. The logging railroads arrived in the 1870s, and by 1880, lumber production had become Del Norte's major industry. Around 1890 a narrow-gauge railroad was built from Smith River to Crescent City to facilitate movement of logs. In the early 1900s a commercial salmon fishery thrived on the Smith River until beach seines and gill nets were declared illegal in the 1930s. Crescent City Harbor served the incoming commercial fishing fleet. Harbor and railroad developments, new highways, and an increase in the price of lumber and fish led to a population boom in the 1920s and 1930s.

The Depression nullified much of the preceding economic growth of the county, but following World War II, the price of lumber rose again; increased lumber employment and the completion of Citizen's Dock in Crescent City in 1950 stimulated a new wave of economic growth. Fish landings at Crescent City doubled from 1950 to 1960, and the cultivation of lilies and daffodils significantly increased the value of agricultural output. Improved highways and higher incomes brought more tourists to the county, and between 1950 and 1960 the population surged.

In the late 1950s, however, the county's economic growth was again arrested; mining and lumber employment declined due to lack of demand, continuing into the 1960s. Timber-related industries, such as trucking and heavy equipment, began to decline as well. Many small mills closed permanently, and the county's population dropped as mill workers left.

Today Del Norte's major industries are lumber, tourism, and agriculture, including flower bulb production, dairy products, livestock production, and field crops. The county's two major rivers, the Smith and the Klamath, support important spawning runs of salmon and steelhead trout, and attract large numbers of anglers year-round. Tourists are also drawn to the county's two redwood state parks and to Redwood National Park.

Fishing at the Klamath River mouth, ca. 1955

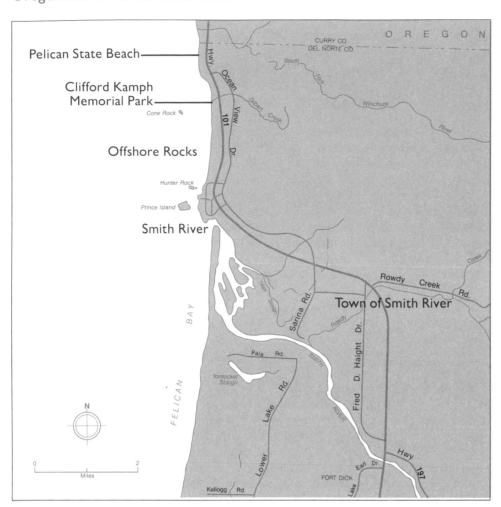

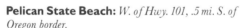

Brandt's cormorant (*Phalacrocorax penicillatus*)
33 to 35 inches long, 4-foot wingspan

Pelican State Beach: *W. of Hwy. 101, .5 mi. S. of Oregon border.*

Pelican State Beach is a five-acre sandy beach with grass-covered dunes and abundant driftwood. The beach, used for beachcombing and surf fishing, is accessible via a steep dirt path off Highway 101 near the Nautical Inn. Coastal scrub and Sitka spruce cover the bluffs and terraces that back the beach, which is habitat for shorebirds and other water-associated birds. Nearshore fish include cabezon, lingcod, and several species of rockfish; surfperch, Pacific sanddab, and starry flounder are found in the surf zone. Fishermen trawl offshore for bottom fish such as bocaccio, flounder, and sole.

Clifford Kamph Memorial Park: *W. of Hwy. 101, 2 mi. S. of Oregon border.*

Popular for surf fishing, the park has picnic tables, wheelchair-accessible restrooms, and a trail and stairway to the beach. The land for the park was deeded to the county as a memorial in 1956; the park was renovated in 1976.

Offshore Rocks: *Offshore, between Kamph Memorial Park and Smith River mouth.*

Cone Rock, Hunter Rocks, and Prince Island are all important rookery and roosting areas for both resident and migratory birds. Forty-six per cent of all seabird nesting sites on coastal rocks in California occur on Hunter Rocks, Prince Island, Castle Rock (north of Crescent City), and False Klamath Rock (near Lagoon Creek).

Cone Rock, offshore of Kamph Memorial Park, is a nesting habitat for western gulls, pel-

agic cormorants, and pigeon guillemots. Hunter Rocks, a cluster of small, relatively barren rocks just north of Prince Island, are an important nesting site for Brandt's cormorants. Pelagic cormorants, western gulls, pigeon guillemots, and black oystercatchers also breed here.

Prince Island, the largest of the rocks, is located a half-mile north of the Smith River mouth. It is held in trust for the Indians of the Smith River Rancheria; the 160-acre rancheria, established in 1908, is located adjacent to the Smith River. Prince Island can be viewed from a parking area at the end of Prince Island Court off Indian Rd., near the small Indian cemetery. The island provides nesting sites for double-crested, Brandt's, and pelagic cormorants, western gulls, pigeon guillemots, black oyster-catchers, Leach's and ashy storm-petrels, and tufted puffins. The island's population of double-crested cormorants is the largest on the Northern California coast. Prince Island is also one of only three California breeding sites for the rhinoceros auklet, whose name is derived from the keratinous "horn" that projects from its bill during breeding season.

Town of Smith River: *Hwy. 101, 13 mi. N. of Crescent City.*

The town of Smith River, located on the north side of Rowdy Creek, started in 1853 as a settlement called Del Norte, which soon began to thrive as an agricultural community. Later called Smith's River Valley after the explorer Jedediah Smith, the name was eventually shortened to Smith River. In 1880 the settlement consisted of a store, hotel, blacksmith shop, and two houses; by 1894 one hundred homes had been built and a narrow-gauge railroad connected the town with Crescent City. A commercial salmon cannery on Tillas Slough at the Smith River mouth continued to thrive until the early 1930s when beach seine and gill net fishing were declared illegal in California. The expansion of the lumber industry stimulated the town's growth during and after World War II. Today the principal industries are dairying, lumber, summer tourism, and commercial growing of lily bulbs. Smith River, where 90 per cent of the nation's lily bulbs are grown, is considered the "Easter Lily Capital of the World" and holds an annual Easter-in-July Festival; call: (707) 464-3174. The first privately owned fish hatchery in California was built in the 1970s by the Smith River Kiwanis Club on Rowdy Creek to perpetuate runs of steelhead and salmon in the Smith River.

Smith River: *Mouth of Smith River Rd., off Hwy. 101.*

This large perennial river, which drains 610 square miles, was explored by Jedediah Smith in 1828 during his expedition through the Pacific Northwest. Now state-classified as a Wild and Scenic River, the Smith is the only completely undammed river in California. The river, with its exceptionally clear waters, is one of California's major sport fishing centers, supporting one of the largest runs of salmon and steelhead in the state. At least 25 species of fish, including the anadromous American shad, cutthroat and steelhead trout, king and silver salmon, green sturgeon, and Pacific lamprey, inhabit the river and delta. Other species include Pacific herring,

northern anchovy, surfsmelt, and starry flounder. In the estuary is a Dungeness crab nursery;
gaper, littleneck, Washington, and soft-shelled
clams are also found here.

The Smith River delta has a diversity of habitats, including riparian woodland, sand dunes,
salt marsh, tidal flats, river channels, and open
water. Riparian vegetation consists of red alder,
willow, blackberry, and salmonberry. Freshwater marshes and isolated sloughs, including
Tillas and Yontocket sloughs, are scattered
throughout the delta and floodplain. There is a
Tolowa Indian village site and cemetery near
Yontocket Slough, an old river channel that
contains resident populations of cutthroat and
rainbow trout; several other Indian settlements
were located at various sites along the Smith
River. Numerous wildlife species inhabit the
floodplain, including black-tailed deer, ringtails,
rabbits, squirrels, and gophers; Roosevelt elk
are occasionally seen, and black bears and
mountain lions inhabit the surrounding forestland. Minks, river otters, muskrats, and beavers
are found in the marshes, streams, sloughs, and
riparian woodlands. Harbor seals, California
sea lions, and Steller sea lions are common in the
ocean waters near the river mouth.

Large numbers of resident and migratory
water birds use the river delta. Waterfowl, especially diving ducks, are the most abundant
species in winter; other birds include shorebirds,
egrets, and gulls. Nesting water birds include
green-backed herons, American bitterns, Virginia rails, American coots, mallards, and cinnamon teals; ospreys fish in the river. In summer
there is a great blue heron rookery in the delta,

Prince Island

and small numbers of nesting rails, shorebirds,
and raptors are found.

Smith River County Park, located at the end
of Smith River Rd. off Highway. 101, is a sand
and pebble beach at the river mouth used for
fishing, picnicking, and bird watching. The
Smith River Public Fishing Access, west of
Highway 101 on Fred Haight Dr., provides a
boat ramp, restrooms, and fishing supplies.
There are other commerical facilities on the
north side of the river, including a dock and
small marina, motel, restaurant and gift shop,
and several mobile home parks.

Clifford Kamph Memorial Park

Pelican Bay: *Between Pyramid Point and Point St. George.*

Pelican Bay is a long, open bay stretching along the coast between the mouth of the Smith River and Point St. George. Redtail surfperch and spawning surf smelt inhabit the nearshore waters. Dungeness crab is taken commercially along the coast, and salmon, shrimp, rockfish, sole, and cabezon are found offshore.

Kellogg Road Beach: *W. end of Kellogg Rd., 5.5 mi. S. of Smith River mouth.*

Kellogg Road Beach, a sand and gravel beach used for surf fishing and beachcombing, is backed by extensive grass-covered dunes and brackish marshes. For information, call: (707) 464-7237. Day use parking and environmental campsites in a natural setting are located north of Kellogg Rd., a half-mile from the beach; call: (707) 458-3310 or 464-9533.

Lakes Earl and Talawa: *W. of Lake Earl Dr., 8 mi. N. of Crescent City.*

These shallow coastal lagoons are connected by a narrow channel, and are periodically drained into the ocean through an outlet from Lake Talawa, which is separated from the ocean by a sandbar. The lakes, part of the Smith River drainage, have a combined surface area of approximately 2,500 acres. Lake Earl, fed by Jordan Creek, is mostly freshwater, whereas Lake Talawa is relatively saline. Much of Lake Talawa is bordered by salt marsh, dominated by saltgrass and pickleweed. Lake Earl is surrounded by bulrush mixed with cattail, spikerush, and hornwort. In summer, much of Lake Earl's surface is covered by blooms of sago pondweed, making power-boating virtually impossible. The lake area contains numerous sloughs, marshland, freshwater wetlands, and extensive sand dunes. The endangered sand

dune phacelia grows in the dunes northwest of Lake Earl and in the Talawa Slough area.

More than 250 species of birds use the lake area, which is situated along the Pacific Flyway, a major West Coast bird migration route; during migration, up to 100,000 birds may be seen here. The shallowness of the lakes permits extensive aquatic plant growth, which provides food for waterfowl such as ruddy ducks, canvasbacks, pintails, and American wigeons; Lake Earl supports the highest wintering population of canvasbacks north of San Francisco. The mudflats provide feeding habitat for wading birds and shorebirds. Other water birds include western sandpipers, dowitchers, American coots, great blue herons, killdeer, grebes, and gulls.

Numerous land birds such as hawks, ravens, sparrows, and owls also use the wetland area, and snowy plovers nest along the beach west of Lake Talawa. Bald eagles and peregrine falcons, both endangered, have been sighted. Endangered Aleutian Canada geese feed in the grassland around Lake Earl during migration. The Department of Fish and Game and the Department of Parks and Recreation control over 8,000 acres in the lake area, 2,000 of which constitute the Lake Earl Wildlife Refuge.

Fifteen species of fish have been found in Lake Earl, including king and silver salmon, and cutthroat and steelhead trout. Soft-shelled clams live in the mudflats of Lake Talawa. At least 50 species of mammals, such as rabbits, mice, gray foxes, and muskrats, and several species of reptiles and amphibians inhabit the area.

Prior to occupation by white settlers in the 1800s, Tolowa Indians inhabited several sites near Lake Earl, subsisting on the abundant wildlife in the area. Jedediah Smith visited Lake Earl in 1828 during his expedition through the northwest. In the late 1800s, a lumber mill operated here, with most of the lumber being shipped to San Francisco; the mill was destroyed by fire in the 1890s.

Public access is via Buzzini Rd. and Lakeview Dr., both of which are off Lake Earl Drive. A parking area at Teal Point on Lake Earl is ac-

---

North Coast Indians

The prehistoric people who inhabited the California coast from what is now the Oregon border to northern San Francisco Bay belonged to four tribes, or language families, comprising eight distinct cultures: the Tolowa, Yurok, Wiyot, Bear River, Mattole, Sinkyone, Pomo, and Coast Miwok. The largest of these cultural groups were the Tolowa and the Yurok, who were neighbors and shared many cultural traits, although they spoke unrelated languages.

In the fog-shrouded redwood forests along the banks of the Smith River stood the redwood plank houses and sweat lodges of the people known to their southern neighbors, the Yurok, as the Tolowa, a Yurok word meaning, roughly, "I speak Athabascan of the Tolowa variety." Regarded as wealthy by the Yurok, the Tolowa reaped an abundant harvest from the sea, the river, and the land; they collected mussels, smelt, and surfperch from the ocean, acorns from the inland valleys and canyons, fished salmon, steelhead, and eel from the Smith River, and snared waterfowl and cormorants from offshore rocks. Their canoes, made of hollowed-out redwood trunks, were used to hunt sea lions from offshore rookeries.

The Yurok lived along the banks of the lower Klamath River and on the coast, from Trinidad Bay to Little River, in present-day Humboldt County. Their name means "downstream" in the language of their neighbors, the Karok, who inhabited the area of the upper Klamath. Yurok geography is oriented to the river, rather than the cardinal points; all directions, in Yurok language, refer to the flow of its waters.

The Yurok esteemed material wealth, and the value of a canoe or a tract of acorn-bearing oaks was measured in dentalium shell money. They cultivated native tobacco, a rare instance of agrarianism among the Indians of California. Yurok healers were women; they cured by removing the offending spirit-object, called a "pain," from the patient. Fees for their services were high, but were expected to be returned if the patient was not cured.

Yurok redwood plank house at Requa, ca. 1928

Saint George Reef Lighthouse

cessible by a public road in the undeveloped Pacific Shores subdivision south of Kellogg Rd.; there is also lake and beach access at the ends of many roads within the subdivision, and off Pala Rd., north of the lakes. The lake area is used for fishing, shallow-draft boating, hunting, and nature study. Call: (707) 464-9533.

Dead Lake: *End of Riverside St., off Washington Blvd., W. of Hwy. 101.*

Formerly a lumber mill pond, Dead Lake is now undeveloped state park property. The small freshwater lake receives its drainage through the sand dunes to the north. Aquatic vegetation includes the yellow pond-lily, claspingleaf pond-weed, and common bladderwort. Shorebirds and waterfowl such as the wood duck use the lake; cutthroat trout are also found here.

Point St. George: *End of Radio Rd., 3 mi. N. of Crescent City.*

Situated at the southern tip of Pelican Bay, the windswept coastal bluff and extensive beach and rocky shore are used for beachcombing, clamming, fishing, and bird watching. A trail leads to the beach from the parking lot of the former Coast Guard Station, built in 1926; there is additional beach access off Radio Rd., one mile to the south. Black oystercatchers and western gulls feed and rest on the beach, which is backed by vegetated dunes. Pelagic cormorants and pigeon guillemots nest along the rocky shore. There is sport and commercial rock fishing and salmon trolling offshore; Pacific halibut is found closer to shore in the channel. The uncommon rocky coast snail occurs near the point; littleneck, razor, and Washington clams are also found here. Sea lions and harbor seals haul out at the point. As early as 300 B.C., ancestors of the Tolowa Indians inhabited the area, which was used as a camping place for shellfish gathering and sea lion hunting.

St. George Reef is a partially submerged chain of rocks extending west of the point to Seal Rocks, which support a pinniped rookery. The St. George Light, located seven miles offshore at the end of the reef, was built in 1892 following the wreck of the steamer *Brother Jonathan* three miles to the south in which 213 passengers lost their lives. The lighthouse was abandoned in 1975 due to the enormous cost of maintenance.

Jedediah Smith Redwoods State Park: *9 mi. E. of Crescent City on Hwy. 199.*

Located along the Smith River, this 9,560-acre park is named after explorer and fur trader Jedediah Smith. The park includes dense stands of virgin coast redwood, with a lush understory of rhododendron and azalea, as well as a variety of other trees such as hemlock, Douglas-fir, cedar, tanbark oak, and madrone. Among the many animals that inhabit the park are woodpeckers, owls, ospreys, belted kingfishers, squirrels, raccoons, river otters, deer, and bears.

The original inhabitants of the area were the Tolowa Indians, who occupied at least two village sites here. In 1828 Jedediah Smith and his party of trappers became the first white men to enter the area. The remains of Camp Lincoln, a military post established in 1862 and now a State Historical Landmark, are located near the northwest corner of the park.

The park is particularly popular for salmon and steelhead sport fishing. Facilities include day-use picnic areas, campsites, trails, a visitor center, and interpretive programs. The Stout Memorial Grove, presented to the state in 1929, is the first of the park's 44 memorial groves and contains the Stout Tree, a 340-foot-high redwood. Call: (707) 464-9533 or 458-3310.

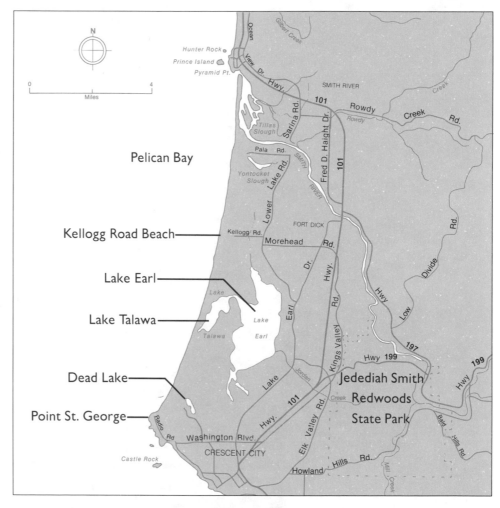

Tolowa dugout redwood canoe on Lake Earl, ca. 1920

Castle Rock

Marhoffer Creek: *N.W. of Crescent City, S. of Washington Blvd.*

Marhoffer Creek, just northwest of Crescent City, drains an extensive marine terrace. Vegetation ranges from willow-dominated marshland in the lower portions of the drainage, to pasturelands of grasses and clovers, brushland of coyote brush and salal, and forest land of Sitka spruce and pine on higher ground. Riparian vegetation includes red alder and blackberry. Egrets, swallows, hawks, kites, quail, California slender salamanders, gopher snakes, western pond turtles, beavers, skunks, feral pigs, and deer inhabit the wetland area.

Castle Rock: *Offshore, 1 mi. S. of Point St. George.*

Now a National Wildlife Refuge, this small offshore island is second in importance only to Southeast Farallon Island as a seabird rookery, supporting the largest breeding colonies of common murres and rhinoceros auklets in the state. Castle Rock also supports large colonies of Cassin's auklets, Leach's and fork-tailed storm-petrels, pigeon guillemots, and tufted puffins. Western gulls, black oystercatchers, and pelagic and Brandt's cormorants also breed here. The island is the primary spring staging ground for endangered Aleutian Canada geese, who roost here at night and feed in nearby fields during the day while en route to their breeding grounds in the Aleutian Islands. The island is a pupping ground for harbor seals, and an important haul-out for California and Steller sea lions. Northern elephant seals have also been spotted here.

Crescent City: *Off Hwy. 101, 79 mi. N. of Eureka.*

Following the discovery of gold on the Trinity River, the first permanent settlement was made at Crescent City in 1852. The town was laid out in 1853, the year Crescent City's first lumber mill was built. Incorporated in 1854, the town swiftly became the chief shipping and distributing center for Southern Oregon and Northern California. It remained a booming mining town as gold discoveries in the nearby hills and on the south fork of the Smith River continued. By the 1870s gold fever had died down, and lumbering became Crescent City's dominant enterprise. There was a population boom in the 1920s and 1930s due to railroad development and the construction of a deepwater harbor, a breakwater, and new highways. In 1964 much of the waterfront area was destroyed by a huge seismic sea wave resulting from an earthquake in Alaska; twelve-foot-high waves hit downtown Crescent City, and 29 city blocks were inundated. Today Crescent City, which has since been rebuilt, is the county seat. Its main industries are lumbering, recreation, dairy farming, commercial fishing, and Easter lily bulb cultivation. Each year the town hosts the World's Championship Crab Races. The Del Norte County Historical Society Museum at 6th and H streets contains Indian artifacts and relics of the pioneer settlements; for information, call: (707) 464-3922.

Pebble Beach Public Fishing Access: *Pebble Beach Dr. and Pacific Ave., N. of Crescent City.*

A stairway provides access from the blufftop parking lot and picnic area to a driftwood-strewn sandy beach and rocky shore where anglers surf cast and rock fish. Shorebirds feed along shore; littleneck clams are found on the beach. A State Historical Landmark at the south end of Pebble Beach, south of Pacific Ave., marks the site of a Tolowa Indian settlement that existed here until the latter part of the 19th century. There is additional beach access at several locations along Pebble Beach Dr. between Point St. George and Battery Point.

Steam schooners Del Norte *and* Mandalay *at Crescent City Harbor, ca. 1910*

Preston Island: *Condor St. and Pebble Beach Dr., Crescent City.*

Preston Island is a rocky spit at the north end of Crescent City, accessible via a paved road down the bluff; the pebble beach is used for beachcombing and fishing. There are tidepools along the rocky shore. Preston Island was quarried nearly to sea level for the Crescent City Harbor breakwaters.

Brother Jonathan Park: *Pebble Beach Dr. and 9th St., Crescent City.*

This grassy park with a playground, a baseball diamond, and restrooms includes a cemetery and a memorial "dedicated to those who lost their lives on the wreck of the Pacific Mail Steamer *Brother Jonathan* at Point St. George Reef July 30, 1865." The cemetery is a State Historical Landmark.

Crescent City Lighthouse: *S. end of "A" St., Crescent City.*

The lighthouse was built in 1856 on a small island off Battery Point, about 200 yards from shore and accessible only at low tide. Also known as Battery Point Lighthouse, it is the oldest surviving light station along California's north coast, and is now a State Historical Landmark. Inside the granite and brick lighthouse is a museum operated by the Del Norte Historical Society that displays Indian artifacts and historic relics; the museum and lighthouse are open April-September, Wed.-Sun., 10 AM-4 PM, tides permitting. Call: (707) 464-3089.

Beach Front Park: *Off Howe Dr., Crescent City.*

Beach Front Park is a 54-acre grassy park with picnic facilities, a playground, shuffleboard court, par course, putting green, restrooms, and views of the harbor. At the corner of Front and H streets is a State Historical Landmark—the remains of the S.S. *Emidio*, which was attacked by a Japanese submarine in 1941 about 200 miles north of San Francisco, drifted northward, and broke up on the rocks off Crescent City. Del Norte County Visitors Center, on Front St., and Redwood National Park Headquarters, at 2nd and K streets, are both just east of the park. County Visitors Center: (707) 464-3174. Redwood National Park: (707) 464-6101.

Crescent City Harbor: *W. of Hwy. 101 and Citizens Dock Rd., Crescent City.*

Now one of the safest harbors on the north coast, Crescent City Harbor is protected by rock jetties reinforced by more than 1,600 huge, 25-ton concrete tetrapods that are shaped like children's jacks. One of the tetrapods is on display on Highway 101 just south of Front St. to mark the first place in the Western Hemisphere where the French-invented tetrapods were used in the construction of a breakwater.

The harbor includes the Small Boat Basin with boat ramps, docks, and guest slips, and Citizens Dock, California's northernmost pier, which was built in 1950 completely with public donations. The pier, used for boat launching and pier fishing, serves the incoming commercial fishing fleet; visitors can watch fishing boats unload shrimp, crab, rockfish, and salmon. Other harbor facilities include fish processing plants, a Coast Guard station, boat rentals, bait and tackle shops, marine supplies, and a fuel dock. Harbor District: (707) 464-6174.

Bayshore Marina, at the southeast end of the harbor, has slips, a boat ramp, a marina, and two trailer parks, and provides access to Whaler Island, a ten-acre rocky headland that was once a small island, but is now connected to the mainland by a filled breakwater. In 1855 a whaling company established a station on the island, where the whales caught along the coast were rendered; whalers headed for Alaska anchored in the lee of the island. The grassy headland provides panoramic views of the harbor and the Pacific Ocean. The remains of two Tolowa Indian villages are located near the harbor.

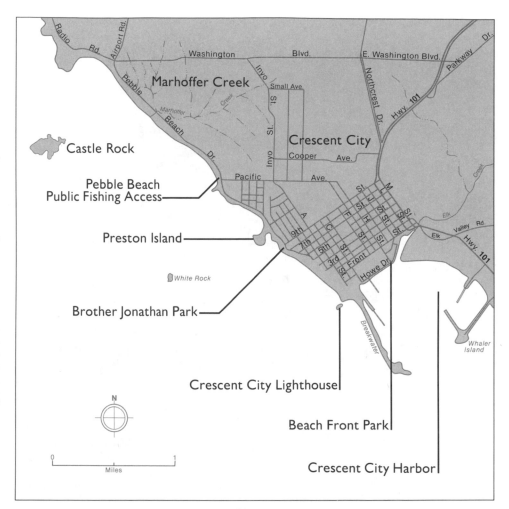

Crescent City Lighthouse

Point St. George

Dead Lake

101

Jordan Creek

JEDEDIAH SMITH
REDWOODS STATE PARK

South Fork

South

Washington Blvd.

Elk Creek

Hwy

Smith River

Castle Rock

CRESCENT CITY

Elk Valley Rd.

Creek

Rd.

Hills

South Fork Rd.

Howland

Humboldt Rd.

Redwood National Park

Crescent Beach———

Hamilton

Rd.

Enders Beach Rd.

East

Fork

Enderts Beach———

Hwy

101

Nickel Creek

West

Del Norte Coast———
Redwoods State Park

Branch

Sister Rocks

Damnation Creek

Wilson

Creek

West

Fork

Wilson Creek Rd.

N

Footsteps Rock

Wilson Creek Beach———

Hwy

High

0   4
Miles

False Klamath Rock

Prairie Creek

Hunter Creek Rd.

Hunter

Creek

101

Elk Creek: *N.E. of Crescent City Harbor.*

The Elk Creek area was originally inhabited by the Tolowa Indians, who fished for salmon near the mouth of the creek, and hunted the abundant elk and deer. In 1871 Hobbs, Wall and Co. established a lumber mill on the creek, using logs transported from harvest sites, first by skid trails and then by flotation down the slough. In the 1880s a railroad was built to transport the logs. There is public beach access along the levee at Elk Creek, through the Shoreline Campgrounds from Sunset Circle Drive.

The creek, which drains 4,120 acres, originates in the upland forests of Jedediah Smith Redwoods State Park and flows southwesterly to Crescent City Harbor. In the lower reaches the creek forms a wetland, vegetated with grasses and clover; upstream in boggy, poorly drained areas is a dense growth of rushes and sedges. Riparian vegetation includes alders, skunk cabbage, and horsetails. Salamanders, Pacific treefrogs, western fence lizards, gopher snakes, shrews, spotted skunks, gray foxes, coyotes, deer, and black bears inhabit the creek and wetland area. The creek area also supports great blue herons, ducks, geese, hawks, kites, and owls; quail and doves are found in brushy areas. Coastal cutthroat trout occur in the creek.

Redwood National Park: *Off Hwy. 101, between Crescent City and Orick.*

The 106,000-acre national park lies within Del Norte and northern Humboldt counties. The park was established in 1968 to preserve virgin forests of coast redwood, *Sequoia sempervirens*, including the world's tallest trees. Within park boundaries are three state parks: Jedediah Smith Redwoods, Del Norte Coast Redwoods, and Prairie Creek Redwoods (in Humboldt). National Park Headquarters are in Crescent City at 1111 2nd St.; call: (707) 464-6101. Visitor information may also be obtained at the Hiouchi Visitor Station on Highway 199.

The park has an average rainfall of 80-135 inches each winter. The rain and coastal fog provide necessary conditions for the redwoods, which grow here in pure stands and in mixed forests along with Douglas-fir, Sitka spruce, western hemlock, grand fir, and tanbark oak. The forest floor is carpeted with ferns, redwood sorrel, yellow violets, and a thick understory of shrubs such as California rhododendron, salal, cascara, and huckleberry. In early spring, trillium blossoms appear briefly, and in May and June, brilliant pink and red rhododendron blooms abound. Farther inland, and at higher elevations, Douglas-fir dominates, interspersed with tanbark oak and madrone. Near the ocean, Sitka spruce mixes with redwoods, and red alder, willow, and coyote brush are prevalent. Alder, maple, cedar, and California bay laurel are found on alluvial flats along streams.

The park, which lies along the Pacific Flyway, attracts over 300 species of birds, about half of which are water-associated, including gulls, black oystercatchers, willets, sanderlings, and seabirds such as cormorants, pigeon guillemots, and marbled murrelets. Bald eagles, peregrine falcons, California brown pelicans, and Aleutian Canada geese, all endangered, are found within park boundaries. Numerous mammals, including black-tailed deer, Roosevelt elk, and elusive mountain lions, inhabit the park; river otters, minks, and beavers are found in and along the creeks. Fifteen of western North America's 22 salamander species are found here, as is the Northern Pacific rattlesnake, a rare poisonous snake inhabiting drier, inland portions of the park. Silver and king salmon, and rainbow, coastal cutthroat, and steelhead trout are caught in streams and rivers within the park.

Within Del Norte County, Redwood National Park includes the following coastal areas: Crescent Beach, Enderts Beach, Lagoon Creek Fishing Access, Requa Overlook, and Coastal Drive.

Crescent Beach: *Off Enderts Beach Rd., 2 mi. S. of Crescent City.*

During the 1849 gold rush, every square foot of Crescent Beach was staked with mining claims. Today, the beach is popular for horseback riding and fishing, and includes a grassy picnic area, parking, and wheelchair-accessible restrooms. Park rangers conduct seashore walks; call: (707) 464-6101. Crescent Beach Overlook, located on the bluffs just south of the beach, affords spectacular views of the coast; gray whales can be seen offshore during migration. A coastal strand community of beach primrose, sea rocket, sand verbena, and beach morning-glory occurs on the upper beach.

Aleutian Canada goose (*Branta canadensis leucopareia*)
22 to 45 inches long

Enderts Beach: *End of Enderts Beach Rd., 3 mi. S. of Crescent City.*

A half-mile-long trail, beginning just south of the Crescent Beach Overlook, leads to the Nickel Creek Primitive Campground and picnic area, and to Enderts Beach, a sandy, driftwood-strewn beach at the base of steep bluffs vegetated with coyote brush, silk tassel, blue blossom ceanothus, and wild plaintain. Popular beach activities include clamming, rock fishing, smelt netting, and surf casting for redtail perch. Tidepools along the rocky shore are inhabited by sea anemones, California mussels, black turban snails, and sea stars, including the unusual sun star and many-rayed star. Park rangers conduct tidepool walks; call: (707) 464-6101. Enderts Beach was once used by the Tolowa Indians for fishing and seaweed gathering.

Del Norte Coast Redwoods State Park: *Hwy. 101, 7 mi. S. of Crescent City.*

The 6,375-acre redwood park of forestland and shoreline extends from the south end of Enderts Beach to the mouth of Lagoon Creek, and includes trails, beaches, and the Mill Creek Campground. The campground, open seasonally, is situated in the redwoods along Mill Creek at the site of the 1920s logging operations of Hobbs, Wall & Co., where second-growth redwood and red alder now abound. The challenging, five-mile-long Damnation Creek Trail, which begins at Highway 101 mile marker 16, winds through dense old-growth redwoods, and Douglas-fir and spruce groves, to a sea cove with a small beach; this trail was used by the Yurok, who gathered shellfish and seaweed at the beach. Tolowa Indians also occupied several sites along the coast in and near the park.

Park vegetation includes redwood, hemlock, Port Orford cedar, alder, and Douglas-fir, as well as tanbark oak, cascara, California bay laurel, and madrone. Rhododendrons, azaleas, and many species of ferns, wild berries, and colorful wildflowers cover the ground. Rabbits, squirrels, chipmunks, skunks, and raccoons inhabit the forested areas; foxes and deer are numerous, and an occasional coyote, bobcat, river otter, beaver, black bear, or mountain lion is seen. Birds include pileated woodpeckers, quail, doves, hawks, great horned owls, great blue herons, kingfishers, and ducks. For information, call: (707) 464-9533 or 458-3310.

Wilson Creek Beach: *W. of Hwy. 101, 15 mi. S. of Crescent City.*

Wilson Creek Beach is a driftwood-strewn sandy beach and rocky shore at the north end of False Klamath Cove; Wilson Creek flows into the ocean at the north end of the beach. Wilson Creek is the old dividing line between Tolowa Indian territory to the north and Yurok territory to the south. A new hostel, scheduled to open by summer of 1987, is located in the historic De-Martin House on Wilson Creek Rd., just across Highway 101 from the beach. The 29-bed hostel is wheelchair accessible and has a kitchen; call: (707) 482-8265.

Redwood trees, Redwood National Park

California rhododendron (*Rhododendron macrophyllum*)
3 to 12 feet tall

Lagoon Creek Fishing Access: *W. of Hwy. 101, 5 mi. N. of Klamath.*

Lagoon Creek feeds a freshwater pond that was formed when the creek was dammed in 1940 to create a log pond; lumber mill operations took place here until 1960, when the county acquired the property. In 1972 the land was deeded to Redwood National Park, and today the pond is stocked with rainbow trout. Yellow pond-lilies, with their heart-shaped leaves, cover large sections of the pond. Red-winged blackbirds, ducks, herons, egrets, salamanders, frogs, rabbits, gophers, river otters, and mountain beavers inhabit the area. Park facilities include picnic tables and wheelchair-accessible restrooms; call: (707) 464-6101. The half-mile, self-guided Yurok Loop Trail winds past picturesque beaches, through a dense forest of willow, spruce, red alder, and oak, and along the windswept bluffs. A four-mile-long section of Redwood National Park's 30-mile Coastal Trail begins at Lagoon Creek and extends south to the Requa Overlook, winding along the high grassy bluffs overlooking the coast.

False Klamath Rock: *Offshore, 5 mi. N. of Klamath.*

Located about 2,000 feet offshore, this large, steep-sided rock is second in importance only to Castle Rock as a Northern California seabird breeding site. False Klamath Rock is used almost exclusively by common murres, which nest here in great numbers each year. Western gulls and Brandt's, double-crested, and pelagic cormorants also breed on the rock. The Yurok dug for the edible *Brodiaea* bulbs, known as "Indian potatoes," that grew here, and called the rock *olrgr*, which is Yurok for "digging place."

Requa: *Hwy. 101, 18.5 mi. S. of Crescent City.*

This tiny town overlooking the mouth of the Klamath River was originally the site of a large Yurok Indian village named Re'kwoi; the Yurok occupied the area for over 2,000 years until they were driven out by white settlers. Still standing on the north bank of the Klamath is a restored Yurok family house built of redwood slabs hewn with an elk horn wedge. In 1876 the first commercial fishery in Requa was established, followed by several fish canneries. A wagon road was built between Crescent City and Requa in 1894, and in 1896 a 1,700-foot-long cable was stretched across the Klamath River and a ferry service was begun. Requa's economic base was commercial fishing and dairying; in 1902 the town had a store, two saloons, a dance hall, a livery stable, and a hotel. Requa's decline began in 1926 when the Douglas Memorial Bridge was built upstream to accommodate increased traffic on the coast road, bypassing Requa. In 1934 commercial fishing was outlawed on the Klamath, and Requa's canneries closed down. Today Requa is a sport fishing and tourist area.

Requa Overlook, on a grassy slope off Patrick Murphy Memorial Dr. 1.5 miles from Requa Rd., has picnic tables, wheelchair-accessible restrooms, and panoramic views of the Klamath River mouth and upland forests; whales can be seen offshore during migration.

Town of Klamath: *E. of Hwy. 101, 21 mi. S. of Crescent City.*

In 1851 a settlement was founded on the south bank of the Klamath River, about three miles from the mouth, and soon became the headquarters for prospectors searching for gold on the river. The settlement, called Klamath City, lasted just a year, since gold was found to be scarce on the lower river, and the shifting sandbar at the mouth of the Klamath River made navigation difficult. Later another town called Klamath grew up on the north bank of the river, developing as a logging and timber community, and later growing to be a resort center. The town's growth was spurred by the completion in 1926 of the Douglas Memorial Bridge, which spanned the Klamath River and connected Del Norte County with the rest of the state.

The Klamath River area suffered great losses in several historic floods, beginning with the first flood of record in 1861-62. The town of Klamath was completely washed away in the disastrous flood of December 1964, which was caused by torrential winter rains and a sudden warm spell that rapidly melted snow in the Siskiyou Mountains. The flood also swept away the Douglas Memorial Bridge, which had been hailed as having "broken the Klamath River barrier"; all that remains today is the southern terminus, flanked by statues of two golden bears, on Klamath Beach Drive. The "new town" of Klamath was established on higher ground east of Highway 101, and today is a small residential community and fishing resort; the town holds an annual Salmon Festival in June, featuring ceremonial dances and craftwork by the local Indians. Numerous campgrounds, trailer parks, and resorts catering to sport fishermen are located in the immediate vicinity.

Klamath River: *Mouth of the river is 20 mi. S. of Crescent City.*

The state's second largest river after the Sacramento, the Klamath drains 15,500 square miles; its major tributaries are the Salmon, Scott, Shasta, and Trinity rivers. The Klamath River originates in the Cascade Mountains of Oregon and flows generally southwestward for 263 miles on its way to the sea, where it widens and forms a large barrier spit at its mouth. The Klamath River is classified as a California State Wild and Scenic River.

The Klamath, which has the largest salmon and steelhead trout runs in California, is a major sport fishing river; anglers fish for king and silver salmon, steelhead trout, surfperch, and sturgeon. The river and estuary also support starry flounder, Pacific lamprey, American shad, cutthroat trout, striped bass, eulachon, and prickly sculpin. Dungeness crab are found near the river mouth. The exposed tidelands of the estuary are

Flint Rock Head, south of the Klamath River mouth

feeding areas for large numbers of shorebirds including godwits, willets, dunlins, plovers, and killdeer; waterfowl such as scoters, mergansers, ruddy ducks, pintails, buffleheads, and greenwinged teals also inhabit the estuary. Endangered bald eagles have been seen here, and osprey and spotted owls nest near the river. Ringtails, deer, mountain lions, and black bears are found inland; the fisher, an uncommon mammal related to the marten, has been sighted in the watershed. Sea lions and harbor seals haul out on the larger offshore rocks just north of the river.

A number of R.V. parks and resorts are situated along both sides of the Klamath River. A scenic turnout on the south side of the river provides views of the river mouth. A toll road leads to the driftwood-strewn sandy beach on the south side of the mouth of the Klamath.

The Klamath River area was historically occupied by the Yurok Indians, who inhabited villages on the banks of the river and along the coast. In 1852 there were approximately 2,500 Yurok in the Klamath River area, subsisting on acorns and fish and living in redwood plank houses; in 1855 many of the Yurok were placed in an Indian reservation along the Klamath, and later were removed to the Hoopa Reservation in Humboldt County.

Coastal Drive: *Alder Camp Rd. and Klamath Beach Rd., off Hwy. 101.*

Coastal Drive is an eight-mile scenic drive that winds along the bluffs between the Klamath River and Prairie Creek Redwoods State Park in Humboldt County; the road is narrow and unpaved in parts.

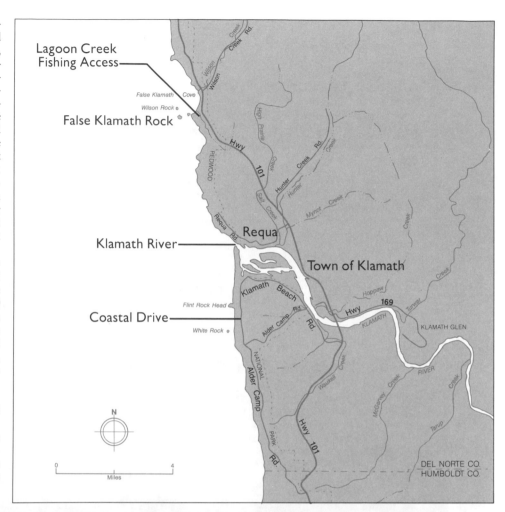

Yurok Indians in a dugout canoe on the Klamath River

Humboldt County
Selected Species of Interest

 Plants: Eelgrass (*Zostera marina*), intertidal flowering plant; largest beds in state occur in Humboldt Bay. **Western azalea** (*Rhododendron occidentale*), found near Humboldt Lagoons State Park and in Azalea State Reserve.

 Trees: Coast redwood (*Sequoia sempervirens*), among the world's tallest trees; grows on coastal mountains, in canyons, and along streams. **Douglas-fir** (*Pseudotsuga menziesii*), common in coastal mountains.

 Insects: Helfer's beach dune grasshopper (*Trimeritriopos helferi*), restricted to Humboldt and Mendocino coasts. **Redwood primitive moth** (*Epimartyria pardeloa*), oldest known moth; found in Fern Canyon.

 Invertebrates: Dungeness crab (*Cancer magister*), commercially important; spawns in Humboldt Bay and Eel and Mad River deltas. **Pacific razor clam** (*Siliqua patula*), edible clam found on exposed sandy beaches.

 Amphibians and Reptiles: Pacific giant salamander (*Dicamptodon ensatus*), inhabits damp forests; only salamander with vocal cords. **Tailed frog** (*Ascaphus truei*), lives in streams; has tail-like copulatory organ.

 Fish: King (chinook) salmon (*Oncorhynchus tshawytscha*), largest salmon species; important commercial and sport fish. **Coastal cutthroat trout** (*Salmo clarkii clarkii*), popular sport fish; found in streams from Alaska to the Eel River.

 Birds: Black brant (*Branta bernicla nigricans*); largest coastal wintering population in California found at Humboldt Bay. **American dipper** (*Cinclus mexicanus*), aquatic, wrenlike bird; dives in streams to feed.

 Land Mammals: Roosevelt elk (*Cervus elaphus roosevelti*), California's largest elk; found in Prairie Creek State Park, near Big Lagoon, and in the King Range. **Black bear** (*Ursus americanus*), inhabits coastal mountains.

 Marine Mammals: Harbor seal (*Phoca vitulina*), breeds on Humboldt Bay mudflats and on offshore rocks. **Harbor porpoise** (*Phocoena phocoena*), small, chunky porpoise; frequents Humboldt Bay and Eel River Delta.

Humboldt County

FROM THE OLD-GROWTH FORESTS of Redwood National Park to the rugged mountains of the King Range, the Humboldt County coast is rich in natural resources. With its extensive redwood and Douglas-fir forests, the county is California's leading timber producer, and wood products operations employ one third of its work force. Humboldt Bay and the productive offshore waters support an important commercial fishery. State and national parklands, numerous rivers, and spectacular shoreline provide visitors with the chance to walk through a grove of towering redwoods, reel in a 20-pound salmon, catch a glimpse of a bald eagle, or hike along a 25-mile stretch of wild beach.

The county's northern coast is characterized by sandy beaches backed by high bluffs, rocky coves and tidepools, three large lagoons, and dense redwood and Sitka spruce forests. Between the Little and Eel Rivers are fertile river floodplains and the lowlands of Humboldt Bay, which support farming and dairy ranching. The county's population is centered around Humboldt Bay, which is one of California's major shipping and commercial fishing ports.

South of False Cape, high coastal mountains drop down abruptly to narrow, exposed beaches. Cape Mendocino and the Mattole Valley contain private grazing land and small farms; most of the primitive King Range, known as the "Lost Coast," is publicly owned forest, chaparral, and grassland. At Shelter Cove, the San Andreas Fault reaches its northernmost onshore extension before trending west to join the Mendocino Fracture Zone. Where the fault and the fracture zone meet is a triple-plate junction between the North American, Pacific, and Gorda Plates.

The original inhabitants of northern Humboldt County were the Yurok Indians, whose residence in the area dates back perhaps 5,000 years. The Humboldt Bay and Eel Delta area was inhabited by the Wiyot Indians, who, like the Yurok, fished for salmon and surfperch, gathered clams and mussels, and hunted sea lions. As in many tribes of the Pacific Northwest, shamanism in the Yurok and the Wiyot was usually practiced by women. The Mattole Indians lived along the Bear and Mattole Rivers, and the Sinkyone occupied the Shelter Cove area. Little is known about these two tribes, as neither survived the arrival of white settlers to the Humboldt coast.

The 1849 gold rush along the upper Trinity and Klamath Rivers stimulated interest in California's north coast, as gold seekers who poured into the area felt the need for a convenient supply port. In the fall of 1849, an exploring party led by writer and frontiersman Josiah Gregg left the Trinity River hoping to find the "lost" Trinidad Bay, which had appeared on old Spanish maps. The first white men to explore the Humboldt coast by land, the Gregg party located both Trinidad Bay and Humboldt Bay, and named the Mad, Elk, and Eel Rivers. Several expeditions by sea followed the news of the party's discovery; in April of 1850, ships anchored at both bays, and settlement of the area began.

The first white settlers to arrive at Humboldt Bay were the members of three land companies, organized with the intent to control land ownership around the bay. The companies identified and surveyed potential townsites, and each member claimed a parcel of land, holding it for the benefit of the others. The companies frequently charged high fees to show survey lines to later arrivals, and threatened those who tried to settle on lands claimed by members. Eventually, all lands were sold off, and the profits divided equally among members.

As trade with the Trinity mines grew during the 1850s, settlement of Humboldt Bay and Trinidad proceeded rapidly. The discovery of gold along the beaches north of Trinidad and oil at Cape Mendocino drew prospectors to those areas as well. Within a few years, the excitement over gold and oil died down, and the new settlers turned to more reliable sources of income. Ranchers and farmers diked the floodplains of the Mad and Eel Rivers and drained the marshes of Humboldt Bay. Loggers began cutting the dense redwood forests, and lumber mills sprang up around the bay. The shipping industry kept pace with logging operations; port facilities were established, navigational channels were dredged, and shipyards were built. Humboldt County was organized in 1853, and was named, as was the bay, for the German scientist and explorer Alexander von Humboldt.

Humboldt County's other major industry began in 1857 when a salmon fishery was established on the Eel River. Among the many species now landed at Humboldt Bay are Dungeness crab, king and silver salmon, Dover sole, English sole, herring, and albacore. The county's fisheries are dependent upon its wetlands and rivers, which provide spawning and nursery grounds for dozens of species. These wetlands also serve as wintering grounds for waterfowl and shorebirds using the Pacific Flyway, one of four continental migration routes.

Patrick's Point State Park

Redwood National Park: *Off Hwy. 101, N. of Orick.*

When a National Geographic team exploring Redwood Creek in 1963 came across the "Mount Everest of all living things," a 367.8-foot coast redwood, the 90-year campaign to create a Redwood National Park finally gained the momentum it needed. Established in 1968 with 58,000 acres, the park was expanded in 1978 to 106,000 acres, comprising three pre-existing state parks and land withdrawn from private ownership. Besides preserving the world's tallest trees, the park protects huge expanses of redwood forests, over half of which are old growth, and includes 40 miles of coast.

The park contains areas of grassland, riparian woodland, freshwater marsh, coastal scrub, and coastal strand. Redwood grows in the canyons along with Douglas-fir, tanbark oak, and rhododendron. Red alders, willows, and ferns grow beside the park's many creeks, whereas strand plants such as beach pea, sand verbena, and European beach grass occur on the shore.

Wildlife includes the mountain beaver, river otter, bobcat, mountain lion, painted salamander, and redwood primitive moth. Roosevelt elk roam the meadows near the beach. The park lies along the Pacific Flyway, attracting shorebirds and waterfowl that overwinter on the beach and along the creeks. The osprey, marbled murrelet, and Virginia rail are also found in the park. King and silver salmon, steelhead, and coastal cutthroat trout spawn in the streams.

Facilities include restrooms, campgrounds, and an extensive trail system. For information on wheelchair-accessible trails and restrooms, call: (707) 822-7611. A new park information center at the mouth of Redwood Creek replaces the center in Orick; call: (707) 488-3461.

Prairie Creek Redwoods State Park: *W. of Hwy. 101, 6.5 mi. N. of Orick.*

The park was established in 1923 on 160 acres donated by the family of lumberman and politician Joseph Russ, the largest landholder in the county in the late 1800s. Seventy per cent of the park's 12,544 acres is virgin redwood forest, mixed with Douglas-fir, Sitka spruce, and western azalea. The park also contains second-growth redwoods, freshwater marsh vegetation, and riparian woodland. Its prairies support oatgrass, fescues, and other native grasses.

Prairie Creek, which flows south along Highway 101 for ten miles before it joins Redwood Creek, contains king and silver salmon and coastal cutthroat trout. The park is also home to California quail, ruffled grouse, foxes, black bears, and three herds of Roosevelt elk. The park provides 75 miles of trails, including a trail for the blind, wheelchair-accessible restrooms, campgrounds, and a visitor's center and museum. Call: (707) 488-2171.

Fern Canyon: *End of Davidson Rd., W. of Hwy. 101.*

Located within Prairie Creek Redwoods State Park, Fern Canyon is a narrow canyon cut by Home Creek through Gold Bluffs. Its 50-foot sheer walls are covered with numerous species of ferns, including sword ferns, lady ferns, and chain ferns. The Pacific giant salamander, tailed frog, American dipper, and winter wren inhabit the canyon; rainbow trout are found in the creek. Facilities include parking, restrooms, and a trail. Call: (707) 488-2171.

Gold Bluffs: *Off Davidson Rd., W. of Hwy. 101.*

In 1850, pioneer Hermann Ehrenberg found gold flakes mixed in the sands below these bluffs. By 1851, enthusiastic prospectors had established a tent city here and were attempting to work the sands. Their yields were poor, but the optimistic name remains. The area is now part of Prairie Creek Redwoods State Park.

Below the steep, redwood-covered bluffs lies 11-mile Gold Bluffs Beach. Songbirds and migratory shorebirds are found here, as well as razor clams, surfperch, and spawning surf smelt. Sea rocket, sand verbena, and bush lupine grow on the extensive dunes. Seabirds breed on Redding Rock offshore. Facilities include restrooms, a campground, and interpretive programs in summer. Call: (707) 488-2171.

Espa Lagoon: *Off Davidson Rd., W. of Hwy. 101.*

Located east of Gold Bluffs Beach in Prairie Creek Redwoods State Park, Espa Lagoon was once the site of an Indian village. The lagoon was open to the ocean until sand build-up at the beach sealed it off. Now a freshwater pond, Espa Lagoon is gradually filling in with red alder, willow, and cattail. Yellow pond-lily and ditch grass grow in the open water, and ferns and grasses cover the shore. Coastal cutthroat and rainbow trout inhabit the lagoon's waters; frogs, waterfowl, songbirds, and river otters are also found here. A picnic area and restrooms are provided. Call: (707) 488-2171.

Redwoods, ca. 1930s

Orick: *On Hwy. 101, 30 mi. N. of McKinleyville.*

Orick's name derives from a Yurok village called Ore'q once located here. The bottom lands surrounding the Redwood Creek estuary have been used since the late 1800s as pasture, supporting beef production and small dairies. To the north on Highway 101 is the Humboldt County Prairie Creek Fish Hatchery, where anadromous fish are raised for release in the county's lagoons and streams.

Redwood Creek: *2 mi. W. of Orick.*

Redwood Creek lost much of its old-growth redwood forest and anadromous fish habitat to intensive logging in its upper watershed and channelization of its estuary. In 1978, the National Park Service added 48,000 acres above the creek to Redwood National Park and began a 15-year project to rehabilitate the creek's watershed. To reduce erosion and runoff from the heavily logged hillsides above the park's Tall Trees Grove, the Park Service is removing old roads, clearing logging debris, and planting the bare slopes with Douglas-fir and redwood. The Park Service has also dredged the creek's north and south sloughs to increase the salmon and steelhead habitat, and is restoring freshwater marsh vegetation along the south slough.

Because Redwood Creek's estuary consists of mostly bare intertidal sand flats, few waterfowl are present. However, herons, egrets, and shorebirds use the lagoon, ospreys nest in the redwoods farther inland, and bald eagles may be spotted along the creek. The creek marks the southern limit of the Del Norte salamander.

Parking for the Orick Beach Fishing Access is on the north side of the creek mouth, at the end of Hufford Road. The road is not recommended for R.V.s or large vehicles; do not trespass on the adjacent private pasturelands. The new Redwood National Park information center is located on the south side of the creek, as is the Redwood Creek Beach Picnic Area, which provides parking, restrooms, and access to a sandy beach; for information, call: (707) 488-3461.

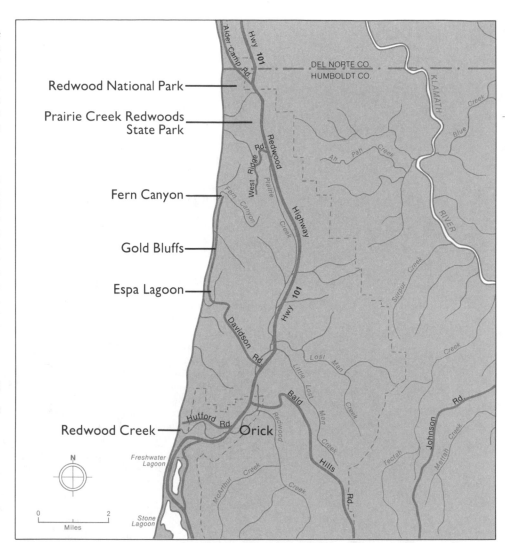

Roosevelt elk at Prairie Creek Redwoods State Park

Freshwater Lagoon: *E. of Hwy. 101, 3 mi. S. of Orick.*

Freshwater Lagoon was sealed off from the ocean in the early 1950s by the construction of Highway 101, which runs along the lagoon's barrier beach. Freshwater marsh vegetation consisting of tule, cattail, and willow provides a breeding area for frogs and salamanders. Red alder, blue blossom ceanothus, and coyote brush grow on the steep east banks, and sand verbena, beach morning glory, and yellow bush lupine occupy the sandy barrier beach. The lagoon is used by waterfowl, mink, and river otters, and is stocked with trout; there is a boat ramp at the north end. West of the highway are restrooms and a parking area that provides access to the beach, which is part of Redwood National Park.

Stone Lagoon: *Off Hwy. 101, 4.5 mi. S. of Orick.*

The former site of a Yurok village called Tsawpewk, Stone Lagoon lies in part within Humboldt Lagoons State Park. A campground is situated on the north shore of the lagoon, and environmental campsites are accessible by boat from the east shore, where a visitor's center is located. The sand spit separating the 521-acre lagoon from the ocean is breached in the winter, allowing saltwater influx. Anadromous fish such as silver salmon, steelhead, coastal cutthroat trout, and Pacific lamprey enter the lagoon to spawn in McDonald Creek, the lagoon's perennial tributary.

Stone Lagoon's diverse vegetation includes red alder, willow, and salal on the east and south shores; coyote brush, Scotch broom, and wax myrtle on west-facing slopes of the rocky point to the south; and sand verbena, beach pea, and lupine on the spit. Brackish marsh vegetation grows around the mouth of McDonald Creek and in a band around the shoreline, with plants such as saltgrass, bulrush, and the endangered Humboldt Bay owl's-clover.

Ducks, geese, and other migratory birds rest and feed at the lagoon in the winter. Grebes, loons, and rails can also be found here, as well as soft-shelled clams, sculpin, and starry flounder. Rabbits, gray foxes, and bobcats inhabit the surrounding woodlands, and snowy plovers nest on the sand spit.

Humboldt Lagoons State Park: *Off Hwy. 101, 6 mi. S. of Orick.*

The Yurok Indians inhabited a village here called Tsotskwi. Gold strikes in 1849 on the Klamath and Trinity Rivers brought the first white settlers to the lagoons; prospectors mined the barrier beaches for gold, and ranchers settled the area in the 1870s. In 1931, the Department of Parks and Recreation bought the Gillis Ranch and created Dry Lagoon State Park, now known as Humboldt Lagoons State Park. The 1,036-acre park includes Dry Lagoon, which is actually a freshwater marsh, the barrier beaches of Stone and Big Lagoons, and much of Stone Lagoon's southern shore. The park preserves important wetland habitats for migratory birds using the Pacific Flyway.

Dry Lagoon's marsh community of tule, cattail, and skunk cabbage provides a habitat for ducks, bitterns, and herons. Coastal strand vegetation grows on the beaches, salt marsh vegetation in the two lagoons, and scrub and riparian woodland on the hills. Park facilities include restrooms, two campgrounds at Dry Lagoon, the campgrounds at Stone Lagoon, and a boat ramp. Call: (707) 445-6547 or 488-5435.

Big Lagoon: *Off Hwy. 101, 9 mi. S. of Orick.*

Big Lagoon's long, sandy barrier beach is part of Humboldt Lagoons State Park. The lagoon's wooded eastern shore and extensive salt marsh compose Harry A. Merlo State Recreation Area, which provides parking and access to fish-

Stone Lagoon

ing and waterfowl hunting at the 1,470-acre lagoon. For information, call: (707) 445-6547.

Four Yurok villages once existed on Big Lagoon's east shore; a small Indian rancheria now occupies the south end. After the 1870s, timber firms held much of the land, but no logging took place until after World War II, when a mill was built near Big Lagoon Marsh, at the lagoon's southeast end. In 1982, the Department of Parks and Recreation acquired 750 acres from the Louisiana-Pacific lumber company, and named the unit for the company's president, Harry A. Merlo.

Big Lagoon's barrier beach is breached several times each winter, and its brackish waters support a large marsh community consisting of tule, sedge, and saltgrass where Maple and Tom Creeks enter the lagoon. Other vegetation includes a coastal strand community of dune tansy, sand verbena, and sea rocket on the sand spit, Sitka spruce forests on the north and southwest shores, coastal scrub on the west-facing hills, and red alder and willow along the creeks. Old-growth redwood grows on the east shore along with Sitka spruce and grand fir. At the south end of the lagoon, east of Highway 101 on Kane Rd., is Stagecoach Hill, which is covered with western azaleas that vary widely in the color, size, and shape of their flowers.

An important link on the Pacific Flyway, the lagoon is a resting and feeding site for thousands of birds during the winter. Some 30 species of fish inhabit the lagoon, including salmon, trout, and starry flounder, as well as Dungeness crab, soft-shelled clams, and bay mussels. Black-tailed deer and black bears inhabit the woodlands, and a herd of Roosevelt elk lives in the marshland and adjacent uplands.

Big Lagoon County Park: *Off Hwy. 101, 12 mi. S. of Orick.*

The park provides access to Big Lagoon Spit and to Agate Beach in Patrick's Point State Park. Facilities include restrooms, a boat ramp, and a campground under a stand of Sitka spruce. Call: (707) 445-7652.

Patrick's Point State Park: *W. of Hwy. 101, 5 mi. N. of Trinidad.*

Established as a state park in 1929, Patrick's Point is named for Patrick Beegan, who homesteaded the area in 1851. The 632-acre park is located on a headland densely forested with Douglas-fir, Sitka spruce, red alder, and pine, with a lush undergrowth of salal, bracken fern, thimbleberry, and azalea. Its varied shoreline consists of scrub-covered rocky promontories, tidepools with abundant algae and invertebrates, and the bluff-backed Agate Beach, scattered with agates and black jade. Offshore rocks provide breeding habitat for pigeon guillemots, black oystercatchers, pelagic cormorants, and western gulls, and hauling-out grounds for sea lions and harbor seals. Several creeks flow through the park, providing habitat for quail, songbirds, and small mammals.

Park facilities include restrooms, a campground, trails, and a visitor's center and museum; many facilities are wheelchair-accessible. The Rim Trail follows an old Indian trail along the bluffs, offering views of Big Lagoon to the north, Trinidad Head to the south, and migrating gray whales offshore. Call: (707) 677-3570.

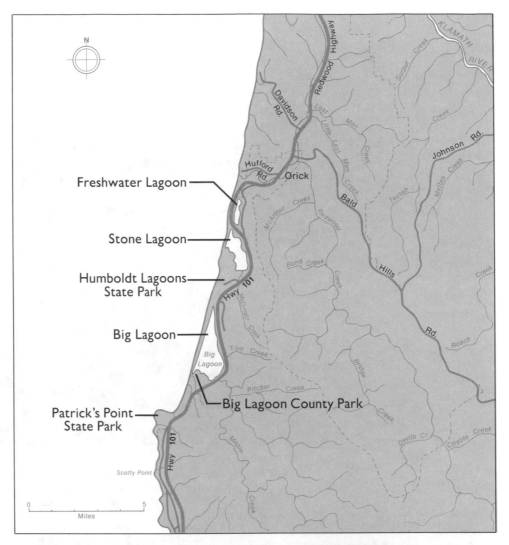

Agate Beach, Patrick's Point State Park

Trinidad State Beach

Offshore Rocks: *Patrick's Point to the Little River.*

Dozens of rocks and small islands are scattered along the Humboldt coast between Patrick's Point and the Little River. Protected from land predators, these offshore rocks provide essential breeding grounds for birds and Steller sea lions, and resting sites for sea lions and seals. Birds breeding on these rocks include the common murre, tufted puffin, western gull, pigeon guillemot, black oystercatcher, and several species of cormorants and storm-petrels.

One of the more important seabird rookeries is Green Rock, located 2,000 feet offshore to the north of Trinidad Head; its common murre colony, estimated at 55,000 birds, is one of the largest in the state. Flatiron Rock, some 4,000 feet northwest of Trinidad, supports six bird species, including 24,000 murres. Little River Rock, 1,600 feet west of Houda Cove, currently supports the largest storm-petrel colony in the state.

Trinidad State Beach: *Off Trinity St., N. of Main St., Trinidad.*

Trinidad State Beach, with 159 acres, provides restrooms, a picnic area, and trails to Trinidad Beach and College Cove, two sandy beaches. The park is situated on a marine terrace covered with Sitka spruce, beach pine, and Scotch broom. Mill Creek, which divides the unit, supports riparian vegetation of red alder and willow, and provides a habitat for numerous songbirds. Coastal scrub vegetation growing on the steep bluffs and on Elk Head to the north includes the Columbia lily and endangered black crowberry, both of which reach their southern limit at Trinidad, and the endangered western lily. Coastal strand vegetation occurs at the base of the bluffs at the two sandy beaches, and tidepools are found below Elk Head.

Pewetole Island, a large, heavily forested rock lying just off Trinidad Beach, is used by black oystercatchers. Perch and rockfish inhabit the nearshore waters, and seals and sea lions haul out on the offshore rocks.

City of Trinidad: *Off Hwy. 101, 14 mi. N. of Arcata.*

Located on a marine terrace above a small harbor, Trinidad is the former site of a Yurok Indian village, Tsurai. The largest and southernmost permanent settlement of the Yuroks, Tsurai was established 5,000 years ago, and was occupied until 1916. The Yuroks used redwood canoes to fish and hunt seals in Trinidad Bay. The village site is now marked by a plaque at the south end of Ocean Street.

The Spanish explorers Heceta and Bodega sailed into the bay in 1775 and erected a cross on Trinidad Head on Trinity Sunday, thereby giving the bay its name. Trinidad Bay was forgotten until gold strikes on the Klamath and Trinity Rivers created the need for a convenient port to supply the mines. Founded in 1850 by a ship's crew, Trinidad had a population of 300 prospectors within three months.

The larger and more protected Humboldt Bay soon became the county's main port. Because it was closer to the mines, Trinidad Bay continued to be an important supply port until the late 1850s, when the gold fever died down. Since then, the town's main industries have been commercial and sport fishing, timber, and tourism. Trinidad is also home to Humboldt State University's Fred Telonicher Marine Laboratory, a teaching and research facility. The laboratory has a wheelchair-accessible visitor's area that contains an aquarium with exhibits of rockfish and tidepools. Call: (707) 677-3671.

Common murre (*Uria aalge*)
1⅓ feet long

Trinidad Head Lighthouse: *South face of Trinidad Head, Trinidad.*

Perched halfway up Trinidad Head, this 25-foot tower has been in continuous operation since 1871. It has also weathered heavy seas; in 1915, a wave striking the headland sent water crashing over the tower, 200 feet above sea level. The light was electrified in 1942 and automated in the early 1970s. In 1948, the Trinidad Civic Club built a replica of the lighthouse above the harbor on Edwards St. at the end of Trinity St. to serve as a memorial to fishermen lost at sea.

Trinidad Harbor: *S. of Trinidad Head, Trinidad.*

Between 1920 and 1926, a whaling station operated in Trinidad Harbor; the bay and nearby waters are now fished commercially for Dungeness crab, silver salmon, king salmon, and bottom fish. Facilities include a privately owned fishing pier that is open to the public, a marine railway for boat launching, and boat moorings. Trails lead from the city to Indian Beach and to tidepools along the bay.

On 362-foot-high Trinidad Head, which juts out on the west side of the harbor, the Tsurai Trail leads through the headland's Sitka spruce, blue blossom ceanothus, and salal to a granite memorial cross. The cross replaces the wooden one placed there by Spanish explorers in 1775. Pelagic cormorants and pigeon guillemots nest on the headland and on the rocks below; dense beds of bull kelp lie offshore. Among the many rocks in the harbor is Prisoner Rock, so named because during the gold rush disorderly citizens were left there overnight; the rock is used by breeding Leach's storm-petrels.

Luffenholtz Beach County Park: *W. of Scenic Dr., 2 mi. S. of Trinidad.*

Named for a mill owner who settled here in 1851, the park is located on a rocky, scrub-covered point, and provides parking, restrooms, and picnic tables. A path along the steep cliffs leads to tidepools and to a sandy beach where smelt and surfperch can be caught.

Houda Point Access: *W. of Scenic Dr., 2.5 mi. S. of Trinidad.*

A parking area on Scenic Dr. provides access to two sandy pocket beaches; rockfish and smelt are fished from shore. The accessway is owned by the Humboldt North Coast Land Trust, a nonprofit land trust that operates several coastal accessways in the area.

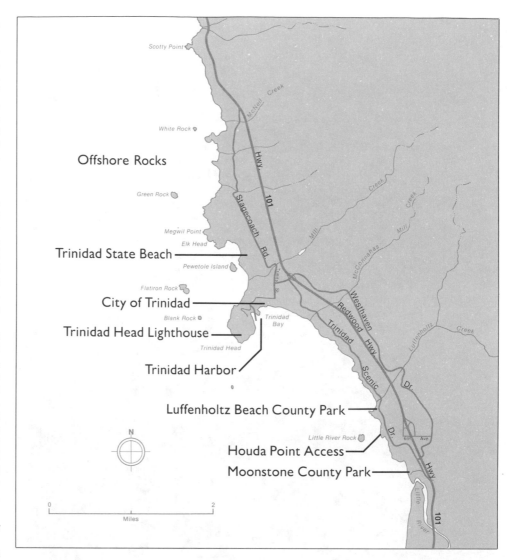

Trinidad Memorial Lighthouse

Moonstone County Park: *W. of Scenic Dr., 3 mi. S. of Trinidad.*

Named for the stones washed in by the waves, this broad, sandy beach is popular with anglers, clam diggers, and surfers. The beach, located north of the Little River, provides a resting and feeding area for gulls, terns, and shorebirds such as the sanderling, dunlin, and willet.

Trinidad Harbor

Little River: *W. of Hwy. 101, 3 mi. S. of Trinidad.*

Although deserving of its name, the Little River has been the site of substantial economic activity for the last 100 years. Its 17-mile watershed, lying entirely within the redwood belt, has been heavily logged since the late 1800s, and much of the upland forest is still owned by timber companies. From 1879 to 1900, the river was dredged for gold, and in 1902, a lumber company built a railroad beside the river. The floodplain is used for livestock grazing and hay production.

The river has been diked to create seasonally flooded farmlands. These pastures and the adjacent riparian woodland are used by hawks, swallows, songbirds, and small mammals. The river and its estuary support seasonal runs of salmon, steelhead, and coastal cutthroat trout; the Humboldt sucker and coast range sculpin are year-round residents.

Dairy ranching along Mad River Road

Little River State Beach: *W. of Hwy. 101, 4 mi. S. of Trinidad.*

Access to this state beach, located on the sand spit south of the Little River, is from a frontage road parallel to Highway 101 or from Clam Beach County Park to the south. The northern portion of the beach lies within the river's floodplain and is sparsely vegetated; the southern portion contains 20-foot dunes covered with yellow bush lupine, beach strawberry, yarrow, and European beach grass. Gulls, shorebirds, and belted kingfishers forage along the beach and in the estuary, and endangered California brown pelicans fish in the nearshore waters, which are inhabited by surfperch and smelt. Razor clams can be found on the sand spit.

Clam Beach County Park: *W. of Hwy. 101, 3.5 mi. N. of McKinleyville.*

Facilities at this broad, dune-backed beach include parking, restrooms, and a picnic area; overnight roadside stops are permitted. Razor clams are found along the water line; insects such as sand wasps and Helfer's beach dune grasshoppers inhabit the dunes. The last 2.5 miles of the Trinidad to Clam Beach Run, which is held each February, are along Clam Beach; for race information, call: (707) 677-3448.

At the base of the bluffs east of Highway 101 are the Clam Beach Ponds, remnant dune hollows donated to Humboldt State University in 1979 for research and recreation. These small freshwater ponds are densely vegetated with pondweed, cattail, and willow, and are used by coots, songbirds, and small mammals. They are periodically stocked with trout.

McKinleyville: *Hwy. 101, 5.5 mi. N. of Arcata.*

Humboldt County's largest unincorporated community, McKinleyville was founded in 1898 when trader and mill owner Isaac Minor built a combination general store, post office, and dance hall on his ranch; Minor's building still stands on Central Ave. as one of McKinleyville's remnants of the Old West. The town was at first called Minorsville, but was renamed in honor of President McKinley after his assassination in 1901. Between 1940 and 1960, the town's population grew with the expanding lumber industry, but then declined as timber employment dropped in the late 1960s.

The town is located on a marine terrace between the Little and Mad Rivers; the adjacent sandy beach is backed by dunes and bluffs. The river bottomlands are used for ranching and hay production. McKinleyville's four creeks support a riparian woodland of black cottonwood, red alder, and willow, providing habitat for amphibians, songbirds, and small mammals. Salmon and trout are found in the creeks.

Mad River: *Mad River Rd., 2.5 mi. W. of Hwy. 101.*

The Mad River was named in 1849 by the exploring party of Josiah Gregg after a dispute between Gregg and the rest of the party. The river, which flows northwest from the Coast Ranges for 110 miles before entering the ocean two miles west of McKinleyville, once flowed into Humboldt Bay; Mad River Slough at the north end of Arcata Bay is part of its former course. The river mouth is still migrating north. In 1855, a canal was built between the river and the slough to float logs into the bay, but was closed by sediment in 1888. Until 1875, the mouth of the Mad River marked the northern boundary of Humboldt County.

The river's rugged watershed is characterized by mixed-conifer forest at higher elevations and redwood forest closer to the coast. Hundreds of migratory waterfowl and shorebirds use the estuary, and snowy plovers nest south of the river mouth, where extensive dunes support dune tansy, sea rocket, and bush lupine. Beach pine, Douglas-fir, and Sitka spruce grow inland of the dunes on the river's eastern bank, and black cottonwood, willow, and salmonberry occur upriver in a band between the river bank and the adjacent fields. Amphibians, rodents, mink, foxes, and black-tailed deer live in the woodlands; the Aleutian Canada goose, bald eagle, and American prairie falcon, all endangered species, may also be spotted in the area.

The Mad River is a major spawning ground and nursery for salmon and steelhead. Other fish inhabiting the river include the Humboldt sucker, rainbow trout, and eulachon, also known as the candle-fish, which reaches its southern limit here. At the state-owned and operated Mad River Hatchery, located east of Highway 101 at the end of Hatchery Rd., salmon and steelhead are raised for release in coastal streams from Del Norte to Santa Cruz Counties. The hatchery is open to visitors; for information, call: (707) 822-0592.

On the north side of the river, the Azalea State Reserve contains dense stands of wild azaleas. Vegetation in the park is controlled to protect the azaleas, which grow best in open areas where there is no competition for space or light. Located east of Highway 101 on North Bank Rd., the 30-acre park provides restrooms, picnic areas, and self-guided nature trails. Call: (707) 677-3570 or 443-4588.

Mad River Beach County Park: *End of Mad River Rd., W. of Hwy. 101.*

The park consists of 150 acres along the sand spit that separates the Mad River estuary from the ocean. There are two parking areas, one adjacent to the river with a wheelchair-accessible restroom and a boat ramp, and one along the sandy ocean beach and high dunes to the west. The river's estuary is a feeding ground for numerous water-associated birds, and supports Dungeness crab, bay shrimp, salmon, and steelhead. Razor clams can be found along the beach, and smelt and surfperch inhabit the nearshore waters, which are popular for surfing.

The county's Hammond Trail Bridge, a recently completed segment of the California Coastal Trail, crosses the Mad River a half-mile east of the park. A former railroad trestle of the Hammond Lumber Company, the bridge is open to hikers, bicyclists, and equestrians. Call: (707) 445-7652.

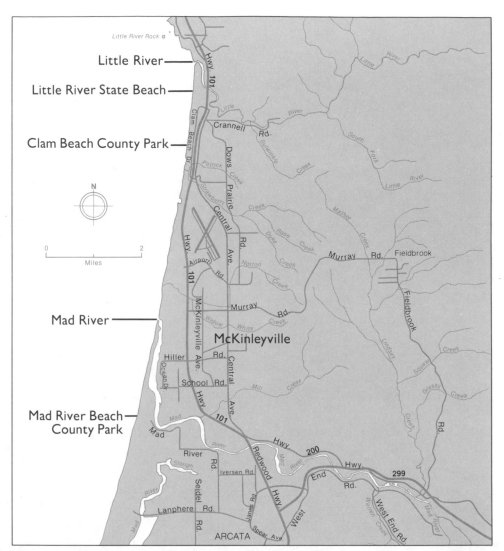

Mad River mouth

Arcata Plaza

City of Arcata: *Off Hwy. 101, 7 mi. N. of Eureka.*

Located on a low plateau north of Humboldt Bay, Arcata was established in 1850 by the Union Company, one of many land companies operating around Humboldt Bay. In 1860 the town's original name of Union was changed to avoid confusion with a town of the same name in El Dorado County; Arcata is said to be an Indian word for "union."

Arcata was a major supply port for the Trinity gold mines during the 1850s; in 1855, a wharf was built across the mudflats to the deeper waters of the bay and was connected to the town by a set of wooden rails, the state's first rail line. Nearby Eurcka, with its more extensive deep-water port, soon surpassed Arcata in importance, replacing it as the county seat in 1856. Arcata's wharf was in use until 1914, when the Northwestern Pacific Railroad reached Humboldt County. Since then, Arcata's main sources of income have been the lumber industry, agriculture, and Humboldt State University.

Arcata's downtown is built around a plaza, and contains many homes built in the Queen Anne and Gothic Revival styles. Many of the town's businesses cater to its large student population. The plaza is the starting point for the Great Arcata to Ferndale Cross-Country Kinetic Sculpture Race, which is held each May; for information, call: (707) 822-3619. The 20-bed Arcata Crew House Hostel, at 1390 I St., is open mid-June to mid-September; call: (707) 822-9995. Redwood Park, located a quarter-mile east of Highway 101 on 14th St., provides picnic areas, a playground, and a playing field. Adjacent to the park is the 600-acre Arcata Community Forest, densely wooded with redwood, Douglas-fir, bracken fern, and redwood sorrel. The forest contains several miles of hiking trails; call: (707) 822-5953.

Humboldt State University: *E. of Hwy. 101 on 14th St., Arcata.*

Located on the slopes of Fickle Hill, Humboldt State University was established in 1913 as the Humboldt State Normal School. The university's programs emphasize natural resources, and the school offers degrees in such fields as forestry, range management, and oceanography. Tours of the campus are available on weekdays; call: (707) 826-4402.

Arcata Marsh and Wildlife Sanctuary: *S. end of I St., Arcata.*

The Arcata Marsh and Wildlife Sanctuary was created in 1979, when the City of Arcata began restoring 65 acres of degraded salt marsh along Arcata Bay. The city built three fresh-

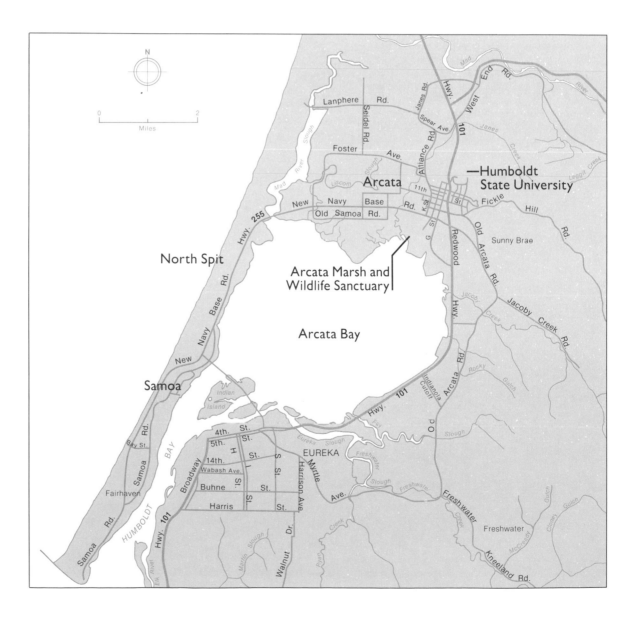

water marshes and a lake at the site, planted the marshes with sedge, sago pondweed, and ditch grass, and stocked the lake with rainbow trout. The sanctuary now supports over 150 species of birds, including migratory ducks and shore-birds, hawks, rails, and warblers. Since 1971, the city has been operating an experimental salmon ranching project at the nearby wastewater treat-ment plant. Juvenile salmon are stocked in the plant's oxidation ponds in a mixture of treated wastewater and bay water.

The marsh provides the only shoreline access in Arcata; facilities include parking, a picnic area, trails along the levees, and a two-lane boat ramp. A second parking area is located on South G St., next to the oxidation ponds, where a trail leads through restored salt marsh. The Au-dubon Society leads nature walks through the marsh each Saturday; call: (707) 822-6918.

Arcata Bay: *Northern part of Humboldt Bay.*

Arcata Bay, or North Bay, is the larger arm of Humboldt Bay, encompassing 8,000 acres. Much of the former marshlands surrounding the bay has been diked for dairy production. These farmed wetlands, including Arcata Bot-toms to the north and Bayside Bottoms to the east, provide winter habitat for herons, egrets, and waterfowl. The bay's remnant salt marsh, much of which is included in the Humboldt Bay National Wildlife Refuge, supports several en-dangered plants, including the Point Reyes bird's beak, Humboldt Bay gumplant, and Humboldt Bay owl's clover. Hundreds of thou-sands of shorebirds and waterfowl, including the endangered Aleutian Canada goose, overwinter in the bay's extensive intertidal mudflats; cor-morants nest on the old pilings of the Arcata wharf. Salmon and trout spawn in Jacoby Creek, which provides riparian habitat for wa-terfowl, raptors, and small mammals. About 45 per cent of California's commercial oyster pro-duction takes place in Arcata Bay; oysters are cultured in beds in the mudflats, and in racks and trays in Mad River Slough.

North Spit: *W. side of Arcata Bay.*

Portions of the ten-mile-long spit that sepa-rates Arcata Bay from the ocean have been in-dustrialized for over a hundred years. In 1872, Danish immigrant Hans Bendixsen built a shipyard that was in use through 1920. Lumber processing facilities were built in 1892, leading to the construction of shipping docks and the establishment of the towns of Manila, Samoa, and Fairhaven.

Dunes extending the length of the spit sup-port a rich coastal strand community of rye grass, beach morning glory, sea rocket, sand-bur, and the endangered Menzies wallflower. On the more stabilized dunes is a forest of beach pine and Sitka spruce, with an understory of California huckleberry and wax myrtle. The Nature Conservancy's Lanphere-Christensen Dune Preserve protects 213 acres of undisturbed dunes, some as tall as 80 feet, and 125 acres of salt marsh. For tours, call: (707) 822-6378.

Manila Community Park, at Peninsula Dr. and Victor Blvd. in Manila, provides picnic areas, playing fields, and access to the bay. The

sandy beach on the ocean side of the spit can be reached from several parking areas off New Navy Base Road. On the bay side is the Samoa Public Access, with restrooms and a boat ramp; camping is permitted. The Coast Guard station at the south end of the spit provides fishing access to the north jetty from May-September. Surfing is popular at the mouth of the bay.

Samoa: *Off Hwy. 255, W. of Eureka.*

Located on Arcata Bay's North Spit, the town of Samoa was originally named Brownsville for an early rancher. In 1889, a group of Eureka businessmen formed the Samoa Land and Im-provement Company, so named because the Sa-moan Islands were in the news at that time, and Humboldt Bay was presumed to resemble the harbor of Pago Pago. The lumber town that soon developed is now owned by the Louisiana-Pacific Lumber Company, and is surrounded by the company's pulp mill operations. The Samoa Cookhouse, a former logging cookhouse, serves family-style meals and contains a small logging museum; call: (707) 442-1659.

Arcata Marsh

Arcata Wharf, ca. 1900

City of Eureka: *Along Hwy. 101, 7 mi. S. of Arcata.*

The largest coastal city in California north of San Francisco, Eureka was established in 1850 by two Humboldt Bay land companies. The name, Greek for "I have found it," had recently been adopted as the state motto, and was an expression popular with miners and traders.

Although Eureka is better situated for shipping, Arcata was at first the county's premier city because it was closer to the Trinity gold mines. However, after the first sawmill was established on Humboldt Bay in 1852, timber ex-

ports created the need for a deepwater port, and Eureka's superior harbor gave it an edge over the other bay towns. In 1856, when trade with the mines was declining, the county seat was moved from Arcata to Eureka; since then, Eureka has been one of California's major ports, serving as a commercial fishing harbor and as the shipping center for export of the county's lumber products and import of its petroleum.

Many of Eureka's older buildings are still standing, including several Victorians in the Queen Anne, Italianate, and Eastlake styles.

The most spectacular example is the majestic Carson Mansion, built by lumberman William Carson in 1886. The three-story redwood building, with its lacy ironwork, stained glass, gables, and turrets, combines characteristics of several styles. Located at 2nd and M Streets, the mansion now houses a private club. Other restored Victorians may be seen in the city's Old Town, a renovated area along the waterfront that features brick-lined streets, sculptured benches, a gazebo, and restaurants and antique shops.

The Clarke Museum, founded in 1960 by high school teacher Cecile Clarke, contains exhibits of Victorian furnishings and clothing, antique toys, and Indian basketry and dance attire. The museum, at 3rd and E Streets, is open Tuesday-Saturday, 10AM-4PM; for information, call: (707) 443-1947. The Humboldt Bay Maritime Museum, at 1410 2nd St., features local shipping artifacts and old photographs. Hours are 11AM-4PM daily; call: (707) 444-9440. The city's 52-acre Sequoia Park, at W and Glatt Streets, includes a grove of virgin redwoods, a zoo, and a playground.

Indian Island: *Off Hwy. 255, Humboldt Bay.*

Also named Gunther Island after Robert Gunther, an early settler, Indian Island is a low, marshy island in southern Arcata Bay. The Wiyot Indians occupied two villages here, and shell mounds dating back 1,500 years have been found. In one of many violent incidents between white settlers and native tribes, 40 Indians who had gathered on the island for a festival were

F Street and Fifth Street, Eureka, ca. 1890

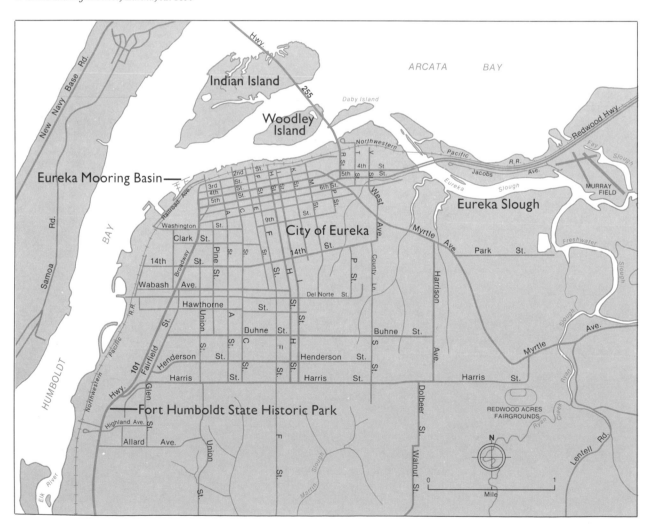

Woodley Island Marina

murdered one night in 1860. The massacre was loudly denounced, but the murderers were never identified or brought to trial.

Although the island was the site of a productive lumber mill and dry dock in the 1870s, and the Samoa Bridge now crosses its northern end, Indian Island remains largely undeveloped; the few homes here are without electricity or water, and are accessible only by boat. The largest single block of salt marsh in Humboldt Bay, Indian Island is part of the Humboldt Bay National Wildlife Refuge. The island supports the northernmost coastal rookery of the American egret; the large white birds can be seen roosting in the Monterey cypress trees. The great blue heron, Virginia rail, and black-shouldered kite (formerly called the white-tailed kite) are also found here. Salt marsh vegetation includes cordgrass and pickleweed, as well as the Humboldt Bay owl's clover and Point Reyes bird's beak, both endangered species.

Woodley Island: *Off Hwy. 255, Eureka.*

Woodley Island was originally covered with salt marsh vegetation. Development began in the 1870s with the construction of a wharf and log booms; in the 1920s, the island was used as a dumping ground for material dredged from channels in the bay. In 1983, completion of a large marina at the southeast shore provided berths for fishing and pleasure boats, a boat hoist, and a restaurant; for information, call: (707) 443-0801. The light tower of the old Table Bluff Lighthouse was moved here in 1984. The rest of the island is a wildlife reserve; birds and small mammals inhabit the cordgrass, arrowgrass, and rushes of the remaining marshland.

Eureka Slough: *S. of Hwy. 101, S. of Arcata Bay, Eureka.*

An intricate system of tidal channels and creeks, Eureka Slough and its tributaries meander through pastureland and marshes at the northern end of Eureka. Although most of the tidal wetlands north of Eureka Slough have been diked for pasture, the area continues to provide seasonal marshland habitat. The sloughs support salt marsh and freshwater marsh vegetation, and are used by anadromous fish, amphibians, waterfowl, and small mammals. Tributary sloughs include Freshwater, Second, Third, Fay, and Ryan Sloughs.

Dead Mouse Marsh, located at the east end of Park St. near Freshwater Slough, is an area of marshland that was restored in 1979. A dike around the restoration area was breached to allow saltwater influx; the area now supports a salt marsh community of cordgrass, pickleweed, and saltgrass. In addition, a new dike was built along a portion of the site that is fed by a spring; protected from the tides, this freshwater marsh is vegetated with willows, sedges, and cattails. Trails along Freshwater Slough lead into the marshland; several species of water birds, raptors, songbirds, and small mammals can be seen in the marshes and surrounding pastures.

Eureka Mooring Basin: *Commercial and 1st Sts., Eureka.*

Most of Eureka's large commercial fishing fleet is based here. Facilities include restrooms, a small boat harbor, a one-lane boat ramp, and fuel docks. The Humboldt Bay Harbor Cruise leaves from the foot of C St., Memorial Day through mid-September; for information, call: (707) 445-1910. The Coast Oyster Company, at the foot of A St., has a self-guided tour of its processing plant; call: (707) 442-2947.

Fort Humboldt State Historic Park: *Off Highland Ave., E. of Hwy. 101, Eureka.*

Hostilities between Indians and whites, and requests for military protection, began shortly after the arrival of white settlers to Humboldt Bay in 1850. In 1853, the U.S. Army established a post on a bluff overlooking the harbor. The fort served for 13 years as an outpost against the Indians and a supply depot for other army units; Ulysses S. Grant was stationed here in 1854. Conflict continued until 1863, when a battalion of volunteers was formed to fight the Indians; within two years, most tribes had surrendered their weapons. The Army withdrew its troops in 1866, and abandoned the fort in 1870.

Only one of Fort Humboldt's original buildings is still standing; however, there are plans to reconstruct the fort. The park features a small museum and a historic logging exhibit with displays of old timber equipment, and provides parking, wheelchair-accessible restrooms, and a picnic area. Call: (707) 443-7952.

Elk River: *W. of Hwy. 101 and Elk River Rd., Eureka.*

Named in 1849 by the exploring party of Josiah Gregg, the Elk River is Humboldt Bay's largest tributary. The stream originates in the steep mountains east of the bay; its watershed, once densely wooded with coast redwood, was heavily logged between 1865 and 1895. The river's floodplain, formerly tidal marshland, has been farmed since the 1870s, when the river was diked; levees extend along the banks for 3.5 miles above the mouth. These pasturelands often flood in the winter, providing freshwater marsh habitat for shorebirds and waterfowl.

A sand spit began to form at the river's mouth in 1930 and now extends over a mile into Humboldt Bay. Reptiles and rodents live on the sparsely vegetated spit, and black-shouldered kites, ospreys, and northern harriers forage there. Several small pockets of salt marsh vegetation occur in the river behind the spit, with plants such as cordgrass, pickleweed, and hairgrass; numerous species of clams can be found in the estuary. The river is a spawning ground for salmon, steelhead, and coastal cutthroat trout.

In 1984, the City of Eureka restored 100 acres of riparian woodland, freshwater marsh, salt marsh, and dunes near its wastewater treatment plant on the west side of the Elk River estuary. A parking area off Hilfiker Lane, west of Highway 101, provides access to trails through the marshland, which is used by waterfowl and small mammals. A second restored area at the south end of the estuary contains seven acres of salt marsh, fenced off to keep out grazing cattle.

King Salmon: *Off Buhne Dr., W. of Hwy. 101.*

In 1983, the heavily eroded shoreline of King Salmon, a small community located on Buhne Point across from the mouth of Humboldt Bay, was restored by the construction of a groin and breakwater and the addition of sand. The breakwater and beach are popular with anglers; boating facilities and equipment, charter boats, and camping are available in King Salmon.

Fields Landing: *Off Hwy. 101, 5 mi. S. of Eureka.*

Named for a longtime resident of the county, Fields Landing was founded in the 1880s as a port and a terminus of the Humboldt Bay and Eel River Railroad. The railroad, owned by the Pacific Lumber Company, hauled timber from the company's mills in Scotia to its docks on Humboldt Bay. The deepwater channel to Fields Landing is dredged regularly, and the town is an active shipping port. The Fields Landing Boat Ramp is located at the foot of Railroad Ave.; facilities include a two-lane public boat ramp on the bay, parking, restrooms, and a grassy picnic area.

The last whaling station in the U.S. was established at Fields Landing in 1939. The station was especially busy during World War II; the sperm whales and humpbacks taken there yielded meat that required no ration stamps, and oil used for making explosives. Amid complaints from residents about the stench, the station closed in 1951.

South Bay: *Southern part of Humboldt Bay.*

The largely undeveloped South Bay provides 4,600 acres of important wildlife habitat, almost all within the Humboldt Bay National Wildlife Refuge. Most of the lowlands surrounding the bay have been farmed since the 1880s; the pasturelands, particularly in the area of Salmon Creek and Hookton Slough, support great numbers of herons, egrets, shorebirds, and ducks. Salt marsh vegetation consisting of cordgrass, pickleweed, and saltgrass occurs below Table Bluff and at the mouth of Hookton Slough, where dikes have been breached to allow former marshland to recover.

Harbor seals use the bay's extensive intertidal mudflats for pupping and hauling out, and shorebirds, terns, and egrets forage there for clams, worms, and fish. Dense eelgrass beds growing in the bay's shallow water serve as a nursery area for Dungeness, red, and rock crabs, and several species of fish. Thousands of black brant, small geese that feed almost exclusively on eelgrass, gather at South Bay during their spring migration. In the open water areas, osprey fish for Pacific herring, sculpin, surfperch, and northern anchovy.

South Spit: *W. side of South Bay.*

In 1891, a jetty was constructed at the north end of the narrow, four-mile-long South Spit. South Jetty Rd. runs the length of the spit, with a public fishing access at the north end, where it is possible to walk out a mile along the jetty. The spit can be dangerous during winter storms, as large waves sometimes wash all the way over the spit and into the bay.

A sparse coastal strand community of yellow bush lupine, European beach grass, beach strawberry, and yellow sand verbena occupies the low dunes on either side of the road. Snowy plovers, songbirds, and rodents inhabit the spit, and are preyed upon by kestrels, northern harriers, owls, and foxes. The sandy beach is frequented by terns, gulls, and shorebirds, and the endangered California brown pelican feeds offshore; gaper clams, littleneck clams, and Washington clams can be found in the tidal mudflats of Humboldt Bay.

Table Bluff County Park: *Table Bluff Rd. off Hookton Rd., W. of Hwy. 101.*

Humboldt Bay is separated from the Eel River to the south by a ridge that terminates above the ocean in a 165-foot-high flat bluff. Early explorers of the bay called the bluff Ridge Point and Brannan Bluff, but by 1851, Table Bluff was known by its present name. Because of its rich soil, Table Bluff has been the site of a small agricultural community since the 1850s; an Indian rancheria is also located here. In 1892, a lighthouse was built on the bluff to replace an older one on the North Spit, and for 80 years, the Table Bluff Lighthouse served ships entering Humboldt Bay. The lighthouse was abandoned in 1972, and its tower is now on display at Woodley Island. Table Bluff County Park provides access to the South Spit, and affords spectacular views of Humboldt Bay and the Eel River Valley. The park is a popular hang gliding area.

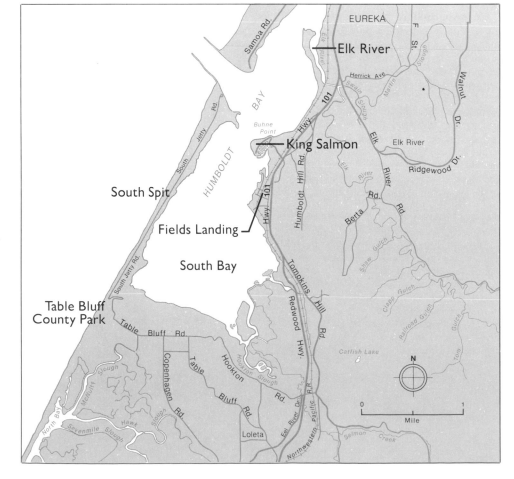

Humboldt Bay

California's second largest enclosed bay, Humboldt Bay consists of two wide arms —Arcata Bay and South Bay—connected by a long channel and separated from the ocean by narrow sand spits. The bay's original inhabitants were Wiyot Indians, who called it "Qualawaloo." With the exception of one visit in 1806, Humboldt Bay was overlooked by early explorers, as its mouth was obscured by sand spits. In 1849, the Josiah Gregg party discovered the bay by land, and in 1850, Douglas Ottinger of the *Laura Virginia* sailed into the bay, naming it for the German scientist Alexander von Humboldt. Settlement began immediately, and timber exports made the area a major shipping center. Most of the shoreline is now developed for industrial, agricultural, and residential purposes.

Dungeness crab (*Cancer magister*)
9¼ inches wide, 6⅜ inches long

To stabilize the width and location of the narrow mouth of the bay, jetties were built off the North and South Spits in the 1890s. Destroyed and rebuilt several times, the jetties were reinforced in 1971 with 5,000 dolosse, which are irregularly shaped, interlocking concrete structures that are extremely resistant to wave force. Humboldt Bay is the first place in the U.S. where dolosse have been used.

As one of the state's major fishing ports, Humboldt Bay provides port facilities, fish receiving and processing plants, and a cannery. Little commercial fishing is done within the bay itself; however, the bay and its tributaries serve as spawning and nursery areas for economically important species such as the Dungeness crab, northern anchovy, Pacific herring, silver salmon, and English sole.

Among the many other fish found in Humboldt Bay are the leopard shark, bat ray, wolf-eel, and several species of rockfish, sculpin, and flatfish. The bay is an important pupping area for the harbor seal; the harbor porpoise can also be seen here. The Humboldt Bay National Wildlife Refuge protects 8,600 acres of marshland, mudflats, and open water. Several areas of diked pastures and industrial lands within the refuge are being restored to wetland. For information on the refuge, call: (415) 792-0222.

View south, Humboldt Bay, ca. 1975

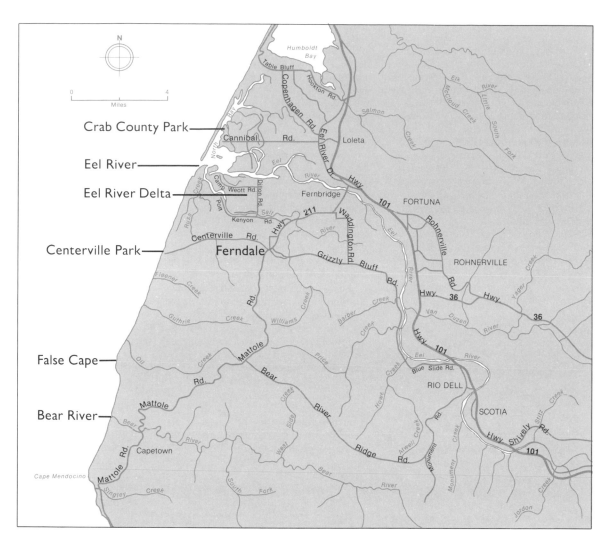

Crab County Park: *W. end of Cannibal Rd., W. of Hwy. 101, Loleta.*

Located on Mosley Island in the Eel River Delta, the park provides boating access to the delta and to its slender north spit, where there is a small wildlife preserve managed by the Department of Fish and Game. Soft-shelled clams, bay shrimp, Dungeness crab, and king and silver salmon are found in the delta; herons, gulls, and shorebirds use the beach; and surfperch and smelt can be caught along the spit.

Eel River: *W. of Hwy. 101 at Fernbridge.*

The Eel River was named in 1849 by the Josiah Gregg party after they spent two days beside the river feasting on lampreys, which they called eels. Both the Eel and its largest tributary, the Van Duzen River, are state and federally classified as wild and scenic rivers. The state's third largest river, the Eel carries ten per cent of California's yearly runoff, and frequently floods its banks. In 1964, the river's largest recorded flood devastated several towns.

The mountainous upper watershed of the Eel River is characterized by mixed-conifer forest; coast redwood and Douglas-fir grow at lower elevations. Some of the tallest living trees are the redwoods in the numerous state parks and recreation areas along the Eel's south fork. The river supports wildlife such as black-tailed deer, mountain lions, and black bears in the upper watershed; Pacific giant and clouded salamanders in the redwood forest; and red-legged frogs, warblers, and ringtails in the riparian woodland. The Eel sustains major runs of salmon and steelhead, ranking second among California rivers in silver salmon and steelhead production, and third in king salmon. The coastal cutthroat trout reaches its southern limit here. Freshwater fish include the Humboldt sucker, brown bullhead, and rainbow trout.

Eel River Delta: *Both sides of the Eel River, W. of Hwy. 101.*

Where the Eel River is joined by the Van Duzen, it emerges from narrow river canyons into a broad, marshy estuary. The first inhabitants of the Eel Delta were Wiyot Indians; in 1851, white settlers arrived and began farming the delta's rich soil, building miles of levees to convert tidelands to pastures. Meat and milk are the delta's major products, but potatoes, corn, and other crops are also grown. Port Kenyon on the Salt River was once an important shipping point, but by 1900, increased siltation had made the river too shallow for ocean-going ships.

Large stands of willow, red alder, and black cottonwood occur along the banks of the Eel and its many sloughs and tributaries. Freshwater marsh vegetation, including bulrush, sago pondweed, and spike rush, is found in the upper reaches of the sloughs. A salt marsh community of saltgrass, alkali bulrush, and cordgrass occurs along the lower Salt River, around the mouth of the Eel, and in McNulty Slough.

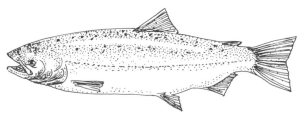

silver salmon (*Oncorhynchus kisutch*)
to over 3 feet long

One of California's largest coastal wetlands, the Eel Delta provides essential habitat for migratory birds using the Pacific Flyway; 10,000 birds are found here at peak periods, including up to 1,000 tundra swans. The delta's raptor population, which includes ospreys, red-tailed hawks, kestrels, and endangered peregrine falcons, is one of the largest along the coast. The delta serves as a spawning and nursery area for ocean fish such as the redtail surfperch, starry flounder, and Pacific herring.

On the north side of the delta, off Highway 101, is the town of Loleta, founded in 1883 as a railroad station. Originally named Swauger for a local landowner, Loleta was given its present name, believed to be an Indian word, in 1893. South of Loleta is Fernbridge, where a seven-arch concrete bridge built in 1911 spans the Eel River. Pedrazinni County Park, off Cannibal Rd. on Seven-Mile Rd., provides parking and a boat ramp.

Ferndale: *5 mi. S. of Hwy. 101, off Hwy. 211.*

Founded in 1852, Ferndale developed as a prosperous farm community and dairying center for the Eel River Delta. The town has remained virtually unchanged since the 1890s, and contains dozens of beautifully preserved Victorians in the Eastlake and Queen Anne styles. Ferndale's distinctive flavor and rural setting have made it a haven for artists, and Main Street is lined with galleries and craft shops.

Ferndale's most popular event is the annual Great Arcata to Ferndale Cross-Country Kinetic Sculpture Race. Participants maneuver their home-made, human-powered vehicles through 36 miles of sand, mud, and marsh, and across Humboldt Bay and the Eel River. For more information, call: (707) 786-4477 or 725-3851. The Ferndale Museum at 3rd and Shaw Streets contains artifacts from the town's history; call: (707) 786-4466. Russ Park, located a half-mile east of town on Grizzly Bluff Rd., provides trails through a dense forest of grand fir and Sitka spruce. The Humboldt County Fairgrounds, west of Main St., offers year-round camping except during the county fair, which is held each August; call: (707) 786-9511.

Centerville Park: *W. end of Centerville Rd., 5 mi. W. of Ferndale.*

During Humboldt County's brief period of oil drilling in the 1860s, Centerville was an important supply depot along the route from Humboldt Bay to the oil fields of the Bear and Mattole Rivers. Centerville Park provides parking, restrooms, and access to ten miles of sand dunes and ocean beach between the Eel River and False Cape. Shorebirds and gulls frequent the beach and dunes; surfperch and smelt inhabit the offshore waters. South of the parking area is a concrete cross erected in memory of the wreck of the *Northerner* in 1860.

False Cape: *5 mi. S. of Centerville Park.*

Named False Cape Mendocino in the 1850s by sailors who often mistook it for the larger headland to the south, False Cape was settled during the 1860s, when oil was found here and along the nearby Bear and Mattole Rivers. The grassy cape provides pastureland for sheep and beef cattle; its creeks support riparian habitat and small runs of salmon and steelhead. A half-mile offshore are the False Cape Rocks, a rookery for several thousand common murres, pigeon guillemots, Brandt's cormorants, and western gulls.

Bear River: *2 mi. N. of Cape Mendocino.*

Originally inhabited by the Mattole Indians, the Bear River area was settled by white ranchers in the 1850s. The discovery of oil here in 1859 led to an influx of settlers; however, when oil extraction proved to be unprofitable, many of the recent arrivals departed, and the area remains sparsely inhabited. The stream's steep upper watershed is heavily timbered with Douglas-fir, madrone, and tanbark oak; the wide floodplain is used primarily as grazing land. The river supports runs of king and silver salmon and steelhead.

Eel River mouth, ca. 1968

Cape Mendocino: *Along the Mattole Rd., 20 mi. S. of Ferndale.*

Named in the 1580s for a viceroy of New Spain, Cape Mendocino is the westernmost point in the contiguous United States. The cape's earliest inhabitants were Mattole Indians; white settlers flocked here after oil was discovered nearby in 1859. When the quality and volume of the oil proved too low to be profitable, the new settlers turned to sheep and cattle ranching along the cape's steep, grassy slopes.

Along the south side of the cape, the Mattole Road parallels four miles of dunes, beaches, and tidepools, accessible at several pull-offs and marked paths; do not trespass on adjacent private lands. The many offshore rocks, including Sugarloaf Island and Steamboat Rock, are a major breeding area for seabirds and Steller sea lions. Sediments from the Mattole River are transported to deep water through the Mendocino Submarine Canyon, located six miles off the cape.

Cape Mendocino Lighthouse: *Off the Mattole Rd., Cape Mendocino.*

With its thick fogs, offshore rocks, and reefs, Cape Mendocino has been the site of hundreds of shipwrecks. In 1868, the Cape Mendocino Lighthouse was built on one of the cape's steep cliffs; it endured for 80 years through high winds, earthquakes, and landslides before being replaced by an automatic light around 1950.

Mattole River and Beach: *W. end of Lighthouse Rd., 5 mi. W. of Petrolia.*

The Mattole River is the site of the state's first commercial oil wells; the oil excitement of the 1860s is reflected in the name of Petrolia, a small community near the river mouth. Many of those who came to the Mattole Valley for its oil remained for its excellent agricultural and grazing land; by 1875, the valley was filled with ranches and small farms.

The upper watershed of the Mattole, which receives some of the heaviest rainfall in the state, has been heavily logged, and much of its Douglas-fir forest has been replaced by tanbark oak and madrone. The lower watershed supports coastal scrub vegetation and Sitka spruce and grand fir forests as well as farms and pasturelands; riparian woodland occurs along the river banks. Salmon and steelhead spawn in the Mattole; red-tailed hawks and endangered golden eagles hunt along the river.

The mouth of the Mattole marks the northern boundary of the King Range National Conservation Area. The sandy beach at the river mouth provides parking, restrooms, and fishing access to the river's estuary, which is used by gulls, shorebirds, and ospreys. Dune habitat extends from the river mouth to Punta Gorda. A trail follows the beach south for 24 miles, past an abandoned lighthouse at Punta Gorda, to Shelter Cove. Call: (707) 822-7648. A.W. Way County Park, on the Mattole Rd. near Petrolia, provides camping and access to the river.

Cape Mendocino Lighthouse

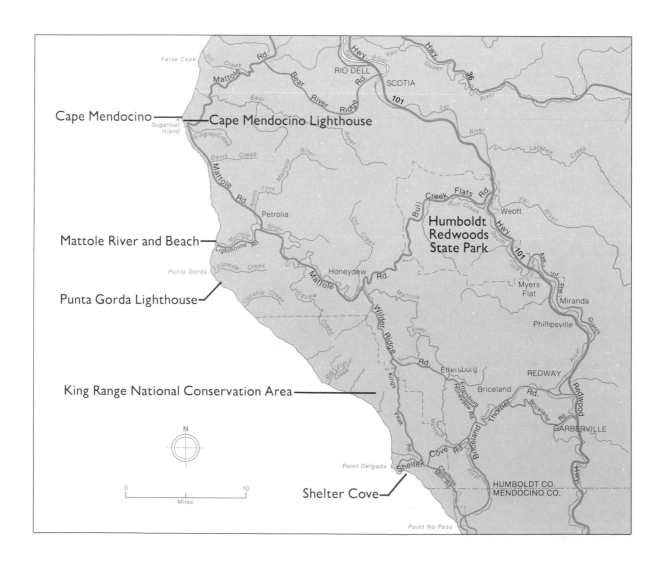

Punta Gorda Lighthouse: *3 mi. S. of Mattole River Beach.*

Punta Gorda, whose name means "massive point," is a high, rounded cape fringed by offshore rocks and reefs. In 1911, after several ships were wrecked off the point, a lighthouse was built on a small flat a mile south of the point. Difficult and costly to maintain, the lighthouse served for only 40 years before it was closed in 1951. The lighthouse is accessible by a beach trail from the Mattole River.

Humboldt Redwoods State Park: *On Hwy. 101, 45 mi. S. of Eureka.*

Northern California's largest state park, Humboldt Redwoods State Park comprises 51,000 acres along the south fork of the Eel River. Half the park consists of spectacular old-growth redwood forests, which support rhododendrons, western azaleas, redwood sorrel, and calypso orchids. The park also contains stands of native grasses, forests of Douglas-fir and madrone, and riparian woodland of red alder and willow.

Wildlife includes blue grouse, black-tailed deer, and bobcats. The Avenue of the Giants, which parallels Highway 101, runs the length of the park through some of the world's tallest trees, and provides picnic areas and trails. The park's facilities, many of which are wheelchair-accessible, include restrooms, campgrounds, horse camping, a visitor's center, and over 100 miles of trails. Call: (707) 946-2311.

King Range National Conservation Area: *Honeydew to Point No Pass in Mendocino County.*

The King Range, part of the "Lost Coast," rises abruptly from sea level to a height of 4,000 feet in less than three miles. The King Range National Conservation Area, administered by the Bureau of Land Management, contains 60,000 acres of rugged mountains and shoreline, including Mattole River Beach and Black Sand Beach. The unit provides campsites, and trails along the beach, on the ridge, and through the Chemise Mountain Primitive Area. Call: (707) 822-7648.

The area's first inhabitants, Mattole and Sinkyone Indians, were killed or driven out by the ranchers and loggers who arrived in the 1850s. Since then, some ranching and timber harvesting have taken place here, but because of the range's steepness, heavy rainfall, and inaccessibility, it has remained relatively wild. Vegetation includes Douglas-fir, sugar pine, madrone, and tanbark oak at higher elevations and on the west slope; chamise, California lilac, huckleberry oak, and manzanita in the Chemise Mountain Primitive Area; native grasses, including the rare leafy reed-grass, near the coast at Big Flat and Spanish Flat; and big-leaf maple, black cottonwood, and California bay laurel along the many creeks.

These diverse habitats support wildlife such as western rattlesnakes, band-tailed pigeons, flying squirrels, black-tailed deer, mountain lions, and black bears. Salamanders, mountain beavers, and otters live near the creeks; California mussels, purple sea stars, and Pacific goose barnacles inhabit the tidepools along the shoreline. Roosevelt elk have been reintroduced to the area, and can be seen in the mountains near Shelter Cove and at Chemise Mountain. Golden eagles, bald eagles, and peregrine falcons, all endangered species, can also be found here.

Shelter Cove: *W. end of Shelter Cove Rd.*

The steep ridges of the King Range drop to a grassy marine terrace at Shelter Cove, which is the only place north of Point Arena where the San Andreas Fault trends onshore. The Sinkyone Indians spent summers here, fishing for salmon, hunting seals, and collecting clam shells for trade with the Northern Pomo Indians. In the 1850s, ranchers came to Shelter Cove to graze their livestock on the fertile grasslands. By 1886, a wharf had been built at the small harbor below, and the cove had become an export center for milk, wool, and produce, and for tanbark, used in tanning leather. Now the site of a small residential community, Shelter Cove provides a harbor for salmon trollers in summer, and is a popular recreational resort.

While Shelter Cove is a privately owned portion of the King Range National Conservation Area, most of the shoreline is open to the public. Beaches include Little Black Sand Beach, Abalone Point, Point Delgada, and the main cove. Rocky tidepools support red abalone, California mussels, purple sea urchins, and several species of algae. Smelt and surfperch can be caught from the beaches, and Dungeness crab, salmon, halibut, and lingcod inhabit the nearshore waters. Restrooms, camping, and a boat ramp are provided; rental boats, marine supplies, and a boat lift are available in summer.

King Range National Conservation Area

Horses at Cape Mendocino

Mendocino County
Selected Species of Interest

 Plants: Western sword fern (*Polystichum munitum*), grows in redwood forest; abundant in Van Damme State Park. **Mendocino coast paintbrush** (*Castilleja latifolia mendocinensis*), endangered; found only in Mendocino County.

 Trees: Pygmy cypress (*Cupressus pygmaea*), dwarf tree, one to ten feet high; found only in Mendocino pygmy forests. **Bolander pine** (*Pinus contorta bolanderi*), dwarf subspecies of beach pine; grows only in pygmy forests.

 Insects: Sand wasp (*Bembix americana comata*); females construct burrows in stabilized sand dunes; visible in dunes near Inglenook Fen. **Lotis blue butterfly** (*Lycaeides argyrognomon lotis*), endangered resident of sphagnum bogs.

 Invertebrates: Sea strawberry (*Gersemia rubiformis*), pinkish soft coral; reaches southern limit at Manchester State Beach. **Great barnacle** (*Balanus nubilus*), grows to four inches in diameter; eaten by Northwest Indians.

 Amphibians and Reptiles: Northwestern salamander (*Ambystoma gracile*), found from mouth of Gualala River northward. **Black salamander** (*Aneides flavipunctatus*), black with gray or green; lives in redwood forest.

 Fish: Silver salmon (*Oncorhynchus kisutch*), important commercial and sport fish; spawns in rivers from summer to late fall. **Bay pipefish** (*Syngnathus leptorhynchus*), lives in eelgrass in the Navarro River estuary.

 Birds: Great blue heron (*Ardea herodias*), up to four feet tall, with blue-gray plumage; nests in colonies along river marshes. **American black oystercatcher** (*Haematopus bachmani*), can be seen foraging on rocky coasts in winter.

 Land Mammals: River otter (*Lutra canadensis*), inhabits upper Albion River. **Townsend's big-eared bat** (*Plecotus townsendii*), has ears more than one inch high, joined across the forehead; seen north of Gualala.

 Marine Mammals: Steller sea lion (*Eumetopias jubatus*), hauls out on offshore rocks; forages in shallow water. **Northern right-whale dolphin** (*Lissodelphis borealis*), slim, blackish dolphin with small but distinct beak; lacks a dorsal fin.

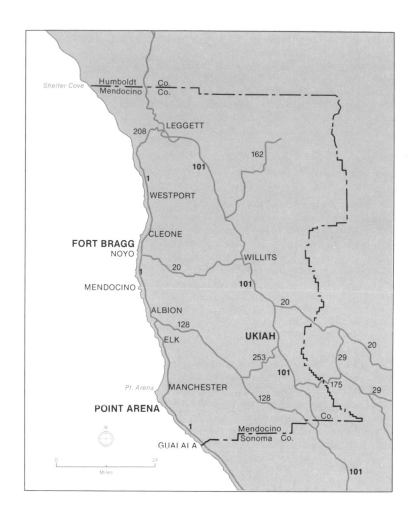

Mendocino County

THE MENDOCINO COUNTY COAST encompasses a diverse geography, from the densely forested Lost Coast of northern Mendocino County to the open grasslands and broad coastal terraces of the Point Arena area. The resources for which the county is best known—redwood trees and salmon—support two of the most important local industries, redwood lumber and commercial fishing. The history of modern settlement and economic development in Mendocino County began with the discovery of gold in California and the subsequent exploitation of Mendocino's vast redwood forests. Commercial and sport fishing, and the most recent important industry—tourism—are evidence of newer patterns of economic activity in the country.

The early history of the coast was shaped by three distinct cultural groups—the Sinkyone, Coast Yuki, and Northern and Central Pomo Indians—who migrated to California as early as 2,000 B.C. Although their languages were different, these groups shared many customs. All three tribes built conical houses of redwood bark and fished the coastal rivers and streams for salmon, using two-pronged harpoons and nets. They built ceremonial dance houses for large gatherings, and constructed sweat houses which the men used for daily cleansing and as a ritual purification before hunting deer. Abalone and other marine life were important food sources; occasionally deer and elk were caught in snares, and acorns, though scarce along the coast, were a diet staple. Although the Pomo built log rafts to cross stream mouths when hunting for mussels or sea lions, none of the Mendocino coast Indians used boats or canoes. Pomo basketry is unique among the woven work of the California Indians; only the Pomo used lattice twining, and were one of the few tribes to use wicker work. Their coiled or twined baskets, often decorated with feathers and abalone shells, are works of exceptional beauty.

Centuries of occupation by Pomo, Yuki, and Sinkyone Indians left little trace on the coastal landscape. However, in the period from 1850 to 1900, sawmills were built on virtually every river and creek, and communities sprouted up at any point along the coast where a schooner could drop anchor and be loaded with lumber. Just prior to the discovery of gold in 1848, San Francisco had a population of 300, and the coast of Mendocino was an expanse of virgin redwood forest. By 1853 San Francisco's population had swelled to 150,000, and within a few years the Mendocino coast was dotted with over thirty sawmills, the result of a surging lumber demand and construction boom in the wake of the gold rush. The first mill in the county was located near the present-day town of Mendocino; by 1853 the Big River mill was turning out 50,000 board feet of redwood a day.

The environmental constraints imposed by Mendocino's rugged coastal topography led to unique developments in the local timber trade. In the 1800s, the lack of paved roads or even adequate trails meant the only practical transportation route was the open ocean, and a specialized shipping trade arose to handle the transportation needs of the budding industry. Sailing ships were fitted with steam engines to better navigate the treacherous rocky coast of the redwood country. The lack of natural harbors made the building of wharves impractical: fierce winter storms, even occasional seismic sea waves, threatened to wash any port constructions away, as often happened to sawmills built at the water's edge. By the 1880s there was a mill on every river, and in every navigable cove a lumber chute was built for loading the schooners; called "doghole ports," these coves were just big enough for "a dog to turn around in." At first, wooden chutes were built with special "aprons" that could be lifted at the ship's deck to regulate the flow of timber sliding down from the mill yard, allowing ships to load while anchored offshore. Later, steel cables with slings replaced the wooden chutes. Even passengers used the slings, sliding from cliff face to ship deck to board for the one-day passage to San Francisco. Steam-powered ships provided the only transportation for lumber until the Union Lumber Company, based in Fort Bragg, completed its rail line to Willits in 1912. Still, the schooners remained in service until the 1930s, when the first paved county roads were constructed.

The lumber industry went into decline with the Depression and most of the mills closed down in the 1930s. Changes such as the introduction of wood pulp products and plywood, as well as continued demand for redwood lumber, have maintained the industry, which continues to employ just under a quarter of the county's workforce. Commercial and sport fishing has become the second major industry in Mendocino County, and Fort Bragg is one of California's four major fishing ports. Almost half of the total value of the county's yearly catch comes from salmon fishing.

The center of the county's tourist industry is the town of Mendocino, renowned for its quaint architecture and spectacular natural setting. Numerous inns dot the northern county coast, attracting visitors year-round, and nine state parks, beaches, and reserves offer a variety of natural environments to explore.

Mendocino

King Range National Conservation Area: *Honeydew in Humboldt County to Point No Pass.*

1,620 acres of the 60,000-acre King Range National Conservation Area are within Mendocino County. Access is via Shelter Cove Rd. and Kings Peak Rd., from Briceland Rd. in Humboldt County. For more information, see Humboldt County.

Sinkyone Wilderness State Park: *Briceland Rd. off Shelter Cove Rd.*

North of Rockport, where Highway 1 turns inland, the Coast Ranges become an almost impenetrable wilderness of steep gorges and narrow ridges blanketed by a vast forestland aptly nicknamed the "Lost Coast." Sinkyone Wilderness State Park encompasses a narrow strip of this remote coast. Once the fishing and hunting grounds of the Sinkyone Indians, the park covers over 7,000 acres of forest and seashore from Whale Gulch along the northern Mendocino coast south to Usal Creek mouth. A trail runs the length of the 15-mile strip of parkland from the mouth of Usal Creek north to Bear Harbor, and connects with the King Range trail system north of Bear Harbor. Hike-in campsites

are located along the coast at Jackass Creek, Little Jackass Creek, and Anderson Gulch; trailhead facilities, including camping areas, will be built at the mouth of Usal Creek. A renovated ranch house at Needle Rock, north of Bear Harbor, provides primitive lodging (no water or cooking facilities) by reservation.

Sinkyone Wilderness offers hikers spectacular views of the crashing surf, offshore rocks, and precipitous cliffs where seabirds such as black oystercatchers, western gulls, pelagic cormorants, and pigeon guillemots make their nests. Offshore of Bear Harbor are beds of giant kelp. A black sand beach, inundated at high tide, stretches north of Bear Harbor to Needle Rock; surf fishing is possible from the beach, and divers find abundant red abalone in the rocky intertidal and subtidal areas. Harbor seals, sea lions, and migrating gray whales can be seen offshore. Commercial crab trapping occurs offshore, from Usal Creek north to Humboldt Bay.

Inland from the coastal bluffs and grassy or scrub-covered marine terraces, the higher ridges are green with Douglas-fir interspersed with groves of tanbark oak, madrone, and California bay laurel. Much of the coast redwood and Douglas-fir has been logged, and only a few pristine groves remain. Black bears, mountain lions, and ringtails are some of the larger mammals inhabiting the wilderness area.

A handful of settlements dotted the Lost Coast during the logging boom in the last half of the 19th century. In 1893 the Bear Harbor Lumber Company built a railroad to carry lumber from the mill on Bear Creek to the company wharf. After nine years of construction, the wharf and portions of the 35-mile-long railroad

were washed away by a seismic sea wave in 1899. The original steam locomotive is now on display at Fort Humboldt State Historic Park in Eureka. Abandoned sheds and a horse barn are all that remain of a settlement at the mouth of Usal Creek.

Sinkyone Wilderness is accessible year-round from Briceland Rd. in Humboldt County, which connects with a dirt road that descends the steep coastal canyons to Bear Harbor. Usal Creek mouth is accessible from Usal Rd., off Highway 1, a few miles north of Rockport. This dirt road was originally a stage line between San Francisco and Eureka in the 1860s and was the only road between these points until the Redwood Highway was completed in the 1920s; it is not recommended for trailers and is impassable for most vehicles during the rainy season. For park information, call: (707) 946-2311 or 986-7711.

Cape Vizcaíno: *W. of Hwy. 1 at Rockport.*

The cape is named for the Spanish explorer Sebastián Vizcaíno, who charted the California coast naming ports from San Diego to Cape Mendocino in Humboldt County. Sandpipers and dabbling and diving ducks winter in the wetland along Cottaneva Creek. Nesting black oystercatchers, western gulls, Brandt's cormorants, pelagic cormorants, and pigeon guillemots populate the rocky coast. Steelhead spawn in Juan Creek, south of the cape; native Thurber's reed grass grows along Highway 1.

The historic settlement of Rockport, a thriving mill town in the late 1880s, lies east of the cape off Highway 1. In the 1870s a 275-foot-long cable suspension bridge spanned the mouth of Cottaneva Creek, connecting the mainland with

Mouth of Usal Creek, Sinkyone Wilderness State Park

a rocky islet in the cove. The bridge served as a loading chute for redwood lumber being carried by schooner to San Francisco and other markets. Several abandoned cottages, the old mill site, and a few residences are all that remain of the settlement.

A large beach at the mouth of Cottaneva Creek, accessible through a private campground, is popular for surf fishing and skin diving. Rockport Bay is a spawning ground for night and surf smelt.

Westport–Union Landing State Beach: *Hwy. 1, 1.5 mi. N. of Westport.*

The beach was the site of a schooner landing in the late 1800s. Steam-powered sailing ships would be loaded with redwood lumber using steel cables suspended between the sea cliff and the ships anchored offshore. The park accommodates recreational vehicles overnight on the blufftop west of Highway 1. Beach access is via trails and stairs from parking and camping areas; there is blufftop wheelchair access. For park information, call: (707) 937-5804.

Abalone Point is a nesting site for western gulls, Brandt's cormorants, pelagic cormorants, and pigeon guillemots. The endangered Mendocino coast paintbrush grows in a narrow strip of coastal strand vegetation on the terrace, which rises 30 feet above the sea.

Westport: *Off Hwy. 1, 15 mi. N. of Fort Bragg.*

Called Beal's Landing in the 1860s, the settlement was renamed Westport in the late 1870s by J. T. Rogers, who built a wharf and loading chute that could handle up to 150,000 board feet of lumber a day. Westport's major exports were shingles, railroad ties, and tanbark, which was the source of tannic acid for San Francisco tanneries. Redwood was used for railroad ties until replaced by creosote-soaked Douglas-fir. The railroad ties were hand-hewn, each from a single log, by "tie-whackers," a local term for the lumberjacks who often worked independently. Today Westport consists of the original saltbox houses of the lumber era, a small cafe, a bed-and-breakfast inn, and a general store where nets for surf fishing may be rented.

Wages Creek Beach, north of Westport and accessible through a private campground west of Highway 1, is popular for fishing. Commercial fishermen trawl for shrimp offshore. There is a day use fee, and reservations are required for camping. Call: (707) 964-2964.

Chadbourne Gulch: *W. of Hwy. 1, 2 mi. S. of Westport.*

A beach which extends north and south of the gulch is accessible from Highway 1 via a dirt road. There is a parking area south of the gulch and trails to and along the bluffs which lead down to the rocky intertidal area; poke-poling, shore fishing, and diving for abalone are popular here. Offshore rocks provide nesting sites for black oystercatchers, western gulls, Brandt's cormorants, pelagic cormorants, and pigeon guillemots; harbor seals haul out on the rocks.

Seaside Creek Beach: *W. of Hwy. 1, .75 mi. N. of Ten Mile River.*

The small beach at the mouth of Seaside Creek is accessible by a roadside turnout adjacent to the beach.

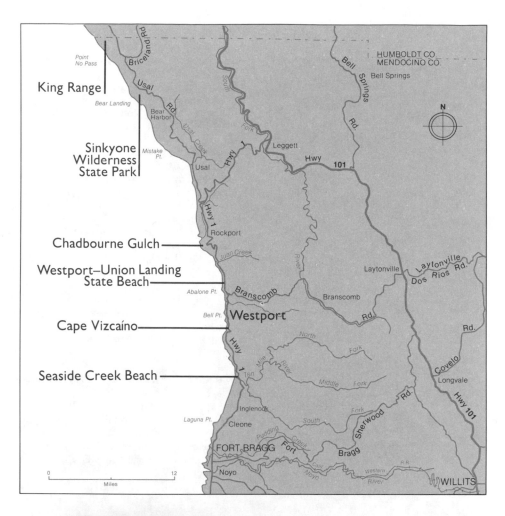

Hauling logs to the railroad, ca. 1880

Ten Mile River: *10 mi. N. of Noyo River.*

So named in the 1850s because it is ten miles north of Noyo River, Ten Mile River and estuary constitute one of the county's largest wetlands. Seventy-five acres of salt marsh lie in back of the dunes at the river mouth. The endangered Menzies wallflower grows in the coastal strand vegetation covering the dunes; nearby are nesting sites for rare snowy plovers. Common mergansers, or fish ducks, nest in the marsh at the river's mouth. The endangered Mendocino coast paintbrush grows on the bluff near the Highway 1 bridge. Silver salmon, steelhead trout, and Pacific lamprey spawn in the north and south forks of Ten Mile River; endangered bald eagles forage in the upstream tributaries during migration.

Ten Mile Beach, one of the longest stretches of dunes in California, extends from the river mouth south for 4.5 miles. Endangered native Thurber's reed grass grows in the dunes back of the beach; surfperch frequent the offshore waters, and night smelt spawn along the beach. Offshore, commercial fishermen catch Dungeness crab.

MacKerricher State Park: *W. of Hwy. 1, 3 mi. N. of Fort Bragg.*

Spanning eight miles of coast, MacKerricher State Park covers almost 1,600 acres of dunes, wetland, and beach, including portions of Ten Mile Dunes, Lake Cleone and Mill Creek, the saltwater marsh along Ten Mile River, and Inglenook Fen.

In 1868 Scottish immigrant Duncan Mac-Kerricher purchased the land around present-day Lake Cleone; his homestead was deeded to the state in 1949, and formed the core of the present state park. Lake Cleone, a tidal lagoon before a road built in the 1940s closed it off from the ocean, is a popular fishing spot and is stocked with rainbow trout. Geese and dabbling and diving ducks winter along Mill Creek, which feeds the lake.

Ten Mile Dunes, MacKerricher State Park

The endangered Mendocino coast paintbrush grows in the dunes north of the lake parking lot. Farther north, Thurber's reed grass and Menzies wallflower, both endangered species, grow in the dunes as do *Ambrosia*, sand verbena, and beach morning glory. The rare globose dune beetle inhabits the dunes.

A short road leads from Lake Cleone to Laguna Point Beach; surf fishing is popular along the rocky shore south to Pudding Creek. Rockfish, lingcod, cabezon, rock cod, and smelt are abundant in the nearshore waters. Offshore, commercial fishing boats trawl for sole and rockfish throughout most of the year; trolling for albacore occurs from August to October, and for salmon between April and September. Laguna Point provides access for abalone divers to rich subtidal waters; there is a harbor seal rookery on the south side of the point.

There are six miles of equestrian trails within the park. Bishop and shore pine shade the park's camping sites; some campsites and restrooms are wheelchair accessible. For park information, call: (707) 964-9112 or 937-5804.

Inglenook Fen: *Within MacKerricher State Park.*

A botanist studying the wetland around Sandhill Lake in the 1960s called the unusual habitat a fen, a word derived from Old English to describe a marsh or swamp. The vegetation of Inglenook Fen is similar to that of bogs and marshes, but contains unusual insect and plant species. Sandhill Lake, at the edge of the fen, is formed by the confluence of two creeks. The dunes surrounding the lake prevent highly acidic runoff from upland redwood and pine forests from entering the marsh, and thus a non-acid environment is created which supports a unique flora.

Within the dunes surrounding Inglenook Fen a diverse biotic community includes at least 30 rare or endemic species of insects and spiders. In the marshy area surrounding but mostly east of Sandhill Lake, plants such as the rein orchid, marsh pennywort, St. John's wort, and brook lime grow among stands of common rushes. The bog or buck bean, rare at this low elevation, grows in the fen's rich soil.

Several species of mammals and salamanders, the California newt, and the ringneck snake inhabit the fen watershed. Great blue herons, cattle egrets, and black-shouldered kites are permanent residents of the fen area; many other birds may be seen from the fen—snowy plovers, black turnstones, kildeer, five owl species, Vaux's swifts, and several species of gulls and hummingbirds.

Fort Bragg: *Off Hwy. 1, 10 mi. N. of Mendocino.*

In 1857, one year after the establishment of the Mendocino Indian Reservation on the Noyo River, a military post was built to oversee the Indian population. Pomo and Yuki Indians as well as members of other tribelets were removed to the reservation, which was abandoned in 1867 after the state legislature condemned it for gross mismanagement. The Indians dispersed to various California reservations, many going to Round Valley Indian Reservation, still in existence, in the county interior.

A walking tour of Fort Bragg, concentrated along Main St., passes by the railroad depot, built in 1924; Shafsky's Ben Franklin Store, dating from the 1880s and the oldest privately op-

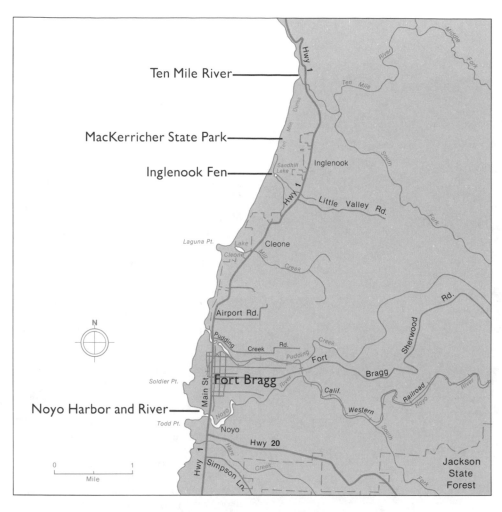

Captain Schuyler Colfax Mitchell, his wife, daughters, and a mate ride sling from schooner Irene *to Noyo Wharf, ca. 1916*

erated business in town; the Fort Bragg Commissary, built in 1857; and remnants of the logging-era Chinese community.

The Georgia-Pacific lumber mill west of Highway 1 dominates the Fort Bragg landscape as well as the area's economy. The mill was built on the site of the old army post in the 1880s to process redwood logged by the Union Lumber Company. It is one of only a few remaining mill operations along the Mendocino coast.

The famous Skunk Train began as the Union Lumber Company's lumber freight train in 1885. Steam passenger service began in 1904 and was extended to Willits by 1911, providing a rail link between the north coast and San Francisco; in 1925 the steam engines were replaced by gas-powered electric cars, nicknamed "skunks" for the noxious fumes they emitted. Today, the Skunk Line employs a diesel locomotive which makes daily passenger runs from Fort Bragg to Willits along Pudding Creek and the Noyo River through 40 miles of dense redwood forests. Call: (707) 964-6371.

Noyo Harbor and River: *Off Hwy. 1, 1.8 mi. S. of Fort Bragg.*

The name Noyo is derived from No-yo-bida, the name of the Pomo Indian village at the mouth of the river. Commercial fishing of silver salmon began here in the 1880s, but the first king salmon was caught by a local fisherman in 1898 using a flasher made from a silver tablespoon. The construction of the Union Lumber Company's railroad to Willits enabled Noyo fishermen to ship their fish, packed in ice, to San Francisco. Today Noyo Harbor is the most important fishing port in Mendocino County; sole, cod, salmon, and other ocean fish caught by Noyo fishermen are shipped frozen to cities across the country.

Smelt spawn at the mouth of the Noyo River; silver salmon and steelhead trout spawn upstream. Dungeness crab, Pacific herring, striped surfperch, and starry flounder inhabit the river estuary, which is also an overwintering area for migrating shorebirds, geese, and dabbling and diving ducks.

Noyo Harbor

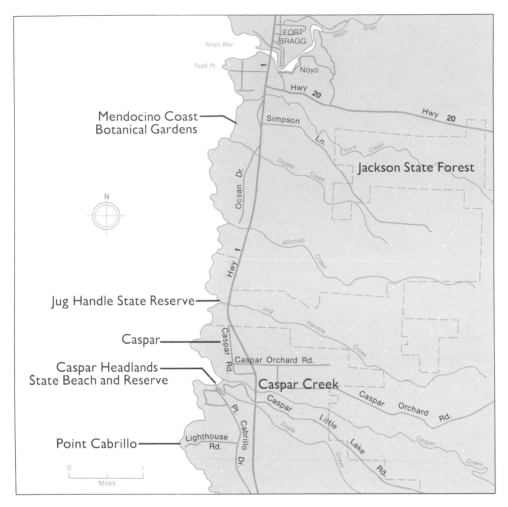

Jug Handle Creek mouth

Mendocino Coast Botanical Gardens: *Hwy. 1, 2 mi. S. of Fort Bragg.*

Located on the marine terrace west of Highway 1, the 47-acre botanical gardens include azalea and rhododendron groves, coastal wildflowers, and a fern canyon. A trail leads from the gardens, across the grass-covered headland, and down to a small sandy beach. Begun in 1960 by the resident landowners, the gardens are now operated by a non-profit organization. For information, call: (707) 964-4352.

Jug Handle State Reserve: *Hwy. 1, 5 mi. S. of Fort Bragg.*

The 700-acre reserve, with 46 acres of ocean frontage and four miles of hiking trails, extends from the beach at the mouth of Jug Handle Creek west of Highway 1, inland to the western boundary of Jackson State Forest. The reserve supports a variety of marine and terrestrial habitats, the most significant of which is the Mendocino pygmy forest. Composed of dwarf pines, cypresses, and shrubs, the pygmy forest grows on the upper steps of the "ecological staircase," a series of marine terraces that rise successively from sea level to a height of about 500 feet, two miles east of Highway 1.

The "staircase" comprises five terraces, each 100,000 years older and 100 feet higher than the one below it. The terraces were formed by the action of waves cutting into the sandstone cliffs as Pleistocene sea level rose and fell. Periodic earth movement related to tectonic plate activity along the Pacific coast caused the terraces to be uplifted; the terraces gradually emerged from the ocean and were covered with sand deposited by winds. This intermittent uplift continues at an average rate of about one inch per century. A sixth terrace is being formed by wave action at the mouth of Jug Handle Creek. The "staircase" is an illustration of coastal ecosystem genesis and evolution; while in most locations the terraces are eroded and no longer distinguishable, here the complete sequence has been preserved.

Plants of the north coastal prairie community are common on the first terrace, including the varicolored lupine and the endangered Mendocino coast paintbrush. Grassland species dominate farther inland, where the underlying soil, a true prairie soil, has accumulated over thousands of years of continuous grass sod decomposition; very few such communities remain on the California coast. The Sitka spruce, which also grows on the terrace, is wind-sculpted and distorted, a phenomenon common at tree-line in alpine forests and named "krummholz"—literally, twisted wood. The second terrace, once covered by virgin redwood forest, is now dominated by second-growth redwood trees. On the third terrace, soil fertility diminishes and pines begin to outnumber redwoods. Growing on the third, fourth, and fifth terraces is the pygmy forest; here mature Mendocino cypresses, Bishop pines, and Bolander pines grow to a height of just five to ten feet. Understory shrubs such as Labrador tea, rhododendron, salal, Fort Bragg and hairy manzanita, and huckleberry are also dwarfed as a result of the shallow, nutrient-poor, and extremely acid soil.

A trail beginning west of Highway 1, at the reserve's parking lot, follows Jug Handle Creek inland through riparian forest. In the creek's upper watershed are several sphagnum bogs—layers of peat in standing water—whose acid soils are much less fertile than other freshwater aquatic habitats. The bog is vegetated primarily with mosses, but the endangered swamp harebell grows here as does *Drosera*, or sundew, an insectivorous plant that uses its sticky leaves to capture its prey.

Jackson State Forest: *E. of Hwy. 1, Noyo to Big River.*

Named after Jacob Green Jackson, founder of Caspar Lumber Company, the forest is a mixture of second-growth redwood, Douglas-fir, grand fir, hemlock, Bishop pine, tanbark oak, alder, and madrone; it has been part of a timber management program since the land was purchased in 1947. The Department of Fish and Game manages an egg collection station within the state forest, where steelhead trout and salmon are caught and their eggs taken for fishery restoration. For camping information, call: (707) 964-5673.

Mendocino Woodlands, within Jackson State Forest, is bisected by the Little North Fork of the Big River. Redwood and mixed-evergreen forest dominate the landscape; animals are abundant and include beavers, pileated woodpeckers, and a variety of amphibians such as Pacific giant, northwestern, and clouded salamanders. Within the woodlands are several group camps built during the Depression under the auspices of the Works Progress Administration. The camps have individual cabins and a central lodge with kitchen. For information, call: (707) 937-5755.

Caspar: *Off Hwy. 1, 3 mi. S. of Noyo Harbor.*

Built on the flat marine terrace inland of Caspar Point, the community's handful of weathered wood buildings cluster near the imposing gothic-style Four Square Lighthouse Church. Now a quiet hamlet, Caspar was once a busy port and mill town during the lumber boom of the last century.

Caspar Creek: *W. of Hwy. 1 at Caspar.*

Caspar Creek, which empties into the ocean at Caspar Point, is an overwintering area for migratory shorebirds, geese, and dabbling and diving ducks. The remains of a sawmill at the mouth of Caspar Creek date from the logging era; built in 1850 by the Caspar Lumber Company, the mill was once the largest lumber manufacturing operation on the Mendocino coast.

Caspar Headlands State Beach and Reserve: *.7 mi. S. of Caspar.*

The small state beach, exposed only at low tide, is located at the mouth of Doyle Creek, along Point Cabrillo Drive. Skin diving and fishing are possible from the beach, often frequented by foraging shorebirds. Harbor seals haul out from offshore rocks, south of the creek mouth.

Caspar Headlands State Reserve comprises four separate parcels of land along the bluff overlooking the state beach. The grassy headlands provide views of the coast, and access to the rocky intertidal areas for fishing and abalone diving. The reserve, which borders private property, is accessible from South Caspar Dr. and Headlands Dr., but permits must first be obtained at Russian Gulch State Park, south on Highway 1. Call: (707) 937-5804.

Point Cabrillo: *W. of Hwy. 1, 1.5 mi. S. of Caspar.*

Black oystercatchers, pelagic cormorants, and pigeon guillemots nest on the rocks offshore of Point Cabrillo. The waters adjacent to the point have been designated a reserve by the Department of Fish and Game, and no fish or other marine life may be taken here. The endangered Lotis blue butterfly completes its life cycle in the restricted locality of small sphagnum bogs within stands of pine near the point.

The Point Cabrillo Lighthouse was built in 1900 by the U.S. Lighthouse Service to guide steam-powered lumber schooners. Three residences and a fog signal were also built at the present site. The unique octagonal tower, Victorian in style, is 47 feet high and sits on a terrace 84 feet above the sea. The Fresnel lens has been out of operation since the light was automated in the 1970s. In 1963 the last civilian lighthouse keeper retired and the Coast Guard now operates the light, which is closed to the public.

Caspar Harbor, ca. 1870

Point Cabrillo Lighthouse

Mendocino Presbyterian Church, State Historical Landmark

bird nesting site; over 1,000 birds, including black oystercatchers, Brandt's cormorants, common murres, and pelagic cormorants, are known to nest here. The endangered Mendocino coast paintbrush grows along Heeser Dr., interspersed with lupine, plantain, and a variety of grasses. Call: (707) 937-5804.

Mendocino: *Off Hwy. 1, 10 mi. S. of Fort Bragg.*

William Kasten, the lone survivor of an 1850 shipwreck off the nearby coast, was the first settler in what later became Meiggsville, now called Mendocino. San Francisco Alderman Harry Meiggs built the county's first redwood lumber mill in 1853 on Big River. He amassed a fortune providing lumber for the booming Barbary Coast of the gold rush era. The last mill in town closed in the 1930s after processing more than seven billion board feet of redwood.

The Masonic Hall, built in 1865, is topped by a sculpture carved from a single block of redwood, with figures based on Freemasonry symbols; the Presbyterian Church, which is now a State Historical Landmark, was constructed in 1867. Another historical landmark, the Temple of Kuan Ti on Albion St., was the cultural hub for the large Chinese community living here at the turn of the century. Mendocino's fortunes waned with the demise of the logging industry in the 1930s; the community later became a favored residence for artists. The Mendocino Art Center was established in 1959 and the flourishing artists' colony attracted an ever-increasing stream of visitors to its numerous galleries and shops.

Big River: *S. of Mendocino.*

The Big River estuary, including mudflats and marsh, covers 1,500 acres, and is one of the largest relatively undisturbed estuaries along the California coast. Starry flounder and Dungeness crab inhabit the river estuary; silver salmon and steelhead trout spawn upstream. Geese, ducks, and endangered bald eagles overwinter in the river's inland watershed.

The sandy beach at the mouth of Big River, a portion of Mendocino Headlands State Park, is accessible from North Big River Rd., east of Highway 1. Big River empties into Mendocino Bay, where brittle stars, sea cucumbers, and sea urchins are found in abundance in the rocky intertidal and subtidal areas. The biologically rich environment of the surge channels, dense with giant kelp, provides habitat for blue and black rockfish, striped perch, kelp greenling, cabezon, buffalo sculpin, and lingcod.

Van Damme State Park: *Hwy. 1, 3 mi. S. of Mendocino.*

The park extends east and west of the highway, from headlands that rise 40 to 60 feet above the sea to second-growth redwood forest along Fern Canyon farther inland. A trail through the canyon traces portions of the logging skid road which dates from the 1880s. A short spur trail near the end of the canyon leads to the pygmy forest loop trail, which is also accessible via Little River Rd., 2.8 miles east of Highway 1. A sign on Little River Rd. indicates the pygmy forest parking area. The campground east of the highway has wheelchair-accessible restrooms. Call: (707) 937-0851 or 937-5804.

The mouth of Little River, just south of the park and visible from the Fern Canyon Trail, is

Russian Gulch State Park: *2 mi. N. of Mendocino.*

West of Highway 1, Russian Gulch empties into the ocean below the scenic headland where a 200-foot-long sea-cut tunnel has collapsed, forming a blow hole. Offshore rocky intertidal and subtidal areas populated by sea urchins and abalone are popular for skin diving. Pine savannah covers the marine terrace east of the headland; a bicycle path winds through the lower canyon of the gulch, which is forested with second-growth redwood, Douglas-fir, and an understory of ferns. Hiking trails lead inland along the gulch to a waterfall, and eventually to the pygmy forest on the upper ridges. Facilities include a recreation hall, group campsites, and horse camps. Call: (707) 937-5804.

Mendocino Headlands State Park: *Along Lansing and Heeser Drives, Mendocino.*

The park is located on the much-photographed headland and marine terrace just west of the town of Mendocino. Hiking and bicycling trails traverse the steep bluffs which rise 50 to 70 feet above sea level and offer views of the rocky offshore islands, blow holes, tidepools, and sandy beach below. Goat Island, a large sea stack a few yards offshore, is an important sea-the site of the historic Little River community. In 1864 Silas Coombs built the lumber mill which is now the recreation hall in Van Damme State Park. The old Coombs mansion south of the park is now the Little River Inn. Little River was a shipbuilding center in the late 1800s; schooners for the coastal lumber trade were constructed here.

Mendocino Pygmy Forests: *Between Ten Mile and Navarro Rivers.*

Mendocino pygmy forests grow in scattered locations on the upper marine terraces along the coast on public and private lands between the Ten Mile and Navarro Rivers. Within Jug Handle State Reserve and Van Damme State Park are public trails through the pygmy forest. Here dwarf cypresses that may be 50 years old are only a foot high and a quarter of an inch in diameter. Six- to eight-foot-high Bolander and Bishop pines also grow here, along with dwarf shrubs such as huckleberry and manzanita. The Bolander pine, genetically distinct from its ancestor, the beach pine, is restricted to the pygmy forest locale.

The dwarf trees and shrubs grow in a nutrient-poor soil called podzol, a Russian word that describes the soil's ash-gray color. As original marine terrace soils were gradually leached of minerals and organic matter, a hardpan was created beneath the surface soil that could not be penetrated by plant roots. The dwarf trees and shrubs have adapted to the shallow, mineral-poor topsoil; in better soil conditions they attain normal heights. Pygmy forest soils are the most acid in the world, with a pH about the same as vinegar.

Albion River: *3 mi. N. of junction of Hwy. 1 and Hwy. 128.*

The river mouth, open to the sea year-round, is a saltwater estuary inhabited by rainbow and rubberlip surfperch, starry flounder, and Dungeness crab. Beds of eelgrass grow along both sides of the channel. Great blue herons build their nests along the river, and migratory geese and dabbling and diving ducks winter here. The river is also an important sport fishing area for silver salmon and steelhead trout. Harbor seals frequent the river mouth, and river otters are common farther upstream.

Albion: *15 mi. S. of Fort Bragg on Hwy. 1.*

Albion was the site of the first water-powered lumber mill in California. Built by Captain William Richards of San Francisco in 1852, the mill provided the basis of a thriving economy until the Depression. Today, Albion is an important commercial fishing port.

Schooner Electra *at Thomas H. Peterson's shipyard, Little River, ca. 1860*

Navarro River, Paul Dimmick State Park

Navarro River: *Junction of Hwy. 1 and 128.*

The river supports anadromous silver salmon, steelhead trout, and introduced striped bass, as well as surfperch and starry flounder. Shorebirds forage at the river mouth, which is a Dungeness crab nursery; migratory waterfowl use the estuary in the winter months. Common egrets are permanent residents along the river, building their nests along the banks. The bay pipefish, which grows to 14 inches and is a relative of the sea horse, lives in the eelgrass beds at the mouth of the river. Red abalone are abundant in the rocky intertidal waters around the Arch of the Navarro at the river mouth. Redtail surfperch inhabit the offshore waters.

The name "Navarro" is probably Pomo in origin, and appears on an Albion land grant map as early as 1844. A historic doghole port called Wendling stood in the deep valley on the south bank of the river; this company town had over 1,000 employees and seven saloons. The company mill closed in the 1930s.

Fifty acres of beach and trails are accessible from the west end of Navarro Bluff Rd., and campsites and restrooms are located on the beach. Shoreline fishing access is from the south bank of the river. Offshore, commercial fishing boats trawl for sole and rockfish.

Paul Dimmick State Park: *8 mi. E. of Hwy. 1 on Hwy. 128 (Navarro Rd.).*

This wayside campground provides access to

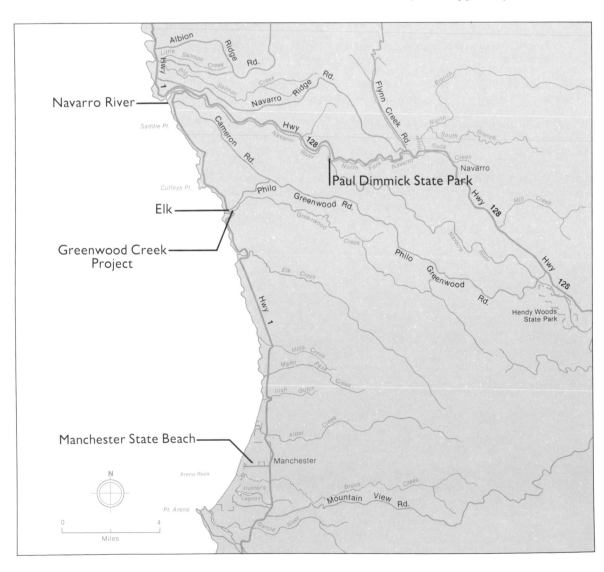

12 acres of Navarro River frontage and is a popular spot for winter steelhead fishing. For information, call: (707) 937-5804.

Elk: *6.2 mi. S. of junction of Hwy. 1 and Hwy. 128.*

The Elk area was settled in the 1840s by the sons of Caleb Greenwood, who ran the first wagon train across the Sierra. Elk River was the original name of the historic doghole port. A sawmill built in the mid-1880s at the mouth of Greenwood Creek, south of present-day Elk, supported a small residential community at nearby Cuffey's Cove. Elk Creek Railroad, built to move logs to the mill at Greenwood Creek in 1890, extended for 24 miles to upper Alder Creek. Between Greenwood and Elk River a trestle was suspended from the sea cliffs within range of the splashing surf. Nothing remains of historic Greenwood; the present-day town of Elk, a few miles north, has a population of about 250 people. Rentals for ocean kayaking are available in Elk.

Greenwood Creek Project: *6.2 mi. S. of junction of Hwy. 1 and Hwy. 128.*

There are no signs to this state-owned beach, which is accessible via a dirt road and parking lot west of Highway 1 at Elk. The park includes the blufftop, beach access, and portions of Greenwood Creek and Bonee Gulch, which joins the creek within the park. For park information, call: (707) 937-5804.

Greenwood Cove and Beach lie beneath a narrow, flat marine terrace; the cove has islets and dome-shaped sea stacks. Lumber was once loaded onto waiting schooners at Casket Wharf by a cable that operated until 1929. The steel cable allowed a sling filled with lumber to be slipped from the cliff to the deck of the schooner anchored some distance offshore. Due to the lack of natural harbors and the treacherous rocky cliffs, this was the only means of transporting lumber from Mendocino County mills to distant markets.

Silver salmon and steelhead spawn in Greenwood Creek after winter rains open the sandbar that closes the creek to the sea during the summer. The creek is a wintering site for migratory geese and dabbling and diving ducks. The offshore rocks from the mouth of Greenwood Creek south to the mouth of Elk Creek support nesting pelagic cormorants and pigeon guillemots. Just south of the park, at the mouth of Elk Creek, is a smelt spawning ground. Steelhead spawn in the upper reaches of the creek. Western gulls, Brandt's cormorants, common murres, and pigeon guillemots nest on the offshore rocks south of the creek mouth.

Manchester State Beach: *1 mi. N. of Manchester.*

The park extends from Alder Creek to one half-mile north of the Garcia River. At the mouth of Alder Creek are smelt spawning beds; steelhead spawn farther upstream. Migratory waterfowl winter along the creek in the freshwater habitat that extends from the creek mouth to two miles upstream. Along the south bank of Alder Creek the main branch of the San Andreas Fault leaves the shore and continues along the ocean floor until re-emerging in Humboldt County. The 1906 earthquake fissure turned seaward at Alder Creek and the bridge that once spanned the creek was destroyed by the tremor. The fault can be traced from the old highway route 1.5 miles north of Manchester.

The park entrance is on Kinney Rd., off Highway 1. Campsites are in the dunes back of the beach. The coastal strand community covering the dunes includes beach morning-glory and sea fig; beach pine growing at the margins of the dunes is at the southern limit of its range here. At the south end of the park, Hunter's Lagoon, a freshwater pond surrounded by marsh within the stabilized dunes, has a canopy of aquatic vegetation including yellow pond lilies; two plants uncommon near the coast, bladderwort and mare's tail, grow in the surrounding marsh. The lake was created during the Pleistocene as dunes formed at the mouths of the rivers that once flowed to the sea from deep inland gorges.

Arena Rock is located offshore, southwest of the beach, its presence indicated only by waves breaking over its submerged crest. A pristine and diverse marine community inhabits the rock's surface and its caves, as well as the surrounding waters. Kelp and coralline algae are abundant near the water surface; sponges, hydroids, bryozoans, and tunicates form a colorful mosaic on the rocky surfaces. This is the southern limit for the soft coral "sea strawberry," more commonly found north of Trinidad Bay in Humboldt County. Overhangs and caves provide habitat for rockfish, china rockfish, and tiger rockfish, a rare species. Large lingcod, which may weigh over thirty pounds, often frequent the caves. For park information, call: (707) 937-5804.

Manchester State Beach

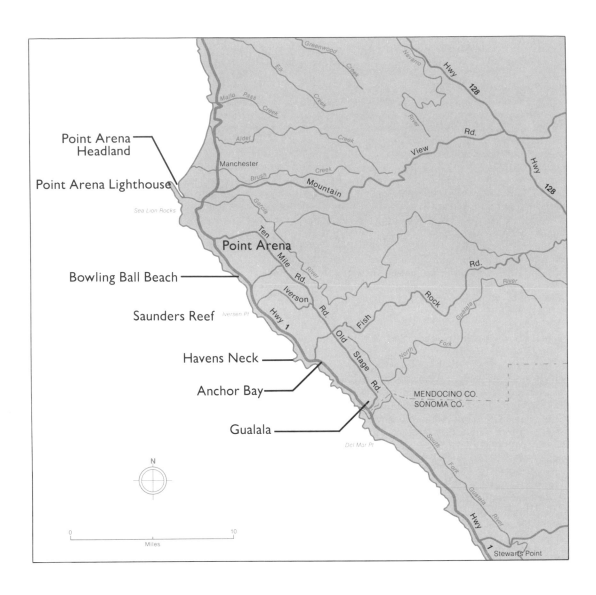

Point Arena Lighthouse

Point Arena Headland: *Lighthouse Rd., off Hwy. 1, 2 mi. N. of Point Arena.*

The prominent headland is the terminus of the Garcia River and the site of the Point Arena Lighthouse. The point is a popular cabezon and rockfish sport fishing spot. Nesting black oyster-catchers, pelagic cormorants, and pigeon guille-mots inhabit the offshore rocks. Steller sea lions and harbor seals frequent the waters just south of the point, where large beds of giant and bull kelp support abundant marine life.

The Garcia River, like the Gualala River far-ther south, runs south to north along the San Andreas Fault zone. The river was named for Rafael Garcia, who built a mill here in 1869. The mill had a wooden flume or chute that allowed logs to be floated from the inland logging areas to the mill. The mill site, called Flumeville, was located near the junction of Highway 1 and Lighthouse Road.

Migratory sandpipers, mallards, and dab-bling and diving ducks winter in the Garcia River estuary, and a flock of tundra swans re-turns here on their yearly migration. This spe-cies, which summers in the Alaskan tundra, usually winters in the Central Valley and is rarely seen on the coast. The river supports spawning runs of silver salmon and steelhead trout. Blue herons nest along Hathaway Creek, a tributary stream. The coast lily and the en-dangered Mendocino coast paintbrush grow along this stream, and endangered peregrine falcons have been sighted in the area where the creek flows into the Garcia River.

Point Arena Lighthouse: *Lighthouse Rd., off Hwy. 1.*

Built in 1870 of brick, the imposing light tower was toppled in the 1906 earthquake which near-ly leveled the town of Point Arena as well. The second tower, built of reinforced concrete, was made by the Concrete Chimney Company of San Francisco, which specialized in factory chimneys. The 115-foot tower contains the origi-nal Fresnel lens, which is over six feet in diame-ter. When in operation, the lens was rated at over 4 million candlepower and was visible for 20 miles. Before the introduction of electric lights, lighthouse keepers had to crank the weight which turned the lens every four hours during their 12-hour shifts.

The lighthouse is now managed by the non-profit Point Arena Lighthouse Keepers, Inc., which conducts daily tours from 11 AM-2:30 PM. Three former keepers' residences are available for rental. For information, call: (707) 882-2777.

Point Arena: *4.3 mi. S. of Manchester.*

Point Arena, once a whaling station, became the busiest town between Eureka and San Fran-cisco at the height of the lumber boom in the late 1800s. By 1880 the town boasted a population of

500, three hotels, three general stores, three churches, a school and fire department, and numerous saloons. Every Wednesday was "steamer day" in Point Arena; local farmers would load their produce onto waiting steam-powered schooners, and travelers would embark on the one-day trip to San Francisco. Point Arena Cove was the site of several attempts to extract oil from bituminous sands in the cove. The first wells were drilled in 1888; recent drilling has not produced any oil.

Bowling Ball Beach: *W. of Hwy. 1, 3.5 mi. S. of Point Arena.*

The beach is named for the rocks visible at low tide, which resemble large bowling balls. The balls, which geologists call concretions, were formed in the Miocene-age strata exposed along the cliff face. Chemical processes created the 5- to 12-foot spheres which gradually "weathered out" from the cliff and fell to the beach below. Parking and trails to the beach are located along Schooner Gulch Road. Roderick's fritillary, a rare lily, grows on the bluff south of Schooner Gulch.

Saunders Reef: *Offshore, 4.6 mi. S.E. of Point Arena.*

The reef is influenced by the circulation of the south-flowing California Current during the summer and early fall. Upwelling, occuring in spring and early summer, brings cold, nutrient-rich water close to shore and stimulates the growth of phytoplankton, the major source of food for marine organisms. The subtidal biota is typical of rocky, wave-exposed nearshore areas along the coast of Central and Northern California. Offshore rocks provide nesting sites for seabirds and a nursery for harbor seals.

Along the grassy terrace at Saunders Landing, a former doghole port, the seaward bluffs are covered with varicolored lupine which, unlike other lupine species, can withstand the higher soil and air temperatures of the summer months. On the rocky cliff outcrops are live-forever, yarrow, columbine, musk flower, and coast buckwheat.

Havens Neck: *W. of Hwy. 1, 5 mi. N. of Gualala.*

The peninsula, privately owned, is awash with colorful wildflowers in the spring, including four subspecies of manzanita, the coast lily, and the calypso orchid. Offshore are picturesque, wind-eroded rocks, habitat for sea palm and red abalone; these waters are also inhabited by California and Steller sea lions.

Anchor Bay: *Hwy. 1, 4 mi. N. of Gualala.*

A single store at Anchor Bay served the surrounding settlements during the height of the lumbering era in the mid-1800s. During Prohibition, rum runners took advantage of the secluded coves from here south to Stewart's Point in Sonoma County.

The rocks exposed in the cliffs at Anchor Bay, west of the San Andreas Fault, are similar to those found on the east side of the fault about

Schooner Gualala, *ca. 1860*

350 miles to the southeast at Eagle Rest Peak in the Temblor Range. The rocks at both sites were once part of a single deposit straddling the San Andreas Fault, but over the last 150 million years tectonic activity has displaced the rocks west of the fault some 350 miles north to their present location at Anchor Bay.

Fish Rocks, located offshore, are a nesting site for black oystercatchers, western gulls, Leach's storm petrels, Brandt's and pelagic cormorants, pigeon guillemots, rhinoceros auklets, and tufted puffins. Fish Rock Beach and Gulch, north of Anchor Bay, are accessible through a private campground.

Gualala: *N. side of Gualala River mouth.*

Gualala was the West Coast's primary lumber port during the early days of the lumber boom. A logging railroad that followed the bank of the North Fork of the Gualala River used the only wide-gauge track in the country. The 68.5-inch-wide tracks were designed to accommodate the broad draft horses used to pull the cars loaded with lumber. When steam engines were introduced, they had to be custom-built to fit the tracks. In operation 50 years, the trains ran from Bourne's Landing south to Robinson Landing, then inland to Mill Bend and Switchville along the Gualala's North Fork. The last engine ceased running in 1930.

Renowned for winter steelhead fly fishing ever since Jack London first came here in 1911, the North Fork of the Gualala River is accessible via Gualala River Rd. (County Road 501). The Gualala Redwood Company owns much of the redwood-covered river frontage and issues permits for access to fishing holes.

Chute for loading vessels at Point Arena, ca. 1880s

Sonoma County
Selected Species of Interest

Plants: Yellow larkspur (*Delphinium luteum*), endangered; grows south of Stewarts Point and along Sonoma Coast State Beaches. **California rhododendron** (*Rhododendron macrophyllum*), grows in Kruse Rhododendron State Reserve.

Trees: Bishop pine (*Pinus muricata*), common conifer growing on windswept bluffs; large stands found at Salt Point State Park. **Red alder** (*Alnus oregona*), native deciduous tree; grows along coastal streams.

Insects: Jerusalem cricket (*Stenopelmatus fuscus*), large, tannish, bulbous ground cricket; burrows in soil. **Saltmarsh caterpillar** (*Estigmene acrea*), black and yellow larva of the acrea moth, which is widespread along the California coast.

Invertebrates: Red abalone (*Haliotis rufescens*), inhabits rocky subtidal areas. **California freshwater shrimp** (*Syncaris pacifica*), endangered; found in only a few streams in Sonoma, Marin, and Napa counties.

Amphibians and Reptiles: California newt (*Taricha torosa*), common in damp woodlands; migrates to ponds and streams to breed. **Northern alligator lizard** (*Gerrhonotus coeruleus*), inhabits woodlands and grasslands.

Fish: Surf smelt (*Hypomesus pretiosus*), spawns on Sonoma County beaches in summer. **Steelhead trout** (*Salmo gairdnerii*), an important sport fish; spawns in the Gualala and Russian rivers and other coastal streams.

Birds: Osprey (*Pandion haliaetus*), large, white-breasted hawk; fishes in coastal rivers. **Brandt's cormorant** (*Phalacrocorax penicillatus*), nests in colonies on Gualala Point Island, Bodega Rock, and coastal cliffs; feeds in flocks.

Land Mammals: Black-tailed deer (*Odocoileus hemionus columbianus*), widespread throughout coastal habitats. **Gray fox** (*Urocyon cinereo-argenteus*), small carnivore; found in dunes, grasslands, and woody and brushy areas.

Marine Mammals: Gray whale (*Eschrichtius robustus*), endangered; seen offshore during migration, particularly from Bodega Head. **Harbor seal** (*Phoca vitulina*), hauls out at the Russian River mouth and on Bodega Rock.

Sonoma County

THE SONOMA COAST, one of California's most sparsely populated and least developed coastal areas, extends for 55 miles from the Gualala River to the Estero Americano. The rugged northern coastline is characterized by broad open marine terraces, steep cliffs, small coves with pocket beaches, sea stacks, and densely forested coastal mountains. South of Fort Ross the marine terrace narrows considerably and is backed by steep cliffs, some rising to elevations of over 1,600 feet. The many offshore rocks provide nesting and roosting areas for seabirds.

South of the Russian River, the marine terrace broadens and forested coastal mountains give way to rolling grass-covered hills. Rocky intertidal areas, low coastal bluffs, and short expanses of narrow, sandy beach dominate the south coast. Bodega Bay is a large, open bay with a rocky shoreline stretching from Bodega Head to Tomales Bay in Marin County. The Valley Ford area, a few miles inland from the coast, supports several dairies on the rolling grassland bordered on the south by the Estero Americano.

The Sonoma County coast has a maritime climate characterized by mild seasonal temperatures, high relative humidity, strong prevailing northwest winds, and low clouds and fog during the summer months. The coast north of Fort Ross to the Gualala River is often called the "banana belt" because it is reputed to have fewer foggy days than the rest of California's north coast.

The predominant geologic feature of the Sonoma coast is the San Andreas Fault, which runs the length of the county along or near the coast. South of Fort Ross, the fault passes out to sea, creating one of the largest landslide masses in California, with steep cliffs rising from sea level to a thousand feet in elevation.

"Sonoma" is derived from "chucuines o sonomas," the name of a local Indian tribe. The name is thought to have come from an Indian word for "nose." One theory is that the Spanish applied a local Indian chief's nickname to the area. Another theory attributes the name to a nose-shaped mountain peak or other geographic feature.

Native Americans occupied the Sonoma coast perhaps as long as 2,000 years ago. The Pomo, who lived on the north coast and along the Russian River, harvested salt, shellfish, and seaweed along the coast, and caught salmon and other fish in the coastal rivers and streams. The Pomo were talented craftsmen and artisans and produced some of the most beautiful and intricate baskets woven by any of the California tribes. The Coast Miwok, who occupied the area south of the Russian River around Bodega Bay, fished in the bay and hunted seabirds in the marshlands around Bodega Harbor.

Spanish galleons passed along the Sonoma coastline on their way from Mexico to the Philippines as early as the 1560s. It was not until 1775, however, that Juan Francisco de la Bodega y Quadra, a Spanish explorer en route to Alaska, anchored in the bay that was to be named for him. No attempt was made to settle the area until a Russian-American Fur Company expedition from Alaska landed at Bodega Head in 1809. The Russian fur hunters established settlements around Bodega Harbor and in the Salmon Creek Valley, and in 1812 built Fort Ross. Decline of the sea otter population and increasingly poor crop yields induced the Russians to abandon their Sonoma settlements in 1841.

Following the Russian departure, the Mexican government divided the county into several large land grants, including Rancho Bodega, a 35,000-acre ranch stretching from the Russian River to the Estero Americano, and Rancho German, which encompassed over 20,000 acres along the northern Sonoma coast.

Before the railroad reached Sonoma County in the 1870s, timber was shipped to San Francisco from small rocky coves which came to be known as "doghole ports" because they were so small "only a dog could turn around in them." Schooners were moored in these rocky coves, while on the bluff above, chutes were set up to send lumber from the bluff sliding down to the ship deck below. The wire chutes were reportedly derived from those used by the forty-niners to extract gold in the Sierra. Settlements like Stewarts Point and Timber Cove grew up around the lumber mills and doghole ports in the 1850s. The gradual depletion of the coastal timber supply and the extension of the railroad to Sonoma County in 1876 caused the decline of the doghole ports. The coastal steamer *Vanguard* was the last ship to load cargo at Stewarts Point in 1929.

The extension of the North Pacific Coast Railroad to Duncans Mills in 1877 established the Russian River area as a popular vacation destination for San Franciscans. Following the opening of Highway 1 in the 1920s, tourism became a major industry in Sonoma County. The dredging of Bodega Harbor in 1943 enabled the town of Bodega Bay to become an important commercial and sport fishing center. Several second-home communities have been developed along the Sonoma coast, notably the Sea Ranch.

The county's economic livelihood today depends upon cattle and sheep raising, timber production, and tourism north of Russian River, and dairy farming and fishing in the Bodega Bay area.

Goat Rock Beach

Gualala River mouth

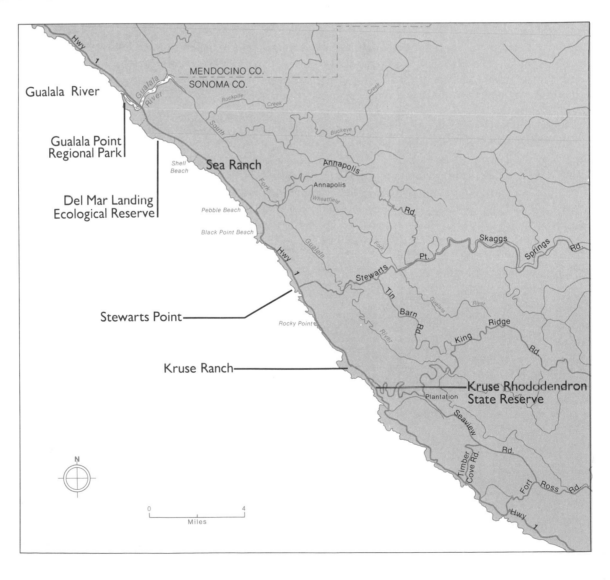

MENDOCINO CO.
SONOMA CO.

Gualala River

Gualala Point
Regional Park

Del Mar Landing
Ecological Reserve

Stewarts Point

Kruse Ranch

Kruse Rhododendron
State Reserve

Sea Ranch

Annapolis

Annapolis

Shell Beach

Pebble Beach

Black Point Beach

Rocky Point

Rockpile Creek

Buckeye Creek

Wheatfield Fork

Skaggs Springs Rd.

Stewarts Pt.

Tin Barn Rd.

King Ridge Rd.

Plantation

Seaview Rd.

Timber Cove Rd.

Fort Ross Rd.

Hwy 1

Gualala River

South Fork

N

0   4
Miles

Gualala River: *Hwy. 1 at Gualala.*

The Gualala River, unlike most West Coast rivers and streams, flows parallel to the coast in a south to north direction along the San Andreas fault line. East of Highway 1, the river is lined by conifer forest, which is habitat for several species of birds including ospreys. The banks of the river provide shelter and den areas for foxes, raccoons, skunks, and ringtails. Near the Highway 1 bridge, several freshwater marshes support rushes and cattails and provide habitat for waterfowl and shorebirds. Sandbars at the mouth of the river are used by egrets, herons, gulls, and shorebirds as resting areas. Sand spits are formed at the river mouth in summer by sediments that are carried northward by ocean currents and then deposited on shore.

The Gualala has sizable runs of anadromous steelhead trout and silver salmon. The river wetlands are nursery areas for smelt, surfperch, flatfish, and spider and market crab. Three species of loon and the common merganser are regularly seen in the area, as are river otters; California sea lions inhabit the offshore waters. The riparian corridor provides an overwintering site for the endangered bald eagle. Gravel mining and logging are the major commercial activities on the river. "Gualala" is the Spanish variant of the Pomo Indian word "Walali," which means "where the waters meet."

Gualala Point Regional Park: *Hwy. 1, 1 mi. S. of Gualala.*

Once a portion of the northernmost Mexican land grant in California, Rancho German, this area was used for cattle grazing and ranching activities until the 1960s. The park contains a variety of plant communities, including coastal strand and grassland along the coast and freshwater marsh and redwood forest along the river. Sea rocket, beach morning glory, and sand verbena cover the dunes. Bracken ferns and lupine are found in the meadows; coast redwood, Douglas-fir, California rhododendron, and sword ferns in the redwood forest; and riparian vegetation of willows, alders, rushes, and cattails along the river.

The large and diverse bird population within the park includes great blue herons, pygmy owls, northern harriers, and Allen's hummingbirds. The sand dunes between the ocean and the river provide habitat for shorebirds. Gualala Point Island south of the park is a major seabird rookery, particularly for Brandt's cormorants. Deer, weasels, jack rabbits, and gray foxes are also found in the park.

Park facilities include parking, camping, and picnic areas, wheelchair-accessible restrooms, and a visitor center. California gray whales can be seen offshore in winter and spring. For information, call: (707) 785-2377.

Del Mar Landing Ecological Reserve: *Hwy. 1, 2 mi. S. of Gualala.*

The offshore reserve extends south from Del Mar Point about 3,000 feet. It was established to protect the rocky intertidal zone, which provides habitat for such marine invertebrates as sea urchins, purple sea stars, California mussels, and black turban snails. Harbor seals often haul out on the offshore rocks. Pelagic cormorants nest in the vicinity of Del Mar Point.

The reserve is presently accessible only with the permission of both the Department of Fish and Game and the Sea Ranch.

Sea Ranch: *Hwy. 1, 29 mi. N. of Jenner.*

Sea Ranch, a planned second-home community, is noted for its unique style of architecture. Condominium I, designed by Moore, Lyndon, Turnbull, and Whitaker, features the shed roof and design elements that have been widely copied across the country and remains the most impressive and celebrated example of the "Sea Ranch style."

Black Point, near the Sea Ranch Lodge, was once a major Pomo Indian settlement. In the 1860s, a town and lumber mill were established there, and by the early 1900s the forests had been completely logged. The area was subsequently abandoned and became grazing land for sheep. In 1963, the land was purchased by Oceanic Properties, Inc., which developed the Sea Ranch.

The Salal Trail, which is lined with native rhododendrons, begins just south of Gualala Point Regional Park and leads to a small cove within the Sea Ranch; parking is available at the Regional Park. There are three new public access trails off Highway 1 leading to Shell Beach, Pebble Beach, and Black Point Beach; restrooms and limited parking are available. Three additional trails, including the Blufftop Trail, are scheduled to be completed by 1987.

Stewarts Point: *Hwy. 1 at Stewarts Point-Skaggs Springs Rd.*

Founded in 1857 by A. L. Fisk, Stewarts Point became one of the major doghole lumber ports of the Sonoma coast. Cut lumber was sent by an aerial chute or cable from the clifftops to schooners in the cove for shipment to San Francisco. Stewarts Point, now designated a Sonoma County Historic District, remains essentially unaltered and is an excellent example of a 19th century coastal settlement. The Stewarts Point School (circa 1860), constructed in the Greek Revival style, is typical of the one-room schoolhouses that were found throughout Sonoma County before the turn of the century. At present, the general store (built in 1868) is the only historic building accessible to the public.

The endangered yellow larkspur grows in the area south of Stewarts Point. Stewarts Point Island is a major roosting site for seabirds.

Kruse Ranch: *Hwy. 1, N. of Kruse Ranch Rd.*

This undeveloped state park land, which includes 1,350 acres, was originally part of a large sheep ranch owned by the Kruse family. The broad marine terrace is covered by Idaho fescue, reedgrass, wild oats, and wildflowers. The gulches that run across the terrace are depressions dug out of the soil by running water and are lined with dense coastal scrub. Bishop pine and tanbark oak predominate in the woodlands east of Highway 1. Trails provide access to the bluff and cove areas west of Highway 1; parking is limited to the highway shoulder.

Kruse Rhododendron State Reserve: *E. of Hwy. 1, off Kruse Ranch Rd.*

This 317-acre reserve comprises a dense mixed forest of native California rhododendrons and second-growth redwood, Douglas-fir, eucalyptus, and tanbark oak. Two stream beds, Chinese Gulch and Phillips Gulch, cross the reserve. The extensive rhododendron growth resulted from a major forest fire that removed most of the existing vegetation. Today the rhododendrons are threatened by the maturing second-growth trees, which are reducing the light available to the plants. The rhododendrons, some reaching 20 feet in height, bloom from mid-April to mid-June. Originally included in the Rancho German, the reserve later formed part of the Kruse Ranch and was extensively logged. Edward Kruse donated the land to the state in 1933 in memory of his father.

Facilities include five miles of hiking trails, parking, and restrooms. For information, call: (707) 865-2391.

Public access trail to Shell Beach at Sea Ranch

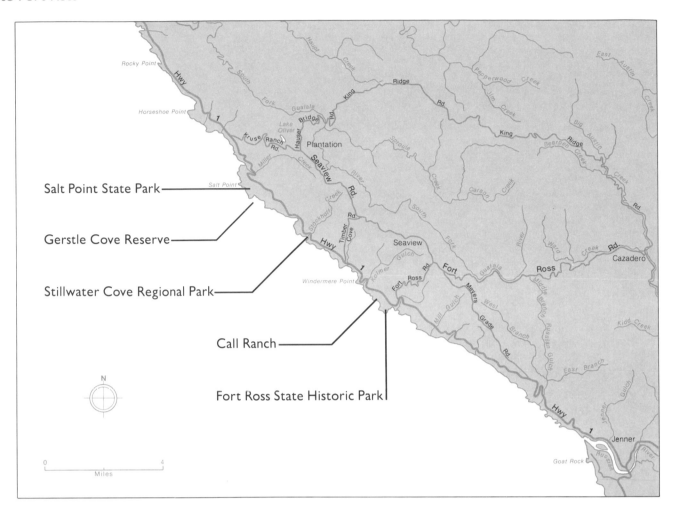

Salt Point State Park

Gerstle Cove Reserve

Stillwater Cove Regional Park

Call Ranch

Fort Ross State Historic Park

Salt Point State Park: *Hwy. 1, 20 mi. N. of Jenner.*

Located on a marine terrace, Salt Point's more than 4,000 acres encompass many diverse habitats, and range from sea level to 1,000 feet in the coastal hills. Plant communities include a pygmy forest of stunted, mature trees such as the Mendocino cypress, which is at the southern extent of its range. The coastline varies from sheltered, sandy coves such as Stump Beach to sharp bluffs and sheer sandstone cliffs at Salt Point and Gerstle Cove. The many tidepool areas along the seven miles of coastline are rela-

tively undisturbed and rich in marine life. The offshore waters are popular for diving.

Wildlife within the park includes black-tailed deer, gray foxes, badgers, feral pigs, pintail ducks, turkey vultures, gulls, terns, and brown pelicans. One of the best locations in the state for observing the breeding behavior of pelagic cormorants is at Stump Beach.

Salt Point was historically used as a summer residence by the Kashia Pomo and Coast Yuki Indians, who gathered abalone, kelp, grasses, and salt there. The name "Salt Point" comes from the large amounts of salt the Indians collected from underwater crevices to use in preserving seafood. The park, which has been designated a National Archaeological District, contains several Indian midden sites. The park also contains the remains of the town of Louisville (circa 1879), which included a hotel, blacksmith shop, and several houses.

Park facilities include day use parking, picnic and camping areas, and wheelchair-accessible restrooms. There are guided whale-watch walks in winter. Call: (707) 847-3221.

Gerstle Cove Reserve: *Hwy. 1, 20 mi. N. of Jenner.*

Located within Salt Point State Park, two acres of the northern part of Gerstle Cove have been designated an ecological reserve. Gerstle Cove, an excellent example of protected rocky habitat, supports a diverse community of fish, invertebrates, and aquatic plants. The ecological reserve was established to allow the recovery of the depleted abalone populations.

pelagic cormorant (*Phalacrocorax pelagicus*)
25 to 30 inches long, 3¼-foot wingspan

Stillwater Cove Regional Park: *Hwy. 1, 3 mi. N. of Fort Ross.*

The park has one of the most spectacular wildflower displays on the northern Sonoma coast; numerous wildflowers, including the vivid deep-blue Douglas iris, bloom in spring on the open grasslands that cover the marine terrace. The adjacent upland area supports a prime example of coastal prairie. Stockhoff Creek, which runs through the park, has anadromous fish runs. The creek drains a steep, forested canyon vegetated with grand fir, alder, rhododendron, western azalea, and such wildflowers as adder's tongue, wild ginger, and calypso orchid. The mouth of the stream opens onto a flat, sandy beach protected by steep bluffs.

Between Salt Point and Stillwater Cove there is a major osprey nesting area. These fish-eating hawks nest in the tops of fir and redwood trees along the ridgelines. Quail, woodpeckers, brush rabbits, and black-tailed deer also inhabit the park. Extensive kelp beds lie offshore.

The Fort Ross School (circa 1885) is situated on a hiking trail along Stockhoff Creek. Originally located at Fort Ross, the one-room red schoolhouse was built in the Greek Revival style and has been restored since being moved to its present site. Park facilities include picnic, camping, and day use parking areas, and wheelchair-accessible restrooms. Call: (707) 847-3245.

Call Ranch: *Hwy. 1, .5 mi. N. of Fort Ross.*

Once a part of the 15,000-acre historical Call Ranch, this area is now a unit of Fort Ross State Historic Park. George W. Call bought Fort Ross and the surrounding land in 1873, and erected the ranch buildings just west of the stockade. Many of the original structures of the fort were utilized by the Calls in their lumbering, farming, shipping, and livestock-raising activities. Goods bound for market in San Francisco or the interior were shipped by schooner from Fort Ross Cove; a 180-foot chute built on the bluff was used to load ships in the cove.

The rocks offshore of Northwest Cape are used as roosting sites by pelagic cormorants, western gulls, and endangered California brown pelicans. The Call Ranch area, which is leased for grazing, is open to day use visitors; there are no facilities.

The Timber Cove Inn at Timber Cove, north of Call Ranch, is the site of a Beniamino Bufano statue, *Peace*. The 85-foot-high statue, a Sonoma County Historic Landmark, was made of concrete and mosaic by Bufano in 1960 and was his last finished work. Timber Cove was a busy doghole lumber port in the mid-19th century.

Fort Ross State Historic Park: *Hwy. 1, 11 mi. N. of Jenner.*

Located on a windswept bluff, Fort Ross was the largest Russian settlement on the California coast. The broad flat marine terrace, calm sheltered cove, high defensible bluff, and upland timbered meadows all played a part in attracting the Russian fur-hunters to choose the site for their colony.

Grasslands made up of Idaho fescue, rye grass, thistle, and wild barley predominate on the coastal plains, while mixed-conifer and redwood forests cover the hills. Farther south the hills and terraces become more open and tree cover is confined mainly to gulches and valleys. Fort Ross Creek is lined with rich riparian vegetation including bay laurel, white alder, willow, wax myrtle, Douglas iris, forget-me-not, and coast redwood. The course of the creek has been displaced some 3,000 feet by movement along the San Andreas Fault. At Mill Gulch, south of Fort Ross, the fault cuts from land to sea, creating the steepest coastal hills in Sonoma.

The one remaining original Russian structure at the fort, the Rotchev House (1836), has been designated a National Historic Building. The other buildings within the stockade are replicas of the original structures. The Fort Ross Living History Program is an annual event which recreates a typical day at the fort in 1836; authentically costumed volunteers portray Russian colonists and foreign visitors to the fort. Demonstrations of threshing, musket and cannon drills, cooking, and other activities are presented, and visitors are encouraged to participate. The new visitor center includes an auditorium and gift shop. Parking and restroom facilities are located within the park. Call: (707) 847-3286.

Sheep at Fort Ross

Fort Ross State Historic Park

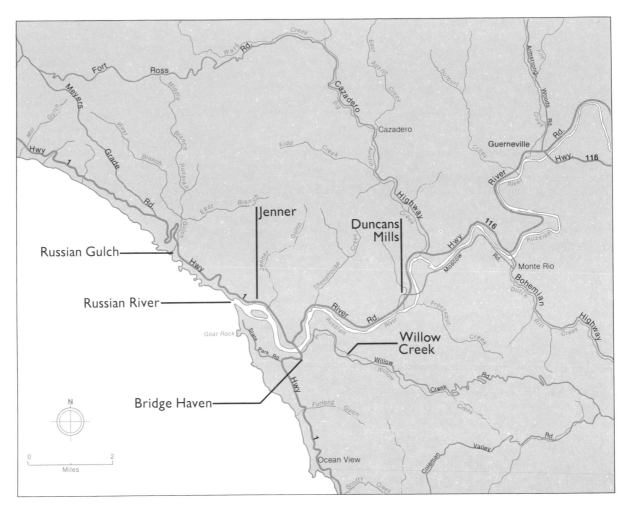

pigeon guillemots (*Cepphus columba*)
12 to 14 inches long

Russian Gulch: *Hwy. 1, 2.5 mi. N. of Jenner.*

Russian Gulch, a unit of Sonoma Coast State Beaches, has a large, accessible beach and is a popular recreation area. Russian Gulch Creek, an intermittent stream, runs through the broad, sheltered valley. Thick riparian vegetation lines the stream bed, providing habitat for several species of songbirds. The creek enters the sea from between high, nearly vertical cliffs; elevations along this stretch of coast range from sea level to over 1,600 feet. Offshore rocks provide nesting and roosting sites for seabirds.

The Russian settlers at Fort Ross established a vineyard at Russian Gulch in the early 19th century. The vineyard was one of the first examples in California of coastal agriculture. In 1845, the Russian Gulch area became part of the Rancho Muniz, which covered much of the Sonoma coastline north of the Russian River. Russian Gulch was acquired by the state in the mid 1970s. There are presently no facilities at the beach, which is open for day use only. Shoulder parking is available along Highway 1.

Jenner: *Hwy. 1, 10 mi. N. of Bodega Bay.*

The Jenner area marks the transition between the steep rugged headlands that extend north from the Russian River and the wide marine terraces of the southern Sonoma coast. The area is noted for serpentine outcrops, which also contain large, unusually beautiful pieces of the metamorphic rock, blueschist. Jenner Pond, located near the intersection of Highway 1 and Highway 116, is a small freshwater marsh visible from the highway. The pond is used extensively by shorebirds, coots, rails, and ducks, notably the cinnamon teal, a dabbling duck.

Located on a steep slope above the Russian River, Jenner is a small, compact coastal town. It became a summer resort area around the turn of the century and contains several bungalows and cottages dating from the early 1900s. The Jenner School (circa 1910) has the gable roof and shingle siding typical of the bungalow era. The Jenner Visitor Center, which is wheelchair accessible, has interpretive displays. For information, call: (707) 875-3483.

Russian River: *Hwy. 1 at Hwy. 116.*

The 110-mile long Russian River, one of the largest north coast river systems, drains a watershed of approximately 1,500 square miles and is fed by several tributaries. The river is thought to have once emptied into San Francisco Bay before geologic upheavals forced the river to change its course. Upland areas of the river basin are wooded with Douglas-fir, redwood, and live oak; manzanita and chaparral are also widespread. The riparian corridor includes white alders, box elders, rushes, and various types of grasses. Gravel bars along the edge of the river support dense stands of willow and cottonwood. Several ponds and freshwater marshes are found along the river.

Ospreys nest in the tops of trees along the river banks and can be seen fishing at the mouth of the river, and shorebirds forage along the sandbar at the river mouth. The shallow waters in the river estuary attract large numbers of birds, sometimes numbering in the thousands. Penny Island, situated near the river mouth, serves as a feeding and resting area for several species of birds, including the endangered California brown pelican.

The earliest known inhabitants of the area were the Kashia Pomo Indians, who called the river "Shabaikai" (long snake). Russian colonists explored the river area in 1809, naming the river "Slavianka" (Slav woman), before establishing a settlement at Fort Ross; the Spanish later called the river "Rio Ruso" (Russian River), referring to the Russians in the area. Settlement of the area increased rapidly during the early 1850s as the lumber industry was established. Farming, logging, and mining activities developed as towns sprang up in the river basin. In 1877, North Coast Pacific Railroad service was extended to the Russian River at

Duncans Mills, and trains began to bring vacationers from San Francisco to the river. Summer camps and resort hotels established the Russian River as a major Northern California resort area, which it remains today.

Duncans Mills: *Hwy. 116, 4 mi. E. of Jenner.*

The town of Duncans Mills grew up around a lumber mill established in 1877 by Alexander Duncan. Duncans Mills was the western terminus of the North Pacific Coast Railroad from San Francisco via Sausalito and an important Sonoma County rail center. Duncans Mills, now classified as a Sonoma County Historic District, contains several historic buildings. B Street, lined by commercial falsefront buildings, has the appearance of a virtually unaltered late-19th-century street. The railroad depot (1910) now serves as a museum with a collection of railroad memorabilia, historical photographs, and three restored wooden railroad cars. The museum is open on Saturdays 10 AM-3 PM and is free to the public.

Bridge Haven: *Hwy. 1 at Willow Creek Rd., 1.5 mi. S. of Jenner.*

One of Sonoma County's first lumber mills along the coast was built in 1860 by Alexander and Samuel Duncan at what is now Bridge Haven. Cut lumber was sent by horse-drawn rail cars to the coast at Duncan's Landing for shipment to San Francisco. A small town grew up around the mill and eventually included a hotel, post office, telegraph office, and store. The town had a population of about 100 in 1877 when Alexander Duncan moved the mill upriver to the present site of Duncans Mills. In the 1920s, the Bridge Haven Resort was constructed on the site; a group of three cottages (circa 1925) are all that remain of the resort.

Willow Creek: *E. of Hwy. 1 at Willow Creek Rd.*

Willow Creek, a perennial stream, is a tributary of the Russian River. Most of the lower Willow Creek watershed has been acquired by the state as a unit of the Sonoma Coast State Beaches. Riparian vegetation, dominated by red alder and willow, lines the banks of the creek. In the upper reaches of the creek are some sheltered pools and several small waterfalls. A freshwater marsh is located just above the junction of Willow Creek and the Russian River. Redwood forest stands occur on the alluvial flats along the creek; swordferns, redwood sorrel, redwood violet, and poison oak line the forest floor. The grand fir reaches its southern limit in the coast ranges in a small stand along Willow Creek.

The creek, which supports runs of steelhead trout and silver salmon, also provides a riparian habitat for waterfowl and other wildlife. The adjacent woods and grasslands provide nesting areas for spotted owls and ospreys, which feed along the creek. Park facilities include environmental campsites, pit toilets, and a parking area. Call: (707) 875-3483.

Russian River mouth

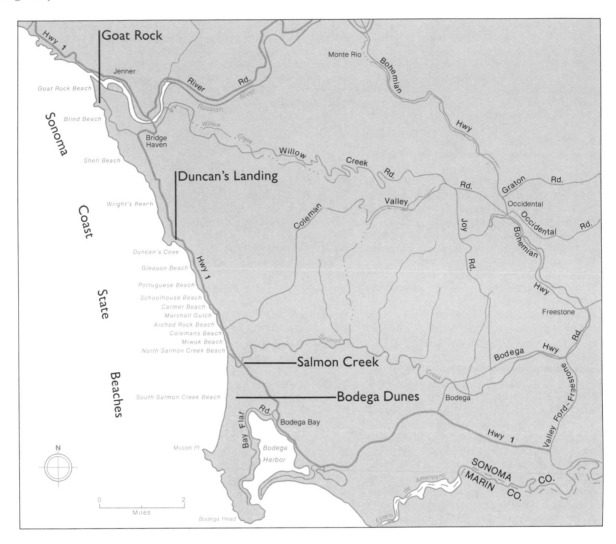

western sandpiper (*Calidris mauri*)
6 to 7 inches long

Sonoma Coast State Beaches: *Hwy. 1, Russian Gulch to Bodega Head.*

Sonoma Coast State Beaches include Russian Gulch, North Jenner Beaches, Willow Creek, Penny Island, Goat Rock, Blind Beach, Shell Beach, Wright's Beach, Duncan's Landing, Duncan's Cove, Gleason Beach, Portuguese Beach, Schoolhouse Beach, Carmet Beach, Marshall Gulch, Arched Rock Beach, Colemans Beach, Miwok Beach, North Salmon Creek Beach, South Salmon Creek Beach, Bodega Dunes, and Bodega Head.

The Sonoma Coast State Beaches encompass approximately 5,000 acres, including 13 miles of coastline characterized by short stretches of sandy beach separated by rocky headlands. In spring, wildflowers such as lupine, Indian paintbrush, western wallflower, and wild strawberry bloom on the coastal bluffs; the endangered yellow larkspur is also found in the area. The diverse intertidal plant and animal communities make the Sonoma Coast State Beaches an important and much studied area.

Large offshore rocks such as Arched Rock (off Blind Beach) and Gull Rock (off Shell Beach) are nesting areas for Brandt's cormorants, western gulls, and pigeon guillemots. The bluffs and upland grasslands provide habitat for raccoons, gray foxes, rabbits, and black-tailed deer.

Most of the beaches have parking areas and many have restroom facilities. Whale talks are given at Goat Rock and Bodega Head on Sundays in winter and spring during the migration of the gray whale. Call: (707) 875-3483.

Goat Rock: *Off Hwy. 1 at Goat Rock Rd., 10 mi. N. of Bodega Bay.*

The mile-long Goat Rock Beach is one of the most popular of the Sonoma Coast State Beaches. The beach forms a sand spit at the mouth of the Russian River; harbor seals haul out on the river side of the sand spit. Coastal strand and scrub species are the dominant vegetation on the bluffs, while European beach grass covers the sand dunes; this non-native grass species was planted in the 1930s to stabilize the dunes. Goat Rock Beach is a popular fishing area for ocean-caught smelt in summer and for steelhead trout in the Russian River in winter. Park facilities include a parking area, picnic tables, and wheelchair-accessible restrooms.

Goat Rock, the large rock situated half a mile south of the Russian River mouth, was once part of the mainland and is now connected by a manmade causeway. In the 1920s, quarried rock was sent by railroad from Goat Rock to the mouth of the Russian River for the construction of a jetty. Goat Rock supports unusually dense and diverse coastal prairie vegetation. Endangered peregrine falcons reportedly once nested in the cliffs on Goat Rock and still occasionally winter in the area.

Duncan's Landing: *Hwy. 1, 5 mi. N. of Bodega Bay.*

This cove was a doghole lumber port in the nineteenth century. From 1862 until 1877, lumber was sent by horse-drawn railroad from the Russian River sawmill of Alexander and Samuel Duncan to Duncan's Landing, where schooners were loaded for shipment to San Francisco. The schooners were anchored in the cove on the south side of Duncan's Point; iron rings used to secure the ships can still be seen.

Duncan's Landing is now a unit of Sonoma Coast State Beaches. The small sandy beach is accessible by a steep trail; coastal scrub vegetation lines the adjacent slopes. Park facilities include a parking area and restrooms.

Salmon Creek: *Hwy. 1, 2.5 mi. N. of Bodega Bay.*

Salmon Creek is an important small coastal stream with a wide variety of wetland habitats, including saltwater and brackish marshes near the creek mouth and freshwater marshes upstream. The marshes near Highway 1 attract several species of waterfowl during migration; tundra swans, not commonly seen in most coastal areas, are found here almost every winter. The lower Salmon Creek watershed is a nesting area for the snowy plover and an overwintering and migratory area for sandpipers and ducks. Salmon Creek has one of the largest populations of the endangered California freshwater shrimp, which is native to only a few streams in Sonoma, Napa, and Marin counties. Silver salmon and steelhead spawn in the stream in winter. A barrier beach forms across the stream mouth in summer, creating a freshwater lagoon.

Salmon Creek Beach is the longest sandy beach on the Sonoma coast, extending for approximately two miles from Salmon Creek to Mussel Point at Bodega Head. Gulls and a variety of shorebirds use the beach as a foraging area. Coastal strand vegetation, including lupine, sand verbena, and beach strawberry,

grows along the dry sand beach. Park facilities include a parking area and restrooms.

A Russian settlement was established in the Salmon Creek Valley in 1809; wheat was cultivated for shipment to the Russian colony in Alaska. The Russians abandoned the settlement in 1841 and the area was acquired by Stephen Smith as part of the Rancho Bodega. In 1843 Smith erected California's first steam-operated sawmill in the valley north of the creek.

Bodega Dunes: *Hwy. 1, .5 mi. N. of Bodega Bay.*

This large sand dune area of approximately 900 acres extends along the coast from Salmon Creek Beach to Bodega Harbor. With elevations approaching 150 feet, the Bodega dunes are some of the highest in the state. The dunes are inherently unstable and subject to wind transport and erosion. By the 1930s, the native vegetation which once covered the dunes, including bush lupine, bromegrass, and rye grass, had been greatly reduced by overgrazing livestock; to stabilize the dunes, European beach grass was extensively planted.

The dunes provide habitat for the northern alligator lizard and coast garter snake, and for black-tailed deer, jack rabbits, mice, voles, foxes, weasels, and badgers. Northern harriers, red-tailed hawks, and short-eared owls prey on mice in the dunes; other species of birds that use the dunes include California quail and the ring-necked pheasant.

The Bodega Dunes unit of the Sonoma Coast State Beaches is located about a mile inland from Salmon Creek Beach and includes a large campground. Monarch butterflies overwinter in the eucalyptus trees near the campfire center. A day use area with parking and wheelchair-accessible restrooms is located at the beach, west of the campground. There is a five-mile riding and hiking loop trail through the dunes, as well as a hiking-only trail that leads to the parking lot at Bodega Head. Call: (707) 875-3483.

bush lupine (*Lupinus chamissonis*)
2 to 6 feet high

Russian River mouth and Goat Rock

Bodega Marine Reserve: *Off Westside Rd., Bodega Bay.*

The 326-acre reserve is a unit of the statewide Natural Reserve System, established by the University of California to preserve areas of undisturbed habitat. The reserve, which comprises a mile of Pacific coastline and a half-mile of shore along Bodega Harbor, includes protected rocky coast, sandy beach, sand dunes, coastal prairie, freshwater marsh, and tidal mudflat. Located within the reserve, Bodega Marine Laboratory provides research and teaching facilities and is open to the public Fridays from 2-4 PM. Call: (707) 875-2211. The marine area extending 1,000 feet offshore along the ocean frontage of the reserve has been designated by the Department of Fish and Game as the Bodega Marine Life Refuge for the protection of the nearshore marine resources.

Town of Bodega

Bodega Head: *End of Westside Rd., Bodega Bay.*

Bodega Head, the southernmost unit of the Sonoma Coast State Beaches, forms the tip of a peninsula that extends south of the Bodega dunes. Bodega Head is located on the Pacific Plate and is geologically related to Point Reyes and the Farallon Islands; the peninsula is the northernmost exposure of coastal granitic rock along the California coast. Geologists believe that Bodega Head was once located 300 miles south near the Tehachapi Mountains and has been carried to its present location by the northward movement of the Pacific Plate along the San Andreas Fault.

Steep cliffs, bluffs, and pocket beaches characterize the topography of the peninsula, which is covered by coastal grassland and scrub vegetation. Wildlife in the area includes California slender salamanders, long-tailed weasels, gray foxes, northern harriers, and great horned owls. Bodega Rock, located offshore about a half-mile south of Bodega Head, supports a breeding colony of Brandt's cormorants and western gulls and is an important haul-out for harbor seals and California sea lions.

Bodega Head is a popular spot for winter whale watching. Park facilities include parking areas, trails, and picnic tables. Westside Regional Park, located on Bay Flat Rd. north of Bodega Head, has a camping area, restrooms, a boat launching ramp, and a day use boating area; for information, call: (707) 875-3540.

Bodega Bay and Harbor: *Off Hwy. 1 and Bay Flat Rd., Bodega Bay.*

Bodega Bay, which stretches from Bodega Head to Tomales Bay, has a shallow sandy bottom and rocky shoreline backed by steep cliffs. Sand or pebble beaches alternate with areas of rocky tidepools. Many of the large offshore rocks are used by brown pelicans, pigeon guillemots, pelagic cormorants, and Brandt's cormorants as roosting areas.

The shallow, 800-acre Bodega Harbor, located north of Doran Spit, includes areas of open water, subtidal channels, freshwater wetlands, tidal mudflats, and salt marshes. Due to

Bodega Harbor

its mild climate and variety of habitats, the harbor attracts shorebirds and waterfowl in great numbers and diversity. At low tide, the extensive mudflats provide a rich foraging area for shorebirds and gulls. Loons, grebes, and ducks can be seen in the open waters of the harbor. The freshwater wetlands provide habitat for long-billed marsh wrens, red-winged blackbirds, sora and Virginia rails, western pond turtles, shrews, and California voles.

The harbor is a popular fishing and clamming area. Rockfish, greenlings, sculpins, and surfperch are found here. At low tide, clammers dig for gaper and Washington clams. Mason's Marina at 1820 Westside Rd. provides berths, docks, a hoist, and marine supplies; Spud Point Marina to the south, used mostly by commercial fishermen, includes berths, a dock, a breakwater, and public parking and fishing access.

Bodega Bay was named for Juan Francisco de la Bodega y Quadra, the Spanish explorer who surveyed the area in 1775. The Bodega Bay and Harbor area has been designated both a National and State Historical Landmark in recognition of its historic and archaeological value.

Town of Bodega Bay: *Hwy. 1, E. of Bodega Harbor.*

The town of Bodega Bay originated as a small fishing port in the late 1870s. In the early 1900s, families from the inland areas of the county began to build summer homes at Bodega Bay, and with the opening of Highway 1 in the 1920s, the town became a tourist destination. The dredging of Bodega Harbor in 1943 stimulated the growth of Bodega Bay's fishing industry.

Today the town of Bodega Bay is a center for both commercial and sport fishing and is the busiest fishing port between Fort Bragg and San Francisco. The area also attracts migrating Monarch butterflies in autumn.

The town contains several interesting examples of 1910-era craftsman bungalows, notably the Bodega Bay Union Church (circa 1910) on Bay View Rd., which has the gabled roof with gable trim and exposed rafters characteristic of this style of architecture.

Doran Regional Park: *Doran Beach Rd., Bodega Bay.*

The park is located on Doran Spit, a narrow, two-mile-long, crescent-shaped sand spit that separates Bodega Harbor from Bodega Bay. Vegetation on the spit includes bush lupine and introduced dune grasses. The beach, backed by low sand dunes, is a feeding and roosting area for several species of shorebirds including sanderlings, snowy plovers, willets, and black turnstones. The park has day use parking areas, camping facilities, restrooms, and a boat launch ramp. Call: (707) 875-3540. The adjacent U.S. Coast Guard station on the spit is open to the public on Saturday and Sunday, 1-4 PM.

Town of Bodega: *Bodega Hwy., 5 mi. E. of Bodega Bay.*

In 1853 the small settlement called Bodega Corners contained a saloon, blacksmith shop, hotel, and two stores. The town quickly became the major trade center for the coastal valleys around Bodega Harbor; lumber and agricultural products, especially the local "Bodega red" potatoes, butter, and cheese, were shipped to San Francisco. In the 1870s Bodega became the largest town in the area, its population reaching 250 in 1877. In 1876 the North Pacific Coast Railroad bypassed Bodega and the town's growth slowly came to an end. The Church of

St. Teresa of Avila, constructed in 1859 of redwood and now the oldest continuously used Catholic church in Sonoma County, is a State Historical Landmark. The Potter School (1873), now the Bodega Gallery Restaurant, was used as the schoolhouse in the 1962 Alfred Hitchcock film *The Birds*.

Valley Ford: *Hwy. 1, 3 mi. S.E. of Bodega.*

Valley Ford is a small farming community named for the ford where the old Indian and Spanish trail from the interior valleys to the coast crossed the Estero Americano. James and Stephen Fowler, the first white settlers in the area, built a house here in 1852. By the early 1860s, the town had a blacksmith's shop, lumber yard, carpenter's shop, and general store.

A 21-foot steel pole used in the construction of Bulgarian artist Christo Javacheff's *Running Fence* stands today on Main Street near the post office to commemorate the artwork; the site is a Sonoma County Historic Landmark. The 18-foot-high, 24-mile-long fence of nylon fabric, steel cables, and steel poles stood for two weeks in September 1976 and stretched from Cotati through Valley Ford to the ocean at Bodega Bay.

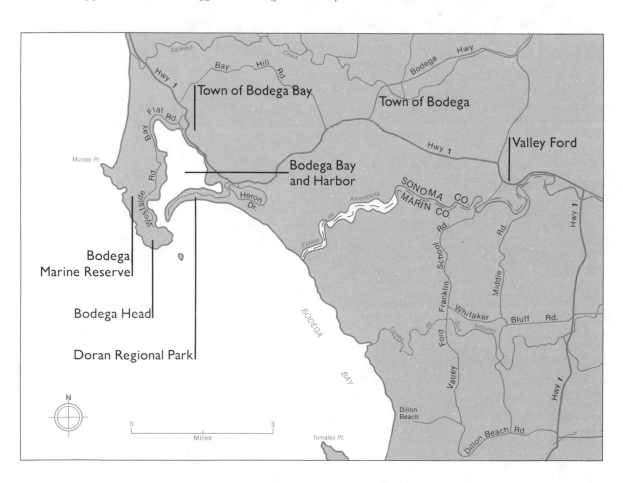

Marin County
Selected Species of Interest

Plants: Douglas iris (*Iris douglasiana*), spring-flowering, purple blooms; grows in clumps on grassy slopes. **California poppy** (*Eschscholzia californica*), California's brilliantly colored state flower; blooms bright orange in spring.

Trees: Madrone (*Arbutus menziesii*), dark-green, shiny-leafed tree; young trees have smooth, terra cotta-colored bark. **California black oak** (*Quercus kelloggii*), deciduous, with deeply lobed, glossy leaves; grows to 80 feet tall.

Insects: Coastal dune fly (*Brennania hera*), predaceous horsefly; larvae live in sand at Pt. Reyes. **Rangeland tiger moth** (*Platyprepia gutta*), broad-winged moth; orange, black, and white woolly caterpillar lives on bush lupine.

Invertebrates: Washington clam (*Saxidomus nuttalli*), has ridged shell with purple tinge; found in gravelly beaches around Tomales Bay. **Ochre sea star** (*Pisaster ochraceous*), common five-rayed variety; occurs in several colors.

Amphibians and Reptiles: Western skink (*Eumeces skiltonianus*), slim lizard with blue tail; found on rocks and in leaf litter. **Western rattlesnake** (*Crotalus viridis*), venomous; wide-ranging in grasslands and woodlands.

Fish: Pacific herring (*Clupea pallasii*), schooling fish, taken commercially for roe. **White shark** (*Carcharodon carcharias*), grows to 20 feet long; feeds on fish and marine mammals; can be dangerous to divers.

Birds: California brown pelican (*Pelecanus occidentalis californicus*), large, endangered bird; plunges bill-first for fish. **Snowy egret** (*Egretta thula*), white wading bird, found in Bolinas Lagoon and Tomales Bay.

Land Mammals: Tule elk (*Cervus elaphus nannodes*), small-statured elk; colony on Tomales Point. **Striped skunk** (*Mephitis mephitis*), nocturnal, omnivorous animal; its powerful scent is used for defense.

Marine Mammals: Harbor seal (*Phoca vitulina*), small, spotted seal; breeds on Pt. Reyes Peninsula. **Gray whale** (*Eschrichtius robustus*), endangered; Point Reyes is good vantage point to view winter migration.

Marin County

MARIN COUNTY contains mountains, bedrock formations, and drowned valleys that are textbook examples of the geologic forces which have created the landscape we see today. Great variations in land elevation and in exposure to wind, sun, and rain have produced an extraordinary range of localized climates and habitats for plants and animals. Many of the resources of coastal Marin County are protected within public parks, such as the Point Reyes National Seashore, the Golden Gate National Recreation Area, and Mount Tamalpais and Samuel P. Taylor State Parks.

The seacoast of Marin County lies astride the great San Andreas rift zone that extends some 650 miles southward from Point Delgada in Humboldt County. To the west of the fault is the Point Reyes Peninsula, sharing the oceanic plate with the Pacific Ocean. To the east of the fault is the continental plate, on which most of the rest of the North American land mass lies. Geologists theorize that the Point Reyes Peninsula has gradually drifted north at an average rate of about one-half inch per year, bringing it several hundred miles north in the last 25 million years. The latest major movement along the rift zone took place in 1906, when up to 20 feet of lateral displacement occurred abruptly at the great earthquake's epicenter, located near Olema. Stories of cows being swallowed in the earth in 1906 may be apocryphal, but it is a fact that an early morning train ready to depart Point Reyes Station for Sausalito was flipped neatly on its side by the quake.

The geology of the Marin coast reflects its location along the San Andreas rift zone. On a map, the rift zone is clearly visible in Tomales Bay and Bolinas Lagoon which trend toward the northwest, and in Inverness Ridge and Bolinas Ridge which rise on either side of the rift. On the ground, one observes the Cretaceous granitic rock formations that underlie the Point Reyes Peninsula, whereas the distinct Franciscan Formation of sandstone, greenstone, and chert is found east of the rift zone. The Point Reyes Peninsula is biologically as well as geologically distinctive; at least six species of plants are known to occur only on the peninsula.

Coastal Marin County has been inhabited since prehistoric times. At least 113 Miwok Indian village sites have been identified on the Point Reyes Peninsula. Near Drakes Bay, mounds have been found that indicate the Miwok relied in part on fish and shellfish for food; some mounds include European and Oriental materials from sixteenth century trade or shipwrecks. The name of the peninsula comes from an early voyage of discovery, that of Sebastián Vizcaíno, who proclaimed it Punta de los Reyes ("Point of the Kings") as he passed in early 1603 on the Feast of the Three Kings of the Nativity. A small Russian colony settled in 1812 in what is now Sonoma County, and Russian trappers explored the coast of Marin County in search of fur seals.

Rancho Punta de los Reyes and Rancho Tomales y Baulenes, together stretching from north of the Point Reyes Peninsula south to Mount Tamalpais, were granted to early settlers in 1836 during California's Mexican period. West Marin County became a provider of lumber, beef, and hogs to gold rush-era San Francisco and later developed into the state's first major dairy district; by the 1870s nearly half of the state's butter was produced in Marin.

Before roads were built, ranch products were moved to San Francisco by sea: ports sprang up quickly at Tomales and Bolinas. Beginning in 1875, a narrow-gauge railroad linked the town of Tomales and the eastern shore of Tomales Bay with a train-ferry in Sausalito, across the bay from San Francisco. Ranches not served by the railroad continued to move butter and hogs by sea. Schooner Bay, the northernmost arm of Drakes Estero on the Point Reyes Peninsula, shipped out produce from the ranches on the peninsula and also became, in the early twentieth century, a commercial fishing base where the ocean catch was processed before delivery to San Francisco.

Today coastal Marin County still provides dairy products, oysters, and fresh vegetables to the metropolitan market. The coast also provides opportunities for recreation and nature study to a broad public. Much of West Marin County is included within federal, state, or local parks. Quiet villages offer historic resources, relaxing accommodations, and a chance to view locally produced arts and crafts, as well as the area's wealth of natural resources.

Drakes Beach

Estero Americano: *Off Hwy. 1, 9 mi. N.W. of Tomales.*

Americano Creek winds through rolling coastal hills, forming the fjord-like Estero Americano. The creek lies in a "drowned valley," the term for an area gradually flooded by a relative rise in sea level. The change in sea level came about either through an actual rise of ocean waters as glaciers melted after the last Pleistocene Ice Age, or through the earth's subsidence, or through a combination of both factors. The Estero Americano, like the several other drowned river mouths in coastal Marin, was most likely created in the last 10,000 years by buckling of the earth's crust along the San Andreas rift zone. The estero is a shallow body of mixed salt and fresh water; the saltwater influence extends up to three miles inland. In summer, reduced freshwater flow allows a sandbar to build, blocking the mouth of the estero and creating heightened salinity behind the bar. The long, narrow configuration of the estero is unusual among California estuaries.

The estero includes more than one square mile of open water and wetlands and contains a wide variety of habitat types, including tidal mudflats, brackish marsh, and freshwater marsh. Pacific herring deposit their eggs on the eelgrass growing in the channel near the mouth of the estero; other fish found in the estero include staghorn sculpin, shiner surfperch, starry flounder, and smelt. The sandy bottom serves as a nursery for juvenile Dungeness crabs.

Wading birds such as great blue herons, black-crowned night herons, and snowy egrets fish in the shallow waters of the estuary. Other water birds such as loons, grebes, cormorants, and endangered California brown pelicans also feed here. Owls and hawks inhabit the surrounding uplands, and endangered bald eagles have been seen in the area. Tundra swans, uncommon along the coast, have also been observed along the upper reaches of the estero. The estero is surrounded by privately owned agricultural land, and although public roads cross Americano Creek several miles inland, there is no direct public access to the estero itself.

Estero de San Antonio: *Off Hwy. 1, 5 mi. N.W. of Tomales.*

The Estero de San Antonio, lying in the drowned valley of Stemple Creek, is a long, narrow estuary similar in form to the Estero Americano. Wading birds feed and rest here. Waterfowl such as pintails, American wigeons, canvasbacks, and ruddy ducks can be seen here, but generally in smaller numbers than at the neighboring Estero Americano which has greater open water area. Western pond turtles commonly bask in the sun along the margins of the Estero de San Antonio.

A half-mile-long remnant of the native coastal grassland community grows along the south bank of the estero. Found here are once-common perennial grasses such as California fescue

and Pacific reedgrass; grazing, clearing, and human activities have caused such species to be replaced elsewhere on the California coast with non-native annual species. There is no public access to the estero, which is surrounded by private land, but the upper end of the estero may be seen from Whitaker Bluff Road.

Tomales: *On Hwy. 1, 4.5 mi. S. of the Sonoma County line.*

The village of Tomales, first known as Keysville, was once an ocean port and one of Marin County's most important towns. The first European settler was John Keys, an Irishman, who built a house in 1850 near the present intersection of Highway 1 and the Tomales-Petaluma Highway, below the present town. Keys started a store which thrived and was joined within ten years by a hotel, post office, and other businesses. A line of warehouses served the ships which carried butter, hogs, beef, and potatoes down Keys Creek to Tomales Bay and thence to San Francisco.

Within 20 years the creek bed had silted in, and ships could sail no closer to Tomales than Ocean Roar at the mouth of Keys Creek. When the North Pacific Coast Railroad reached Tomales in 1875, linking the area to the rail-ferry wharf in Sausalito, transportation of farm produce was greatly improved. A new Tomales soon grew up on higher ground, with two hotels, a bank, saloons, and a cheese factory. A number of 19th century structures remain near the intersection of Main St. and Dillon Beach Road. The Church of the Assumption, located just south of the present business section, was built in 1860 and restored after the 1906 earthquake.

Dillon Beach: *End of Dillon Beach Rd., 4.1 mi. W. of Tomales.*

This resort community is named for George Dillon, an Irish rancher who arrived in 1859. Rows of modest cottages dating from the 1920s line the narrow streets. Day use of the privately owned sandy beach is available for a fee. Clinging to the rocks at the north end of the beach is a rich assortment of intertidal species, such as sea palms, sea anemones, California mussels, goose barnacles, and ochre sea stars. The tidepools support a wide variety of algae.

Lawson's Landing: *1 mi. S. of Dillon Beach via the toll road.*

Prominent sand dunes stretch nearly a mile and a half south from Dillon Beach to Lawson's Landing in rows perpendicular to the prevailing northwest winds. Hang gliders ride the winds from the tops of the dunes, some of which are 150 feet high. Privately owned Lawson's Landing Resort near Sand Point at the mouth of Tomales Bay offers camping, boating, and fishing. Clammers are ferried from the landing at low tide to the flats surrounding Hog Island in search of Washington and horseneck clams.

Walker Creek: *W. of Highway 1, S. of Tomales.*

Walker Creek with its tributary, Keys Creek, is the second largest of the streams feeding Tomales Bay. Although its flow is reduced by siltation, the stream still supports runs of silver salmon and steelhead. The Walker Creek delta includes over 100 acres of marsh and mudflats where salt marsh plants predominate. Large

Estero Americano, ca. 1965

numbers of shorebirds use the marsh, including whimbrels, short-billed dowitchers, and occasional long-billed curlews. A dominant insect of marine-influenced marshes such as the Walker Creek delta is the midge fly. The larval and pupal stages of midges provide an important food source for nearshore fish and waterfowl. Mudflats with abundant algal material, like the Walker Creek delta, are home to insects such as the long-legged shore fly; wading shorebirds feed on the fly larvae. The endangered yellow larkspur may be seen growing in spots along Highway 1 between the Walker Creek delta and Stemple Creek.

Keys Creek Fishing Access: *Hwy. 1, 1.6 mi. S.W. of Tomales.*

This small public fishing access area has picnic tables and restrooms. Silver salmon and steelhead are caught in the creek from late fall until spring.

Hog Island: *N. end of Tomales Bay, S.W. of Walker Creek delta.*

Hog Island lies in the middle of Tomales Bay near the mouth of Walker Creek. Harbor seals haul out on the shores of the island and its tiny neighbor, Duck Island. Wintering black brant feed on the surrounding eelgrass. The islands are a wildlife sanctuary owned by Audubon Canyon Ranch; call: (415) 383-1644.

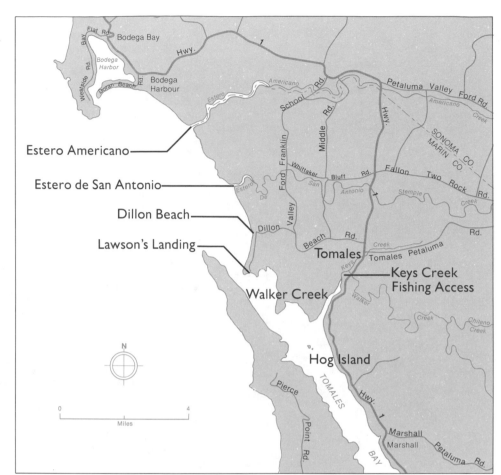

Dillon Beach

Pacific oyster (*Crassostrea gigas*)
shell to 11¾ inches long

rock oyster or jingle shell (*Pododesmus cepio*)
to 3 inches in diameter

Tomales Bay: *N.W. of Pt. Reyes Station.*

When Spaniard Sebastián Vizcaíno sailed homeward from Cape Mendocino on a voyage of exploration in 1603, he mistook the mouth of Tomales Bay for the outlet of a great river and named it Rio Grande de San Sebastián. It was not until 1793 that another Spaniard, Captain Juan Matute, scouted the interior of the bay, which he called Puerto Nuevo. Matute and his fellow explorers were greeted by peaceful Miwok Indians who lived in shoreline settlements. Although the 1793 expedition recommended creation of an outpost on the bay, it was not until 1817 that a Spanish mission was built in what is now Marin County; that mission was built not on Tomales Bay, but at what is now the town of San Rafael.

Tomales Bay lies in a drowned rift valley formed by earth movement along the San Andreas fault. The name Tomales may come from a Miwok Indian word for bay, or it may derive from the Spanish word for the food tamales. The bay is 13 miles long, one mile wide, and very shallow: the south end is less than ten feet deep, and wide expanses of mudflats are exposed at low tide. The three main streams which feed the bay—Walker/Keys Creek, Lagunitas Creek, and Olema Creek—are relatively small, and the amount of fresh water entering the bay is modest. The bay is not a true estuary, where substantial mixing of fresh water and salt water takes place; however, localized estuarine conditions do exist at scattered points along the shoreline. Both salt and freshwater marshes are found along the edges of the bay.

Bottom materials in Tomales Bay include gravel or coarse sand near the mouth of the bay and fine sand, silt, or mud at the upper, or southern, end. The range of coarse to fine bottom materials encourages a great variety of inhabitants; over 1,000 different species of worms, clams, snails, crabs, and other marine and estuarine invertebrates have been identified.

Some of these invertebrates are exotic species: in 1928, what are now called Pacific oysters were introduced to Tomales Bay from Japan, and many types of tiny clinging and boring invertebrates were introduced inadvertently along with the oysters. Pacific oysters are raised commercially in Tomales Bay, where the larvae of the oysters do not survive to replace harvested adults. Instead, seed oysters are imported and attached to large oyster shells suspended from racks or rafts, where they grow to harvestable size. Rows of racks are visible at low tide at several points along the east shore of the bay, and oysters are offered for sale along Highway 1.

In the extensive eelgrass beds in the shallow waters near the mouth of Tomales Bay, black brant feed and Pacific herring deposit their eggs. The herring have supported an important commercial fishery since gold rush days in California. At first, the fish themselves were sold on the domestic market, but in the last 20 years the principal target of the fishery has been the herring roe which is exported to Japan as a delicacy. Herring boats cast their nets in the bay during the annual season beginning each January; the fishing season is brief in order to avoid depleting the herring population.

Bird watchers have identified nearly 100 species of water-associated birds at Tomales Bay, including species that winter in the area and those that pass through along the Pacific Flyway. Shorebirds commonly seen include marbled godwits, willets, black turnstones, and dunlins. Waterfowl seen include buffleheads, white-winged scoters, surf scoters, and ruddy ducks. Great blue herons, common egrets, and snowy egrets wade in the shallow waters of the bay in search of fish. There is a heron rookery in a grove of eucalyptus trees located on private land south of Miller Park along Highway 1.

The varied resources of Tomales Bay, which are largely unaffected by urban or industrial development, are highly popular with recreational users. Anglers in boats or on the rocky shore catch perch, flounder, and sand dabs. Rock crabs, Dungeness crabs, and clams, such as littlenecks, are also found in the bay. The shelter from wind and fog provided by Inverness Ridge makes the westside sandy beaches, such as Heart's Desire in Tomales Bay State Park, popular with swimmers.

Miller Park: *Hwy. 1, 3.6 mi. N. of Marshall.*

This small county park offers two boat launching ramps, picnic tables in a grove of trees on the bluff, and fine views of Hog Island, Inverness Ridge, and the bay.

Livermore Marsh: *Hwy. 1, .8 mi. N. of Marshall.*

A fresh-to-brackish water marsh is located near the bay's edge at the Cypress Grove property owned by Audubon Canyon Ranch. Insects such as mosquitoes, dance flies, and stiletto flies inhabit the brackish marsh. Pintails and wigeons are seen in the marsh. Entry is by appointment only; call: (415) 383-1644.

Marshall Marsh: *Hwy. 1 at Marshall-Petaluma Road.*

This small freshwater willow swamp and brackish marsh is owned by Audubon Canyon Ranch; call: (415) 383-1644. The wooded areas

Tomales Bay north of Inverness

around the marsh, where stream-side litter, logs, and rocks accumulate, are home to amphibians such as the California newt, California slender salamander, western toad, and the Pacific tree frog. Common reptiles found in the area of the marsh include the western fence lizard, aquatic garter snake, western terrestrial garter snake, and western rattlesnake.

Marshall: *Hwy. 1, 9.5 mi. N. of Pt. Reyes Station.*
Four Irish brothers named Marshall began ranching in this area in the early 1860s, and the first commercial building in the new town appeared in 1867. The town became an important transfer point between ocean-going schooners and the North Pacific Coast Railroad. Today Highway 1 occupies the old railroad right-of-way at Marshall. Commercial and recreational fishing continues in the area; boat repair and service facilities are located just south of town.

Marconi: *Hwy. 1, 7.7 mi. N. of Pt. Reyes Station.*
Early explorers of Tomales Bay reported that numerous Miwok Indian villages were located along the shoreline of the bay; one such village was located at the cove at Marconi. In 1913 the 28-room Marconi Hotel was built by the Marconi Wireless Company to house workers at what was the first Trans-Pacific radio transmission facility. Radio Corporation of America took over the radio facility in 1920 and moved it to the Point Reyes Peninsula nine years later. On the blufftop above the cove the old hotel stands unused; renovation of the buildings for a retreat and conference center has been proposed.

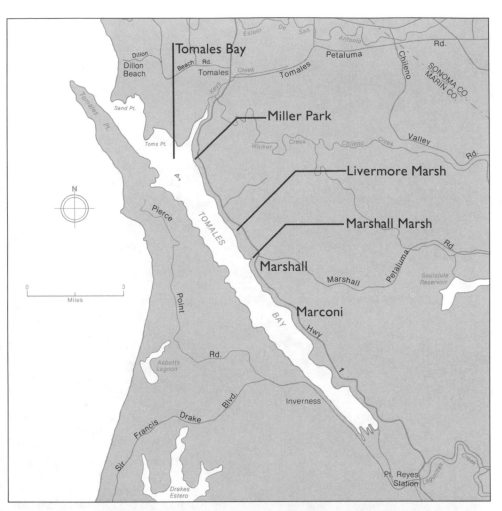

View north from above Tomales Bay, ca. 1965

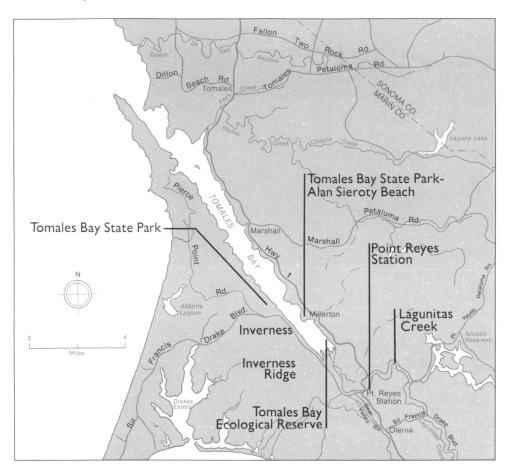

Tomales Bay State Park includes the following areas: Alan Sieroty Beach, Inverness Ridge unit, Heart's Desire Beach, Indian Beach, Pebble Beach, and Shell Beach. For information, call: (415) 669-1140.

Pacific razor clam (*Siliqua patula*)
shell 6¾ inches long

Tomales Bay State Park-Alan Sieroty Beach: *Hwy. 1, 4.7 mi. N. of Pt. Reyes Station.*

Millerton Point, and Tomasini Point to the north of it, are part of Tomales Bay State Park. A parking lot, picnic area, and toilets are located at the southern end of Millerton Point. From the tip of Millerton Point fine views of the bay are available. Immediately south of the point is a small salt marsh in the delta of Millerton Gulch.

Point Reyes Station: *Highway 1 at Point Reyes-Petaluma Road.*

Point Reyes Station was originally a stop on the North Pacific Coast Railroad, which linked Sausalito in southern Marin County to northern Marin and Sonoma counties. In 1875 the line reached the town of Tomales, and by 1877 it extended north to the lumber mills on the Russian River. Southeast of Point Reyes Station, the narrow-gauge tracks ran through dense redwood forest along Lagunitas Creek; north of town the tracks ran mostly on a trestle along the eastern shore of Tomales Bay. The railroad hauled lumber, farm produce, commuters, and weekend sightseers on trips that were not without their mishaps; more than one locomotive left the tracks and landed in the creek or upside down in the bay mud.

The townsite of Point Reyes Station was laid out in 1883, and the town grew up around the railroad station. Buildings on the south side of "A" Street date from around the turn of the century, including the red brick Mission Revival style Grandi Building, now in disrepair, at the corner of 2nd Street. After train service to Point Reyes Station ceased in 1933, commercial structures were built on the north side of "A" Street

on the former railroad right-of-way; the old depot now serves as the post office.

Lagunitas Creek: *Hwy. 1 at Pt. Reyes Station.*

Lagunitas Creek, also called Paper Mill Creek, drains the northern slopes of Mount Tamalpais and flows through redwood forest and riparian woodland before entering the south end of Tomales Bay. The creek is the largest of the streams feeding Tomales Bay. The endangered California freshwater shrimp inhabits the creek upstream of Point Reyes Station.

Steelhead and silver salmon return annually to spawn in Lagunitas Creek and its tributary, Olema Creek. White House Pool is a public fishing access point near the junction of the two creeks, at Sir Francis Drake Blvd. and Bear Valley Road. Anglers fish for silver salmon from late October to December and for steelhead from December through April. A 22-pound silver salmon, the largest recorded in California, was caught in 1959 in White House Pool.

Tomales Bay Ecological Reserve: *Southern portion of Tomales Bay.*

Where Lagunitas Creek enters the shallow southern end of Tomales Bay is the largest wetland and marsh system found within the bay. Although some of the historic marsh has been diked off and is used as grazing land, an extensive wetland area remains. The Tomales Bay Ecological Reserve, held by the State Wildlife Conservation Board, includes some 500 acres at the southern end of the bay. Dominant plants in the salt marsh along the bay's edge are pickleweed and arrowgrass. The tidal channels and mudflats are a feeding ground for many species of shorebirds, including killdeer, western sandpipers, and black-bellied plovers.

Bird watchers use pull-outs on Highway 1 along the bay, such as the one-time railroad flagstop called "Bivalve," located 2.6 miles north of Point Reyes Station. On the west side of the bay, the William Page Shields Salt Marsh overlook, located on Sir Francis Drake Blvd. 3.4 miles north of Point Reyes Station, also provides views of the ecological reserve. Due to the sensitive nature of the resources, entry into the reserve is not encouraged.

Inverness Ridge: *W. side of Tomales Bay.*

The steep, forested Inverness Ridge that runs parallel to the drowned rift valley of the San Andreas Fault beneath Tomales Bay presents a sharp contrast to the rolling grassy hills on the east side of the bay. The highest point on Inverness Ridge at 1,407 feet is Mount Wittenberg, located southwest of Point Reyes Station. A dense canopy of Douglas-fir covers the southern end of Inverness Ridge; Bishop pine grows on the northern end.

Near the point where Sir Francis Drake Blvd. crosses the crest of the ridge is a dwarf Bishop pine forest where severely acidic soils cause stunting; the trees here, however, are not as dwarfed as those in the Mendocino pygmy forest. Found in association with the Bishop pine forest on Inverness Ridge is the rare Mount Vision ceanothus; this is the only known location for this species of plant. The forest on Inverness Ridge harbors the southernmost colony in the coastal range of the native mountain beaver, an elusive, cat-sized, nocturnal rodent. Ospreys nest in snags on the ridge, and blue Steller's jays are abundant. Much of the bay side of Inverness Ridge is privately owned; Point Reyes National Seashore and units of Tomales Bay State Park compose the rest.

Inverness: *Sir Francis Drake Blvd., 3.1 mi. N. of Bear Valley Rd.*

Inverness was created as a resort community in 1889 by James McMillan Shafter, who, along with his family, owned most of the Point Reyes Peninsula. Shafter recalled his Scottish heritage with street names such as Argyle, Aberdeen, and Dundee. The community at first consisted primarily of summer homes built by San Francisco Bay Area residents. Today the steep wooded slopes of Inverness Ridge overlooking Tomales Bay hold both year-round and summer

dwellings, and there are several small bed-and-breakfast inns and a number of eating places along Sir Francis Drake Boulevard.

Tomales Bay State Park: *Off Pierce Point Rd., 3.8 mi. N. of Inverness.*

The Tomales Bay State Park unit lying northwest of Inverness includes two miles of bay shoreline with four sandy beaches where swimming is possible in the sheltered bay waters. The main parking and picnic areas are at Heart's Desire Beach, reached off Pierce Point Road. Indian Beach and Pebble Beach are accessible by half-mile-long trails from Heart's Desire Beach. Shell Beach can also be reached by a 4.1-mile long trail from Heart's Desire or from a separate parking area at the end of Camino del Mar (outside the park). Spotted owls have been

sighted in the Bishop pine forest that hugs the shoreline, and Pacific tree frogs are common. The clamming at Heart's Desire and Pebble Beach is among the best in Tomales Bay.

Tomales Bay State Park also includes property on Inverness Ridge near the community of Inverness Park; the property is undeveloped except for trails. Information is available at the Heart's Desire Beach entrance station.

The San Andreas Fault

The San Andreas Fault is one of the most studied geologic features in the world. The fault is not a single fracture; rather, it is a zone laced with many smaller faults stretching from Shelter Cove in Humboldt County southeast for approximately 650 miles to the Salton Sea in Imperial County. Along the coast, obvious features of the fault are long, parallel, northwest-trending valleys and ridges, including the submerged valleys of Bodega Bay in Sonoma County, Tomales Bay in Marin County, and San Andreas Lake in San Mateo County. Other indicators of past fault activity are offset stream channels and fences, and differences in the composition of abutting rock formations on opposite sides of the fault zone.

The origin of the San Andreas Fault can be explained by the geologic theory of global, or plate, tectonics, which describes the movement of massive plates that together form the earth's outer crust. The San Andreas Fault is an impact zone between the Pacific Plate, which underlies much of the Pacific Ocean, and the North American Plate, which underlies North America and roughly half the Atlantic

Ocean. Geologists infer that when these two plates first collided 150-200 million years ago, the Pacific Plate moved under the North American Plate, initiating a phase of mountain-building that created the Sierra Nevada.

Approximately 20 million years ago, the direction of movement changed: the Pacific Plate then began a northwesterly movement, and the North American Plate slid past it to the southeast. In California, movement between these two plates occurs along the San Andreas Fault, as well as along parallel faults, such as the

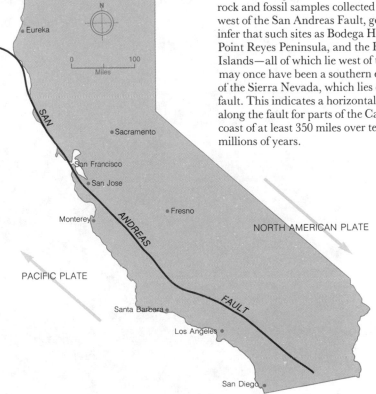

Hayward and Calaveras faults. Movement between the plates continues today at an average rate of several centimeters per year.

Periodic movement along the San Andreas Fault can be immense; for example, the 1906 San Francisco earthquake ruptured the fault surface for 200 miles and caused 20 feet of slippage at the north end of Tomales Bay. In 1857 an earthquake at Fort Tejon in Southern California caused 29 feet of displacement. In some areas, movement along the fault is more often a slow creep: near Hollister in San Benito County, earth displacement averages one half inch per year, without sizable earthquakes. Based on analysis of rock and fossil samples collected east and west of the San Andreas Fault, geologists infer that such sites as Bodega Head, the Point Reyes Peninsula, and the Farallon Islands—all of which lie west of the fault—may once have been a southern extension of the Sierra Nevada, which lies east of the fault. This indicates a horizontal slippage along the fault for parts of the California coast of at least 350 miles over tens of millions of years.

The Point Reyes National Seashore, administered by the National Park Service, encompasses most of the Point Reyes Peninsula. The following are within the National Seashore: Tomales Point, McClures Beach, Kehoe Beach, Abbotts Lagoon, North and South Beaches, Point Reyes Lighthouse, Point Reyes Headlands, and Drakes Beach.

Tomales Point: *End of Pierce Point Rd., 9.3 mi. N.W. of Sir Francis Drake Blvd.*

A four-mile-long trail leads from a parking area at the old Upper Pierce Ranch to Tomales Point. Rock outcroppings along the trail hold associations of spring-flowering Douglas iris, California buttercup, cow-parsnip, and the endangered Point Reyes blennosperma. Dramatic views of Tomales Bay, Bodega Head, and Point Reyes are available from the trail. Bird Rock, near the ocean side of the point, is a rookery for several species of seabirds, including the ashy storm-petrel, and is a major harbor seal pupping area. Great white sharks are frequently observed in the ocean near Tomales Point; divers have been attacked in this area. Granite cliffs at the point are covered with sheets of orange-colored algae, actually a variety of green alga in which a red pigment masks the chlorophyll. A short trail leads from the Tomales Point trailhead to White Gulch on Tomales Bay.

A small herd of native tule elk was reintroduced to the Tomales Point area in 1978 by the National Park Service after an absence of over 100 years. Dogs are not permitted on Tomales Point.

McClures Beach: *End of Pierce Point Rd.*

Exposed to the full force of storms and waves rolling in off the open ocean, this is one of the most dramatic sections of the Marin coast; it is also extremely unsafe for swimming. Backed by steep bluffs, the beach is a broad sandy crescent; portions are covered with rocks smoothed by the surf. Endangered California brown pelicans, cormorants, and common murres are often seen on the granite sea stacks off the south end of the beach. Surf scoters ride the ocean waves. Abundant rocky intertidal life here includes giant green anemones and sturdy sea palms. A steep half-mile-long trail leads from the parking lot to the beach; dogs are not permitted.

Kehoe Beach: *Off Pierce Point Rd., 5.5 mi. N.W. of Sir Francis Drake Blvd.*

A half-mile-long trail, partly a cow path, leads along the edge of a freshwater marsh from the road to the sandy beach. A stand of Point Reyes bent grass, an endangered native species, is found on rock outcroppings near the trailhead. Spring wildflowers include California poppies, baby blue eyes, wild hollyhock, phacelia, and cream cups.

Abbotts Lagoon: *Off Pierce Point Rd., 3.4 mi. N.W. of Sir Francis Drake Blvd.*

The lower lagoon is brackish, since the sandbar at the mouth is breached occasionally by winter storm waves and high tides. The upper lagoon is freshwater. Shorebirds that are uncommon elsewhere, such as Baird's sandpipers and semipalmated sandpipers, are found seasonally around the lagoon. Western grebes and pied-billed grebes are frequently sighted; Caspian terns may be seen in the summer. A one-mile-long trail leads from the parking area to the lagoon, where hikers may continue to the sand dunes and the beach.

North Beach and South Beach: *Off Sir Francis Drake Blvd.*

This 12-mile-long sandy beach is served by two parking areas with wheelchair-accessible restrooms. In the wide dune field behind the beach are stands of endangered Point Reyes lupine, along with colorful, non-native ice plant. Huge breakers pound this windward shore; look out for hazardous sneaker-waves.

Along Sir Francis Drake Blvd. near the beach are antenna fields operated by RCA Global Communications, AT&T, and the U.S. Coast Guard. These are receiving antennas for overseas telephone calls and for radio transmissions from ships at sea all over the Pacific.

Point Reyes Lighthouse

McClures Beach

Point Reyes Lighthouse: *End of Sir Francis Drake Blvd., 15 mi. S.W. of Inverness.*

The tip of the Point Reyes Peninsula, thrusting seaward some 20 miles from the main shoreline and subject to persistent winds and fogs, has been the site of numerous shipwrecks. The earliest recorded was in 1595 when the *San Agustin*, a Spanish galleon loaded with cargo from the Philippines and captained by Sebastián Rodríguez Cermeño, went aground in what is now called Drakes Bay. In 1870 the Point Reyes Lighthouse was built on the bluff face 294 feet above sea level. An automated light and foghorn were installed in 1975, although the original lighthouse and Fresnel lens remain. Some 400 steps lead from the parking area down the bluff to the lighthouse. The point receives up to 2,700 hours of fog annually, but it gets relatively little rainfall, less than 20 inches per year.

Gray whales pass near Point Reyes on their annual winter migration south to Baja California, where calving takes place in warm lagoons. Point Reyes is a favorite whale-watching spot; prime viewing months are December through early April. Parking at the lighthouse is limited; during peak whale-watching months, the National Park Service may operate a shuttle from the Drakes Beach parking area.

Point Reyes Headlands: *End of Sir Francis Drake Blvd.*

The headlands extending from the Point Reyes Lighthouse east to Chimney Rock form a massive granite promontory up to 600 feet high. The submarine topography is similarly steep: depths of 150 feet and more are found close to shore. Along the shoreline at the base of the headlands are sea stacks, smooth granite rocks, wave-carved sea caves, and coarse sandy pocket beaches. The variety of surfaces makes the area attractive to many different kinds of clinging plants and invertebrates. The subtidal zone is home to giant green anemones, rose anemones, and red sea urchins. Red abalone fasten to undersea rocks where they feed on kelp.

Censuses have shown that the headlands area is the principal location in the county for breeding birds. Particularly numerous are common murres, which nest on the rocks almost directly below the lighthouse, and Brandt's and pelagic cormorants. California sea lions occupy offshore rocks, and there is a breeding colony of Steller sea lions in one of the coves. The headlands from the lighthouse east to Chimney Rock are designated as a marine reserve that is off-limits to all but approved researchers. The waters surrounding the Point Reyes Peninsula are also part of the Gulf of the Farallones National Marine Sanctuary.

Drakes Beach: *Drakes Beach Rd., off Sir Francis Drake Blvd., 10.3 mi. S.W. of Inverness.*

Drakes Bay is thought by some historians to be the site of English explorer Francis Drake's landing in 1579. White cliffs rise behind the bay, and summer fog often envelops the shore, matching the description left in Drake's journal. Cermeño, a Portuguese who explored these shores in 1595 on behalf of Spain, named the bay "San Francisco," causing later confusion with the bay now carrying that name. Beach facilities include a visitor center with exhibits, wheelchair-accessible restrooms, and picnic tables.

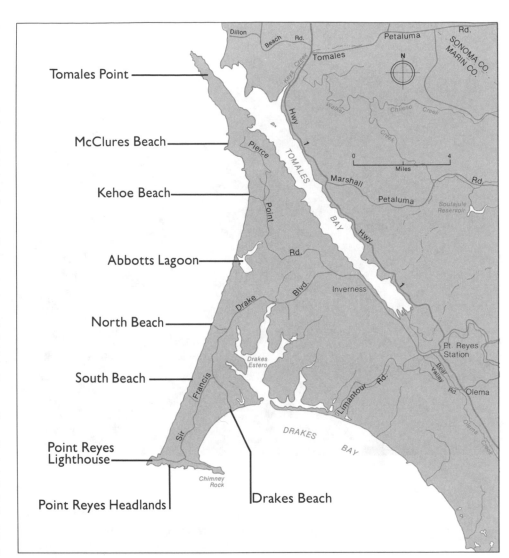

Upper Pierce Ranch

View east, Point Reyes Peninsula

Olema Marsh: *S.E. corner, intersection of Sir Francis Drake Blvd. and Bear Valley Rd.*

This 40-acre marsh, the largest of the freshwater marshes around the edge of Tomales Bay, is formed by Olema Creek upstream from its junction with Lagunitas Creek. Cattails and tules are found in the marsh. This is the only known site in Marin County of the bur marigold.

Over 150 species of birds have been observed at Olema Marsh, including the yellow warbler, the Virginia rail, and the sora, an uncommon relative of the rail. The threatened California black rail has also been seen here. Western pond turtles are found in abundance. Most of the marsh is owned by Audubon Canyon Ranch as a research and wetland restoration project; for information, call: (415) 383-1644. Although public entry to the marsh is not permitted, many birds may be seen from the roadside.

Olema: *Hwy. 1, 2 mi. S. of Pt. Reyes Station.*

Olema was established in 1859 and soon became a busy commercial center. When the North Pacific Coast Railroad was built in 1875, the nearest stop was located two miles away at Olema Station, later known as Point Reyes Station, and the town of Olema soon began to fade in importance. A few historical structures remain, including the Olema Inn in a restored 1877 building at the corner of Sir Francis Drake Blvd. and Highway 1. The name Olema is taken from the Miwok name Olemaloke, meaning Coyote Valley.

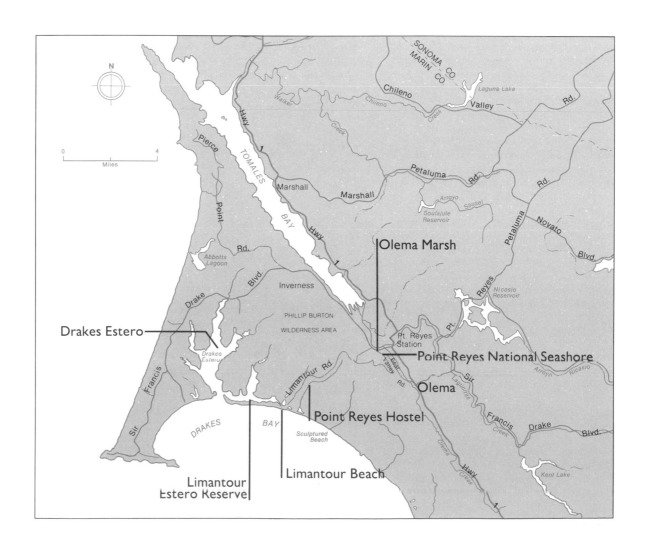

The following are within the Point Reyes National Seashore: Bear Valley Headquarters, Phillip Burton Wilderness Area, Point Reyes Hostel, Limantour Beach, Limantour Estero Reserve, and Drakes Estero.

Point Reyes National Seashore: *Headquarters on Bear Valley Rd., .6 mi. N.W. of Olema.*

The Point Reyes National Seashore encompasses most of the land mass west of the San Andreas rift zone, excluding Tomales Bay State Park and the communities of Bolinas and Inverness. The seashore is noteworthy for its great diversity of ecosystems: although the Point Reyes Peninsula is only a tiny fraction of California's total land area, over 15 per cent of California's plant species are found here. Along Limantour Rd., sticky monkeyflower, lupine, and other perennials are showy in the springtime. Annual wildflowers carpet the open grasslands at Tomales Point and along the road to the Point Reyes Lighthouse. East of the lighthouse are clusters of the endangered yellow Point Reyes meadowfoam.

Point Reyes also exhibits tremendous avian diversity; some 360 species of birds have been observed at the National Seashore. Significant species include land birds such as the western flycatcher, Anna's hummingbird, warbling vireo, and Wilson's warbler, all of which breed in the area, as well as water birds such as transient Forster's terns, California gulls, and arctic loons. Peregrine falcons and southern bald eagles, both endangered, are occasionally seen here.

The Bear Valley Headquarters includes a large visitor center with interpretive exhibits. Nearby is a picnic area and the wheelchair-accessible Earthquake Trail, which provides a close-up view of the effects of earth movement on the San Andreas Fault. The Morgan Horse Farm offers demonstrations of the care and riding of these animals; the farm also provides mounts for trail patrol in the National Seashore. Horses are available for rental at Bear Valley Stables; call: (415) 663-1570. Near the visitor center is a display of Coast Miwok structures, such as tule houses and acorn granaries, reproduced as they might have appeared 200 years ago. The 4.4-mile-long Bear Valley Trail

and connecting trails link the visitor center to the shoreline of the seashore and to four hike-in camps available to individuals or groups; for information and reservations, call: (415) 663-1092. Among the beaches reached by the trail system is Sculptured Beach, named for the high cliffs which have eroded into graceful spires.

Within the National Seashore boundaries are several historic ranches where dairy and beef cattle still graze under lease agreements. The Phillip Burton Wilderness Area composes nearly half of the National Seashore's 71,000 acres. No pavement or structures are found in the designated wilderness area; a network of trails leads through it. Seashore visitors are warned to use caution near strong ocean currents, sneaker-waves, and precipitous cliffs.

Point Reyes Hostel: *Off Limantour Rd., 6 mi. from Bear Valley Rd.*

For information and reservations for this 40-bed hostel, call: (415) 663-8811. Nearby is the Clem Miller Environmental Education Center with overnight facilities for school groups; call: (415) 663-1920.

Limantour Beach: *End of Limantour Rd., 7.7 mi. from Bear Valley Rd.*

A long sandy crescent, backed by dunes, stretches east from the mouth of Drakes Estero. Due to the sheltering effect of the Point Reyes headlands, wave action is generally calmer here than on the west-facing beaches of the Point Reyes Peninsula.

Limantour Estero Reserve: *End of Limantour Road.*

Extending along the north side of the two-mile-long Limantour Spit is the 500-acre Limantour Estero Reserve. Pickleweed grows in the salt marsh on the margin of the estero, and eelgrass grows in deeper water. Water birds such as white pelicans and black brant feed and rest in the estero, and harbor seals haul out on shore. Numerous invertebrates are found in the mudflats, including blue mud shrimp and giant moon snails. Within the reserve, removal of all life forms is prohibited without permits.

Drakes Estero: *Estero Trail off Sir Francis Drake Blvd., 4.6 mi. W. of Inverness.*

This is the largest of the saltwater lagoons along the Marin coast. The shallow estero receives freshwater flow only from minor streams, and broad mudflats are exposed at low tide. Invertebrates found in the mudflats include giant geoduck clams, now uncommon elsewhere, and abundant phoronids, or "stringworms." The rocky intertidal area of the estero is inhabited by limpets, sea anemones, ochre sea stars, and several varieties of crabs. The estero harbors rays and leopard sharks and also serves as a nursery for fish such as lingcod. Uncommon water-associated birds, such as Caspian terns and Canada geese, use the estero.

Located on a dirt road off Sir Francis Drake Blvd. at the north end of Drakes Estero is Johnson's Oyster Company. For over 50 years, Pacific oysters have been raised commercially on leased tidelands within the estero, and oysters are available for sale here. Southwest of the estero near the beach is Drakes Lagoon, a mainly freshwater marsh containing cattails and tules. The marsh is habitat for pied-billed grebes and other water birds.

Reconstruction of Miwok hut, Bear Valley

Limantour Estero Reserve

Duxbury Reef

Bolinas

Samuel P. Taylor State Park: *Sir Francis Drake Blvd., 5.2 mi. E. of Olema.*

The state park includes 2,600 acres of wooded canyons along Lagunitas Creek and its tributaries some eight miles upstream from Tomales Bay. The creek is also known as Paper Mill Creek, after the first paper mill on the Pacific Coast, built in 1856 in what is now the state park by gold prospector and businessman Samuel P. Taylor. Taylor used his earnings from the gold fields to set up a water-powered mill which produced newsprint for dailies in San Francisco, fine quality paper, and a new creation—square-bottomed, folding paper bags. A resort hotel and campground were added in the 1870s, making the canyon one of California's early weekend recreational areas. Samuel P. Taylor State Park offers picnic areas and campsites, including some for backpackers and bicyclists, and a group camp suitable for use by equestrians. Call: (415) 488-9897.

Five Brooks Trailhead: *Hwy. 1, 3.6 mi. S. of Olema.*

From the Five Brooks Trailhead, trails lead to the southern shore of the Point Reyes National Seashore and to the Palomarin Trailhead near Bolinas. Horses may be rented from a concessionaire at Five Brooks; for information, call: (415) 663-8287.

Bolinas: *End of Bolinas-Olema Rd., off Hwy. 1, 9.1 mi. S. of Olema.*

When San Francisco grew explosively after the discovery of gold in 1848, Bolinas shared the boom in a modest way. Redwoods on the hills surrounding Bolinas were cut to build the wooden row houses of San Francisco, and smaller trees were cut for household fuel. From sawmills near the shore, lumber was loaded on flat-bottomed lighters in Bolinas Lagoon and transferred to ships anchored offshore. In the U.S. Census of 1850, the first to include California, two-thirds of Marin County's few hundred residents lived in the Bolinas area.

In the 1880s, summer homes began to appear in Bolinas near the shore, and tents were put up on the sandy beach, which was much wider at that time than it is now. Some 19th-century buildings remain, particularly near the old downtown along Wharf Road. Part of Smiley's Bar dates from 1852, the Gibson House building dates from 1875, and St. Mary Magdalen Catholic Church from 1878. Hundreds of thousands of Monarch butterflies overwinter in Bolinas in a grove of eucalyptus trees on Audubon Canyon Ranch property.

Duxbury Reef: *S.W. shoreline of Bolinas Mesa.*

Duxbury Reef is California's largest exposed shale reef. The reef lies at the base of the headlands known as the Bolinas Mesa, also formed of Monterey shale. At low tide, a mile-long stretch of reef is exposed. The shape of the reef is continuously changing, as the waves erode the edges of the reef and the adjacent cliffs. The relatively soft shale is habitat for an unusual assemblage of rock-boring clams and worms.

The intertidal area includes gooseneck barnacles, ochre sea stars, and huge beds of California mussels. Shallow gravel tidepools contain a type of acorn worm that is apparently unique to the Duxbury Reef, and a small burrowing anemone, *Halcampa crypta*, found only here and at Puget Sound in Washington State. Gumboot chitons and giant pink sea stars inhabit the subtidal area and are occasionally washed onshore by storm waves. The entire reef is a marine reserve; marine life may not be removed without permission from the Department of Fish and Game.

Agate Beach: *End of Elm Rd., Bolinas.*

This county park includes a small beach at the edge of Duxbury Reef. Rocks around the beach that are splashed by the waves hold associations of barnacles, limpets, and periwinkles.

Point Reyes Bird Observatory: *Mesa Rd., 4.2 mi. N.W. of Bolinas.*

The Point Reyes Bird Observatory is a nonprofit research, conservation, and education organization which maintains a field station near the Palomarin Trailhead. The field station is the location of a major land bird research program; wrentits, rufous-sided towhees, song sparrows, and other birds are captured, examined, banded, and released. Banding takes place every morning from April to November and on Wednesdays, Saturdays, and Sundays during the winter months; visitors are welcome to observe. Call: (415) 868-1221 for more information.

Displays of the observatory's research projects are contained in a small museum, open daily to the public. A half-mile-long self-guided nature trail leads through coastal scrub habitat and the small canyon of Arroyo Honda. In addition to the field station, the Point Reyes Bird Observatory operates an estuarine research program centered on Bolinas Lagoon and maintains a permanent staff on the Farallon Islands, where research focuses on seabirds.

Palomarin Trailhead: *End of Mesa Rd., 5 mi. N.W. of Bolinas.*

The Palomarin Trailhead provides access to the southern end of the Point Reyes National Seashore, including Double Point, two Monterey shale outcroppings which enclose a small bay. A large breeding colony of harbor seals resides on this beach; do not disturb the seals. Kelp clings to the intertidal reef, along with acorn barnacles and unusually large California mussels. Purple and giant red sea urchins lie in the crevices, and porcelain crabs and red rock crabs are common on the reef. Rocks north and south of Double Point, particularly Stormy Stack off North Point, are important feeding and roosting sites for Brandt's cormorants, common murres, grebes, and endangered California brown pelicans. On top of the bluff is Pelican Lake, drained by a stream flowing down to the beach. Four nearby freshwater lakes, named Bass, Crystal, Ocean, and Wildcat, contain small marshy areas and provide habitat for waterfowl. Alamere Falls cascades down the bluff north of Double Point.

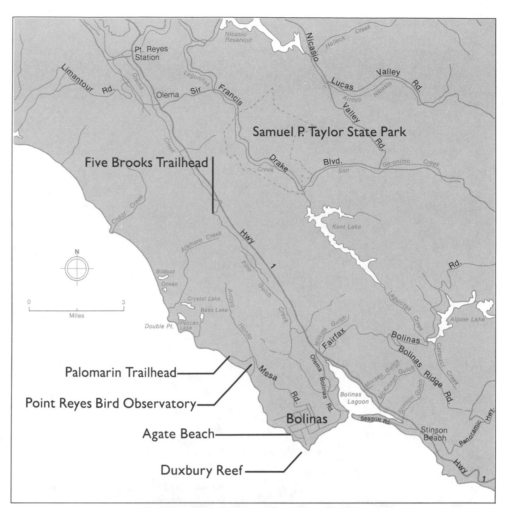

Smiley's Bar, Bolinas

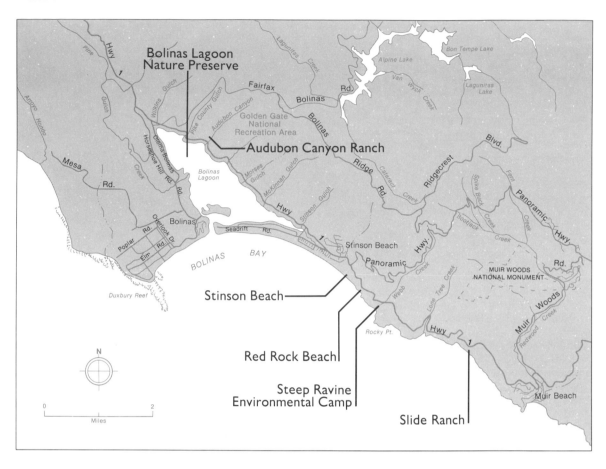

great blue heron (*Ardea herodias*)
42 to 52 inches high, 6-foot wingspan

Bolinas Lagoon Nature Preserve: *Along Hwy. 1, N. of Stinson Beach.*

Bolinas Lagoon, a county-owned nature preserve, includes over 1,200 acres of sheltered water, salt marsh, and mudflat. In winter, when freshwater runoff is relatively high, the lagoon is an estuary; in summer it is essentially a saltwater lagoon. The shallowness of the lagoon has resulted from siltation due, in part, to historic logging on the surrounding hills. The lagoon serves as a nursery for fish such as starry flounder, cabezon, and several varieties of perch.

The lagoon's extensive mudflats attract large numbers of shorebirds. Plovers, sandpipers, herons, and egrets are abundant. Surf scoters, ruddy ducks, greater scaups, avocets, and pintails are also commonly seen. Uncommon, but occasionally present, are Virginia rails. During the migration season at the lagoon, as many as 30,000 to 35,000 waterfowl and shorebirds have been counted, representing over 60 species.

Around the perimeter of the lagoon are several salt marshes in which cordgrass, pickleweed, and saltgrass are present. Small freshwater marshes exist where streams open into the lagoon. The major perennial stream flowing into Bolinas Lagoon is Pine Gulch Creek, which drains the upper Bolinas peninsula; silver salmon and steelhead spawn in the stream. A dense stand of native bay laurel and alder trees is located where Stinson Creek enters the lagoon near Highway 1.

Near the mouth of Bolinas Lagoon is Kent Island, a low-lying islet barely separated from the Bolinas peninsula at low tide. Harbor seals haul out on the island. Pull-outs along Highway 1 allow views of the lagoon.

Audubon Canyon Ranch: *Hwy. 1, 3.1 mi. N. of Stinson Beach.*

Inland of Highway 1 near Bolinas Lagoon are several heavily wooded canyons separated by grass-covered ridges. High in the redwood trees in one of the canyons is a large nesting colony of great blue herons and great egrets. Audubon Canyon Ranch operates a reserve centered on the heron rookery. A half-mile-long trail leads to an overlook on the hill where fixed telescopes allow close-up views of all the activities of a nesting colony of great blue herons, including courtship, mating, incubation, feeding, and fledgling flights. Two three-mile-long loop trails and a self-guided nature trail into other canyons are also available.

Facilities at Audubon Canyon Ranch include an exhibit hall, nature bookshop, and picnic area adjacent to the 1875 home of Captain Peter Bourne. In a neighboring canyon, the ranch operates a wildlife education center in another ranch house built in the 1870s. The ranch is open from March through mid-July; the public is welcome on weekends and holidays from 10 AM–4PM, and school and other groups may visit Tuesday through Friday by appointment. For information, call: (415) 383-1644.

Stinson Beach: *Off Hwy. 1, .3 mi. N. of Panoramic Highway.*

Stinson Beach is a long sandy crescent facing Bolinas Bay. Its location below the slopes of Mount Tamalpais gives it more summer sunshine than other, less sheltered, Marin County beaches. The main part of the beach, parking area, and support facilities lie within the Golden Gate National Recreation Area. There are picnic facilities, wheelchair-accessible restrooms, and a snack bar. Call: (415) 868-0942 or 868-1922. Upton's Beach, a county beach where dogs are permitted, extends two-thirds of a mile upcoast from the GGNRA beach.

Early settler Alfred D. Easkoot promoted Stinson Beach as a destination for campers and swimmers; his 1875 house, now restored, is located on Highway 1 just west of the village center. Around 1900, a summer tent colony called Willow Camp appeared in the dunes near the beach. Cabins and houses began to be built after a subdivision was created by Nathan H. Stinson in 1906. Early day visitors to Stinson Beach arrived by stagecoach or buggy via a road around the north side of Mount Tamalpais; a 1911 plan to extend the Mount Tamalpais and Muir Woods Railway from Mill Valley was never carried out.

Introduced eucalyptus and Monterey pine trees in the village are winter resting areas for colonies of Monarch butterflies. Easkoot Creek, bordered by dense riparian vegetation, flows through the center of town and feeds Bolinas Lagoon. The former creek mouth was located on the beach, emptying directly into the bay.

Red Rock Beach: *Hwy. 1, 1 mi. S. of Stinson Beach.*

From an unpaved parking lot a trail leads down the steep, red chert bluff to a remote sandy beach within Mount Tamalpais State Park.

Steep Ravine Environmental Camp: *Hwy. 1, 1.3 mi. S. of Stinson Beach.*

A mile below Highway 1 at the base of Steep Ravine on Rocky Point are ten cabins overlooking the sea. The simple redwood cabins were built in the 1930s for Congressman William Kent and his family. Today the area is part of Mount Tamalpais State Park, and the cabins provide modest accommodations for the public. Outdoor environmental campsites are also available nearby. For reservations, write the Reservations Office, Department of Parks and Recreation, P.O. Box 2390, Sacramento, CA 95811, or phone: (800) 952-5580. Parking at the cabins is for registered campers only; day users hike down from Highway 1.

On the beach north of Rocky Point is a subsurface thermal spring in the low intertidal area. The spring causes warm water to bubble up through the pebbles on the beach, but it is accessible only during exceptionally low tides.

Slide Ranch: *Hwy. 1, .5 mi. N. of the Muir Beach Overlook.*

Slide Ranch is a privately owned day use area and environmental education center for groups, located down a gravel drive; call: (415) 383-0358 for information. Serpentine outcroppings form steep, unstable cliffs in this area. Tidepools inhabited by sponges, bryozoans, and tunicates are found at the shoreline.

Steep Ravine Environmental Camp

View to Stinson Beach from Highway 1

Mount Tamalpais State Park: *Off Panoramic Highway, southwestern Marin County.*

The name Tamalpais may stem from the Miwok word *tamal* for bay plus the Spanish *pais* for mountain or country. To early settlers, the mountain's flat profile seen from the ocean off Point Reyes suggested the name Table Mountain, which appears on some 19th-century maps. Seen from the east side of San Francisco Bay, the shape of the mountain has been described more colorfully as resembling a sleeping maiden. The highest peak reaches 2,604 feet; the range of habitats found on the slopes includes redwood forest, mixed-evergreen forest, chaparral, mountain meadow, and riparian. Coast live oak, California black oak, bay laurel, madrone, and tanbark oak grow in the mixed-evergreen forest. Chaparral, which grows on well-drained sunny slopes, includes ceanothus, chamise, chaparral pea, and silk-tassel bush. The rare Mount Tamalpais thistle and Tamalpais jewel flower are found only on this mountain. Northern alligator lizards, western fence lizards, and Pacific gopher snakes are common here. Spotted owls nest on the mountain, and wrentits are abundant. Mountain lions and feral pigs roam the area, but are seldom seen.

Mount Tamalpais State Park includes mainly the south and west sides of the mountain, extending to the sea between Muir Beach and Stinson Beach. Some 250 miles of trails link the beaches with the top of the mountain and the town of Mill Valley on the inland side. Hiking and day-use recreation are also permitted on Mount Tamalpais on watershed lands surrounding a series of reservoirs operated by the Marin Municipal Water District. The Steep Ravine and Cataract trails follow streams with waterfalls. Trail maps are available at local bookstores or at the Water District office at 220 Nellen Ave., Corte Madera 94925.

Steam trains of the eight-mile-long Mount Tamalpais and Muir Woods Railway climbed an incredibly crooked line from Mill Valley to East Peak between 1896 and 1930. The outdoor Mountain Theater in a natural bowl overlooking San Francisco Bay is the scene of the Mountain Play in May of each year. On Panoramic Highway leading to the top of the mountain is the restored Mountain Home Inn, which offers a restaurant and bed-and-breakfast accommodations. Information on camping and other activities within Mount Tamalpais State Park is available at Pan Toll Headquarters on Panoramic Highway; call: (415) 388-2070.

The Golden Gate National Recreation Area, administered by the National Park Service, includes the following areas: Muir Beach, Muir Woods National Monument, Tennessee Cove, and the Coastal Trail.

Muir Beach: *Hwy. 1 at Muir Woods Rd.*

Redwood Creek and its tributaries drain the southern slopes of Mount Tamalpais and flow through Franks Valley to the ocean adjacent to the community of Muir Beach. The creek is a spawning stream for steelhead and silver salmon and also supports crayfish. Big-leaf maples, which turn golden in the fall, grow along the stream, as do red alders.

Where Franks Valley and Green Gulch meet at the shoreline is a lagoon formed by Redwood Creek, and a large sandy beach with rocky areas and tidepools at both ends. Between mid-October and mid-March Monarch butterflies overwinter in a grove of Monterey pines on land owned by Audubon Canyon Ranch near the entrance to the GGNRA beach parking area.

One and a half miles north of Muir Beach, seaward of Highway 1, is the Muir Beach Overlook. Once a World War II gun emplacement and now a county park, the overlook affords views of the steep serpentine cliffs to the north and south. Offshore due south is the Potato Patch Shoal, where the sea at low tide is little more than 20 feet deep, causing turbulence and occasional freak waves that threaten boaters.

coast redwood (*Sequoia sempervirens*)
tree: 200 to 325 feet high
cone: ½ to 1⅛ inches long
needles: ⅜ to ¾ inches long

Mount Tamalpais from Sausalito, ca. 1890

Muir Woods National Monument: *Muir Woods Rd., 3 mi. N. of Hwy. 1.*

The virgin redwood forest in the canyon of Redwood Creek was donated to the federal government in 1907 by Congressman William Kent, who requested that it be named for naturalist John Muir. Muir Woods is the only remaining old-growth redwood forest close to San Francisco; other nearby groves were cut for lumber in the 19th century. Some bay laurel and tanbark oak trees are found here, but fewer than if the redwood overstory had been subject to past timber cutting, thus allowing more sunlight to reach seedlings on the forest floor. Low-growing plants in the understory include western azalea, huckleberry, redwood sorrel, and redwood violet. Horsetails and lady ferns grow in moist areas, and sturdy sword ferns thrive on drier slopes. California hazelnuts produce nuts favored by western gray squirrels and Sonoma chipmunks. In the winter, colorful displays of fungi sprout from the forest floor.

Common reptiles include the rubber boa, western yellow-bellied racer, and garter snake. Pacific giant salamanders are occasionally seen in dark, moist places. In the summer, masses of convergent ladybug beetles sometimes cluster on shrubs or fallen logs. Pileated woodpeckers have been sighted in the redwood forest. A quarter-mile-long wheelchair-accessible nature trail leads past plant species of interest, and other trails connect to those in Mount Tamalpais State Park. Muir Woods National Monument offers a visitor center, gift shop, and snack bar. For information, call: (415) 388-2595.

Tennessee Cove: *Off Hwy. 1, end of Tennessee Valley Rd.*

Tennessee Valley Rd. ends two miles short of the cove; a well-worn trail leads through the valley to the shore. The coastal hills are covered with grassland and coastal scrub. Horses may be rented at the trailhead at the privately owned Miwok Livery; for information, call: (415) 383-8048. At Tennessee Cove, a small natural lagoon is located just inland of a coarse sand beach that is flanked by greenstone outcroppings to the north and south. Pelagic cormorants nest along the steep cliffs.

The cove is named for the side-wheel steamship *Tennessee*, which carried fortune hunters from Panama to gold rush-era San Francisco, making a round trip in 15 days. On March 6, 1853 the fully loaded *Tennessee* overshot the Golden Gate in heavy fog and ran aground on this beach. There was no loss of life or cargo, although the ship broke up in the surf. The steam engine still lies buried deep beneath the sand.

Coastal Trail: *East Fort Baker to the Point Reyes Peninsula.*

A series of trails traverse the Marin Headlands. One of these, the Coastal Trail, begins at East Fort Baker near Sausalito on the San Francisco Bay side of the headlands and generally follows the shore northwest, linking Rodeo Beach, Tennessee Valley, Muir Beach, Mount Tamalpais State Park, and the Point Reyes Peninsula. Other trails criss-cross the headlands, connecting units of the Golden Gate National Recreation Area, Muir Woods National Monument, and Mount Tamalpais State Park. Maps and information are available at the Rodeo Beach ranger station; call: (415) 331-1540.

Muir Beach

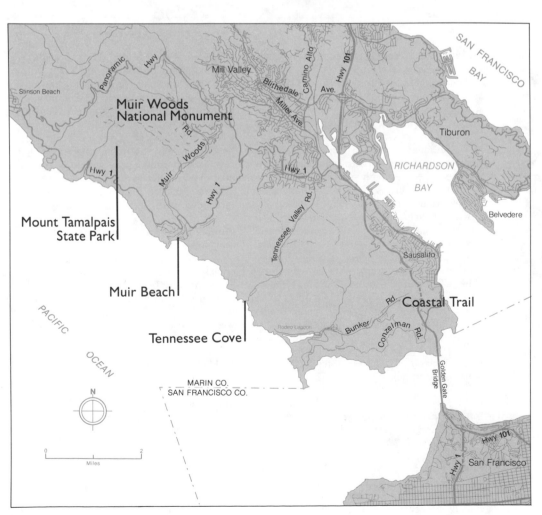

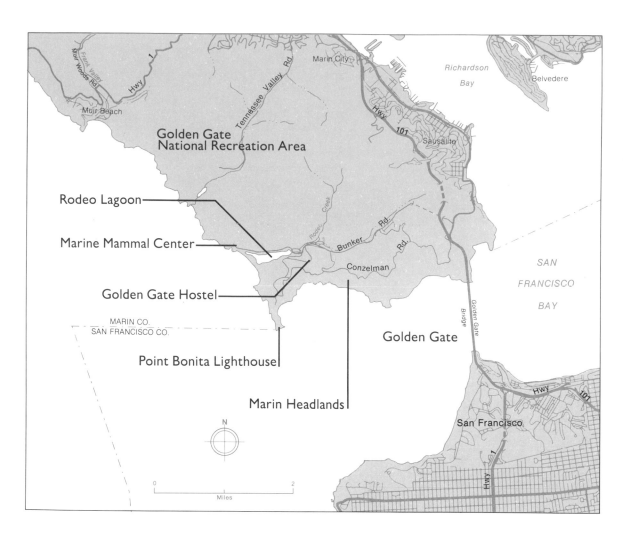

Point Bonita Lighthouse

Golden Gate National Recreation Area:
Marin Headlands, W. of Hwy. 101.

The recreation area, known as GGNRA, stretches from Tomales Bay in Marin County south through San Francisco to Sweeney Ridge in San Mateo County, encompassing public lands and private cattle ranches operated under lease. Although located in three highly urban counties, the recreation area holds surprisingly wild and open hills, canyons, and beaches. In the Marin Headlands, GGNRA includes three military reservations: Forts Baker, Barry, and Cronkhite. Picnic sites are located in Rodeo Valley and at Battery Wallace, an abandoned artillery emplacement overlooking the Golden Gate. There are hike-in camps at several locations near the headlands, and group camps are available at Kirby Cove (summer only) and Battery Alexander. Call: (415) 331-1540 for information and reservations. The YMCA Point Bonita Center offers overnight facilities for conferences and groups; call: (415) 331-9622. The Headlands Institute located on the north side of Rodeo Lagoon provides environmental education programs; call: (415) 332-5771.

The following are included within the Golden Gate National Recreation Area: Rodeo Beach, Marine Mammal Center, Golden Gate Hostel, Point Bonita Lighthouse, and the Marin Headlands.

Rodeo Lagoon: *End of Bunker Rd. off Hwy. 101.*
This brackish lagoon is separated from the sea by a pebble barrier beach that is only occasionally breached. Offshore near the southern end of the beach is Bird Rock, a resting and breeding place for pelagic cormorants. Uncommon tufted ducks and harlequin ducks winter on the lagoon, and endangered California brown pelicans may be sighted during the summer. An uncommon fish known as the tidewater goby is found in the lagoon. On the upstream edges of the lagoon are freshwater marshy areas in which cattails and tules grow; a willow and alder swamp borders the stream that feeds the lagoon. The National Park Service offers nature walks in the Rodeo Valley area; call: (415) 331-1540.

Marine Mammal Center: *End of Bunker Rd., near Rodeo Lagoon.*
This non-profit organization rescues injured or sick marine mammals that become stranded along the coast between Oregon and Monterey. After treatment, animals are returned to their natural habitats. The Marine Mammal Center welcomes visitors, and education programs are offered. Call: (415) 331-7325.

Golden Gate Hostel: *On Bunker Rd. in Rodeo Valley.*
A 60-bed hostel is located in Rodeo Valley in a historic former military officers' headquarters. Call (415) 331-2777 or write Building 941, Fort Barry, Sausalito, CA 94965.

Point Bonita Lighthouse: *S.W. tip of Marin Headlands, end of Conzelman Rd.*
Until it was automated in 1980, the 1877 lighthouse was the last of the manually operated lighthouses in California. It is located on a

treacherous point reached only via a tunnel hewn through solid rock and a suspension bridge over crashing surf. The original lighthouse at Point Bonita was built in 1855 and proved to be an inhospitable place: seven different tenders were employed in the first nine months of operation. In 1856 an iron cannon was installed as a fog signal, the first on the Pacific Coast. The keeper of the fog signal found his task somewhat onerous, as he was required to fire the cannon every 30 minutes during continuous fogs, which last sometimes for days on end. The cannon was abandoned after a couple of years, and a foghorn was built in 1902. Call (415) 331-1540 for information on visiting hours at the lighthouse.

Marin Headlands: *Coastline west of the Golden Gate Bridge.*

The coastline from Tennessee Cove to the Golden Gate Bridge consists of steep sea cliffs with beaches located between rocky outcroppings. The ridges and outcroppings are mostly composed of rocks of the Franciscan Formation, including chert, greenstone, and a type of sandstone known as graywacke, which were formed perhaps 100 million years ago during the late Cretaceous Period. These rocks can be observed in many exposed locations in the headlands.

Chert is a thin-bedded sedimentary rock found in uncharacteristically thick ribbons in the headlands, usually layered and folded in angular patterns. Red chert is exposed in road cuts along Conzelman Rd., which winds along the top of the headlands west of the Golden Gate Bridge. The basalt found in the headlands, called greenstone, is of volcanic origin, often with a greenish cast due to the presence of the minerals chlorite and pumpellyite. Bird Island, the large rock lying just offshore the south end of Rodeo Beach, is a greenstone formation. Cavities in the greenstone are filled with pillow lavas or with various minerals, such as red jasper,

visible on the cliffs around the beach at Kirby Cove, or orange chalcedony, which weathers and contributes pebbles, known as carnelians, to Rodeo Beach. Graywacke is a type of sandstone made up of various-sized angular grains, probably formed originally in a deepwater environment. The rocky cliffs at the north end of Rodeo Beach are composed of graywacke, ranging in color from gray at the bottom to a weathered soft brown at the top.

The various components of the Franciscan Formation in the Marin Headlands have been folded and faulted in complex ways. Numerous landslides caused by steep slopes, pounding of ocean waves, and earthquakes have left exposed cliffs of chert, greenstone, and sandstone and have dumped piles of these rocks onto the beaches, where weathered particles form a large proportion of the beach sands and pebbles.

Chert deposits along Conzelman Road

Golden Gate: *Between Marin and San Francisco headlands.*

Early explorers of the Northern California coast, including Cermeño in 1595 and Vizcaíno in 1602-1603, apparently steered west of the rocky Farallon Islands and missed sighting the entrance to San Francisco Bay. The bay was not discovered by Europeans until 1769 when it was seen by a scouting party led by Sergeant José Francisco de Ortega of the Portolá overland expedition. Captain John C. Frémont, in an 1848 report to Congress on his explorations with the U.S. Topographical Engineers through Mexican California, called the opening of San Francisco Bay "Chrysopylae," or "golden gate." Within the year, gold-seekers bound for the Sierra Nevada foothills began to pour into the bay, and they quickly adopted Frémont's uncannily appropriate label.

San Francisco Bay is the drowned mouth and floodplain of the Sacramento-San Joaquin rivers. The Golden Gate is the river outlet eroded by the Sacramento River during interglacial periods of the Pleistocene Epoch, around three million years ago. Although San Francisco Bay is relatively muddy and shallow, the floor of the Golden Gate is swept of sand and silt by strong tidal action; the depth of the sea at the gate is 341 feet. The San Francisco Headlands on the south side of the Golden Gate are underlain by the Franciscan Formation of chert, sandstone, and basalt, much like the Marin Headlands, but the radically different angles of the deposits on the two shores indicate that a major rift zone lies beneath the floor of the gate.

Rodeo Lagoon

157

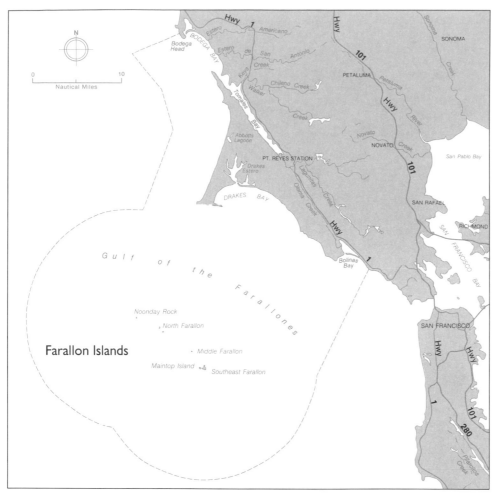

Farallon Islands

Common murres and Brandt's cormorants on the north side of Southeast Farallon

Farallon Islands: *27 nautical mi. W. of Point Bonita, Marin County.*

On a clear day, the craggy peak of Southeast Farallon Island, one of the seven Farallon Islands, is visible due west from almost any high vantage point in the San Francisco Bay area. The islands are part of the 100-acre Farallon Islands National Wildlife Refuge, established in 1972 and managed by the U.S. Fish and Wildlife Service and the Point Reyes Bird Observatory. In 1982, the Gulf of the Farallones National Marine Sanctuary was established to protect the waters adjacent to the coast between Bodega Head in Sonoma County, Rocky Point in Marin County, and the Farallon Islands, extending offshore for 6 nautical miles and including the waters within 12 nautical miles of the Farallones. Also included within the sanctuary are Bodega Bay, Tomales Bay, Drakes Bay, Bolinas Bay, Bolinas Lagoon, Estero Americano, and Estero de San Antonio on the mainland.

The Farallones rise from the edge of the continental shelf, which is wider here than at any other place along the California coast. The jagged, rocky outcroppings are the wave-eroded crests of a granite fault-block mountain, uplifted during the mid-Ice Age. Southeast Farallon, with an area of 65 acres, is the largest of the seven islands, and its 350-foot peak is the highest. The island's soil—a mix of decomposed granite and guano—severely limits the number and diversity of plants able to grow here. Southeast Farallon's most ubiquitous plant is the endemic Farallon weed, a member of the sunflower family, which grows on rocky cliffs and terraces in thick mats up to a foot and a half tall.

The Farallon Islands are the most important seabird nesting site on the California coast, with more than 300,000 individuals of 12 species arriving annually to breed on the islands. Eighty per cent of the state's nesting Cassin's auklets are found here, as are the world's largest nesting populations of ashy storm petrels, Brandt's cormorants, and western gulls. Over 350 species of land birds, shorebirds, and seabirds use the islands as a stopover during migration. The Farallones are the northernmost breeding site of northern elephant seals, which appeared here in 1972 for the first time since their near-extinction by commercial seal hunters in the mid-19th century. Over 600 seal pups have been born on the islands since recolonization by the elephant seals in 1984. Before they were exterminated from the Farallones by sealers in the 19th century, northern fur seals also bred here; they have recently been sighted near Southeast Farallon Island, but currently breed only on San Miguel Island in the Channel Islands. Harbor seals, Steller sea lions, and California sea lions also breed on the Farallones.

The waters that surround the Farallon Islands support a highly productive and biologically diverse marine ecosystem. A phenomenon called upwelling contributes to the abundance of marine life in these waters. Beginning in spring, northwesterly winds push the warmer surface water offshore, causing cold water from below the ocean surface to upwell. This brings to the surface nutrients from the ocean floor that nourish microscopic marine plants called phytoplankton—the primary link in the marine food chain. Zooplankton such as krill—small, shrimplike crustaceans that graze on the marine plants—appear in abundance in summer, and are an important food for breeding birds such as Cassin's auklets that nest on the Farallones. Large schools of fish also feed on the zooplankton, and the fish are eaten by seals and sea lions, as well as by seabirds; whales linger here to feed during their annual northward migration. In 1983, a warming current called El Niño disrupted the normal pattern of upwelling, and as a consequence only half the breeding seabirds on the islands produced eggs, presumably because of decreased marine food supplies.

It is possible that the first European to visit Southeast Farallon Island was the Spanish explorer Ferrelo in 1543; however, Francis Drake, who landed on rocky Southeast Farallon in 1579, was the first to record the "plentifull and great store of Seales and birds" on the island, which he named the "Ilands of Saint James." In 1775 Juan Francisco Bodega y Quadra gave the islands their present name, calling them "Los Farallones de los Frayles" (headlands of the friars) after the founders of Mission Dolores. In the 1820s, Russian and Aleut sealers continued the decimation of the islands' seal and otter populations that had begun with the West Coast expeditions of Boston-based sealers in the early 1800s. The Americans reportedly collected over 150,000 seal skins in a three-year period, selling the valuable pelts in the Canton fur market.

In 1850, the demand for fresh eggs in gold rush San Francisco resulted in the near-extinction of the Farallon Islands' bird populations. Until the 1880s, when chicken farming was introduced in Petaluma, Sonoma County, common murre eggs from Southeast Farallon Island were a staple in the diets of thousands of San Franciscans. An estimated 14 million murre eggs were taken by commercial egg companies in the last half of the 19th century. In response to this depredation, the director of the California Academy of Sciences initiated an effort to protect the birds' nesting site, and the order to make the island a bird reservation was signed by President Taft in 1909. By 1911, public concern over the islands' wildlife resulted in creation of the Farallon Reserve, the first of several statutory protections; at that time the sea otter, fur seal, and elephant seal were extinct from the island, and the murre population, along with populations of other seabirds such as Cassin's auklets and tufted puffins, was in steep decline.

Today, biologists from the Point Reyes Bird Observatory inhabit Southeast Farallon Island year-round to monitor bird and marine mammal populations, which still face serious threats not only from natural occurrences such as the cyclic El Niño ocean current, but also from human activities. In 1977, rusting barrels of atomic waste were discovered at a dumping site on the ocean floor near the islands, and an oil tanker explosion in 1984 spilled over 100,000 gallons of oil into the waters surrounding the Farallones; more recently, gill nets used by commercial fishermen have entrapped thousands of diving seabirds. Overfishing and the diversion of fresh water from the San Francisco Bay estuary also affect the islands' marine ecosystem.

The Farallon Light, perched atop Southeast Farallon Island, is one of the principal maritime beacons on the California coast, directing mariners to the often fog-shrouded entrance to San Francisco Bay. The first permanent lighthouse, completed in 1854, had a unique wave-powered foghorn; waves entering a cove forced air through a blowhole near the base of the lighthouse site, causing a steam-locomotive whistle to shriek loudly. The present foghorn is a modern diaphone whose low-pitched moan can be heard for miles.

For information on whale-watching trips and boat trips in the marine sanctuary, call the Oceanic Society at (415) 441-1106, or the Whale Center at (415) 654-6621. For information on the marine sanctuary, call: (415) 556-3509; for the Farallon Islands, call the Point Reyes Bird Observatory: (415) 868-1221.

Southeast Farallon, off East Landing

Southeast Farallon, view southeast to Saddle Rock

San Francisco County
Selected Species of Interest

 Plants: Presidio clarkia (*Clarkia franciscana*), endangered endemic; grows on serpentine soils of the Presidio. **Yerba buena** (*Satureja douglasii*), ubiquitous native coastal mint; the "good herb" of Spanish settlers.

 Trees: Coast live oak (*Quercus agrifolia*); original oaks preserved in N.E. corner of Golden Gate Park. **Eucalyptus** or **blue gum** (*Eucalyptus globulus*), native to Australia, introduced in California in the late 1800s.

 Insects: San Francisco tree lupine moth (*Grapholitha edwardsiana*), endangered; tree lupine is host for larvae. **Mission blue butterfly** (*Icaricia icarioides missionensis*), endangered; inhabits Twin Peaks.

 Invertebrates: Franciscan bay shrimp (*Crangon franciscorum*), dried and exported by Chinese fishermen, 1850-1950; now used only for bait. **Bay mussel** (*Mytilus edulis*), small, native mussel found in S.F. Bay; toxic from bay pollutants.

 Amphibians and Reptiles: Pacific treefrog (*Hyla regilla*), inhabits the Presidio, Golden Gate Park, and Lake Merced. **Western aquatic garter snake** (*Thamnophis couchii*), has a wide, greenish-yellow dorsal stripe; found near water.

 Fish: Striped bass (*Morone saxatilis*), Eastern U.S. native, introduced to San Francisco Bay in 1879; populations declining due to Delta water projects and pollution. **Bat ray** (*Myliobatis californica*), digs in mudflats for mollusks.

 Birds: Sanderling (*Calidris alba*), small, gray shorebird that feeds in flocks on sandy beaches, just out of reach of the surf. **Canvasback** (*Aythya valisineria*), migratory diving duck that winters in the bay; feeds in large flocks.

 Land Mammals: Salt marsh harvest mouse (*Reithrodontomys raviventris* ssp.); Suisun Marsh and San Francisco Bay subspecies are endangered. **Black-tailed deer** (*Odocoileus hemionus columbianus*), lives on Angel Island.

 Marine Mammals: California sea lion (*Zalophus californianus*), hauls out on Seal Rocks; the Spanish called them *lobos marinos*, or sea wolves. **Humpback whale** (*Megaptera novaeangliae*), sometimes strays into the bay.

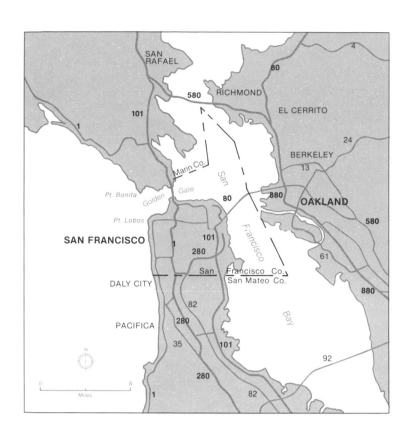

San Francisco Bay:

San Francisco Bay is not within the jurisdiction of the California Coastal Commission. The Bay Conservation and Development Commission (BCDC) regulates bay tidal wetlands (non-tidal wetlands are regulated by the U.S. Army Corps of Engineers). For information, call BCDC: (415) 557-3686.

For Information on San Francisco Bay:

The Oceanic Society, Fort Mason, San Francisco: (415) 441-5970.

Save San Francisco Bay Association, Berkeley: (415) 849-3044.

North Bay: For San Pablo Bay National Wildlife Refuge: (707) 792-0222. Suisun Bay and Marsh, Petaluma River and Marsh, and Napa River and Marsh: (707) 944-2011. Richardson Bay Wildlife Sanctuary: (415) 388-2524. Bay Model: (415) 332-3870. China Camp State Park: (415) 456-0766.

East Bay: For Martinez Regional Shoreline, George Miller Regional Shoreline, Alameda's Crown Beach, San Leandro Bay Shoreline Preserve, Hayward Regional Shoreline, Coyote Hills Regional Park, and Berkeley waterfront, call the East Bay Regional Park District: (415) 531-9300.

South Bay: For San Francisco Bay National Wildlife Refuge and Environmental Education Center: (415) 792-3178 or 792-0222. Palo Alto Baylands and Lucy Evans Interpretive Center: (415) 329-2506. Coyote Point Museum: (415) 342-7755.

San Francisco County

SAN FRANCISCO lies at the northern tip of a 50-mile-long peninsula separating the Pacific Ocean from the waters of San Francisco Bay. The city's windswept western shoreline turns abruptly eastward at Land's End, forming the entrance to the bay, where the Golden Gate Bridge straddles the narrow channel between San Francisco and Marin County. From the promontory of Fort Point to the western terminus of the San Francisco-Oakland Bay Bridge, the city spreads southward from the waterfront in a pastel jumble of low-lying buildings; rising abruptly from the city's northeast corner are the towering glass and steel monoliths of the Financial District.

San Francisco is the urban core of a nine-county metropolitan area clustered along the hundred-mile shoreline of San Francisco Bay. Beginning about 4,000 years ago with the encampments of California Indians, the bay has been a focus of settlement. Exploitation of the bay's abundant marine life supported some of San Francisco's earliest industries. In the mid-1800s, the bay was the site of several Chinese shrimp camps, where the catch was dried and prepared for export. Commercial fishing in the bay was well established by the time the city built the first Fisherman's Wharf in 1900, in part due to the introduction of the trawling net and lateen-rigged fishing boats by Genoese and Sicilian immigrants. The bay is perhaps the state's largest single natural resource; its 460-square-mile surface provides life-sustaining habitat for many species of wildlife, in particular for millions of waterfowl on their annual migrations along the Pacific Flyway.

San Francisco Bay contributes to the area's unique weather patterns, primarily due to the sea-level breach in the coastal mountain barrier formed by the Golden Gate. Oceanic air masses enter through this gap to meet continental air masses over the bay, producing a cool summer breeze. Westerly winds condense over the ocean, creating thick summer fogs in the bay that disperse in winter as the Pacific High pressure system moves south.

English sea captain Sir Francis Drake on his voyage of 1579 may have been the first European to enter San Francisco Bay, but Juan Manuel de Ayala, who sailed into the bay 200 years after Drake, was the first to map it and name its major features. A safe harbor for early Spanish and Mexican inhabitants, San Francisco Bay proved to be a favorable location for English expatriate William A. Richardson, who established a trading post at Yerba Buena Cove in 1835. Richardson's enterprise was a magnet for the English, Russian, and American ship captains who came to exchange manufactured goods for California hides and tallow. In July of 1846, the American flag was raised at Yerba Buena, and six months later the outpost was renamed San Francisco—one year prior to the discovery in 1848 of a gold nugget at John Sutter's sawmill on the American River in the Sierra Nevada. Almost overnight the tiny settlement of San Francisco was transformed into an international port of call as gold seekers arrived by the thousands, decamping on the shores of Yerba Buena Cove to make the up-river journey to Sacramento—a day's horseback ride away from the gold fields.

From 1848 to 1849, San Francisco's official population swelled from 600 to 25,000. With the arrival of more than 40,000 gold seekers, an "instant city" of tents, shacks, and shanties sprang up at the foot of Telegraph Hill. By 1860, the city's 56,000 residents were distributed among already distinct neighborhoods, from the stylish settlement of South Park and adjacent Rincon Hill, to Italian North Beach, and nearby Chinatown, crowded with Asian immigrants whose exclusion from the gold mines forced them to seek their fortune by other means. The invention of the cable car by Andrew Hallidie in 1873 enabled the new "nabobs" such as Leland Stanford, Mark Hopkins, Collis Huntington, and James Flood to erect ostentatious mansions on Nob Hill, most of which were destroyed by the fire that followed the 1906 earthquake. Many of San Francisco's lesser Victorian residences survived both earthquake and fire, and now add to the eclectic appearance of several of the city's outlying neighborhoods.

San Francisco was a major military, manufacturing, and shipping center during World War II. The influx of wartime factory workers to the city and the surrounding bay communities contributed to a population boom in the post-war years; since the 1960s, construction of the skyscraping monoliths in San Francisco's downtown has continued apace. Although the city's heavy manufacturing, shipbuilding, and port activities have dwindled to a very small percentage of its total economy, the city retains some of the aura of the last century in its piers and historic Fishermen's Wharf area, where 19th-century industrial buildings such as the Ghirardelli Chocolate Factory and The Cannery have been converted and restored to serve the tourist trade.

Golden Gate Bridge

San Francisco Bay and Estuary: *From the Sacramento and San Joaquin River Delta to the Pacific Ocean.*

Through a narrow gap in the Coast Ranges, the waters of the Pacific Ocean flow into San Francisco Bay, which is the terminus of a vast river network draining almost half the land area of California. Fourteen tributaries of the Sacramento and San Joaquin rivers contribute to the inflow that reaches San Francisco Bay via the Sacramento-San Joaquin Delta, where fresh water mixes with salt water. The bay estuary's aquatic and wetland habitats range from the brackish water of the lower Delta and Suisun Bay to the dilute salt water of San Pablo Bay, San Francisco Bay's northern "wing," and the shallow, highly saline waters of the South Bay.

Just 15,000 years ago San Francisco Bay was dry land—a series of gorges and valleys carved by the rivers that rushed through Carquinez and Raccoon straits and into the 350-foot-deep gorge of the Golden Gate before emptying into the sea at a point near the Farallon Islands. When melting glaciers raised worldwide sea level 10,000 years ago, the river valleys of what are now San Francisco, San Pablo, and Suisun bays flooded, and over thousands of years sediments gradually accumulated along the estuary margins, forming marshes and mudflats.

Evidence of human settlement around San Francisco Bay dates back at least 4,000 years. When the first Spanish explorers arrived in the mid-1700s, they saw hundreds of Indian villages along the bay margins. The abundance of wildlife that supported the native people was noted with amazement by the gold-seeking Americans and Europeans arriving nearly a hundred years later—flocks of waterfowl darkened the sky, and tidal channels were so thick with ducks that a single gunshot brought down several at once. Whales were said to be so plentiful that one spouted every half minute, and on the shore herds of pronghorns, deer, and elk grazed, and grizzly bears fished for salmon or feasted on whale carrion. By 1900, most of the wildlife and the Indians were gone. Of the more than 400 shell mounds that marked the village sites of generations of Coast Miwok and Ohlone Indians, only two remain—on Brooks Island, and in Coyote Hills Regional Park.

As the crucial water link between coastal and interior California in the late 1800s, San Francisco Bay bustled with the commerce of a maritime metropolis. Side-wheel paddle steamers plied bay and Delta waters, carrying passengers and cargo the 75 miles from San Francisco to Sacramento. In the late 1800s, wheat grown in the San Joaquin Valley was transported down the Delta to San Francisco Bay ports, where hundreds of two-masted schooners were loaded with grain bound for Europe and Asia; Port Costa, in the Carquinez Strait, was America's foremost grain depot. Flat-bottomed scow schooners laden with produce from Santa Clara Valley farmlands shuttled between Alviso and the booming port of San Francisco. Between 1882 and 1908, the world's whaling center was in San Francisco Bay; ships headed out of the bay into Arctic waters in search of valuable bowhead whales. Point Richmond, the last whaling station in the bay, closed in 1971.

Since the first landfill was dumped into Yerba Buena Cove in 1848 by landowners eager to profit from the skyrocketing value of waterfront lots, schemes to fill and develop San Francisco Bay and its wetlands have abounded. One proposal in the 1940s would have dammed San Pablo Bay and the South Bay, created a land bridge between Oakland and San Francisco to accomodate four six- to eight-lane freeways, and would have "reclaimed" 36 square miles of wetland—reducing the size of San Francisco Bay by 85 per cent. Congress funded a study of the plan, including construction of a hydraulic model of the bay; the Bay Model, located in a Sausalito warehouse, is still used for research and is open to the public.

Since 1850 half of San Francisco Bay's open water and tidal marshes have been filled or cut off from tidal action by dikes and levees, eliminating 95 per cent of the original wetland habitats. Concern over rampant filling of the bay in the 1960s led to creation of the Bay Conservation and Development Commission (BCDC) in 1965, in order to regulate bay filling and shoreline development. However, 16,000 acres of diked wetlands along the perimeters of the bay and estuary lie outside the Commission's jurisdiction, and this valuable wildlife habitat and open space is in danger of disappearing beneath a new wave of development.

Since the 1850s, dams and water projects for flood control, irrigation, and public water sup-

View north, entrance to San Francisco Bay

ply have reduced by half the historic freshwater inflow to San Francisco Bay. Circulation of water in the bay and estuary, which flushes wastes and pollutants from the bay system, depends upon the mixing of fresh water from the Delta with salt water from the bay. The denser salt water, drawn upstream by gravity along the bottom of the estuary channel, returns to the bay diluted by the freshwater inflow, and is then distributed throughout the bay by the action of tides, winds, and currents. Because of this mixing, water in the bay is about 25 per cent less salty than ocean water. In the South Bay, which has no large freshwater inflow and is cut off from the main circulation route of the bay's currents, it may take five months for tidal currents and winds to completely flush the shallow, salty waters. Water circulation is important for the transport of nutrients to the bay's aquatic habitats, for maintenance of dissolved oxygen levels in bay waters, and for dispersion of aquatic organisms, including fish eggs and larvae, that breed in the bay.

San Francisco Bay and estuary contains 90 per cent of California's remaining coastal wetlands. The bay is an important stop on the Pacific Flyway for millions of migrating waterfowl. Almost the entire California population of migrating northern shovelers winters in the bay, as do two-thirds of the state's canvasbacks and greater and lesser scaups. Even larger numbers of shorebirds inhabit bay marshes, particularly in the South Bay where snowy plovers, black rails, and endangered California clapper rails nest, and nesting and breeding American avocets and black-necked stilts are common. Endangered California least terns breed on the South Bay's salt flats, and two subspecies of the endangered salt marsh harvest mouse inhabit the bay's salt and brackish water marshes.

Northern anchovy, Pacific herring, flatfish, and bay shrimp are common in the bay estuary, and soft-shelled clams and Japanese littleneck clams are abundant in East Bay mudflats. However, the bay's historic salmon and steelhead trout fisheries have virtually disappeared due to loss of their ancestral spawning grounds to dams and water projects; the once plentiful striped bass is also becoming scarce, and its flesh now contains high levels of mercury. The shrimp, mussels, and Dungeness crab that once supported lucrative fisheries are gone or too contaminated by industrial pollutants to be edible.

Major preserves and shoreline parks of San Francisco Bay include Suisun Bay Marsh, with many duck hunting preserves; San Pablo Bay National Wildlife Refuge and Tubbs Island, accessible by boat; and Point Pinole Regional Shoreline. China Camp State Park, along the southwest shore of San Pablo Bay, preserves a historic Chinese shrimp fishing village; Coyote Hills Regional Park and San Francisco Bay National Wildlife Refuge protect important wetland acreage in the South Bay for wintering waterfowl. Bay ecology displays and educational programs are offered at the Audubon Wildlife Sanctuary in Richardson Bay, San Mateo County's Coyote Point Park and Museum, the Palo Alto Baylands Interpretive Center, and the Environmental Education Center in Alviso. Many other small parks, piers, and marinas also provide access to the bay or its shores.

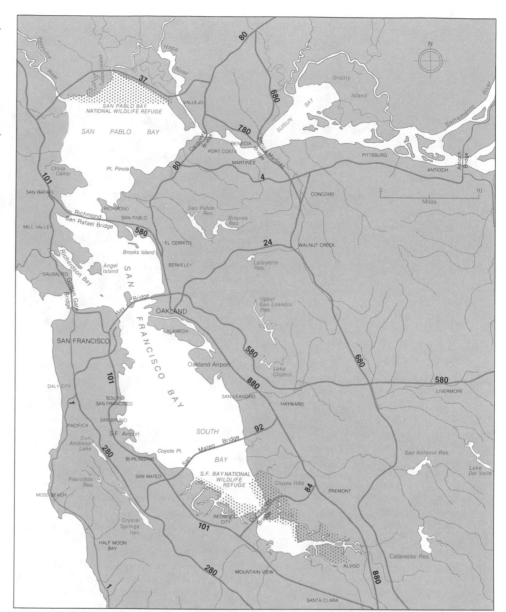

Great egret, San Francisco Bay

Historic ships at the Hyde Street Pier

City of San Francisco: *S.E. of the Golden Gate.*

Cosmopolitan San Francisco, situated at the tip of a peninsula between the Pacific Ocean and San Francisco Bay, was once a windswept stretch of sand dunes and rocky hills. In 1776, seven years after members of Portolá's expedition sighted San Francisco Bay from the hills of present-day Pacifica, Captain Juan de Anza established a colony on the north end of the peninsula, but for the next 50 years the colonial outpost consisted of little more than a mission and a presidio. In 1835 William A. Richardson, an Englishman turned hide and tallow merchant, was permitted by the Mexican government to set up a trading post on the shores of Yerba Buena Cove at the foot of present-day Telegraph Hill. This tiny port formed the nucleus of the modern city's business district.

Mission San Francisco de Asis: *Dolores and 16th streets, San Francisco.*

Although officially named for St. Francis of Assisi, founder of the Franciscan order, the mission takes its more familiar name of Mission Dolores from the lake and stream that once bordered it. In 1776 Anza named the lake "Nuestra Señora de los Dolores," and designated the adjacent land for the establishment of the sixth Alta California mission. The mission, built in Mexican Baroque Ecclesiastical style, combines Moorish and Hispanic architectural styles. Call: (415) 621-8203.

yerba buena (*Satureja douglasii*)
8 to 24 inches high

Bay Waterfront: *Hunter's Point to Aquatic Park.*

In the mid-1800s the cove known as Mission Bay extended from Mission Rock south to Hunter's Point and inland to present-day Mission Street, then a plank road crossing the marsh between the cove and Mission Dolores. Hunter's Point shipyard, now a marine machine shop, was the site of World War II steel works. India Basin is named for the ships of the India trade that docked here in the late 1800s. In Central Basin, near the floating dry docks of Todd Shipyards, is the site of the Union Iron Works, where iron-hulled men-of-war and steel steamships were built from 1884 to 1906. China Basin was the anchorage for the "China Clipper" sailing ships of the 1860s; Mission Rock, which now forms the base of Pier 50, once marked the center of Mission Bay harbor. In 1934, one of the biggest labor disputes in U.S. history began at Pier 30-32 where 800 striking longshoremen battled with National Guard troops. In the 1950s and 1960s this pier complex was one of the busiest on the West Coast, and remains the center of the Port of San Francisco's dwindling shipping trade.

North of the Bay Bridge, the Ferry Building's landmark clock tower, modeled after Giralda Tower in Seville, Spain, once presided over one of the world's busiest ferry terminals. The building, completed in 1898, served 40 million ferry passengers a year in its heyday. The opening of the Bay Bridge in 1936 was the beginning of a rapid decline of the ferry system, and by 1958 all commuter service had ceased. San Francisco's northern waterfront rests on landfill composed of rubble and the hulks of abandoned ships left in Yerba Buena Cove as passengers and crew alike rushed to the gold fields. Before landfill extended the waterfront, a sandy beach known as North Beach stretched northwest from Telegraph Hill, then a promontory marking the western end of Yerba Buena Cove. Along the Embarcadero, the arched entrance to Pier 35 berthed the Matson Navigation Company's famed *Lurline* that sailed between San Francisco and Honolulu; passenger cruise ships still dock at the pier. Fisherman's Wharf, built in 1900, is home to a small commercial fishing fleet.

Aquatic Park: *Northern end of Van Ness Avenue, San Francisco.*

Aquatic Park has benches, lawns, a sandy beach on the bay, and showers and lockers for swimmers. The Golden Gate Promenade, a 3.5-mile scenic walk, begins here and follows the shoreline to Fort Point. The 1,850-foot Municipal Pier curves out into the bay and is a favorite place to fish for smelt, flounder, and sculpin. In the mid-19th century, this cove was a popular swimming spot with makeshift bathhouses along the waterfront. A public bathhouse, built here in the 1930s using WPA funds, now houses the National Maritime Museum.

National Maritime Museum: *Northern end of Polk St., San Francisco.*

The museum, which contains an extensive collection of model ships, photographs, and the remnants of old San Francisco Bay vessels, includes the Hyde Street Pier and the sailing ship *Balclutha*. Since 1951 the museum exhibitions have been housed in the nautical-design public bathhouse; the 37 mural panels, sculptures, and terrazzo marble floors that adorn the interior were created for the bathhouse complex. The museum library, in Building D at Fort Mason, contains historic newspaper articles, books, ships' logs, charts, maps, and over 100,000 photographs; call: (415) 556-8177. The historic ships *Eureka* and *C.A. Thayer* are berthed at the Hyde Street Pier. From 1890 to 1957, the paddlewheel ferryboat *Eureka* shuttled between San Francisco and Marin County; the sail schooner *C.A. Thayer*, built in 1895, carried North Coast redwood lumber to the South Sea Islands and Mexico until 1950. Call: (415) 556-6435. The *Balclutha*, at Pier 43, was built in Glasgow, Scotland in 1886. The square-rigged sailing ship carried wine, whiskey, wool, rice, and coal "around the Horn" until the early 1900s, then sailed as the *Star of Alaska* with the Pacific Coast salmon fleet. For tours, call: (415) 982-1886.

Alcatraz Island: *Access via ferry from Pier 41, San Francisco.*

The site of the first lighthouse on the Pacific Coast, Alcatraz later became a military prison for Civil War, Indian, and World War I prisoners. A maximum security prison from 1934 to 1963, it housed such notable incorrigibles as Robert Stroud—the "Birdman of Alcatraz"—Al Capone, and Machine-Gun Kelly. In 1969, 80 American Indians landed on Alcatraz, claiming their right to the island on the basis of an 1868 U.S. treaty with the Sioux Nation. The three-year occupation was ended in 1971 when the Indians were evicted by U.S. Marshals. In 1972 "The Rock" became part of the Golden Gate National Recreation Area; for ferry schedules and tour information, call: (415) 546-2805.

Angel Island State Park: *Access via ferry from Tiburon or San Francisco.*

At various times San Francisco Bay's largest island was a seafarer's anchorage, a Mexican rancho, the kitchen gardens for Alcatraz prison, a prisoner-of-war camp, and a U.S. Quarantine and Immigration Station. The 740-acre island has picnic areas, environmental campsites, and bicycle and hiking trails. Slips and mooring buoys are available; call: (415) 435-1915. Ferries leave from San Francisco's Pier 43 1/2. For information, call: (415) 435-1915.

Yerba Buena Island and Treasure Island: *Mid-span, San Francisco-Oakland Bay Bridge.*

The Bay Bridge's large-bore, two-level tunnel slices through Yerba Buena Island, called Goat Island until 1931; the northern addition to the natural island was created from landfill for the 1939-1940 Golden Gate International Exposition. Treasure Island is now a Navy base; its military museum, open to the public, exhibits photos of the Exposition. Call: (415) 765-6182.

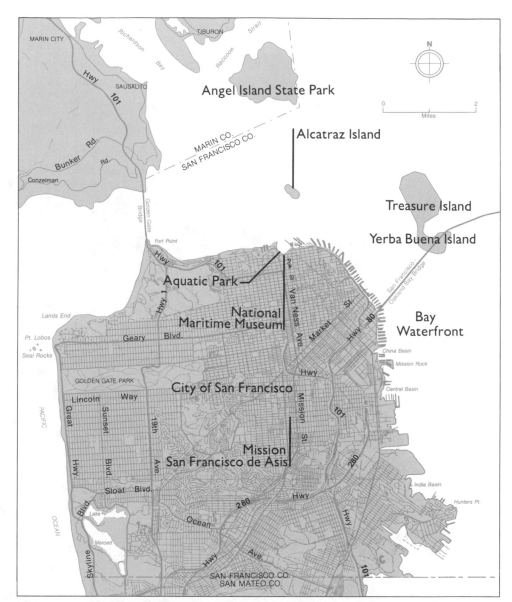

View of San Francisco Bay from Telegraph Hill, 1889

165

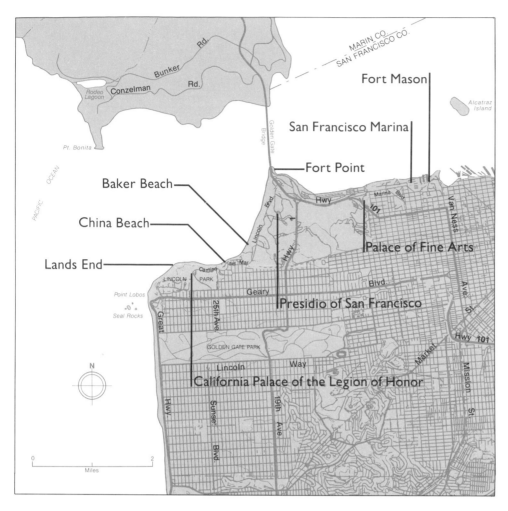

Fort Mason: *Marina Blvd. off Buchanan St., San Francisco.*

Established in 1848 and later named for Colonel Richard Mason, military governor of gold rush California, Fort Mason was a port of embarcation for soldiers shipping out for Pacific battlefronts during World War II. The fort now houses special exhibitions, galleries, museums, theater groups and art workshops, and headquarters for several environmental organizations. The U.S.S. *Jeremiah O'Brien*, the last of the World War II Liberty ships, is moored here. Fort Mason is headquarters for the Golden Gate National Recreational Area (GGNRA), which encompasses 31,000 acres in San Francisco and Marin counties. In San Francisco this urban national park, which includes Alcatraz Island, extends west from Fort Mason along the shore of San Francisco Bay, and south from the Golden Gate along the ocean coast to Fort Funston. For information, call: (415) 556-2920.

San Francisco International Hostel, in Building 240 at Fort Mason, opened in 1980 on the site of a Civil War-era army dispensary. The hostel, which accommodates 130 guests, sits on a bluff overlooking the Golden Gate Bridge and the distant Marin Hills. For reservations and information, call: (415) 771-7277.

San Francisco Marina: *Along Marina Boulevard, San Francisco.*

The San Francisco Marina, home of the St. Francis Yacht Club, has 732 berths and is host to aquatic events including yacht parades and races. The adjacent Marina Green—created originally from landfill for the 1915 Panama-

Fort Mason and San Francisco Marina

Pacific Exposition—is a grassy waterfront recreation area popular for jogging, kite flying, and frisbee tossing.

Palace of Fine Arts: *Off Hwy. 101 at Richardson Blvd., San Francisco.*

Designed by architect Bernard Maybeck, the Palace of Fine Arts was built for the Panama-Pacific International Exposition of 1915, which celebrated the completion of the Panama Canal, the rebuilding of San Francisco after the 1906 earthquake and fire, and the 400th anniversary of Balboa's historic Pacific Ocean voyage. After the Exposition closed, the Palace housed tennis courts, and was used to store city equipment and army vehicles. Intended to be a temporary exhibit, it was built of chicken wire and plaster, and was crumbling into ruins by the 1960s; it was then rebuilt in concrete, using the original molds for the figures and decorative motifs.

The Exploratorium, located at the Palace of Fine Arts, is a privately directed and funded science museum founded in 1969 by physicist Frank Oppenheimer. The museum, open to the public, has innovative exhibits that explore plant and animal behavior and the human senses using light, sound, and motion. For information, call: (415) 563-3200.

Presidio of San Francisco: *Lincoln Blvd. at 25th Ave., San Francisco.*

The park-like Presidio, covering 1,542 acres, is a U.S. military reservation. Its historic buildings, trails, and picnic areas are open to the public. The renovated adobe Presidio Officer's Club was built in 1776. Guided tours of the Presidio begin at the Army Museum; for information, call: (415) 561-3319.

The Presidio's groves of cypress, Monterey pine, and eucalyptus, planted a century ago, have replaced much of the native vegetation, although native California poppy, yerba buena mint, buckwheat, coffeeberry, and wax myrtle still grow here. Presidio manzanita, Presidio clarkia, and San Francisco lessingia are endangered endemics that grow only in the Presidio's serpentine soils.

Crissy Field, a former military airstrip, was the destination of the first transcontinental airmail flight in 1924. Independence Day firework displays and other public events are held here. Crissy Field is known as a world-class windsurfing spot; launching their sailboards from the beach north of the field, expert windsurfers skim the waves just inside the Golden Gate.

Fort Point: *Off Lincoln Blvd., San Francisco.*

In 1794, Spanish colonists built an adobe block fort, Castillo de San Joaquin, overlooking the Golden Gate. The old fort was demolished in 1853 and replaced by the present structure. The 27-foot-high iron lighthouse tower perched atop the fort ceased operating in 1934 when the partly completed Golden Gate Bridge obscured its beam. From 1933 to 1937, Fort Point was the base of operations for construction of the Golden Gate Bridge. It is now a National Historic Site; call: (415) 556-1693. The Coastal Trail begins at the dirt road above Fort Point and winds along the cliff tops, through chaparral and cypress groves, southwest to Lands End.

1880 view of San Francisco Bay from Black Point, which is now part of Fort Mason

U.S.S. Jeremiah O'Brian *moored at Fort Mason*

Baker Beach: *Off Lincoln Blvd., San Francisco.*

The sandy beach southwest of the Golden Gate is named for a prominent San Francisco lawyer killed in the Civil War. Dune vegetation includes California poppy, sea rocket, and beach primrose; a small stand of mock heather grows on the hillside. The tree lupine, a native coastal strand species that grows near dunes, is a host plant for larvae of the endangered San Francisco tree lupine moth. A cypress grove shelters several picnic areas inland of the beach.

Western gulls rest and forage onshore; seabirds such as Brandt's cormorants, pigeon guillemots, and endangered California brown pelicans are seen offshore. For information on weekend tours of the adjacent Battery Chamberlin, a former coastal defense site with a 95,000-pound cannon, call: (415) 556-8371.

China Beach: *Seacliff Ave. and El Camino del Mar, San Francisco.*

Formerly called James D. Phelan Beach for the San Franciscan who left part of his fortune to aid California writers and artists, the 600-foot-long sandy beach was the site of a Chinese fishing camp before 1900. A lifeguard is on duty at this popular swimming beach. Facilities include picnic areas, restrooms, and a sun deck. For information, call: (415) 556-7894.

California Palace of the Legion of Honor: *Legion of Honor Dr. at El Camino Del Mar, San Francisco.*

Modeled after the Palace of the Legion of Honor in Paris, the art museum was presented to the city in 1924 by Alma de Bretteville Spreckels and Adolph Spreckels as a memorial to California soldiers who lost their lives in World War I. The museum features the largest collection of French art in the U. S.; its 19 galleries display porcelains, tapestries, antique furniture, sculptures, prints, and paintings.

Lands End: *Pt. Lobos Avenue and 48th Avenue, San Francisco.*

The Coastal Trail leads northwest along the bluffs from Lincoln Park to the precipitous promontory at Lands End, and descends to a small beach that faces northwest across the Golden Gate to Point Bonita and the stark Marin Headlands. South of Lands End, a 12-acre portion of GGNRA includes Fort Miley, named for an officer of the Spanish-American war, and adjacent West Fort Miley, which has picnic tables, restrooms, and a parking area. For information, call: (415) 556-8371.

Cliff House: *Point Lobos Ave. and Great Highway, San Francisco.*

Seal Rock House, built in 1863, was the first of two predecessors to today's Cliff House. The first roadhouse was frequented by wealthy San Franciscans who made the journey to the remote blufftop in private carriages. In 1881 Comstock millionaire and philanthropist Adolph Sutro bought Seal Rock House with the intention of making the seaside site accessible to San Francisco's working class residents. In 1888, he built a steam railway to the coast from downtown San Francisco; the one-way fare to Seal Rock cost a nickel. Fire destroyed Sutro's roadhouse and another he built to replace it in 1896. The present Cliff House, built in 1909, includes the Musee Mechanique, the Camera Obscura, a gift shop, and a restaurant. The Golden Gate National Recreation Area (GGNRA) visitor information center features a collection of historic photographs and interpretive displays.

Seal Rocks, visible offshore of the Cliff House lookout platform, have been eroded from the mainland by wave action. The rocks are a haul-out area for Steller and California sea lions, the latter distinguished by their raucous barking; gulls and cormorants also roost here.

Northeast of the Cliff House are the ruins of the Sutro Baths. Built in 1890 by Adolph Sutro, the complex covered more than three acres and consisted of six saltwater swimming pools and a freshwater plunge, a restaurant, conservatories, galleries, and a museum. The baths attracted large crowds who came to see the Roman-like splendor of the public spa. As the popularity of public natatoriums waned, the baths fell into

Cliff House, ca. 1900

disuse, and in 1937 the largest pool was converted to an ice-skating rink. In 1966 the property was sold to land developers. Within the same year a spectacular fire destroyed all but the foundation walls of the pools, visible today as water-filled ruins. The site became part of the GGNRA in 1980.

Sutro Heights Park, at Point Lobos and 48th Ave. within GGNRA, is the landscaped grounds of the mansion built by Adolph Sutro in 1879 and since razed. Groves of Monterey pine, fir, and Norfolk Island pine grow on the terrace overlooking the Cliff House and the ocean.

Ocean Beach: *West of the Great Highway, San Francisco.*

Ocean Beach is a four-mile-long sandy strand between the Cliff House and Fort Funston. Surf fishing for redtail surfperch and striped bass is popular year-round; anglers catch halibut and seabass offshore. Western gulls and black oystercatchers feed and rest on the beach, and Brandt's cormorants, pigeon guillemots, and endangered California brown pelicans can be seen offshore. The seawall that runs from the Cliff House south to Lincoln Way was built in the late 1920s. Alongside the seawall is the Esplanade, a concrete pedestrian path.

Golden Gate Park: *E. of the Great Highway, between Fulton St. and Lincoln Way, San Francisco.*

In 1868, the city of San Francisco acquired over 1,000 acres of sand dunes that extended three-and-a-half miles inland from present-day Ocean Beach. In 1871, William Hammond Hall drew up preliminary plans for a "natural" urban park in the English garden style with meadows, lakes, and waterfalls. John McLaren took over as park superintendent in 1877 and devoted 56 years of his life to the development and maintenance of Golden Gate Park. Within the park are the M.H. de Young Memorial Museum, Japanese Tea Garden, California Academy of Sciences, Conservatory of Flowers, Strybing Arboretum, and Stow Lake. Adjoining the de Young Museum, which has collections of European and American art, the Asian Art Museum houses the Avery Brundage Collection of Asian bronzes, paintings, ceramics, sculpture, and jade. Next to the museum, the Japanese Tea Garden is a reproduction of a traditional Japanese teahouse and garden built for the "Midwinter Fair" of 1894. The California Academy of Sciences, across the Music Concourse from the de Young Museum, houses a natural history museum, Steinhart Aquarium, and Morrison Planetarium. The park's oldest structure is the domed, Victorian-style Conservatory, modeled after the glass conservatories in London's Kew Gardens. Built in New York in 1878, it was shipped around the Horn in pieces and assembled in San Francisco.

San Francisco Zoological Gardens: *Sloat Blvd. and Skyline Blvd., San Francisco.*

Development of the 63-acre Zoological Gardens site began in 1922. Today, over 1,000 animals are on exhibit, including snow leopards, polar bears, elephants, and pygmy hippopotamuses. Special attractions are the Penguin Pool, Gorilla World, Lion House, Insect Zoo, Children's Zoo, Koala Exhibit, and the Primate Discovery Center; complete with lush atriums, meadows, and pools, the Primate Center's naturalistic habitats shelter 16 species of rare and endangered monkeys and prosimians, such as the fat-tailed lemur and Francois' leaf-monkey. For information, call: (415) 661-4844.

Lake Merced: *E. of Skyline Blvd. and the Great Highway, San Francisco.*

Lake Merced was a tidal lagoon until formation of a barrier beach closed it off from the sea, creating the five-acre freshwater lake. In the 1870s, the lake was owned by the Spring Valley Water Company, whose monopoly of the city's water supply lasted until the facilities were sold to the city and county in 1930. Lake Merced is now a popular recreation site for city residents. A path for bicycling, walking, and jogging circles the lake, which is stocked with trout and largemouth bass. The lake has a 168-foot-long fishing pier, small boat berths, and boat rentals.

Fort Funston: *W. of the Great Highway and Skyline Blvd., San Francisco.*

Built at the turn of the century, the former military reservation was named for Presidio Commander Frederick Funston. During World War II it was a Nike missile installation site and is now a unit of the GGNRA. Sand verbena and wild buckwheat cover the windswept blufftops overlooking the sandy beach. The wheelchair-accessible Sunset Trail makes a 1.5-mile loop through the uplands; a steep unmarked trail leads to the beach. There is a picnic area and observation deck on the blufftop, which is an official hang gliding launch site.

Phillip Burton Memorial Beach: *S. of Fort Funston, San Francisco.*

The sandy beach extends south of Fort Funston into San Mateo County and is a popular spot to fish for striped bass and redtail surfperch. San Francisco Congressman Phillip Burton, for whom the beach is named, was instrumental in the creation of the Golden Gate National Recreation Area (GGNRA). Call: (415) 556-0560.

Ocean Beach

Humpback whale, 57 feet long, on Ocean Beach, ca. 1900

San Mateo County
Selected Species of Interest

Plants: Bush lupine (*Lupinus arboreus*), native perennial, blooms April- July; common along the roadside and on stabilized dunes. **Sea palm** (*Postelsia palmaeformis*), annual intertidal marine plant; inhabits high-wave-energy rocky shore.

Trees: California buckeye (*Aesculus californica*), found in riparian canyons; toxic seeds were used by the Ohlone for fishing. **California bay laurel** (*Umbellularia californica*), widely distributed throughout the county.

Insects: San Bruno elfin butterfly (*Callophrys mossii bayensis*), endangered; endemic to northern San Mateo County. **Bay checkerspot butterfly** (*Euphydryas editha bayensis*); larva feeds on owl's clover.

Invertebrates: Tube worm (*Dodecaceria fewkesi*), builds large calcareous structures; found at Año Nuevo. **California brackish water snail** (*Tryonia imitator*), lives near Pescadero and Butano Creek mouths.

Amphibians and Reptiles: San Francisco garter snake (*Thamnophis sirtalis tetrataenia*), endangered; endemic to a few coastal streams and marshes in the county. **Western fence lizard** (*Sceloporus occidentalis*), found on rocky outcrops.

Fish: Striped bass (*Morone saxatilis*), anadromous; an important sport fish; found in the offshore waters of San Mateo's north coast. **Blue rockfish** (*Sebastes mystinus*), swims in large numbers; found offshore in kelp beds.

Birds: Pelagic cormorant (*Phalacrocorax pelagicus*), builds nests on narrow ledges of vertical sea cliffs. **California black rail** (*Laterallus jamaicensis coturniculus*), threatened marsh bird; inhabits Pescadero Marsh.

Land Mammals: Black-tailed jack rabbit (*Lepus californicus*), inhabits open grassy fields and chaparral. **California ground squirrel** (*Spermophilus beecheyi*), burrows in open fields, pastures, and hillsides.

Marine Mammals: Northern elephant seal (*Mirounga angustirostris*); largest mainland rookery in the world at Año Nuevo. **Steller sea lion** (*Eumetopias jubatus*); California's largest population breeds on Año Nuevo Island.

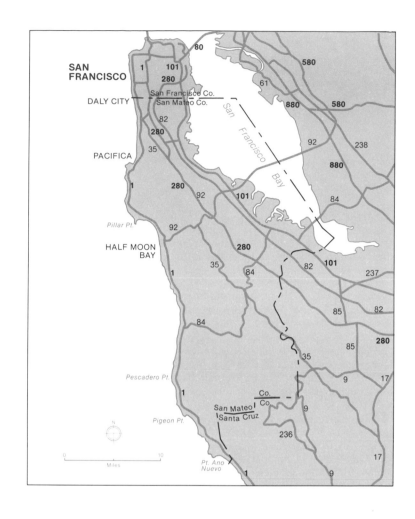

San Mateo County

SAN MATEO COUNTY was first formed in 1856. In 1868 its southern boundary was extended to include the northern portion of what was then Santa Cruz County, including San Gregorio, Pescadero, and Año Nuevo. Often referred to as the Coastside, the San Mateo County coast offers many cultural and natural resources.

Many beaches in San Mateo County have hazardous surf conditions with rip currents and cold water temperatures, and swimming can be dangerous. Extensive intertidal reefs along the coast offer close-up viewing of marine life. The principal geologic feature in the area is the San Andreas Fault, which enters the sea at Mussel Rock. Ongoing geologic processes of the California Coast Ranges can be observed in the landscapes of Año Nuevo, Devil's Slide, and the Fitzgerald Marine Reserve.

In search of Monterey Bay, and not knowing they had passed it, the Portolá Expedition camped at several San Mateo beaches in 1769 and were the first Europeans to make contact with the Ohlone Indians. The Spanish called them "Costeños" (coast people), and English-speaking settlers mispronounced it "Costanos"; the name was finally twisted into "Costanoans." Descendants of these indigenous people prefer to call themselves Ohlone, which may have been the name of a village along the San Mateo coast or a Miwok word meaning "western people." Related culturally and linguistically to the Coast Miwok, the Ohlone were made up of forty or so tribelets that seasonally migrated between the interior valley and the coast. They were a nomadic hunting, gathering, and fishing people who lived on abalone, smelt, salmon, mussels, clams, sea urchins, seals, sea otters, and beached whales.

During the Mexican period, from 1822 to 1846, eight ranchos were formed along the San Mateo coast. These were resurveyed and taken over by American settlers in the 1850s and 1860s; the land was leased to lumber companies, dairymen, and farmers. Logging operations in the redwood canyons of the Santa Cruz Mountains took place between the 1850s and 1920s. The most active logging areas were the watersheds of Purisima, Tunitas, San Gregorio, Pescadero, and Gazos creeks. During the 1870s, the increase in exporting grain and produce coincided with the rise in timber export. In response to this, several chutes and wharves were built along the coast at places like Tunitas Creek, Año Nuevo, and Half Moon Bay, where goods were transferred onto ships. Seafaring Portuguese islanders from the Azores began arriving in the 1860s, and operated whaling stations at several locations, including Pillar Point and Pigeon Point, until the 1880s.

The coastal terraces were once covered with lush, perennial native grasses that were destroyed by overgrazing during the Spanish and Mexican periods and replaced by invading European annual grasses. Monterey cypress and Monterey pine were planted to replace the chaparral that originally grew there. Eucalyptus trees were introduced from Australia and planted as a windbreak for agriculture. Artichokes were first commercially planted in California near Half Moon Bay in 1898. Today, agriculture, floriculture, and horticulture play a significant role in the coast's economy.

Promoters of the Ocean Shore Railroad advertised it as a scenic link between San Francisco and Santa Cruz; their slogan was "It Reaches The Beaches." Track-laying began in 1905 and eventually the line ran down the coast to Tunitas Creek, south of Half Moon Bay, where a Stanley Steamer (a steam-powered automobile) transported passengers 26 miles farther south to Swanton; another train carried them to Santa Cruz. The promoters intended to open up the coast for real estate development, and whole communities, such as El Granada, were created. However, in 1920, as finances weakened and competition from the automobile became too strong, the railroad company was forced out of business. Today, remnants of the railroad are still visible; for example, Vallemar Station in Pacifica, once a railroad depot, has since been remodeled into a high-tech video sports bar and restaurant.

Post-World War II demands for housing in San Mateo County resulted in suburban development spilling over onto the coastline around Daly City and Pacifica. With the exception of Half Moon Bay, the area south of Montara Mountain just below Pacifica is sparsely populated. Between 1890 and 1940, Half Moon Bay registered no gain in its population of 1,000; today, however, suburbia has infiltrated this once remote town. South of Half Moon Bay, the Santa Cruz Mountains drop down to rolling pastures and cultivated farmland on marine terraces. Redwood forests are found inland at several locations, including Butano State Park. Oak woodland and chaparral grow on exposed hillsides. Creeks flow out of riparian canyons to sandy beaches and rocky coastline. The rural environment of the southern San Mateo coast contrasts sharply with the nearby San Francisco Bay Area, one of the most populous urban regions in the nation.

Northern elephant seal, Año Nuevo State Reserve

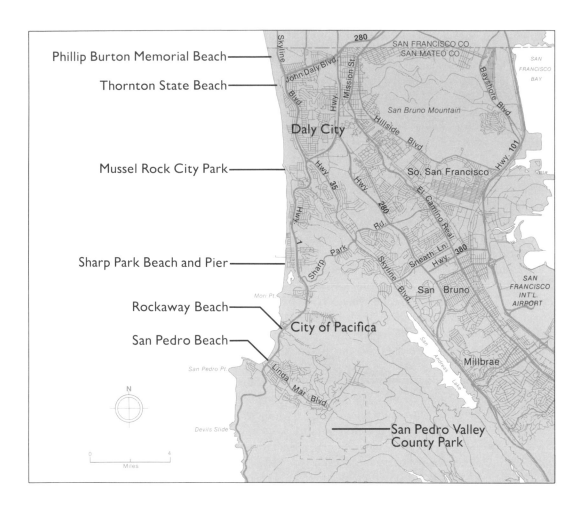

ochre star (*Pisaster ochraceus*)
to 10 inches in diameter

Phillip Burton Memorial Beach: *.5 mi. N. of Thornton State Beach, Daly City.*

Named after former San Francisco Congressman Phillip Burton, this beach is accessible from the north at Fort Funston in San Francisco. An equestrian trail along the bluff leads down to the sandy beach. Call: (415) 556-0560.

Thornton State Beach: *End of Thornton Beach Rd., Daly City.*

Once owned by former county supervisor and farmer Robert S. Thornton, this sandy beach is a popular kite flying and model glider area; it is also used for surf fishing and clamming for razorback clams. There is a hiking trail along the bluff to the north, where bank swallows nest. The upland area is closed due to extensive landslide damage from the storms of 1982 and there is no projected re-opening date. Beach access is from Burton Beach to the north, or from Mussel Rock to the south. Call: (415) 557-4069.

Daly City: *Hwy. 1, S. of San Francisco.*

Incorporated in 1911, Daly City was named for dairyman John D. Daly, whose ranch became a refuge for people fleeing the 1906 San Francisco earthquake and fire. Today, the residential community is an urban extension of San Francisco. Toward the coast, the nearly identical rows of stucco houses uniformly lining the streets have a regimented, "ticky-tacky" look that inspired Malvina Reynold's hit tune "Little Boxes." San Bruno Mountain, rising out of the urban landscape and stretching four miles across the peninsula, is the dominant physical feature east of the coast; the mission blue butterfly and San Bruno elfin butterfly, both en-

dangered, are found here. Palisades Park, along Palisades Dr. at Westridge Ave., provides a northward view of the coast toward the Golden Gate. Northridge City Park, along Northridge Dr. at Carmel Ave., offers two vista points that overlook the ocean and the steeply eroded Daisaku Ikeda Canyon.

The Broderick-Terry Dueling Site near Lake Merced is a State Historical Landmark that commemorates a famous duel: The duel that ended duels in California. On September 13, 1859, in an attempt to settle an argument over which side California should join in the impending Civil War, California Supreme Court Justice David S. Terry shot and killed U.S. Senator David C. Broderick.

Mussel Rock City Park: *End of Westline Dr., off Skyline Dr., Daly City.*

The beach is popular for fishing. Along the bluff face, silty clay and gravel deposits known as the Merced Formation have been subject to earthquake and storm activity, causing landslides that have exposed Pliocene marine fossils. Whale bones have been found in the roadcut of the abandoned Ocean Shore Railroad. Mussel Rock, covered with California mussels, is a harbor seal haul-out. The San Andreas Fault enters the ocean just north of Mussel Rock.

Sharp Park Beach and Pier: *Beach Blvd. and Santa Rosa Ave., Pacifica.*

Sharp Park Beach is a popular surfing and surf fishing area, particularly for striped bass. The L-shaped Pacifica Municipal Pier, opened in 1973, extends 1,110 feet out from the sandy beach at the foot of Beach Boulevard. Fishermen catch surfperch, smelt, cabezon, lingcod, halibut, king salmon, striped bass, and several species of sharks and crabs. The hexagonal concrete pilings angling out from the pier provide an ideal habitat for a number of invertebrates such as stalked barnacles, California mussels, and ochre sea stars. Migrating California gray whales can be seen offshore in winter and spring. The pier, open 24 hours a day, has a bait and tackle shop with concessions and wheelchair-accessible restrooms. South of the pier is Laguna Salada, a freshwater lagoon and marsh area that is a known habitat for the endangered San Francisco garter snake.

City of Pacifica: *Hwy. 1, 15 mi. S. of San Francisco.*

In 1957, the nine communities of Edgemar, Pacific Manor, Westview (now Pacific Highlands), Sharp Park, Fairway Park, Vallemar, Rockaway Beach, Linda Mar, and Pedro Point became unified under the name Pacifica.

Near the coast, the endangered endemic San Francisco wallflower is found in the coastal scrub vegetation along with annual grasses and spring wildflowers such as buttercup, seaside daisy, and California poppy.

The Sanchez Adobe on Linda Mar Blvd. near Adobe Lane in Pacifica is a State Historical Landmark. The two-story adobe brick ranch house was completed in 1846 during the Mexican era by Don Francisco Sanchez, commandant of the San Francisco Presidio and former mayor of San Francisco. Previously, the site was an Ohlone village; it later became the agricultural outpost of Mission Dolores. Within the adobe, saddles, spinning wheels, butter churns, Ohlone artifacts, and other relics are displayed. Huge Monterey pine, Monterey cypress, and eucalyptus trees surround the building. For information, call: (415) 359-1462.

Rockaway Beach: *End of Rockaway Beach Ave. at San Mario Way, Pacifica.*

Located in a hill-sheltered cove, this narrow sandy beach is popular for surfing and surf fishing, particularly for rockfish, striped bass, and ocean perch. At the north end of the beach a limestone and greenstone quarry has been in operation since 1904 beside Calera (Spanish for "lime") Creek where, 200 years ago, lime pits furnished whitewash for the newly built Presidio of San Francisco.

East of Rockaway Beach is the Sweeney Ridge Skyline Preserve, a National Historical Landmark. In November 1769 a scouting party led by Sargeant José Francisco de Ortega of the Portolá Expedition first sighted San Francisco Bay from Sweeney Ridge; the bay had not been previously sighted from sea because of its narrow opening and the persistent coastal fog. Sweeney Ridge is now part of the Golden Gate National Recreation Area. For information on hiking trails that lead to the 360-degree panorama and discovery site, call: (415) 556-8371.

San Pedro Valley County Park: *Off Oddstad Blvd., Pacifica.*

San Pedro Valley County Park is a 1,500-acre upland park that offers hiking trails, an interpretive center, and shaded picnic tables. Wheelchair-accessible facilities include restrooms and a self-guided nature trail. Live oak, Douglas-fir, redwood, creek dogwood, arroyo willow, and several species of ferns provide habitat for abundant wildlife, including scrub jays, red-tailed hawks, gray foxes, brush rabbits, deer, coyotes, bobcats, and California garter snakes. The San Bruno Mountain manzanita and the Montara Mountain manzanita, both endangered endemics, occur in the thick coastal scrub. Steelhead trout spawn in the middle fork of San Pedro Creek. For information, call: (415) 355-8289.

San Pedro Beach: *Hwy. 1 between Crespi Dr. and Linda Mar Blvd., Pacifica.*

San Pedro Beach is a popular surfing and fishing spot, where basket cockles, gaper clams, and littleneck clams are found. Facilities include wheelchair-accessible restrooms, skiff rentals, and a boat ramp. In 1769 Portolá camped near the mouth of San Pedro Creek beside an Ohlone village; his soldiers named the point to the south Punta de las Almejas (Mussel Point) from the abundant supply of mussels they feasted on. Juan Crespí later named it Punta del Ángel Custodio (Guardian Angel). San Pedro was the name of the land grant.

Sanchez Adobe, Pacifica

View south to Burton Beach from Fort Funston

Devil's Slide: *Hwy. 1, 1 mi. S. of San Pedro Pt.*

South of Pacifica, Highway 1 cuts through the rock as it winds along the edges of spectacular sea cliffs that drop hundreds of feet to the ocean below. Although the view is breathtaking, the narrow roadway can be hazardous, especially during storms or fog. The cliffs here reveal much about the region's geologic history. Built up by marine sedimentation over hundreds of thousands of years, these once flat sedimentary layers have been bent, upturned, and tightly folded as a result of seismic activity. This is very noticeable along the road cut where ground water and earthquakes have loosened the sedimentary layers, causing entire sections of the cliff to collapse during rainstorms. The chute-like rock slide descends precipitously over 800 feet to the ocean below. The slide consists of Paleocene sandstone and shale, mixed with granitic boulders that date back to the Cretaceous period. During the 1906 San Francisco earthquake most of the roadbed of the Ocean Shore Railroad and much of the company's equipment was pushed into the ocean along this stretch.

Black oystercatchers, western gulls, pelagic and Brandt's cormorants, common murres, and pigeon guillemots nest along the cliffs and on offshore islets.

Gray Whale Cove State Beach: *Hwy. 1, .5 mi. S. of Devil's Slide.*

This privately managed state beach, formerly called Edun Cove, is also referred to as Devil's Slide Beach. A stairway leads from a bluff down the steeply eroded Green Valley Creek canyon to a protected sandy beach that offers sun-bathing, surf fishing, and volleyball; clothing is optional. Atop the hill at the north end of the beach are the weathered remains of a Base End Station, used for observation during World War II. California gray whales often swim close to shore here during their northern migration. Facilities include a parking lot east of Highway 1, and restrooms on the beach. For information, call: (415) 728-5336.

Montara State Beach: *Hwy 1. and 2nd St., Montara.*

The half-mile-long sandy beach is popular for picnicking, surfing, and surf fishing. Restrooms, a small parking lot, and access trails are located at the south end of the beach; Martini Creek is at the north end. Call: (415) 726-6238.

Montara Mountain, east of Highway 1, is the northern extension of the Santa Cruz Mountains; it is composed of 90-million-year-old granitic rock, largely quartz diorite. Martini Creek supports riparian vegetation such as willow, red alder, horsetail, and mugwort. Coastal scrub vegetation includes coastal sage, sticky monkeyflower, ceanothus, and California huckleberry. Both plant communities provide habitat for the barn owl, American kestrel, brown towhee, junco, northern harrier, California quail, chipmunk, bobcat, jack rabbit, and deer. The peregrine falcon and the San Bruno elfin butterfly, both endangered, also inhabit the area. East of Highway 1 and north of Martini Creek is the McNee Ranch State Park, which offers a network of trails for hiking, horseback riding, and mountain biking.

hermit crab in black turban snail shell
(*Pagurus samuelis* in *Tegula funebralis*)
crab: ¾ inch long
shell: 1 inch long

Devil's Slide

Montara Lighthouse: *Hwy. 1 and 16th St., between Montara and Moss Beach.*

In 1875 a steam whistle was installed on the bluff above Montara Point to warn ships of the sunken rocks that lie west of the point. An oil lamp light was added in 1900. In 1928, a 30-foot conical metal tower was constructed on the bluff; later a Fresnel lens was added. Today, the small, white New England-style Point Montara Fog Signal and Light Station is fully automated; it is also on the list of National Historic Places.

The historic buildings next to the lighthouse include a Stick-Eastlake style Victorian house which is now the Montara Lighthouse Hostel. Facilities include 30 beds, kitchen facilities, a volleyball court, an outdoor hot tub, beach access, a whale-watching area, and bicycle rentals. For hostel information, call: (415) 728-7177.

James V. Fitzgerald Marine Reserve: *Off California Ave. and N. Lake St., Moss Beach.*

Established in 1969, the reserve includes three miles of rocky coastline interspersed with sandy beaches. The reserve is one of the richest intertidal areas on the California coast; 25 species new to science have been discovered at the reserve, and 49 species reach the extent of their northern or southern ranges here. Extensive intertidal shale reefs provide habitat for abundant marine life such as giant green anemones, limpets, chitons, barnacles, spiny purple sea urchins, sea palms, surfgrass, feather boa kelp, and several species of crabs and snails. Kelp greenling, cabezon, lingcod, rockfish, and red abalone are found in offshore kelp beds.

Abalone and scuba diving are allowed in the reserve, and surf fishing is permitted for a few selected species; tidepool life is protected and may not be removed. Facilities include picnic tables in a sheltered cypress grove, restrooms,

Montara Lighthouse

and a parking area. An interpretive exhibit and program are available, and tidepool walks are given at low tides. For information, call: (415) 728-3584 or 573-2595.

North of the entrance to the reserve, Monterey cypress, coyote brush, and introduced annuals such as foxtail barley and English plantain grow along the bluff area. South of the entrance there are hiking trails along grassy bluffs near the shoreline, where overwintering and migratory shorebirds such as the American avocet and black-necked stilt are found. Along these trails, native plants such as yellow bush lupine, wild buckwheat, sea lettuce, lizardtail, and beach strawberry grow on top of marine terrace sediment deposits of sand and gravel.

The Seal Cove earthquake fault passes through the reserve just north of San Vicente Creek, near the steps at the entrance to the reserve; southwest of the fault, 7-million-year-old siltstone beds have been pushed against 70,000-year-old terrace deposits on the fault's northeast side. A few hundred feet to the north a trough-shaped depression, known as a syncline, can be seen in the rocks exposed in the ocean at low tide. The Seal Cove Landslide, south of San Vicente Creek, is a classic example of a large, slow-moving landslide. Rotated slide blocks with distinct slip surfaces step down from the bluff to the beach.

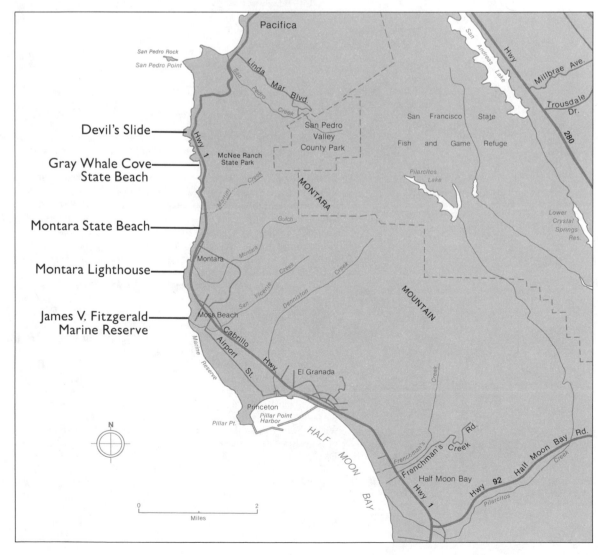

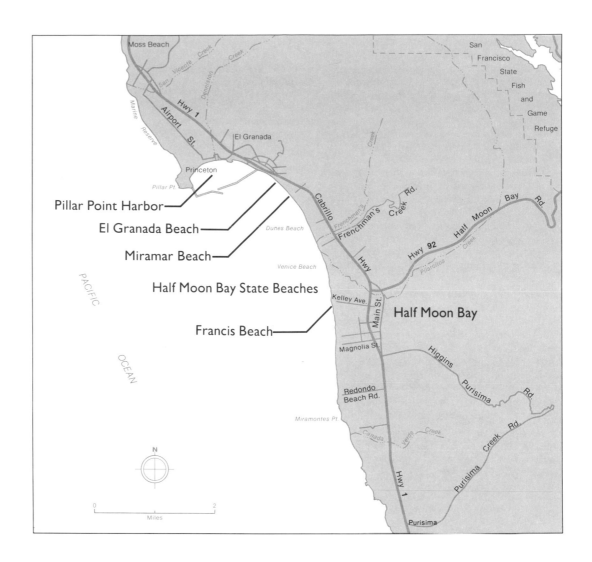

Pillar Point Harbor: *W. of Hwy. 1 and Capistrano Rd., Princeton.*

Located just west of Princeton, Pillar Point is a granitic headland that shelters the only protected harbor between San Francisco and Santa Cruz. The point was originally part of the extensive Rancho Corral de Tierra (The Earth Coral) under the Republic of Mexico. From 1860 until the 1890s, the sandy cove was used as a whaling station by Portuguese sailors from the Azores, who rendered their catches of humpback and California gray whales on the shore. In 1961, the harbor's east and west breakwaters were completed, providing additional wave protection for the anchorage; the west breakwater was extended in 1967.

The town of Princeton, formerly known as Old Landing, is a commercial fishing and boat building center. Salmon, halibut, and kingfish are harvested commercially, and rockfish, starry flounder, and flatfish are caught at Johnson Pier. Located off Capistrano Rd., the pier is open 24 hours a day and offers charter fishing boats, whale-watching trips, a picnic area, bike path, wheelchair-accessible restrooms, boat ramp, dinghy hoist, and several seafood restaurants. For information, call: (415) 728-3377.

The Princeton Inn, located at Capistrano Rd. and Prospect St., was constructed as a resort hotel in 1908 in the Mission Revival architectural style by the promoter of Princeton-by-the-Sea. The building served as a center for illegal rum-running during Prohibition, and today has been remodeled into a restaurant; it is listed in the National Register of Historic Places.

Denniston Creek empties into the harbor; the grassy and marshy areas along the creek are a known habitat for the endangered San Francisco garter snake.

El Granada Beach: *Between East Breakwater and Mirada Rd., Half Moon Bay.*

El Granada Beach is a sandy beach below the rock riprap along Highway 1. East Breakwater, located at the north end of the beach, is a rock jetty that is popular for rock fishing and surfing. Restrooms and a parking lot are available.

Originally intended to rival Atlantic City and Coney Island as a beachside resort, the town of El Granada was laid out in anticipation of the Ocean Shore Railroad boom that never fully developed. The community was subdivided in 1906 in a Beaux-Arts design of radial and semi-circular landscaped streets by architect and city planner Daniel Burnham; this street pattern predominates today.

Miramar Beach: *End of Magellan Ave. off Hwy. 1, Half Moon Bay.*

Miramar Beach, whose name is Spanish for "behold the sea," is a sandy beach popular for surfing. In 1868, Josiah Ames built a wharf here to accommodate the growing export of local grain, lumber, vegetables, and dairy products. The wharf, which extended 1,000 feet beyond the surf, no longer exists.

Half Moon Bay State Beaches: *W. of Hwy. 1, Half Moon Bay.*

Beginning at East Breakwater, Half Moon Bay's shoreline gently curves southward and forms a long, sandy beach that is accessible at several points off Highway 1. The following beaches are within the Half Moon Bay State Beach system: Roosevelt Beach, Dunes Beach, Venice Beach, and Francis Beach, all of which provide restrooms and parking. Highly eroded bluffs and sand dunes with coastal strand vegetation, including cordgrass, seaside daisy, and introduced New Zealand spinach, are typical of the area. Shorebirds feed and rest along the beaches. An equestrian trail runs from Dunes Beach to the bluff area of Francis Beach. Horse rentals are available at two stables located off Highway 1; call: (415) 726-9871 or 726-2362. Picnicking, kite flying, and surfing, as well as surf fishing for starry flounder, rock cod, and surfperch, are popular activities at the beaches. For beach information, call: (415) 726-6238.

Roosevelt Beach, also known as Naples Beach, is located at the end of Roosevelt Boulevard. A flat, sandy trail leads to the beach through dune vegetation such as wild radish and sea fig; red-winged blackbirds are commonly seen. Dunes Beach, at the end of Young Ave., has a path that leads from the bluff area to the sandy beach. Frenchmen's Creek is to the south. Venice Beach, at the end of Venice Blvd., also has a path leading to the sandy beach. Pilarcitos Creek is to the south; the name Pilarcitos means "little stone pillars."

Francis Beach: *Foot of Kelly Ave., Half Moon Bay.*

Headquarters for Half Moon Bay State Beaches, Francis Beach is popular for surfing, and provides parking, picnic tables that overlook the ocean, and a campground. Beach access and restrooms are wheelchair-accessible.

Main Street, Half Moon Bay, ca. 1915

Half Moon Bay: *28 mi. S. of San Francisco at Hwy. 1 and Hwy. 92.*

Originally called San Benito and later Spanishtown, Half Moon Bay was settled by Spanish immigrants in 1840; it is the oldest town in San Mateo County. Surrounding the town are broad marine terraces with rich alluvial deposits. These prime agricultural soils, in combination with a long, cool, fog-moistened growing season, provide ideal conditions for growing specialized crops such as artichokes, Brussels sprouts, broccoli, and pumpkins. Floriculture and horticulture operations grow indoor plants and cut flowers, such as carnations, roses, tulips, and irises. In the inland canyons where it is warmer and sunnier, Christmas trees and kiwi fruit are grown. Other agricultural products include wool, livestock, and honey.

The Pilarcitos Creek bridge, built in 1900, was the first reinforced-concrete span in the county. Historic Johnston House, built out of redwood in a New England saltbox style by James Johnston in 1853, is an architectural landmark that stands in a field near Higgins Rd. and Main St.; recently restored, it is one of the few Atlantic Seaboard Design houses in California.

There are three annual celebrations in Half Moon Bay: the Great Pumpkin and Art Festival in October, the Coastside County Fair in July, and the Portuguese Chamarita (or Holy Ghost Festival) in the spring. For information on festivals and the historic walking tour of downtown Half Moon Bay, call: (415) 726-5202.

Johnson Pier, Pillar Point Harbor

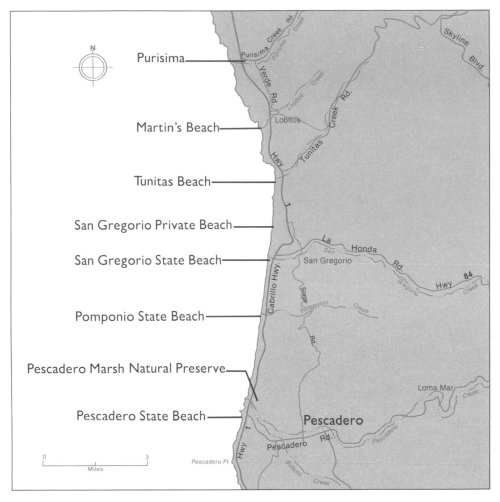

Purisima

Martin's Beach

Tunitas Beach

San Gregorio Private Beach

San Gregorio State Beach

Pomponio State Beach

Pescadero Marsh Natural Preserve

Pescadero State Beach

Purisima: *Hwy. 1 and Verde Rd., 4 mi. S. of Half Moon Bay.*

In 1769, Portolá camped on the south bank of Purisima Creek; the Ohlone village on the north bank was named "Las Pulgas" (The Fleas) by the army engineer with the party because the soldiers who occupied some abandoned Indian huts became covered with fleas. The first American settlement in the Half Moon Bay area was established here around 1853. The historic town of Purisima, whose name means "immaculate," no longer exists. In its heyday, it was a stagecoach stop with stores, hotel, school, saloon, dance hall, and blacksmith shop, serving farmers and loggers in the surrounding area. With the growth of Half Moon Bay as the produce shipping center of the region, the town declined, and by the 1930s Purisima had become a ghost town. All that remains today is the cemetery.

Martin's Beach: *Toll Rd. off Hwy. 1, 6 mi. S. of Half Moon Bay.*

Named after rancher and former owner Nicholas Martin, this privately managed sandy beach offers surf fishing and netting for surf smelt; net rental is available. Harbor seals haul out on the rocks at the north end of the beach, where black oystercatchers, pigeon guillemots, and pelagic cormorants nest. Sea palms, crabs, and barnacles inhabit the intertidal zones. Beach facilities include picnic tables, restrooms, and parking. Call: (415) 726-9943.

East of Highway 1, the historic town site of Lobitos is situated along Lobitos Creek, which flows through a lush riparian canyon and empties onto the beach; steelhead trout spawn upstream.

Tunitas Beach: *Hwy. 1 at Tunitas Creek bridge.*

Tunitas Beach was formerly inhabited by the Ohlone Indians; the Portolá Expedition camped here in 1769. In 1872, Alexander Gordon built Gordon's Chute at a 45-degree angle from the 100-foot-high bluff to the north; produce and lumber were sent down the chute and transferred to ships waiting below. The chute was demolished by a storm in 1885. Beneath the Tunitas Creek bridge in a thick riparian habitat are remnants of pilings from the original Ocean Shore Railroad. Access to Tunitas Beach is from San Gregorio Private Beach to the south.

San Gregorio Private Beach: *Off Hwy. 1, 1 mi. N. of San Gregorio Rd.*

Also known as Nude Beach or Bare-Bottom Beach, this is a privately run sandy beach. A freshwater pond, located on the blufftop, is surrounded by tule and wildflowers such as yellow bush lupine. A path leads from the high bluff down to the beach. Look for the white gate just north of San Gregorio Road.

San Gregorio State Beach: *Hwy. 1 and San Gregorio Rd., 5 mi. S. of Half Moon Bay.*

A bronze plaque commemorates the 1769 Portolá camp that was located at an Ohlone village near the mouth of San Gregorio Creek. A path and stairs lead from the parking lot down to the sandy beach and rocky shore where surf fishing for rockfish and surfperch is popular. Picnic tables and restrooms are available.

Martin's Beach

The beach is an overwintering area for plovers and other shorebirds. The highly eroded bluffs to the north provide a good vantage point for whale watching. Inland of the beach is the San Gregorio Creek estuary and freshwater marsh, which supports water-associated birds such as herons and egrets. Silver salmon, steelhead trout, and Pacific lamprey spawn upstream in gravel beds. For beach information, call: (415) 726-6238.

Surrounded by rolling hills, the tiny town of San Gregorio is about a mile inland from the beach; the town was a popular resort at the turn of the century before the redwoods were logged out. The Peterson & Alsford General Store, located at Route 84 and Stage Rd., was built in 1889 in the California Mission Revival style and rebuilt after a fire in 1930. Stage Road, an inland scenic link between San Gregorio and Pescadero, was the old stagecoach route from 1865 until 1905.

Pomponio State Beach: *Hwy. 1 at Pomponio Creek, Pescadero.*

A dirt path leads from the parking lot down to a sandy beach where surf fishing is popular. Facilities include picnic tables and restrooms. For information, call: (415) 726-6238.

Inland from the beach, a freshwater marsh and lagoon area, created by Pomponio Creek, supports birds such as plovers, herons, and egrets. Pomponio Creek is named for Chief Pomponio, an Ohlone Indian who attacked Spanish settlers and repeatedly escaped from the missions; his mountain hideout was at the headwaters of the creek, where he made a desperate stand as his people and culture were destroyed.

Pescadero State Beach: *Hwy. 1 at Pescadero Rd.*

The Portolá Expedition camped at this beach in 1769. Once a favored launching site for whaling boats, the mile-long sandy beach and rocky shore is covered with large, active sand dunes where leaf litter of coastal scrub vegetation provides habitat for the rare globose dune beetle.

Western gulls, California gulls, Heermann's gulls, and shorebirds such as sandpipers, dowitchers, godwits, and willets inhabit the area. Tidepools are located at the south end of the beach, where poke-poling for monkey-face eels is popular; farther south there is a harbor seal and Steller sea lion haul-out at Pescadero Point. Beach facilities include picnic tables, restrooms, and parking. Call: (415) 726-6238.

Pescadero Creek flows into the ocean here; steelhead trout, silver salmon, and Pacific lamprey migrate upstream from the ocean into the creek to spawn in fresh water. The creek widens at the juncture with Butano Creek, forming a lagoon and estuary behind the beach. A riparian woodland flourishes along both creeks.

Pescadero Marsh Natural Preserve: *E. of Hwy. 1, N. of Pescadero Rd., Pescadero.*

East of Pescadero State Beach is a 510-acre protected wildlife sanctuary, which includes two large brackish ponds. Pescadero Marsh is the largest coastal marsh between San Francisco Bay and Elkhorn Slough, providing an important habitat for a variety of animals such as deer, raccoons, foxes, skunks, black-shouldered kites, yellow-throated warblers, Allen's hummingbirds, and overwintering dabbling and diving ducks. The San Francisco garter snake and peregrine falcon, both endangered species, also inhabit the area. In the hills above the marsh, large stands of eucalyptus provide roosts for great blue herons and snowy egrets. Over 180 species of birds, 50 species of mammals, 33 species of amphibians, and 380 species of plants have been sighted in the area.

Informal access for bird watching is permitted along the dirt fill levees off Pescadero Rd., and along the interpretive trails off Highway 1 at the north end of the preserve near Pescadero Creek. The northernmost trail is closed from March 15 to September 1 to prevent hikers from disturbing breeding birds; best bird watching is during the late fall and early spring. No hunting or pets are allowed at the marsh. Facilities include picnic tables and restrooms.

Pescadero: *Off Pescadero Rd., 2 mi. E. of Hwy. 1.*

Pescadero means "fishing place," probably referring to Pescadero Creek, where the Ohlone Indians used to fish. When the S.S. *Columbia* wrecked on the rocks nearby in 1896, its cargo of white paint was salvaged and used by the local residents to paint the town. Today, descendants have kept the white paint tradition. Farmers, mostly of Italian and Portuguese descent, grow Brussels sprouts, beans, lettuce, artichokes, and strawflowers; there is also some cattle grazing. The Portuguese Chamarita Festival is held in the spring and the Artichoke Festival in August.

Built in 1867 and now a California Historical Landmark, the Pescadero Community Church expresses in wood the Greek Revival architectural style. Duarte's Restaurant is a traditional meeting place for local townfolk and nearby farmers as well as visitors from the San Francisco Bay Area. Along Pescadero Rd., just east of Pescadero, stands the largest Monterey cypress in the United States; 120 feet tall and approximately 40 feet in circumference, it is estimated to be 150 years old.

Gordon's Chute at Tunitas Beach, ca. 1872

Pescadero State Beach

Pebble Beach

Bean Hollow State Beach: *Hwy. 1 at Bean Hollow Rd., 5 mi. S. of Pescadero.*

A rocky outcrop separates two sandy coves; tidepools are located at the north end, and surf fishing for rockfish is popular. Facilities include picnic tables and restrooms. Call: (415) 726-6238. Arroyo de los Frijoles, "Creek of the Beans," drains into Lake Lucerne east of Highway 1, and is an important freshwater habitat for overwintering dabbling and diving ducks.

Butano State Park: *7 mi. S. of Pescadero on Cloverdale Rd.*

A 2,200-acre park in the Santa Cruz Mountains, Butano State Park offers hiking, picnicking, fishing, and nature study exhibits. Butano is an Indian word meaning "a gathering place for friendly visits." The land was selectively logged during the 1880s, but second-growth redwoods and a varied hardwood forest remain. Alders, tanbark oaks, sword ferns, blackberries, and trillium abound. Steller's jays, pygmy nuthatches, chestnut-backed chickadees, winter wrens, rabbits, deer, and bobcats inhabit the forest. Silver salmon and steelhead trout are found in Butano Creek. Facilities include a campground and wheelchair-accessible restrooms. For information, call: (415) 879-0173.

Pigeon Point Lighthouse: *Pigeon Point Rd., 7 mi. S. of Pescadero.*

In 1853, the Boston clipper ship *Carrier Pigeon* drifted aground on the headland then known as Punta de la Ballena, or Whale Point; after the wreck it became known as Pigeon Point. A whaling station was located on the point during the late 1800s, and lumber and produce were shipped from Pigeon Point Wharf until the

Pebble Beach: *Hwy. 1, between Hill Rd. and Artichoke Road.*

Stairs lead from the bluff down to a small cove where wave-broken quartz rocks from an offshore reef are tumbled, polished, and finally deposited as small stones on the shore; it is illegal to remove any pebbles. A major resort hotel, known as "Coburn's Folly," was built here during the 1890s; it was a financial disaster and was destroyed by fire in the 1920s. Tidepools are located south of the beach; fossils can be seen in the cliffs. Facilities include picnic tables, restrooms, and a self-guided nature trail along the blufftop that features spring wildflowers such as blue iris, seaside daisy, and California poppy.

Pigeon Point Lighthouse

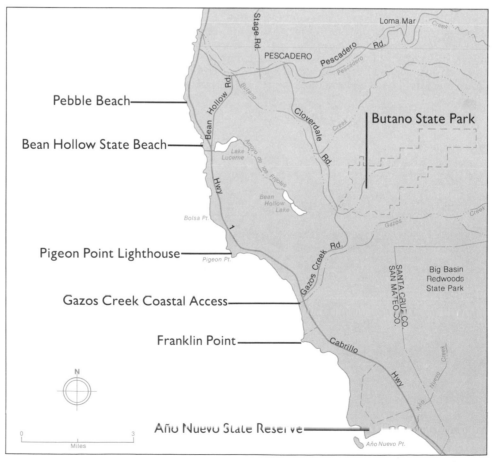

1920s. After numerous shipwrecks, a steam-operated fog signal with a 12-inch whistle was installed on the bluff in 1871. The 115-foot-high brick lighthouse was built the following year; its 9-foot Fresnel lens has 1,008 pieces of glass.

Tidepools are located north of the lighthouse along the rocky shoreline, where surf fishing is popular from sandy pocket beaches. Steller sea lions can be seen on offshore rocks. Located adjacent to the lighthouse is a 40-bed hostel. For information on the hostel and lighthouse tours, call: (415) 879-0633.

Northern elephant seal, Año Nuevo State Reserve

Gazos Creek Coastal Access: *Hwy. 1, N. of Gazos Creek Rd., Pescadero.*

The name Gazos is probably a corruption of the word Garzas, which means "heron," or "crane." Portolá camped near the mouth of Gazos Creek in 1769. The creek is stocked with rainbow trout during the summer fishing season; silver salmon and steelhead trout spawn upstream. A wheelchair-accessible path leads to the sandy beach, where surf fishing for rockfish and surfperch is popular. Facilities include parking and restrooms.

Franklin Point: *W. of Hwy. 1 between Gazos Creek and Año Nuevo State Reserve.*

The point got its name in 1865, when the clipper ship *Sir John Franklin* out of Baltimore smashed into the rocks. A trail leads out to the point through active dune fields where shorebirds such as snowy plovers overwinter. Tidepools are accessible along the rocky shoreline. The harbor porpoise is seen offshore between Franklin Point and Año Nuevo Point.

Año Nuevo State Reserve: *Hwy. 1, off New Years Creek Road.*

Punta del Año Nuevo, "New Years Point," was named by the chaplain of Spanish explorer Vizcaíno, who sighted it on January 3, 1603. At that time the region was occupied by Ohlone Indians whose first contact with Europeans didn't occur until 1769 when the Portolá Expedition explored the area. The Ohlone harvested fish and shellfish for food and trade.

Año Nuevo has had many owners including the famous mountain man Isaac Graham, Daniel Boone's cousin, who served as a model for the western frontiersman myth. In 1862 the Steele Brothers dairy empire was established and soon became famous throughout the west. Several historic structures remain, including the restored 1880s Flora Dickerman Steele dairy barn, now an interpretive center.

In 1872, a fog whistle was installed on Año Nuevo Island, and in 1890, a five-story light tower was added, replaced by an automated buoy in 1948. In 1958 Año Nuevo became a reserve, and today encompasses 1,200 acres of coastal bluffs, sandy beaches and dunes, and tidepools. Wheelchair-accessible restrooms and parking are available; no dogs allowed. Hiking permits may be obtained at the ranger station.

The reserve is open year-round; however, from December 1 to April 30 it is open to guided walking tours only, in order to protect the largest mainland population of northern elephant seals in the world. Año Nuevo is the only location where visitors can view large numbers of northern elephant seals close-up during their breeding season; for reservations, call after October 1: (415) 879-0227 or 879-0595.

California's largest population of Steller sea lions inhabits Año Nuevo Island; elephant seals and harbor seals also breed here. California sea lions are the largest visiting population to the reserve, but do not breed here.

Año Nuevo Island was part of the mainland as recently as 150 years ago; it has since been separated from the land by wave erosion and faulting. Textbook examples of complicated geologic relationships are preserved in the irregular patterns of several rock formations exposed in the sea cliffs along the shore. At Año Nuevo Point, thousands of tiny black polychaete worms build massive calcareous mounds that are among the largest found on California's coast.

The sand dunes at Año Nuevo are some of the few remaining active dunes on the California coast. Evidence of Indian occupation has been discovered here, including flint and chert chipped tools and kitchen midden deposits; these shell mounds stretch from the dunes of Año Nuevo Point north to Gazos Creek. Dune vegetation includes beach morning glory, European beach grass, yellow sand verbena, and beach strawberry, whose most abundant growth outside of Alaska occurs here.

The reserve is a nesting area for the California thrasher, western gull, common bushtit, cliff swallow, red-tailed hawk, California quail, and common flicker. Bird watching is popular during spring and fall migrations.

East of the reserve is a closed-cone pine forest that contains one of only four native stands of Monterey pine in the world. Coast redwood, Douglas-fir, coast live oak, knobcone pine, and wildflowers such as wild radish are also present. The Santa Cruz long-toed salamander and the San Francisco garter snake, both endangered species, inhabit the marsh area. Año Nuevo Creek, near the entrance to the reserve, supports red alder, California bay laurel, and coffeeberry, as well as numerous small herbs and perennial wildflowers.

Northern elephant seal, Año Nuevo State Reserve

181

Santa Cruz County
Selected Species of Interest

Plants: Silver-leaved manzanita (*Arctostaphylos silvicola*), endangered; endemic to Santa Cruz County; found in pine forest and chaparral. **Santa Cruz wallflower** (*Erysimum teretifolium*), endangered; occurs in Bonny Doon area.

Trees: Ponderosa pine (*Pinus ponderosa*), normally found inland; occurs along coast from Bonny Doon to Scotts Valley. **Santa Cruz cypress** (*Cupressus abramsiana*), endangered; endemic to Santa Cruz Mountains.

Insects: Monarch butterfly (*Danaus plexippus*), overwinters at several areas in the county; largest wintering population in U.S. at Natural Bridges State Beach. **Brine fly** (*Ephydra riparia*), swarms along shores of coastal lagoons.

Invertebrates: Pismo clam (*Tivela stultorum*); Santa Cruz County is northern extent of its range. **Giant green anemone** (*Anthopleura xanthogrammica*), common in tidepools; color comes from symbiotic green algae.

Amphibians and Reptiles: Santa Cruz long-toed salamander (*Ambystoma macrodactylum croceum*), endangered; endemic to Monterey Bay area. **California legless lizard** (*Anniella pulchra*), live-bearing lizard of south county dunes.

Fish: Leopard shark (*Triakis semifasciata*), important commercial and sport fish; abundant in bays and along sandy beaches. **Lingcod** (*Ophiodon elongatus*), found in nearshore waters along kelp beds and rocky reefs.

Birds: Marbled murrelet (*Brachyramphus marmoratus*), nests in redwoods in Big Basin Redwoods State Park. **Black swift** (*Cypseloides niger*), nests in cliffs at Big Basin and along West Cliff Drive in the city of Santa Cruz.

Land Mammals: Bobcat (*Lynx rufus*), found at Big Basin, at the Forest of Nisene Marks, and throughout the Santa Cruz Mountains. **Narrow-faced kangaroo rat** (*Dipodomys venustus*), endemic to Central California coast.

Marine Mammals: Southern sea otter (*Enhydra lutris nereis*), threatened; feeds and rests in offshore kelp beds. **Gray whale** (*Eschrichtius robustus*), endangered; seen offshore from Davenport bluffs during migration.

182

Santa Cruz County

SANTA CRUZ COUNTY, with its mild climate, miles of sandy beaches, acres of parklands, and bike route that extends the length of the county, is a popular tourist and recreation area. The county is located in one of the most geologically active regions in the world, the California Coast Ranges; These mountains are a physical boundary between the Pacific and North American plates. The plates move along active faults, causing earthquakes. In Santa Cruz County, the San Andreas fault system extends northwest and southeast, paralleling the coastline.

The Santa Cruz Mountains, forming the backbone of the county's northern coastal region, are relatively young and still rising; the mountain crests are composed of igneous and metamorphic rocks overlain by thick layers of sedimentary material uplifted from the ocean floor and ancient shoreline zone. There is a series of uplifted marine terraces, most apparent in the north county, indicating a continued uplift of the region and fluctuation of sea levels. Sheer cliffs with sandy pocket beaches form at the mouths of coastal streams. As the coastline stretches southward along the crescent-shaped Monterey Bay, wide, sandy beaches and dunes become more prominent.

In 1602, Monterey Bay was discovered and named by the Spanish explorer Sebastián Vizcaíno. At the time, the area was inhabited by the Ohlone Indians, also called Costanoans. These nomadic coast dwellers traveled in small numbers, and lived by hunting, fishing, and gathering seeds and acorns. The Ohlone population in the Santa Cruz area was estimated at nearly a thousand before the arrival of the Spanish.

The Spanish settlement of California, which began in 1769, altered the way of life for many Native Americans. In 1791, Father Fermín Francisco de Lasuén founded Misión la Exaltación de la Santa Cruz; Christian Indians from Santa Clara and the Ohlone from Santa Cruz were used as labor for construction of the mission. Villa de Branciforte, a small settlement established on the east bank of the San Lorenzo River in 1797, provided grain and manufactured goods for the mission and nearby presidios. Named in honor of the viceroy of Mexico, the Marquis de Branciforte, it was one of three pueblos established by the Spanish to prevent Russian advancement from Alaska. Branciforte was a separate community until 1907, when it became part of the City of Santa Cruz.

The growth of Santa Cruz following the Spanish and Mexican occupation stimulated the development of industry. Because of the area's natural resources and close proximity to San Francisco, Santa Cruz became a major shipping center and primary supplier of lumber, lime, leather goods, grain, potatoes, and whaling products.

The development of railroad lines from San Francisco and surrounding areas in the late 1800s made the City of Santa Cruz more accessible to tourists. Following the construction of the casino and boardwalk complex in 1904, the beach front area became a popular resort. By the 1920s, with the increased use of the automobile, the improvement of the highway from the San Jose area, and new amusements at the beach and boardwalk, tourism had become one of Santa Cruz's major industries.

The development of the City of Santa Cruz can be traced through its architecturally significant buildings. In the 1700s, Santa Cruz was a small-farm community with commercial centers expanding outward from the mission site. Buildings were made from adobe and designed to resemble the late baroque architecture common in Mexico and Spain. The 1840s were the beginning of "Yankee" dominance in Santa Cruz; new industries and, later, a prosperous Gold Rush economy stimulated growth. As building materials and skills improved, architectural design gradually changed from the simple Pioneer style to the more elegant and decorative Greek Revival, Italianate, and Gothic Revival styles.

In the 1890s, the tourist industry was an integral part of the city's economy. Residential areas reflected this new prosperity; building designs were more elaborate and ornamental features such as building façades, chimneys, and bay windows were common. The shingle, Queen Anne, Eastlake, and Colonial Revival styles are examples of these designs.

During the 1930s, many chicken and flower farms within the city were sold for residential development. New architectural designs emerged, creating a style unique to California. Arches, tiled roofs, plastered walls, and balconies were common features of the adapted Mission Revival style. The California bungalow style was characterized by a rustic exterior, often stained rather than painted. Today, the unique character of Santa Cruz County has been preserved in its variety of architectural styles.

Santa Cruz Beach Casino, ca. 1912

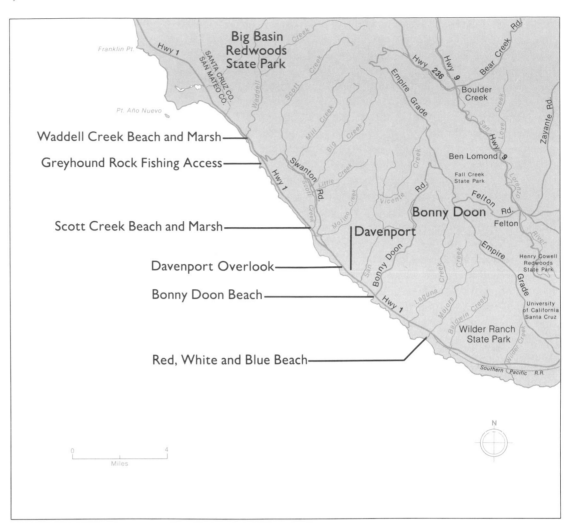

Waddell Creek Beach and Marsh

Greyhound Rock Fishing Access

Scott Creek Beach and Marsh

Davenport Overlook

Bonny Doon Beach

Red, White and Blue Beach

Big Basin, ca. 1900

Waddell Creek Beach and Marsh: *Hwy. 1, 1 mi. S. of San Mateo County line.*

In 1769, Portolá camped at Waddell Creek, naming it Cañada de la Salud (Canyon of Health), where the expedition rested and the sick recovered. Waddell Creek Beach, now a unit of Big Basin Redwoods State Park, was named after William Waddell, who built a sawmill along the creek in the 1860s. Gulls, waterfowl, and shorebirds such as the marbled godwit, willet, and sanderling overwinter at the sandy beach and dune area. The beach marks the terminus of the scenic Skyline-to-the-Sea Trail, which begins inland at Castle Rock State Park and continues through Big Basin to the coast. The park is also a popular windsurfing and hang gliding spot.

Waddell Creek Marsh, an extensive wetland on the inland side of Highway 1, lies within the Theodore J. Hoover Natural Preserve and provides habitat for many water birds, including avocets, stilts, herons, and egrets. Silver salmon and steelhead trout can be found seasonally in Waddell Creek. There is a harbor seal rookery south of the beach.

Big Basin Redwoods State Park: *14 mi. N. of Santa Cruz on Hwy. 9, 7 mi. N.W. on access road.*

Located in the Santa Cruz Mountains, this 14,000-acre park, created in 1902 to preserve the virgin redwood stands, is the oldest park in the California State Park System. It contains over 40 miles of hiking trails, numerous waterfalls, and a variety of wildlife, including deer, bobcats, raccoons, skunks, squirrels, Steller's jays, and California woodpeckers. Big Basin also provides nesting habitat for the black swift and the marbled murrelet. The coast redwood, Douglas-fir, huckleberry, western azalea, and salal grow in the canyon areas. The mixed-evergreen forest includes madrone, wax myrtle, California nutmeg, and several species of oak; knobcone pine also grows within the park.

The Nature Lodge Museum at Park Headquarters off Highway 236 houses historical and natural science exhibits. Park facilities include parking, restrooms, a grocery store, and a campground. Call: (408) 338-6132.

Greyhound Rock Fishing Access: *W. of Hwy. 1 at Swanton Rd., 3 mi. S. of San Mateo County line.*

This popular rock fishing spot is named for the shape of the large rock extending into the water. Giant kelp grows offshore. Parking is available on the bluff; a trail leads to the beach.

Scott Creek Beach and Marsh: *Hwy. 1, 6 mi. S. of San Mateo line.*

Named for the successful gold miner Hiram Scott, Scott Creek Beach is a sandy beach with dunes, tidepools, and a lagoon. North of the creek is an intertidal reef with such flora and fauna as sea anemones, chitons, sea urchins, surfgrass, and kelp. The large freshwater marsh inland of Highway 1 supports overwintering shorebirds, ducks, and grebes; the adjacent riparian community contains willows, tules, and cattails. Silver salmon, steelhead, and Pacific lamprey are found in the creek. Parking is limited to the highway shoulder.

Davenport Overlook: *W. of Hwy. 1 and the R.R. tracks, 8 mi. S. of San Mateo County line.*

A promontory overlooking the ocean, Davenport Overlook provides an excellent vantage point for watching the migration of California gray whales. The area is vegetated with grasses and mature cypress trees; sheer cliffs drop to the sea. To the north, remnants of the old steel pier built in 1934 by the Santa Cruz Portland Cement Company provide a nesting and roosting area for cormorants.

Davenport: *E. of Hwy. 1, 8 mi. S. of San Mateo County line.*

Davenport is a historic whaling community, originally founded around 1870 in a cove a mile and a half north of its present site. John P. Davenport built a wharf in the 1880s as a shipping point for lime, whaling, and lumber products. The present town site was developed in 1906 when the Santa Cruz Portland Cement Company began operation. Two of Davenport's historically significant buildings are still standing and in good condition: the old jail, built in 1914, and the St. Vincent de Paul Catholic Church, built in 1915 and still in use.

Bonny Doon Beach: *Hwy. 1 and Bonny Doon Rd., 12 mi. N. of Santa Cruz.*

There is an unpaved parking area off Highway 1 below the railroad tracks. The sandy beach and dunes are in a sheltered cove beneath the bluff. Giant kelp, rockfish, and lingcod are found offshore.

Bonny Doon: *Between Bonny Doon Rd. and Empire Grade, 10 mi. N.W. of Santa Cruz.*

In the 1870s limestone quarries operated on the road between Bonny Doon and the coast. The Bonny Doon area contains several endangered species, including the Santa Cruz wallflower and silver-leaved manzanita. Some of the only ponderosa pines found near the coast in Santa Cruz occur in Bonny Doon; the narrow-faced kangaroo rat, unique to the Central California coast, also lives here.

Red, White and Blue Beach: *5021 Hwy. 1, off Scaroni Rd., 5.5 mi. N. of Santa Cruz.*

Turn off Highway 1 at the red, white, and blue mailbox to get to this private, clothing optional beach. The beach is located at the mouth of Majors Creek, where gulls and shorebirds can be found resting and feeding. Parking, restrooms, and camping are available.

Scott Creek Beach

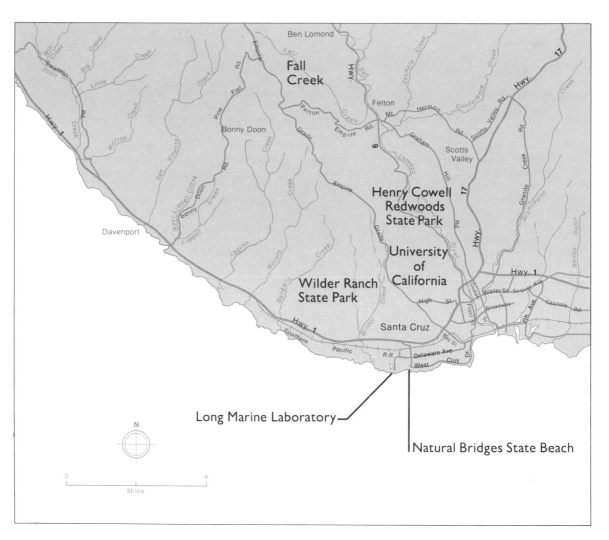

Long Marine Laboratory

Natural Bridges State Beach

N

0   4
Miles

Wilder Ranch State Park: *Both sides of Hwy. 1, 4.5 mi. N.W. of Santa Cruz.*

This new state park, not yet open to the public, includes more than 4,000 acres of extensive uplands, coastal terraces, streams, beaches, and offshore submerged lands. Vegetation ranges from chaparral along the ridgetops to coastal redwood forest and mixed-evergreen forest in the canyon areas, riparian forest along the streams, saltwater marsh near the creek mouths, and freshwater marsh along creeks and reservoirs. Wilder Beach contains the best preserved coastal strand vegetation in the northcoast area of the county. Wildlife such as coyotes, foxes, salamanders, and squirrels are found here. Currently, the only public access is at Four Mile Beach, located off Highway 1, four miles northwest of Santa Cruz. Call: (408) 688-3241.

Fall Creek: *Felton and Hwy. 9, 5 mi. N. of Santa Cruz.*

Located on Ben Lomond Mountain, the Fall Creek unit of Henry Cowell Redwoods State Park contains 2,335 acres. The park, given to the state by the Samuel H. Cowell Foundation in 1972, includes nearly the entire drainage of both forks of Fall Creek. Douglas-fir and second-growth redwood dominate the canyons; tanbark oak, live oak, and madrone are also abundant. A lush growth of ferns and other shade-loving plants such as big-leaf maple and red alder occur along the creek banks, where slime molds and liverworts also grow. Silver salmon and steelhead trout spawn in the creek.

Remnants of old wagon and logging roads that once led to a limestone kiln and a barrel mill are now used for park trails; in the 1870s the IXL Company produced 30% of the lime used in California. At the turn of the century, Henry Cowell took over the operation, which produced much of the lime for the bricks and cement used in rebuilding San Francisco after the 1906 earthquake. Cowell built a water-powered mill in 1912, used to make redwood barrels for storing and shipping the lime. The area was logged for the wood to build these containers and to fire the limekilns. In 1919, the kilns were shut down and in 1925 the barrel mill closed.

Henry Cowell Redwoods State Park: *Hwy. 9, 3 mi. N. of Santa Cruz.*

In the 1860s, Joseph Warren Welch and Henry Cowell Sr. bought property of the Rancho Cañada del Rincón, an original Mexican land grant of 1843. Both men shared similar views on protecting the coast redwood trees.

Redwood Grove, originally called the Big Trees Grove, was sold by Welch along with another 80 acres to Santa Cruz County in 1930 for a local park. In 1954, this land was combined with more than 1,500 acres given to the state by Cowell's son, Samuel.

Now the park comprises 4,000 acres and includes coast redwoods, purple needlegrass, manzanita, Douglas-fir, madrone, tanbark oak, and ponderosa pine, which usually grows farther inland. Facilities include over 15 miles of hiking trails, campgrounds, and a day use area. Call: (408) 335-9106. The San Lorenzo River, which crosses the park, provides a popular spot for both swimmers and fishermen; steelhead trout and silver salmon spawn in the river.

University of California, Santa Cruz: *Bay Dr. and High St., Santa Cruz.*

In 1849, Albion Jordan and Isaac Davis began producing lime from quarries located on what is now the U.C. Santa Cruz campus; the lime was used to manufacture bricks which supplied the San Francisco area with a new building material. These land holdings were purchased in 1865 and 1888 by Henry Cowell, who developed a lime and cement company and a cattle ranch on the site.

In 1961, a 2,000-acre parcel of the Cowell Ranch was acquired by the University of California Regents for construction of a unique campus. To preserve its natural and historical elements, the campus buildings were clustered and architectural features were designed to blend with the natural environment. Historic structures including the ranch house, the first quarry, limekilns, and a horse barn have been restored to maintain the character of the area.

The campus lands support a variety of vegetation, including redwood forest, mixed-evergreen forest, ponderosa pine, chaparral, and grassland, which provide habitats for such wildlife species as jays, squirrels, California quail, red-tailed hawks, black-tailed deer, coyotes, bobcats, western fence lizards, gopher snakes, and brush rabbits. Salamanders, newts, broadhanded moles, and various owl species are also present but seldom seen.

Long Marine Laboratory: *End of Delaware St., western edge of the City of Santa Cruz.*

This 40-acre site, donated by Marion and Donald Younger to the University in 1974, includes a beach, wetlands, and a marine terrace. The Joseph M. Long Marine Laboratory was opened in 1978 and provides year-round facilities for faculty, researchers, and students. The Marine Aquarium is open to the public for docent tours 1-4 PM Tuesday-Sunday. Younger Lagoon, which is closed to the public due to the sensitive ecology of the area, supports a wide variety of birds and coastal plant communities.

Whale vertebrae, Long Marine Laboratory

Natural Bridges State Beach: *2531 W. Cliff Dr., Santa Cruz.*

This large pocket beach is named for its natural sandstone bridges; today, only one of the bridges remains. The rocky intertidal region adjacent to the beach is a rich habitat for tidepool animals such as sea anemones, chitons, limpets, sea urchins, sea stars, barnacles, and California mussels. Endangered California brown pelicans, cormorants, snowy plovers, and gulls frequent the sandy beach area.

A eucalyptus grove in the center of the park, accessible by trail, is the largest Monarch butterfly overwintering site in the United States; the butterflies can be seen here from September through December. Natural Bridges is the only state park with an interpretive program about Monarch butterflies.

A self-guided ¾-mile nature walk begins at the Monarch trail. The Secret Lagoon, dependent on winter rains, attracts a variety of birds ranging from great blue herons to red-winged blackbirds; mallard ducks can be seen swimming through duckweed, a tiny freshwater flowering plant. Coyote brush and rattlesnake grass are found in drier, more exposed areas. A grove of Monterey pines marks the end of the trail. Park facilities include parking and wheelchair-accessible restrooms. Guided tidepool tours are provided during most of the year. For information, call: (408) 423-4609.

La Feliz, aground off Natural Bridges State Beach, 1924

City of Santa Cruz: *W. of Capitola.*

Seventy-five miles south of San Francisco, overlooking Monterey Bay, is the seaside city of Santa Cruz. In 1769, the Portolá party planted a cross on the bank of the San Lorenzo River, establishing the site for the city. Twenty-two years later, Father Fermín Francisco de Lasuén dedicated the same site for a mission, Misión la Exaltación de la Santa Cruz (the exaltation of the Holy Cross).

The mission plaza soon become the site for the first businesses. Farming and commercial centers thrived, supported by shipments of food crops, cattle hides, and bags of tallow to whaling crews and merchants. In 1846, with the beginning of the Yankee dominance, new residents brought skills producing a variety of new industries such as lumber, lime, gun powder, and leather goods.

Today, the city serves as an attractive tourist spot, providing an amusement park, miles of sandy beaches, and the Pacific Garden Mall, a popular shopping area.

Lighthouse Field State Beach: *Along W. Cliff Dr., at Point Santa Cruz.*

This 36-acre park is located on a coastal terrace, with small pocket beaches at the base of 30-40 foot bluffs. Planned facilities include nature observation areas, interpretive trails, picnic sites, restrooms, parking, and beach access stairways.

Lighthouse Field is historically important because of a successful citizen opposition to a proposed convention center on the property, which was the city's last major oceanfront open space. The property was eventually purchased by the state for use as a park.

The original lighthouse at Point Santa Cruz was constructed in 1869 by the U.S. Government and was removed in 1948. The present lighthouse was built in 1965 by Chuck and Esther Abbott in memory of their son Mark, who died in a surfing accident, and is "dedicated to all youth whose ideals are beacons to the future." The Santa Cruz Surfing Museum is housed within the lighthouse; call: (408) 429-3773. Steamer Lane, one of the most famous surfing spots on the coast, is just offshore of the point. The point, which is the headland to Monterey Bay, provides a good spot for viewing sea otters, endangered California brown pelicans, and several species of whales. The black swift, which nests in only 14 sites in the state, and the Monarch butterfly are also found here.

Neary's Lagoon City Park: *Off California St., N. of Bay St., Santa Cruz.*

Neary's Lagoon is a freshwater marsh located near the center of town. Prior to human disturbance, the lagoon and marshlands covered approximately 45 acres. In 1876, James and Martin Neary purchased the property and converted portions of the lagoon into farmlands; draining and filling of the lagoon's outlet provided additional land for development of railroad tracks, streets, and a sewer plant.

The lagoon, one of the last sizable open and undeveloped portions of land within the city, attracts wildlife such as herons, coots, willets, and mallards and supports freshwater marsh and stream vegetation such as bulrush, cattail, willow, and red alder.

Park facilities include a wildlife sanctuary, a floating platform for wildlife viewing, restrooms, tennis courts, and a parking lot.

Cowell Beach: *W. Cliff Dr. and Bay St., Santa Cruz.*

Once owned by Henry Cowell, one of the state's wealthiest men, the beach was sold to the City of Santa Cruz in 1954. It is now a popular site for volleyball games and other beach activities. Gulls and common shorebirds such as sanderlings and willets use the beach for feeding.

Santa Cruz Municipal Wharf: *End of Washington St. and Beach St., Santa Cruz.*

The present wharf, constructed in 1913, is the fifth and longest of the wharves built in Santa Cruz. The first wharf, built in 1853 by the Renfield Brothers, was located at the foot of Bay St. and was used to ship and receive goods; later wharves were used by the lumber and fishing industries. Until around 1960, the primary use of the present wharf was for commercial fishing. The wharf is now a tourist attraction with its many restaurants and shops.

The fishing pier at the end of the wharf attracts many fishermen, who catch flounder, bonita, blue shark, lingcod, halibut, and crab. Sea lions haul out on the timbers below the wharf.

Santa Cruz Surfing Club, 1941

Santa Cruz Beach and Boardwalk: *E. of Municipal Wharf, Santa Cruz.*

In the late 1860s, the development of summer cottages, hotels, and bathhouses made Santa Cruz Beach a popular tourist spot; today, the sandy, mile-long beach continues to be popular for swimming. Gulls, sandpipers, sanderlings, willets, and other shorebirds use the beach for resting and feeding. Steller and California sea lions swim and feed offshore.

In 1904, Santa Cruz Beach was the site of a casino and boardwalk designed by Fred Swanton to resemble those at Coney Island. A fire destroyed the original casino in 1906, but one year later a new casino building, an indoor swimming pool, a pleasure pier, and a boardwalk were constructed. The boardwalk, one of the first amusement parks erected on a beach, offers rides, arcades, snack bars, restaurants, and gift shops. Call: (408) 423-5590.

Santa Cruz Mission: *Emmet St. and High St., Santa Cruz.*

In 1791, Father Fermín Francisco de Lasuén founded the mission at the lower end of the San Lorenzo Valley. To protect against flooding, the mission was relocated in 1793 to a mesa above the San Lorenzo River. The new church was built from native stone and adobe, with other buildings added as needed, forming an open square. The mission church and priest's quarters were sited on what is now High Street. The mission guard headquarters, on the other side of School St., is the oldest building in the City of Santa Cruz. Known today as the Neary-Hopcroft house, it became a State Historical Monument in 1959.

The earthquake of 1857 caused the mission to collapse; in 1931 a replica was built on Emmet St. identical in proportions, but only half the size of the original structure. The mission site is now a State Historical Landmark.

The mission chapel is open daily from 9 AM-5 PM. A donation is requested. The mission gift shop, including a display of vestments and books, is open daily from 2:30-5 PM.

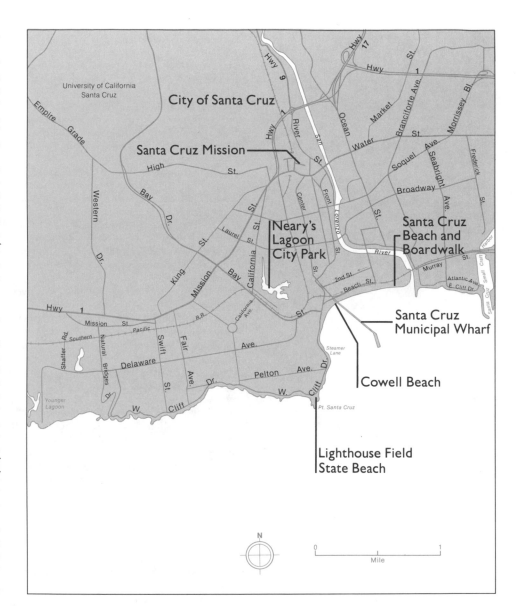

Pelicans, Santa Cruz Municipal Wharf, ca. 1940

San Lorenzo River: *City of Santa Cruz.*

The San Lorenzo River originates 22 miles inland from the coast. The upper watershed is dominated by redwood and fir forests, while nearer the coast the dominant plant species include sycamore, willow, cottonwood, box elder, and poplar trees. The willow thickets are important foraging areas for migratory warblers and other songbirds, as well as for leaf-feeding insects.

Within the city boundaries of Santa Cruz, the river is dredged periodically to serve as a flood-control channel. The open water and sandflats characteristic of the lower river provide feeding and resting areas for resident and migratory birds such as gulls, terns, plovers, and sanderlings. The river supports the largest steelhead trout and silver salmon runs south of San Francisco Bay.

In the summer of 1895 and 1896, the river delta was the site of the Venetian Water Carnival; the mouth of the river was dammed to create a lagoon for the display of floats. The river continues to be used for fishing, hiking, and biking along the shore.

Seabright Beach: *E. Cliff Dr. off Murray St., Santa Cruz.*

Seabright Beach is also called Castle Beach; until the 1950s, the Scholl Mar Hotel, a beach resort designed to resemble a castle, was located adjacent to San Lorenzo Point. Gulls and shorebirds such as sandpipers and sanderlings feed and rest on the beach. At dusk, the black-crowned night heron, a wading bird, can sometimes be seen feeding near shore.

Santa Cruz City Museum: *1305 E. Cliff Dr., Santa Cruz.*

After William Tyrell died in 1913, his house and property in Seabright were deeded to the City of Santa Cruz for a park and museum. In 1954, the old Tyrell house was demolished and the museum collections were relocated to the present museum site, originally the Seabright Branch Library. Exhibits include displays of Native Americans of Central California; natural history of local fossils, plants, and animals; and a touch tidepool tank.

A spring Wildflower Show takes place in April, and a winter Fungus Fair in December.

Tours are by appointment 9 AM-5 PM Tuesday-Friday; call: (408) 429-3773.

Santa Cruz Small Craft Harbor: *Eaton St. at Lake Ave., Santa Cruz.*

In 1958, Woods Lagoon was dredged and reshaped to form a harbor; two years later, because of high demand for additional berthing, the harbor was expanded into Arana Gulch.

Inland and adjacent to Arana Gulch is Arana Marsh; dominant plant species in the marsh include pickleweed, bulrush, and cattail, while south near the harbor entrance eucalyptus, pine, and cypress trees are found. Shorebirds, such as plovers, sandpipers, turnstones, and terns, and waterfowl, including mallards and coots, frequent the site for food and rest.

The harbor provides areas for boat launching, berthing, and boat repair; there is a pedestrian/bike path around the perimeter. Call: (408) 475-6161.

Twin Lakes State Beach: *7th Ave. at E. Cliff Dr., Santa Cruz.*

In the late 1880s, Twin Lakes was developed as a Baptist summer resort. In the 1890s, a hotel was built and the surrounding area was used for camping. Prior to the development of the Santa Cruz Small Craft Harbor, Woods Lagoon and Schwan Lake formed the Twin Lakes complex.

The beach provides valuable resting and feeding habitats for many water-associated birds including gulls, terns, sandpipers, and plovers. Facilities include a picnic area, restrooms, and volleyball nets. There is fishing from the harbor jetty. Call: (408) 688-3241.

Schwan Lake: *E. Cliff Dr. and 9th Ave., Live Oak.*

Schwan Lake was named after the pioneer Jacob Schwan and his family. Once a mixed saltwater/freshwater lagoon, Schwan Lake is now a freshwater lake bounded by a marsh. Saltwater exchange is controlled by a tide gate at East Cliff Drive. The diverse plant communities in and around the lake include a marsh community of tules, cattails, and willows, with numerous exotics such as eucalyptus in the upper portions of the marsh; saltbush, yerba reuma, bulrush, and saltgrass at the southern end of the lake; sea fig along the eastern shore; and a dense shrub and oak woodland community con-

Sardine fishing boats, Santa Cruz, 1939

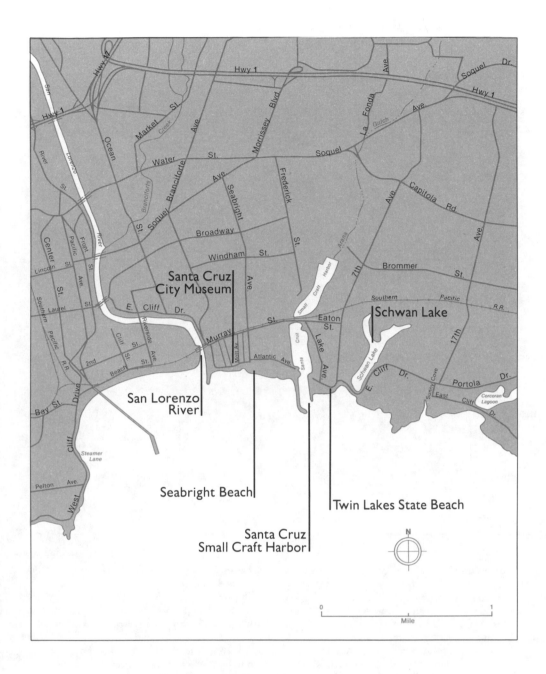

Santa Cruz City Museum

Schwan Lake

San Lorenzo River

Seabright Beach

Twin Lakes State Beach

Santa Cruz Small Craft Harbor

taining coast live oak, poison oak, and dwarf coyote brush farther north along the shore.

This high diversity of habitats permits a correspondingly high diversity of bird and wildlife species. Tremendous numbers of waterfowl use the lake for feeding and resting, especially during migration. Schwan Lake's freshwater marshes are particularly important to gulls, who need fresh water for preening and drinking, and to the Virginia rail and sora rail for nesting and feeding. In the oak woodland community the scrub jay, chestnut-backed chickadee, and brown towhee are found. Six species of swallow use the lake as an insect hunting area, while belted kingfishers hunt for fish in the lake. The drainages into the lake, with their willow thickets and dense vegetation, provide an important habitat for many migratory species, particularly warblers and flycatchers. The various habitats also support many species of mammals, amphibians, and reptiles.

Schwan Lake, which has a birdwatching platform, is also used for canoeing and kayaking. The small sandy beach south of E. Cliff Drive is part of Twin Lakes State Beach.

western gull (*Larus occidentalis*)
24 to 27 inches long

191

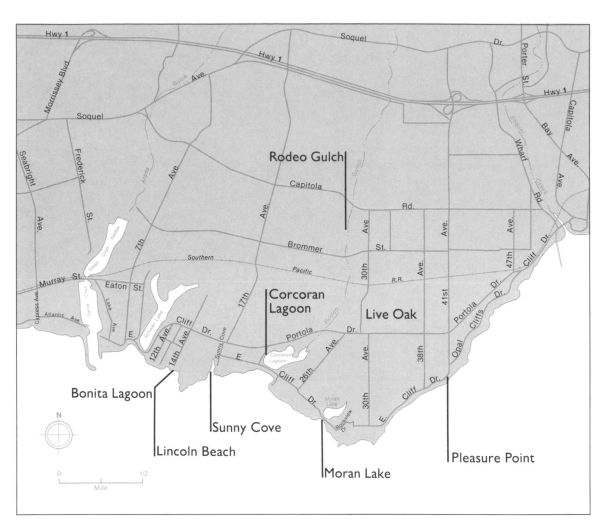

Bonita Lagoon: *S.W. of E. Cliff Dr., between 14th and 16th Avenues, Live Oak.*

Bonita Lagoon is a small freshwater lagoon that receives its water through a culvert at the north end; coastal strand vegetation such as sea fig and sea rocket is found at the south end. Other vegetation surrounding the lagoon includes red willow, curly dock, poison oak, pampas grass, and Spanish thistle. Due to the sparse vegetation along the shoreline, wildlife is limited to mallards and coots year-round and migrating birds in fall.

Lincoln Beach: *S.W. of E. Cliff Dr., between 14th and 16th Avenues, Live Oak.*

A privately owned sandy beach seaward of Bonita Lagoon, Lincoln Beach is managed as a unit of Twin Lakes State Beach and is accessible to pedestrians via the end of 14th Ave. or by a stairway at the end of 12th Avenue. There is very limited on-street parking along 14th Ave. and there are pit toilets at the beach.

Sunny Cove: *End of Sunny Cove Dr., Live Oak.*

Sunny Cove is a privately owned pocket beach without facilities, accessible via Sunny Cove Dr. or Johann's Beach Dr.; the extent of public and private rights is undetermined and subject to further investigation.

Some rocky intertidal habitats occur in the vicinity of Black Point just east, between 17th Ave. and 20th Ave., where a wide variety of biota may be found, including algae, sea anemones, snails, mussels, shore crabs, and shorebirds such as oystercatchers, turnstones, and plovers.

Corcoran Lagoon: *Off E. Cliff Dr., E. of 21st Ave., Live Oak.*

Named after the Corcoran family, early settlers in the Live Oak area, this coastal lagoon receives periodic saltwater influx and freshwater inflow. The lagoon extends under East Cliff Dr. toward the beach and is sometimes connected to a small pond to the east.

Beach sagewort, sea fig, and sea rocket grow near the sandy beach, while abundant pickleweed, yerba reuma, saltgrass, and jaumea oc-

Moran Lake

Pleasure Point Overlook

cur along the shoreline and around the pond. Farther away from shore, shrubby plants such as dwarf coyote brush, poison oak, and California blackberry predominate. The lagoon itself, with its constantly changing salt concentrations, supports such organisms as phytoplankton, copepods, mussels, and water boatmen. Western pond turtles, tidewater gobies, and the threespine stickleback also inhabit the lagoon.

Numerous species of waterfowl and shorebirds, including the pied-billed grebe, greenbacked heron, mallard, and bufflehead, a small diving duck, use the lagoon as a feeding and resting area, mostly in winter. Such mammals as the opossum, muskrat, and Norway rat are also found here.

There is no parking at the lagoon, but there is a pedestrian walkway leading from East Cliff Dr. to a sandy ocean beach.

Rodeo Gulch: *N. of Corcoran Lagoon, Live Oak.*

Historically, Rodeo Gulch was a typical Central California freshwater stream and watershed emptying directly into Corcoran Lagoon, but development in the area has reduced its size and types of vegetation. Habitats range from riparian vegetation such as horsetail and bracken in the creek bed to oak woodland-grassland communities including coast live oak and coyote brush along the border and, where it is moister, redwood communities including redwood sorrel and coast redwood. The strip along the western side of the gulch is one of the largest of the remaining oak woodland sites in the Live Oak area. The riparian corridor ends abruptly at Portola Dr. where saltwater influence from Corcoran Lagoon creates a small marsh habitat comprised of bulrush.

Common wildlife species living in the area include the Pacific treefrog, southern alligator lizard, gopher snake, fox squirrel, brown towhee, house finch, and deer mouse.

Moran Lake: *E. Cliff Dr., W. of Lake Dr., Live Oak.*

Due to landfill, storm runoff, sewage dumping, and inadequate tidal flushing, Moran Lake was severely degraded and lacking in vegetation and wildlife species prior to 1981. During recent restoration, the entire lake was dredged, a new tide gate built, and the area revegetated in an effort to return the lake to a functioning coastal wetland.

Salt marsh vegetation includes pickleweed and saltgrass, while the area surrounding the lagoon supports various grasses, sea fig, and eucalyptus. Waterbirds such as ducks, coots, and sandpipers use the lagoon; mourning doves, Anna's hummingbirds, black phoebes, and song sparrows are also found here. Monarch butterflies winter in some of the eucalyptus trees surrounding the lake.

New facilities include parking, wheelchair-accessible restrooms, a bike path, and a nature trail. There is a wide, sandy beach across East Cliff Dr. to the south.

Live Oak: *S. of Hwy. 1, between Santa Cruz and Capitola.*

Live Oak gets its name from the once predominant coast live oak; non-native eucalyptus has since replaced the oak woodland in many areas. Now primarily residential, Live Oak has a varied history. In 1769 the Portolá land expedition passed through the Live Oak area while trying to find Monterey Bay. Following the establishment of the Villa de Branciforte near the San Lorenzo River in 1797, the Live Oak area was used mostly for cattle grazing. Over the years, lumbering and agriculture became major industries, while residential and resort growth occurred near the coast. In the early part of the 20th century, the Live Oak area became the freesia (a fragrant flower) capital of the world. Many other small industries also flourished, such as farms, dairies, apple-drying, and chick-en ranching; what is now 41st Ave. was then called "Chicken Alley" because of the large number of chicken coops found there.

Pleasure Point: *S. of E. Cliff Dr., between 32nd and 41st Avenues, Live Oak.*

Steep coastal bluffs along East Cliff Dr. provide sweeping vistas of Monterey Bay; sea otters can be seen rafting in the kelp beds offshore. Pleasure Point is a popular spot for surfing, skin diving, rock fishing, and clam digging; rock crab and red abalone are also found here. There is parking and a scenic overlook at East Cliff Dr. and 41st Ave., and a stairway down the bluff to a pocket beach with tidepools at 35th Avenue.

The overlook at the foot of Rockview Dr. to the west of Pleasure Point has suffered severe storm damage and there is no longer a parking area or stairway to the beach; harbor seals are found offshore.

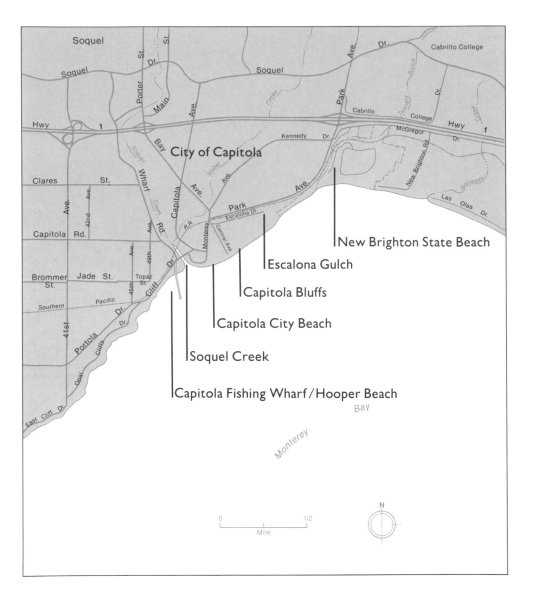

New Brighton State Beach

Escalona Gulch

Capitola Bluffs

Capitola City Beach

Soquel Creek

Capitola Fishing Wharf / Hooper Beach

The Venetian Court, Capitola

City of Capitola: *S. of Hwy. 1, 3 mi. E. of Santa Cruz.*

Said to be the oldest seaside resort on the Pacific Coast, Capitola was founded in 1869 by a local lumberman named F. A. Hihn and was incorporated in 1950 with a population of 1,848. Previously, the site was occupied by Ohlone Indians, then became part of two Mexican land grants; later, Soquel Landing at the mouth of Soquel Creek was used for shipping lumber and ranch products. Hihn named the resort "Camp Capitola" hoping to convince the State Legislature to move from hot and dusty Sacramento to the coast.

Capitola Village, with its shops, restaurants, galleries, and distinctive character, is a popular visitor destination. The Venetian Court, which fronts on Capitola Beach, is one of California's earliest condominium-type subdivisions. With its 1920s-style pastel stucco construction, tiled roofs, and ornate decorations, the Venetian Court is a unique architectural site. Other historic sites near the coast include the "Six Sisters," six Victorian houses built in a row along the Esplanade behind Capitola Beach, and the old railroad depot at the corner of Monterey Ave. and Escalona Dr., now a private home; a small city park with benches is located in front of the site.

An annual event in Capitola is the Begonia Festival each September featuring boat races, aquatic shows, and a parade of begonia-covered floats on Soquel Creek.

Capitola Fishing Wharf: *Foot of Wharf Rd., Capitola.*

In 1856, the first Capitola wharf was built as a commercial pier in Soquel Cove, just west of the mouth of Soquel Creek; lumber and farm products from the Soquel Valley were loaded onto ships and sent to San Francisco. Once railroad service began from Watsonville to Santa Cruz, commercial use of the wharf dropped off. Through the years, the wharf has been used to launch fishing boats, store boat trailers, and store and dispense rental boats.

In 1962 a bait and tackle shop, outboard motor repair facility, and snack counter were in operation, and between 1967 and 1968 two party boats operated from the pier. Storm damage closed the pier in 1978, but it has since been restored and is now used for sport fishing; facilities include restrooms, a view deck, a restaurant, and a bait and tackle shop. For fishing and weather reports, call the bait and tackle shop: (408) 462-2208.

Hooper Beach: *Foot of Wharf Rd., Capitola.*

Hooper Beach is a privately owned sandy beach west of the wharf, leased to the City of Capitola. Access is either via the end of Wharf Rd. or from a wooden stairway on the pier.

Soquel Creek: *E. of Wharf Rd., Capitola.*

Soquel Creek is a perennial stream rich in riparian flora; the woodland along the east bank of the creek is the best example of a riparian corridor in an urban setting in Santa Cruz County. The creek supports an important steelhead run and provides habitat for a diverse group of wildlife species such as the Pacific treefrog, western toad, brown towhee, barn owl, California mouse, dusky-footed woodrat, and the opossum.

Common vegetation found near the lower section of the creek includes arroyo willow, black cottonwood, big-leaf maple, red willow, yellow willow, coast redwood, California blackberry, Himalaya berry, periwinkle, and poison oak. In the stream bed common plants include Spanish clover, curly dock, and bracken fern.

The mouth of the creek forms a lagoon; in the late 1800s and early 1900s a small boat rental business operated near the Stockton Avenue bridge. The lagoon is winter habitat for mallards, grebes, coots, and gulls. Farther upstream, east of the intersection of Wharf Rd. and Clare St. on the steep west side of the creek, there is a Monarch butterfly grove; Monterey pines, redwoods, and acacia are interspersed among the eucalyptus trees within the grove.

Soquel, located in a valley on Soquel Creek just inland, was once a booming lumber town and is now a residential community. In 1769, Portolá marched toward Soquel Creek and saw "low hills well forested with high trees of a red color, not known to us . . . because none of the expedition recognizes them, they are named redwoods from their color."

Capitola City Beach: *S. of the Esplanade and Monterey Ave., Capitola.*

A popular sandy beach at the mouth of Soquel Creek, located east of the wharf. A groin at the east end of the beach traps sand drifting downcoast and has helped re-establish the sand supply depleted during the late 1960s, probably due to the construction of the Santa Cruz Harbor jetty. Giant kelp grows offshore.

Capitola Bluffs: *Between Capitola Beach and New Brighton State Beach, Capitola.*

Located below Depot Hill, this section of eroding bluffs contains an important paleontological resource; large numbers of prehistoric shells are embedded in the layers of rock and can be seen at low tide.

Escalona Gulch: *Off Escalona Dr., between Southern Pacific R.R. tracks and the ocean.*

Escalona Gulch is heavily forested with eucalyptus trees and some Monterey pines and cypresses; poison oak is also prevalent. The area is an overwintering site for Monarch butterflies. A footpath runs from the end of Escalona Dr. down through Escalona Gulch and up to Grove Lane on the east side of the gulch.

New Brighton State Beach: *1500 Park Ave., off Hwy. 1, 4 mi. S. of Santa Cruz.*

The park provides day use parking, wheelchair-accessible restrooms, interpretive nature trails, beach access, and a campground on the bluffs; there are interpretive programs in summer. The upland area is heavily forested with Monterey pines, and a small community of coastal strand plants is found at the base of the bluffs. Many species of birds, and wildlife such as raccoons, opossum, and deer, inhabit the park. The park also contains an overwintering site for Monarch butterflies, located between New Brighton Rd. and the park campground. There is fishing for California halibut offshore. Call: (408) 475-4850.

Capitola Fishing Wharf, ca. 1942

Concrete ship Palo Alto *at Seacliff State Beach*

Forest of Nisene Marks State Park: *Off So-quel Dr., 4 mi. N. on Aptos Creek Rd.*

Covering nearly 10,000 acres, the Forest of Nisene Marks is one of the largest state parks in Central California. Previously owned and extensively logged by the Loma Prieta Lumber Company during the 40-year lumber boom (1883-1923), the property was sold in the 1950s to the Marks family, a prominent Salinas Valley farming family. In 1963 the three Marks children donated the land to the State of California in memory of their mother, Nisene. As specified in the deed, the park is managed as a semi-wilderness.

The roads within the park are unpaved and facilities are limited to picnic areas, pit toilets, and thirty miles of hiking trails. The existing trail system follows a portion of the old railroad grade; some historic ruins of Chinese labor camps still remain. Hike-in camping is permitted by reservation only, with parking at the trailhead. Horses are prohibited upstream of the steel bridge. Call: (408) 335-4598 or 335-9106.

The park, with elevations ranging from 100' to 2,600', contains a variety of habitats, including redwood and mixed-evergreen forests, chaparral, riparian vegetation, and grasslands. The redwood forest is a good example of natural revegetation as it is almost all second growth, having been virtually clear-cut by 1923. Douglas-fir, madrone, California bay laurel, and tanbark oak are found in the mixed-evergreen forest; chaparral with knobcone pine in the higher elevations; and riparian vegetation with willows, alders, ferns, and liverworts along the many creeks.

Wildlife is also diversified and includes chipmunks, raccoons, black-tailed deer, coyotes, gray foxes, bobcats, mountain lions, and feral pigs, as well as many species of birds. Silver salmon and steelhead spawn in the larger creeks, such as Aptos and Hinckley Creeks, and prickly sculpin and lamprey can also be found. Steelhead fishing is permitted downstream of the steel bridge during open winter season.

Seacliff State Beach: *5.5 mi. S. of Santa Cruz on Hwy. 1; foot of State Park Dr., Rio del Mar.*

Seacliff State Beach, situated on Monterey Bay, has nearly two miles of ocean frontage below steep sandstone cliffs. Gulls and shorebirds rest and feed along the shore. Several clam species are found at the beach, which is the northern limit of the Pismo clam. Sea lions, seals, and sea otters are found offshore.

The 500-foot wooden fishing pier extending into the bay leads to a concrete supply ship, the *Palo Alto*, built in 1918 for use during WWI. However, the ship remained unused until 1929 when it was bought by the Cal-Nevada Stock Co., which towed it to Seacliff, flooded its holds so it would sink, remodeled it, and operated it for two years as an amusement center with a dance floor, cafe, pool, and carnival booths.

Today both the pier and the ship are used extensively for fishing; perch, kingfish, sole, flounder, halibut, and many other coastal species are taken from shore or from the ship. Many species of seabirds and shorebirds use the end of the ship as a resting and roosting site. Offshore is a trammel net fishery for halibut, Dungeness crab, leopard shark, skates, soupfin shark, and white seabass.

Both the pier and park restrooms are wheelchair accessible; the park also has day use parking, picnic facilities, en route and regular trailer campsites adjacent to the beach, and an interpretive center with natural history displays. Call: (408) 688-3222 or 688-3241.

Aptos: *Off Hwy. 1, E. of Capitola.*

In 1833 Rancho Aptos was granted to Rafael Castro by Governor Figueroa; late in the 19th century Claus Spreckels, who built a large sugar beet refinery near Watsonville and founded California's first sugar dynasty, bought most of Rancho Aptos and built an estate there with a mansion and racetrack. Today Aptos is primarily residential. The word "aptos" means "the meeting of the streams."

Rio Del Mar Beach: *End of Rio Del Mar Blvd., Aptos.*

Rio Del Mar Beach is the southern end of Seacliff State Beach; facilities include restrooms, parking, a cement seawall at the esplanade, and a pedestrian/bike path leading to Seacliff. The mouth of Aptos Creek crosses the beach.

Aptos Creek: *Santa Cruz Mountains to Rio del Mar Beach, Aptos.*

Aptos Creek is a perennial coastal stream originating within the Forest of Nisene Marks State Park in the Santa Cruz Mountains. The creek surfaces along Santa Rosalia Ridge, is joined by Bridge Creek, and at the bottom of a steep-sided canyon in the lower reaches of the park drains into Monterey Bay at Rio del Mar Beach, where it forms a small lagoon. A few water-associated birds, primarily gulls, can be found in the open water of the lagoon; the creek mouth also provides some habitat for shorebirds. The dense riparian vegetation consists mostly of alder with some big-leaf maple.

Valencia Lagoon: *Off Hwy. 1 and Rio del Mar Blvd., Rio del Mar.*

Valencia Lagoon, a freshwater marsh of about three acres, is one of the two main breeding sites of the endangered Santa Cruz long-toed salamander, and is now an ecological reserve administered by the California Department of Fish and Game.

Dominant vegetation in the lagoon includes cattails and bulrushes, whereas willows grow around the lagoon; surrounding vegetation also includes coastal scrub and various exotics. The summer habitat of the salamander, located south of the lagoon, consists primarily of oak woodland. Valencia is also important as a waterfowl, amphibian, and rodent habitat.

Freeway construction in the 1950s and 1960s drastically disturbed the Santa Cruz long-toed salamander's habitat; two artificial breeding ponds were constructed in the 1970s to help perpetuate the endangered amphibian.

Ellicott Station Ecological Reserve: *4 mi. W. of Watsonville on San Andreas Rd.*

Ellicott is the second of the two main habitats of the Santa Cruz long-toed salamander; vegetation includes grassland with coyote brush and a dense willow-blackberry thicket. In winter and early spring there is a pond near the KOA campground which is used by the salamanders as a breeding site. Waterfowl, other amphibians, and rodents are also found in the area.

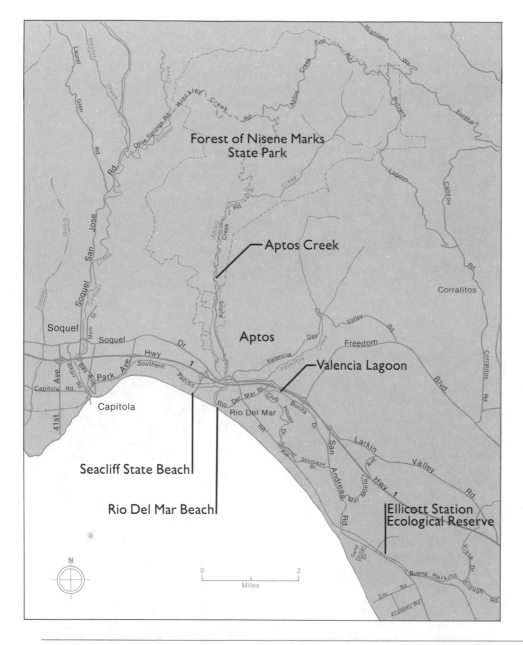

Santa Cruz Long-toed Salamander

The Santa Cruz long-toed salamander, *Ambystoma macrodactylum croceum*, is three to six inches long and black with prominent yellow and faint white spots. Named for its long toes, it is one of 25 species of salamanders in California and is a relict form of a species that probably lived throughout much of California during and just after the last Pleistocene ice advance 10,000-12,000 years ago. As the climate became drier, several populations of this salamander were isolated near Santa Cruz; due to unique habitat conditions the Santa Cruz population evolved into a distinct subspecies.

The salamander has a moist, scaleless skin and prominent tail; body temperature depends on the surroundings rather than internal heat. To keep cool, it lives in burrows and under vegetation on steep, shady hillsides and is rarely seen. This amphibian eats a variety of insects, snapping them up with its sticky tongue.

Long-toed salamanders breed in ponds; Valencia Lagoon and Ellicott Pond are the major breeding sites. With the onset of the rainy season, the mature adults (three to four years old) migrate on cool, moist nights from wooded hillsides to the ponds, where they pair up, conduct their courtship rituals, and breed.

Eggs are deposited on aquatic plants singly or sometimes in small clusters. After about a week, the eggs hatch into polliwog-like larvae. Several months later during metamorphosis the larvae are transformed into miniature forms of the adult. Bullfrogs and fish are the main predators of young salamanders.

Neither eggs nor larvae are tended by the adults; after egg-laying the adult salamanders begin their migration back to the vegetated slopes. Exactly how far these creatures wander from the breeding ponds is unknown, but they seem to return to the same general area every summer and breed in the same ponds each winter.

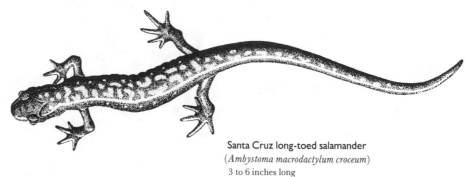

Santa Cruz long-toed salamander
(*Ambystoma macrodactylum croceum*)
3 to 6 inches long

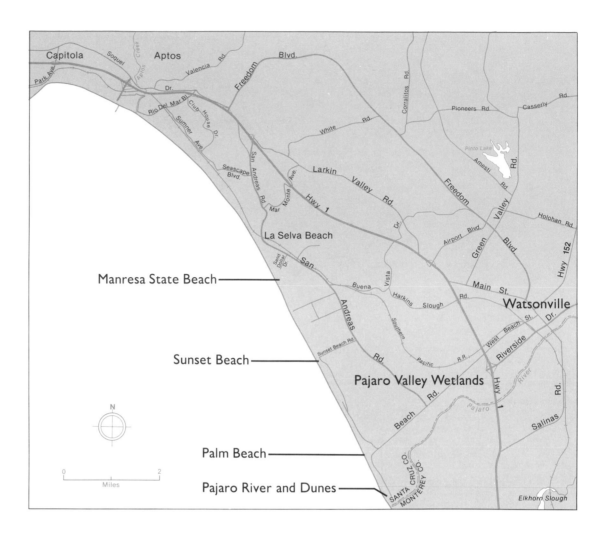

sticky monkey-flower (*Mimulus aurantiacus*)
2 to 4 feet high

Manresa State Beach: *W. of San Andreas Rd. across R.R. tracks, S. of La Selva Beach.*

Manresa State Beach is a wide, sandy beach, backed by steep cliffs, with a day use parking lot at the north end of San Andreas Rd.; additional beach access is off Sand Dollar Drive.

The vegetation at Manresa has been disturbed by past agricultural land use and is not in a natural condition. The bluff and adjacent border of the coastal terrace supports a narrow band of coastal sage scrub, including coyote brush, California sagebrush, and lizardtail, and provides habitat for such wildlife as the Allen's hummingbird, lesser goldfinch, rufous-sided towhee, and brush rabbit.

The intertidal area of the beach is inhabited by such marine invertebrates as the sand crab, purple olive snail, beach hopper, and Pismo clam. There is commercial and sport salmon trolling in the area, and sea otters swim and feed offshore. During their migration, California gray whales can also be seen. For park information, call: (408) 724-1266.

Sunset Beach: *201 Sunset Beach Rd., S.W. of Watsonville.*

A wide, sandy beach with high dunes and a freshwater lagoon, Sunset Beach is the northern unit of Sunset State Beach. The largest and most diverse coastal strand community in the county, including European beach grass, mock heather, and sea rocket, is found in the extensive dune formation beginning at the parking lot at the north end of the beach and extending south to the Pajaro River mouth. Several rare, endemic plants, including Monterey paintbrush, robust spineflower, and the endangered coast wallflower, grow here; the California legless lizard also uses the dunes.

Coastal scrub, including dwarf chaparral broom, sticky monkey flower, and bush lupine, is found in the fixed dune formation. In the uplands, eucalyptus, Monterey cypress, coyote brush, and Monterey pine occur. The upper sandy beach area serves as nesting habitat for the endangered California least tern and the snowy plover, and gulls and shorebirds such as the godwit and willet rest and feed along the shore. Sea otters can be seen offshore.

Park facilities include parking, restrooms, and en route and regular campsites. For information, call: (408) 724-1266 or 688-3241.

Palm Beach: *Foot of Beach Rd., W. of Watsonville.*

The southern unit of Sunset State Beach, Palm Beach is a wide, sandy beach with active and stabilized dunes. Where Watsonville Slough traverses the south end of the beach before entering the ocean there is a brackish marsh habitat containing pickleweed, alkali heath, and saltgrass. As at the Sunset Beach unit, extensive coastal strand vegetation as well as coastal scrub grows in the dunes, and numerous shorebirds and seabirds use the beach for resting and feeding.

Park facilities include parking, restrooms, and a grass picnic area surrounded by eucalyptus trees. Call: (408) 724-1266 or 688-3241.

Pajaro River and Dunes: *Santa Cruz / Monterey County line.*

Meaning "River of the Bird," the Pajaro River was crossed by the Portolá land expedition in 1769 during their search for Monterey Bay and named after a straw-stuffed bird left by the Indians at the river's edge as an offering.

Pajaro Landing, located at the river mouth, was the southernmost landing along the Santa Cruz coast and was used in the 19th century as a shipping point for produce and passengers before the advent of the railroad; a warehouse was also built there to store grain and produce.

Channelized by levees in 1949 for flood control, the lower 11 miles of the river flow through intensely developed agricultural lands; as a result much of the historic riparian and marsh vegetation no longer exists. In the wetland area near the river mouth, resident and migratory waterfowl and other water-associated birds are found, as well as the California brown pelican and California least tern, both endangered, who use the river mouth seasonally. Pheasants, raptors, and several species of reptiles, amphibians, and small mammals also live here.

The Pajaro dunes, located near the river mouth, are part of an extensive dune formation beginning at the north end of Sunset State Beach; the dune area is one of only four areas along the Santa Cruz coast where the snowy plover nests. Private residential development in the area has greatly altered and reduced the dune habitat.

Pajaro Valley Wetlands: *W. of Watsonville.*

Comprised of 21 square miles of freshwater sloughs, the Pajaro Valley Wetlands is the largest and most significant intermittent wetland in coastal Santa Cruz County and includes Struve, Gallighan, Hanson, Harkins, and Watsonville Sloughs. Upper portions of the system, especially near Harkins Slough Rd., remain in a natural condition, although other sections of several of the sloughs have been channelized for agricultural use.

Native rushes, sedges, common marsh perennials, and wildflowers provide resting, feeding, and breeding habitat for a variety of water-associated birds. Harkins Slough has historically been the principal breeding area in the county for the black-shouldered kite; cuckoos, tree swallows, yellowthroats, chats, and American goldfinches breed in the dense willow thickets in Gallighan Slough and upper Harkins Slough. Herons, egrets, shorebirds, gulls, and raptors also use the sloughs as habitat. Surrounding and separating the sloughs is an extensive grassland which supports large numbers of raptors and is also habitat for the endangered Santa Cruz tarplant.

Watsonville Slough is a northern extension of the marsh at the mouth of the Pajaro River and receives freshwater inflow from the river; there is a tide gate on Shell Road. An important link in the Pacific Flyway, the slough is also one of only a few major snowy plover nesting areas.

Watsonville: *Off Hwy. 1, both sides of the Pajaro River.*

Watsonville was named after Judge John H. Watson who, along with D. S. Gregory, laid out the town in 1852. The first apple orchard was planted in 1853; today Watsonville is renowned for its apple industry, as well as other fruits, vegetables, and flowers.

In the 19th century, bull and bear fights took place in the plaza in the center of town. Located in the plaza is the cannon that fired the first salute on October 18, 1850 from the Pacific Mail Steamship *Oregon* as it entered San Francisco Bay announcing the news of California's admission to the Union.

Some historic buildings in Watsonville include the Tuttle Mansion at 723 East Lake Dr., built in 1899; the Silliman House at 508 Riverside Rd., built in 1850 and supposedly the oldest frame house in the Pajaro Valley; and Mansion House, at 418 Main St., built in 1871 and once Watsonville's leading hotel.

Plaza at Watsonville

Manresa State Beach

Pajaro dunes

Monterey County
Selected Species of Interest

Plants: Bull kelp (*Nereocystis luetkeana*), grows in offshore beds; its bulbous, gas-filled floats may be mistaken for heads of sea otters. **Mock heather** (*Haplopappus ericoides*), perennial dune species; blooms yellow in late summer.

Trees: Monterey cypress (*Cupressus macrocarpa*); only remaining native stands are in the Del Monte Forest and at Point Lobos. **Monterey pine** (*Pinus radiata*); one of four native stands in the world occurs at Point Lobos.

Insects: Monarch butterfly (*Danaus plexippus*), overwinters in great numbers in Pacific Grove. **Smith's blue butterfly** (*Euphilotes enoptes smithi*), endangered; restricted to a narrow coastal strip in Monterey County.

Invertebrates: Market squid (*Loligo opalescens*), spawns in southern Monterey Bay. **Fat innkeeper** (*Urechis caupo*), worm inhabiting Elkhorn Slough mudflats; shares its burrow with four other animal species.

Amphibians and Reptiles: Black legless lizard (*Anniella pulchra nigra*), burrows in dunes on Monterey Peninsula. **Santa Lucia slender salamander** (*Batrochoseps pacificus* ssp.), inhabits leaf-litter of forested canyons.

Fish: Kelp greenling (*Hexagrammos decagrammus*), inhabits shallow rocky bottom of offshore kelp forests. **Albacore** (*Thunnus alalunga*), pelagic; an important sport fish that is commercially harvested from Monterey Bay.

Birds: California clapper rail (*Rallus longirostris obsoletus*), endangered; resident of salt marsh at Elkhorn Slough. **Willet** (*Catoptrophorus semipalmatus*), shorebird found on mudflats, sandy beaches, and rocky shores.

Land Mammals: Mountain lion (*Felis concolor*), primarily nocturnal; inhabits rugged Santa Lucia Mountians along Big Sur Coast. **Dusky-footed woodrat** (*Neotoma fuscipes*), builds large nests at Point Lobos State Reserve.

Marine Mammals: Minke whale (*Balaenoptera acutorostrata*), seen from Point Lobos in summer. **Southern sea otter** (*Enhydra lutris nereis*), threatened; frequents kelp beds; uses rocks as tools for feeding on invertebrates.

Monterey County

MONTEREY COUNTY's north coast is characterized by broad, sandy beaches backed by an extensive dune formation that rims the inner curve of Monterey Bay. The rural area between the Pajaro River and the city of Marina is made up of large tracts of rich agricultural land that stretch inland to the Salinas Valley on a flat coastal plain and along gentle rolling hills. Elkhorn Slough, adjacent to Moss Landing, is an estuarine complex with extensive mudflats and one of the largest salt marshes on the California coast. Sand dunes extend south through the Fort Ord Military Reservation and the cities of Sand City, Seaside, and Del Rey Oaks to the developed waterfront of the city of Monterey, where the shoreline becomes rocky with sandy pocket beaches. The community of Del Monte Forest and the cities of Monterey, Pacific Grove, and Carmel-by-the-Sea are located on the hilly Monterey Peninsula, which supports Monterey pine and Monterey cypress trees.

South of the Monterey Peninsula is the Big Sur Coast; noted for its spectacular landscape, the sparsely populated coast has remained relatively undeveloped due to its rugged topography. The Santa Lucia Mountains, the largest of the southern Coast Ranges, rise abruptly from the ocean to heights of over 5,000 feet. Nearly 50 streams flow down the western slopes of the forested mountains through steep canyons to rocky and sandy pocket beaches. The coast redwood reaches the southernmost limit of its natural range just inland from the coast near the southern end of the county. Narrow marine terraces along the Big Sur Coast are used as pasture for cattle grazing.

The Ohlone, or Costanoan, Indians inhabited the Monterey Bay area for at least 10,000 years prior to Spanish settlement. Large midden deposits of shells and bones reveal that the Ohlone diet included clams, abalones, fish, birds, and sea otters. The Big Sur Coast was occupied by the Ohlone, Esselen, and Salinan Indians. The Esselen were one of the smaller indigenous groups in California, numbering between 500 and 1,300; they were also the first California Indians to become extinct. The Salinan Indians, named after the Salinas River by the Spanish, loaned shell money to each other at 100 per cent interest per day, a unique custom among California Indian groups.

From his description of the "Bay of Pines" in 1542, it is assumed that Portuguese navigator Juan Rodríguez Cabrillo, sailing for Spain, sighted the Monterey Peninsula, but did not go ashore. Sebastián Vizcaíno, also sailing for Spain, landed here in 1602 and named the bay "Monterey" in honor of the viceroy of Mexico, the Conde de Monterey, who sponsored his trip. In 1770, Gaspar de Portolá and Father Junípero Serra established the second presidio and mission in California at the southwest end of Monterey Bay. This area of settlement evolved into the town of Monterey.

During the Spanish period, Native Americans were concentrated in rancherias, where missionaries converted them to Christianity. The Indian population was eventually decimated by introduced European diseases. In 1834, the mission lands along most of the Monterey County coast were divided into Mexican land grants, or ranchos. Monterey developed into a bustling port of trade and was the capital of California under Spanish and Mexican rule from 1777 until 1846, when U.S. Navy Commodore John Drake Sloat claimed California as part of the United States, with Monterey its capital. The Constitutional Convention met in Monterey in 1849 to set up a government for California, which achieved statehood in 1850. Monterey County, one of California's original 27 counties, was established at this time.

Commercial fishing activities on Monterey Bay, centered around Moss Landing and the city of Monterey, were pioneered by Chinese immigrants beginning in the 1850s. Cannery Row, along the city of Monterey's waterfront, is the historic site of a world-famous sardine canning industry that developed in the early 1900s and peaked in 1945. Today, northern anchovy, Pacific herring, albacore, salmon, and squid are harvested from Monterey Bay.

The Big Sur Coast was homesteaded in the 1870s. Logging and limestone mining took place in the Santa Lucia Mountains during the 1880s; lumber, tanbark, and lime were transferred onto ships from several small landings along the coast. Tourism developed around the Monterey Peninsula in the 1880s with the extension of the Southern Pacific Railroad and the construction of the Del Monte Hotel. In 1965, Highway 1 from Carmel River south to the county line was designated California's first Scenic Highway. There are six underwater reserves and refuges along the Monterey coast, which protect the area's sea otters, extensive kelp beds, and other abundant marine life. Los Padres National Forest and four state parks encompass a large portion of the Big Sur Coast and inland mountains.

Cypress Grove Trail, Point Lobos State Reserve

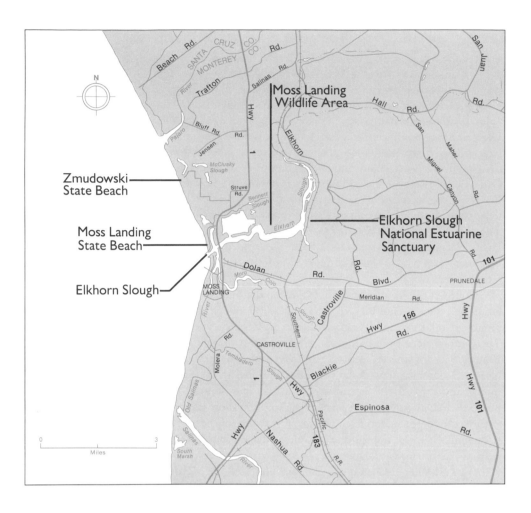

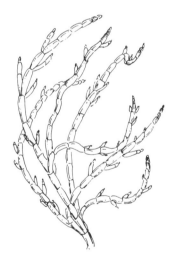

pickleweed (*Salicornia virginica*)
8 to 25 inches high

Zmudowski State Beach: *End of Giberson Rd., off Struve Rd., N. of Moss Landing.*

A steep path over sand dunes leads to Zmudowski State Beach, named after former land owner Mary Zmudowski. The sandy beach is used for beachcombing and surf fishing; horses are permitted only on the beach—not on the dunes. Coastal strand vegetation in the dunes includes yellow bush lupine, mock heather, and European beach grass. Snowy plovers nest and breed on the beach as far north as the Pajaro River mouth. Great blue herons, snowy egrets, and several species of ducks can be seen at Zmudowski Slough and McClusky Slough to the east. Beach facilities include restrooms and a parking lot. Call: (408) 649-2836.

Moss Landing State Beach: *End of Jetty Rd., off Hwy. 1, N. of Moss Landing.*

Moss Landing State Beach, popular for surfing, is also called Jetty Beach because the North Jetty of Moss Landing Harbor marks the south end of the beach. The rock jetty provides a fishing access where anglers catch rockfish, flounder, sharks, surfperch, and sculpin. It is possible to walk or ride horses north along the sandy beach all the way to the mouth of the Pajaro River. Restrooms and limited parking are available. Call: (408) 649-2836.

Jetty Rd., which skirts Moss Landing's north harbor, is considered one of the best bird watching spots in Central California. During low tides, shorebirds, gulls, and terns congregate on exposed mudflats. The Monterey Bay Area Rare Bird Alert is a recorded message of weekly sightings in the region; call: (408) 449-6100. The west bank of the north harbor provides access for windsurfing; kayaks and canoes can also be launched from here into Elkhorn Slough. Bennett Slough, to the north, provides habitat for the rare California brackish water snail.

Elkhorn Slough: *E. of Hwy. 1 at Moss Landing.*

One of the few relatively undisturbed coastal wetlands remaining in California, Elkhorn Slough is a tidal embayment that extends inland for over seven miles from Moss Landing to Watsonville. This complex ecosystem comprises pasture and agricultural land, freshwater and brackish water marsh, salt ponds, grassland, riparian and oak woodland, and 2,500 acres of tidelands that include mudflats and salt marsh; the slough area is used extensively for research, recreation, and education.

The name "Elkhorn" may have originated because herds of tule elk were once abundant in the area, or, possibly, because the contour of the slough is antler-shaped. Scattered kitchen middens of the Ohlone Indians, who occupied the slough area probably beginning 10,000 to 15,000 years ago, reveal that their diet included shellfish, sea otters, waterfowl, and tule elk. Historic Hudson's Landing, at the head of the slough, once served as the port for the Watsonville area. Early American settlers shipped grain and vegetables from the Pajaro and Salinas valleys via barges and steamboats along the slough channel to Moss Landing, where shipments were transfered onto schooners bound for San Francisco. With the extension of the Southern Pacific Railroad in the 1870s and, later, the creation of dairy pastures, hundreds of acres of slough wetlands were diked off from tidal action. In 1908, farmers diverted the Salinas River away from the mouth of the slough to reclaim large parcels of land for agricultural use; this, and the creation of Moss Landing Harbor in 1946, resulted in higher salinity of slough waters. Since major streams no longer flow into the slough, it is considered a "seasonal estuary," as fresh water mixes with the sea only during the rainy season.

Elkhorn Slough supports nearly 260 species of birds and is an important link in the Pacific Flyway. Tremendous numbers of birds congregate here during the peak of the migration season in winter and spring. At low tides, exposed mudflats run the length of the slough and provide a rich source of food for resident and migratory shorebirds and wading birds such as sandpipers, stilts, avocets, dowitchers, marbled godwits, willets, plovers, long-billed curlews, herons, and egrets. Waterfowl includes northern shovelers, green-winged teals, and cinnamon teals. The endangered California clapper rail, a permanent resident, is dependent on the perennial pickleweed that makes up almost all of the salt marsh vegetation. Brass buttons grow near freshwater seeps and ponds, providing colorful contrast to the pickleweed; the ponds are also habitat for the endangered Santa Cruz long-toed salamander.

The slough channel and tidal creeks serve as nursery grounds for many species of fish, some of which are commercially important such as the northern anchovy, Pacific herring, English sole, starry flounder, surfperch, jack smelt, and halibut; leopard sharks and bat rays also breed here. Sea otters sometimes visit the slough, and harbor seals haul out regularly on the mudflats at low tide. Over 400 species of invertebrates have been identified in the slough, including pea crabs, ghost shrimp, horseneck clams, predatory moon snails, and fat innkeeper worms.

Moss Landing Wildlife Area: *Hwy. 1 at Struve Rd., Moss Landing.*

The Moss Landing Wildlife Area, located on the north bank of Elkhorn Slough, includes the salt ponds of the old Monterey Bay Salt Company. Constructed in the late 1800s, the ponds at one time supplied salt to the Moss Landing and Monterey canneries. Now abandoned, these evaporation ponds provide the most important roosting grounds north of Point Conception for over 5,000 endangered California brown pelicans during the summer and fall. Access facilities soon to be completed will feature a boardwalk and trail system. For information, call: (408) 649-2870.

Elkhorn Slough National Estuarine Sanctuary: *1700 Elkhorn Rd., off Hwy. 1. and Dolan Rd.*

In 1979, 900 acres on the south and east sides of Elkhorn Slough became the state's first National Estuarine Sanctuary (since renamed "National Estuarine Research Reserve"). Also a State Ecological Reserve, the area has since grown to 1,300 acres. A visitor center, open Thursday through Sunday, offers interpretive displays including a raised-relief model of the deep Monterey Submarine Canyon; wheelchair-accessible restrooms and parking are available. The visitor center is adjacent to 4.5 miles of hiking trails that feature a marsh restoration project, old dairy barns, eucalyptus groves, and stands of native coast live oak. Common upland plants along the trails include coyote brush, chicory, poison hemlock, California poppy, field mustard, lupine, and blue dicks.

The North American record for the most species of birds seen in one day from one spot was set here on the Five Fingers Loop Trail in 1982 with 116. The golden eagle and peregrine falcon, both endangered species, and the osprey and merlin are regularly seen here. For information on docent-led walking tours or kayak and canoe trips through the slough, call: (408) 728-2822.

Kirby Park is a fishing access with a parking area and small boat launching ramp (use subject to tidal variation); it is located on the northeast side of Elkhorn Slough, off Kirby Rd., west of Elkhorn Road. Call: (408) 633-2461. The Nature Conservancy's 500-acre Elkhorn Slough Preserve, located just north of Kirby Park, is accessible by appointment only. For information on guided walking tours, call: (415) 777-0541.

Elkhorn Slough National Estuarine Research Reserve

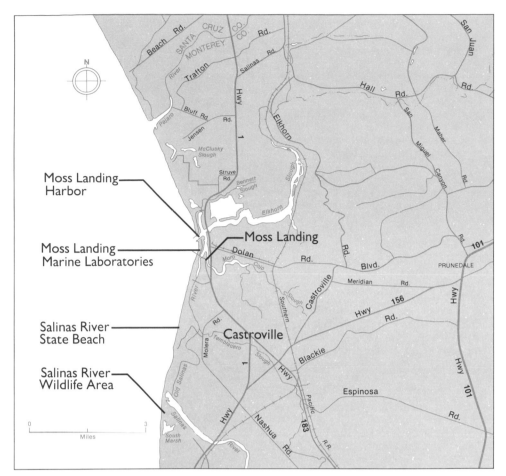

transformed into magnesium oxide and pressed into refractory bricks for high-temperature ovens in the glass, steel, and cement industries.

Moss Landing: *Sandholdt Rd. and Moss Landing Rd., W. of Hwy. 1, 15 mi. S. of Santa Cruz.*

Moss Landing was named after Charles Moss, a New England sea captain who built a wharf here in 1865 along with Cato Vierra, a Portuguese whaler from the Azores. Shore whaling took place in the late 19th century, until it became economically less profitable. With the advent of modern equipment in 1919, whaling was resumed and continued into the 1920s; an average of 300 whales were killed a year. In the late 1800s, the Pacific Coast Steamship Company offered steamer service to San Francisco; the company's historic building, now a private residence, is off Moss Landing Road.

Access to Moss Landing Island, a sand spit known locally as "The Island," is via the one-lane Sandholdt Bridge. In addition to marine supply stores, ship building yards, and fish-packing plants, there are several historic cannery buildings that date back to the Monterey Bay sardine fishery which peaked in the mid-1940s. "Island Beach," along the north end of the peninsula, is accessible from the South Jetty fishing access at the end of Sandholdt Rd.; surf fishing is popular south to Sandholdt Pier. Moss Landing is known for its antique shops and flea markets; the annual Antique Fair and Flea Market is held the last Sunday in July. Call: (408) 633-5202.

Moss Landing Marine Laboratories: *W. of Sandholdt Rd. off Hwy. 1, Moss Landing.*

Moss Landing Marine Laboratories is a marine sciences research facility and educational institution that offers undergraduate and master's degree programs through a consortium of six state universities. Open house, held each spring, features lectures, slides shows, films, and exhibits, including a touch tank with marine life. A stairway at the south end of the parking lot leads over sand dunes to a sandy beach. For information, call: (408) 633-3304.

Salinas River State Beach: *End of Potrero Rd., off Hwy. 1, Moss Landing.*

A trail leads through a fragile sand dune community to Salinas River State Beach. The sandy beach is a snowy plover nesting habitat. Popular for surf fishing and horseback riding, the beach is also accessible from Monterey Dunes Way, south of Tembladero Slough, off Highway 1 and Molera Road. Restrooms and parking are available at both sites; horses are not permitted on the dunes. Call: (408) 649-2810.

East of the beach is the old Salinas River channel, which runs between Moss Landing and the Salinas River Wildlife Area to the south. Snails, nudibranchs, and other invertebrates, as well as Pacific herring, attach their eggs to beds of eelgrass in the channel; the eelgrass also provides habitat for surfperch and long, slender pipefish. The Salinas River was once the major source of fresh water for Elkhorn Slough, as it flowed north past Moss Landing before entering the ocean. In 1908, farmers altered its course to reclaim land for agricultural use, and today the mouth of the river is adjacent to the Salinas

South Harbor, Moss Landing

Moss Landing Harbor: *W. of Hwy. 1, off Sandholdt Rd., 15 mi. S. of Santa Cruz.*

Situated at the mouth of Elkhorn Slough and the head of the Monterey Submarine Canyon, the harbor was created in 1946 by dredging out a portion of the old Salinas River channel and digging a new entrance. The presence of the deep submarine canyon reduces wave energy and refracts large swells away from the harbor, making it one of the safest refuges between San Francisco and Los Angeles. The T-shaped harbor is divided into North and South Harbors; the North Harbor has 100 recreational slips and is popular for windsurfing and clamming. Facilities include wheelchair-accessible restrooms, parking, and a boat ramp. Elkhorn Slough is accessible by boat under the Highway 1 bridge.

The South Harbor is a boat-building center with 500 slips and is used by one of the largest commercial fishing fleets in the state; fishermen catch northern anchovy, Pacific herring, albacore, tuna, squid, crabs, and salmon. There are several seafood restaurants and fresh fish markets around the harbor. Facilities include dry dock storage areas, a boat ramp, restrooms, and parking. Call: (408) 633-2461.

On the south bank of Elkhorn Slough across Highway 1 from the harbor is the Moss Landing Power Plant. Built in 1952, it is the second largest fossil fuel thermal electric power plant in the world. Its twin 500-foot-high cement boiler stacks can be seen from miles away; sailors use the towers as a navigational aid. At a factory just south of the power plant, dolomite from a quarry near Salinas is mixed with sea water to produce chemical grade milk of magnesia that is

River Wildlife Area. Moro Cojo Slough is a brackish marsh east of the old Salinas River channel, and is a migratory and overwintering area for shorebirds and waterfowl.

Castroville: *Junction 183 and Hwy. 1, 3.5 mi. S. of Moss Landing.*

Founded by Juan Bautista Castro in 1863, Castroville is the second oldest town in Monterey County. The cool, foggy summers and mild winters of this region, in combination with the rich, fast-draining soil, are conducive to growing artichokes, which were first planted here by Italian immigrant farmers in the early 1920s. The perennial green globe artichoke is a member of the sunflower family and native to North Africa and the Mediterranean. Although the sign over Main St. proclaims, "Castroville— The Artichoke Center of the World," in reality, Italy, Spain, France, Argentina, and Algeria out-produce Castroville; however, the area does produce the major U.S. crop. Artichokes are harvested year-round, with the peak of the production season March through May; the annual Artichoke Festival is held the first weekend in September. Call: (408) 633-2465.

Salinas River Wildlife Area: *.7 mi. W. of Del Monte Ave. exit off Hwy. 1.*

The wildlife area is used for fishing, hiking, and bird watching. A dirt road to the parking area passes agricultural fields, which provide habitat for the black-shouldered kite, northern harrier, and short-eared owl. Trails lead to the Salinas River, South Marsh, and a sandy beach that is a snowy plover nesting area. The endangered Smith's blue butterfly feeds and nests on two species of buckwheat in the sand dunes; it is restricted to several locations along a narrow coastal strip in Monterey County, from the Marina dunes to Lucia on the Big Sur coast.

The Salinas River, one of the longest rivers in the state, flows northwest for 170 miles from its headwaters in San Luis Obispo County to its mouth at the Salinas River Wildlife Area. It is unusual both in flowing north and in being one of the largest submerged rivers in the U. S., with most of its water flowing beneath the surface. Large numbers of gulls, terns, and endangered California brown pelicans congregate along the lower river. Stilts, avocets, and gadwalls nest on small islands in the river. South Marsh, just south of the river mouth, is a brackish water pond and marsh with vegetation such as salt grass and pickleweed; sandpipers, herons, and egrets can be seen. South Marsh is separated from the ocean by a dune barrier that is occasionally breached by storm-driven waves. The best remaining example in the area of undisturbed dunes and stabilizing native vegetation stretches south of here on private property to Dunes Dr. in Marina. Call: (408) 649-2870.

artichoke (*Cynara scolymus*)

Submarine Canyons

Many areas of the continental shelf and slope offshore of California are incised by submarine canyons. These deep underwater gorges are winding and rock-walled, with V-shaped profiles. They are thought to have been formed over time by a series of complex processes including fluctuation of sea level, uplift and faulting of land masses, and, in some cases, cutting and shaping by ancient rivers. Turbidity currents, which are avalanches of sand and mud in suspension, scour the canyon walls and enlarge the canyon as this sediment is transported to deep sea basins.

Some of the larger canyons off the California coast include the Mattole, Mendocino, Delgada, Carmel, Redondo, Newport, and Scripps canyons, but none matches the size of Monterey Canyon.

The Monterey Submarine Canyon, located at the center of Monterey Bay just offshore of Moss Landing, is one of the largest submarine canyons in the world; it is comparable to the Grand Canyon of the Colorado River in cross-section, width, and length. Just a half-mile offshore, the Monterey Canyon is 300 feet deep; the canyon extends more than 90 miles out from the coastline, cutting through the continental shelf to a depth of nearly two miles at the abyssal sea floor.

Monterey Canyon cuts through the granite rocks of the Salinian Block—a geologic basement terrain on the Pacific Plate that has been moving northward along the coast at the rate of several inches per year. Scientists have proposed that 30 million years ago the Monterey Canyon region was probably west of what is now Santa Barbara, where the canyon began to form as a small onshore gully.

During the season of upwelling from March through September, cold, nutrient-rich water is funneled up through the Monterey Canyon, contributing to the high biological productivity in Monterey Bay. The canyon was explored in 1970 and 1985 by a manned submersible and found to harbor an entire community of unusual, luminescent deepwater creatures, many new to science.

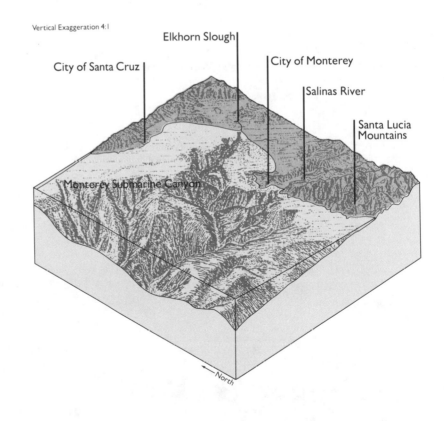

Vertical Exaggeration 4:1

City of Santa Cruz

Elkhorn Slough

City of Monterey

Salinas River

Santa Lucia Mountains

Monterey Submarine Canyon

North

Marina State Beach: *End of Reservation Rd., off Hwy. 1, Marina.*

This sandy beach features a hang glider take-off ramp and concession that offers lessons and equipment rentals; call: (408) 384-2622. All hang gliders must register before launching. Marina State Beach is also accessible via Reservation Rd. at the end of Lake Dr., where a steep, sandy trail leads to the top of a huge dune that is a model glider flying area and hang glider take-off spot. Call: (408) 649-2836.

The southern Monterey Bay dune complex—one of the most extensive dune systems on the West Coast—stretches from Sunset State Beach in Santa Cruz County to the Monterey City Marina. Within this region, between the Salinas River mouth and the U. S. Naval Postgraduate School, are some of the tallest sand dunes on the California coast. These parabola-shaped dunes are habitat for the globose dune beetle, black legless lizard, ornate shrew, and endangered Smith's blue butterfly. A wheelchair-accessible boardwalk leads from the parking lot at the northern unit of Marina State Beach through a dune restoration project that features native plants such as the rare, endemic Monterey paintbrush and coast wallflower. The Monterey Bay slender-flowered gilia, Monterey spine-flower, and Menzies wallflower, all endangered endemics, also occur here; their habitat is seriously threatened due to development, foot traffic, and encroaching exotic plants such as Hottentot fig, an ice plant native to South Africa.

Eleven vernal pools occur within or near the City of Marina where small depressions in the sand dunes are underlain with an impermeable hardpan layer that traps water. These rare formations support an unusual assortment of plants, most of which are native species. At one time a true vernal pool, Marina Freshwater Marsh, east of Highway 1 off Reservation Rd., supports plants associated with vernal pools such as alkali heath and fleshy jaumea.

Fort Ord: *Off Hwy. 1, Fort Ord Main Entrance off-ramp, 2.5 mi. S. of Marina.*

The Ford Ord Military Reservation was named after Major General Edward Ortho Cresap Ord, who converted the Presidio of Monterey from a Mexican post to an American post in 1847. Fort Ord was a major staging area for U. S. Army units deployed to the Pacific during World War II, and a basic training center for soldiers in the Vietnam War. There is no public access along Fort Ord's 4.5-mile stretch of beach; a paved bicycle path next to Highway 1 leads over sand dunes from Marina through Fort Ord to Seaside. For information on the Fort Ord Museum, call: (408) 242-4905.

Sand City: *4.5 mi. S. of Marina.*

Since the early 1900s sand mining activities have been concentrated along two stretches of Monterey Bay's shoreline, one in Marina and the other in Sand City. The specialty sands mined and produced at these sites are commercially valuable because of their unusual characteristics of hardness, amber color, jagged particle shape, and wide range of usable grain sizes. Specialty sand is used in sand blasting, foundry casting, pool filters, and the manufacture of glass. The mining occurs on the dune fields, and in the surf zone where cables anchored offshore pull a dragline of buckets shoreward along the beach face. The sand is deposited on a conveyor belt and carried inland to be washed and then trucked to a processing plant where it is sorted; railroad cars transport tons of sand daily to destinations around the country. Of the other specialty sand producing areas in the state, only one—Oceanside in San Diego County—approaches Monterey Bay's sand quality. Most of the dunes in Sand City have been disturbed and are characterized by shifting sand with sparse plant life; however, east of Highway 1, the stabilized dunes contain a variety of native species, including the rare Monterey ceanothus and endangered sandmat manzanita.

Roberts Lake: *Roberts Ave. and Canyon Del Rey, Seaside.*

Roberts Lake and Laguna Grande were once a single brackish lagoon with an outlet to the ocean; over the years, filling for development and transportation purposes divided the lake and cut off tidal action from the formerly estuarine complex. The reeds on the east side of Roberts Lake, opposite a small grassy picnic

alkali heath (*Frankenia grandifolia*)
6 to 12 inches high

Sand mining, Sand City

area, are habitat for green-backed herons and pied-billed grebes. A popular model boat racing area, the freshwater lake was named for Dr. John Roberts, who founded the Seaside Post Office in 1890. Beach access in Seaside is located at the foot of Humboldt Street. A bicycle/pedestrian pathway follows the old Southern Pacific right-of-way parallel to the shoreline from Roberts Ave. to Pacific Grove.

Laguna Grande Regional Park: *Del Monte Ave. and Canyon Del Rey, Seaside.*

Laguna Grande is a freshwater lake that is lined with tules and cattails, a habitat for redwinged blackbirds. A paved path around Laguna Grande crosses the lake via a bridge; grassy picnic areas, playgrounds, wheelchair-accessible restrooms, and parking are available on both east and west sides. Additional access is located off Del Monte Ave. at Virgin Ave. and Montecito Avenue. Call: (408) 899-6270.

Frog Pond Natural Area: *2 mi. S. of Del Monte Ave., off Hwy. 218, Del Rey Oaks.*

The seasonal freshwater Frog Pond, located opposite and just south of the Del Rey Oaks City Hall, is a habitat of the Pacific treefrog. Hiking trails lead through surrounding marsh, meadow, scrub, grassland, and oak woodland; vegetation includes arroyo willow, sagebrush, wild oat, and coast live oak. Common birds are kinglets, warblers, bushtits, titmice, and rufous-sided towhees. Call: (408) 394-8511.

Monterey State Beach: *End of Sand Dunes Dr., off Hwy. 1, Monterey.*

The wide, sandy beach and fragile dunes that border the southern end of Monterey Bay are historically known as Del Monte Beach; Monterey State Beach encompasses two separate areas along this continuous stretch of beach. The northern unit at Sand Dunes Dr. features a wooden cross, commemorating the Portolá expedition of 1769. The southwesterly unit is accessible off Del Monte Ave. at the foot of Park Avenue; parking is limited at both locations. Call: (408) 649-2836.

Del Monte Lake: *Off Del Monte Ave. and Sloat Ave., Monterey.*

Located on the grounds of the U. S. Naval Postgraduate School, the freshwater Del Monte Lake is lined with tules and provides habitat for overwintering waterfowl. Herrmann Hall, the school's headquarters, is nearby in the former Del Monte Hotel. The historic hotel played a major role in converting the Monterey Peninsula into a resort area in 1880, when the Southern Pacific Railroad was extended from Castroville to Monterey. The "Big Four" railroad tycoons (Charles Crocker, Leland Stanford, Mark Hopkins, and Collis P. Huntington) purchased over 7,000 acres of land including the Del Monte Forest, 17-Mile Drive, and a site for the Del Monte Hotel. Built in a Stick Style Victorian design, the huge luxury hotel attracted prominent figures and soon became internationally famous; it featured a glass-roofed bathing pavilion at Del Monte Beach and several landscaped gardens, one with a seven-foot-high cypress hedge maze. The hotel was rebuilt in Swiss-Gothic and later in Spanish Colonial Revival styles after twice being destroyed by fire,

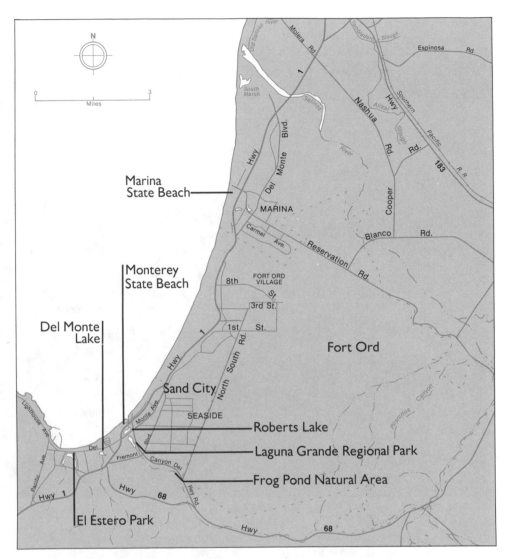

in 1887 and 1924. The school's grounds are open daily; call: (408) 646-2411.

El Estero Park: *Del Monte Ave. and Camino El Estero, Monterey.*

U-shaped El Estero Lake, a freshwater habitat for ducks, is surrounded by El Estero Park. Facilities include paddleboat rentals, a par course, swimming pool, baseball field, group picnic area, parking, and wheelchair-accessible restrooms. Dennis the Menace Park, off Pearl St., is a playground designed by Hank Ketcham, creator of the famous comic strip character. Call: (408) 646-3866.

Marina State Beach

207

Monterey fishing fleet, ca. 1945

City of Monterey: *25 mi. S. of City of Santa Cruz.*

Capital of California under Spanish and Mexican rule from 1777 until 1846, Monterey was California's social and political center until the gold rush of 1849, when San Francisco became the major port of trade. Incorporated in 1851, the city of Monterey is the hub of the Monterey Peninsula, located at the southwest end of Monterey Bay. Once a port for New England hide and tallow traders, it was also the site of a Portuguese shore whaling operation, a Chinese fishing village, and, later, a world-renowned sardine canning industry. Monterey developed into a residential and resort area with tourism its biggest industry; a free shuttle runs between Fisherman's Wharf, Cannery Row, and the Monterey Bay Aquarium. The Monterey

Peninsula Museum of Art is located at 559 Pacific St.; call: (408) 372-7591. The Monterey Peninsula Youth Hostel, open during the summer, has no permanent facility; call (408) 373-4167 for location.

The world-famous Monterey Jazz Festival is held each September at the Monterey County Fairgrounds, off Highway 68 and Fairground Road. In 1967 the fairground was the site of the three-day Monterey Pop Festival, which featured performers such as Janis Joplin, Jefferson Airplane, and the Grateful Dead. The festival marked a turning point in rock music as it introduced Jimi Hendrix to America, and was the nation's first huge outdoor rock concert.

Jacks Peak Regional Park at the end of Olmstead County Rd. off Highway 68 was named for Scottish immigrant David Jacks, whose local dairies produced "Monterey Jack" cheese, the only native California cheese. The Monterey pine-forested park offers panoramic views of Monterey and Carmel bays via hiking and equestrian trails. Call: (408) 424-8611.

Municipal Wharf No. 2: *Foot of Figueroa St. off Del Monte Ave., Monterey.*

Built in 1926, Wharf No. 2 is the site of an active commercial fishing operation where sand dab, sole, squid, shrimp, salmon, rockfish, northern anchovy, and Pacific herring are unloaded. Pier facilities include a boat hoist, fuel dock, restrooms, and bait and tackle supply store. Adjacent Monterey Beach Park is a wide, sandy beach used for picnicking and surf fishing; California grunion spawn on the beach.

Monterey Marina: *Between Municipal Wharf No. 2 and Fishermen's Wharf, Monterey.*

The 425 berths of the Monterey Marina are protected by a concrete seawall. Boat rentals, charter boats, marine supplies, and a boat ramp are available. Call: (408) 646-3950.

Fisherman's Wharf: *Foot of Olivier St., Monterey.*

Built in 1870 by the Pacific Coast Steamship Company, the pier became known as Fisherman's Wharf after expansion of the sardine industry in the late 1900s. Also called "Wharf No. 1," the wharf is now a popular tourist spot featuring souvenir shops, fish markets, seafood restaurants, and art galleries; sea lions can be seen in the water below the pier. Parking and wheelchair-accessible restrooms are available. Shoreline Park is a paved bicycle/pedestrian path that extends along the waterfront to the Coast Guard Pier.

Monterey State Historic Park: *20 Custom House Plaza, off Olivier St., Monterey.*

The park consists of nine historic adobe buildings, and the 1602 landing site of Sebastián Vizcaíno, located off Pacific St. near Presidio Gate. In 1770 Father Junípero Serra landed at the same site, joining the overland Portolá Expedition in establishing the Presidio of Monterey, and founding Mission San Carlos de Borromeo. Guide maps and brochures are available at Park Headquarters, next door to the Custom House. Most of the buildings are open daily; several are shown by guided tour only. Call (408) 649-2836 for specific days and hours.

Larkin House, at 510 Calle Principal, was designed and built in the mid-1830s by Thomas O. Larkin, the only American consul to California; his house served as the prototype for the Monterey Style of architecture. Its design consists of a basic American Colonial structure, with a redwood frame, adobe walls, a second story with a broad veranda on all sides, and a low-hipped roof with shingles.

Stevenson House, at 530 Houston St., was built in the 1830s and later named after author Robert Louis Stevenson, who rented a room in this two-story adobe home in the fall of 1879; his essay "The Old Pacific Capital" contains his impressions of Monterey. Open daily and shown by guided tours only, the adobe boasts the largest collection of Stevenson memorabilia in the United States.

The Monterey Path of History is a self-guided walking tour through the historic downtown area. Marked by a trail of painted blue dots, it incorporates Monterey State Historic Park and features many additional sites, including the Old Whaling Station, which was a boarding house for Portuguese shore whalers in the mid-1800s and has a sidewalk made of whalebone; Casa Amesti and the Cooper-Molera Adobe, which exemplify the Monterey Style of architecture; Colton Hall, the site of the California Constitutional Convention in 1849; the Allen Knight Maritime Museum, which portrays local fishing, whaling, and naval history through a collection of maritime artifacts including the 1887 Fresnel lens from the Point Sur Lighthouse; and the Royal Presidio Chapel, built in 1794, the oldest structure in Monterey and part of the original Presidio. For more information, call: (408) 649-2836. The Monterey History and Art Association sponsors the annual Adobe Tour each spring; call: (408) 372-2608.

Presidio of Monterey: *Artillery St. off Pacific St., Monterey.*

The original Presidio, whose ruins are located downtown off Church and Figueroa streets, was built in 1770; it was one of four major Spanish military forts built in California between 1769 and 1797. El Castillo was a fortification built in 1792 on a hill overlooking Monterey Bay to protect the Presidio. In 1818, the Presidio was destroyed by fire when Hippolyte de Bouchard, a French-born privateer, attacked Monterey. El

Castillo was used by the Mexicans from 1822-1846. The American Fort Mervine was built up the hill from El Castillo in 1847.

The present Presidio was built in 1902 by the U.S. Army on the site of El Castillo and Fort Mervine. The Presidio now houses the Defense Language Institute, one of the world's largest language schools. A self-guided walking tour of the Presidio grounds features archaeological sites of the Rumsen tribelet of Ohlone Indians. The Sloat Monument commemorates U.S. Navy Commodore John Drake Sloat, who in 1846 claimed California as part of the United States, with Monterey its capital. The U.S. Army Mu-

seum, open Monday-Friday, traces the history of the Presidio Hill site; call: (408) 647-5414.

Coast Guard Pier: *Southeast end of Cannery Row, Monterey.*

Also called "the Breakwater," the Coast Guard Pier is a popular staging area for scuba divers; San Carlos Beach on the north side provides a sandy beach entry. Sea lions haul out on the rock jetty extension of the pier. Facilities include parking, wheelchair-accessible restrooms, and a boat ramp. For information, call the Monterey Coast Guard: (408) 375-2278.

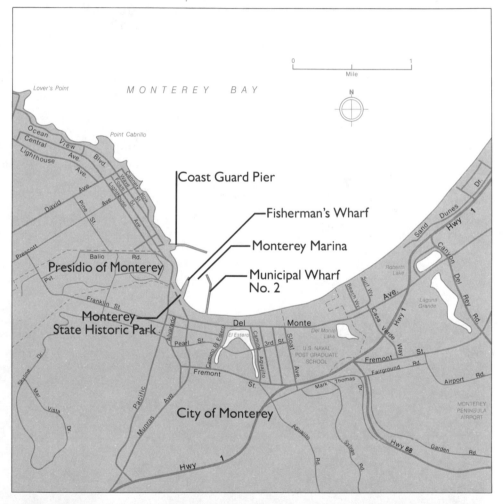

Stevenson House

Larkin House

Macabee Beach: *Between Prescott and Hoffman Avenues, Monterey.*

Developed in the early 1890s as a tourist resort with a bathhouse and, later, the Ocean View Hotel, Macabee Beach is a rocky and sandy beach used for diving access. A bust of the Nobel and Pulitzer prize-winning author John Steinbeck stands in the beach parking lot at the foot of Prescott Avenue. Steinbeck lived at several locations in Monterey and Pacific Grove and vividly chronicled the area during the 1930s and 1940s in his novels *Tortilla Flat, Cannery Row,* and *Sweet Thursday.*

Cannery Row: *Cannery Row, between Coast Guard Pier and David Ave., Monterey.*

Originally the site of the largest Chinese fishing village on Monterey Bay, the area eventually became the center of a thriving sardine canning industry pioneered by Frank Booth, who built the first fish-packing plant near Fisherman's Wharf in 1902. In 1905 Knute Hovden from Norway modernized packing methods here and developed a system for steam-cooking sardines that revolutionized the industry. Pietro Ferrante from Sicily introduced the lampara net in 1911, which greatly increased the sardine catch. Sardines were canned almost exclusively for human consumption until the end of World War I, when the price fell so low that an additional use was developed by Booth. Sardine by-products, previously considered waste, were reduced to fish meal for animal feed, and oil for manufacturing soap, tires, paint, vitamins, and glycerine. As a result of this more efficient use of the fish, and the introduction of the purse seiner boat in 1928, the annual sardine catch jumped from 3,000 tons in 1916 to 250,000 tons in 1945.

The sardine industry peaked in 1945—the same year that John Steinbeck's novel *Cannery Row* was published; at that time 23 canneries and 19 reduction plants occupied nearly one mile of shoreline. The "silver harvest" continued, despite warnings of overfishing, until the sardines virtually disappeared in 1951. Why the Pacific sardine fishery collapsed is not fully understood; biologists believe it may have been due to overfishing during a down cycle. Recent studies suggest that there may be a resurgence of sardines occurring.

Originally a stretch of Ocean View Ave., the street was not officially named "Cannery Row" until 1953 when the canneries were already closing. Today, Cannery Row is a tourist attraction with souvenir shops, art galleries, restaurants, and the Monterey Bay Aquarium. The small, sandy Aeneas Beach is accessible from a stairway opposite the Monterey Plaza Hotel at the south end of Cannery Row. Reeside Access at the foot of Reeside Ave. provides diving access via a sandy beach.

Monterey Bay Aquarium: *886 Cannery Row, at David Ave., Monterey.*

Located at Point Alones in "the footprint" of the old Hovden Cannery is one of the most innovative marine aquariums in the world. Opened in 1984, the Monterey Bay Aquarium is unusual in that almost all its exhibits focus on the local marine ecosystem. The aquarium features 83 habitat tanks that contain more than 5,500 specimens representing 525 species of invertebrates, plants, fish, birds, and mammals native to or found in and around Monterey Bay.

The three-story, 335,000-gallon underwater Kelp Forest exhibit is the centerpiece of this $50 million facility, offering a view previously available only to divers. Towering stands of giant kelp, *Macrocystis pyrifera,* one of the world's largest and fastest growing plants, form a can-

Pacific sardine (*Sardinops sagax*)
4 to 8 inches long

San Carlos Cannery, ca. 1952

opy under which numerous species of marine plants and animals thrive.

The Monterey Bay exhibit is a cross-section of wharf pilings, sandy sea floor, shale reefs, deep reefs, and open sea; inverted bubble-shaped viewing windows offer visitors a fisheye camera lens perspective. The tank is 90 feet long and hourglass-shaped to give the several species of sharks the longer glide path they require. The Marine Mammal Gallery features life-size models of marine mammals suspended from the ceiling. Sea otters can be viewed above and below the water in a split-level tank.

The Sandy Shores exhibit, modeled after nearby Elkhorn Slough, is a walk-through, open-air shorebird aviary; snowy plovers, stilts, avocets, and killdeers can be viewed close-up in a cross-section that represents the bay shoreline, from salt marsh and estuary to vegetated sand dunes and a wave-swept sandy beach.

The Ed Ricketts exhibit displays artifacts from his Cannery Row laboratory. Ricketts was a local marine biologist and inspiration to friend John Steinbeck, who immortalized him as the key character "Doc" in the novels *Cannery Row* and *Sweet Thursday*. Ricketts produced the pioneer study *Between Pacific Tides* in 1939, in which he proposed a standard system for the identification of four distinct vertical habitat zones along the rocky Pacific Coast, with predictable associations of plants and animals adapted to each.

The aquarium's Cannery Museum focuses on the heritage of Monterey's canning days; the Hovden Cannery was the largest sardine cannery on Cannery Row and was the last to close, canning squid until 1972. The Kelp Lab provides close-up views of kelp forest inhabitants. Additional attractions include a bat ray touch tank, a touch tidepool, an indoor/outdoor coastal stream exhibit, and a bookstore and gift shop.

Raw sea water flowing in from the bay at 2,000 gallons a minute provides food for the aquarium's marine life; the water is filtered during visitor hours for clarity. Architecturally, the aquarium building was designed with emphasis on strong industrial lines to preserve and reflect the historic flavor of Cannery Row. Marine education and research programs are conducted on an ongoing basis. Open from 10 AM-6 PM daily, the entire complex is wheelchair accessible. For information, call: (408) 375-3333. Advanced tickets are recommended; call: (408) 247-7469.

Hopkins Marine Station: *End of Dewey Ave, along Ocean View Blvd., Pacific Grove.*

In 1892, the first marine biological laboratory on the Pacific Coast was built on Point Aulon (now called Lover's Point) by the Leland Stanford Junior University. Hopkins Seaside Laboratory was moved to Point Almeja (now called Mussel Point, China Point, or Cabrillo Point) and named Hopkins Marine Station in 1916. The site includes the historic Monterey Boat Works building, where many of the fishing boats of the sardine era were built; the building now houses research facilities. The Hopkins Marine Life Refuge, offshore between 3rd St. and Eardley Ave., is the second oldest marine life refuge in California, established in 1931. The refuge includes Bird Rocks, where gulls and shorebirds roost and harbor seals haul out. The marine station and refuge are restricted to researchers by special permit. Call: (408) 373-0464.

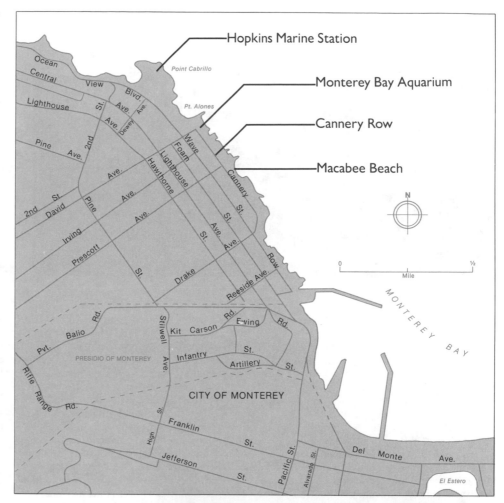

Monterey Bay Aquarium

Perkins Park

Shoreline Park: *Ocean View Blvd., between Pt. Cabrillo and Lovers Pt., Pacific Grove.*

Shoreline Park extends along the blufftop above the rocky coast. The Monterey Peninsula Recreational Trail is a paved bike path and pedestrian trail that runs the length of the park, passing Andy Jacobsen, Berwick, and Greenwood parks.

Pacific Grove: *N.W. of the City of Monterey.*

This residential community at the northern end of the Monterey Peninsula was founded as a Methodist retreat and tent city in 1875 and incorporated in 1889. The sale of alcohol in Pacific Grove was prohibited, except for medicinal purposes, until 1969 when voters ended the restriction in what was California's last "dry town." The first Chautauqua in the West was organized here in 1879—a nationwide summer educational program with lectures and entertainment; Chautauqua Hall at 16th and Central Ave. is a State Historical Landmark. From 1890 to 1923 the Monterey and Pacific Grove Street Railway ran along Lighthouse Ave.; originally horse-drawn, the trolley was electrified in 1902. The annual Victorian Home Tour, held in April, visits some of the 260 Pacific Grove homes built before 1910; call: (408) 646-3551. The Pacific Grove Art Center at 568 Lighthouse Ave. features several galleries; call: (408) 375-2208. Pacific Grove is one of the few cities in the state that owns its own shoreline, which is made up almost entirely of coastal parks.

Beginning in October, hundreds of thousands of Monarch butterflies overwinter here in several groves of native Monterey pine and cypress trees and in introduced eucalyptus trees, collectively called "butterfly trees." Pacific Grove protects these insects under law and promotes itself as "Butterfly Town U.S.A." Monarch viewing areas include George Washington Park along Alder St. and Pine Avenue. Development and tree removal in and around the nesting sites is threatening the habitat and microclimate required by the insects.

Pacific Grove Museum of Natural History: *165 Forest Ave. at Central Ave., Pacific Grove.*

The museum emphasizes the natural history of the Monterey area, with exhibits on shells, fish, mammals, and Indian artifacts; the bird collection is made up of over 400 mounted specimens—all collected in Monterey County. The Annual Wildflower Show, held here the third weekend in April, features over 500 species of local flora. The museum is open Tuesday-Sunday, 10 AM-5 PM; call: (408) 372-4212.

Lover's Point: *End of 17th St., along Ocean View Blvd., Pacific Grove.*

Formerly called Point Aulon, Lover's Point is a rocky granite headland with a grassy blufftop picnic area surrounded by Monterey cypress trees. The park features a granite statue of a Monarch butterfly. Facilities include picnic tables, wheelchair-accessible restrooms, and a sand volleyball court that is located on the site of a historic bathhouse dating from the early 1900s. Stairways lead to Otter Cove, Lover's Point Beach, and Pacific Grove Beach, used for surfing and diving access; call: (408) 372-2809. The Pacific Grove Recompression Chamber at 600 Pine Ave., just east of Lover's Point, is the main treatment facility between Seattle and Los Angeles for injured scuba divers suffering from "the bends." Call: (408) 372-6660.

The Pacific Grove Marine Gardens Fish Refuge is offshore of Ocean View Blvd. between the Monterey Bay Aquarium and Asilomar State Beach; the refuge extends from the mean high tide line out to the 60-foot depth contour, and surrounds the Hopkins Marine Life Refuge off Point Cabrillo. Within the marine gardens, large stands of giant kelp provide habitat for sea otters, harbor seals, and invertebrates such as brown turban snails and nudibranchs. All ma-

Lover's Point, ca. 1890

rine life is protected and may not be disturbed or removed, except for finfish such as cabezon, rockfish, and salmon, which may be taken with a sport license. Call: (408) 649-2870.

Perkins Park: *Ocean View Blvd., between Sea Palm Ave. and Asilomar Ave., Pacific Grove.*

This landscaped blufftop park was named after local resident Hayes Perkins who introduced *Drosanthemum floribundum* as a ground cover in 1943; known locally as the "Magic Carpet," the colorful lavender and pink ice plant blooms late April through August along a path that runs the length of Perkins Park. Stairways lead to small beaches at the foot of Coral St., Beach St., Shell Ave., and Sea Palm Avenue.

Point Piños Lighthouse Reservation: *Between Asilomar Ave. and Lighthouse Ave., Pacific Grove.*

In 1602, Vizcaíno named the southern tip of Monterey Bay "Punta de Piños" (Pine Point). The rocky, low-lying point, backed by dunes, is a refuge for marine life. Snails, sea stars, black abalone, and marine algae inhabit the tidepools; several times a year great numbers of pelagic red crabs are washed ashore here and on nearby beaches. Whales and pelagic birds can be seen from the point. Adjacent freshwater Crespi Pond at the edge of a golf course is a sanctuary for nesting coots and migratory gulls.

Point Piños Light Station, built in 1855, is the oldest continuously operating lighthouse on the West Coast. The lighthouse features a small Coast Guard museum, open Saturday and Sunday from 1 PM-4 PM; call: (408) 372-4212.

Asilomar State Beach and Conference Center: *Along Sunset Dr., Pacific Grove.*

Asilomar State Beach consists of stretches of fine-grained white sand—derived from local granitic rock—along a rocky shore; tidepools are inhabited by limpets, chitons, and sponges. Waves break offshore over a reef, creating good surfing conditions. A boardwalk leads from the beach to the Asilomar Conference Center grounds across dunes that have been transformed into a vegetated landscape in a classic example of plant succession. Inland from the beach, bare sand has been colonized by native "pioneer" species such as beach sagewort and sand verbena. These plants have stabilized the dunes and created a soil in which larger species such as coyote brush and coffeeberry have become established; these in turn are being replaced by Monterey pine and coast live oak, which represent the final stage in plant succession. To protect native dune plants such as Tidestrom's lupine and Menzies wallflower—both endangered endemics—Hottentot fig, an encroaching exotic, has been removed.

The Asilomar Conference Center at 800 Asilomar Blvd. off Sunset Dr. was established as a YWCA retreat in 1913. It has been the site of many notable events, including a meeting in 1971 that resulted in guidelines for Proposition 20, the Coastal Initiative, and the 1975 worldwide conference on genetic engineering. The name Asilomar is derived from Spanish to suggest "refuge by the sea." Architect Julia Morgan designed the original Conference Center buildings, which now include over 50 lodging and meeting facilities. For information and reservations, call: (408) 372-8016.

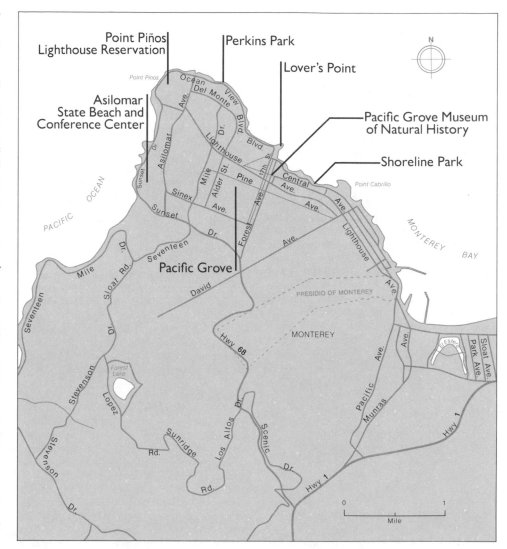

Point Piños Lighthouse

213

17-Mile Drive: *Coastal toll road between Pacific Grove and Carmel, Del Monte Forest.*

Seventeen-Mile Drive originated in 1881 when the Pacific Improvement Company opened a road to be used for sightseeing tours for its Del Monte Hotel guests. Horsedrawn coaches, called tallyho's, made a 17-mile round trip from the City of Monterey along the coast of Pacific Grove south to the Carmel Mission, and back over Carmel Hill to Monterey. The wooded area between Pacific Grove and Carmel became known as the Del Monte Forest.

Today, 17-Mile Drive is a scenic toll road that winds along the coast through the Del Monte Forest portion of the original Seventeen-Mile Drive. Samuel Morse, the grandnephew of the inventor of Morse code, acquired the Del Monte Forest in 1919. Morse subdivided the land while preserving much of the Monterey pine and cypress tree forest. Today, the 8,400-acre Del Monte Forest is a private community managed by the Pebble Beach Company and developed with elaborate homes of many styles, seven golf courses, and hiking and equestrian trails. There are five toll gates to 17-Mile Drive including one in Pacific Grove via Sunset Dr. off Highway 68, and one in Carmel via San Antonio Ave. off Ocean Avenue. Call: (408) 649-8500.

The following areas are located off 17-Mile Drive: S. F. B. Morse Botanical Reserve, Moss Beach, Seal and Bird Rocks, Fanshell Beach, Cypress Point Lookout, the Lone Cypress, Pescadero Point, Pebble Beach, and Stillwater Cove Access.

S. F. B. Morse Botanical Reserve: *Bird Rock Rd. and Congress Rd., Del Monte Forest.*

Dedicated to Samuel Morse for his preservation of the Del Monte Forest, the 86-acre reserve lies within the Huckleberry Hill Natural Habitat Area, which offers hiking trails and features an unusual association of closed-cone coniferous trees. It is the only place in the world where Monterey pines and Bishop pines grow together. The old wave-cut marine terraces of Huckleberry Hill contain Pleistocene deposits of poor-draining claypan soil and acidic podsol that support a stunted community, or "pygmy forest," of Bishop pine and the endangered endemic Gowen cypress. The Gowen cypress is known to occur only at this location and at Point Lobos State Reserve. Eastwood's ericameria and Monterey clover, both endangered endemics, occur within the area, which also supports western harvest mice, jack rabbits, mule deer, and an occasional mountain lion.

Spanish Bay: *Along Spanish Bay Rd., off 17-Mile Drive, Del Monte Forest.*

A broad, fine-grained sandy beach known as Moss Beach fronts Spanish Bay and stretches north to Asilomar State Beach. Moss Beach, due to its variety of underwater habitats, has the greatest diversity of marine algae on the Monterey Peninsula, which itself has the largest number of algal species on the West Coast. The beach was historically backed by sand dunes and Monterey pines; this combination of coastal dunes and maritime pine forest is uncommon in

Central and Southern California. Recent development and sand mining have resulted in the destruction of dune fields and native vegetation. A large-scale dune restoration project can be seen inland from the beach; the reconstructed dunes near the Spanish Bay Resort Golf Course will be planted with indigenous species.

Point Joe, southwest of Moss Beach, marks the south end of Spanish Bay. Site of several shipwrecks, the area directly offshore here has been dubbed "The Restless Sea" for the unusual wave patterns and turbulence resulting from ocean bottom topography and the meeting of ocean swells and currents. Pacific Grove clover and Monterey milk vetch, both endangered endemics, grow on the coastal terrace to the south.

Seal and Bird Rocks: *Bird Rock Rd. and 17-Mile Drive, Del Monte Forest.*

Harbor seals, California sea lions, and Steller sea lions haul out on offshore Seal and Bird Rocks, which provide roosting sites for gulls and seabirds. The Indian Village natural habitat area, located east of 17-Mile Drive at Seal Rock Creek, supports Hickman's cinquefoil and Monterey clover, both endangered endemics.

Fanshell Beach: *Signal Hill Rd. and 17-Mile Drive, Del Monte Forest.*

Sea otters frequent the crescent-shaped cove offshore of this sandy beach, which is used for picnicking and fishing. Pink sand verbena and the endangered Menzies wallflower occur on the dunes, which provide habitat for the black legless lizard.

Cypress Point Lookout: *W. of Portola Rd. and 17-Mile Drive, Del Monte Forest.*

The lookout provides one of the most spectacular views along 17-Mile Drive: on a clear

The Lone Cypress

day one can see Point Sur, located 20 miles to the south along the Big Sur Coast. Black oyster-catchers, western gulls, and cormorants nest on offshore rocks.

Crocker Cypress Grove, southeast of Cypress Point off 17-Mile Drive, is a 13-acre reserve that contains some of the largest and oldest Monterey cypress trees in existence. Native stands of Monterey cypress occur at only two places in the world: between Cypress Point and Pescadero Point, and at Point Lobos State Reserve.

The Lone Cypress: *.75 mi. S. of Cypress Point, off 17-Mile Drive, Del Monte Forest.*

The Lone Cypress, one of California's most familiar landmarks, is a popular attraction for tourists, artists, and photographers. The solitary, wind-blown Monterey cypress grows on a granite headland just north of Midway Point.

Pescadero Point: *1.5 mi. S. of Cypress Point off 17-Mile Drive, Del Monte Forest.*

Pescadero Point, a blufftop overlook with a rocky shore and tidepools below, marks the northern tip of Carmel Bay. The Ghost Tree and Witch Tree are located on opposite sides of 17-Mile Drive just north of the point; these Monterey cypress trees are named for their bleached-white twisted trunks and gnarled branches shaped over time by wind and sea spray. Author Robert Louis Stevenson described Monterey cypress trees as "ghosts fleeing before the wind."

Pebble Beach: *Cypress Dr. off 17-Mile Drive, Del Monte Forest.*

From 1868 to 1912, Pebble Beach was the site of a Chinese fishing village. The Pacific Improvement Company built a log cabin here in 1908 for its Del Monte Hotel guests, adding a row of cottages in 1912. The cottages, referred to as the Pebble Beach Lodge, were destroyed by fire in 1917. Two years later, the Del Monte Lodge was built here; the lodge eventually became a world-famous resort hotel, and was renamed The Lodge at Pebble Beach in 1977. The Concours d'Elegance is a classic car show held here each August. Adjacent Pebble Beach Golf Links, site of the 1972 and 1982 U. S. Open and the 1977 PGA Championships, hosted the Bing Crosby National Pro-Am Tournament from 1947 until 1985. Call: (408) 649-8500.

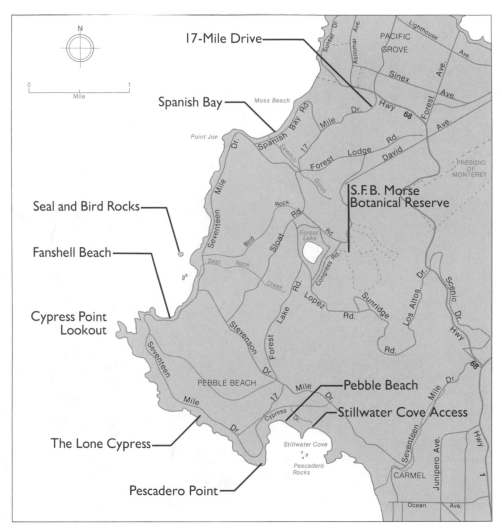

Stillwater Cove Access: *End of Cypress Dr., off Hwy. 1, Del Monte Forest.*

A small, sandy beach and a pier with a boat hoist are located at the southwest end of the private Beach Club parking lot, just south of The Lodge at Pebble Beach. The beach provides diving access to Stillwater Cove, which is protected from northwest swells by Pescadero Point. The rocky substrate of the cove supports giant kelp, puffball sponges, sunflower stars, plume worms, and sea hares. Harbor seals haul out on offshore Pescadero Rocks.

Seal and Bird Rocks, off 17-Mile Drive

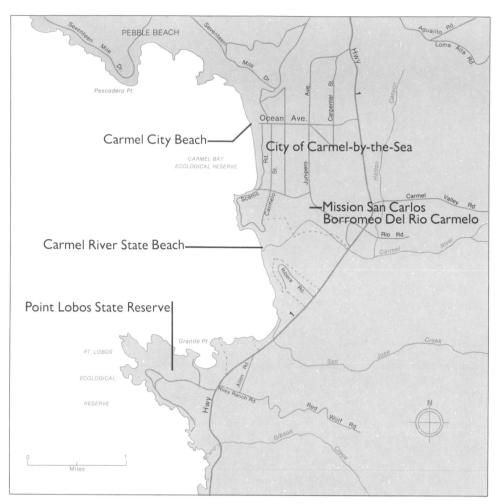

Carmel City Beach

City of Carmel-by-the-Sea

CARMEL BAY ECOLOGICAL RESERVE

Mission San Carlos Borromeo Del Rio Carmelo

Carmel River State Beach

Point Lobos State Reserve

City of Carmel-by-the-Sea: *Off Ocean Ave., W. of Hwy. 1, 2 mi. S. of City of Monterey.*

Carmel City was the name of the townsite established in 1888, which was succeeded in the early 1900s by a subdivision, Carmel-by-the-Sea. In 1904, under the influence of poet George Sterling and author Mary Austin, Carmel became a Bohemian colony, attracting other writers and artists including photographer Arnold Genthe and painter Xavier Martinez. Carmel was incorporated in 1916. Today, Carmel retains a number of unusual features; for example, houses are given individual names, instead of street numbers, and all trees are registered and may not be cut down without permission. Carmel is known for its boutiques and over 75 art and photography galleries; call: (408) 624-2522. Carmel achieved notoriety in 1986 when movie actor Clint Eastwood was elected mayor. The annual midsummer Bach Festival, held at the outdoor Forest Theater, features music of many classical composers played by top performers; call: (408) 624-1521.

Carmel City Beach: *Off Hwy. 1, foot of Ocean Ave., Carmel.*

This fine-grained, white sandy beach is popular for picnicking, swimming, and surfing. The beach, composed of eroded granite with quartz and feldspar, is backed by a large dune and bluff that supports Monterey cypress. Annual events include the Kite-Flying Contest, held each May, and the Sand Castle Contest in early fall. Wheelchair-accessible restrooms and parking are provided. Call: (408) 624-3543.

Scenic Road winds around Carmel Point past Walker House, designed by Frank Lloyd Wright, and Butterfly House, a private residence named for its wing-shaped roof. Poet Robinson Jeffers moved to Carmel in 1914 and wrote about the Big Sur Coast and its people. Jeffers' Tor House, which he built out of granite boulders, is located off Scenic Rd. at Ocean View Ave. and Stewart Way; for tour information, call: (408) 624-1813.

Mission San Carlos Borromeo Del Río Carmelo: *W. of Hwy. 1 at Rio Rd., Carmel.*

Mission San Carlos Borromeo was founded by Father Junípero Serra in Monterey in 1770, and was moved to its present location near the Carmel River in 1771, where it became known as the Carmel Mission. The mission, which was the second established in California, fell into ruins after secularization in 1833 and was not

Carmel River State Beach

Robinson Jeffers' Tor House

fully restored until 1936. Over 3,000 Indians are buried in the cemetery beside the mission church in which Fathers Serra and Crespí are interred. The church is noted for its star-shaped window and Moorish tower. The mission features two museums; call: (408) 624-3600. Mission Trail Park to the east provides access to the Lester Rowntree Memorial Arboretum.

Carmel River State Beach: *Scenic Rd. at Carmelo St., Carmel.*

Carmel River and Bay were named by Vizcaíno in 1602 for the three Carmelite friars on his expedition. The north end of Carmel River State Beach is used for diving access to underwater kelp forests; the rocky bottom supports sea lemons, strawberry anemones, and California hydrocoral. The adjacent Carmel River Bird Sanctuary at the mouth of the Carmel River is a brackish water lagoon and marsh habitat where gulls and shorebirds rest and feed; steelhead trout spawn upstream. Wheelchair-accessible restrooms and parking are available. Additional beach access is located south of Carmel River off Highway 1 and Ribera Road.

The southernmost stretch of the state beach, off Highway 1 just north of Point Lobos, is known as Monastery Beach for the nearby Carmelite Monastery, or as San Jose Creek Beach for adjacent San Jose Creek. Upwelling from the Carmel Submarine Canyon, located just offshore, supplies nutrients for the rich marine life of Carmel Bay; the deep canyon also contributes to the dangerous surf conditions of this steep, coarse-grained sandy beach. The safest diving access is from the extreme north end of the beach near a rocky area and the adjoining kelp forest. Restrooms and limited parking are available. Call: (408) 649-2836.

Offshore, the Carmel Bay Ecological Reserve stretches from Pescadero Point in the Del Monte Forest south to Granite Point in Point Lobos State Reserve. Marine invertebrates and plants within the undersea reserve are protected and may not be disturbed or removed. The California Sea Otter Game Refuge, which protects the threatened species, extends from the Carmel River south to Santa Rosa Creek in San Luis Obispo County. The Sea Otter Education Center, located east of Carmel off Highway 1 and Rio Rd. at 3750 The Barnyard, provides information on sea otters; call: (408) 625-3290.

Point Lobos State Reserve: *W. of Hwy. 1 at Riley Ranch Rd., Carmel.*

Established in 1933, the 1,300-acre state reserve encompasses a forested rocky headland, grassy meadows, sandy coves, tidepools, pebble beaches, a creek, and the underwater area surrounding the point. The reserve's six-mile-long coastline is composed of granite and a sedimentary rock formation of sandstone and gravel called Carmelo conglomerate. The point was originally named Punta de los Lobos Marinos, "Point of the Sea Wolves," for the California sea lions that haul out on offshore rocks. Point Lobos contains shell mounds of the Rumsen tribelet of Ohlone Indians; the area has also been the site of a Chinese fishing village, a whaling station, and an abalone cannery. Author Robert Louis Stevenson visited Point Lobos in 1879, and used the landscape here as inspiration for the setting of his novel *Treasure Island*.

Point Lobos features one of two native stands of Monterey cypress in the world; the other occurs north of Carmel. The endangered Gowen cypress grows only here and in the Del Monte

Forest. The reserve also contains one of the world's four native stands of Monterey pine. In addition to numerous wildflowers, such as sun cups and brodiaea, the area contains bluff lettuce, lace lichen, and fly agaric, a poisonous mushroom. Mound Meadow, which supports purple needlegrass, is the southernmost example of the north coastal prairie plant community. Wrentits and white-crowned sparrows nest in coastal scrub vegetation such as California sagebrush and lilac. Bobcats, mule deer, and dusky-footed woodrats also inhabit the reserve.

In 1960, the first underwater reserve in the U.S. was established on 750 submerged acres off Point Lobos; this area was designated the Point Lobos Ecological Reserve in 1973. Blue whales and minke whales are occasionally seen from shore. Harbor seals haul out on offshore islets, which provide roosting sites for numerous seabirds, and sea otters raft in large stands of giant kelp. The kelp forms an extensive floating canopy under which numerous marine species thrive, including abalone, rockfish, kelp greenling, and lingcod. All marine life within the reserve is protected, and fishing of any kind is prohibited. Diving is permitted only in Whalers and Bluefish coves and is limited to ten pairs of divers per day by permit only, available at the entrance gate; the Whalers Cove parking area provides diving access via a boat ramp.

Point Lobos is maintained as a pristine area, and all plants, rocks, wood, sea shells, and animal life are protected and may not be disturbed, removed, or collected. Dogs are not allowed in the reserve, and visitors are required to stay on hiking trails, except at several beaches. Facilities include picnic areas and wheelchair-accessible restrooms. Guide maps and docent-led walking tours are available. Call: (408) 624-4909.

Point Lobos State Reserve

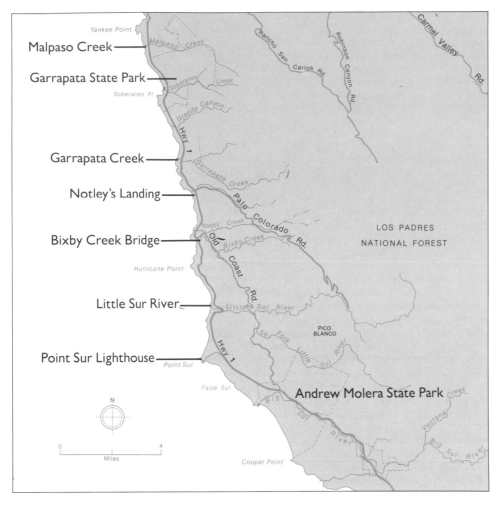

Malpaso Creek

Garrapata State Park

Garrapata Creek

Notley's Landing

Bixby Creek Bridge

Little Sur River

Point Sur Lighthouse

Andrew Molera State Park

Malpaso Creek: *Hwy. 1, 2 mi. S. of Point Lobos State Reserve, Carmel Highlands.*

The area known as the Big Sur Coast extends from Malpaso Creek 70 miles south to San Luis Obispo County. East of Highway 1, Monterey pines grow on the sides of the creek gorge. Nature photographer and environmentalist Ansel Adams, who photographed the Big Sur Coast, lived nearby until his death in 1985.

Garrapata State Park: *Hwy. 1, 2 mi. S. of Malpaso Creek, Big Sur Coast.*

Established in 1983, the park offers a number of coastal blufftop trails. Interpretive panels just south of Soberanes Creek provide information on local marine life. A trail leads to Soberanes Point, a popular whale-watching spot, where western gulls and pelagic cormorants roost. Restrooms and roadside parking are available. For information, call: (408) 667-2316.

The Granite Canyon Marine Resources Laboratory of the Department of Fish and Game is south of Soberanes Point off Highway 1 at the mouth of Granite Creek. An annual open house the first weekend in May features a display on sea otters and a marine life "touch tank." Red and pink abalone, which the mariculture lab cultivates for experimental seeding programs, can be viewed during their various stages of development. For information on tours for school groups, call: (408) 624-0255.

Garrapata Creek: *Hwy. 1, 1.5 mi. S. of Granite Canyon, Big Sur Coast.*

One of the larger streams in the Big Sur region, Garrapata Creek flows down a deep canyon that supports alder thickets and a redwood forest. The mouth of the stream empties out through a sheer granite gorge covered with orange lichen into a small estuary; steelhead trout spawn upstream. The steep, sandy Garrapata Beach is visible from the Highway 1 bridge.

Notley's Landing: *Along Hwy. 1, S. of Palo Colorado Canyon, Big Sur Coast.*

This historic settlement was named after the Notley brothers, Bill and Godfrey, who operated a timber mill here from 1898 to 1907. The remains of Notley's Landing include the homestead building made of redwood logs, the ruins of a barn, and the old Palo Colorado schoolhouse. West of Highway 1 is the foundation of what is thought to be part of a winch mechanism used for transferring lumber and tanbark onto ships offshore. Pigeon guillemots and western gulls nest on the cliffs below the road. Palo Colorado Road, just north of the Rocky Creek Bridge, is a narrow, winding road that leads eight miles inland to the Bottcher's Gap Campground of Los Padres National Forest, which provides access to the Ventana Wilderness.

Bixby Creek Bridge: *Hwy. 1 and Old Coast Rd., 1 mi. S. of Rocky Creek, Big Sur Coast.*

The concrete arch of Bixby Bridge—originally called Rainbow Bridge—spans the creek and canyon of the same name. Rancher Charles Bixby homesteaded here near the mouth of Mill Creek, later called Bixby Creek. This area became known as Bixby Landing. In 1904, Bixby sold his land to the Monterey Lime Company, which excavated limestone and produced lime

Bixby Creek Bridge

that was transported in kegs via cables and chutes from Long Ridge down to warehouses at Bixby Point; production ceased in 1910 when the deforested canyon could no longer supply a cheap source of fuel to fire the lime kiln.

At the time of its construction in 1932, Bixby Bridge was the highest single-arch bridge in the world, reaching 260 feet in height. The Bixby Canyon cabin of poet Lawrence Ferlinghetti was frequented by many Beat Generation writers in the late 1950s, including Jack Kerouac, whose novel *Big Sur* describes his visits.

Bixby Creek supports alders and maples. Tufted puffins and common murres nest on the cliffs around Hurricane Point to the south, which provides spectacular views of the Big Sur Coast. Old Coast Road, which begins at the north end of Bixby Bridge, is a scenic inland drive that rejoins Highway 1 at Andrew Molera State Park to the south.

Little Sur River: *Hwy. 1, 3.5 mi. S. of Bixby Bridge, Big Sur Coast.*

Originally called El Río Chiquito del Sur, "The Little River of the South," the Little Sur River is now part of the State Protected Waterway System and will remain undammed. The endangered endemic Little Sur manzanita grows near the coast. Steelhead trout spawn upstream. The headwaters of the Little Sur River support the densest and most extensive redwood forest in the Big Sur area; a trail through the forest is located off Old Coast Rd. a half-mile south of the bridge that crosses the south fork of the river.

The white top of Pico Blanco, a 3,709-foot mountain visible to the east, consists of meta-morphosed limestone, or calcium carbonate, that is unusually close to the surface. Pico Blanco held religious significance for the Esselen Indians, who occupied an area along the coast between Point Sur and Big Creek. During the late 19th century, limestone was mined from several locations in the Big Sur region; recently, exploratory mining of Pico Blanco was conducted to determine the economic feasibility of a larger scale open-pit mining operation.

Point Sur Lighthouse: *W. of Hwy. 1, 1.5 mi. S. of the Little Sur River, Big Sur Coast.*

In 1889, the Point Sur Light Station was built 270 feet above the ocean on the Point Sur headland. The initial light source for its Fresnel lens was a whale oil lantern. The lighthouse became fully automated in 1975. For tour information call: (408) 667-2316. Point Sur is an island of basaltic rock that is connected to the mainland

Point Sur

by a large sandbar; this rare geologic formation is called a tombolo. Snowy plovers nest on the sandy beach, which is backed by low-lying dunes. The Navy dirigible *Macon* crashed off Point Sur in 1935. False Sur to the south is named for its resemblance to Point Sur when viewed from sea; a small naval research facility is adjacent to Point Sur.

Andrew Molera State Park: *Off Hwy. 1, 21 mi. S. of Carmel, Big Sur Coast.*

The Molera Ranch was formerly part of Rancho El Sur, an 1834 Mexican land grant of 8,949 acres that was acquired in 1855 by Juan Bautista Rogers Cooper, a sea otter fur trader. His granddaughter Frances Molera gave a large portion of the Molera Ranch to the state in 1965 in memory of her brother Andrew. Opened in 1972, the park's 4,749 acres include meadows, mountains, ten miles of hiking trails, a walk-in campground, and two and a half miles of sandy beach. The Big Sur River flows through the park and supports vegetation such as thimbleberry, big-leaf maple, and coast redwood. A trail parallels the river and leads through a eucalyptus grove, where Monarch butterflies overwinter, to the river mouth; shorebirds such as willets, sanderlings, and northern phalaropes frequent a shallow lagoon. Turkey vultures, black-shouldered kites, coyotes, bobcats, and mule deer also inhabit the park. Coastal prairie plants include rattlesnake grass, little quaking grass, and Italian rye. Park facilities include parking and restrooms. Guided hikes are offered during the summer; call: (408) 667-2316.

Andrew Molera State Park

Pfeiffer Beach

Big Sur River: *River mouth is 2.5 mi. S. of Point Sur, Big Sur Coast.*

Originally called El Río Grande del Sur, "The Big River of the South," by Spanish missionaries in Carmel, the Big Sur River is now part of the State Protected Waterway System. The river, which flows through the Santa Lucia Mountains, supports vegetation such as red alder, willow, and coast redwood, and also provides habitat for the two-striped garter snake and the American dipper, a resident bird; steelhead trout spawn upstream. The river mouth, accessible via Andrew Molera State Park, is a good bird-watching spot.

Big Sur Valley: *Off Hwy. 1, 25 mi. S. of Carmel.*

The Big Sur Valley is a rural community located a few miles inland from the coast between Andrew Molera State Park and the Ventana Inn. The valley was homesteaded in the late 1860s by American settlers, including the Pfeiffers and the Posts. Several privately-run campgrounds and resorts are located off Highway 1 in redwood groves along the Big Sur River, including Big Sur, Riverside, and Fernwood campgrounds.

Pfeiffer Big Sur State Park: *E. of Hwy. 1, 26 mi. S. of Carmel, Big Sur Coast.*

Established in 1934, the 821-acre state park is named after John Pfeiffer, the son of Michael Pfeiffer, who homesteaded in the Big Sur Valley in 1869. The park offers hiking in the redwoods, picnicking, fishing in the Big Sur River, and camping; group campsites are also available. Riparian vegetation along the Big Sur River, which flows through the park, includes coast redwood, sycamore, black cottonwood, and bigleaf maple trees. Common birds include Steller's jays, canyon wrens, dark-eyed juncos, chestnut-backed chickadees, band-tailed pigeons, red-tailed hawks, and belted kingfishers. Coast horned lizards, California mountain kingsnakes, wild pigs, and mule deer also inhabit the park. Pfeiffer Falls, accessible via a trail, is situated in a fern-lined canyon. Docent-led nature walks are given in the summer. The Big Sur Lodge, located within the park, offers cabins; call: (408) 667-2171. For park information and reservations, call: (408) 667-2316.

Los Padres National Forest/Ventana Wilderness: *Santa Lucia Mtns., between Mt. Carmel and the San Luis Obispo County line, Big Sur Coast.*

Los Padres National Forest, which comprises 1,753,000 acres in five counties, is popular for hiking, camping, and backpacking. The largest coastal section of the national forest consists of 325,000 acres within the rugged Santa Lucia Mountains along the Big Sur Coast. The mountains are vegetated with coast live oak, madrone, ponderosa pine, knobcone pine, and Douglas-fir. The rare endemic Santa Lucia fir occurs naturally only in these mountains on steep, rocky slopes. The dry southward-facing slopes support chaparral plants such as chamise, ceanothus, toyon, cascara, manzanita, and yucca. Coast redwoods grow on the cool northward-facing slopes of deep canyons, which receive year-round moisture. The Santa Lucia slender salamander inhabits the deep leaf-litter of redwood and mixed-evergreen forests. Southern

sea otter (*Enhydra lutris*)
4 to 4½ feet long

rubber boas, western rattlesnakes, coast horned lizards, wild pigs, mule deer, and mountain lions also inhabit the forest area.

The Ventana Wilderness consists of 164,503 acres within the Big Sur section of Los Padres National Forest. Its rugged terrain is characterized by V-shaped valleys separated by steep-sided ridges, with elevations up to 5,862 feet at Junipero Serra Peak. The Marble Cone fire of 1977 was started by lightning and burned over 90 per cent of the wilderness; most of the vegetation has since grown back. More than 235 miles of trails provide access to remote campsites in the wilderness, including the Pine Ridge Trail at the Big Sur Ranger Station, located east of Highway 1 just south of the entrance to Pfeiffer Big Sur State Park. Call: (408) 385-5434.

Pfeiffer Beach: *W. of Hwy. 1, end of Sycamore Canyon Rd., Big Sur Coast.*

The sandy beach, included in Los Padres National Forest, is at the end of the unmarked Sycamore Canyon Rd., which is the second right turn off Highway 1 one mile south of the entrance to Pfeiffer Big Sur State Park. The narrow, winding, two-mile-long road parallels Sycamore Creek, which supports a redwood forest and riparian vegetation such as ferns, California bay laurel, and sycamore. A sandy trail leads to the creek mouth at Pfeiffer Beach that is frequented by gulls and sandpipers. Picturesque sea stacks and arches are visible just offshore. Wheelchair-accessible restrooms are available. For beach information, call: (408) 385-5434.

South of the Big Sur Valley, west of Highway 1, is a restaurant called Nepenthé, which has a deck 800 feet above the ocean; known as a popular hang-out for artists and writers during the 1960s, Nepenthé is named after the drug mentioned in Homer's *Odyssey* that cured grief, pain, or sorrow. The Henry Miller Memorial Library, located a half-mile south of Nepenthé, features reference materials and memorabilia on author Henry Miller, who lived nearby on Partington Ridge from 1944 until 1962; call: (408) 667-2574.

Deetjen's Big Sur Inn, south of the library, is a rustic resort with redwood cabins that typify Big Sur architecture; the resort was built by Norwegian Helmuth Deetjen in the early 1920s. The Coast Gallery, which displays local art, occupies two huge redwood water tanks at the mouth of Lafler Canyon; call: (408) 667-2301. The Highway 1 bridge across Torre Canyon to the south affords a bird's-eye view of the top of a redwood forest. The De Angulo Trail, which leads into the Ventana Wilderness of Los Padres National Forest, begins one mile south of Torre Canyon and east of Highway 1.

Julia Pfeiffer Burns State Park: *Hwy. 1, 37 mi. S. of Carmel, Big Sur Coast.*

The mountainous, 2,405-acre state park, which is named after John Pfeiffer's sister, features a picnic area in a redwood grove and hiking trails; walk-in environmental campsites are located in a cypress forest on a blufftop overlooking the ocean. A trail leads under Highway 1 through a tunnel to the edge of a 100-foot-high bluff overlooking a small cove; the McWay Creek waterfall spills into the ocean here. Vegetation in the park includes wood mint, redwood sorrel, ferns, trillium, poison oak, tanbark oak, and madrone. Southern alligator lizards, Mon-

terey ringneck snakes, and gray foxes inhabit the area. Facilities include restrooms and parking. The scar from the massive landslide of April 1983, which blocked through-traffic along Highway 1 for over a year, is south of the park entrance. The historic site of Anderson's Landing, from which James Anderson shipped redwood lumber and tanbark during the 1860s, is south of the slide at the mouth of Anderson Canyon.

The 1,680-acre Julia Pfeiffer Burns Underwater Area, offshore between Partington Point and McWay Creek, was established in 1970.

Kelp forests provide habitat for sea otters and for abundant marine life such as abalone, tubesnouts, and lingcod. A trail where Highway 1 crosses Partington Creek leads down Partington Canyon, through a 110-foot-long tunnel in the rock, and emerges at Partington Cove. During the 1880s John Partington, who homesteaded in the area in 1874, operated Partington Landing at the cove; lumber and tanbark were transferred from the landing onto ships. The rocky shoreline provides diving access to the underwater area. Call: (408) 667-2315.

Big Sur Coast

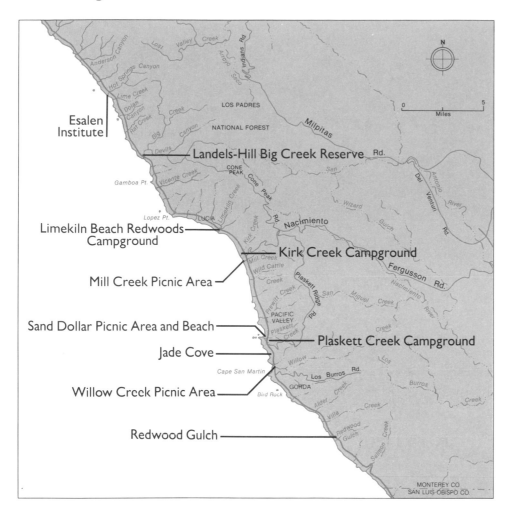

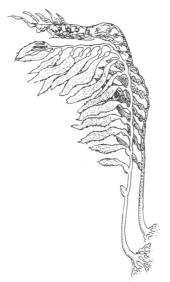

giant kelp (*Macrocystis pyrifera*)
to 250 feet long

reserve. The rocky bottom offshore supports owl limpets, small brooding chitons, and a forest of giant kelp, in which sea otters can be seen.

Big Creek, which runs through the reserve, was the boundary between the Esselen Indians, who lived as far north as Point Sur, and the Salinan Indians, whose territory stretched south into San Luis Obispo County. The Rat Creek Fire of 1986 was started by lightning and burned the entire reserve; much of the vegetation has resprouted and is growing back. The Nature Conservancy offers docent-led walks of the reserve by reservation only; call: (415) 777-0541. The endangered Smith's blue butterfly reaches the southernmost extent of its range near the small community of Lucia, five miles south of Big Creek.

Limekiln Beach Redwoods Campground: *Off Hwy. 1, 2 mi. S. of Lucia, Big Sur Coast.*

The privately-run sandy beach and campground are situated at the mouth of the redwood-forested Limekiln Canyon. Popular activities include hiking, surf fishing, and trout fishing in Limekiln Creek; call: (408) 667-2403. The creek mouth is the historic site of Rockland Landing, from which lime was shipped during the 1870s; a short trail leads to four historic lime kilns. Limekiln Canyon is one of the steepest coastal canyons in the U.S., rising 5,155 feet to Cone Peak in less than three and a half miles. Within this gradient, twelve different plant communities have been identified, from coastal strand to alpine forest.

The following units of Los Padres National Forest are located along Highway 1 south of Limekiln Creek: Kirk Creek Campground, Mill Creek Picnic Area, Sand Dollar Picnic Area and Beach, Plaskett Creek Campground, Jade Cove, Willow Creek Picnic Area, and Redwood Gulch. Most have parking, restrooms, and/or picnic and camping facilities. Call: (408) 385-5434.

Kirk Creek Campground: *W. of Hwy. 1, 2 mi. S. of Limekiln Creek, Big Sur Coast.*

The campground is located on a 100-foot-high bluff planted with non-native pampas grass and eucalyptus. A steep trail leads down to a sandy beach where anglers surf fish for jacksmelt and surfperch. The narrow, winding Nacimiento Fergusson Road to the south provides the only access to the Big Sur Coast from the Salinas Valley. Mission San Antonio De Padua is located 20 miles inland.

Mill Creek Picnic Area: *W. of Hwy. 1, 1 mi. S. of Kirk Creek, Big Sur Coast.*

The picnic area is adjacent to a small rocky and sandy beach, which provides diving access to offshore beds of giant and bull kelp. Marine life includes black abalone, rockfish, and cabezon. The Vicente Trail begins north of Mill Creek and leads inland past sagebrush, coyote brush, ceanothus, and chamise.

Pacific Valley is a small community about seven miles south of Lucia on a prominent marine terrace between Wild Cattle Creek and Plaskett Ridge Road. Blufftop trails within Los Padres National Forest are accessible west of Highway 1. Hang gliders, who launch from Plaskett Ridge, use the blufftop as a landing site. All hang gliders must register with the Pacific Valley Ranger Station; call: (805) 927-4211.

Esalen Institute: *W. of Hwy. 1, 3 mi. S. of Julia Pfeiffer Burns State Park, Big Sur Coast.*

Around 1870, Thomas Slate acquired the hot sulfur springs located here on the cliffs above the rocky shore and built a resort called Slate's Hot Springs. In 1910, Dr. Henry Murphy bought the resort, which became known as Big Sur Hot Springs. Michael Murphy (a relative of Dr. Murphy) and Dick Price founded the Esalen Institute on the site of the resort in 1961. Best known as an early center for the "human potential" movement, Esalen is a retreat that offers classes and workshops on education, religion, philosophy, and the physical and behavioral sciences. Progressive thinkers and writers such as Alan Watts, Aldous Huxley, Abraham Maslow, Gregory Bateson, and Ken Kesey have all held seminars at the institute. The hot springs are open to the public for a fee every morning from 1–5 AM. For information on programs and lodging, call: (408) 667-2335.

Landels-Hill Big Creek Reserve: *Hwy. 1, 4 mi. S. of the Esalen Institute, Big Sur Coast.*

The mountainous, 3,858-acre reserve is part of the University of California Natural Reserve System and is managed by the University's Santa Cruz campus, which uses it for teaching and research. The reserve supports wild oats, coffeeberry, Coulter pine, ponderosa pine, coast redwood, and the rare endemic Hoover's manzanita and Santa Lucia fir; the endangered Hutchinson's larkspur also occurs here. Spotted owls, black swifts, side-blotched lizards, wild pigs, mule deer, and mountain lions inhabit the

Sand Dollar Picnic Area and Beach: *W. of Hwy. 1, 4 mi. S. of Mill Creek, Big Sur Coast.*

A trail leads from the picnic area across a grassy meadow to the edge of a blufftop overlooking a crescent-shaped bay. The sandy beach that fronts the bay is accessible via a steep trail. Pacific sanddab, white croaker, and flounder inhabit the nearshore waters. Gulls roost on offshore rocks at the south end of the bay.

Plaskett Creek Campground: *E. of Hwy. 1, S. of Sand Dollar Picnic Area, Big Sur Coast.*

The campground, which has been planted with Monterey pine and cypress, features a large grassy picnic area and a hiking trail; group campsites are also available. Scrub jays and red-tailed hawks inhabit the area.

Jade Cove: *W. of Hwy. 1, .3 mi. S. of Plaskett Creek, Big Sur Coast.*

A trail leads from Highway 1 to the edge of a blufftop overlooking Jade Cove. The small rocky beach is accessible via a steep path that leads down the serpentine cliff face. Removal of jade or any rock is prohibited above the mean high tide level. The Big Sur Jade Company, which collects and sells jade, is located three miles south in the small community of Gorda.

Willow Creek Picnic Area: *W. of Hwy. 1, 1.5 mi. S. of Plaskett Creek, Big Sur Coast.*

A paved road at the southeast end of the Willow Creek Bridge leads down to a rocky beach. Vegetation includes arroyo willow, sagebrush, and wild buckwheat. Offshore kelp beds provide habitat for harbor seals and sea otters. Gulls and cormorants roost around Cape San Martin, a rocky point to the south.

Los Burros Rd., an unmarked dirt road about a mile south of Willow Creek, winds inland six miles to the Alder Creek Campground in the national forest. The campground is within the historic Los Burros Mining District, where W.D. Cruikshank discovered gold in 1887. Near the campground is the site of Mansfield, originally called Manchester, which in the late 1800s was a boom town with over 200 people, a hotel, post office, and five saloons; it was destroyed by fire in 1909. Gold and silver mines, now abandoned, operated in the area until 1915.

Redwood Gulch: *E. of Hwy. 1, 5 mi. S. of Willow Creek, Big Sur Coast.*

The coast redwood reaches the southernmost limit of its natural range near Redwood Gulch. The following hiking trails lead inland from Highway 1 to remote campsites within the national forest: Cruikshank Trail, which begins north of Redwood Gulch; Soda Springs Trail, located one mile south of the gulch; and Salmon Creek Trail, two miles south of the gulch. Salmon Creek features a large waterfall and supports riparian vegetation such as ferns, alders, and California bay laurel. Western skinks, salamanders, and mule deer inhabit the area.

Willow Creek Picnic Area

Sand Dollar Beach

San Luis Obispo County
Selected Species of Interest

 Plants: Giant coreopsis (*Coreopsis gigantea*), blooms bright yellow on Coreopsis Hill in the Nipomo Dunes February to March. **Nipomo Mesa lupine** (*Lupinus nipomensis*), endangered endemic of Nipomo Mesa.

 Trees: Santa Lucia fir (*Abies bracteata*), rarest fir in North America; grows in Santa Lucia Mountains. **Monterey pine** (*Pinus radiata*), found in Cambria; one of four relict populations in the world.

 Insects: Morro blue butterfly (*Plebejus icarioides morroensis*), lays eggs on bush lupines near Morro Bay. **Sand dune grasshopper moth** (*Areniscythris brachypteris*), flightless moth found in Nipomo Dunes among giant coreopsis.

 Invertebrates: Pismo clam (*Tivela stultorum*), endemic to Central California; inhabits the surf zone; once abundant in Pismo Beach area. **Geoduck clam** (*Panopea generosa*), found in mudflats of Morro Bay; has huge siphon.

 Amphibians and Reptiles: Foothill yellow-legged frog (*Rana boylii*), native California frog. **Two-striped garter snake** (*Thamnophis hammondii*), aquatic; rare black type found only at Montana de Oro and south to Oceano.

 Fish: Jacksmelt (*Atherinopsis californiensis*), commercial and sport fish, similar to grunion; caught from Morro Bay piers. **Prickly sculpin** (*Cottus asper*), mottled black or brown freshwater fish, found in Los Osos Creek.

 Birds: Peregrine falcon (*Falco peregrinus anatum*), endangered due to DDT poisoning in 1960s; now recovering. **Snowy plover** (*Charadrius alexandrinus*), nests in dry, sandy areas of Morro Spit; eats sand crabs and beetles.

 Land Mammals: Morro Bay kangaroo rat (*Dipodomys heermanni morroensis*), endangered; inhabits Baywood Park area. **Desert cottontail** (*Sylvilagus audubonii*), nocturnal, long-eared inhabitant of Nipomo Dunes.

 Marine Mammals: Harbor seal (*Phoca vitulina*), breeds on offshore rocks along county coast. **Southern sea otter** (*Enhydra lutris nereis*), near southern end of range in the county; inhabits kelp beds beyond surf zone.

San Luis Obispo County

SAN LUIS OBISPO COUNTY'S northern coast is a pristine landscape of forested mountains carved by numerous perennial streams that wind their way to the sea across narrow, grassy marine terraces. Prominent headlands at Ragged Point, Point Sierra Nevada, and Piedras Blancas Point separate long stretches of rocky coast where seabirds nest on offshore rocks, shorebirds forage along the water's edge, and passing whales or playful otters can frequently be seen beyond the surf line. Highway 1, cut into the steep slopes of the Santa Lucia Mountains, traverses the jagged north coast shoreline south to the gradually broadening coastal terrace at San Simeon, Cambria, and Cayucos.

Morro Bay lies at the midpoint of the San Luis Obispo County coast and is an important wildlife sanctuary. The bay, really an estuary that is sheltered from the ocean by a four-mile-long sand spit, is dominated by the looming presence of Morro Rock, a navigational landmark from the time of the first explorers along the California coast. Rising 581 feet above the ocean at the entrance channel to the bay, the rock is an ecological reserve protecting the endangered peregrine falcon.

South of Morro Bay the San Luis Mountains, part of the southern Coast Ranges, form a barrier to travel between the bay and the southern county coast. In these mountains, Montana de Oro State Park provides access to a largely undisturbed landscape with spring wildflower displays, rare geologic formations, and remote canyons where the Chumash Indians once walked. The coast south of the bulging headland of Point Buchon is inaccessible as far as the northern rim of San Luis Bay.

At Morro Bay the coast highway turns inland, skirting the northern flanks of the seven volcanic peaks, sometimes referred to as the "Seven Sisters," that form a chain southeast to San Luis Obispo. From San Luis Obispo, Highway 101 joins the coast highway, which turns west again and reaches the coast at San Luis Bay. Continuing south, the coast broadens into a wide plain edged with sandy beaches and undulating dunes from Pismo Beach to the Santa Maria River.

Chumash Indians greeted the first Spanish explorers to the San Luis Obispo coast, as noted in the diaries of Cabrillo, Portolá, and de Anza. Morro Bay marked the northern boundary of this populous Indian tribe whose territory extended south to what is now Ventura County. Middens and archaeological sites around Morro Bay and within the Nipomo Dunes are evidence of the Chumash presence here over the last 9,000 years.

The establishment of the mission at San Luis Obispo in 1772 initiated the era of Spanish settlement. By the mid-1850s, much of the coast was parceled into ranchos. Hides and tallow formed the basis of an extensive sea trade; Yankee and Mexican sailing ships regularly landed at the trading ports of San Simeon Point, Cayucos, and Cave Landing in San Luis Bay. A severe drought in the mid-1860s ended the ranching era, but American and European settlers began to arrive in increasing numbers, buying up cheap rancho land and establishing dairy and crop farms. A small mining boom in the Santa Lucia Mountains in the 1860s led to rapid growth in the villages of Cambria and Cayucos.

Until the intrastate railroads were built, beginning in the 1870s, coastal overland travel was hazardous and slow, and the coastal towns of San Luis Obispo County depended upon the sea for transportation, trade, and communication with the metropolitan centers of California. But the state's booming economy, ignited by the gold rush, was fast outgrowing the capacity of the coastal shipping trade, and the completion of the transcontinental railroad in 1869 ushered in a new era of economic expansion. The Southern Pacific Railroad line, completed in 1894, shifted the locus of development and trade from coastal port towns to San Luis Obispo, on the inland rail route.

Today San Luis Obispo County's economy depends largely upon agriculture and oil production. Over 65% of the county's coastal land is used to grow field crops and graze cattle. The most intensively cultivated land lies in the Santa Maria River floodplain in southern San Luis Obispo County and supports a variety of speciality crops, feed crops, and pastureland. The Santa Maria River basin is also the site of extensive oil refining facilities for nearby offshore oil reserves.

The county's fishing industry contributes nearly half the total annual Southern California fish catch—mostly rockfish, sole, and cod—caught by fishermen from Morro Bay and Avila.

The county's scenic resources attract large numbers of visitors, especially to the former Hearst family mansion in San Simeon, now a State Historical Monument, and to Morro Bay State Park and Pismo State Beach.

Morro Rock, Morro Bay

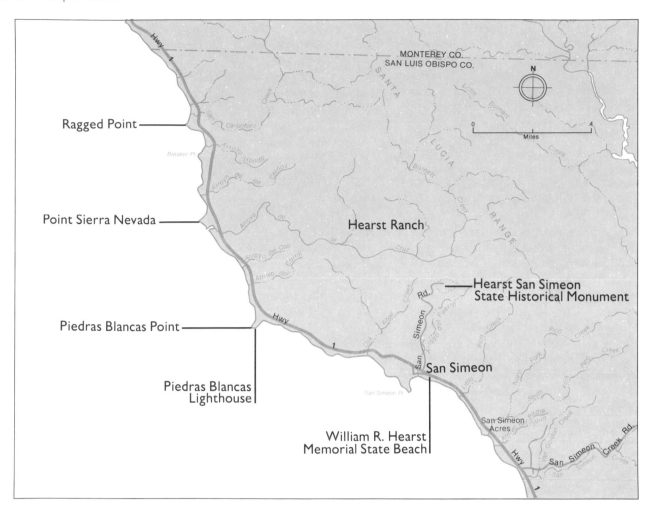

Piedras Blancas Lighthouse

Ragged Point: *W. of Hwy. 1, 12 mi. N.W. of San Simeon.*

The scrub-covered point terminates in a ragged spine of surf-washed rocks, bounded on either side by small sandy beaches. The intertidal rocks host colonies of mussels and other mollusks that provide food for foraging American black oystercatchers. The sea cliffs harbor nesting western gulls, pelagic cormorants, and pigeon guillemots.

San Carpoforo Creek, a spawning run for steelhead, empties into the ocean north of the point. A small freshwater wetland at the creek mouth extends inland, east of the Highway 1 overpass. It was at this creek mouth that Portolá's expedition camped for several days before attempting to cross the rugged Santa Lucia Mountains on the way to Monterey Bay. The Santa Lucia fir, the rarest fir in North America, grows along the creek in the higher ridges.

North of Ragged Point, Ragged Point Trail begins behind Ragged Point Inn at the edge of the lawn and descends the steep cliff face to a small beach cove.

Point Sierra Nevada: *W. of Hwy. 1, 3.5 mi. S. of Ragged Point.*

Arroyo de la Cruz empties into the ocean just south of the point. A small freshwater marsh west of the highway is frequented by migratory shorebirds such as sandpipers and yellowlegs, as well as by grebes and dabbling ducks; resident herons and egrets also forage in the marsh. Hickman's onion and the adobe sanicle, both endangered plants, grow near the creek mouth in the grassland on the mesa. The endangered endemic dwarf goldenstar and Arroyo de la Cruz mariposa-lily grow on the coastal bluff.

Piedras Blancas Point: *W. of Hwy. 1, 7 mi. S. of Ragged Point.*

The explorer Cabrillo noted the guano-covered rocks just south of the point on his voyage up the California coast in 1542, and called them "piedras blancas," or "white rocks." The rocks at the point are a California sea lion and harbor seal hauling-out ground, as well as a rookery for Brandt's cormorants.

A small population of the Salinan Indian tribe once inhabited the coast near Piedras Blancas Point, establishing seasonal camps along the coastal bluffs in winter and migrating a few miles inland to collect acorns, seeds, and berries in the summer. After they were gathered into the mission system at Mission San Antonio de Padua, located in what is now southern Monterey County, the coastal Salinans were employed to supplement the mission's meager winter food supplies. Indian runners were dispatched daily over 30 miles of rugged terrain to the coast to collect fish and shellfish.

Piedras Blancas Lighthouse: *On Piedras Blancas Point.*

In 1864 a crow's nest lookout was built on the point to alert whalers at nearby San Simeon of approaching leviathans, and a lighthouse was built on the same site in 1874. In 1949 the Fresnel lens and iron lanternhouse were removed from the top of the lighthouse tower and are now on display in nearby Cambria; an exposed aero-marine beacon replaced the original light. There is no public access to the lighthouse.

The U.S. Fish and Wildlife Service operates a sea otter research station at the lighthouse. The highest concentration of sea otters along California's coast is from Monterey Bay south to Point San Luis; otters can often be seen floating in the kelp canopy just beyond the breaking waves.

Hearst Ranch: *E. and W. of Hwy. 1 between Ragged Point and San Simeon.*

The private 86,000-acre Hearst Ranch straddles the Santa Lucia Mountains east of Highway 1, and extends along the coast from Ragged Point south to San Simeon Creek. Acquired by mining millionaire George Hearst in the latter half of the 19th century, the ranch comprises most of former Ranchos Piedra Blanca, San Simeon, and Santa Rosa. Hearst purchased the land after the drought of 1863-64 devastated Spanish livestock and forced many of the rancheros to sell land to pay their debts. The ranch, a cattle-raising operation, is managed by the Hearst Corporation.

Numerous perennial creeks and seasonally wet arroyos drain the western slopes of the Santa Lucia Mountains within the Hearst Ranch property, and empty into the sea west of Highway 1. Many rare and endangered endemic plants grow along the north slope of Arroyo de la Cruz; above the arroyo among thick stands of coyote brush are Hearst's and maritime ceanothus, Hearst's and Arroyo de la Cruz manzanita, and the compact cobweb thistle. Several species of reptiles and amphibians live in the moist environment of the arroyo, including garter snakes and yellow-legged frogs. Egrets, herons, American bitterns, wood ducks, coots, belted kingfishers, dippers, and bank swallows reside in the marshy area east of Highway 1. Steelhead spawn in Arroyo de la Cruz, and in several of the perennial streams that traverse the ranch lands.

Hearst San Simeon State Historical Monument: *E. of Hwy. 1 on San Simeon Rd., San Simeon.*

Originally part of the vast Hearst Ranch, William Randolph Hearst's castle-like estate was deeded to the state by Hearst's heirs in 1958. The only child of George and Phoebe Apperson Hearst, William Randolph inherited his father's mining and real estate fortune, as well as the extensive newspaper and radio empire, when his mother died. He earned renown as the builder of "La Cuesta Encantada," the mansion atop the "enchanted hill" overlooking the Pacific. The estate, designed by Julià Morgan in collaboration with Hearst, combines eclectic architectural styles into an overall Mediterranean theme; construction began in 1919 and continued for over 30 years. Hearst's retreat served both as an entertainment center for prominent politicians, businessmen, and movie stars of the day, and as a showcase for his immense art collection—all of it imported from abroad. The paintings, sculpture, furniture, and even exotic animals formed one of the largest private collections in the world. Four different tours of the estate include views of the rooms, gardens, and pools. Call: (805) 927-4621.

San Simeon: *Hwy. 1, at San Simeon Rd.*

Originally part of Rancho San Simeon, the village was a whaling station in 1864. When George Hearst bought the rancho in 1865 he constructed a wharf, a store, warehouses, and a pier from which he exported tallow, hides, grain, and quicksilver from cinnabar mines on the ranch land. Hearst built a new pier in 1878, expanding his export business to include local dairy products, dried seaweed, and abalones. The Sebastian General Store in San Simeon, little altered since it was established in 1873 and still in operation today, offers the visitor a glimpse of life here a century ago.

William R. Hearst Memorial State Beach: *W. of Hwy. 1 at San Simeon Rd.*

The eight-acre park has a fishing pier, picnic facilities, and a protected beach. For information, call: (805) 927-4621.

Schoolhouse, San Simeon

Hearst San Simeon State Historical Monument

San Simeon State Beach: *5 mi. S. of San Simeon.*

The state beach includes a campground at San Simeon Creek east of Highway 1; Moonstone Beach at Leffingwell Cove, west of Highway 1; and Santa Rosa Creek day use area, south of Leffingwell Cove. Call: (805) 927-4509.

The campground nestles in the hilly oak woodland north of San Simeon Creek. South of the creek, vernal pools appear in late spring where permanent depressions in the grassland fill with winter rains; as the water evaporates, the pools are transformed into concentric rings of contrasting color by blooming plants specially adapted to this microhabitat.

Moonstone Beach, south of San Simeon Creek, is named for the milky white agates that can be found in the sand; the moonstones, jaspers, and agates that make up the beach sands here are types of quartz. Originally part of larger rock formations, the quartz pebbles were eroded out of coastal mountains and carried by streams to the beach, where the constant washing of the surf ground and polished the stones. Tidepools border the beach at low tide; the bluffs provide a place to observe whales and sea otters. Resident herons and migratory grebes, ducks, and shorebirds frequent the small freshwater lagoon at the mouth of Santa Rosa Creek, south of the beach. The creek mouth marks the southern boundary of the California Sea Otter Game Refuge, which extends north to the Carmel River in Monterey County. Historically, the area now called Moonstone Beach was called Leffingwell Cove or Landing, after William Leffingwell, an early settler of Cambria.

Cambria Pines: *N.E. of Hwy. 1, Cambria.*

A real estate boom in 1927 resulted in the creation of this subdivision and a new commercial area on Main St., west of the original business district. Hillcrest Dr., off Main St., winds up a tree-covered ridge to the unusual residence built by local contractor Art Beal, also known as "Captain Nitwit." The several-storied house, with paths and terraces covering the hillside plot, was constructed of cement and embedded with bits of shell, old auto parts, glass, beer cans, and other found objects. Described as a "20th century folk art environment," the home is a California Historical Landmark.

Shamel County Park, off Highway 1 on Windsor Rd. south of Santa Rosa Creek, has a playground, picnic tables, and a swimming pool. Trails to the beach lead to tidepools and rock and surf fishing spots.

Along Windsor Rd., west of Highway 1, is a 380-acre area of native Monterey pines located within a low-density residential area. Although the Monterey pine is widely cultivated in many parts of the world, this stand is one of only four naturally occurring Monterey pine groves in the world; the other three such groves are in Monterey County, Santa Cruz/San Mateo counties, and Baja California.

Cambria: *On Hwy. 1, 10 mi. S. of San Simeon.*

In 1861 William Leffingwell built a saw pit on Leffingwell Creek, which supplied Cambria with lumber for the next two decades. A year later cinnabar ore, from which quicksilver, or mercury, is extracted, was discovered in the Santa Lucia Mountains east of the town, and the resultant mining boom caused rapid growth of the area. Copper, quicksilver, dairy products, and cattle hides were loaded onto schooners at nearby San Simeon Bay until Leffingwell built a pier in the cove at Cambria in 1874. In 1894 a rail line from San Luis Obispo was extended to Cambria, ending the coastal shipping trade. The town remained an isolated outpost until 1937 when the coast highway was finally completed between Cambria and Carmel.

Nitwit Ridge, State Historical Landmark, Cambria Pines

Mouth of San Simeon Creek, San Simeon State Beach

Estero Bay: *Point Estero to Point Buchon.*

Estero Bay was first sighted by Cabrillo in 1542 during his exploration of the California coast. The estero, or estuary, refers to Morro Bay, which it contains. In 1769 Portolá's expedition camped at the mouth of Villa Creek, in the northern crook of the bay.

Rocks of the Franciscan Formation visible in the cliffs near the mouth of Villa Creek were formed by volcanic activity deep beneath the mid-Pacific Ocean millions of years ago; tectonic movement caused the portion of sea floor containing these rocks to move eastward and eventually to collide with the North American Continental Plate. As subduction—slipping of the sea floor beneath the continental land mass—occurred, these rocks were scraped off and deposited at their present site.

From the late 1800s until China closed its ports at the end of World War II, seaweed was harvested along Estero Bay for commercial export. Local Chinese gathered the alga called sea lettuce, even cleaning selected rocks to induce its growth. The harvested seaweed was sun-dried and tied into 40-pound bales for shipment to San Francisco and China, where it was used in Chinese medicines. The residence of the last seaweed farmer, who continued his trade into the 1970s, stands on the wind-swept coastal terrace at China Point in the north end of Estero Bay.

At Cayucos Point, coralline algae and many marine invertebrates, including abalones, inhabit the tidepools that dot the shore. A favorite food of sea otters, abalones became abundant after the near extinction of the otters due to fur hunting in the 1700s and 1800s, and were commercially harvested in large quantities along this coast in the following decades. As the otter population re-established itself, humans have had to compete with the sea mammals for a dwindling supply of abalones. Today, a commercial mariculture operation in Estero Bay raises abalone artificially.

Cayucos Beach: *S.W. of N. Ocean Ave., Cayucos Creek to E. St., Cayucos.*

The beach includes restrooms, picnic facilities, and Cayucos Pier, which replaced the 940-foot pier built in 1875 by Captain James Cass. The original pier was a regular stop for the Pacific Steamship Company's ships. Captain Cass's redwood Victorian residence, built between 1867 and 1875, is located a block east of the pier entrance. Call: (805) 549-5200.

Named after Rancho Moro y Cayucos, the town of Cayucos was a dairy farming center when it was founded in 1875. In the early 1900s an abalone-drying enterprise operated on the site of the present-day Veteran's Building. Abalones were soaked in salt for 24 hours, then briefly boiled and set out to dry. About three tons per year were exported to San Francisco and Japan, where the dried meat sold for as little as two hundred dollars a ton. Several stairways in the residential area lead to Cayucos Beach.

Morro Strand State Beach: *W. of Studio Dr., 24th St. to Chaney Ave., Cayucos.*

The long, sandy beach is popular for beachcombing and surf fishing; facilities include restrooms and picnic tables. Call: (805) 772-2560.

Black turnstones in winter plumage, Moonstone Beach

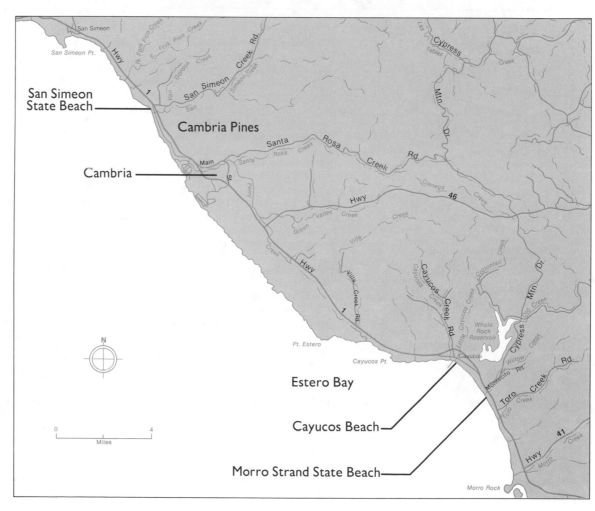

229

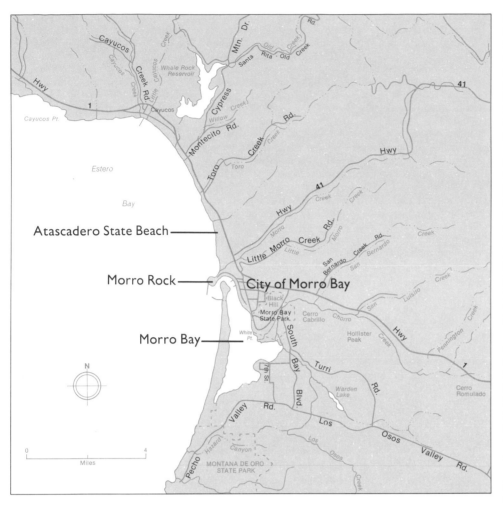

Atascadero State Beach

Morro Rock

Morro Bay

N

0   4
Miles

Atascadero State Beach: *W. of Hwy. 1, Yerba Buena Dr. to Atascadero Rd., Morro Bay.*

The broad, sandy beach fronts Estero Bay, and is a clamming, surf fishing, and surfing spot; there is a campground at the west end of Yerba Buena Drive. The dunes behind the beach offer excellent views of Morro Rock to the south. For information, call: (805) 772-2560.

Morro Rock: *W. end of Coleman Dr., Morro Bay.*

In 1542 explorer Juan Rodríguez Cabrillo named the distinctive dome-shaped rock "El Moro." Two centuries later, Portolá's land expedition camped along the north end of Morro Bay and recorded the presence of "a rounded morro," or promontory, at the entrance to the estuary. Between 1880 and 1969 more than a million tons of hard basaltic rock were quarried from Morro Rock; the rock was used to build breakwaters at Morro and San Luis bays.

In 1969 a 30-acre ecological reserve was established to protect the rock from further quarrying, and to preserve the nesting site of the endangered peregrine falcon. The falcon's worldwide population fell to a hundred pairs in the 1940s as a result of eggshell thinning and consequent fledgling mortality caused by pesticide contamination; by 1970 there were only ten peregrine falcons in California. After laws were passed banning use of the pesticides, artificial nesting boxes were used on Morro Rock and at other sites in an attempt to revive the population. As a result of these efforts, by 1977 there were 14 adult falcons and 25 fledglings in California. Currently there are over 80

nesting pairs in the state, including one pair that nests on Morro Rock. Falcons nest in March and April, usually on a ledge or cliff face. They do not build their own nests but use those of ravens, vultures, or eagles. Peregrine falcons are remarkable for their flight speed, estimated at 275 mph when "stooping," or diving, to catch their prey in midair. The falcon preys on any bird close to its size, including shorebirds, coots, cormorants, auklets, pigeons, and ducks.

Morro Rock is a volcanic "plug," the remnant of volcanic activity that took place 22 to 24 million years ago. It is one of a chain of volcanic peaks that extends west of Morro Rock to include one or more submerged plugs, and southeast to San Luis Obispo where the remaining nine peaks line the north rim of the Los Osos Valley. The igneous rock called dacite that forms Morro Rock is a remnant of the original volcanic intrusion which probably never reached the surface to form a true volcano. The soft sedimentary rock and volcanic ash once covering the volcanic plug have eroded away, leaving the 581-foot-high core that is visible today.

Morro Rock was once an island 1,000 feet offshore, and the entrance to Morro Bay was a channel north of the rock. In the late 1800s the north channel was partially closed by the construction of a revetment and by sand shoaling that resulted from efforts to widen and deepen the south channel; by 1938, further construction completed the closure, forming a "tombolo"— the geographic term for a sand spit that connects an island to the mainland.

Morro Bay: *Hwy. 1, 13 mi. N.W. of San Luis Obispo.*

Within Morro Bay's intertidal areas, over 400 acres of eelgrass beds provide essential forage for thousands of migrating waterfowl. The bay has historically been an important winter stop for the black brant, a small goose that migrates from northern Canada. In the past, as many as 12,000 black brant could be seen at one time on Morro Bay, but since 1960 the number of overwintering brant has declined drastically, probably due to disturbances associated with hunting and urban development along the bay.

The extensive and diverse habitats of Morro Bay attract many bird species, and in winter the bay is teeming with birds. Particularly common are migratory waterfowl such as pintails, green-winged teals, lesser scaups, wigeons, ruddy ducks, and buffleheads. Shorebirds are abundant along the bay margins, and species such as marbled godwits, willets, and sandpipers number in the thousands. Other shorebirds seen here are curlews, dunlins, dowitchers, and sanderlings. Terns, pelicans, grebes, and loons are also winter visitors. Wading birds—herons and egrets—inhabit the bay year-round.

Numerous marine invertebrates live in the mudflats of Morro Bay. Mud shrimp, lugworms, and fat innkeeper worms share their burrows with crabs and segmented worms. Washington clams and geoducks are still collected in the mudflats; shells found in nearby Indian middens indicate that at one time gaper and bent nosed clams, basket cockles, littleneck clams, and native oysters also were found here.

There are four public piers in Morro Bay. The 190-foot-long North T-pier, adjacent to the power plant, accommodates fishing boats, dock-

American peregrine falcon (*Falco peregrinus anatum*)
15 to 21 inches long, 3¼- to 3¾-foot wingspan

Morro Rock, view from Morro Bay State Park

side fishermen, and crab trappers. The South T-pier has slips and moorings for commercial and pleasure boats, and boats can be rented for ocean fishing. The "clam taxi," a motor-powered skiff, transports passengers to the sand spit from the Morro Bay Marina. A third pier, at Dunes St. and Embarcadero, provides benches and picnic tables. The Second Street Pier is at the south end of Second St. in Baywood Park. Anglers catch northern anchovy, lingcod, and black perch from the pier; the bay's eelgrass beds are spawning and nursery areas for California halibut, jacksmelt, and surfperch.

City of Morro Bay: *12.5 mi. N.W. of San Luis Obispo.*

Two wharves existed for the export of local dairy and ranching products when the town of Morro Bay was established in 1870. Lumber schooners landed in the bay, bringing redwood and pine from Santa Cruz County. By the turn of the century Morro Bay, like many Central and Southern California coastal villages, was attracting vacationers who came by train or car to camp on the sandy beaches.

In the 1940s Morro Bay began to develop as a commercial fishing port, and today it is one of the more important fishing centers along the California coast; trawlers harvest halibut, sole, rockfish, and lingcod, and trollers catch salmon and albacore from the ocean waters outside the bay. In the past, Morro Bay was the center of an abalone industry that has declined as a result of heavy commercial harvesting and sea otter predation. Only one processing plant now operates in the area.

The Morro Bay Power Plant east of Morro Rock uses oil to fuel turbines that produce electricity by converting ocean water to steam; 470,000 gallons of heated water per minute are then recycled back to the ocean via an outfall canal north of Morro Rock. The surface temperature of the water near the canal may be as much as 15 to 20 degrees above normal. Built in 1956, the plant is one of 23 thermal electrical generating plants in the state.

Morro Rock before 1933, when causeway construction was begun to connect the rock to the mainland

Abalone processing, ca. 1930s, at Pierce Fisheries, Morro Bay

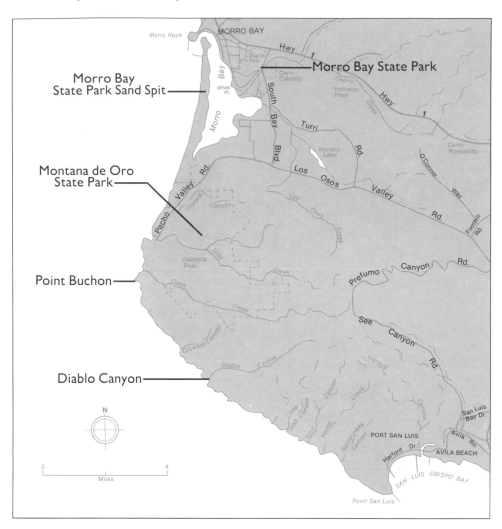

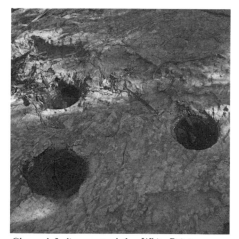

Chumash Indian mortar holes, White Point

nels that drain salt water from the marsh. With each low tide, the bay is reduced to a main channel surrounded by mudflats and exposed eelgrass and algae that provide food for the bay's wildlife. The salt marsh is gradually expanding as eelgrass from the deeper waters of the bay decomposes and forms soil that is eventually colonized by pickleweed. Baywood Park Beach, south of Morro Bay State Park, is reached via Pasadena Dr.; the sandy beach has picnic tables and parking. Sweet Springs Marsh, accessible from Ramona St., is a 25-acre wetland with two freshwater ponds upland of a saltwater marsh along the bay. Monarch butterflies overwinter in the eucalyptus trees that grow along with Monterey cypress in the wetland area.

Morro Bay State Park: *South Bay Blvd. and State Park Rd., Morro Bay.*

The park's more than 1,500 acres include salt marsh, sandy beach, the wetlands of Los Osos and Chorro creeks, and portions of Black Hill and Hollister Peak, east of the bay. Within the park are campsites, a group campground, a boat launch and boat basin, a golf course, and the Morro Bay Museum of Natural History. For park information, call: (805) 772-2560.

From the museum, visitors have a sweeping view of the baylands and Morro Rock. Exhibits focus on the bay's ecology and importance to thousands of migrating shorebirds and waterfowl. The museum has an extensive library, and docent-led museum tours and field trips are available by reservation. A "hands-on" display with braille explanations is changed every six weeks. For information, call: (805) 772-2694.

The eucalyptus grove just north of White Point is a protected rookery for a colony of great blue herons. Herons can be observed in their tree-top nests between February and June. Trails from the point provide access to volcanic Black Hill, the extensive marshlands of Chorro Delta, the Chorro Creek estuary, and several archaeological sites that are evidence of Indian habitation in the Morro Bay wetlands centuries before the Spanish arrived in California.

Chorro Delta, the marshland created by Chorro and Toro creeks, is patterned by meandering distributary channels that carry fresh water from the creeks to the bay, and tidal chan-

Morro Bay State Park Sand Spit: *Ocean side of Morro Bay.*

The sand spit can be reached by boat from Morro Bay; a motorboat taxi leaves from the marina on Embarcadero Road. A hiking trail to the spit begins from the parking lot at Shark Inlet, off Pecho Valley Road. The three-mile-long spit is ridged with 85-foot-high dunes vegetated with silvery lupine, mock heather, coyote brush, and lizard tail. Snowy plovers nest on the spit, laying their eggs in fist-sized scrapes of pebbly sand; camouflaged by their gray and white coloring, the small birds are virtually invisible unless a sudden intrusion into their territory prompts the flock to scurry across the sand, cheeping and whistling in warning. South of the spit is a small preserve for the endangered Morro Bay kangaroo rat.

Montana de Oro State Park: *Pecho Valley Rd., 4 mi. S.W. of Los Osos.*

The park is named for 1,347-foot Valencia Peak, which is transformed into a "mountain of gold" by spring- and summer-blooming poppies and mustard. Hazard Canyon Reef begins offshore at the north end of the park and extends south for more than nine miles. The reef's surge channels are rich with hydroids, sponges, rock-boring clams, crabs, sea stars, and other marine invertebrates. Abalones are abundant, and there are over 90 fish species and 100 species of algae in the reef area.

Spooner's Cove has picnic tables and a parking area. Across the road from the cove, the old Spooner Ranch house serves as park headquarters; behind the house and along Islay Creek is the campground. Call: (805) 528-0513. Islay Creek Trail begins at the campground and continues inland for 1.3 miles to a secluded waterfall and the old Spooner Ranch barn.

Valencia Peak Trail begins just south of the Spooner Ranch house, crossing marine terraces covered with coastal sage scrub and native bunchgrass. These Pleistocene marine terraces overlay hills of steeply dipping Monterey shales that are exposed in contorted strata along the sea cliffs. Distinctive mounds of hard volcanic rock are visible on the terrace, created by erosion of the softer sedimentary rock that once surrounded them. Offshore, the same process has produced "sea stacks," tiny islands of volcanic rock left standing after waves eroded the shoreline. The bedrock upon which the marine terrace sits was formed by the decomposition and bonding together of extremely abundant

one-celled marine plants called diatoms; a three-inch-thick layer of this diatomaceous rock may be as much as a thousand years old.

The Coon Creek Trail at the end of the park road follows the creek bed, meandering through groves of black cottonwood, oak woodland, and chaparral, where rare Pecho manzanita grows. The rare, dark-colored two-stripe garter snake inhabits the park, its range extending only a few miles south to Oceano.

Corallina Cove, at the south end of the park, is reached by a bluff trail from the parking area. An offshore reef provides protection from wave action and a surface for a rich diversity of algae to attach to. In the cove's intertidal zone are invertebrates such as periwinkles, limpets, mussels, sea stars, sea urchins, anemones, and abalones that depend, directly or indirectly, on the algae for food and shelter.

Point Buchon: *8 mi. S.W. of Morro Bay.*

Near Point Buchon is the site where Portolá's expedition encountered a Chumash chief with a prominent goiter; the soldiers called the site "el buchón," which means "the one with the goiter." From the point south to Diablo Canyon, the coast is a pristine natural landscape, little changed since it was occupied by Chumash Indians more than a thousand years ago. In the mid-1800s this land was part of Rancho Cañada de los Osos y Pecho y Islay—literally, the valley of bears, bravery, and wild cherry—and continues as a cattle ranch today.

The exposed headland of Point Buchon is composed of minerals found only here and at a site in Santa Barbara County. The augite, analcite, calcic feldspar, and iron oxide minerals are layered in a rock formation called an ophiolite; these rocks were formed by volcanic activity in

Spooner's Cove, Montana de Oro State Park

the mid-Pacific Ocean and deposited on the California coast as a result of tectonic plate movement between one and two hundred million years ago.

Diablo Canyon: *4 mi. S. of Point Buchon.*

This remote coastal canyon was once the hunting grounds of ancestors of the Chumash Indians who inhabited it beginning 9,000 years ago. In 1968 construction began on the Diablo Canyon Nuclear Plant, and continued for over a decade amid controversy and mass demonstrations over the building of the plant near an active earthquake fault. The plant began operating in 1986. Its two units are designed to produce over 2,000 megawatts of power, contributing five per cent of the state's peak energy demand forecast for 1989. There is no public access to this portion of the coast.

View from Morro Bay Museum of Natural History at White Point

Los Osos Oaks State Reserve: *S. of Los Osos Valley Rd. at Palomino Dr., Los Osos.*

A self-guided trail winds through the reserve past contorted oaks, chaparral, and a Chumash midden. The ancient grove of California live oaks, some estimated to be from 600 to 800 years old, represents the last stage in a cycle of plant succession that began some 30,000 years ago during the last glacial period. Then, worldwide sea level was much lower, and a massive dune field extended inland to where these oaks now stand. As seaweed and microscopic zooplankton were deposited on the sterile sand by wind and waves, a soil developed from the decomposed plant and animal matter, and "pioneer" species such as sea rocket, verbena, and silver lupine colonized the dunes. Over thousands of years the pioneer dune plants at Los Osos were succeeded by coyote brush and coastal sage scrub. After the succession of three plant communities —coastal strand, coastal sage, and chaparral— over many thousands of years, oaks became established in the old dunes. The oak grove is unique both for its great age and as an example of how plant succession transforms landscapes.

Some of the Los Osos oaks growing on the dune crest are dwarfed, probably due to poor soil fertility. The ground here is littered with shell fragments and traces of charcoal, reminders that Chumash Indians once camped in these groves, gathering acorns from the oaks; the manzanita, sage, and coffeeberry growing here were also useful to the Chumash, providing firewood, medicines, and food.

Los Osos Oaks State Reserve

Los Osos Creek, which forms the eastern boundary of the reserve, is a perennial stream shaded by western sycamore, bay laurel, yellow willow, and black cottonwood trees. Freshwater fish inhabiting the creek include the riffle sculpin and prickly sculpin. The chaparral that covers nearly a quarter of the reserve provides habitat for many small animals, including brush rabbits, jack rabbits, coyotes, and an occasional bobcat. Several species of mice, voles, and possibly the endangered Morro Bay kangaroo rat also live here. Western fence lizards and alligator lizards are common, and the spotted night snake, western rattlesnake, and western whiptail may also be found in the reserve. Birdlife is abundant in the grassland and chapparal, with California quail, California thrashers, towhees, Bewick's wrens, plain titmice, common bushtits, chestnut-backed chickadees, and Anna's hummingbirds commonly seen.

Within the oak grove, the wood rat may be the most common animal species; this secretive rodent builds nests of piles of sticks, often several feet high. In the canopy of the oak trees are birds such as black phoebes, western flycatchers, and orange-crowned warblers, and rufous-sided towhees may be seen grub-hunting in the leaf litter beneath the trees.

Los Osos Valley: *Los Osos Valley Rd., from Morro Bay to San Luis Obispo.*

"In this valley we saw troops of bears, which kept the ground plowed up and full of holes which they made searching for roots which con-

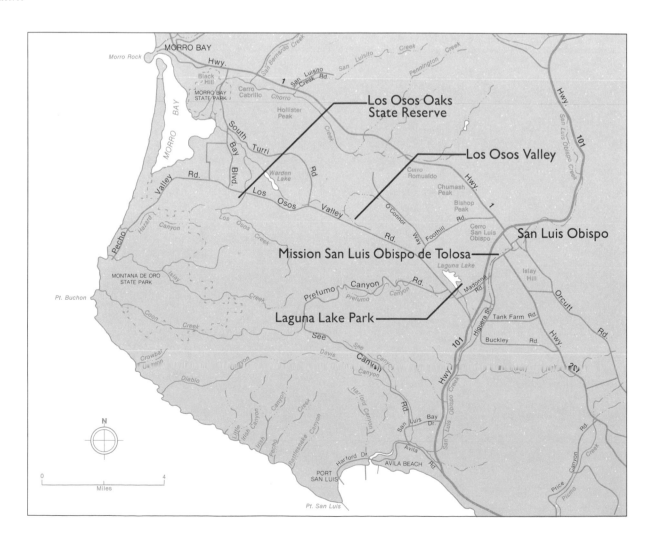

stitute their food, and on which the heathen also live, for there are some which have a very good flavor and taste." This entry from Father Juan Crespí's diary describes the place where Portolá's expedition camped on September 7, 1769; the bears of which he writes were California grizzly bears, extinct since the mid-1800s, but at that time abundant throughout most of the state. It was the grizzlies for which the valley was named by the soldiers of Portolá's expedition: *los osos* is Spanish for "bears."

The valley was part of the 32,000-acre Rancho Cañada de los Osos y Pecho y Islay in the early 1800s, and was farmed and used for cattle grazing, as much of the valley is today. Urban development, however, is rapidly encroaching on both ends of the valley.

A chain of volcanic peaks rims the northern edge of the valley; Black Hill, Cerro Cabrillo, and Hollister Peak are visible from Turri Road. Cerro Romualdo and Chumash Peak can be glimpsed from Los Osos Valley Rd., and Bishop Peak and Cerro San Luis Obispo can be seen from the town of San Luis Obispo and along Foothill Road. Southeast of San Luis Obispo is the inland-most volcanic peak in the chain, Islay Hill. Morro Rock and several submerged plugs west of the rock are also part of this chain. The peaks were formed by volcanism over 20 million years ago; time and weather have eroded the overlying sedimentary rock to expose the "plugs" of igneous rock that cooled after the intrusion of magma occurred.

San Luis Obispo: *Hwy. 1, 14 mi. S.E. of Morro Bay.*

The town of San Luis Obispo developed around Mission San Luis Obispo de Tolosa, becoming a merchandising and market center for the surrounding ranchos in the 1840s and 1850s. The town, incorporated in 1856, has been the county seat since San Luis Obispo County was established in 1850. A walking tour of the streets surrounding Mission Plaza includes the Murray adobe, the County Historical Museum, and the Ah Louis store, the first Chinese store in the county. The store served as counting house, bank, and post office for the 2,000 Chinese who were brought here to excavate the eight tunnels through Cuesta Pass for the Southern Pacific Railroad between 1884 and 1894. The adobe home of French vinyardist Pierre Dallidet on Pacific and Toro streets, built in the early 1850s, is open to the public on Sunday afternoons. Well-preserved Victorian mansions within the town include the Biddle home on Pismo St., and the Erickson home on Islay Street. The latter, built between 1888 and 1897, has an unusual round tower with a bell-shaped roof.

On the outskirts of town is California Polytechnic State University, founded in 1901. Trails wind through the university's botanical garden, located in Poly Canyon, where there is a large display of native California plants.

Mission San Luis Obispo De Tolosa: *782 Monterey St., San Luis Obispo.*

Founded by Father Serra in 1772, Mission San Luis Obispo de Tolosa was the fifth mission to be built in Alta California. The first buildings, constructed of saplings, tules, adobe, and tar, were replaced by the present mission, completed in 1794. Almost 800 Chumash converts to Christianity lived at or near the mission in 1798; by 1859 what remained of the Indian population at the mission had succumbed to a cholera epidemic. From 1875 to 1933 the mission was sheathed in wooden siding and shingles, and a New England style wooden belfry was added. The bell tower was removed, and the courtyard, church, and padres' quarters were restored to their original appearance in the late 1930s.

Laguna Lake Park: *On Madonna Rd., off Hwy. 101, S. of San Luis Obispo.*

The 150-acre park includes one of the few remaining natural lakes in the county. Rails, great blue herons, and grebes nest in the lake area, and dabbling and diving ducks use the lake during winter migration. Fishing and windsurfing are popular activities; campsites and picnic tables are available.

View of Cerro Cabrillo and Hollister Peak from Turri Road

Morro Bay Kangaroo Rat

The endangered Morro Bay kangaroo rat, *Dipodomys heermanni morroensis*, is the largest member of a family of small rodents that includes kangaroo mice and pocket mice. Kangaroo rats are nocturnal and survive without drinking water, obtaining moisture instead from seeds and plants. Not related to either marsupials or Old World rats, the kangaroo rat derives its common name from its resemblance to the kangaroo. The rodent has short, stubby front limbs; long, powerful hind legs capable of propelling it several feet into the air; and a tail one and a half times as long as its body. Kangaroo rats are native to arid and semi-arid habitats throughout North America. The Morro Bay subspecies is found only in the area of Baywood and Los Osos along the southeastern perimeter of Morro Bay in San Luis Obispo County.

The Morro Bay kangaroo rat is inactive during the rainy months, remaining in its shallow underground burrow and living on seeds gathered in the dry season. Its main predators are the gray fox and the great horned owl. When pursued, the kangaroo rat can leap six feet into the air and is able to change directions mid-jump by using its tufted tail as a rudder. The rat requires a sparsely vegetated area in which to maneuver, such as the native coastal sage scrub and strand habitats of Morro Bay; the succulent species of these plant communities also supply the rat with moisture and nourishment. However, this habitat is rapidly disappearing.

Substantial increases in its human population have transformed Morro Bay into a densely developed residential area, and periodic wildfires that once thinned the plant cover have been prevented. As a result, the low-growing, sparse vegetation is being succeeded by dense, woody growth unsuitable for the rat's escape methods. Now one of the most endangered mammals in the state, the Morro Bay kangaroo rat's numbers have declined from an estimated 8,000 in 1958 to perhaps less than a hundred today.

Morro Bay kangaroo rat (*Dipodomys heermanni morroensis*)
head & body: 4⅔ inches long
tail: 6⅞ inches long

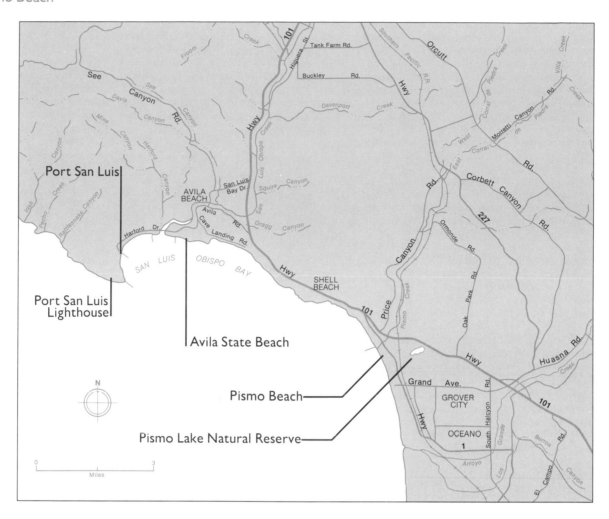

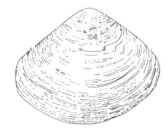

Pismo clam (*Tivela stultorum*)
6 inches long

Port San Luis: *1.5 mi. W. of Avila State Beach.*

Pedro de Unamuno, commander of a Manila galleon that sailed along the California coast in 1587, was the first to record the presence of San Luis Bay, noting the protected landing in the curve of the bay where Port San Luis is located today. In 1867 a steam railroad was built between San Luis Obispo and the bay, eventually connecting to the wharf built by John Harford in 1873. Steamships, each carrying as many as 90 passengers and 200 tons of freight, arrived at the wharf (then called Port Harford) several times a week during its heyday. The wharf was destroyed by a seismic sea wave in 1878. The port's economic vitality declined in the 1890s after the completion of the inland Southern Pacific rail line to San Luis Obispo. During the 1940s the port was revitalized by the oil extraction operations in the Santa Maria River basin to the south, becoming a major West Coast oil port during World War II.

Today Port San Luis is a sport and commercial fishing center; crab, bottom fish, and albacore are the main catch. Facilities include a pier, fish markets, and a sport fishing shop; party boat charters leave from the pier. The harbor provides boat hoists, a launch, a carpentry shop, moorings for large vessels, and 170 private moorings (300 in summer).

Port San Luis Lighthouse: *On Point San Luis, S.W. of Port San Luis.*

Originally named the Port Harford Light, the Victorian-style redwood structure was completed in 1890 at a cost of $50,000. It is one of seven West Coast lighthouses designed from a single plan; the intricate millwork was done on Mare Island in San Francisco Bay, and the pieces assembled on site. The Port Harford Light's Fresnel lens was shipped piecemeal from France on four separate vessels so the entire lens would not be lost in the event one ship sank; upon arrival, the heavy crystal prisms were pulled up the rocky point to the lighthouse site by mules.

When the lighthouse was built, Port Harford was a thriving whaling station, and whale oil to fuel the light was in good supply. Eventually kerosene and then electricity replaced the whale oil, and today the Coast Guard maintains an automatic beacon and photoelectrically activated foghorn near the old lighthouse.

Avila State Beach: *S. of Front St., off Avila Rd., Avila Beach.*

Facilities at this sandy beach include restrooms, volleyball standards, and playground equipment. The public fishing pier, destroyed by a storm in 1983, has been rebuilt and is now open to the public. Call: (408) 595-2381.

The town of Avila Beach was named in 1867 for Miguel Avila, the original grantee of Rancho San Miguel. The port town was a rival of neighboring Port Harford (now Port San Luis) for steamship passenger and freight business in the last half of the 19th century. People's Wharf, built in 1868 near the present wharf site, was the western terminus for a rail line between Avila Beach and San Luis Obispo. For 70 years the steam train carried freight and passengers; in 1941 rail workers pulled up the tracks behind the last car on its final trip to San Luis Obispo. Today this small beach community is a popular destination for swimmers and sun lovers who flock to its protected white sandy beaches during the summer months.

Located about a half-mile east of Avila Beach off Cave Landing Rd., Cave Landing, also known as Mallagh Landing, is a rock that juts out 150 feet into the water and forms a natural pier. The Chumash Indians once fished from the rock, and buried their dead in the shallow caves of the east-facing cliffs. The padres of Mission San Luis Obispo carted hides and tallow produced at the mission to this landing for export, and in 1860 sea captain David Mallagh built a warehouse on the rock summit and a wooden chute for shipboard loading of local produce.

Pismo Beach: *Hwy. 101, 11.3 mi. South of San Luis Obispo.*

The name "pismo" is derived from *pismu,* the Chumash word for the asphaltum tar that seeps through natural fissures in the ground and sea floor of Central California. The Indians used the tar to caulk their plank canoes and to make baskets watertight. The City of Pismo Beach is located within the original land grant, called Rancho Pismo, established in 1840. The town was founded in 1891 as Pismo; "Beach" was added in 1904, when it was becoming a popular destination for summer vacationers.

The Pismo clam for which the area is famous was so abundant in the late 1800s that local farmers used the clams for animal feed, harvesting them by plowing the beach. By 1911 depletion of the seemingly endless supply resulted in the imposition of a 200-per-day limit. From 1916 to 1947, an estimated 100,000 pounds of clams were commercially harvested yearly; sport clammers took even more. In 1947, the commercial harvest had declined substantially and was soon prohibited; today the sport limit is ten clams per person per day.

Margo Dodd City Park is located in the community of Shell Beach within the Pismo Beach city limits. The park overlooks an islet and offshore rocks that are hauling-out grounds and a

nursery for harbor seals, and a rookery for several species of shorebirds. Endangered California brown pelicans can be seen roosting here, and pigeon guillemots nest on the sea cliffs and offshore rocks.

The Pismo Beach public fishing pier, at the end of Pomeroy and Hinds avenues, is nearly unchanged since it was built in 1881. The pier was used by local farmers to export their produce; originally 1,600 feet long and 27 feet above low tide level, the pier had a hand-car track along its length that facilitated the loading of goods onto waiting ships. From 1895 until the 1920s there was a dance pavilion at the foot of the pier. During the summer months the pavilion was surrounded by a tent city; tents could be rented for eight dollars a week.

Pismo Lake Natural Reserve: *N. 4th St. and Five Cities Dr., Pismo Beach.*

The fifty-five-acre reserve is an important waterfowl habitat and overwintering site. Ten years ago the surface of Pismo Lake covered ten acres but has since shrunk to about two and a half acres of water due to both natural causes and increased development; surrounding residential development has resulted in the proliferation of non-native plants that require large volumes of water and deplete the groundwater reserves that feed the lake. Shorebirds using the marsh include overwintering sandpipers, plovers, and yellowlegs; herons, egrets, and rails are permanent marsh residents, and waterfowl such as grebes, dabbling ducks, and diving ducks use the marsh during their migration.

Port San Luis Lighthouse, 1894

Migrating sooty shearwaters off Shell Beach

Pismo State Beach: *W. of Hwy. 1, 2 mi. S. of City of Pismo Beach.*

Situated within the Nipomo Dunes, the state park spans seven miles of beachfront, including over 800 acres of dunes in the Pismo Dunes State Vehicular Recreation Area that are accessible to off-road vehicles. Hiking trails traverse the 40-acre Pismo Dunes Natural Preserve, south of Arroyo Grande Creek, which is off-limits to vehicles. Campsites are located at the North Beach Campground, at the end of Dolliver St., and at the Oceano Campground; primitive campsites along the beach begin ¾ mile south of Arroyo Grande Creek. For park information, call: (805) 489-2684, 549-3433, or 549-3452.

Nipomo Dunes: *Arroyo Grande Creek to Point Sal, Santa Barbara County.*

The dunes cover an 18-square-mile area, bisected by the Santa Maria River, from Oceano south to Mussel Rock in Santa Barbara County; the dunes extend inland east of Oceano to Nipomo Mesa, and to Orcutt Mesa, southeast of the river. This wind-sculpted, or "eolian," landscape is one of the few undeveloped coastal dune ecosystems in California. The dunes, freshwater lakes, riparian habitats, and saltwater marshes support a large number of rare endemic plants. More than 80 water bird species frequent the wetlands, and over 100 land bird species, many mammals, and a number of reptiles and amphibians inhabit the Nipomo Dunes.

The Nipomo Dunes are divided into three distinct topographic areas, called dune fields or dune "sheets." The Callender Dunes sheet forms a wide crescent from Arroyo Grande Creek inland to Nipomo Mesa, and south to Oso Flaco Lake. The Guadalupe Dunes sheet spreads out along the Santa Maria River floodplain south of Oso Flaco Lake, and the Mussel Rock Dunes sheet extends south of the river to Point Sal in Santa Barbara County.

The Nipomo Dunes represent several stages of dune building that began 18,000 years ago. The oldest dunes, dating from the last glacial period, lie on top of Nipomo and Orcutt mesas. Now stabilized and covered with plants, these dunes were created from wind-borne sand carried inland from the beach and deposited in characteristic parabola-shaped mounds, now barely visible on the mesas. Between Nipomo Mesa and the beach, younger dunes, created

Pismo State Beach

Oso Flaco Lake

since the end of the Pleistocene, form a series of sparsely vegetated ridges and hollows. Still actively moving in the direction of prevailing northwest winds, these dunes are vulnerable to the effects of vehicle and foot traffic, forming "blow outs" when the fragile plant cover that stabilizes them is destroyed. Denuded of vegetation, dunes are dispersed by the wind, and rapidly migrate inland.

Callender Dunes: *Nipomo Dunes, Arroyo Grande Creek to Oso Flaco Creek.*

Nipomo Indian paintbrush and comet's plume grow in scattered locations along the Nipomo Mesa ridge. In the foredunes near the beach, dune mint, sand verbena, and native dune grass continue the process of stabilizing the wind-driven sands, creating hillocks a foot or two high. In the dune swales—concavities created by the scouring action of the wind —larger plants such as willow, salt bush, and wax myrtle grow, their roots tapping the surface groundwater that lies beneath the dunes.

During the Depression, the Callender Dunes just west of the village of Oceano were home to a collection of artists, writers, and astrologers called the "Dunites," who published a literary magazine called *Dune Forum.* Shifting sands have buried all traces of the driftwood dwellings of the Bohemian village.

Dune Lakes: *Nipomo Dunes, W. of Hwy. 1, 7 mi. S. of Pismo Beach.*

From north to south, the dune lakes are: Big Pocket (dry), Willow, Pipeline, Celery, Hospital, Big Twin, Small Twin, Bolsa Chica, White, Mud, and Black lakes; all are privately owned. Jack Lake, at the southern reaches of the Callender Dunes sheet, is accessible on foot. Nestled in the dunes, these lakes are among the last remaining coastal freshwater lakes in California and provide resting and foraging areas for migrating waterfowl and shorebirds. Endangered California least terns hunt on the lakes, and herons, rails, and grebes are residents of the marshy lake perimeters.

The lakes were formed in the troughs between the dunes about 16,000 years ago, and were fed by groundwater seeping seaward from the nearby mesa. Black Lake—so named for the color of the water, which is blackened by 40-foot-thick peat deposits on the lake bottom—once received runoff from the stream that runs through Black Lake Canyon. The construction of a railway bed across the canyon, and the tapping of groundwater reserves for agriculture and urban development, have curtailed the inflow of water to the lakes; only in extremely wet years does natural runoff feed the lakes, which are otherwise filled by agricultural wastewater.

Clustered on the surface of many of the dune lakes is the yellow pond lily, at the southern limit of its range here. Endangered Nipomo lupine, numbering only a few plants, grows in the drier sandy soils of the dunes along Nipomo Mesa, east of the lakes. In the meadow surrounding Jack Lake are endangered La Graciosa thistle and fragrant dune mint, along with silver dune lupine, yellow bush lupine, and coast tidy tips. Mock heather, sky-blue larkspur, and curled fiddlenecks bloom in spring, and in winter the meadow is colored by white wreathe flowers and brilliant goldfields.

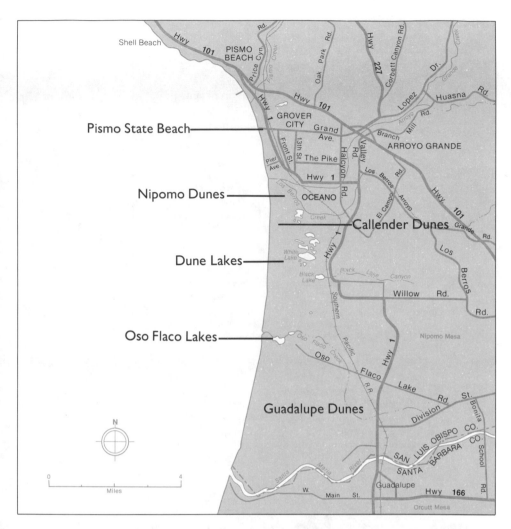

Oso Flaco Lakes: *Off Oso Flaco Lake Rd., 3 mi. W. of Hwy. 1.*

Oso flaco, or "lean bear" in Spanish, is the name the soldiers of Portolá's expedition gave to the lake site where, in 1769, they encamped and shot a grizzly bear; the bear, which was ten feet long and weighed 375 pounds, fed 62 men.

Herons, rails, and grebes nest along the edge of the lakes. The endangered California least tern is sometimes seen foraging nearby, and sandpipers and dabbling and diving ducks overwinter here. Along Oso Flaco Creek, rushes, entwined with endemic Gambel's watercress, grow in dense clusters with goldenrod and evening primrose. Wild beach strawberry grows in the upper marsh as do gooseberry, sedge, and silver weed.

A dune blow out has formed at the western edge of the larger lake, where the precipitous "slip face," or moving front, of the dune has encroached upon the lakeshore. Fences have been installed and native dune species planted to arrest the process of dune destabilization. No ORV'S are allowed, but cars may be parked at the end of Oso Flaco Lake Rd. where entry to the lakes and dunes may be made on foot.

Guadalupe Dunes: *From Oso Flaco Lake to the Santa Maria River.*

The Guadalupe Dunes lie at the seaward end of the Santa Maria River floodplain, encompassing 6,000 acres north of the river. Coreopsis Hill, a prominent dune ridge south of Oso Flaco Lake, is covered with the lacy foliage and sunflower-like blossoms of the giant *Coreopsis* from February to April; the plants grow to eight feet here, several feet higher than most mature individuals of this species.

giant coreopsis (*Coreopsis gigantea*)
1½ to 5 feet high

Santa Barbara County
Selected Species of Interest

 Plants: Giant kelp (*Macrocystis pyrifera*), commercially harvested brown alga; one of California's largest kelp beds is offshore of Point Conception. **Dune mint** (*Monardella crispa*), fragrant, endangered endemic of the dunes.

 Trees: Coast live oak (*Quercus agrifolia*), most common coastal oak. **Southern California black walnut** (*Juglans californica*), scattered along creeks from Carpinteria west to Santa Barbara, and at the mouth of Jalama Creek.

 Insects: Flat-backed kelp fly (*Coelopa vanduzeei*), flattened, dark gray fly; found swarming over beached kelp; the flies are eaten by the **California black tiger beetle** (*Omus californicus*), a flightless, slow-moving, nocturnal beetle.

 Invertebrates: Red abalone (*Haliotis rufescens*), California's largest marine snail, prized as food; commercially harvested. **California spiny lobster** (*Panulirus interruptus*), from Point Conception to lower Baja; commercially harvested.

 Amphibians and Reptiles: Ringneck snake (*Diadophis punctatus*), has yellow or orange neck band; found in oak woodlands and riparian habitats. **Red-legged frog** (*Rana aurora*), native California frog; fully aquatic.

 Fish: California halibut (*Paralichthys californicus*), important commercial and sport fish, from Southern Washington to Baja. **Kelp bass** (*Paralabrax clathratus*), predominant fish in kelp beds from Point Conception to Baja.

 Birds: Black-shouldered kite (*Elanus caeruleus*), protected species; nests on More Mesa; eats rodents and insects. **Light-footed clapper rail** (*Rallus longirostris levipes*), endangered; year-round resident of Carpinteria Marsh.

 Land Mammals: Gray fox (*Urocyon cinereoargenteus*); habitat is open grasslands along the coast. **California vole** (*Microtus californicus*), small rodent; prey of black-shouldered kite and short-eared owl.

 Marine Mammals: Harbor seal (*Phoca vitulina*), hauls out along the coast at secluded pocket beaches and rocky shores. **Common dolphin** (*Delphinus delphis*), swims in large groups in offshore waters.

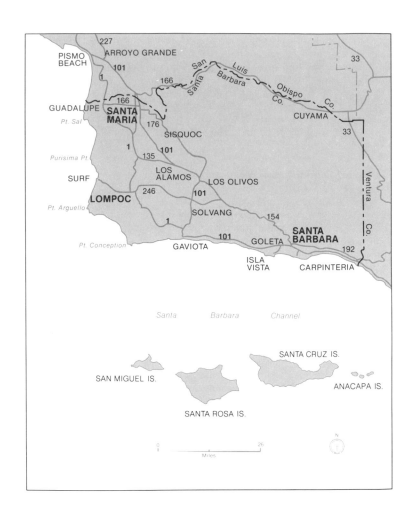

FROM THE NIPOMO DUNES at the mouth of the Santa Maria River to the rugged cliffs of Point Conception, the northern coast of Santa Barbara County is largely undisturbed and undeveloped. Broad marine terraces, rolling hills, and precipitous bluffs continue from Point Conception east to the City of Santa Barbara. The southern county coast, from Gaviota to Rincon Point, is characterized by a wide, urbanized coastal plain with scattered parcels of farmland.

At Point Conception the coastline turns sharply as the Transverse Ranges rise eastward. The only mountains in California running east and west, the Transverse Ranges include the San Bernardino Mountains to the east and the Santa Ynez and Santa Monica Mountains in the west; the Northern Channel Islands are an extension of the Santa Monica Mountains. The abrupt reorientation of the coastline creates a gyre or eddy in the Santa Barbara Channel, forming the Southern California Countercurrent. This countercurrent typically bathes the coast south of Point Conception with water about two degrees warmer than that north of the point. A unique intermingling of northern and southern plant and animal species occurs in this transition area.

About 10,000 years ago humans established permanent residence in the Santa Barbara area. The Chumash, descendents of this ancient hunter-gatherer culture, became one of the largest of the California Indian tribes. It is estimated that over 13,000 Chumash were living in the region when Cabrillo landed on the California coast in 1542. The Chumash were the most sea oriented of the California Indians; they fished the rich channel waters in wooden plank canoes caulked with asphalt from local tar seeps, and colonized the nearby islands. Archaeological excavations of Chumash villages and midden sites as well as extensive accounts by diarists of the early Spanish land expeditions provide us with many details of Indian life.

Spanish settlers introduced cattle ranching, and the Spanish missionaries organized rancherias where Indian converts to Christianity were taught agricultural skills. In 1821 over 12,000 bushels of grain and vegetables were produced by Indian farmers at Mission Santa Barbara. The Spanish rancheros traded their cowhides and tallow for scarce items such as dishes, tools, and shoes from Yankee ship captains who put in at the small wharves along the Santa Barbara coast. The hides and tallow were unloaded in Boston where they would be made into shoes and candles. Increasing numbers of Europeans and Americans began to immigrate to the Santa Barbara area in the mid-1800s, many becoming farmers. The era of the ranchos ended with the California gold rush. The small port in the town of Santa Barbara that existed during the Spanish and Mexican eras was expanded to support the increasing traffic in agricultural goods, timber, and asphaltum that went to pave the streets of San Francisco. By the turn of the century agricultural commerce was becoming less important as Santa Barbara's fame as a health resort spread.

Santa Barbara's Spanish heritage is enshrined in the adobe homes and structures preserved from the colonial era and in the Spanish Colonial Revival style of the city's civic and commercial buildings. The elaborate turn-of-the-century resort hotels for which Santa Barbara became world famous have all disappeared, but homes remaining from the Victorian era are scattered throughout the city.

The Santa Barbara Channel is located in the northwest corner of the Southern California Bight; a gentle inward curve in the coastline from Point Conception to the Mexican border marks the bight, which extends from the mainland shore to the continental slope and includes eight islands. A large portion of the state's commercial fish and shellfish hauls come from the rich waters of the Santa Barbara Channel and coast. Extensive offshore kelp beds near Point Conception and around the Channel Islands contribute to the abundance and diversity of marine life and also are harvested for commercially valuable extractions from the prolific brown algae. As a consequence of the region's unique geologic history, oil and gas resources of the county, in particular the offshore oil reserves of the Santa Barbara Channel, are an important industry. An estimated 85,000 barrels of petroleum per day are pumped from the tidal and submerged lands of the channel.

Commercial flower and flower seed farming in the Lompoc, Santa Maria, and Carpinteria Valleys continue to be important agricultural industries. Lemon and avocado orchards, planted over fifty years ago, occupy land once grazed by cattle.

In part due to the mild Mediterranean climate, Santa Barbara's beaches are renowned for their beauty and suitability for bathing and surfing. Many coastal sites are popular for surf fishing, skin diving and, in the offshore reefs, scuba diving. The county's coastal parks include drifting dunes, spectacular sea cliffs, extensive marshlands, and wide, flat beaches.

Windsurfer off Jalama Beach County Park

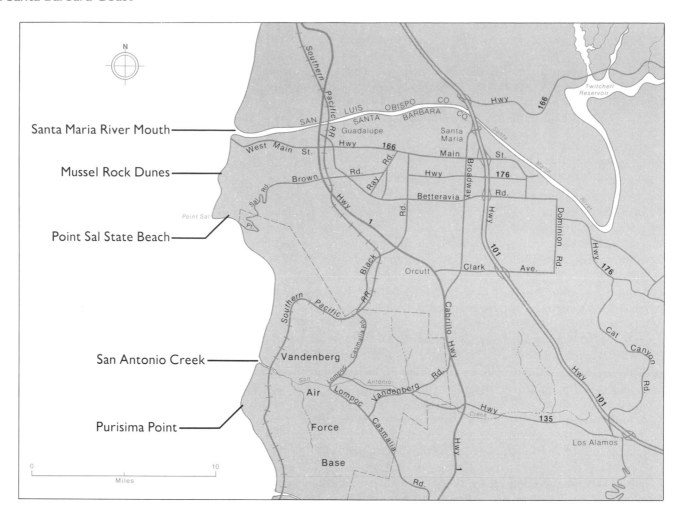

Santa Maria River Mouth: *Off Highway 1 at Guadalupe.*

The massive dune complex extending north and south of the river mouth is a portion of the Nipomo Dunes, one of the least disturbed of the remaining dune systems in California. A 365-acre wetland at the river mouth provides habitat for migrating shorebirds and waterfowl as well as year-round marsh residents. The endangered California least tern nests in the barren foredunes and forages in the lagoon; endangered California brown pelicans flock on the beach. The endangered endemic La Graciosa thistle grows in the marsh north of the river; its name, a Spanish word meaning "the beautiful," refers to a village founded nearby in 1868 and destroyed by an earthquake in 1877.

The floodplain and riparian vegetation of the Santa Maria River provide habitat for mule deer, the long-tailed weasel, and the gray fox. The coast garter snake, a subspecies with an uncharacteristic dark coloring that has been studied by scientists for clues to species evolution, is at the southern limit of its range here. Occasionally, an endangered peregrine falcon hunts in the freshwater marsh, and the bald eagle, also endangered, has been sighted in the area during fall and spring migration.

Millions of years ago the Santa Maria Valley was the bay of an ancient sea. Fossils of large birds and whales are embedded in diatomites, sedimentary rock deposits found in the area. A mild coastal climate provides favorable conditions for commercial flower growing, earning the area the name "Valley of the Gardens." The

town of Guadalupe, founded in the 1840s and named after a former Mexican rancho, has retained its Mexican-American character; small cafes serve produce and beef from local farms and ranches.

Mussel Rock Dunes: *West end of Main St., Guadalupe.*

Bounded on the north by the Santa Maria River and on the south by Mussel Rock, these dunes are a continuation of the Nipomo Dune complex. The area is a transitional zone between northern and southern biotic communities. Coastal strand plants such as sand verbena, sea rocket, and beach morning glory grow in the sparsely vegetated dunes nearest the beach; these plants, which must adapt to constantly shifting sand, are pioneers in the dune stabilization process, creating hillocks a few feet high. On the stabilized inland dunes, mock heather and dune lupine grow, as well as several endangered species including the soft-leaved paintbrush, surf thistle, dune mint, and San Luis Obispo monardella, a mint whose characteristic curly leaves emit a strong odor when crushed. Mussel Rock, a promontory composed of an ancient dune deposited on the rock formation, stands 450 feet high and is located at the southern end of the dune complex.

Rancho Guadalupe County Park, located south of the Santa Maria River Mouth, provides the only access to the dunes. Ocean fishing for surfperch and California halibut is popular. For park information, call: (805) 937-1302.

Point Sal State Beach: *End of Brown Rd. and Point Sal Rd., W. of Guadalupe.*

From the ridge behind the secluded, undeveloped beach is a spectacular view of the coastline looking south toward Point Arguello. The point was named after the commandant of the San Francisco Presidio, Hermenegildo Sal, by George Vancouver. Vancouver was the English ship captain who named several coastal sites after officers and priests he met in the Spanish ports he visited along the California coast between 1782 and 1783. In the late 1800s a port at Point Sal, consisting of a warehouse and wharf, served as an export point for grain grown in the Santa Maria Valley.

The intertidal zone south of the beach is inhabited by crabs, rock scallops, red and black abalones, and Pismo clams. Lion Rock, south of the beach, is a sea lion and harbor seal haul-out area. Coastal bluff vegetation, including the spring-blooming giant *Coreopsis*, grows near the point; two species of native needlegrass also grow in the area.

The Point Sal area displays a varied geology with excellent exposures of unique features. The Point Sal Ridge is the top segment of the Point Sal Ophiolite, a rock assemblage originating in the mid-Pacific ocean during the Jurassic Period, 125 to 175 million years ago, and deposited on the coast as a result of tectonic plate movement. Pillow lavas, spheroid-shaped lava created by rapid cooling in sea water, are scattered throughout the ridge.

The endangered endemic black-flowered figwort and Hoffman's sanicle grow in the riparian woodland of Corralitos Canyon along Point Sal Road. The road, unmaintained and impassable in storms, is closed during missile launches at Vandenberg Air Force Base. For road information, call: (805) 733-3713.

San Antonio Creek: *Within Vandenberg AFB.*

The mouth of San Antonio Creek, one of several coastal estuaries in northern Santa Barbara County, includes a pristine saltwater lagoon. California least terns nest in the barren dunes closest to the ocean. Virginia and sora rails, the common yellowthroat, and the long-billed marsh wren live in the salt marsh.

East of the lagoon and salt marsh, a small freshwater marsh contains the western pond turtle and an endangered native freshwater fish, the unarmored threespine stickleback. The male of this unique species constructs a nest for its young and guards the eggs until they hatch.

Barka Slough, upstream of San Antonio Creek, is one of the largest wetlands in Santa Barbara County. Fed by upwelling groundwater, the slough covers over 500 acres; an extensive riparian woodland in the western portion of the slough comprises thick groves of arroyo willow, red willow, and box elder. Uncommon plants such as swamp cress, wax myrtle, and water pimpernel also grow here. Regionally rare birds nest in the riparian habitat, including Cooper's hawks, tree swallows, blue grosbeaks, and Swainson's thrushes. The slough is visible from San Antonio Rd., off County S20, which parallels the creek.

Purisima Point: *Within Vandenberg AFB.*

An endangered endemic plant, the Lompoc yerba santa, grows at the point; in the dunes near the beach are soft-leaved paintbrush and surf thistle, endangered coastal strand plants. Vandenberg Air Force Base provides limited public access along the blufftop from Purisima Point south for 3.5 miles; trails lead down the bluffs to pocket beaches. Fishing and abalone gathering are permitted. Weekend beach access is limited to 50 people per day and visitors must obtain a pass from the Game Warden on the base. Call: (805) 866-6804.

Vandenberg Air Force Base encompasses 35 miles of coastline from Point Sal to Jalama Creek. Except for two public beach accesses, the base is limited to nature and scientific study by non-military personnel.

Lompoc yerba santa (*Eriodictyon capitatum*)
to 8 feet high

San Antonio Creek mouth

Windsurfer off Jalama Beach County Park

Santa Ynez River Mouth: *Ocean Park Rd., 10 mi. W. of Hwy. 1.*

The lagoon at the mouth of the Santa Ynez River includes nearly 400 acres of salt and freshwater marshes, mudflats, and open water. There is a nesting colony of endangered California least terns at the river mouth. Several species of amphibians, including the foothill yellow-legged frog, red-legged frog, tiger salamander, California newt, and bullfrog, live in the freshwater lagoon east of the river mouth. The wetland is an important resting and foraging site for migrating shorebirds and waterfowl and provides habitat for raptors such as the northern harrier and the osprey, which hunts along the river. The Santa Ynez River supported the largest runs of spawning steelhead trout in Southern California before Cachuma Dam was built in the 1950s; today rainbow trout and a small number of steelhead are found only in Salsipuedes Creek, a tributary stream.

Ocean Beach County Park includes 36 acres of broad sandy beach and a portion of the lagoon. Vandenberg Air Force Base provides unlimited beach access that extends 1.5 miles north and 3.5 miles south of the park. Fishing is allowed from the public pier north of the beach. Migrating California gray whales pass near shore in the winter and spring. For park information, call: (805) 963-7109.

Point Pedernales, south of the river mouth, is a harbor seal haul-out and seabird nesting site. Ringneck snakes and California lyre snakes inhabit the area. The point was named by members of the Portolá Expedition in 1769 when flints, or *pedernales,* were found here.

Point Arguello: *Within Vandenberg AFB.*

Named by Vancouver after a commandant of Monterey Presidio, the promontory is topped by a lighthouse overlooking the treacherous waters below, the site of numerous shipwrecks. One of the more spectacular occurred in 1923 when seven U.S. destroyers, following their lead ship, foundered upon rocks in the fog and sank within minutes of each other. The point is a nesting area for seabirds, including pigeon guillemots, pelagic cormorants, and rhinocerous auklets.

Over two thousand years ago, Chumash Indians inhabited the area near the point, catching spiny lobsters, crabs, and shore and marine birds for food. Nocto, one of several villages located along the shore, lagoons, and rivers of the area, is one of the most significant archaeological sites in California. In 1974 excavations uncovered cultural artifacts that identified Nocto as the site of important Chumash ceremonies. When the Portolá Expedition passed through the area in 1769 there were about 70 Chumash still living in the village.

Lompoc: *Hwy. 1 and Ocean Ave. (Hwy 246).*

Originally a Chumash village, the townsite was part of a land grant given to the Carillo brothers in 1874. The founding of Misión de la Purísima Concepción de María Santísima in 1787 marked the beginning of Spanish occupation of the valley. The original mission was destroyed by earthquake in 1812, but ruins exist today at the south end of F Street in Lompoc. A gash in the hillside behind the ruins is visible evidence of the quake fault. A new mission was built nearby a few years later and was restored in the 1930s as a State Historic Park.

Lompoc Oil Field, located in the Purisima Hills north of the old mission ruins and the town of Lompoc, is the site of a State Historical Landmark, Well "Hill 4." This well was the first to use modern oil pumping techniques that increased the productive life of oil wells. Located along the crest of the Purisima Hills and visible from Highway 1 are stands of the closed-cone Bishop pine; the cones of this species are fire-adapted and remain closed until the heat of a fire opens them. Nearby, a small relict population of Douglas-fir grows on a north-facing slope; it is the only stand in the county and represents the southern limit of the species.

The town of Lompoc is also the site of the largest commercial diatomite mining operation in the world. In the diatomaceous earth are rare fossil deposits of fish, pelagic birds, and marine invertebrates dating back 25 million years, including fossils of extinct cormorants, boobies, and shearwaters. The deposits are several hundred feet thick and have been mined commercially since the turn of the century; specimens are sold for artistic and educational collections. Diatomaceous earth without fossils is used in many commercial products.

Jalama Creek mouth

La Purisima Mission State Historic Park:
Purisima Rd., 3 mi. N.E. of Lompoc.

Originally located in the town of Lompoc, La Purisima Mission is the only California mission to be restored as a complete complex, including padres' residences, church, soap factory, and tannery. A self-guided tour enables visitors to gain detailed knowledge of a typical mission establishment of the Spanish period. For information, call: (805) 733-3713.

La Purisima Mission was one of the most prosperous of the missions until secularization under Mexican rule. It was also the site of one of the only Indian uprisings in mission history. After starting at nearby Mission Santa Inés in 1824, the revolt spread to La Purisima, where Indians captured the mission and held it for several weeks until soldiers from the Monterey Presidio were sent to quell the uprising.

The area surrounding the mission consists of upland and wetland habitats, including chaparral, grassland, oak woodland, and marsh plant communities. Over 200 native plants have been collected in the area. The mission garden contains many plants introduced during the settlement of California by the Spanish, and native plants known to the mission's Indians.

Jalama Creek: *Jalama Rd. off Hwy. 1, 5 mi. N. of Point Conception.*

Jalama Road crosses Jalama Creek several times as it winds through the hills and over Jualachichi Summit, the headwaters of the creek. Jualachichi Basin is an important biological area containing stands of native Southern California black walnut. A mixed-evergreen forest growing in the area is a relict community and rare in Southern California; the forest includes tanbark oak, madrone, California bay laurel, big-leaf maple, and California huckleberry, species common in Northern California forests.

The mouth of Jalama Creek lies within Jalama Beach County Park, a 28-acre park with a sandy beach, campground, and wheelchair-accessible restrooms. Vandenberg Air Force Base provides one mile of unlimited beach access west of the park. The Amtrak Coast Starlite can be seen on the cliffs high above the beach as it crosses the trestle spanning the creek. An offshore reef protects the nearshore waters from turbulent wave action, creating a popular sport fishing and surfing spot. For park information, call: (805) 736-6316 or 736-3504.

La Purisima Mission

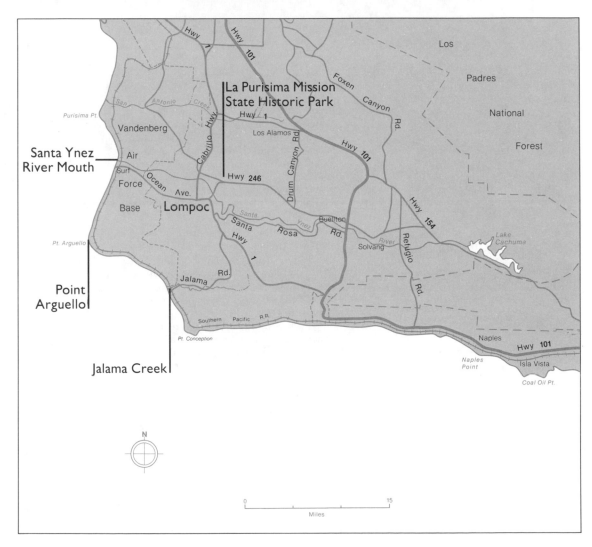

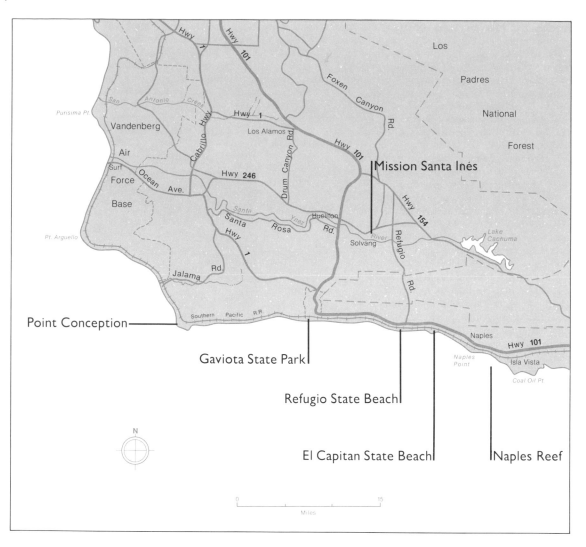

Point Conception Lighthouse

Point Conception: *15 mi. W. of Gaviota.*

In Chumash legend Point Conception is known as the "Western Gate." The Indians believe that all land visible from the point is sacred, and disaster will befall anyone who disturbs the land. Mariners called the coast from Point Arguello to Point Conception "Cape Horn of the Pacific Coast," because of its treacherous waters, fogs, and storms.

The coastline bends sharply at the point, changing from a north-south to an east-west direction. Near Point Conception, the cold, southward-flowing California Current sweeps westward, while the warmer, nearshore Southern California Countercurrent typically flows northward. This ocean circulation pattern combined with seasonal upwelling creates a transition zone that allows a complex terrestrial and marine flora and fauna to flourish. Plants and animals typical of southern climates are found in conjunction with northern species. The offshore waters support one of the most productive fishing grounds as well as one of the largest commercially harvested kelp beds in California. From the point, California gray whales can be seen migrating south to breeding grounds from November through March and returning to Arctic waters between February and May.

Point Conception is an ancient marine terrace with sheer bluffs reaching as high as 160 feet. The stabilized dunes on top of the terrace were part of a massive dune complex in the late Pleistocene. The endangered surf thistle and the rare Ida Mae's aster grow on the terrace.

A lighthouse was built on the top of the headland in 1856; because fog obscured its light it was relocated to the rocky point below in 1881, where it remains in operation.

East of the point, privately owned Hollister Ranch includes the remote canyons and beaches west of Gaviota State Park. Hollister Ranch was once part of a 200,000-acre cattle ranch, owned by the Hollister family, which stretched along the coast from Monterey to Santa Barbara. In the early 1960s the ranchland south of Point Conception was subdivided into 140 hundred-acre parcels to create the Hollister Ranch community; the area continues to be used for cattle ranching. The rich fishing grounds and exceptional surfing spots along this part of the coast are presently accessible only by boat.

Gaviota State Park: *Hwy. 101 at Gaviota Beach Rd.*

The park includes 5.5 miles of shoreline, the mouth of Gaviota Creek, and portions of the inland canyon north of the beach; Gaviota Pass, the historic settlement of Las Cruces three miles inland, and an undeveloped hot sulphur spring off Highway 101 northeast of the beach are also within the park boundaries. A trail leads from the hot spring into Los Padres National Forest. Day use and camping facilities are located along the beach; some restrooms are wheelchair accessible. For information, call: (805) 968-0019.

Gaviota Creek cuts through an uplifted ridge of the Santa Ynez Mountains to form the gorge at Gaviota Pass. The creek, lined with dense riparian woodland, supports a small, sporadic steelhead spawning run. The perennial stream also provides habitat for the foothill yellow-legged frog and red-legged frog.

Remnants of a Chumash village along the beach have been excavated by archaeologists. In 1542 Cabrillo stopped at this village during his explorations of the California coast, and in 1769 Portolá's expedition camped here. It is recorded in the expedition diary that Portolá's soldiers shot a seagull, or *gaviota*, in the pass, and today the coast retains this name. In 1874, Colonel William Hollister and the Dibblee brothers built a wharf at Gaviota. From the wharf, locally produced wool, grain, and lumber were loaded onto sailing ships and exported to Boston and other ports.

Fishing for yellowtail, sanddab, and rockfish is popular from Gaviota Pier, and scallops, abalones, and clams are collected in the nearshore waters. There are harbor seal hauling-out grounds and rookeries along the coast, as well as dense offshore kelp forests.

Mission Santa Inés: *Hwy. 246, E. of Solvang.*

The 19th of 21 missions built along El Camino Real, Mission Santa Inés was founded in 1804 and named after Saint Agnes, a fourth-century martyr. In 1812 an earthquake, now estimated to have reached an intensity of 8 or 9 on the Richter scale, destroyed most of the buildings. Rebuilt in 1817, the mission was again damaged during the Indian uprising of 1824. Restoration of the mission was begun in 1904. The mission is operated by the Franciscan Capuchin Fathers.

Refugio State Beach: *Hwy. 101 on Refugio Rd., 15 mi. W. of Goleta.*

The park includes rocky shore and tidepool habitats and a wide, sandy beach. There are day use and camping facilities, and some restrooms are wheelchair accessible. Call: (805) 968-1350 or 968-0019.

Originally part of Rancho Nuestra Señora del Refugio, the surrounding coastal land was granted to Sargeant José Ortega, a member of the Portolá Expedition. The small cove at Refugio was for a while the chief contraband port on the Southern California coast. Yankee traders, forbidden to trade with the Spanish in California, loaded hides, tallow, wine, and leather goods processed at the Ortega Ranch onto their sailing ships bound for Boston.

Refugio Road, originally a trading route for the Chumash and later a wagon road in the 1800s, cuts across the ridge of the Santa Ynez Mountains, connecting Refugio State Beach with the Santa Ynez Valley inland.

Mission Santa Inés

El Capitan State Beach: *S. of Hwy. 101, 20 mi. N.W. of Santa Barbara.*

The park includes a narrow beach at the mouth of El Capitan Creek, and day use and camping facilities located upland from the beach. Some restrooms are wheelchair accessible. Call: (805) 968-1411 or 968-0019.

Along El Capitan Creek are extensive riparian woodlands. The ringtail cat can be found here, and in the fall, Monarch butterflies congregate and breed in trees here and along the coast south of Gaviota. At the mouth of Cañada del Capitán are remnants of a Chumash village, called Ahwin or Ajuahuilashmu by the Chumash, which was excavated in 1957.

The coastal hills west of Highway 101 support extensive avocado orchards, which flourish due to the area's mild coastal climate and the well-drained soils of the marine terrace.

Naples Reef: *1 mi. offshore, S.W. of Ellwood Pier.*

The reef is a unique habitat that supports large numbers of surfperch, rockfish, lingcod, and cabezon as well as kelp bass, California sheephead, Pacific barracuda, spiny lobster, and abalone. Dense giant kelp forests cover the reef and the kelp understory provides shelter from predators for young fish. The reef has been the site of scientific research, including studies on grazing habits and territoriality of resident fish species, and the effects of El Niño and the resulting severe storms on the reef ecosystem.

Naples Reef is an important sport and commercial fishing site. Boats from Santa Barbara harbor visit the area regularly; scuba divers collect lobster and abalone, and commercial divers harvest abundant sea urchins.

Hollister Ranch

Coal Oil Point Reserve: *University of California, Santa Barbara, West Campus.*

The reserve, which includes Coal Oil Point and adjacent Devereux Lagoon, contains a salt marsh, grasslands, and coastal sand dunes. An offshore reef provides habitat for sea stars, crabs, spiny lobsters, octopuses, and mollusks. Kelp bass, rockfish, Pacific bonito, California halibut, cabezon, and California sheephead are typically found in the offshore waters. Forty-five-acre Devereux Lagoon, northeast of the point, provides habitat for egrets, curlews, plovers, sanderlings, terns, sandpipers, cormorants, great blue herons, and black-crowned night herons. The Coal Oil Point Reserve is part of the University of California's statewide Natural Reserve System, and is administered through the Santa Barbara campus. The system was created to preserve plant and animal communities, geologic and soil features, and fresh and saltwater areas of California.

Dune vegetation at Coal Oil Point exemplifies the biological and geological transition between Northern and Southern California flora. The dunes are the northern limit for the southern beach primrose and the southern limit for the northern bush lupine.

Bat ray on beach near Goleta Point

University of California, Santa Barbara and Isla Vista: *Off Clarence Ward Memorial Blvd.*

At one time part of Rincon Ranch, and the site of an asphaltum mine in the late 19th century, the Santa Barbara campus site was a Marine training station just prior to its inclusion in the University of California system in the 1950s. The station was declared surplus after World War II and sold to the University of California Regents for ten dollars. The Marine camp included buildings, paved streets, and an Olympic-sized swimming pool.

Isla Vista County Park, along Del Playa Dr., is built on cliffs that were formed in four successive stages of uplifting of the ancient sea floor, rising sea level, and wave erosion. A stairway leads from the blufftop to the beach and tidepools below.

There are several vernal pool sites in Isla Vista. Vernal pools are rare microhabitats found in only a few places outside of California. As a result of standing water that accumulates in soil depressions during the winter and spring, a unique vegetation flourishes. The Del Playa sites, located half a mile east of Coal Oil Point on Del Playa Dr., are typically only a few feet across and from nine to ten inches deep. *Eryngium armatum* is a rare plant that reaches its southern limit at these pools. Another vernal pool, located about a mile northeast of Coal Oil Point at the juncture of Camino Corto and El Colegio Rd., contains the rare pillwort, a small fern. Other plants typically found at these pool sites include *Plagiobothrys undulatus*, a member of the borage family, and *Stachys ajugoides*, of the mint family.

Campus Lagoon is a brackish water pond adjacent to Goleta Point on the Santa Barbara campus. Covering 25 to 30 acres, it is the site of the Marine Science Institute. The institute conducts research on California wetlands and offshore reefs. Northeast of Goleta Point is a heavily used, wide sandy beach, a popular spot for skin diving and surfing. Goleta Point is a hauling-out ground for sea lions, and was the site of a whaling camp from 1870 to 1890. Whales were towed ashore and their fat and oils rendered in huge kettles over driftwood fires.

Goleta Slough: *8 mi. W. of Santa Barbara.*

Goleta Slough, which includes over 350 acres of wetland, is fed by several freshwater streams that carry runoff from the Santa Ynez Mountains. The majority of the slough is owned by the City of Santa Barbara, but a small portion is part of the Santa Barbara campus of the University of California. The slough is an important feeding and nesting area for migrating land birds and waterfowl, and a breeding area for many fish and marine organisms.

The earliest inhabitants of the Goleta Slough area were the Oak Grove peoples, who lived there about 5,000 B.C. Their descendents, the Chumash, had long established villages in the slough area when the Spanish first arrived in the mid-1700s. The Spanish found more than 1,000 Indians living on Mescalitan Island, in the center of a natural harbor that is now the slough. The harbor was used by ocean-going vessels during the Spanish period and the remains of a wrecked sailing ship in the estuary, noted in documents from the period, are perhaps the origin of the slough's name; *goleta* is the Spanish word for "schooner." An unusually severe flood in 1861 caused 14 feet of silt from inflowing creeks to be deposited in the harbor, creating a lagoon. Siltation over the last 50 years created the present slough.

In 1928 a runway was built across a portion of the marsh, and by 1941 the municipal airport was completed, filling 400-500 acres. Mescalitan Island and the remains of the Chumash village were bulldozed to provide fill for the airport. The sand spit at the mouth of the slough was a hauling-out ground for a large population of harbor seals until the construction of a bridge across the creek and marsh in 1930 caused the seals to abandon the site.

Goleta Beach County Park: *5990 Sandspit Rd., Goleta.*

The county park includes the outlet stream of Goleta Slough, used for canoeing and birdwatching. The park is a popular recreational area with a pier and restaurant. 1,450-foot Gole-

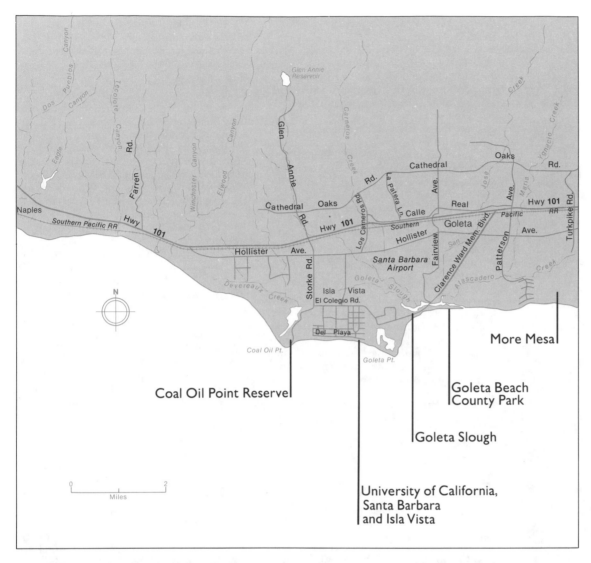

Coal Oil Point Reserve

More Mesa

Goleta Beach
County Park

Goleta Slough

University of California,
Santa Barbara
and Isla Vista

ta Pier has a boat launch and is a popular spot for sport fishing. Offshore reefs provide habitat for spiny lobsters, California halibut, and white seabass. The beach is the site of one of several seasonal grunion runs in the county, and on three or four nights after the full or new moon in March through September, the grunion swim ashore to deposit their eggs on the beach; the eggs are washed out to sea at the next high tide.

More Mesa: *End of Puente Dr. off Hollister Ave., 1.5 mi. S.E. of Goleta.*

The mesa, bounded on the north by Hollister Ave. and on the south by the ocean, is an up-lifted marine terrace encompassing close to 300 acres of undeveloped land. Several archae-ological excavations on the mesa have un-covered 3,000 to 6,000-year-old artifacts. The mesa was once part of Rancho La Goleta; Thomas More bought 400 acres in 1857 and began cattle ranching on the land. More also mined the tar seeps of the mesa sea cliffs; some of the asphaltum was used to pave San Francisco's streets in the 1860s. The Southern Pacific Rail-road crossed the mesa in 1887; today a natural gas pipeline that carries gas from deposits dis-covered in the 1930s follows the old rail bed.

More Mesa is important for its biological re-sources. Black-shouldered kites, northern har-riers, merlins, and burrowing and short-eared owls use the mesa for roosting and foraging. The mesa is particularly important to the black-

shouldered kite; now a fully protected species, this raptor was common in Southern California before 1895, but was nearly extinct by the 1920s due to hunting, egg collection, and habitat de-struction. The northern harrier also has suffered a declining population in this century due to loss of its habitat. Only two to four individuals winter along the southern coast of Santa Barba-ra County each year. The merlin, a falcon, is rare in the state; a few individuals overwinter on the mesa. The mesa area is the only known hab-itat in Santa Barbara County for the migratory short-eared owl.

black-shouldered kite (*Elanus caeruleus*)
15 to 17 inches long, 3⅓-foot wingspan

249

Arroyo Burro Beach County Park: *2981 Cliff Dr., Santa Barbara.*

Arroyo Burro Creek runs through the park and empties into the ocean at the eastern end of the beach. Oak and lemonade berry grow in the relatively undisturbed riparian woodland extending inland along the west bank of the creek. The ripe fruit of the lemonade berry shrub was used by Indians and early settlers to make a cooling drink.

A variety of invertebrates typical of the central California coast live in the waters below the rocky headlands west of the park. Excavation of a well-preserved Chumash midden east of the park produced shellfish remains, bones, and artifacts such as flake tools, hammerstones, and projectile points.

Park facilities include restrooms, parking, and a picnic area. Call: (805) 687-3714.

La Mesa Park: *Shoreline Dr., Santa Barbara.*

La Mesa Park, a nine-acre neighborhood park with picnic tables and restrooms, overlooks the Santa Barbara channel from La Mesa Bluff. In 1856 a 30-foot lighthouse was built on top of the bluff. Destroyed by the 1925 earthquake that devastated Santa Barbara, the lighthouse was replaced by an automated light.

Shoreline Park: *Shoreline Dr., Santa Barbara.*

Situated on a marine terrace, this 14-acre grassy strip along La Mesa Bluff overlooking the Pacific Ocean is a popular whale watching site; on a clear day the Channel Islands are visible offshore. The bluff face is actually a fault scarp that was created by displacement of the earth's surface along Mesa Fault. In 1925, movement along this fault may have been the origin of a devastating earthquake that almost leveled the city of Santa Barbara.

Leadbetter Beach: *Shoreline Dr., Santa Barbara.*

Situated below the knoll that is now the site of Santa Barbara City College, the park includes 27 acres of sandy beach. The knoll was the site of Punta del Castillo, a mansion built in 1886 by Thomas Dibblee. Leadbetter Beach was created in 1929 after construction of the harbor breakwater caused large amounts of sand to be deposited upcoast from the breakwater.

City of Santa Barbara: *90 mi. N.W. of Los Angeles.*

The city of Santa Barbara was the site of a Royal Spanish Presidio, established in 1782, the last of four presidios founded by the Spanish in Alta California. The outlines of the original rectangular complex are traced by the present State, De la Guerra, Santa Barbara, and Canon Perdido streets. The remaining Presidio buildings are part of a State Historic Park. El Cuartel, located on East Canon Perdido St., was the Presidio barracks, and is the oldest building in Santa Barbara.

El Paseo, a shopping and restaurant complex, was designed in the Spanish style by architect James Osborne Craig in the 1920s; it incorporates the Orena adobes, built in 1849 and 1858, and the restored *casa grande*, or main house, of Casa de la Guerra, built in 1819-1826. El Paseo is now a State Historical Landmark.

Included among the many historic buildings in Santa Barbara that have been preserved are the adobe homes of prominent citizens of the Spanish and Mexican periods. The Covarrubias Adobe, in the courtyard of the Santa Barbara Historical Museum, was built in 1817 and is a State Historical Landmark. The Trussel-Winchester adobe on West Montecito St. was built in 1854 by a sea captain using timbers from the wrecked steamship, the *S.S. Winfield Scott*. It is an example of the architectural transition between the adobe construction of the Spanish and Mexican periods and frame construction of the early American period. Alongside it is Fernald Mansion, built in the 1860s; both the Trussel-Winchester adobe and Fernald Mansion are open to the public on Sundays.

In the late 1800s and early 1900s, State Street in downtown Santa Barbara was lined with ornate Italianate and Eastlake style buildings built during the city's rise to prominence as a

Presidio of Santa Barbara

Covarrubias Adobe

health resort. After the 1925 earthquake destroyed most of these buildings, the city instituted a mandatory design review to establish a Spanish or Mission style of architecture. State Street was transformed by the construction of continuous arcades, and was widened by moving the sidewalk under the arcades.

The Santa Barbara Museum of Natural History was founded in 1916. The museum, situated on 11 acres, houses exhibits, conducts educational programs, and supports research programs that focus on the geology, zoology, and ethnographic history of the southern and central California coast and the Channel Islands.

Mission Creek, which originates on the south slopes of the Santa Ynez Mountains, winds along a six-mile course through the center of downtown Santa Barbara. Sections of the stream and its tributaries remain relatively undisturbed and support remnant stands of riparian vegetation, including sycamores and coast live oak. The Santa Barbara Botanic Garden at 1212 Mission Canyon Rd. contains 60 acres of native plants along upper Mission Creek representing major native California habitat regions. Rattlesnake Canyon Park contains three miles of hiking trails leading to the creek's upper watershed.

Mission Santa Barbara: *Upper Laguna St., Santa Barbara.*

The tenth mission to be established in Alta California, Mission Santa Barbara was dedicated in 1786, four years after the establishment of the Royal Presidio. The site was selected by Father Junípero Serra, who died before the first church was built.

Several churches have been built on the present site. The first simple adobe structure was replaced by a more substantial building made from local sycamore and laurel trees. Construction of the present church was begun in 1812 after a severe earthquake destroyed the previous building, and was completed in 1870. Built of sandstone blocks, the church's neoclassical façade is a replica of a design from a Renaissance architectural pattern book.

Over 8,000 Chumash Indians were living in the area when the Spanish arrived. In 1798 a village of over 250 adobe huts was built to house the Indian converts to Christianity. The mission Indians grew grain, vegetables, fruit trees, and grapes, and manufactured adobes and tiles in the mission pottery, as well as making shoes and wool cloth. A dam, located two miles up Mission Creek in what is now the Botanic Garden, was built by Indian labor in 1807; the Indians also built a mill, tanning vats, reservoir, and filter on the mission grounds. The 640,000-gallon holding tank of the reservoir is still in use as part of Santa Barbara's water system.

Mission Santa Barbara

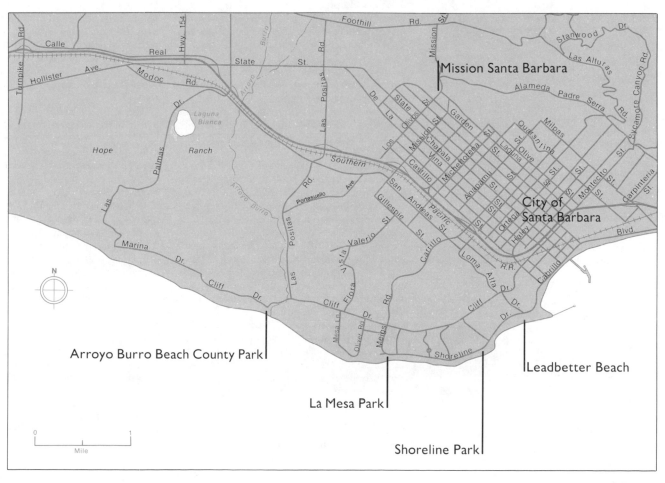

Arroyo Burro Beach County Park

La Mesa Park

Shoreline Park

Leadbetter Beach

Mission Santa Barbara

City of Santa Barbara

City of Santa Barbara, ca. 1905, Los Banos Del Mar left foreground, Potter Hotel upper left

Santa Barbara Harbor: *Foot of State St., Santa Barbara.*

In 1929 a detached breakwater was built to protect the harbor. However, the breakwater caused sand build-up, creating what is now Leadbetter Beach and resulting in loss of sand at downcoast beaches. The breakwater was extended to Point Castillo to alleviate the problem, and in 1938 a pipeline was built to carry dredged sand to a spit in the harbor and to a downcoast "feeder beach." Sand from the feeder beach is eventually carried downcoast to other beaches by longshore currents. A walkway along the 2,400-foot breakwater affords scenic views of the Santa Barbara Channel. Surfing conditions are good outside the harbor.

Marina facilities within the harbor include boat slips, marine specialty shops, restaurants, sport fishing boat rentals, and a yacht club. Call: (805) 963-1737.

Los Banos Del Mar, one of Santa Barbara's two public swimming pools, is located adjacent to the harbor on West Cabrillo Boulevard. One of California's largest annual swim competitions, Semana Nautica, is held here. The pool is on the site of an elaborate bathhouse, built by the city in 1901, that included an indoor pool, bowling alley, billiard parlor, and outdoor bandstand. For pool information, call: (805) 966-6119.

Ambassador Park/Burton Mound: *129 W. Mason St., Santa Barbara.*

Half-acre Ambassador Park, located on a small rise that overlooks the harbor and beach front, was the site of an Indian village at the time of Cabrillo's arrival in 1542. A large adobe house, built in the early 1800s, stood atop the rise or "mound" for nearly a century and was last occupied by Don Luis Burton until 1879. The site, which retains Burton's name, is a State Historical Landmark.

The block-long park is bordered by palm trees planted at the turn of the century when a promenade extended from the entrance of the opulent Potter Hotel, which was built on the site of the Burton adobe, to the beach boulevard. The Potter Hotel, renamed the Ambassador in 1918, burned to the ground in 1921. A major archaeological excavation conducted in the still-smoldering ashes of the hotel uncovered skeletal remains of what proved to be pre-Columbian Indians. Artifacts of three distinct Indian cultures were removed from the mound, including sandstone bowls and *ollas*, or water jugs, as well as Venetian glass beads and wine bottles from the Spanish period.

West Beach: *Seaward of W. Cabrillo Blvd., Santa Barbara.*

The 11.5-acre sandy beach extends from the Santa Barbara Harbor parking lot to Stearns Wharf. Cabrillo Blvd., which borders the beach, is lined with palms planted by the city in 1902 in the style of European boulevards of the era.

Stearns Wharf: *Foot of State St., Santa Barbara.*

When first completed in 1872 by local lumber merchant J. P. Stearns, the wharf was the longest deepwater pier on the California coast between San Francisco and Los Angeles. Stretching 1,500 feet long in 40 feet of water, the pier was built to serve both passengers and freight arriving by steamship. With construction of the pier the practice of "lightering" was ended. This was a marine taxi service that took passengers, for about 50 cents apiece, from ships anchored beyond the surf line to the shore. People were loaded into surf boats, or "lighters," and rowed through the surf where they would then be carried ashore on the backs of sailors.

Between 1876 and 1896 a horse-drawn streetcar and then electric tram cars ran from downtown Santa Barbara to the foot of the wharf. In 1878 a storm caused extensive damage to the wharf. Stearns rebuilt it in 1880, adding an additional pier, or "dogleg," that ran to a railroad spur on shore. A restaurant built on the wharf in 1941 marked the end of the wharf's use for shipping and transportation. A fire in 1973 severely damaged the wharf, which was closed until restoration began in 1979, and reopened in 1981. Now shops and restaurants occupy the three-block-long wharf.

The Santa Barbara Museum of Natural History, in a joint project with the Channel Islands Marine Sanctuary, operates the Sea Center marine exhibit hall. Located on the remains of the "dogleg" pier, the exhibits focus on the marine resources of the Channel Islands National Park. Next to the Sea Center, The Nature Conservancy maintains administrative offices and exhibits of its California preserves; the exhibits are open to the public daily and are free.

Stearns Wharf is used both for commercial and recreational fishing. An open-air market sells fish and shellfish caught in the Santa Barbara Channel, which is an important state fishery; 90 percent of the total Southern California catch of abalone and shrimp, and 70 percent of the barracuda landings come from channel waters. For information, call: (805) 963-1979.

Palm Park: *E. Cabrillo Blvd., Santa Barbara.*

The park has a mile of beach frontage, including a strip of turf bordered by palm trees. Facilities include a playing field, the Palm Park Cultural Center, picnic tables, restrooms, a walkway, and a bike path.

By the late 1880s and early 1900s, business development related to wharf activities began to replace the palm-thatched beach cottages that were rented by winter visitors to Santa Barbara. Local citizens, concerned that the area would become an eyesore, sought to make the site a city park. Palm Park was created in 1931 on the site of J. P. Stearns' old lumber yard adjacent to Stearns wharf.

East Beach: *1400 E. Cabrillo Blvd., Santa Barbara.*

The 44-acre park with a half-mile of sandy beach includes a wading pool, children's play equipment, turfed picnic area, and volleyball courts. Cabrillo Pavilion, built in 1925, includes a youth recreation center and public bathhouse; call: (805) 965-0509. Cabrillo Arts Center, located on the beach, is an art and cultural activities center; call: (805) 962-8956.

Stearns Wharf

Santa Barbara Zoological Gardens: *1300 E. Cabrillo Blvd., Santa Barbara.*

In 1947 the City of Santa Barbara acquired the mansion called Vega Mar, built on this site in 1896. It was removed in 1957 to make way for the zoological gardens.

The zoological gardens are located atop a prominent knoll, overlooking East Beach and the harbor area. Over 500 animals in 50 exhibits are displayed in the zoo. There is also a small nature theatre, a children's train and play area, and picnic facilities. Access to the zoological gardens is from Niños Drive. For information, call: (805) 962-6310.

Andree Clark Bird Refuge: *E. Cabrillo Blvd. and Hwy. 101, Santa Barbara.*

The Andree Clark Bird Refuge, a 42-acre wildlife refuge, has a varied population of resident and migrating birds, including cormorants, coots, egrets, gulls, herons, and many species of ducks. Close to 200 species of birds use the 30-acre lake and three islands.

The saltwater marsh and surrounding lowlands were purchased by the City of Santa Barbara in 1909. In 1928, additional funds were donated by the owner of the neighboring estate to excavate the marsh and create an artificial freshwater lake. The refuge is named in memory of the donor's daughter, Andree Clark. A bike path skirts the refuge on the southern and eastern perimeters.

Montecito: *2 mi. E. of Santa Barbara Harbor.*

Montecito is an unincorporated residential community comprised mostly of large estates, many built in the 1870s when the area was a fashionable neighborhood for the resort town of Santa Barbara. Set in rolling oak woodlands between the foot of the Santa Ynez Mountains and the Pacific Ocean, the community was called *El Montecito*, the little woods. Montecito's architectural heyday was from 1900 to the 1930s, when its Mission and Classical Revival style mansions were built. The Santa Barbara Biltmore Hotel, located on the Montecito waterfront, is an example of the Spanish Colonial Revival style. It was designed by architect Reginald D. Johnson and built in 1926.

There are several examples of restored Spanish and Mexican-era adobes in Montecito. The Pedro Massini Adobe, built in the mid-1800s, is one of two remaining Monterey-style adobes in the area. The adobe, a private residence, is located at the junction of Sheffield Dr., Ortega Hill Rd., and North Jameson Lane, north of Highway 101.

Montecito is the location of the first West Coast house designed by architect Frank Lloyd Wright. Stewart House was built in 1909-1910 and is a cruciform Prairie house, a style associated with Wright.

A private 40-acre estate, Madam Ganna Walska's "Lotusland," contains one of the most diverse horticultural displays in the area. The Music Academy of the West, the Brooks Institute of Photography, and Westmont College are also located in Montecito.

Hammond's Meadow, along the Montecito waterfront, covers 22 acres of rolling grassland with a low bluff overlooking the ocean, and some woodland. The meadow contains an important archaeological resource which is included on the National Register of Historic Places. Access to the meadow is from the beach south of Channel Drive. There are views of the Santa Ynez Mountains from the bluff and the beach.

Public access to the Montecito beach area is via Channel Dr.; there is also a pedestrian accessway under Highway 101 at the south end of Butterfly Lane, and a ramp at the end of Eucalyptus Lane.

Chumash

The Chumash were the largest Indian tribal group in California at the time of Cabrillo's arrival in 1542. Abundant food supplies allowed the Chumash to enjoy a stability and material wealth rare among the California Indians. Some permanent villages along the Santa Barbara coast had as many as a thousand residents and served as centers of culture and trade within larger provinces. Fish and shellfish from the Santa Barbara Channel were the foundation of the Chumash economy, providing a major food source. A variety of plants and animals were also utilized. Edible bulbs and roots were dug up in the spring, and acorns, pine nuts, walnuts, and chia seeds were harvested in the fall and stored, along with dried meat, for the lean winter months. Small mammals, deer, and birds were caught year-round, and even kelp was dried and eaten. The surplus of food enabled an extensive trade network to develop between the mainland and Channel Island Chumash, and with neighboring tribes. Clam-shell disk bead currency made by the Chumash was highly valued and widely distributed,

facilitating the exchange of foodstuffs, utensils, and ornamental and ceremonial objects among the culturally diverse tribes.

Chumash material culture was innovative as well as complex. Chumash houses were large, up to 50 feet in diameter and capable of housing several extended families. They were framed with willow poles planted in the ground in a circle and tied at the top to form a dome, then covered with tules. The only California Indians to use beds, the Chumash constructed raised platforms and covered them with rush mats. Also

unique to the Chumash was the use of the tomol, or plank boat, for fishing and for transportation between the mainland and Channel Islands. The planks were hewn directly from upland pine trees and carried to coastal villages where carpenters would split them using wedges made of whale ribs with blades of abalone shell. The planks were then sewn together with plant fibers and caulked with asphalt from local tar seeps. The Chumash were the only California Indians to use fishhooks; carved from abalone shell, the hooks were used to catch quantities of bonito, yellowtail, albacore, and bluefin.

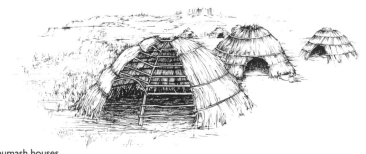

Chumash houses

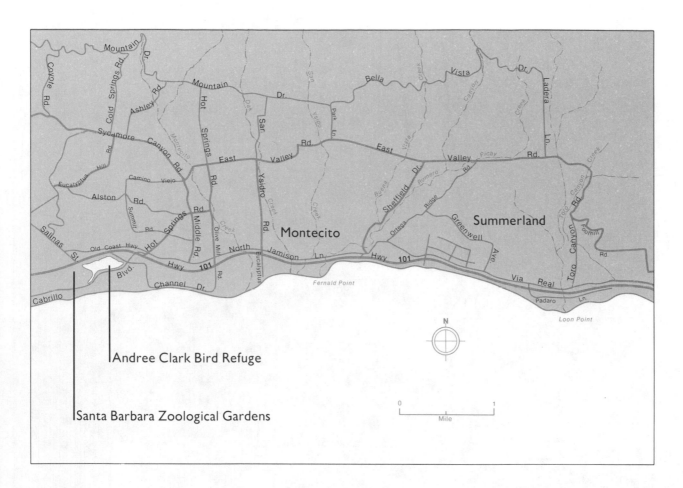

Andree Clark Bird Refuge

Santa Barbara Zoological Gardens

Summerland: *4 mi. E. of Santa Barbara.*

Summerland takes its name from spiritualist literature. At the turn of the century, revival meetings were conducted here in tents pitched on vacant lots. The Summerland Presbyterian Church, on the northeast corner of Lillie and Valencia Streets, is an example of turn-of-the-century Gothic Revival architecture.

This small, hillside beach community with views of the ocean and the Channel Islands is the site of the first offshore oil drilling rig. Erected in 1896, the drill was a simple device, attached to the end of a wooden pier extending offshore. By 1906 more than 400 wells drilled in the area covered the beaches of Summerland. Although the wells were drilled into submerged lands, the oil field was actually an extension of an onshore oil deposit. Average daily oil production from these wells was two barrels per day per well. New wells drilled within the Santa Barbara Channel today produce 800 to 1400 barrels of oil per day per well.

In 1958 the first offshore drilling platform on state tidelands was erected. Located two miles offshore from Summerland in 100 feet of water, the platform was named "Hazel." Over 20 wells were eventually drilled from this platform. Offshore oil drilling and production platforms "Hazel" and "Hilda" are visible from the Summerland area. In 1969 a blowout of an oil well five miles offshore blackened Santa Barbara beaches with residue from thousands of barrels of crude oil.

Lookout County Park, located on Lookout County Park Rd., is a small blufftop park with restrooms, a picnic area, volleyball courts, and a children's play area. There is a ramp leading to the sandy beach below. Call: (805) 969-1720.

Summerland, oil wells, ca. 1911

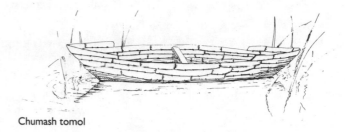

Chumash tomol

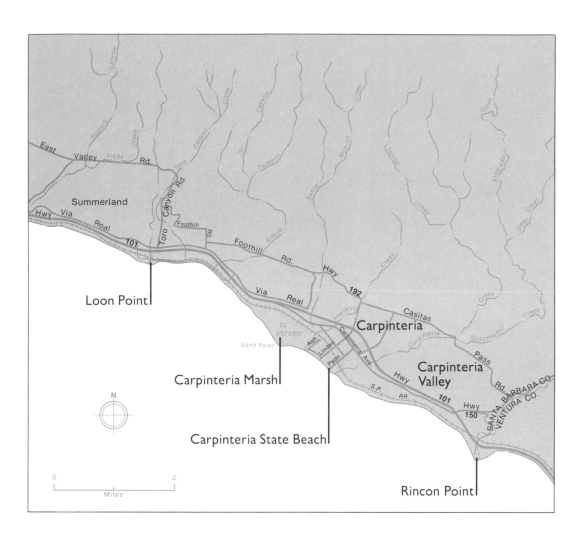

coast live oak (*Quercus agrifolia*)
tree: 30 to 75 feet high
leaves: ¾ to 2½ inches long
acorns: 1 to 1½ inches long

Loon Point: *2 mi. E. of Summerland.*

Dense stands of coast live oak and sycamore grow along the coastal stream that parallels Toro Canyon and empties into the ocean at Loon Point. Introduced eucalyptus and Monterey cypress provide habitat for roosting and mating Monarch butterflies. Kelp beds grow a half-mile offshore of Loon Point.

Carpinteria Marsh: *W. of Hwy. 101, Carpinteria.*

The coastal lagoon and salt marsh complex cover 230 acres, most of which are included in the statewide University of California Natural Reserve System. The marsh, also known as El Estero, is fed by Santa Monica and Franklin creeks, which drain the Santa Ynez Mountains and the Carpinteria Valley. Historically, a seasonal sandbar separated the marsh from the ocean; since the construction of flood control channels in 1966, the marsh is open to the sea year-round.

A narrow strip of freshwater marsh supports willows, alkali bulrushes, and cattails. The salt marsh vegetation is dominated by pickleweed. Native species include saltgrass, saltbush, alkali heath, and sea-blite. The marsh contains an endangered plant, salt marsh bird's beak.

Thousands of shorebirds and migratory waterfowl, including at least 49 different species of birds, use Carpinteria Marsh. Two endangered birds, the light-footed clapper rail and Belding's savannah sparrow, are permanent marsh residents. Clapper rails prefer to nest in cordgrass, but also inhabit pickleweed in the low marsh. Because its habitat is often inundated, the clapper rail builds a platform nest of dead plant material, including a ramp that floats with the rising tide. The clapper rail feeds on crabs, insects, shrimp, snails, and crayfish.

Belding's savannah sparrow is distinguished from other sparrows by its darker coloring and heavy streaks on the throat, breast, and sides. The sparrow prefers the higher salt marsh habitat, using pickleweed for nesting, for perching, and as a food source. This marsh-adapted species is able to concentrate chlorides in its system, enabling it to drink and process sea water.

Herons and egrets are permanent marsh residents. Several land birds consistently use the marsh, including Say's phoebes, loggerhead shrikes, swallows, and kestrels, which hunt in the marsh. Hundreds of migrating ducks have been recorded arriving daily, including pintails, American wigeons, shovelers, cinnamon teals, and green-winged teals. Grebes, cormorants, coots, and ducks can be seen in the channels and ponds, whereas shorebirds such as sandpipers, dowitchers, willets, and dunlins feed on exposed mudflats. Eight species of gulls and five species of terns are also found in the marsh.

Archaeological investigations in Carpinteria Marsh in 1929 revealed that a succession of Indian cultures once inhabited the marsh area, beginning with the Oak Grove peoples and concluding with the Chumash Indians, who occupied the marsh from about 500 A.D. until the mid-19th century.

Carpinteria: *9 mi. E. of Santa Barbara.*

Located in a narrow coastal plain between the ocean and the Santa Ynez Mountains, the city of Carpinteria was founded in 1863. The beach-oriented community is the urban center for the predominantly agricultural Carpinteria Valley.

Carpinteria City Beach, located at the ends of Linden and Ash avenues, includes a quarter-mile of sandy beach. Access to the beach and limited parking are available at the ends of Ash, Holly, Elm, and Linden avenues.

Carpinteria State Beach: *Foot of Palm Ave., Carpinteria.*

The park contains 84 acres and two miles of ocean frontage. Facilities include restrooms, parking, a picnic area, and campsites, some of which are wheelchair accessible. For information, call: (805) 684-2811.

Carpinteria Creek bisects the park and supports a remnant stand of riparian woodland, including sycamores and willows, above the tidal zone. A sandbar forms a tidal lagoon at the mouth of the creek during the summer months. A small intertidal reef is exposed at low tides; the reef is habitat for a diverse invertebrate community that includes several species of mollusks and crustaceans.

The park was once the site of a Chumash village. The village, named Mishopshnow, was a center for construction of the wooden plank canoes, called *tomols*, used by the Chumash for travel to and from the Channel Islands. When Portolá visited the village in 1769 he recorded the presence of 38 huts and 300 inhabitants. Portolá called the village site *La Carpinteria*, or carpenter shop.

Large deposits of tarry asphaltum lie underneath the beach and cliff area a half-mile east of Carpinteria Creek. Some of the tar seeps are still active. The Chumash used the tar to caulk canoes and waterproof cooking vessels. In the 1920s fossils were recovered from open tar pits on the beach; they proved to be Pleistocene plants, mammals, birds, insects, and marine invertebrates.

A half-mile east of the park is a small pocket beach that is a major harbor seal haul-out. The seals use the beach, usually at night, for resting or sleeping. Up to 150 individuals have been seen using this site.

Carpinteria Valley: *From Toro Canyon Rd. to Rincon Creek.*

The Carpinteria Valley contains some of the best agricultural land in the state for growing specialty crops. Mild temperatures, little wind, and a north-south orientation favor the growing of avocados, lemons, and flowers. Of the almost 4,000 acres in agricultural production, over half are used to grow avocados, one quarter are lemon orchards, and the remaining land is used for greenhouse and nursery operations.

Rincon Point: *Bates Rd. exit, off Hwy. 101.*

This low, tree-lined point is the boundary between Santa Barbara and Ventura counties. The point is an alluvial fan composed of cobble material washed down from the coastal mountains by Rincon Creek. The cobble is erosion-resistant and has created a stable landform at the point. Waves refracting off Rincon Point create ideal surfing conditions. Rincon Beach County Park, located north of the point, has a parking lot at the end of Bates Rd., a picnic area, and a stairway to the beach.

Largest grapevine in Carpinteria, ca. 1900

Carpinteria State Beach

257

Channel Islands
Selected Species of Interest

Plants: White-felted paintbrush (*Castilleja hololeuca*), endangered endemic of the northern Channel Islands. **Island barberry** (*Mahonia pinnata insularis*), endangered endemic of Anacapa, Santa Cruz, and Santa Rosa islands.

Trees: Santa Cruz Island ironwood (*Lyonothamnus floribundus asplenifolius*), a relict species; endangered endemic of three Channel Islands. **Island oak** (*Quercus tomentella*), endemic to the Channel Islands; grows in canyons.

Insects: Channel Islands ironwood moth (*Ypsolopha lyonothamnae*), endemic to two islands; larva lives on ironwood. **Darkling beetle** (*Phaleria rotundata*), nocturnal; feeds on kelp washed onto beaches.

Invertebrates: Pink abalone (*Haliotis corrugata*), abundant offshore of Santa Barbara and San Clemente islands. **Allopora californica**; rare, red or pink hydrocoral found offshore Santa Barbara and Santa Cruz islands.

Amphibians and Reptiles: Santa Cruz gopher snake (*Pituophis melanoleucus pumilis*), a dwarf relative of the mainland gopher snake. **Island night lizard** (*Klauberina riversiana*), endemic to three of the Channel Islands.

Fish: Blacksmith (*Chromis punctipinnis*), inhabits kelp beds around all Channel Islands; eats parasites off other fish. **Giant sea bass** (*Stereolepis gigas*), abundant in Channel Island waters; lives to age 70, weighs up to 500 pounds.

Birds: Santa Cruz Island scrub jay (*Aphelocoma coerulescens insularis*), an endemic subspecies found only on Santa Cruz Island. **Xantus' murrelet** (*Synthliboramphus hypoleucus*), breeds only on Santa Barbara Island.

Land Mammals: Island fox (*Urocyon littoralis*), threatened; endemic to six Channel Islands. **Pygmy mammoth** (*Mammuthus exilis*), extinct subspecies of Ice Age mammoth; fossils found on northern Channel Islands.

Marine Mammals: Northern fur seal (*Callorhinus ursinus*), breeds on San Miguel Island. **Northern elephant seal** (*Mirounga angustirostris*), breeds on several Channel Islands; protected in California.

Day trips to Santa Cruz Island:
The Nature Conservancy
Santa Cruz Island Project
213 Stearns Wharf
Santa Barbara, CA 93101
(805) 962-9111.

Landing permits for western 90 percent of Santa Cruz Island:
Santa Cruz Island Company
P.O. Box 71940
Los Angeles, CA 90071
(213) 485-9208

Access to San Miguel, Santa Rosa, Anacapa, and Santa Barbara islands:
Channel Islands National Park: (805) 644-8262.
Channel Islands National Marine Sanctuary: (805) 644-8464.

San Nicolas Island:
San Nicolas Island is a military reservation.
Access is by special arrangement only; call: (805) 989-7259.

Anchorage permits for San Clemente Island:
San Clemente Island is a military reservation.
For restricted anchorage permits: (619) 437-6011, ext. 3311.

Landing permits for East Santa Cruz Island:
P. Gherini (805) 966-4155 or
F. Gherini (805) 483-8022.
No camping.

Channel Islands

EIGHT ISLANDS off the coast of Southern California constitute the Channel Islands. The four northern Channel Islands—San Miguel, Santa Rosa, Santa Cruz, and Anacapa—form a chain that is the southern boundary of the Santa Barbara Channel. San Nicolas, Santa Barbara, Santa Catalina (see Los Angeles County), and San Clemente compose the southern Channel Islands. The unique combination of geographic formations, wind patterns, and water currents has created a diverse and exceptionally productive ecosystem in the Santa Barbara Channel. Near Point Conception, the cold southward-flowing California Current veers to the southwest and, typically, the warmer Southern California Countercurrent flows north closer to shore. This ocean circulation pattern and resulting change in water temperature has created a transition zone that supports marine life indigenous to both northern and southern waters.

Six species of pinnipeds breed or haul out on the islands. Eleven species of seabirds nest on the Channel Islands and, because intensive development on the mainland has eliminated many of their nesting and breeding grounds, these island rookeries are critical to their reproduction. A total of 64 land and marine bird species use the islands for nesting and feeding.

Several animals and many plants found on the islands are endemic species that have adapted in special ways to their island environment. The island fox, found on six of the eight islands, is a dwarf relative of the mainland gray fox; by contrast the Santa Cruz Island scrub jay is 25 per cent larger than the mainland scrub jay. There are over 80 endemic plant species on the Channel Islands and more than 60 of them are endangered or rare.

During the Ice Ages, a drop in sea level exposed a "super-island" geologists call Santarosae, which was composed of the combined four northern Channel Islands. As a result of the drop in sea level, the Santa Barbara Channel was greatly narrowed, perhaps to less than four miles; today the channel is thirteen miles at its narrowest. Fossils of dwarf mammoths dating from the Ice Ages have been discovered on Santa Rosa and San Miguel islands; researchers speculate that the mammoths reached the islands by swimming across the narrowed channel.

Both the Chumash and Gabrielino Indians established permanent and temporary settlements on the Channel Islands, where they hunted otter, fished in plank canoes, and manufactured implements and utensils from chert and steatite found on the islands. There is evidence that the island people traded these products with the mainland Indians for acorn meal and other scarce food staples such as venison.

Channel Islands National Park, established by Congress in 1980, extends one nautical mile around San Miguel, Santa Rosa, Santa Cruz, Anacapa, and Santa Barbara islands. The history of the park begins with the declaration of Santa Barbara and Anacapa islands as a National Monument in 1938, and in 1949 the extension of the monument boundary to include the surrounding waters. Today, the National Park Service manages San Miguel, Santa Rosa, Anacapa, and Santa Barbara islands; Santa Cruz Island is privately owned. Most of Santa Cruz Island is in the process of being transferred to The Nature Conservancy, a national conservation organization that will acquire ownership by the year 2008. Marine resources within the park are owned and managed by the State of California in cooperation with the National Park Service, which enforces state regulations within the park and conducts research. Scuba diving and commercial and sport fishing are permitted uses.

The Channel Islands National Marine Sanctuary, which extends six nautical miles around the five park islands, includes the shallow shelf surrounding each of the islands that extends three to six miles offshore with an average depth of 300 feet. A highly variable submarine topography, in combination with complex current regimes, makes this one of the richest marine environments on the California coast.

In the waters surrounding the islands, forests of the large brown seaweed *Macrocystis pyrifera* grow in dense stands, anchored to the rocky sea floor by root-like "holdfasts"; the plants grow as high as 200 feet to reach the water surface where they create a canopy. Nearly 1,000 plant and animal species flourish in the kelp beds. Gray whales with calves can sometimes be seen in the kelp beds, which are thought to offer protection from rough seas.

In the deeper waters of the sanctuary are 20 species of dolphins, porpoises, and whales. Common and Pacific white-sided dolphins travel in large herds and often accompany boats as they cross the channel. Whale-watching trips are scheduled daily during the gray whale migration.

East Anacapa Island, Channel Islands National Park

Channel Islands
San Miguel Island and Santa Rosa Island

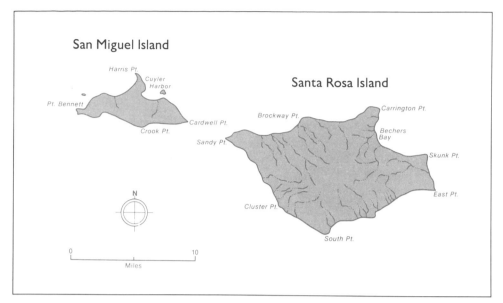

San Miguel Island

Santa Rosa Island

Harris Pt.
Cuyler Harbor
Pt. Bennett
Cardwell Pt.
Crook Pt.
Sandy Pt.
Brockway Pt.
Carrington Pt.
Bechers Bay
Skunk Pt.
East Pt.
Cluster Pt.
South Pt.

N

0   10
Miles

the millions, this rare seal was exploited by sealers in the late 1800s and was believed to be extinct by the turn of the century; a breeding colony was found on Guadalupe Island, Mexico in the 1950s and today there is a good chance for the seals' revival.

The most common pinnipeds on the island are the California sea lions, which breed at Point Bennett and Adam's Cove. The northern fur seal was once thought to breed only in the Pribilof Islands of the Bering Sea, but in the 1960s a breeding colony was discovered on San Miguel, which is now a protected rookery. Harbor seal rookeries are on the south coast of the island. Castle Rock offshore is a breeding and pupping site for the California sea lion, northern fur seal, and Steller sea lion.

The largest and most diverse marine bird rookeries in the Southern California Bight are found on Prince and San Miguel islands; significant numbers of Brandt's cormorants, western gulls, ashy storm-petrels, and pigeon guillemots breed on these two islands. Prince Island has the largest population of nesting Cassin's auklets in the Channel Islands.

San Miguel Island's proximity to the upwelling waters near Point Conception contributes to an increased number and rich diversity of subtidal and intertidal marine biota. Westcott Shoal on the north side of the island has a subtidal community dominated by giant kelp. On the rocky subtidal slopes are southern sea palms, anemones, sea urchins, and giant keyhole limpets, whose shells were used by the coastal Indians for wampum.

Coastal strand and coastal scrub vegetation cover more than half of San Miguel, while the rest remains barren. A caliche "forest" formed by a combination of calcium carbonate and rainwater that calcifies on the roots of trees and

San Miguel Island: *38 nautical miles S.W. of Santa Barbara.*

San Miguel, only 14 square miles in area, is a windswept plateau reaching 500 feet at its highest, with two central, low-lying hills, and beaches of shifting dunes. San Miguel has one of the world's most outstanding wildlife displays and is a major breeding area for pinnipeds and marine birds. Extensive offshore kelp beds provide habitat for an abundance of fish and invertebrates.

San Miguel is the only location in the country where breeding populations of five pinniped species occur, and is the southern limit of the Steller sea lion and northern fur seal. At Point Bennett the northern elephant seal and Steller sea lion breed, and the threatened Guadalupe fur seal is occasionally seen. Once numbering in

California sea lions and northern elephant seals, Point Bennett, San Miguel Island

other plants covers the sandy slopes above Cuyler Harbor. The aster *Malacothrix indecora*, an island endemic found only on San Miguel and Santa Cruz islands, grows on the mesa and rocky knoll at the west end of Cuyler Harbor.

Ten Channel Island endemics are found on San Miguel as well as several rare and endangered species. The rare island deerweed growing on the cliffs and sandy areas of San Miguel is found only here and in Baja California. The endangered white-felted paintbrush, island bedstraw, and island phacelia, as well as the rare San Miguel Island buckwheat and red-flowered buckwheat, are all Channel Island endemics found on San Miguel. The endangered island mallow grows at the western end in stabilized dunes, as does the giant *Coreopsis*, which produces masses of brilliant yellow blooms in the spring.

Over 500 archaeological sites, including numerous shell middens, have been uncovered on San Miguel Island. A monument to Juan Rodríguez Cabrillo, erected in the 1930s, overlooks Cuyler Harbor; though his grave has never been found, it is generally believed that Cabrillo died here from an infected broken arm after a fall on the island in 1543.

The island has been occupied by Chumash Indians, fur hunters, and ranchers, as well as Alaskan Aleuts brought to the island by Russian fur traders to hunt marine mammals in the 1800s. The adobe built in the 1850s by rancher George Nidever is possibly the earliest structure built on the Channel Islands. San Miguel Island was used by the Navy as a bombing range during the Korean war.

Santa Rosa Island: *28 nautical miles S.W. of Santa Barbara.*

With 84 square miles of land, Santa Rosa Island is slightly smaller than Santa Cruz Island, the largest Channel Island. Fifteen rare or endangered plant species and three endemic species grow here. There are eight different species of trees, including oaks, pines, cottonwood, and the Santa Cruz Island ironwood, an endangered endemic found only here and on Santa Cruz and San Clemente islands. The Torrey pine grows only on Santa Rosa Island and on the mainland near San Diego. Marine flora and fauna are very diverse due to the influence of both north-flowing and south-flowing ocean currents along the island's coasts.

Significant archaeological sites located on Santa Rosa Island, including human remains, date back at least 10,000 years. The charred bones of dwarf mammoths, at least 12,000 years old, were found in ancient fire pits that may have been used by humans as many as 37,000 years ago. Archaeological evidence of 12 villages found here indicates that the island was probably a major Chumash settlement from the 16th to the 19th century.

In 1843 Santa Rosa Island was granted to Carlos and José Antonio Carrillo, who established a livestock ranch on the island. In the 1860s and 1870s, T. W. More, who had bought the ranch from descendents of the Carrillo brothers in 1858, developed a large sheep ranch operation. Walter Vail and J. W. Vickers bought the ranch from More in 1902 and introduced elk and deer, which remain there today. In 1950 a small military air base was built at Johnson's Lee. In 1987 the island became part of Channel Islands National Park.

Island vegetation includes wooded areas with stands of Torrey pines, oaks, and Santa Cruz Island ironwood. The Torrey pine, which was once more extensive in Southern California in the geologic past, is today the rarest pine tree in the world, with only about 6,000 individuals remaining. The woodland chaparral community found in inland canyons and ridges contains unique endemics such as Catalina cherry, the rare Channel Island tree poppy, island ceanothus, and a rare subspecies of manzanita that grows exclusively on Santa Rosa.

Nesting colonies of Brandt's and pelagic cormorants and pigeon guillemots dot the northeast coast from Brockway Point to Carrington Point. In the subtidal waters offshore from Brockway Point are forests of giant kelp; the dominant invertebrates here are tunicates, purple and giant red sea urchins, and giant sea stars, species associated with the cooler upwelling waters of Santa Rosa Island's north coast. Black and striped surfperch are the dominant fish species in the nearshore waters; china rockfish, kelp bass, and blacksmith are also common. Giant spined sea stars, leather stars, pile perch, and monkeyface eels live in the warmer subtidal waters at Cluster Point on the south coast of Santa Rosa Island.

The island is a breeding and pupping area for the harbor seal and California sea lion. Whales pass near the coast during migration, and the Pacific white-sided dolphin, Dall's porpoise, common dolphin, and northern right whale inhabit the waters surrounding the island.

Monument to Cabrillo, overlooking Cuyler Harbor, San Miguel Island

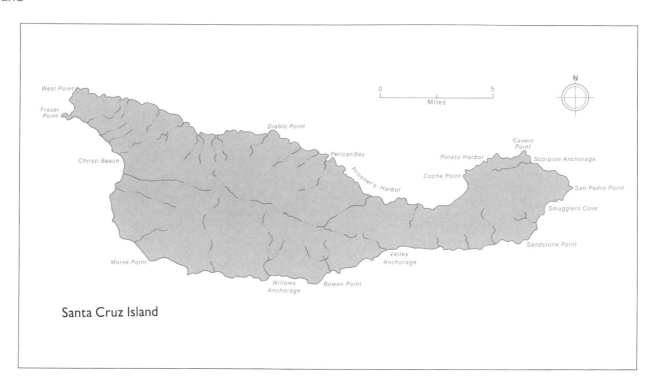

Santa Cruz Island

Santa Cruz Island: *22 nautical miles S.W. of Santa Barbara.*

Largest and most environmentally diverse of all the Channel Islands, Santa Cruz has two mountain ranges surrounding an interior valley, and encompasses 96 square miles. Santa Cruz Island has the largest number of island endemics of all the northern Channel Islands; over 40 species and subspecies are endemic to the Channel Islands, and 8 are found only on Santa Cruz Island. Over 50 species of land and marine birds breed here.

Chumash Indians established permanent villages on the island, estimated at their peak to have over 2,000 inhabitants. Called "Limu" by the Chumash, Santa Cruz Island was a regional center for the coastal Indians. The Chumash fished and hunted otter in the rich Channel waters, using wooden plank canoes called "tomols." Numerous shell middens and manufactured implements are evidence of the once thriving community that existed on the island for thousands of years.

Juan Rodríguez Cabrillo sailed past Santa Cruz in 1542, and was perhaps the first European to see the island. Juan Pérez, a member of the Portolá Expedition of 1769, gave Santa Cruz Island its name.

The first endemic species to be reported on Santa Cruz Island was the Santa Cruz Island ironwood in the late 1800s. This endangered tree is a relict species which was widespread in western North America before the Ice Ages; it is now found only in the canyons and ravines on Santa Cruz, Santa Rosa, and San Clemente islands.

Some of the island trees and shrubs represent disjunct populations, species whose ranges once extended much farther south; the presence of such species as madrone, big-leaf maple, California huckleberry, and chaparral currant is evidence that the island's climate was once wetter and cooler than it is today. Fossil remains of Douglas-fir trees found on the island dating back 14,500 years indicate that a flora typical of colder climates once existed on the island. As the Ice Ages came to an end, temperatures rose and warmer-climate species such as red willow, coyote brush, and prickly-pear cactus became established on the island. Temperatures gradually cooled again about 3,000 years ago, and most of the warm-climate species disappeared.

There are several plant communities on Santa Cruz Island that contain unique species. Oak woodland and chaparral communities in the vicinity of Pelican Bay include island endemics such as the rare Santa Cruz Island manzanita, Santa Cruz Island ironwood, and a hybrid pine related to the closed-cone or Bishop pine. The island oak, a relict species common on the mainland in the geologic past, now grows only on Santa Cruz and several other Channel Islands.

Rare and endangered flowers growing on Santa Cruz include the island barberry, an endemic found in the interior of Santa Cruz Island and on Santa Rosa and Anacapa islands, and a variety of the island deerweed, which grows only on Santa Cruz. The Santa Cruz Island lace pod is a rare endemic herb found only on this island.

island fox (*Urocyon littoralis*)
length, nose to tail: 2 to 2½ feet

Nature Conservancy tour group in grove of Santa Cruz Island pines

Santa Cruz Island has the most animal species of all the northern Channel Islands. Animals found here include the island fox and the Santa Cruz Island scrub jay. A subspecies of the gopher snake and the western spotted skunk live only here and on Santa Rosa Island.

At the eastern end of the island are the Gherini Ranch and, on the north coast, several marine bird rookeries at Scorpion Anchorage and Potato Harbor. There are extensive offshore kelp beds, harbor seal rookeries and hauling-out grounds, and marine bird nesting grounds along the south coast, from San Pedro Point to Sandstone Point.

The small tidepools at the east end of Prisoners' Harbor contain turban snails and aggregating sea anemones, an olive-green anemone with white, pink, or purple tips that forms dense mats on the rocks. In the intertidal zone at the western rocky point is the channeled *Nassa*. The largest of its species on the west coast, this snail is common from British Columbia to Baja California. The black turban snail, which may live up to 25 years, also lives here. In the subtidal zone is "oar weed," a species of brown alga that was burned by early settlers to use in making soap and glass. The burned ashes of the oar weed were called "kelp," a name now used to refer to all brown algae.

Surfgrass grows in the subtidal zone and in the cove near Fraser Point; it is the favored habitat of the spiny lobster and a species of limpet which lives only on the blades of the marine grass. The rich intertidal biota at Fraser Point includes California mussels, acorn and gooseneck barnacles, turban snails, anemones, abalones, purple or orange ochre sea stars, and rock crabs. The rock crab is considered as tasty as the Dungeness crab; it is caught by hand or by using a baited hoop.

A rich and diverse intertidal community at Willows Anchorage on the south coast of Santa Cruz Island contains hermit and rock crabs and the parchment tube worm, a marine worm that lives inside a self-made casement and exudes a parchment-like substance with which it nets its food. The rock louse lives under rocks or kelp during the day and comes out at night to scavenge. Very common in intertidal zones from Sonoma County to Central America, this crustacean dies if it is continuously submerged; the species represents a transition in the evolutionary process from aquatic to land habitation. The green abalone in the intertidal zone at Christi Beach is only found between Point Conception and Baja California; it is considered the most beautiful of all the abalones, with an olive-green to dark red-brown outer shell and an iridescent rainbow of dark green, blue, and lavender on the inner shell.

Pelican Bay, Santa Cruz Island

Channel Islands

Anacapa Islands, Santa Barbara, San Nicolas, and San Clemente Islands

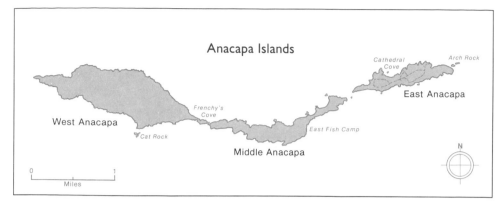

Anacapa Islands

Cathedral Cove • Arch Rock

East Anacapa

West Anacapa

Frenchy's Cove

Cat Rock

East Fish Camp

Middle Anacapa

N

0 1
Miles

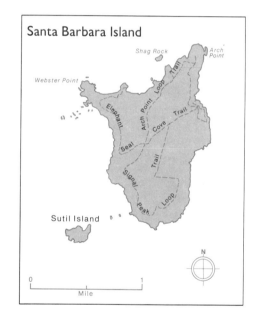

Santa Barbara Island

Shag Rock

Arch Point

Webster Point

Elephant Seal Arch Point Loop Trail Cove Trail

Signal Peak Loop Trail

Sutil Island

N

0 1
Mile

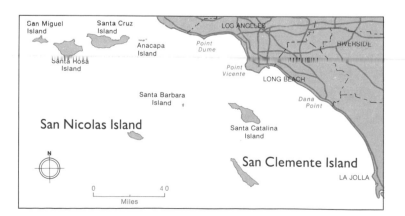

San Miguel Island

Santa Cruz Island

LOS ANGELES

Anacapa Island

Point Dume

RIVERSIDE

Santa Rosa Island

Point Vicente

LONG BEACH

Santa Barbara Island

Dana Point

San Nicolas Island

Santa Catalina Island

N

San Clemente Island

LA JOLLA

0 40
Miles

and the sea hare, a marine slug with two antennae that resemble rabbit's ears; it is eaten by the giant green anemone, which consumes it whole but expels the slug's toxic digestive gland by regurgitating its meal. Sea cucumbers and orange puffball sponges live in deeper subtidal waters.

Vegetation on the island is limited; small patches of coastal strand, including buckwheat, live-forever, ice plant, and the brilliant yellow-blooming *Coreopsis*, grow behind Frenchy's Cove on West Anacapa. The south slopes of the islets are covered with coastal sage and prickly-pear cactus. At the heads of the canyons are Catalina cherry, toyon, and native island oak.

Endemic birds on the Anacapas include subspecies of the horned lark, loggerhead shrike, orange-crowned warbler, house finch, rufous-crowned sparrow, and song sparrow. There are also lizards, salamanders, rats, and deer mice.

Sheep were herded on the islets in the early 1900s but removed in 1938 when Anacapa became part of the Channel Islands National Monument, a predecessor to the Channel Islands National Park. The lighthouse built in 1912 on East Anacapa was replaced by the present light in the early 1930s and has been automated since 1966.

Santa Barbara Island: *63 nautical miles S.E. of Santa Barbara.*

Located 38 miles west of San Pedro Harbor, Santa Barbara Island is one of the southern Channel Islands. Only one square mile in area, it is the smallest Channel Island. One of the principal rookeries of the California sea lion is found on Santa Barbara Island, where the northern elephant seal also breeds. Santa Barbara Island is the second most important seabird nesting site in the Channel Islands, after the San Miguel/Prince Island complex. The black storm-petrel, the rarest breeding seabird on the California coast, nests here. On Santa Barbara Island and tiny Sutil Island are nesting western gulls, three cormorant species, Cassin's auklets, and three species of storm-petrel. Santa Barbara Island has the largest known breeding colony in the world of rare Xantus' murrelets. Pink abalones, which are abundant in the subtidal waters, have been harvested commercially since World War II. Almost all pink abalones come from the waters surrounding Santa Barbara and San Clemente islands.

The island flora is highly endemic; six of the forty species growing on Santa Barbara Island are found only on the Channel Islands. The island night lizard, a threatened endemic, lives here and on San Clemente and San Nicolas islands. It is related to a species that disappeared from the mainland millions of years ago and has survived on these islands probably due to lack of predators or other competitors, as well as a mild island climate that shielded the lizard from the changes that led to extinction of the mainland species.

In the 1700s Spaniards used the island as a base from which to chase pirates. In 1846 goats were pastured on Santa Barbara Island and by 1915, fields were plowed and a ranch built. By 1916 the land was cleared by burning and domestic farm animals were introduced; the native flora was consequently destroyed and the resident bald eagles disappeared.

Anacapa Islands: *32 nautical miles S.E. of Santa Barbara.*

Actually three islets, the Anacapas are landscaped by rugged cliffs and edged with sea caves. The name Anacapa is taken from the Chumash word "Eneeapah," meaning deception, perhaps referring to the deceptively large size of the islets from a northern perspective. Fishing and diving are popular here. There is a lighthouse, a museum, and ranger station as well as a campground. West Anacapa is a research and natural area except for the public day use area at Frenchy's Cove; it is the only consistently used brown pelican nesting site in the western United States. Rich subtidal waters have a high diversity and abundance of marine life. There are ranger-guided walks of the middle island by reservation. The wreck of the ship *Winfield Scott* lies just off the northeast shore of the middle islet.

Anacapa's intertidal communities are some of the richest on the southern California coast, including barnacles, periwinkle, the rock louse, the parchment tube worm, and the spotted unicorn limpet. Chitons, crabs, and the black abalone live in the mid to deep subtidal waters.

Anacapa has an extremely varied subtidal biota, including surfgrass and the giant red urchin, an uncommon species that is much larger than the others in its genus and may live up to twenty years. The deep orange or red bat star, a sea star, lives among rocks overgrown with surfgrass and feeds by extending its stomach over dead or living surfgrass, algae, or tunicates. In deeper waters are the white sea urchin, small red anemone, the giant spined sea star,

Lighthouse on East Anacapa Island

San Nicolas Island: *68 nautical miles S.E. of Santa Barbara.*

Sculpted by wind and sand, San Nicolas Island presents a desolate landscape. Piles of human skulls and many large middens are evidence of the Indian populations that had lived on San Nicolas for centuries before Cabrillo landed there in 1542. The island was taken over by the U.S. Navy in the 1930s and is now part of the Pacific Missile Range.

The island's vegetation is sparse and several endemic species have become extinct in the last 50 years due to military activities and overgrazing by sheep. The San Nicolas Island buckwheat, an endangered endemic, can still be found here. Tufted puffins breed on the island, and six pinniped species frequent the surrounding waters, including the California sea lion, which breeds here. Offshore kelp beds are extremely abundant and are a major harvesting site for shellfish such as abalones, spiny lobsters, and sea urchins, as well as for the kelp itself, which accounts for about one-quarter of the total Southern California annual kelp harvest.

San Clemente Island: *40 nautical miles S.W. of Long Beach.*

San Clemente Island is a low, treeless plateau, vegetated primarily by chaparral and scrub. Forests were once abundant on the island, which was denuded of most of its vegetation in recent times by feral goats. Twenty million years ago the island was an area of diverse marine habitats; fossils of the tiniest marine diatoms and largest vertebrates such as sharks and whales have been found here.

San Clemente has some of the best examples of marine terraces in the world, with over 20 distinct terrace levels. Caliche deposits, calcified castings of tree limbs and roots, dot the dunes.

A true oceanic island, having never been connected to the mainland, San Clemente has a rare assemblage of endemic plants. With over 13 species found only on San Clemente Island, it has the largest number of endemics of all the California islands. However, since the introduction of goats on the island in the 1800s, many of its unique species have disappeared. Today, of the remaining endemics, seven are endangered, including the San Clemente Island larkspur, the San Clemente Island woodland star, and the San Clemente Island bush mallow.

California Brown Pelican

The California brown pelican, *Pelecanus occidentalis californicus*, one of six subspecies of the brown pelican, breeds only on the offshore islands of Southern California and Mexico and in the mangrove swamps of mainland Mexico. Once abundant, this bird is now endangered; northern populations dropped 95 per cent within two decades. This decline was brought about by egg thinning and resulting reproductive failure caused by high levels of DDT compounds in Southern California coastal waters in the 1960s and 1970s. DDT is now banned in the U.S., and pelican populations are slowly increasing.

Visitors to California's coast will often see California brown pelicans plunging for fish, or roosting and loafing on breakwaters, piers, and offshore rocks. Weighing eight to ten pounds, this bird has a wingspread of seven to eight feet. Large webbed feet, short, stout legs, silver-brown body, and a long pouched bill make the brown pelican a distinctive bird. The expandable throat pouch, suspended from the lower mandible, is about six inches deep and can hold up to two gallons. The base of the brownish pouch turns bright red during the breeding season.

Plunging from heights up to 60 feet (more typically 30 feet), pelicans dive and scoop up fish in their pouches; squeezing the water out of the pouch, the pelican swallows the fish whole. Air sacs between the skin and the skull cushion the bird's forceful contact with the water and provide flotation and thermoregulation. Anchovies make up the bulk of a pelican's diet, though they also eat sardines and mackerel. Pelicans migrate from south to north following these small schooling fish.

Brown pelicans are gregarious, but almost silent birds. The pelicans sometimes fly in V-shaped formations like geese, but are probably the only birds to favor single file flight with synchronized wing beats following a leader's cues.

Anacapa Island is the only stable breeding colony of the California brown pelican in the United States, but since 1984 some pelicans have successfully bred and hatched young on Santa Barbara Island. West Anacapa, where the birds usually nest, has steep, heavily vegetated slopes and is closed to the public to protect the nesting habitat.

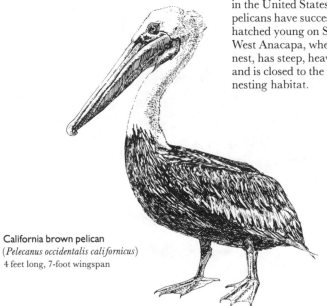

California brown pelican
(*Pelecanus occidentalis californicus*)
4 feet long, 7-foot wingspan

Ventura County
Selected Species of Interest

 Plants: Salt marsh bird's beak (*Cordylanthus maritimus maritimus*), endangered; inhabits salt marsh at Mugu Lagoon and Santa Clara River mouth. **California sagebrush** (*Artemisia californica*), common in coastal sage scrub.

 Trees: Western sycamore (*Platanus racemosa*), found in Sycamore Canyon, along Ventura River, and in other canyons in the Santa Monica Mountains. **Arroyo willow** (*Salix lasiolepis*), grows along rivers and creeks.

 Insects: Pictured rove beetle (*Thinopinus pictus*), wingless predator found under kelp on sandy beaches. **Tule beetle** (*Agonum funebre*), common near rivers and in wetlands along Central and Southern California coast.

 Invertebrates: Littleneck clam (*Protothaca staminea*), abundant in rocky beaches and in Mugu Lagoon. **Sand dollar** (*Dendraster excentricus*), occurs in offshore beds, especially off Ormond Beach and Mugu Lagoon.

 Amphibians and Reptiles: Southern alligator lizard (*Gerrhonotus multicarinatus*), preys on invertebrates, lizards, and small mammals. **California red-sided garter snake** (*Thamnophis sirtalis infernalis*), widespread along coast.

 Fish: White seabass (*Atractoscion nobilis*), important food fish found over sandy bottoms. **California sheephead** (*Semicossyphus pulcher*), spends first part of life as female, becoming male when it attains a length of about one foot.

 Birds: American coot (*Fulica americana*), black, duck-like water bird common in large flocks in ponds, marshes, and estuaries. **Western gull** (*Larus occidentalis*), only gull species that breeds along the California coast.

 Land Mammals: Western harvest mouse (*Reithrodontomys megalotis*), abundant in grassy areas near Mugu Lagoon; eats seeds and insects. **Long-tailed weasel** (*Mustela frenata*), preys on rodents and other small animals.

 Marine Mammals: Common dolphin (*Delphinus delphis*), often seen swimming alongside boats. **Pacific white-sided dolphin** (*Lagenorhynchus obliquidens*), frequents nearshore waters in winter and spring.

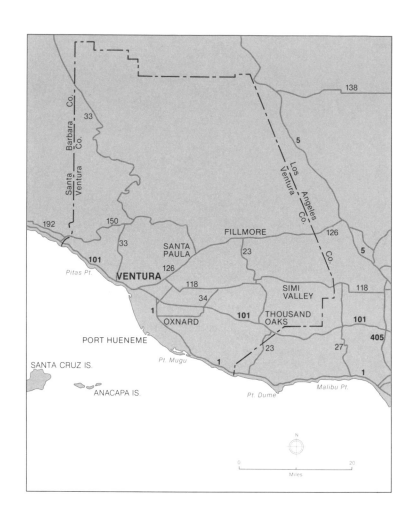

Ventura County

VENTURA COUNTY, situated in the east-west trending Transverse Ranges, comprises 43 miles of shoreline, and also includes two Channel Islands, Anacapa and San Nicolas islands. The steep slopes of the Santa Ynez Mountains form the county's northern coast; in the south coast, the Santa Monica Mountains rise above a narrow, rocky shoreline. Agriculture and urban development are concentrated in the flat central coast on the Oxnard Plain, a 22-mile-wide floodplain traversed by the Santa Clara River. Within this extremely productive agricultural region are the coastal cities of Ventura (officially the City of San Buenaventura), Oxnard, and Port Hueneme. The coastline here is characterized by wide, sandy beaches, with wetlands at the mouths of the Ventura and Santa Clara rivers. At the southern end of the plain is Mugu Lagoon, one of the largest remaining salt marshes in Southern California.

Before the arrival of Spanish missionaries, the Chumash Indians inhabited several large permanent villages along the Ventura County coast. Villages at the present-day City of Ventura and at Mugu Lagoon served as mainland canoe ports for trade with the Chumash of the Channel Islands. After the establishment of San Buenaventura Mission in 1782, the Chumash were inducted into the mission, where their numbers were diminished by European diseases, low birthrates, and poor living conditions. In 1834 Mexico secularized the vast mission lands, and the surviving Chumash were absorbed into Mexican ranchos and nearby settlements.

The Mexican government granted the vast mission lands to ranchers, who prospered through the 1860s raising cattle, grain, corn, and beans. The village that developed around the former mission was incorporated in 1861 as the City of San Buenaventura; in 1872, the city became the county seat of the new Ventura County, created from the eastern portion of Santa Barbara County.

A drought in 1863 caused a drastic decline in cattle ranching, and a succession of crops was introduced to the fertile, frost-free Oxnard Plain. With its deep, rich soils, ample groundwater, and cooling summer fog, Ventura County's central coast provides ideal growing conditions for such vegetables as celery, tomatoes, lettuce, and broccoli. Lemons thrive on the Oxnard Plain and in the lower Santa Clara River Valley because of the area's mild temperatures, high humidity, and freedom from the damaging Santa Ana winds that ravage citrus groves in other parts of Southern California. The county is the nation's leading producer of lemons, lima beans, cabbage, romaine lettuce, and spinach; other major agricultural products include avocados, strawberries, and cut flowers. However, urban development on the Oxnard Plain now competes with agriculture for available land.

Ventura County's petroleum industry got its start in 1864, when Thomas R. Bard and tycoon Thomas A. Scott arrived to investigate the area's oil prospects. Bard purchased 227,000 acres of former ranch land and began exploratory drilling along the coast. Although Bard, who later founded the Union Oil Company, drilled his first successful oil well in 1865, the oil industry did not achieve prominence until the 1920s, when large petroleum fields were discovered north of the City of Ventura. Today, the extraction and processing of oil is one of the county's main sources of income and employment.

The onset of World War II brought the military to coastal Ventura County, and in 1942 the Navy appropriated the Port of Hueneme and established a base that was a major supplier of personnel and equipment to the Pacific Fleet; Port Hueneme is now the site of the Naval Construction Battalion Center. The Navy also acquired Mugu Lagoon, establishing the Pacific Missile Test Center there in 1958. Post-war growth of industry and government employment has resulted in extensive residential development.

Ventura County is known for its mild climate, varied shoreline, and pleasure harbors at Ventura and Channel Islands Harbor. Wetlands at Mugu Lagoon and at the Ventura and Santa Clara rivers provide essential habitat for a diverse array of plants, invertebrates, fish, birds, and mammals. The inland northern portion of the county, almost all of which is included in Los Padres National Forest, is within the current range of the endangered California condor; the Sespe Condor Sanctuary, located northeast of Ventura in the Topatopa Mountains, preserves 53,000 acres of rugged, inaccessible mountains used by condors as nesting sites.

Oil Piers Beach

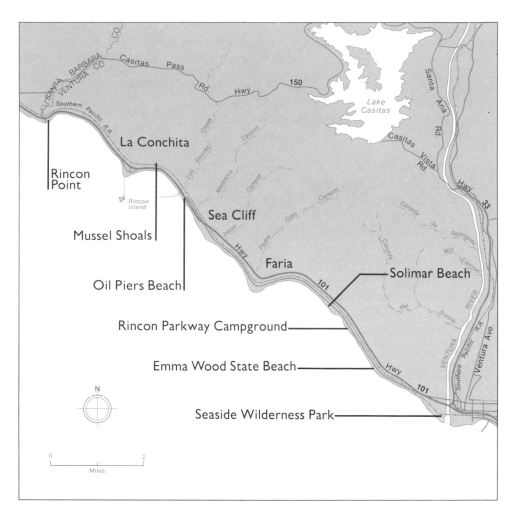

Rincon Point

Rincon Point: *Bates Rd., off Hwy. 101 at Ventura County line.*

Rincon Point is an alluvial fan formed along the creek bed of Rincon Creek, a perennial stream arising in the Santa Ynez Mountains. The downcoast beach is predominantly cobble with a rocky offshore reef. Rincon Point became famous for its association with the Battle of San Buenaventura, fought in 1838 between rival factions of Californians.

Rincon Point Parkway, located south of the locked-gate residential community of Rincon, provides parking and access to one of the most famous surfing spots in the state. Riparian vegetation is found along Rincon Creek north of Highway 101. Shorebirds and gulls rest and feed along the beach, and the intertidal area supports littleneck clams and other marine invertebrates. Common dolphins and Pacific white-sided dolphins may occasionally be seen from the point.

In the early 1900s a plank causeway was built just south of Rincon, completing the first highway between Santa Barbara and Ventura counties. The causeway included three sections constructed on pilings over the ocean. The previously constructed railroad had left little available land between the steep cliffs and the ocean for construction of a conventional highway.

La Conchita: *Off Hwy. 101, .5 mi. N.W. of Mussel Shoals.*

Once home to oil field workers, La Conchita, whose name is Spanish for "little seashell," is a residential community that was subdivided in 1924. Shoreline access to various pocket beaches is from the Highway 101 shoulder down the riprap revetment.

Mussel Shoals: *Seaward of Hwy. 101 at Punta Gorda.*

Located on a point of land called Punta Gorda, Mussel Shoals is a small residential community subdivided in 1924. The shoreline consists of a sandy beach north of the point and a rocky beach with tidepools to the south. Rincon Island, an artificial island located offshore of Punta Gorda and connected to land by a private causeway, was built in 1958 for oil extraction. The concrete tetrapods protecting the island from the surf have become habitat for algae, sponges, sea anemones, and rock scallops.

Oil Piers Beach: *1 mi. S.E. of Mussel Shoals.*

A popular surfing area is located along a wide, sandy beach backed by a rock revetment, between piers housing oil drilling rigs. These are the most visible of northern Ventura County's numerous facilities for onshore and offshore extraction, processing, and shipment of oil and gas. Three oil fields—Rincon, which extends offshore, San Miguelito, and Ventura—are located in an area where tightly undulating folds of the earth trap the oil.

Sea Cliff: *Old Pacific Coast Hwy., adjacent to Sea Cliff interchange.*

The locked-gate residential beach community of Sea Cliff is located northwest of Hobson County Park, a small, oceanfront day use and overnight camping area. For information, call: (805) 654-3951. Inland of the Old Pacific Coast Highway and Sea Cliff is a 45-acre remnant of the once extensive flower farms eliminated by construction of Highway 101.

Rincon Parkway Campground: *Old Pacific Coast Hwy., between Hobson County Park and Emma Wood State Beach.*

There is limited day use, and overnight camping for self-contained R.V.s in county-designated areas along the sandy beach seaward of the old Pacific Coast Highway; the beach is backed by a rock revetment. A bicycle path is designated between the roadway and the campsites. For information, call: (805) 654-3951.

Faria: *Old Pacific Coast Hwy., S. of Pitas Point.*

Faria is a residential beach community named for Manuel Faria, who settled here in 1908 because the area reminded him of his native Azores. Faria was at one time a resort and summer home area. To the north is Faria County Park, which provides day use and camping areas along a cobble and sand beach. For information, call: (805) 654-3951.

Pitas Point is the former site of a Chumash Indian village that was called Los Pitos, or "the whistles," by members of the Portolá expedition. The party camped near the village in 1769, and the Indians kept them awake all night by playing reed whistles. Soft shale in the intertidal area houses numerous rock-boring invertebrates, including piddock clams and date mussels. Western gulls, which breed on Anacapa Island to the south, rest and feed on shore.

Solimar Beach: *Old Pacific Coast Hwy., .5 mi. S.E. of Faria.*

Solimar, named for the Spanish "sol y mar" meaning "sun and sea," is a locked-gate residential beach community subdivided in 1934. A sandy beach used by gulls and migratory shorebirds fronts the community. An artificial reef offshore provides habitat for several species of rockfish, California sheephead, and garibaldi.

Emma Wood State Beach: *Old Pacific Coast Hwy. at Hwy. 101, Ventura.*

The 100-acre state beach includes cobble and sand beaches, dunes, coastal sage scrub, a small freshwater marsh, and riparian vegetation. The oceanfront campground, restored after extensive storm damage in 1983 and now operated by the county, provides day use and overnight camping. For information, call: (805) 654-4611; for reservations, call: (800) 446-7775. The group campground is located off Main St. near the Ventura River; call: (805) 643-7532.

Coastal strand vegetation on the beach includes ice plant and sea spinach. A small marsh community of tules and cattails occurs at the south end of the state beach at the former second mouth of the Ventura River. Willets, curlews, and other shorebirds rest and feed along the shore. Fishermen catch surfperch, cabezon, and California corbina; common dolphins and Pacific white-sided dolphins may be seen offshore.

Seaside Wilderness Park: *S. of Emma Wood State Beach, Ventura.*

Seaside Wilderness Park, also known as "Hobo Jungle," is a 22-acre undeveloped park with a quarter-mile of sand and cobble beach frontage; the only access is from Emma Wood State Beach to the north. Remnants of World War II gun emplacements have been used as shelters by transients. A grove of Monterey cypress serves as a roosting area for double-crested cormorants.

Emma Wood State Beach

Ventura River: *S. of Hwy. 101, W. of Fairgrounds.*

The Ventura River drains a 220-square-mile area including the Santa Ynez Mountains and Sulphur Mountain. The steep upper watershed is characterized by mixed-conifer forest, chaparral vegetation, and riparian woodland. The lower reaches of the river have been developed for agriculture and industry, notably apple, orange, lemon, and avocado orchards, and oil extraction and processing plants. Some natural habitat remains, including riparian vegetation such as arroyo willow, black willow, and tree tobacco, and coastal sage scrub including salt bush, California sagebrush, and coyote brush.

The Ventura River supports probably the largest of the remnant runs of steelhead trout in Southern California. The wetland area at the river mouth, vegetated with tules and cattails, supports such fish as Santa Ana sucker and arroyo chub, and provides habitat for waterfowl, coots, grebes, great blue herons, and endangered Belding's savannah sparrows. Hawks, owls, western pond turtles, bullfrogs, muskrats, red foxes, and skunks also inhabit the area.

San Buenaventura Mission: *N. end of Figueroa Street Plaza on Main St., Ventura.*

The ninth California mission and the last founded by Father Junípero Serra, the mission was dedicated in 1782 and named after Saint Bonaventure, an Italian Franciscan monk, philosopher, and educator. The mission was completed in 1809 as part of a large quadrangle of 60 structures. The present mission church dates from 1790; massive buttresses were added to the church façade after an earthquake in 1815. Frescoes, a wooden pulpit, and confessionals were crafted by the Indian neophytes. The present grounds are a small remnant of the once-extensive mission gardens and orchards praised by Richard Henry Dana, the well-known American author, as "the finest in the whole country." The mission is open daily from 7 AM-5 PM, except Sundays, when it is open from 10 AM-4 PM.

La Loma de la Cruz, or "Hill of the Cross," is located in Grant Memorial Park 300 feet above the mission, and provides views of the city and coastline. The cross was erected in 1933 to commemorate the original cross raised by the Franciscans; a portion of the original cross is on display at the County Historical Museum.

City of Ventura: *25 mi. S.W. of Santa Barbara.*

The City of Ventura, known officially as San Buenaventura, is located along the northwest edge of the Oxnard Plain, between the Ventura and Santa Clara rivers. When Cabrillo landed here in 1542, a sizable Chumash village called Shisholop existed near the site of the present-day mission; the village declined with the establishment of the mission in 1782. Subsequent to mission secularization, the former mission lands were subdivided in 1850. Settlers from Italy, France, Prussia, and Greece, as well as Yankees, replaced the adobe buildings with wood frame and brick structures. A Chinatown existed between 1870 and 1905, including a joss house (temple) and fire brigade.

The Mission Historic Area contains the Chinatown site; the mission reservoir water filtration building; the site of the San Miguel Chapel, the original church that preceded the mission; the Ortega Adobe, sole remnant of the many adobes along Main St.; and other buildings in the Italianate and Queen Anne styles.

The Albinger Archaeological Museum at 113 East Main St. provides an audio-visual show and contains artifacts from Chumash, Spanish, Chinese, and Yankee cultures of early Ventura. The Ventura County Historical Museum at 100 East Main St. features a collection of Ventura County artifacts, an exhibit of antique farm implements, and the George Stuart Collection of Historical Figures. Both museums are open Tuesday-Sunday, 10 AM-5 PM.

The Downtown Historic Area contains numerous residences and commercial buildings built in the Queen Anne, Colonial Revival, Spanish Colonial Revival, Beaux Arts, California bungalow, and Zigzag Moderne styles. The

---

Missions of Alta California

The 21 Alta California missions, established in the 18th and 19th centuries under the auspices of the Franciscan religious order, marked the northernmost reach of the Spanish empire in the New World. The founding of Mission San Diego by Junípero Serra in 1769 began the Sacred Expedition in Alta California, which was to carry out the dual purpose of Christianizing the Indians and replacing their culture with the social, political, and economic institutions of Spain. The expedition that included Serra and 100 others was led by Capt. Gaspar de Portolá, who was to carry out the secular aims of the expedition by establishing presidios at strategic locations along the coast of the new colony.

The mission-presidio system was not unique to Alta California. It had been in use for more than 200 years of Spanish colonization in the Americas, notably following the conquest of the Inca and Aztec civilizations. But unlike the highly centralized and culturally homogeneous agrarian native societies of Peru and Mexico, the native population of Alta California was a mosaic of culturally distinct and geographically dispersed tribelets that, with one exception, did not practice agriculture.

In the utopian vision of the mission founders, the California wilderness was to be transformed into a landscape of farming settlements inhabited by Christianized natives, educated by Franciscan friars and trained by lay craftsmen. In theory, the mission lands were not owned by the church, but were held by the missions in trusteeship, to be parceled out to each mission neophyte at the end of a ten-year apprenticeship.

During 65 years of Spanish occupation of Alta California, four presidios and 21 missions were built on the coastal plains and in nearby inland valleys from San Diego Bay to San Francisco Bay, but the territory in between these colonial outposts remained sparsely settled. Though nearly 81,000 native people had been baptized and apprenticed as mission neophytes during this time, by 1834 fewer than 15,000 had survived the ravages of disease and psychological malaise that resulted from the dismantling of the spiritual and material structure of their native cultures. The era of the missions ended shortly after Mexico gained both its independence from Spain and the territory of Alta California; the missions were secularized by the new Mexican government in 1834.

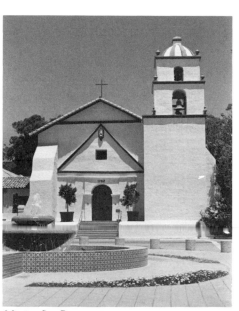

Mission San Buenaventura

Bard Hospital was built in the Mission Revival style in 1902. The Mitchell Block, facing Plaza Park, is the only intact row of turn-of-the-century buildings, including brick and wood Italianate, Gothic Revival, and Dutch Colonial Revival styles. Nearby, the Ventura County Church of Religious Science built in 1931 combines Mayan and Zigzag Moderne design; a model of a sacrificial altar serves as the lectern.

The Ventura City Hall at 501 East Poli St., formerly the County Courthouse, was completed in 1912 in the Neo-Classic style. Prominent features include a terra cotta exterior with whimsical friars' head gargoyles, a marble entrance lobby, mahogany and walnut paneling, and stained glass domes. The Father Serra statue in front of City Hall, overlooking California St., was a Depression-era project of the Finnish sculptor John Palo-Kangas.

Ventura County Fairgrounds: *S. of Hwy. 101, between Ventura Ave. and Ventura River, Ventura.*

The Ventura County Fairgrounds is the site of the County Fair, held each year in early October; other events are held almost every weekend. For information, call: (805) 648-3376. The rock and cobble beach, reached by Surfer's Point Park at the foot of Figueroa St., supports littleneck and chione clams, and is used by shorebirds and western gulls for resting and feeding. Offshore is a popular surfing area.

Ventura Pier: *Off Harbor Blvd., E. of California St., Ventura.*

The Ventura Pier was built in 1872, and lumber and petroleum products were unloaded here until 1940. Now part of San Buenaventura State Beach, the pier houses a snack bar and restaurant, and is popular for strolling and fishing; anglers catch Pacific bonita, surfperch, white seabass, and California corbina. Promenade Park begins near the foot of the pier and runs west to Surfer's Point Park and the Ventura County Fairgrounds.

San Buenaventura State Beach: *From the Ventura Pier S. to Marina Park, Ventura.*

San Buenaventura State Beach, which extends along two miles of broad sandy beach, is popular with swimmers, surfers, and anglers; facilities include parking, restrooms, picnic areas, a snack bar, and a beachfront bicycle path. For information, call: (805) 654-4611.

Hottentot fig grows on a low dune ridge along Harbor Boulevard. The narrower southern part of the beach fronting the Pierpont residential community is protected by large rubblemound groins inhabited by worms, mussels, barnacles, and sea stars. Sanderlings and western gulls frequent the beach; endangered California brown pelicans can be seen fishing offshore. Surfperch, rockfish, California halibut, and northern anchovy inhabit the nearshore waters.

The state beach includes Allesandro Lagoon, a former brackish water marsh that was cut off from the ocean and partially filled during construction of Highway 101. Located across the highway from the beach, the freshwater lagoon, vegetated with cattails and tules, is used by waterfowl such as green-winged teals, mallards, and wigeons, as well as grebes, coots, egrets, and domestic fowl.

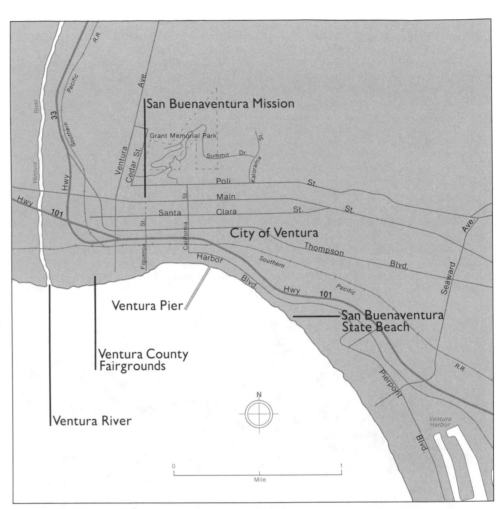

San Buenaventura, ca. 1885, Mission in center foreground

Ventura Harbor: *W. of Harbor Blvd., between Peninsula St. and Spinnaker Dr., Ventura.*

The Ventura Harbor, completed in 1963, was dredged from part of the Santa Clara River estuary. The harbor serves 1,500 pleasure boats, and provides boat charters, a fuel dock, boat storage and repair, transient docking, a launching ramp, pedestrian walkways and bike paths, and sailboat and fishing equipment rentals. The Fiesta del Sol, held in the harbor each year in late spring or early summer, offers sports and aquatic events and entertainment. For information, call: (805) 642-8538.

Beach recreation areas are located along both peninsulas that form the harbor entrance. Marina Park, on the north peninsula, provides restrooms, picnic areas, play equipment, beach access, and a small boat dock. Peninsula Beach, on the south peninsula, provides parking and restrooms, and is popular with surfers; Marina Cove is an ocean swimming area protected by

breakwaters. Vegetation in these areas includes European beach grass, lupine, red flowering ice plant, and acacia.

Inland of Ventura Harbor, along Harbor Blvd., is a row of eucalyptus trees used by Monarch butterflies as a winter resting place. Below these trees are stands of malva rosa, or tree mallow, which closely resembles and is related to hibiscus.

Channel Islands National Park Headquarters: *1901 Spinnaker Dr., Ventura Harbor.*

The Channel Islands National Park Headquarters and Visitor Center, which also serves the National Marine Sanctuary, contains exhibits of island natural history, an audio-visual show, a bookstore, and a garden of unique island plants. The headquarters tower affords views of the harbor, the City of Ventura, the Channel Islands, and the Santa Monica Mountains. Whale-watching trips and trips to the islands

leave from nearby docks. Headquarters are open daily, 8 AM-5 PM. Call: (805) 644-8262.

Olivas Adobe: *Olivas Park Rd., 1.5 mi. E. of Ventura Harbor, Ventura.*

Built in 1837 and now a State Historical Monument, the Olivas Adobe is one of the best restored adobes in the Ventura area. The adobe, a long, two-story building with a balcony and veranda, is located on land granted to Don Raimundo Olivas, a prosperous cattle rancher. On the grounds are picturesque gardens, and exhibits including a Chumash dwelling. The adobe is open daily; call: (805) 644-4346.

Santa Clara River: *S. of Ventura Harbor.*

The Santa Clara River, named in 1769 by the Portolá Expedition, arises in the San Gabriel Mountains north of Los Angeles, and flows west for 70 miles to the ocean. A major source of beach sand, the river is almost dry for six months of the year, with much of the flow at its mouth coming from reclaimed wastewater and agricultural runoff. The lower river, now confined by levees, once meandered across the fertile Oxnard Plain, a 22-mile-long coastal plain formed by the river delta between the Santa Ynez and Santa Monica Mountains. Where the river crosses the Oxnard Plain, the areas along the river bank are used for landfill, row crops, citrus orchards, and sand extraction.

The river banks support a riparian habitat of sandbar willow, black cottonwood, and giant reed, and a coastal sage scrub community of salt bush, coyote brush, and California sagebrush. Freshwater marsh plants such as tule, cattail, and bulrush grow in the river channel. Wildlife along the river includes painted lady butterflies and anise swallowtail butterflies, California red-sided garter snakes, southern alligator lizards, hummingbirds, thrushes, brush rabbits, and raccoons. Pacific lamprey and remnants of the Santa Clara River's once abundant steelhead population spawn upstream.

The mouth of the Santa Clara River lies within McGrath State Beach, and is a State Wildlife Refuge. Construction of the Ventura Harbor destroyed much of the river's historic wetlands; however, a 20-acre salt marsh community persists, with pickleweed, jaumea, alkali heath, and the endangered salt marsh bird's beak. The salt marsh attracts birds such as herons, egrets, ducks, coots, raptors, shorebirds, and endangered Belding's savannah sparrows. Seasonal fencing protects nesting areas of the endangered California least tern. Wastewater treatment ponds north of the river mouth are also used by waterfowl; these ponds are known as "Snoopy Ponds" because their shape, as seen from the air, resembles the comic strip character.

McGrath State Beach: *Along Harbor Blvd., 1.2 mi. S. of Spinnaker Dr., Oxnard.*

The 295-acre state beach stretches along two miles of shoreline south of the Santa Clara River and includes stabilized dunes, sandy beach, the marsh at the river mouth, and a small freshwater lake. Facilities include a day use area, wheelchair-accessible restrooms, a campground, and a nature trail. For information, call: (805) 985-1188 or 654-4611; for reservations, call: (800) 446-7275.

The dunes are vegetated with sea fig and sand verbena, and provide a nesting area for the Cal-

Santa Clara River mouth at McGrath State Beach

California least tern (*Sterna antillarum browni*)
8½ to 9½ inches long, 20-inch wingspan

ifornia least tern; behind the dune area is coastal sage scrub of California sagebrush and coyote brush. McGrath Lake, in the southern part of the park, is a haven for a variety of birds and small mammals. The lake's depth is maintained artificially by pumps, and because the water level is fairly constant, the shoreline has a well-established marsh community of willow, bulrush, and tule. Kelp flies, tiger beetles, Pismo clams, and littleneck clams can be found on the beach; surfperch, rockfish, and bass inhabit the offshore waters. Grunion spawn on the beach in spring and summer.

Mandalay County Park: *5th St. and Mandalay Beach Rd., Oxnard.*

Presently undeveloped, 90-acre Mandalay County Park contains foredunes vegetated with beach primrose, sea rocket, and sea fig. The backdune area contains arroyo willow, rushes, coyote brush, and yerba mansa. Western gulls, terns, and shorebirds may be seen on the beach, which is popular for fishing and surfing.

The nearby Mandalay Generating Station, at 393 Harbor Blvd., provides electric power from oil or gas-fired generators, or from jet engines, using jet fuel. In combination with the Ormond Beach Generating Station, power is provided to a 50,000-square-mile service area serving 3.4 million customers. Water, used for cooling, is taken in from the Edison Canal and discharged to the ocean at the rate of 176,000 gallons per minute. Tours may be arranged on two-week notice; call: (805) 486-0413.

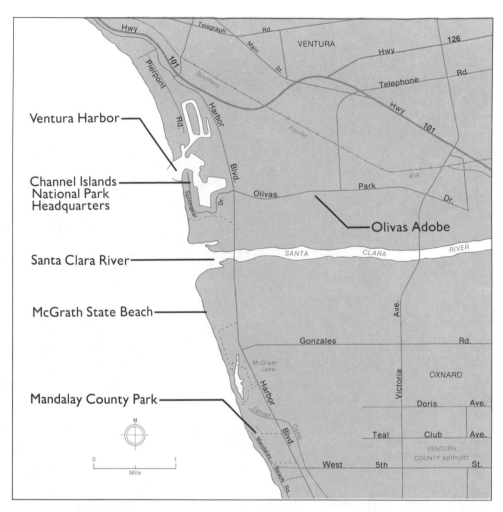

Ventura Harbor, view east from Channel Islands National Park Visitor Center

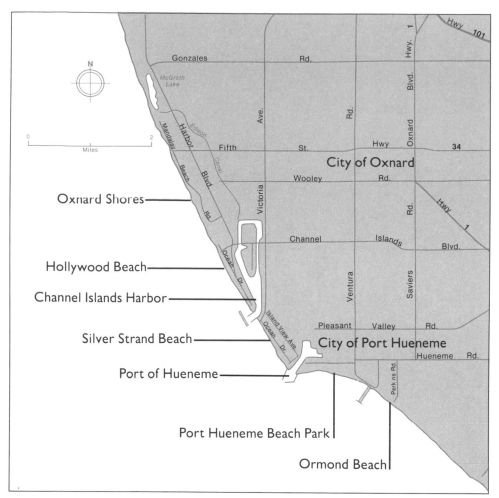

Map labels: Gonzales Rd., McGrath Lake, Ave., Rd., Hwy. 1, Hwy 101, Mandalay Beach Rd., Harbor Blvd., Ecrson Canal, Fifth St., Hwy, Oxnard Blvd., 34, City of Oxnard, Oxnard Shores, Wooley Rd., Victoria, Ocean Dr., Hollywood Beach, Channel, Islands, Rd., Hwy 1, Blvd., Channel Islands Harbor, Ventura, Saviers, Silver Strand Beach, Island View Ave., Ocean Dr., Pleasant Valley Rd., Port of Hueneme, City of Port Hueneme, Hueneme Rd., Perkins Rd., Port Hueneme Beach Park, Ormond Beach, N, 0 Miles 2

City of Oxnard: *7 mi. S. of Ventura.*

Oxnard was founded in 1898 when the Oxnard brothers established a beet sugar refinery in the heart of a productive agricultural region. Incorporated in 1903, the city remained fairly small until World War II, when the Naval Construction Battalion Headquarters was established nearby. Now Ventura County's largest city, Oxnard is a center for government and for manufacturing, which has replaced the processing of agricultural products as the main industry. Visitor attractions include Plaza Park and its pagoda-shaped pavilion, and the 1906 Chamber of Commerce Building, formerly the Carnegie Library. For information, call the Carnegie Cultural Art Center: (805) 984-4649.

Oxnard Shores: *W. side of Harbor Blvd., between Channel Way and Beach Way.*

Oxnard Shores is a residential beachfront community; a beach resort hotel, protected dune area, bicycle path, and public park are located in the area between Oxnard Shores and Hollywood Beach. Dune vegetation includes European beach grass and ice plant.

Hollywood Beach: *Along Ocean Dr., between Channel Islands Blvd. and San Miguel Ave.*

Hollywood Beach is located north of the Channel Islands Harbor entrance; access is via street ends along Ocean Drive. Restrooms are provided.

The unincorporated residential beach communities of Hollywood Beach and Hollywood-by-the-Sea, located north of the Channel Is-

lands Harbor, and Silver Strand, south of the harbor, were laid out in the 1920s and 1930s and served as isolated retreats for Hollywood movie stars such as Clark Gable; the towns' vacation cabins and homes are now being replaced by large beach residences.

Channel Islands Harbor: *W. of Victoria Ave., S. of Channel Islands Blvd., Oxnard.*

Channel Islands Harbor, once dune fields and wetlands, was excavated in 1960 as part of a U.S. Army Corps of Engineers project that used the unearthed materials to restore beaches at Point Mugu and Port Hueneme. The Corps also constructed entrance jetties and a half-mile-long detached breakwater across from the harbor entrance. The harbor contains approximately 2,500 boat slips, commercial fishing facilities, boat ramps and hoists, sport fishing and whale-watching services, and bicycle and pedestrian paths along the waterfront. The City of Oxnard holds a strawberry festival here each spring with crafts, food, and entertainment.

Silver Strand Beach: *Along Ocean Dr., between San Nicholas Ave. and Sawtelle Ave.*

Main access to Silver Strand Beach is at the foot of San Nicholas Ave.; facilities include parking and restrooms. At the south end of the sandy beach is the rock-filled shipwreck of the ocean liner *La Jenelle*, which has been converted to a fishing jetty.

Peninsula Park, near the south end of Peninsula Rd., provides a playground, tennis courts, and boat docks. Channel View Park, located at the north side of the harbor mouth, affords views of harbor activities. Channel Islands Beach Park, a small, protected sandy beach with wheelchair-accessible restrooms, is located at the south end of Victoria Ave. near the south side of the harbor entrance. Several small parks are found along the east side of Harbor Blvd., across from the harbor. For park information, call: (805) 984-4640.

Port of Hueneme: *W. end of Hueneme Rd., Port Hueneme.*

The Port of Hueneme, the only deepwater port between San Francisco and San Pedro, was dredged from 300 acres of land donated by Richard Bard, and opened in 1940. In 1942, the Navy appropriated and enlarged the harbor; during World War II, the Port of Hueneme shipped out 200,000 military personnel and 2 million tons of supplies and equipment. After the war, the Harbor District gradually re-acquired a small portion of the harbor from the Navy. The port, which is the major support base for offshore oil facilities in the Santa Barbara Channel, handles a variety of cargo, including automobiles, lumber, wood pulp, oil, offshore drilling equipment, fruit, and eggs. Commercial and sport fishing boats are also based at the port. Offshore is the Hueneme Submarine Canyon, where much of the sand moving downcoast is lost to deeper waters.

On the south side of the harbor mouth is the Port Hueneme Lighthouse, originally built in 1874 and rebuilt in 1941; the light was automated in 1972. Just east of the harbor is the 1,600-acre U.S. Navy Construction Battalion ("Seabee") Center. The Bard Mansion, a historical landmark built in Classical and Spanish

Colonial Revival styles, is located on the base. The Seabee Museum, at the base's Ventura Rd. entrance gate, contains a wide variety of artifacts and displays, including war memorabilia and dioramas. Call: (805) 982-5163.

City of Port Hueneme: *N.W. of Port of Hueneme.*

Port Hueneme is the former site of a Chumash Indian village named Wene'me, meaning "halfway" or "resting place." In 1871 the first major wharf between Santa Cruz and San Pedro was built here by Thomas Bard. This led to the development of Port Hueneme as a prosperous shipping center; throughout the late 1800s, grain, beans, potatoes, honey, and livestock from the area's farms were shipped from the wharf. Teams of horses pulled flatcars along the pier, and steamers called for passengers. However, the town lost its trade after 1898, when the railroad bypassed it for nearby Oxnard.

Port Hueneme has since redeveloped considerably; condominiums and a cultural center have been constructed along the shoreline. The Port Hueneme Historical Museum at 220 N. Market St. contains information and exhibits on the city; hours are 10 AM-3 PM weekdays. Call: (805) 488-2023.

Port Hueneme Beach Park: *Along Surfside and Oceanview Drives, Port Hueneme.*

The park features a wide, sandy beach with wheelchair-accessible restrooms, a playground, picnic facilities, a bike path, and a snack bar. A 1,200-foot-long recreational pier, built in 1978, has replaced the original Hueneme wharf. The pier, which is wheelchair accessible, is used for fishing and strolling, and offers views of the Santa Monica Mountains to the east and the Channel Islands offshore.

Ormond Beach: *Foot of Perkins Rd., S. of Port Hueneme.*

Ormond Beach, with three miles of broad, undeveloped beach, is backed by extensive dunes which provide nesting sites for the endangered California least tern. Pismo clams can be found along the shore; offshore is a dense bed of sand dollars. Approximately 130 acres of wetlands inland of the beach contain salt and brackish water marsh, mudflats, and open water. Marsh vegetation of saltgrass and pickleweed provides habitat for a variety of birds, including shorebirds, coots, and endangered Belding's savannah sparrows. A number of sportsmen's clubs maintain ponds nearby which provide habitat for migratory waterfowl.

Inland of Ormond Beach is the Ormond Beach Generating Station, which has two 750 megawatt generating units powered by oil, gas, or a combination of both.

Harvesting sugar beets near Oxnard, ca. 1890s

Port Hueneme harbor, ca. 1908, White Fleet on horizon

Mugu Lagoon: *S.W. of Hwy. 1, between Middle Point and Point Mugu.*

Located at the southeast edge of the Oxnard Plain, Mugu Lagoon is one of Southern California's largest remaining wetlands. The 1,800-acre saltwater lagoon, which is contained entirely within the U.S. Navy's Pacific Missile Test Center, is now half its original size.

Mugu Lagoon is fed by Calleguas Creek, and is protected from the surf by two sand spits. The lagoon contains over 900 acres of salt marsh vegetation, including pickleweed, sea-blite, alkali heath, and the endangered salt marsh bird's beak. Eelgrass, ditch grass, and green algae grow in deeper areas of the lagoon. Dunes on the barrier beaches are vegetated with sand verbena and European beach grass; the nearby upland areas support giant *Coreopsis*, California sagebrush, and a variety of introduced plants.

Mugu Lagoon attracts fish such as sharks, halibut, turbot, and topsmelt; killifish, mudsuckers, and staghorn sculpin are year-round residents. The lagoon contains a rich invertebrate fauna, including polychaete worms, snails, clams, crabs, shrimp, and tiger beetles. Harbor seals haul out in the lagoon, and California sea lions are frequent visitors.

The lagoon is used by thousands of migratory shorebirds and waterfowl, and is home to Belding's savannah sparrows and California least terns, both endangered. Threatened California black rails and endangered light-footed clapper rails may be seen here. Hawks and owls hunt in the area, and quail and pheasants inhabit the scrublands. Other wildlife includes reptiles, rodents, gray foxes, and coyotes.

Mugu Lagoon is named for Muwu, a large Chumash village located where Calleguas Creek enters the lagoon. Native Americans occupied the lagoon area for 7,000 years, and several villages have been uncovered here. A nearby nationally registered archaeological site has yielded California's best sample of Chumash artifacts, providing a comprehensive picture of this native culture.

The lagoon can be viewed from a roadside station on Highway 1, a half-mile north of Point Mugu Rock. Group tours may be arranged with the Navy Public Affairs Office, and reservations should be made up to several months in advance during birding season (October to March). For information, call: (805) 989-8094.

Mugu Submarine Canyon, which is a half-mile deep and over nine miles long, lies offshore to the west of Point Mugu. The canyon's meandering upper portion was probably formed by Calleguas Creek during the late Pleistocene.

Point Mugu Beach: *At Pt. Mugu Rock, S. of the Navy Firing Range.*

Off-road parking provides access to a sandy beach east of Point Mugu. Gulls, terns, and shorebirds frequent the beach; bass and rockfish inhabit the nearshore waters; and common dolphins and California sea lions may be seen offshore. There are numerous pocket beaches along the rocky shore between Point Mugu and La Jolla Beach to the east, accessible off Pacific Coast Highway.

Point Mugu State Park: *Point Mugu E. to Sycamore Canyon.*

Point Mugu State Park, located at the western end of the Santa Monica Mountains, consists of 13,360 acres, with five miles of shoreline and over 70 miles of trails. Most of the area east of Big Sycamore Creek is included in Boney Mountain State Wilderness Area. For park information, call: (805) 499-2112.

Among the park's diverse plant communities are coastal strand, with beach primrose and sea rocket; coastal sage scrub including giant *Coreopsis* and California buckwheat; grassland of tarweed and needlegrass; chaparral including chamise and ceanothus; oak woodland of coast live oak and toyon; and riparian woodland of California sycamore, black walnut, arroyo willow, and California bay laurel.

Gulls, shorebirds, and endangered California brown pelicans are found along the coast. Farther inland, hawks, owls, prairie falcons, and golden eagles hunt for reptiles, small birds, and rodents. After an absence of several decades, endangered peregrine falcons are being re-established on Boney Ridge. Also found in the park are lizards, snakes, badgers, gray foxes, bobcats, southern mule deer, and mountain lions. The nearshore waters support sand dollars, white seabass, and California sheephead. Common dolphins can be seen offshore.

La Jolla Valley: *La Jolla Canyon turnoff, 2 mi. W. of Sycamore Canyon.*

La Jolla Valley, part of Point Mugu State Park, contains an excellent example of California's vanishing tall-grass prairie. Among the native grasses found here are purple needlegrass, foothill needlegrass, melica grass, and goldfields. The least Bell's vireo, an endangered songbird, inhabits the narrow La Jolla Canyon. A pond near the walk-in campground provides habitat for ducks and coots. There is also a group camp, and trail access into the La Jolla Valley Natural Preserve and into other areas of the state park.

screech owl (*Otus kennicottii*)
7 to 10 inches long

Sycamore Canyon, Point Mugu State Park

La Jolla Beach: *W. of Hwy. 1, 1.5 mi. N. of Sycamore Cove.*

La Jolla Beach, part of Point Mugu State Park, provides trailer and tent camping on a long sand and cobble beach. The beach's low, active dunes support a strand community of beach primrose and sea rocket. Anglers catch white seabass, rockfish, and kelp bass; Pismo clams can be found in the sand.

Sycamore Canyon: *E. of Hwy. 1 and Sycamore Cove.*

The stream courses of Sycamore Canyon, which extends seven miles into the Santa Monica Mountains, support diverse riparian woodland vegetation. Western sycamore is abundant here, as well as Fremont cottonwood, big-leafed maple, dogwood, chain fern, and bracken fern. Associated birds include red-tailed hawks, woodpeckers, and canyon wrens; other animals living in the canyon are California red-sided garter snakes, western rattlesnakes, black-tailed deer, and bobcats. The canyon is a unit of Point Mugu State Park; facilities include a campground and trail access into the park. Call: (805) 499-2112.

Sycamore Cove: *9000 Pacific Coast Highway.*

Point Mugu State Park Headquarters are located at Sycamore Cove, which provides a day use area and access to a sandy pocket beach flanked by rocky points The beach is used for fishing and swimming, and is frequented by western gulls, terns, and migratory shorebirds. For information, call: (805) 499-2112.

Solromar: *1 mi. N.W. of Ventura County line.*

Solromar, whose name is derived from the Spanish to suggest "golden sunset of the sea," is a small residential community. An endangered plant, the Santa Monica Mountain dudleya, occurs in nearby Little Sycamore Canyon. A number of recorded archaeological sites are in the vicinity, including the nationally recognized Little Sycamore Shell Mound.

Leo Carrillo State Beach North: *40000 Pacific Coast Hwy.*

A portion of Leo Carrillo State Beach, including a day use area with parking and restrooms, extends into Ventura County from Los Angeles County. Across Highway 1 from Solromar is another segment of the state beach, called Yerba Buena Beach or County Line Beach, which is popular for surfing and windsurfing.

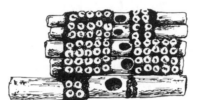

Chumash flute
Made of hollow bird bones and asphaltum tar, with olivella shell bead decoration.

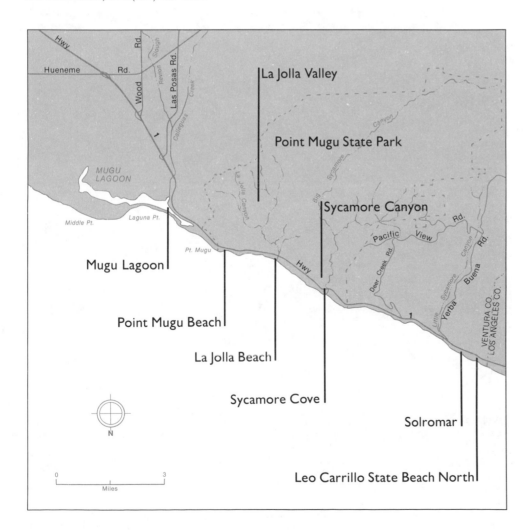

Los Angeles County
Selected Species of Interest

Plants: Coast cholla (*Opuntia prolifera*), erect, bushy cactus found on coastal bluffs and hillsides. **California scrub oak** (*Quercus dumosa*), densely branched evergreen shrub characteristic of chaparral-covered slopes.

Trees: Catalina ironwood (*Lyonothamnus floribundus floribundus*), endangered evergreen; endemic to Santa Catalina Island. **Big-leaf maple** (*Acer macrophyllum*), tall, broad-crowned tree common along stream banks.

Insects: El Segundo blue butterfly (*Euphilotes battoides allynii*), endangered; endemic to El Segundo Dunes. **Avalon hairstreak** (*Strymon avalona*), small butterfly endemic to Santa Catalina Island; common on brushy slopes.

Invertebrates: Chestnut cowrie (*Cypraea spadicea*), brown-shelled snail found on subtidal rock ledges and sandy mud. **Rock scallop** (*Hinnites giganteus*); adults attach to pilings and rocky substrates.

Amphibians and Reptiles: Coast horned lizard (*Phrynosoma coronatum*), cream-colored with a spiny head. **California mountain kingsnake** (*Lampropeltis zonata*), colorful snake inhabiting Santa Monica Mountains.

Fish: Barred surfperch (*Amphistichus argenteus*), prized game fish; abundant in surf zone along sandy beaches. **Pacific mackerel** (*Scomber japonicus*), important commercial and sport fish; schools in nearshore waters.

Birds: California gull (*Larus californicus*), winters along the California coast. **California quail** (*Callipepla californica*), resident of the Santa Monica Mountains; a larger, darker subspecies inhabits Santa Catalina Island.

Land Mammals: Western gray squirrel (*Sciurus griseus*), large, gray squirrel; nests in trees. **Pacific kangaroo rat** (*Dipodomys agilis*), dark brown, nocturnal burrower; has long hind legs for jumping; inhabits brushy areas.

Marine Mammals: Bottle-nosed dolphin (*Tursiops truncatus*), dark-colored, with a chunky build; travels in small groups near shore. **Short-finned pilot whale** (*Globicephala macrorhynchus*), often seen near Santa Catalina Island.

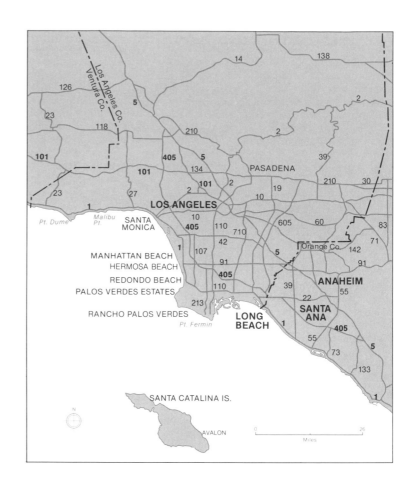

278

Los Angeles County

LOS ANGELES COUNTY, which includes 75 miles of mainland coast as well as Santa Catalina and San Clemente islands, is California's most populous county and contains its largest city. The northwest coast of Los Angeles consists of the rugged, largely undeveloped Santa Monica Mountains, part of the Transverse Ranges, which descend to a narrow ribbon of rocky and sandy shoreline. East of the mountains lies the intensely urbanized Los Angeles Basin, a broad, flat coastal plain formed by the Los Angeles, San Gabriel, and Santa Ana rivers and Ballona Creek. Located here are the beach communities of Santa Monica, Venice, Manhattan Beach, Hermosa Beach, and Redondo Beach, where wide beaches line crescent-shaped Santa Monica Bay.

The hills of the Palos Verdes Peninsula mark the southern end of Santa Monica Bay. The peninsula comprises a series of 13 marine terraces, and is characterized by headlands, steep cliffs, rocky beaches, and sandy coves. East of Palos Verdes is San Pedro Bay, which once contained extensive wetlands at the mouths of the Los Angeles and San Gabriel rivers. The bay is now the site of one of the world's largest industrial harbor complexes, which includes the ports of Los Angeles and Long Beach. Several miles of broad, sandy beach stretch from Long Beach southeast to Alamitos Bay.

The original inhabitants of the county's northwestern coast were the Chumash Indians, whose territory extended southeast to Topanga Canyon. The rest of the coast was home to the Gabrielino, so named by Spanish missionaries for their proximity to Mission San Gabriel. The seafaring Gabrielino also colonized Santa Catalina and San Clemente islands. Like the Chumash, the Gabrielino subsisted by fishing, hunting, and gathering.

The first European contact came in 1542 when navigator Juan Rodríguez Cabrillo sighted San Pedro Bay. The Portolá Expedition passed through the area in 1769, and in 1771, Junípero Serra founded Mission San Gabriel. Settlement did not begin until 1781, when Governor Felipe de Neve established the Pueblo de Nuestra Señora la Reina de Los Angeles de Porciúncula. The pueblo of Los Angeles was for many years California's most populous town, and during the 1820s-1830s, nearby San Pedro Bay was a major trading point for cattle hides and tallow. Mission San Gabriel, where California's first large orange grove was planted, was one of the most agriculturally productive of all the missions.

After secularization in 1834, the mission lands were granted to Mexican cattle ranchers. In 1850, when California became a state,

Los Angeles became the seat of the county of the same name. As the city grew, Phineas Banning and others began efforts to develop a port and a transportation system. In 1876 Southern Pacific Railroad completed a rail line from San Francisco to Los Angeles, thus connecting Southern California with the East Coast; both Southern Pacific and Santa Fe railroads completed direct lines from the east in the early 1880s. Competition between the two rail companies helped launch the great real estate boom of the 1880s: low train fares coupled with exaggerated tales of the area's beneficent climate lured thousands of midwesterners to Southern California. Dozens of resorts, suburbs, and subdivisions were created, and by the time the boom ended, the city's population had swelled. The rail connection to the east also boosted local agriculture; soon oranges, whose commercial cultivation had begun in the 1870s, and other crops were being shipped across the country.

The county's growth picked up again in the 1890s, following Edward Doheny's discovery of oil in 1892, and the designation of San Pedro as the official harbor for Los Angeles in 1897. In the early 1900s, beachfront development was spurred by the Pacific Electric Railway, which linked inland cities with the coast. To accommodate Los Angeles's growing population and expanding agriculture, the city's water supply was increased in 1913 by the diversion of the Owens River via the Los Angeles Aqueduct. In the 1920s the discovery of oil fields at Signal Hill and elsewhere led to further real estate booms. The Southern California motion picture industry, which began in 1906 with the establishment of Los Angeles's first film studio, flourished in the 1920s-1930s. During World War II, Los Angeles became a center for shipbuilding, airplane manufacturing, and shipping. The postwar years have seen the growth of the television and other entertainment industries, expansion of the ports, development of the electronics and aerospace industries, and an ever-increasing population.

The Los Angeles County coast affords a wide variety of recreational opportunities to the millions of visitors who come here annually. Parks within the Santa Monica Mountains offer hiking and equestrian trails, interpretive programs, and campgrounds in a natural setting. Visitors to the county's beaches enjoy such activities as volleyball, swimming, fishing, and diving. Surfing, introduced to California at Redondo Beach in 1907, and popularized in the 1960s by surfing movies and the music of the Beach Boys, remains a favorite sport at Los Angeles beaches.

Surfer off Hermosa Beach

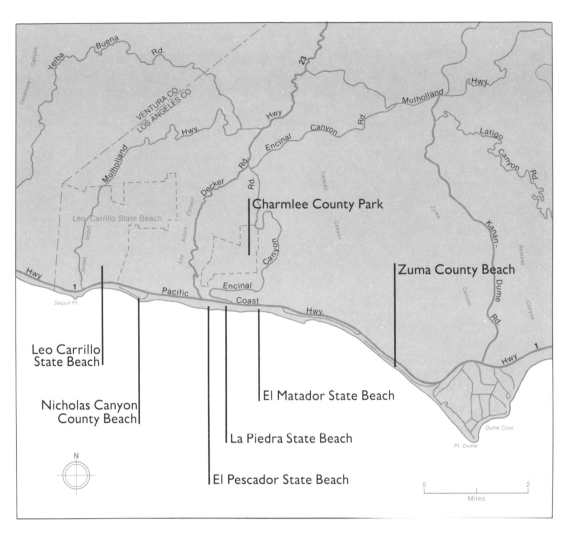

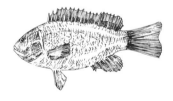

opaleye (*Girella nigricans*)
to 2 feet long

Leo Carrillo State Beach: *36000 Pacific Coast Hwy., Malibu.*

The 2,190-acre state beach encompasses steep mountains and bluffs, Arroyo Sequit canyon and creek, and several sandy beaches. Facilities include parking, restrooms, three campgrounds—one of which is wheelchair accessible—and a hiking trail that climbs to an elevation of 1,600 feet into the mountains. The beach attracts swimmers, surfers, anglers, and skin and scuba divers. Call: (818) 706-1310.

The mile-long stretch of beach is divided by Sequit Point, a rocky promontory with shallow caves and tunnels. Arroyo Sequit drains into the ocean here, scattering cobblestones and gravel on the beach. The tidepools along the rocky shore near Sequit Point, which are accessible at low tide, support sea anemones, snails, crabs, and many species of algae. Beds of giant kelp grow offshore, providing habitat for opaleye, kelp rockfish, olive rockfish, halfmoon, and cabezon, as well as an array of invertebrates. Gulls and migratory shorebirds feed and rest on the beach; offshore rocks provide resting sites for sea lions, seals, and seabirds. Docent naturalists give tidepool walks on selected weekends, and offer special walks for school groups; for information, call: (818) 888-3440. Sunday whale-watching programs are held at the beach from November to May, during the annual migration of California gray whales.

The park area was originally inhabited by the Chumash Indians; a Chumash archaeological site has been found near the mouth of the creek.

The inland portion of the park is vegetated with coastal sage scrub and chaparral plants such as California sagebrush, laurel sumac, chamise, and mountain mahogany, as well as coast live oak and California sycamore. Wildlife includes mice, squirrels, skunks, raccoons, bobcats, deer, and numerous species of reptiles and birds. Arroyo Sequit has been known to support spawning runs of steelhead trout.

Los Angeles–born actor Leo Carrillo, for whom the state beach was named, was a descendent of a prominent California ranching family and a son of the first Santa Monica mayor. Carrillo was well known for his television role as Pancho, Cisco Kid's sidekick.

Nicholas Canyon County Beach: *Pacific Coast Hwy., 1 mi. N. of Decker Rd., Malibu.*

The beach entrance is located across from the Malibu Riding and Tennis Club. Stairways from the bluff lead to the sandy beach, known as Point Zero by local surfers. The beach is a popular skin and scuba diving area; parking and restrooms are provided. Call: (213) 457-9891.

Charmlee County Park: *Encinal Canyon Rd., 4.5 mi. N. of Pacific Coast Hwy., Malibu.*

A portion of the 461-acre regional park was donated by ranchers Charmaine and Leonard Swartz, for whom the park was named. Located in the Santa Monica Mountains, the park is used for hiking, riding, and picnicking. Trails lead from the oak-shaded picnic area through meadows to the bluffs. Migrating whales can be observed from the blufftops, which offer a panoramic view of the coast and the Malibu community. Coyotes, bobcats, mule deer, and squirrels can be seen in the park. Spring wildflower displays have been spectacular in an area cleared of chaparral vegetation by a large fire in 1985. The park has a nature center, and offers guided hikes; a group campground is planned. Call: (213) 457-7247 or (818) 888-3440.

The Robert H. Meyer Memorial State Beaches include El Pescador, La Piedra, and El Matador State Beaches. The Memorial Beaches, opened to the public in 1984, were named after Robert H. Meyer in recognition of his work with the Department of Parks and Recreation in expanding and improving the State Park System. For information, call: (818) 706-1310. Private property adjoins the beaches; do not trespass.

El Pescador State Beach: *32900 block of Pacific Coast Hwy., Malibu.*

Pescador is Spanish for "fisherman." A parking lot, restrooms, and picnic tables are located on the bluff, and a trail leads down the bluff to the sandy, ten-acre beach. Gulls, plovers, willets, and sanderlings feed along the shore.

La Piedra State Beach: *32700 block of Pacific Coast Hwy., Malibu.*

Piedra means "stone" in Spanish. La Piedra is a nine-acre sandy beach used for sunbathing and swimming. A parking lot, picnic tables, and restrooms are located on the bluff.

El Matador State Beach: *32350 block of Pacific Coast Hwy., Malibu.*

Eighteen-acre El Matador State Beach is the largest of the three memorial beaches. The picnic area, located near the parking lot, provides panoramic views of the coast and of the Channel Islands offshore. Giant coreopsis, a tall shrub that produces clusters of large, yellow flowers in spring, grows near the picnic area and along the trails. Whimbrels, sandpipers, and other shorebirds feed along the water's edge. The rocky bottom offshore supports beds of giant kelp, and provides habitat for invertebrates such as gorgonian coral, anemones, keyhole limpets, and rock scallops. Kelp bass, señorita, California halibut, white seabass, and California sheephead also inhabit the nearshore waters. Sunbathing, swimming, scuba diving, and surf fishing are popular beach activities. Rangers lead educational beach walks and offer talks on Chumash Indian life; call: (818) 888-3440.

Zuma County Beach: *30000 block of Pacific Coast Hwy., Malibu.*

The 105-acre white sand beach is Malibu's largest beach, attracting sunbathers, joggers, swimmers, and surfers by the thousands during the summer months. The beach also affords shore fishing and scuba diving. The Department of Beaches and Harbors operates an all-day surfing area near lifeguard tower Number 11 where surfing is permitted at all times. Swimmers and surfers should be cautious of the rough waters and hazardous rip currents. From mid-March to late August, grunion spawn at the water's edge for several nights following a new or full moon. Anglers catch California corbina, opaleye, barred surfperch, and shiner surfperch. Park facilities include a playground, volleyball courts, restrooms, food concessions, and parking. For information, call Lifeguard Headquarters: (213) 457-9891.

One mile upcoast of Zuma County Beach, public accessways at the 31300 and 31200 blocks of Broad Beach Rd. lead to a beach known as Broad Beach. Private property adjoins the accessways; there are no beach facilities.

El Matador State Beach

Malibu: *Pacific Coast Hwy., W. of Pacific Palisades.*

Malibu is an unincorporated area of Los Angeles County that extends along Pacific Coast Highway for 27 miles, from the Ventura County line to Pacific Palisades. The Malibu area was originally home to the Chumash and Gabrielino Indians; human habitation of the area dates back perhaps 7,000 years. *Maliwu* is believed to have been the name of a Chumash village that was located at the mouth of Malibu Canyon. In 1805 13,316 acres of shoreline and adjacent mountain land were granted by the Spanish government to Jose Tapia, a former soldier, as Rancho Topanga Malibu Sequit. Frederick and May Rindge purchased the ranchland in 1887, and soon began a fierce battle with the state government to seclude Malibu and to prevent construction of a public highway. May Rindge continued the fight after her husband's death, building a private railroad and pier to exclude the Southern Pacific Railroad, hiring armed guards to keep out trespassers, and dynamiting contruction attempts. She eventually exhausted her financial resources in court battles, which she lost. The state opened the Pacific Coast Highway, first known as the Roosevelt Highway, through Malibu in 1929.

Development of the famous and secluded Malibu Colony soon followed when Rindge began leasing her shoreline property to writers and entertainers such as Anna Nillson, John Gilbert, Dolores Del Rio, and Barbara Stanwyck, who built summer cottages along the beach. Further growth began in 1940 when Rindge's Marblehead Land Company posted sale of property on both sides of Pacific Coast Highway. In the 1960s and 1970s, development soared with the construction of condominiums, houses, shopping centers, and mobile home lots in the Malibu area. State and county agencies have been acquiring beach and park property for the past 20 years, and the Malibu coast is now divided into private and public land, including a number of county-operated accessways to the shore. The Malibu Colony continues to be an exclusive community inhabited by movie stars, musicians, and other celebrities.

Point Dume State Beach: *S. end of Westward Beach Rd., Malibu.*

Point Dume, at the northwestern end of Santa Monica Bay, was named in 1782 by George Vancouver, the 18th-century English explorer, for Father Dumetz of Mission San Buenaventura. Point Dume consists of a mass of basaltic lava backed by a low, triangular-shaped plain. The basaltic hill was once an offshore island, and was later connected to the mainland by a tombolo. Traces of two marine terraces, formed during the Pleistocene, can be observed near the point at about 150 and 250 feet above sea level.

Point Dume State Beach includes the rocky shoreline below the point and a 34-acre sandy beach westward of the point. Sunbathing, swimming, tidepool exploring, surf fishing, and diving are popular activities. Restrooms and parking are provided. Call: (213) 457-9891.

The 215-foot-high bluffs of the Point Dume Headlands are vegetated with coastal sage scrub plants such as bladderpod, purple sage, coyote brush, and giant coreopsis; the live-forever *Dudleya caespitosa*, a green succulent with yellow to red flowers, reaches the southern extent of its range here. Rocky tidepools support brown algae, coralline algae, surfgrass, giant green anemones, and sea stars. Extensive kelp beds grow on the rocky reef offshore of Point Dume, providing habitat for kelp bass, grass rockfish, olive rockfish, halfmoon, and mackerel. Cormorants and endangered California brown pelicans roost on offshore rocks. Migrating gray whales can be seen between November and May from the Point Dume Whale Watch at the top of a stairway located at the intersection of Birdwatch Rd. and Westward Beach Road.

Paradise Cove: *28128 Pacific Coast Hwy., Malibu.*

Paradise Cove was used in the filming of the television series *The Rockford Files:* in the series, private investigator Jim Rockford lived in a mobile home on the beach. The privately owned cove, open to the public for a fee, has a beach, a restaurant, and a 220-foot-long pier. Pier fishing, sunbathing, picnicking, and scuba diving are popular at the cove. Anglers catch opaleye, sargo, and several species of rockfish and surfperch, including olive rockfish and shiner surfperch. For information, call: (213) 457-2511.

Paradise Cove is the site of California's first artificial reef. In 1958 the Department of Fish and Game sank 20 old automobile bodies in 50 feet of water to form an artificial reef, in an effort to improve coastal fishing by creating increased habitat for a variety of fish. The reef is now mostly deteriorated.

California grunion (*Leuresthes tenuis*)
to 7 inches long

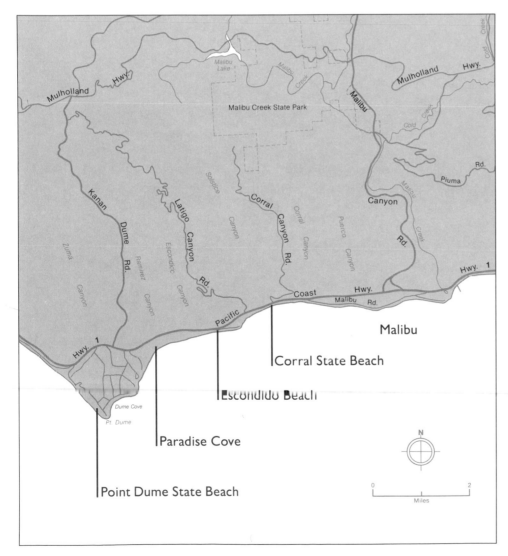

Escondido Beach: *27200 block of Pacific Coast Hwy., Malibu.*

Escondido means "hidden" in Spanish. The beach, popular for diving, is located at the mouth of Escondido Creek and is accessible by a stairway. Sanderlings, willets, and whimbrels feed on the beach. Parking is limited to the highway shoulder.

Located near Escondido Beach at 27400 Pacific Coast Highway is a two-story motel designed in 1950 by Richard J. Neutra, a Southern California architect who worked in the International Style during the 1940s-1950s. The building is sheathed in board and batten, and the balconies are supported by L-shaped riggers.

Corral State Beach: *Pacific Coast Hwy. and Corral Canyon Rd., Malibu.*

A narrow, four-acre beach, located between Corral and Solstice canyons, Corral State Beach is a popular location for sunbathing, picnicking, surf fishing, and scuba diving. Parking is limited to the highway shoulder. The beach is a spawning area for grunion; California halibut, cabezon, rockfish, and Pacific barracuda inhabit the nearshore waters. Call: (213) 457-9891.

Paradise Cove

Dume Cove at Point Dume Headlands

283

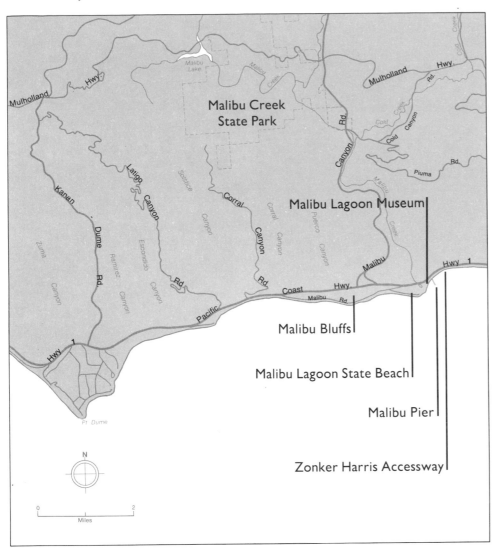

Malibu Creek State Park

Malibu Lagoon Museum

Malibu Bluffs

Malibu Lagoon State Beach

Malibu Pier

Zonker Harris Accessway

Pt. Dume

N

0 _____ 2
Miles

Malibu Creek State Park: *28754 Mulholland Dr., Agoura.*

Located within the Santa Monica Mountains, Malibu Creek State Park encompasses some 5,000 acres of chaparral-covered hillsides, steep, wooded canyons, and outcrops of volcanic rock. The park includes Century Lake, portions of Malibu Creek and other perennial streams, and Kaslow, Udell Gorge, and Liberty Canyon natural preserves. The diverse vegetation includes red-heart, scrub oak, manzanita, California sagebrush, coast live oak, and California bay laurel. Riparian woodland of big-leaf maple, black cottonwood, and willow flourishes along Malibu Creek and other streams; uncommon plants such as stream orchids, brown dogwood, and giant chain ferns grow in Fern and Mendenhall canyons. The endangered Santa Monica Mountain live-forever occurs along mossy creek banks.

Arroyo chub, Pacific lamprey, and California killifish inhabit Malibu Creek, which is believed to support California's southernmost steelhead spawning run. Frogs, kingsnakes, horned lizards, quail, endangered golden eagles, ravens, squirrels, raccoons, foxes, bobcats, and mountain lions are among the numerous inhabitants of the park. Insects found here include California live oak gall wasps, California oak moths, and blind snout beetles.

The park area was inhabited by the Chumash until the mid-1800s, and was first homesteaded by white settlers around 1860. Twentieth Century Fox Studios once owned over 2,000 acres in Malibu Canyon, and used the area, then called Century Ranch, for the filming of movies and television series such as *M*A*S*H*, *The Dukes of Hazzard*, and *South Pacific*. The land was acquired by the state in 1974; television series, commercials, and movies are still filmed here.

The park is used for picnicking, horseback riding, and hiking, and a small nature center is open on weekends. A campground is currently being developed. Hiking trails connect Malibu Creek State Park with Topanga State Park and Will Rogers State Park. Call: (818) 706-1310 or 706-8809.

Malibu Bluffs: *Malibu Canyon Rd., between Pacific Coast Hwy. and Malibu Rd., Malibu.*

Malibu Bluffs, part of Malibu Lagoon State Beach, comprises 90 acres on the bluffs south of Pacific Coast Highway. Little league fields and soccer fields are situated on the bluffs. For information, call: (818) 706-1310. Beach access is provided nearby via public stairways at the 25100, 24700, 24500, 24400, and 24300 blocks of Malibu Road, located below the bluffs. Private property adjoins the stairways; do not trespass.

Malibu Lagoon State Beach: *Pacific Coast Hwy. and Cross Creek Rd., Malibu.*

The 166-acre Malibu Lagoon State Beach comprises Malibu Bluffs, Malibu Lagoon, the Malibu Lagoon Museum, the Malibu Pier, and a 35-acre sandy beach known as Surfrider Beach. Popularized by surfing movies of the 1950s and 1960s, the beach is still a favorite surfing spot, especially during summer when strong southwest swells refract around a rock reef at Malibu Point and break over a gently sloping sandy bottom. The waves offer rides of 300 yards or more, giving Surfrider Beach its reputation as one of the finest surfing spots in California. Volleyball courts, parking, and restrooms are available at the beach. For information, call: (818) 706-1310 or (213) 457-9891.

Malibu Lagoon is a small, brackish lagoon at the mouth of the perennial Malibu Creek. The Chumash once fished in the lagoon and harvested mollusks here. The lagoon area was opened to the public in 1983; facilities include parking and picnic areas, trails, and interpretive panels. The picnic area, restrooms, and some viewing spots are wheelchair-accessible. For information on walks and bird-watching tours, call: (213) 456-9497 or (818) 888-3440.

Malibu Lagoon supports salt marsh vegetation consisting primarily of two species of pickleweed. The lagoon lies along the Pacific Flyway, and is used by migratory birds for resting and feeding. Over 200 species of birds have been observed here, including grebes, great horned owls, elegant terns, belted kingfishers, red-winged blackbirds, and American goldfinches. Arrow gobies, California killifish, topsmelt, and shiner perch inhabit the lagoon.

Malibu Lagoon Museum: *23200 Pacific Coast Hwy., Malibu.*

In 1928 an Andalusian-style beach house was built for Frederick Rindge's daughter Rhoda upon her marriage to Merritt Adamson; designed by architect Stiles Clement on a 13-acre site, the Adamson House is now a museum and

Malibu Lagoon

a State Historical Landmark. It has colorful tiles, no two of which are identical, that were specially designed for the fountains, courtyard, pool, bathhouse, and bedrooms. The house is occasionally used for filming commercials and television shows, including portions of *Dallas*. Free tours of the house and grounds are provided for school and community groups; there are also special group tours for the disabled. The museum is open to the public Wednesday-Saturday; for information and reservations, call: (213) 456-8432 or (818) 706-1310.

Malibu Pier: *23000 Pacific Coast Hwy., Malibu.*

The pier is located in a cove named "Keller's Shelter" after its first American owner, Matthew Keller, who bought the cove in 1860. Frederick Rindge purchased the property in 1891, and in 1903 he built a 400-foot-long pier to serve as a loading dock for ranch supplies. In 1943 William Huber bought the cove and built the present pier to replace Rindge's, which had been destroyed by storms. Huber sold the 700-foot-long pier and the adjoining shoreline property to the state in 1980.

Malibu Pier, which is wheelchair accessible, is a popular spot for watching surfers at Surfrider Beach and for fishing; catches include kelp bass, halibut, yellowtail, and rockfish. The bait and tackle shop rents fishing equipment, and excursion, charter, and fishing boats are available from the Malibu Sport Fishing Landing. Call: (213) 456-8030.

In 1960 the Department of Fish and Game deposited quarry rock, concrete pilings, and deteriorated car bodies and streetcars offshore in 60 feet of water to create an artificial reef. The reef is located approximately one mile southeast of the Malibu Pier.

Zonker Harris Accessway: *22548 Pacific Coast Hwy., Malibu.*

Named after Zonker Harris, a beach and sun fanatic from the comic strip "Doonesbury," the Zonker Harris Accessway was opened in 1980. This walkway was the first public accessway to the beach in Malibu to be opened since 1972. There are no beach facilities.

Malibu Creek

Las Tunas State Beach: *Pacific Coast Hwy., 1 mi. W. of Topanga Canyon Blvd., Malibu.*

Spanish explorers named this area "Las Tunas" after the numerous prickly pear cacti growing in the nearby canyon; *tuna* is the Spanish word for the prickly pear cactus. A sandy area along the narrow, rocky beach provides diving access to an offshore reef, inhabited by spiny lobsters and halibut. Other marine life such as red and brown algae, surfgrass, and gooseneck barnacles live on the rocks, and on the steel groins that are the remains of a 1929 erosion control program. Anglers surf fish here for barred surfperch and California corbina. Castle Rock at the east end of the beach marks the dividing point between Las Tunas State Beach and Topanga State Beach. Parking is limited to the highway shoulder. Additional accessways to the beach are located at the 20300 and 19960 blocks of Pacific Coast Highway. For information, call: (213) 457-9891.

Topanga State Beach: *Pacific Coast Hwy. and Topanga Canyon Blvd., Malibu.*

"Topanga" is a Gabrielino Indian place name. The Los Angeles Athletic Club once owned what is now Topanga State Beach and granted leases to individuals to build beach houses until 1969, when the club sold the beach to the state; the houses were removed and in 1973 the mile-long, narrow, sandy beach was opened to the public. Topanga Creek empties into the ocean midway along the beach. California gulls, and shorebirds such as sandpipers and killdeer, rest and feed along the shore. Rock scallops, sea urchins, and numerous other invertebrates inhabit the rocky bottom offshore. The beach is popular for sunbathing, swimming, and surfing; wheelchair-accessible restrooms and parking are available. Call: (213) 451-2906.

prickly pear (*Opuntia littoralis*)
to 4 feet high

J. Paul Getty Museum: *17985 Pacific Coast Hwy., Malibu.*

In 1945, international businessman J. Paul Getty, who amassed a fortune in the oil industry, purchased a 65-acre citrus farm in Malibu where he housed his growing art collections in a ranch house. Getty opened part of the house as a museum in 1953 with five galleries and soon thereafter expanded it to nine galleries. In 1968, he began work on a new museum to accommodate his entire collection. Opened in 1974, the new building is a reproduction of an ancient and lavish Roman country house, Villa dei Papiri, which stood outside the city of Herculaneum; the original villa was buried by the volcanic eruption of Mount Vesuvius in 79 A.D., and was excavated by Swiss archaeologists in the 18th century. The museum has five gardens, which duplicate those of Villa dei Papiri in style, arrangement, and flora. The frescoes and bronze statues in the gardens are copies of originals from Villa dei Papiri and other Roman villas. Getty died in 1976, leaving a trust that has directed millions of dollars to be spent annually in acquiring art objects, and has established several art programs and institutes.

The 38-gallery museum has seven collections: Greek and Roman antiquities, paintings, sculpture, drawings, illuminated manuscripts, European decorative arts, and photography. The antiquity collection includes Greek and Roman sculptures, mosaics, and vases. The painting collection emphasizes Renaissance and Baroque art, but all major periods of Western European art from the late 1200s to the early 1900s are represented. The decorative arts collection of mostly 18th century French objects is displayed in re-created rooms of the period.

The museum is open Tuesday-Sunday, 10 AM-5 PM, and admission is free; parking reservations are required. The entire facility is wheelchair accessible. Call: (213) 458-2003.

Topanga State Park: *20825 Entrada Road, Topanga.*

The pristine, 9,000-acre park is situated in the Santa Monica Mountains; 35 miles of trails and fire roads wind through canyons and along ridges that support chaparral, oak woodland, riparian woodland, grassland, and coastal sage scrub vegetation. The park is popular for hiking, horseback riding, and picnicking. Three major trails, including a self-guided nature trail, begin at the parking lot near the ranger station at Trippet Ranch. A 1.5-mile trail through Santa Ynez Canyon leads to a 20-foot-high waterfall, where plants such as tiger lilies and stream orchids grow. Other vegetation within the park includes California poppy, Indian paintbrush, California scrub oak, coast live oak, chamise, toyon, laurel sumac, manzanita, big-pod ceanothus, and purple nightshade, a perennial herb. Wildlife includes coast horned lizards, California mountain kingsnakes, California pocket mice, desert cottontails, gray foxes, coyotes, bobcats, and mule deer. Wrentits, quail, scrub jays, and turkey vultures also inhabit the park area.

Park facilities include hike-in and equestrian campsites, a picnic area, wheelchair-accessible restrooms, and parking. Rangers and docents lead educational hikes; call (213) 455-2465 or (818) 706-1310 for schedules and trail maps.

Façade, J. Paul Getty Museum

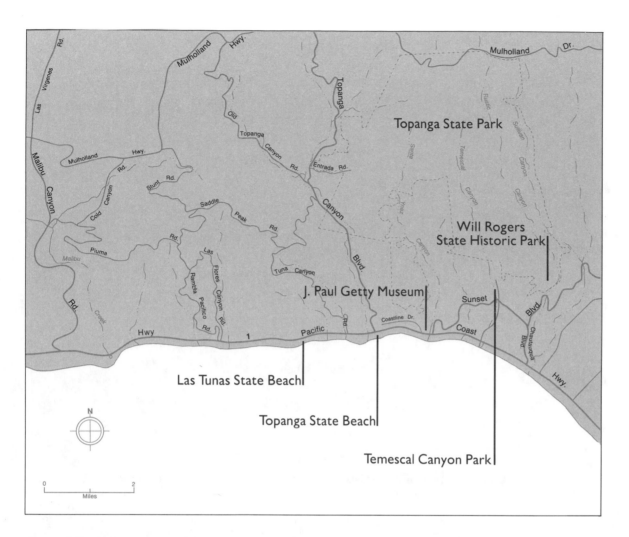

Some of the higher trails provide panoramic views of the Pacific Ocean and the San Fernando Valley. The Santa Monica Mountains Backbone Trail extends into the park, linking other parks in the region.

Will Rogers State Historic Park: *14235 Sunset Blvd., Pacific Palisades.*

Will Rogers, for whom the park is named, began his show business career as a trick roper for traveling rodeos. Rogers came to Hollywood in 1919, and later became known as the "Cowboy Philosopher." In 1928 he built a ranch to accommodate his family on property located above Sunset Boulevard. In 1935 Rogers, by then a popular radio commentator, newspaper columnist, and film actor, was killed in a plane crash in Alaska. The Rogers family donated the 187-acre ranch to the state park system in 1944. The grounds and ranch house have not been altered, and memorabilia and family possessions are displayed inside. The park also features a polo field that hosts equestrian events.

Facilities include a nature center with exhibits and interpretive panels, a picnic area, parking, wheelchair-accessible restrooms, and hiking trails that lead into adjacent Topanga State Park. Call (213) 454-8212 for park information and group tour reservations.

Temescal Canyon Park: *Temescal Canyon Rd. and Sunset Blvd., Pacific Palisades.*

Early Spanish explorers applied the word *temascal*, a Mexican word derived from Aztec for bathhouse, to describe the sweathouses of the California Indians. Twenty-two-acre Temescal Canyon Park includes picnic areas, parking, and restrooms, as well as hiking trails that traverse steep, chaparral-covered hills and lead into Topanga State Park and Will Rogers State Historic Park. Temescal Creek is a perennial stream that features several waterfalls and supports riparian vegetation such as sycamores and ferns. For information, call: (818) 888-3440. The Y.M.C.A. operates a public swimming pool adjacent to the park; call: (213) 454-5591.

Will Rogers State Historic Park

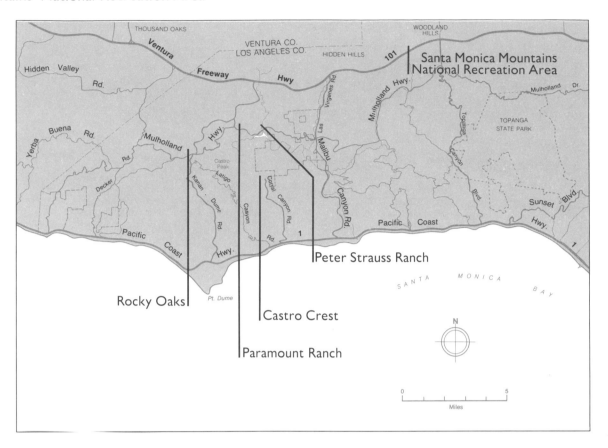

poison oak (*Toxicodendron diversiloba*)
4 to 8 feet high

Santa Monica Mountains National Recreation Area: *Headquarters and Information Center at 22900 Ventura Blvd., Woodland Hills.*

Established in 1978, the Santa Monica Mountains National Recreation Area comprises 150,000 acres of mountains and seashore, including the coastal area from Point Mugu to Santa Monica. The east-west trending Santa Monica Mountains, part of the Transverse Ranges, rise abruptly from the Oxnard Plain in Ventura County, forming a dramatic chain of ridges that stretch 60 miles to the center of metropolitan Los Angeles at Griffith Park in Hollywood. Only about one-third of the designated Recreation Area is in public ownership; the remainder is privately owned. The National Park Service manages the following park units: Rocky Oaks, Paramount Ranch, Castro Crest, and Diamond X Ranch. Other parks and beaches within the Recreation Area are operated by state, county, or private agencies.

The Santa Monica Mountains, which are largely undeveloped, feature deeply incised canyons, streams, upland meadows, jagged peaks, and rolling hills covered with an array of grasses, flowers, shrubs, and trees. Chaparral is the most common plant community in the mountains; other vegetation types include coastal strand, coastal sage scrub, oak woodland, and riparian woodland. The valley oak reaches its southernmost distribution in California here. The abundant wildlife within the mountains includes lizards, ring-tailed cats, mountain lions, and endangered golden eagles, which nest in the cliffs. The steep, rugged mountain terrain was formed by folding and faulting of complex rock formations composed primarily of sandstone, granite, slate, and schist. Malibu Canyon, a spectacular gorge 1,400-1,800 feet deep, bisects the mountain range, which reaches

a height of 3,111 feet at Sandstone Peak at the eastern end of Boney Ridge. The mountains drop down to sandy beaches with occasional rock outcrops along the coast; in most places, narrow beaches are backed by high bluffs. The estuarine Mugu and Malibu lagoons support coastal salt marsh plants and attract numerous migratory birds.

The National Park Service is presently constructing the Backbone Trail, which, when fully completed, will run 55 miles along the crest of the Santa Monica Mountains from Point Mugu to Will Rogers State Historic Park, linking all the parks in the Recreation Area by an extensive trail system. The various parks offer such facilities as interpretive centers, educational programs, horse and bicycle trails, and tent and equestrian campsites. Call: (818) 888-3770.

Rocky Oaks: *Corner of Mulholland Hwy. and Kanan Dume Rd., Agoura.*

Located in upper Zuma Canyon, this 200-acre park features trails that wind past numerous spring wildflowers, and a picnic area surrounded by stands of coast live oak. Riparian vegetation includes willow, sycamore, and big-leaf maple. A nearby half-acre freshwater pond supports cattails and sedges, and provides habitat for ducks, coots, and insects such as damselflies and water boatmen. The adjacent grassland community contains native perennial bunchgrasses and *Chaetopappa lyonii*, a sunflower native to Los Angeles County that occurs on the mainland and on Santa Catalina Island. Barn and horned owls, Cooper's hawks, brush rabbits, and coyotes inhabit the chaparral area.

Volcanic rock formations within the park include outcrops of pillow basalt, formed millions of years ago during the early Cenozoic Era when the area was submerged. Pillow basalt is formed as lava flows out onto the sea floor through cracks or fissures and is chilled by ocean water, causing the distinctive shaping that gives this rock its name. Park facilities include parking and wheelchair-accessible restrooms. Rangers lead hikes on selected weekends; call park headquarters for schedules: (818) 888-3770.

Paramount Ranch: *Cornell Rd. at Mulholland Hwy., 2.5 mi. S. of Ventura Fwy.*

The ranch, once encompassing 4,000 acres, was extensively used by Paramount Studios in the early 1920s to the mid-1940s. Today, Paramount Ranch is a 336-acre park of chaparral, grassland, and oak woodland, and is open for hiking, horseback riding, and picnicking. A self-guided nature trail leads up Coyote Canyon in the shadow of Sugarloaf Mountain, a volcanic outcrop of basalt; brochures on the natural history and geology of the canyon are available at the trailhead kiosk. Western Town is a movie set on the site that is still used for filming television shows, commercials, and movies. On weekends, rangers and docents lead hikes through the park and conduct tours of the movie set; call: (818) 888-3770. The Renaissance Pleasure Faire, an annual spring event held on private land adjacent to the park, features the crafts, food, plays, and music of the Renaissance period.

Castro Crest: *Off Pacific Coast Hwy., at the end of Corral Canyon Rd., Malibu.*

Castro Crest, an 800-acre park adjacent to Castro Peak, offers extensive hiking trails, including a four-mile loop trail and portions of the Backbone Trail, which afford sweeping views of the inland Santa Susana Mountains and the offshore Channel Islands. Large areas of the park are composed of reddish-purple sandstone that is embedded with smooth, round rocks; the sandstone is part of the Sespe Formation, which was formed 30 million years ago during the Oligocene. Western fence lizards, gray foxes, badgers, and mule deer inhabit the oak woodland. At Castro Peak the endangered endemic Santa Susana tarplant grows in chaparral areas on sandstone outcroppings. For information on ranger-led hikes, call: (818) 888-3770.

Peter Strauss Ranch: *30000 Mulholland Hwy. at Troutdale Rd., Agoura.*

Now a 64-acre recreation area operated by the Santa Monica Mountains Conservancy, the property was originally developed by automobile designer Harry Miller in 1923 as a private retreat with an aviary, fruit trees, and a zoo. In the late 1930s, Charles Hinman purchased the property and converted it to a weekend resort that featured what was then one of the largest outdoor swimming pools west of the Rockies. The resort drew record crowds from Los Angeles for swimming, picnicking, camping, and dancing. The area became known as Lake Enchanto after the damming of Triunfo Creek in the 1940s, which created a ten-acre lake; high water broke the dam in 1969 and drained the lake. The land was purchased by actor/producer Peter Strauss in 1977. In 1983, the Santa Monica Mountains Conservancy acquired the ranch and opened it as a public park with picnic facilities and hiking trails.

Steep hillsides support chaparral vegetation including scrub oak and red-heart. Coast live oak, coffeeberry, and poison oak grow on the lower hillsides. Triunfo Creek is a perennial stream at the base of the hills that provides habitat for aquatic insects, bullfrogs, birds, and a riparian flora of ferns, alder, and sycamore. Great blue herons are occasionally seen along the creek. Gopher snakes, red-tailed hawks, brush rabbits, and mule deer inhabit the hills and meadows. Concerts and Shakespearean plays are performed in the outdoor amphitheater; the main building serves as a classroom, conference room, and art gallery. Docents and park rangers give educational talks and lead walks through the park. The park is open for public use on the first and third weekends of every month and at all other times by reservation only. For information and reservations, call: (818) 706-8380.

Eagle Rock, Santa Monica Mountains

Mulholland Scenic Parkway Corridor: *Hollywood Freeway 101 to Leo Carrillo State Beach.*

The Mulholland Scenic Parkway Corridor, which comprises all of Mulholland Drive and Highway, lies within the Santa Monica Mountains National Recreation Area. The 50-mile scenic drive winds westward from the Hollywood Freeway along the crest of the Santa Monica Mountains and ends at Leo Carrillo State Beach. Mulholland Drive becomes Mulholland Highway outside the Los Angeles city limits. One stretch of the road just north of Topanga State Park remains unpaved. The original road was completed in 1924 under the direction of William Mulholland, the chief engineer of the Los Angeles Water Department. Mulholland is known for constructing Los Angeles' first major aqueduct, which brought water from the Owens Valley to the city and contributed to Los Angeles's rapid development. Director Roman Polanski depicted Mulholland working on Water Department projects in the Academy Award-winning film *Chinatown.*

The drive along the Mulholland Scenic Parkway Corridor offers spectacular vistas of the San Fernando Valley, the rugged Santa Monica Mountains, and the Malibu coastline. The section of the road between Topanga Canyon Blvd. and Las Virgenes/Malibu Canyon Rd. affords views of steep and rugged terrain, chaparral-covered mountains, heavily wooded upper Cold Creek Canyon, and scattered residences in the Malibu Creek watershed. Along the corridor between Las Virgenes/Malibu Canyon Rd. and Kanan Dume Rd., sandstone outcroppings, Malibu Lake, and Peter Strauss Ranch are visible. Volcanic peaks, riparian and oak woodlands, and the Malibu coast can be seen from the road between Kanan Dume Rd. and Pacific Coast Highway. Scenic overlooks along the drive feature interpretive displays. For information, call the National Park Service Headquarters: (818) 888-3770, or the Santa Monica Mountains Conservancy: (213) 620-2121.

Tapia County Park: *Las Virgenes/Malibu Canyon Rd., 5 mi. S. of Hwy. 101, Agoura.*

In 1805, the Spanish government granted José Tapia property that stretched along the Malibu coast and extended into the Santa Monica Mountains. Tapia County Park, located on a portion of the former Tapia ranch property, covers 94.5 acres and falls within the boundaries of Malibu Creek State Park. Hiking and equestrian trails wind along the banks of Malibu Creek, which supports oak and sycamore trees. Facilities include picnic tables, a group campground, a sports field, restrooms, and parking. Call: (213) 738-2961.

Diamond X Ranch: *Mulholland Hwy., E. of Las Virgenes/Malibu Canyon Rd., Agoura.*

Formerly owned by cowboy film star Rex Allen, this 18-acre ranch was obtained by the National Park Service in 1981, and the ranch house was converted into a ranger station and maintenance headquarters. The former main dining room is now available for community meetings; for reservations, call: (818) 888-3770.

Stunt Ranch: *Stunt Rd., 1.5 mi. S. of Mulholland Hwy., Agoura.*

In 1889, the Stunt family built a summer cottage in Cold Creek Canyon. They used the house as their permanent residence after the 1930s and added the fourth and final ranch structure in 1955. The ranch and property were donated to Occidental College in 1980, and in

California quail (*Callipepla californica*)
9 to 12 inches long

Saddle Peak, Santa Monica Mountains

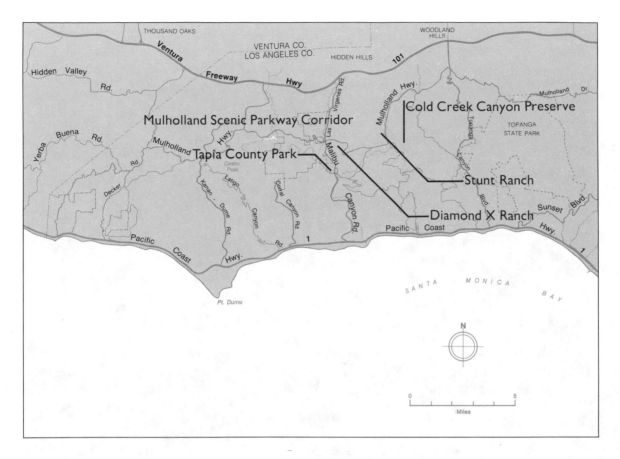

1982 the Santa Monica Mountains Conservancy obtained the 309-acre property and opened it to the public for hiking and nature programs. The University of California is planning to incorporate the majority of the property into its reserve system, but public use will continue.

Stunt Ranch supports plant communities typical of the Santa Monica Mountains such as chaparral, oak woodland, grassland, and riparian woodland. Vegetation within the canyon includes native perennial grasses, red shank, flowering ash, milkwort, coast live oak, and ceanothus. Cold Creek, a major upland tributary of Malibu Creek, supports mosses, fungi, and ferns. Coast Range newts, California side-blotched lizards, rattlesnakes, red-tailed hawks, piñon mice, western gray squirrels, long-tailed weasels, broad-footed moles, raccoons, brush rabbits, and mule deer inhabit the area.

Over 10,000 Indian artifacts, dating from 3000 B.C. to 1000 A.D., were removed in the early 1980s from Stunt Ranch; a building used for seminars presently occupies what was the main archaeological dig site. Stunt High Trail connects with the Backbone Trail, which links other parks in the Santa Monica Mountains Recreation Area. For information and reservations, call: (818) 884-6025.

Cold Creek Canyon Preserve: *Stunt Rd., 1.1 mi. S. of Mulholland Hwy., Agoura.*

In 1970, Kathleen Murphy donated the Murphy Ranch property in Cold Creek Canyon to the Nature Conservancy in memory of her mother, Ida Haynes Murphy. The Nature Conservancy established the 545-acre Cold Creek Canyon Preserve; in 1984, it was transferred to the Mountains Restoration Trust, which protects the preserve, maintains the trails, and provides educational programs.

The preserve contains a complete cross-section of flora and fauna of the Santa Monica Mountains. All six species of ceanothus, or California lilac, that occur in the Santa Monica Mountains grow here. Along perennial Cold Creek and its spring-fed tributaries, oak woodland and riparian woodland vegetation flourish. California bay laurel and walnut occur in the upper woodland on north-facing slopes, and big-leaf maple, sycamore, arroyo willow, and oak are abundant in the lower woodland. Year-round surface water from Cold Creek provides moisture for red shank, stream orchid, yellow iris, red mimulus, Humboldt lily, lichens, mosses, liverworts, and fungi. Cold Creek is the last remaining watershed in the Santa Monica Mountains to support three species of stoneflies, a group of aquatic insects that are particularly sensitive to pollution.

Hummingbirds, finches, swallows, woodpeckers, roadrunners, and hawks are common in the preserve, and endangered golden eagles are occasionally seen. Many species of amphibians and reptiles, such as California slender salamanders, Pacific treefrogs, and coast horned lizards, are found in the preserve. Bobcats and mountain lions have also been sighted.

A self-guided nature trail loosely follows Cold Creek to an old stone-boulder hunting cabin, built in 1909, and continues to the lower gate at the bottom of the property. Other trails include a short loop trail, a trail to a waterfall, and a trail that connects with the Backbone Trail. Docents conduct natural and cultural history programs on a regular basis. The preserve is private property and visitors are required to obtain a permit. For information and reservations, call: (213) 456-5627 or (818) 888-9363.

greenbark ceanothus (*Ceanothus spinosus*)
6 to 20 feet high

291

Santa Monica Municipal Pier, ca. 1920s

Pacific Palisades: *17 mi. W. of Los Angeles.*

Named for its jagged shoreline cliffs, Pacific Palisades was a popular resort area in the 1860s for vacationers from Los Angeles. It remained a summer beach colony until 1921 when a group of Methodists founded a community here to serve as a "new Chautauqua," a place for educational and recreational assembly. During the 1920s-1940s, Pacific Palisades became the art center of Los Angeles, where writers, artists, actors, and architects pursued their creative talents. Under the direction of John Entenza, the editor and publisher of *Arts and Architecture* magazine, some of the most advanced Modernist architectural styles were developed by noted architects, including Neutra and Soriano. The Case Study House Program (1945-1960), a proj-

ect that encouraged architects to employ the latest building techniques and materials, is exemplified in the Eames House at 203 Chautauqua Blvd., a glass and steel structure incorporating interior furnishings as part of the design.

In 1950, followers of Paramahansa Yogananda, the founder of the Self-Realization Fellowship, built a non-denominational open-air temple at 17190 Sunset Blvd., where visitors can meditate and stroll in the gardens. A spring-fed lake is surrounded by native chaparral, exotic plants, and grassy lawns; the Golden Lotus Archway, a monument symbolizing the soul of man, faces the lake. Ducks, swans, and turtles can be seen from a walkway along the lake.

Will Rogers State Beach: *16000 block of Pacific Coast Hwy., Pacific Palisades.*

The three-mile-long sandy beach was named for Will Rogers, actor, radio star, and humorist known as the "Cowboy Philosopher." Swimming, diving, surfing, and bodysurfing are popular; surfperch, halibut, and bonito are caught from shore. Commonly seen birds include gulls, sanderlings, and willets. A bike path and pedestrian promenade extend along the shore from Chautauqua Blvd. to Temescal Canyon Road. Call: (213) 394-3266.

Santa Monica: *15 mi. W. of Los Angeles.*

In 1769, an expedition led by Gaspar de Portolá to establish a chain of missions in California camped at a spring in west Los Angeles. According to legend, these waters reminded Father Juan Crespí, who accompanied Portolá, of Saint

Monica's tears that were shed for her heretic son St. Augustine, and Crespí named the coastal area in her honor. In 1828, the grasslands of Santa Monica were granted to Francisco Sepúlveda, the former alcalde, or mayor, of Los Angeles, for the raising of cattle. Colonel Robert Baker bought the Sepúlveda ranch lands in 1872 to use for sheep grazing, but he soon realized the area's potential as a terminus for a transcontinental railroad; in 1875, he and John Jones, a wealthy senator from Nevada, laid plans for building a town, wharf, and the Los Angeles and Independence Railroad at Santa Monica. In 1877, they sold their railroad to Collis Huntington's Southern Pacific Railroad, and the wharf at Santa Monica was deliberately destroyed so it would not compete with Huntington's own commercial port at Wilmington.

In 1894 a large, curved wharf called the Long Wharf was built one mile northwest of Santa Monica by the Southern Pacific Railroad, and plans were drafted to make Santa Monica Bay the Port of Los Angeles. Although Santa Monica continued as a busy port, in 1897 the federal government designated San Pedro as the official deepwater harbor for Los Angeles. By 1896, an interurban trolley line stretched west from Los Angeles to Santa Monica, luring inland residents to the beach and to the bathhouses and amusement piers built at Santa Monica and Ocean Park.

Since the 1950s, Santa Monica has become more urbanized and has undergone many architectural changes. In 1965 a downtown pedestrian mall was developed to revitalize the area, and in 1980, Santa Monica Place, an enclosed shopping mall designed by Frank Gehry and Associates with glassed-in galleries and striking use of chain link fencing, was built. Today Santa Monica, immortalized by Raymond Chandler as "Bay City," is a pleasant seaside community.

Palisades Park: *Ocean Ave., between Colorado Ave. and Adelaide Dr., Santa Monica.*

This popular urban park stretches for two miles atop eroding cliffs, providing panoramic views of the Pacific Ocean. Two rows of Washington palms line the winding path that extends the length of the park. The Visitor Assistance Stand near Arizona St. has free maps, brochures, and tour information on Santa Monica. Additional facilities include shuffleboard courts and a Senior Recreation Center; the Camera Obscura near Arizona St. is open daily.

Santa Monica State Beach: *W. of Pacific Coast Hwy., Santa Monica.*

One of the most popular beaches in Los Angeles, this wide, sandy beach extends for three miles south from Will Rogers State Beach to Venice City Beach. Facilities include picnic tables, volleyball courts, and playground and gymnastic equipment. Muscle Beach, south of the Santa Monica Municipal Pier, was originally named for the mussels attached to the pier pilings. In the 1930s, a WPA project turned the beach into a workout area for Depression-era children. Later, UCLA gymnasts, circus performers, and weightlifters practiced on the beach, which came to be called Muscle Beach. Today, Venice Beach claims the name.

In the early 1920s, luxurious beach cottages were built along the shore just west of Pacific Coast Highway, which was then known as Palisades Beach Road. Celebrities including Cary Grant, Mary Pickford, and Marion Davies resided in these cottages, which were collectively nicknamed the "Gold Coast."

The 19-mile-long South Bay Bicycle Trail, which provides a scenic coastal route along the beaches from Santa Monica to Torrance, begins at California Ave. and extends south to Torrance. Call: (213) 394-3266.

Santa Monica Municipal Pier: *Colorado and Ocean Aves., Santa Monica.*

In the early 1870s, the Shoo-Fly Landing was built at the present site of the pier. Brea, or tar, from the La Brea Tar Pits in Los Angeles was shipped from the landing to pave San Francisco's streets. Five years later, the Los Angeles and Independence Railway replaced the landing with a 1,700-foot-long wharf and passenger depot for coastal steamers.

The Long Wharf, which extended 4,720 feet, was built in 1894 to replace the demolished Los Angeles and Independence wharf; the Long Wharf was torn down in 1920. In the early 1900s, the Santa Monica Municipal Pier was built. The pier actually consists of two adjoining piers: the long and narrow municipal pier, with its commercial boat facilities and public fishing areas, and the shorter but wider Newcomb Pier, built in 1916 as a privately owned amusement center. The Newcomb Pier still offers an amusement park with a world-famous carousel, arcades, and curio shops.

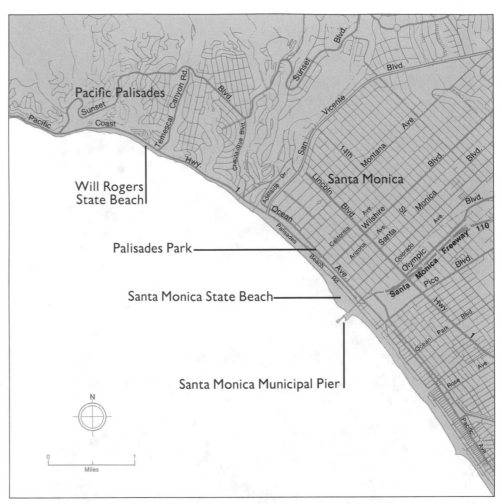

Severe storms in 1983 destroyed the boat facilities, harbormaster's office, and visitor center at the west end of the municipal pier. Popular activities include roller-skating, bicycling, and fishing from the end of the pier for mackerel, bonito, halibut, and rock cod. Carousel Park, just east of the pier, is wheelchair accessible and provides a children's play area and a viewing area. Pier Office: (213) 458-8689.

View of Santa Monica State Beach from Palisades Park

Windward Street, Venice, ca. 1906

Venice: *3 mi. S.E. of Santa Monica.*

In 1904, cigarette magnate Abbot Kinney purchased 160 acres of coastal marshland just south of Santa Monica (once part of the Ballona Wetlands) with the intention of developing a "Venice of America." Architects Norman Marsh and C.H. Russell, commissioned by Kinney to design his project, created the Grand Canal, two networks of smaller canals, and a central lagoon from wetlands that were historically used for hunting and fishing. Gondoliers and gondolas imported from Italy, arched Venetian bridges joining the canals, and the St. Mark's Hotel added authenticity and romance to the venture. Visitors were drawn to the beachfront promenade and the pier with its cafes and an auditorium for lectures and concerts, where such notables as author Helen Hunt Jackson, actress Sarah Bernhardt, and the Chicago Symphony performed. However, attendance soon waned at these cultural events, and from 1910 to 1920, visitors flocked to Venice's roller coasters, casinos, parades, and bathhouse instead. The decline of Venice began after the death of Abbot Kinney in 1920 with problems resulting from flaws in the design of the canals and the sewage system: the canals were often dirty and stagnant, the sewer system was inadequate for the growing population, and the narrow streets were designed primarily for pedestrians and not automobiles. In 1929, the canals in northern Venice were filled in and the amusement park was dismantled; by 1930, all but four canals were paved over.

Following the discovery of oil in Venice in 1929, oil derricks dotted the residential area. By the late 1950s Venice had become the beatnik capital of Southern California, and in the 1960s, hippies made it their home. Today, long-time residents of Venice, including poets, writers, artists, and those seeking low rents and alternative lifestyles, are faced with gentrification of the canal neighborhoods. Peoples Park, at Sherman Canal and Dell Ave.; quiet walk streets, including Amoroso and Marco courts; and the pagodas along Ocean Front Walk offer a respite from the surrounding urban setting and contribute to the uniqueness of the community.

Venice City Beach: *Between Marine St. and Spinnaker St., Venice.*

Almost three miles long, this wide, sandy beach was one of the first Southern California beaches since the 1920s to have full-time professional lifeguard protection. Venice City Beach is popular for swimming, surfing, diving, and kite-flying; facilities include a playground and volleyball courts. Fish caught from shore include rockfish, California halibut, and seabass. From mid-March through late August grunion spawn on the beach several nights a month immediately following a new or full moon. Sanderlings, gulls, and willets rest and feed on the beach. Call: (213) 394-3265.

Ocean Front Walk, an asphalt walkway paralleling Venice City Beach, extends from Navy St. to Washington Boulevard. Built in 1905 by Abbot Kinney, Ocean Front Walk is today a popular promenade with a medley of street merchants, artists, musicians, and beachfront stores and cafes. Popular activities include strolling, jogging, roller-skating, and skateboarding; a bikepath parallels Ocean Front Walk.

Ocean Park: *2.5 mi. S.E. of Santa Monica.*

What is today the community of Ocean Park was once a large expanse of sand dunes and marshes. The area was developed as a small seaside resort in 1892 by Abbot Kinney, Francis Ryan, and A.R. Fraser. Six years later, Kinney erected Ocean Park's first wharf, which was abandoned in 1904. The wharf was rebuilt in 1910 as "Fraser's Million Dollar Pier," modeled after its namesake in Atlantic City. Until the 1930s, Ocean Park welcomed thousands of visitors, who strolled along the beachfront promenade and played in the arcades. During the Depression, the crowds and the revenue generated by the amusement pier began to decline, and by the 1940s and 1950s, Ocean Park's neighorhoods had changed; many of its residents moved to the newer suburbs, and members of the working class, the elderly, minorities, and beatniks, attracted by the low rents, settled in the area. Pacific Ocean Park, an amusement pier that included nearly a half-mile of cafes, arcades, rides, and the legendary roller coaster above the sea, was built in 1958 to stimulate new economic growth. The park was demolished in 1975 after years of declining crowds.

The Venice Pavilion, at the foot of Windward Ave., has picnic tables, an auditorium, and a rollerskating area, and is wheelchair accessible by ramp. The Venice Pavilion was built in 1961 on the beach where the old Venice Pier once stood; it now serves as a community recreation center. The pavilion's large concrete panels, painted in 1973, form a series of murals depicting the history of Venice.

Venice Fishing Pier: *Foot of Washington St., at Ocean Front Walk, Venice.*

In the summer of 1905 a pier, pavilion, ship-hotel, and auditorium were built at the end of Windward Avenue. The pier served as a meeting place and as a site for society dances. The pier was destroyed by fire in 1920, and was later rebuilt as an amusement midway lined with rides and concessions. The last scene in Mack Sennett's 1914 comedy *Tillie's Punctured Romance*, featuring the Keystone Kops and Charlie Chaplin, was filmed here.

After a series of disastrous fires, the pier was demolished in 1947. The new, 1,100-foot-long concrete fishing pier was constructed in 1965. Food concessions, fish-cleaning facilities, and a bait and tackle shop are located at the end of the pier. Strolling, roller-skating, and fishing are popular; fish commonly caught from the pier include bonito, mackerel, and jacksmelt. The pier is currently closed for renovation.

Ballona Lagoon: *Between Hurricane St. and marina entrance channel, adjacent to Esplanade Way, Venice.*

The name Ballona is derived from the name of the city of Bayona in northern Spain; Bayona was the ancestral home of the Talamantes family, who were granted land in Southern California under the name Ballona de las Carretas. Ballona Lagoon is a remnant of the once-extensive Ballona Creek wetlands. In 1960, wetlands adjacent to and east of the lagoon were developed as the Marina del Rey Harbor.

Ballona Lagoon is one of the last remaining coastal wetlands in Los Angeles County. Fish found here include topsmelt, California killifish, and longjaw mudsuckers. Bridge pilings and intertidal areas provide habitat for invertebrates such as barnacles and bay mussels. Horn snails, crabs, and California sea hares are also abundant in the lagoon and in the canals. The lagoon is a foraging and resting area for wading birds and shorebirds, including the endangered California least tern; western grebes, blue herons, willets, and domestic geese and ducks are commonly seen. There is a public walkway on the east side of the lagoon.

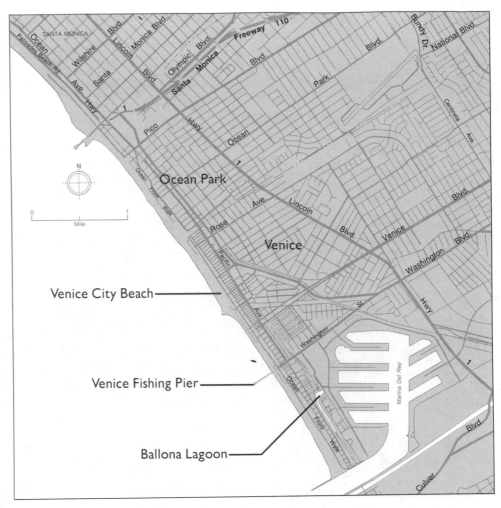

Windward Street, Venice

Bathhouse at Ocean Park, ca. 1906

Marina del Rey Harbor: *South of Venice, Marina del Rey.*

This area was originally inhabited by the Gabrielino Indians, who occupied villages along the edges of the marshlands, and used the area for hunting game, collecting shells, fishing, clamming, and gathering medicinal herbs. What is now the marina was once known as the Playa del Rey inlet, where, from 1815-1825, the Los Angeles River emptied into the Pacific Ocean. In the late 1800s, lodges were built in the area to accommodate hunting expeditions by Spanish, Mexican, and American settlers. As early as 1887, Moses Wicks, a real estate speculator, began construction of a commercial harbor where the Playa del Rey inlet had formed, but when the real estate market collapsed, the project was abandoned. Oil was discovered here in the mid-1920s, but the wetlands proved too swampy for exploitation; portions of the wetlands were later converted to agricultural and residential uses. In 1954 Congress passed a law that authorized dredging the wetlands for construction of the recreational harbor. Dredging began in 1960, and in 1962 the harbor opened.

Marina del Rey Harbor, one of the largest artificial harbors in the world, encompasses 375 acres of land and 405 acres of water, and provides boat slips, marine supplies, hoists, and fuel docks. There is public access along most of the bulkheads in the harbor. A public beach at the end of Basin D is open all year; a ramp for the disabled leads to the beach, and wheelchairs are provided free of charge for use on the ramp. Admiralty Park, with a view of the marina, is a linear, grassy park that extends along Admiralty Way between Lincoln Blvd. and Washington St.; the Marina del Rey Bike Path parallels one

Marina del Rey

edge of the park. Burton Chace Park, an eight-acre park with a panoramic view of the main channel, offers transient boat docks, a picnic shelter, a water tower, a fishing dock, and fish cleaning facilities. Anglers fish offshore for white croaker, California halibut, and spotted sand bass. For information, call the Marina del Rey Chamber of Commerce: (213) 821-0555.

Fisherman's Village: *Basin H, Fiji Way, Marina del Rey.*

Fisherman's Village, built to resemble a New England–style fishing village, extends along the waterfront and features shops, restaurants, and galleries. Boat charters and rentals, fishing licenses, and bait and tackle are available; call: (213) 823-5411. For harbor cruises from the Boat House, call: (213) 822-1151.

Ballona Wetlands: *Along Ballona Creek, S. of Marina del Rey.*

The Ballona Wetlands were formed at a time of lowered sea level during the last Ice Age by the gradual infilling of an incised river valley. The Gabrielino called the Ballona Wetlands *pwinukipar*, meaning "full of water." Prior to development, the wetlands covered 1,700 acres of marshlands, lagoons, and ephemeral ponds. In the early 1800s the wetlands served as a drainage basin for the Los Angeles River, and at times for Ballona and Centinela creeks. After the early 1900s, the wetlands were converted to agricultural uses; partial urbanization followed. By 1928, the remaining lagoons had been drained, leaving a reservoir called Los Angeles Lake and a waterway that is today referred to as Ballona Lagoon. In addition, oil derricks and gas wells

Fisherman's Village, Marina del Rey

were constructed in the wetlands. Ballona Creek was channelized for flood control in 1930 by a WPA project, which reduced the tidal flow into the wetland and altered the composition of the flora and fauna. Further development has moved the marsh edge westward, reducing the wetlands to a few hundred acres.

Today, the Ballona Wetlands serve as a refuge for migratory birds, provide a breeding habitat for endangered species, and offer recreation and open space. The Belding's savannah sparrow and the California least tern, both endangered, use the wetlands for resting, foraging, and breeding; pickleweed provides habitat for the sparrows, and salt pans within the wetlands are one of the only significant least tern breeding sites between Long Beach and Malibu. The scrub and chaparral communities at the eastern boundary of the wetlands support rabbits, gophers, and mice. Areas in agricultural production serve as habitat for birds, including raptors such as marsh hawks and short-eared owls, which concentrate here seasonally to feed. Yellow shore crabs, polychaete worms, and horn snails are found in tidal channels in the wetlands. A plan to restore 175 acres of the wetlands, including a 50-acre buffer zone and future development of an interpretive center by the Audubon Society, has been proposed.

Westchester YMCA: *8015 S. Sepulveda Blvd., Los Angeles.*

The YMCA is located approximately three miles northeast of Dockweiler State Beach. The facility serves as a hostel mid-June through mid-September. Call: (213) 776-0922.

Del Rey Lagoon Park: *6660 Esplanade, off Culver Blvd., Playa del Rey.*

Thirteen-acre Del Rey Lagoon, a remnant of the once-extensive Ballona Wetlands, is surrounded by a grassy park. Facilities include picnic tables, a playground, a baseball diamond, and basketball courts. There is a small boat launch on the lagoon; swimming is not permitted. There is access to the beach along Ballona Creek. Domestic geese and ducks feed and rest at the lagoon.

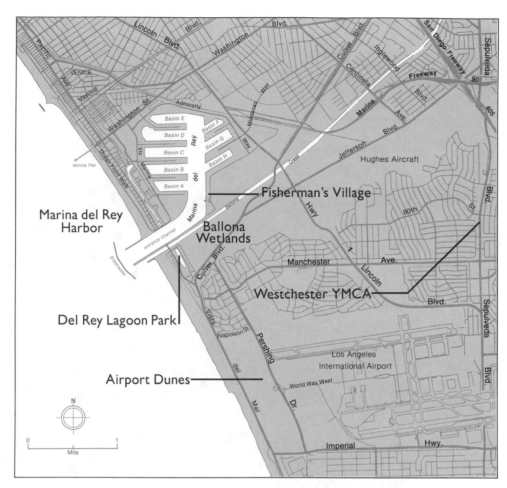

Del Rey Lagoon Park

Airport Dunes: *W. of Los Angeles International Airport, between Napoleon St. and Imperial Hwy.*

Two remnants of the El Segundo Dunes, which once covered 36 square miles of coast from Playa del Rey to Palos Verdes, exist today —the 1.6-acre dune remnant on the El Segundo Chevron Oil refinery site, and the 302-acre Airport Dunes. The remainder has been developed into the communities of Manhattan Beach, Hermosa Beach, and Redondo Beach. The Airport Dunes is the only sizable remaining coastal strand plant community between San Luis Obispo County and the Mexican border. By the mid-1960s, most of the site had been developed into a residential community. However, due to safety hazards from overhead jets, the houses were condemned and purchased by the City of Los Angeles and the Department of Airports, and the last homes were removed in 1975; remnants of the development, including streets and sidewalks, still remain. The native dune ecosystem has recently begun re-establishing itself. The southern section, an area of about 40 acres, has never been developed and remains in a relatively undisturbed natural state.

The Airport Dunes provide habitat for a wide variety of native flora and fauna, including several rare and endangered species. The endangered El Segundo blue butterfly depends entirely on a species of buckwheat endemic to the El Segundo Dunes; both the larvae and adults feed on the flowers of this buckwheat. Lora Aborn's moth and Henne's Eucosman moth are two additional rare species that are endemic to the El Segundo Dunes. The endangered pholisma, a fleshy, scaly herb that is parasitic on the roots of shrubs, is also native to the sandy beach and dunes. Five insects and one mammal, the Pacific pocket mouse, that inhabit the El Segundo Dunes are known to occur only in coastal dunes in Southern California and have been designated as candidate species for listing under the Federal Endangered Species Act. Native reptiles such as the coast horned lizard and the California legless lizard, which are increasingly rare in California, are also found here. Black-bellied plovers and sanderlings forage and nest in the dunes; the introduced red fox hunts for small prey in the dunes.

Statue at Hermosa Beach

is regularly planted with buckwheat, and non-native vegetation is removed.

City of Manhattan Beach: *Along Pacific Coast Hwy., between El Segundo and Hermosa Beach.*

Manhattan Beach was laid out as a seaside resort in the late 1890s and named by developer Stewart Merrill, a native New Yorker, after Manhattan Island. The town, situated on a low bluff above the ocean, featured narrow streets, wooden and stucco bungalows, and a plank boardwalk above the beach. Real estate sales were stimulated in 1903 by the arrival of the Pacific Electric Railway's "Big Red Cars," which ran along the beach from Playa del Rey to Redondo Beach. The city was incorporated as Manhattan in 1912; the word "Beach" was added to its name in 1927. In 1918 a new concrete boardwalk, known as the Strand, was completed, and bathhouses and pavilions were built to accommodate visitors from Los Angeles. As the city grew, its extensive dunes were leveled for development, and in the 1920s much of the sand was shipped to beaches in Hawaii.

The Manhattan Beach Historical Society, located at 425 15th Street, features historic photographs and artifacts. Hours are 9 AM-3 PM, Tuesday and Thursday; call: (213) 545-1624. Parque Culiacan, at 27th St. and Manhattan Ave., is a grassy park with benches and ocean views; it is named for Manhattan Beach's sister city, Culiacán, Mexico. In the early 1920s the park was the site of a bathhouse and lodge for black visitors. Strong anti-black sentiment led to the burning of the structures, and to the city's condemnation of the lodge site in 1924.

Manhattan State Beach: *W. of the Strand, Manhattan Beach.*

The state beach encompasses the entire Manhattan Beach shoreline. The sandy beach, once rather narrow, widened considerably after breakwater construction began at Redondo Beach to the south in 1938. The beach is popular for swimming, surfing, and fishing; facilities include parking, restrooms, wheelchair ramps, and volleyball courts. Pedestrians, joggers, and roller skaters use the Strand, below which is a paved bicycle path that was built over the tracks of the Pacific Electric Railway. Anglers catch barred surfperch, California halibut, and jacksmelt. Shorebirds and gulls frequent the beach, and western grebes and endangered California brown pelicans feed in the nearshore waters. Call: (213) 372-2166.

Manhattan Beach Municipal Pier: *Foot of Manhattan Beach Blvd., Manhattan Beach.*

Manhattan Beach's first pleasure pier was a 900-foot-long structure built around 1900. Referred to as the "Old Iron Pier" because its pilings were made from rail ties, the pier was destroyed by winter storms in 1913; seven years later, the present-day pier was built at the same location. The new pier, also 900 feet long, is supported by concrete pilings, and terminates with a round platform. In 1921 an octagonal pavilion was built at the seaward end of the pier, and a bathhouse and restaurant were erected at the beach end. In 1928 the pier was extended by 200 feet, but storms in 1941 demolished the extension. Today, the pier's pavilion houses the Roundhouse Marine Studies Lab, which con-

Dockweiler State Beach: *W. of Vista del Mar, Marina del Rey Channel to Grand Ave.*

The 255-acre state beach, which fronts Los Angeles International Airport, was established in 1947 and named for Isidore B. Dockweiler, a state park commissioner. The wide, sandy beach provides parking, a picnic area, wheelchair-accessible restrooms, volleyball courts, wheelchair ramps to the beach, and an R.V. campground; a paved bicycle path runs the length of the beach. The state beach extends north of the harbor channel to Reef St. in Venice. Endangered California least terns nest in a protected area of the beach north of the channel, and feed in nearby Ballona Lagoon. For beach information, call: (213) 322-5008.

City of El Segundo: *Along Pacific Coast Hwy., S. of Los Angeles International Airport.*

El Segundo, whose name is Spanish for "the second," was named in 1911 for Standard Oil's second oil refinery in California. El Segundo is a major port for the shipping of petroleum products, which are pumped from tankers offshore through pipes to an oil pier. A bicycle path parallels the city's narrow shoreline.

Located within the property of the Chevron Oil refinery is a 1.6-acre dune remnant of the once-extensive El Segundo Dunes. The protected dune area is one of only two sites where the endangered El Segundo blue butterfly is still found. This tiny, blue and orange butterfly, with a wingspan of only three quarters of an inch, feeds exclusively on a species of wild buckwheat. To protect the endemic butterfly, the dune area

tains displays on marine life and offers classes in marine biology and oceanography for school groups; for information, call: (213) 379-8117. Pier facilities include parking and wheelchair-accessible restrooms. Anglers fish from the pier for California halibut, walleye surfperch, and mackerel. Endangered California gray whales are occasionally seen from the pier during their annual migration.

Hermosa City Beach: *W. of the Strand, Hermosa Beach.*

The city of Hermosa Beach was subdivided in 1901 as a residential community; *hermosa* is Spanish for "beautiful." After construction of the Pacific Electric Railway in 1903, Hermosa Beach developed as a family resort for Angelenos, who were attracted by the city's wide, sandy beach. The beach provides parking, restrooms, and volleyball courts, and offers swimming and surfing. The cement Strand, which begins in Manhattan Beach, and the South Bay Bicycle Trail continue south along the Hermosa Beach shoreline. Anglers surf fish on the beach for barred and walleye surfperch, spotfin croaker, and shovelnose guitarfish, which is a type of ray. Shorebirds such as sanderlings, willets, and dunlins feed along the beach. For beach information call: (213) 372-2166.

Hermosa Beach Municipal Pier: *Foot of Pier Ave., Hermosa Beach.*

Hermosa Beach has been the site of three public fishing piers, the first of which was built in 1904, shortly after the city was founded, and destroyed by storms in 1913. A second pier met a similar fate. The present pier, completed in 1965, is 2,140 feet long, and provides parking, restrooms, and a bait and tackle shop. Fish commonly taken at the pier include halibut, mackerel, opaleye, and several species of surfperch. Gulls, grebes, coots, scoters, and pelicans can be seen in the nearshore waters.

Hermosa Beach

Hermosa Beach

299

City of Redondo Beach: *Along Pacific Coast Hwy., just S. of Hermosa Beach.*

Redondo Beach was founded in 1881 during the land boom of the 1880s, when a rate war between the transcontinental railways brought droves of newcomers to Southern California. Although the city is situated on the former Rancho San Pedro, its name is probably derived from the adjacent rancho, Sausal Redondo ("Round Willow Grove"). A narrow-gauge railway connected the city with Los Angeles in 1888. After the completion of its first wharf in 1890, Redondo Beach became a small seaport. Ships were able to anchor close to shore in the calm waters created by the Redondo Submarine Canyon, which begins just offshore. The fashionable Hotel Redondo was built near the harbor in 1891. In 1903 Henry Huntington's Pacific Electric Railway was extended to Redondo Beach; two years later, Huntington bought the Redondo Land Company, becoming owner of 90 per cent of the city's property and thus launching a frenzied but short-lived boom in real estate sales and raising hopes that a major port would be built here.

Redondo Beach's seaport was soon overshadowed by the port at San Pedro, and shipping gradually ceased here. However, the city thrived as a beach resort, attracting visitors with its pleasure pier, theater, roller coaster, pavilion, and sandy beach. To promote a new saltwater plunge, Huntington sponsored exhibitions in 1907 that featured Hawaiian surfer George Freeth. Freeth's demonstration of surfing at Redondo Beach marked the first appearance of the sport on the California coast. Although a commercial port was never built at Redondo Beach, initial work on King Harbor, a small-craft harbor, was completed in 1939.

Redondo Beach

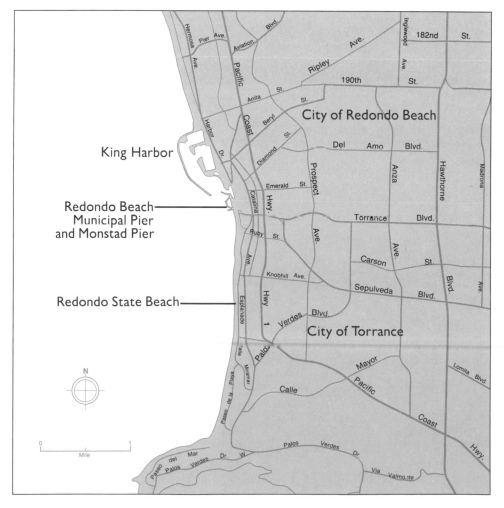

King Harbor: *W. of Harbor Dr., Redondo Beach.*

This small-boat harbor, which consists of three boat basins, was first built in 1939. At that time, it was protected on the northwest by a half-mile-long, arc-shaped breakwater, which cut off the sand supply to the beach area between the breakwater and the municipal pier to the south. The Redondo Submarine Canyon, which begins near the harbor entrance just offshore of the pier, causes waves to concentrate north and south of the head of the canyon; this, combined with the reduced sand supply, caused the shoreline area north of the pier to suffer severe erosion—a section of the boardwalk and a whole block behind it were destroyed. In 1958, to prevent further erosion, the breakwater was extended a half-mile to the southeast, and a jetty was built at the south end of the harbor.

King Harbor provides boat slips, hoists, fuel docks, marine supplies, charter boat rentals, parking, restrooms, and restaurants. A paved bike path follows the perimeter of the harbor. For harbor information, call the Harbormaster: (213) 372-1175 ex. 239. Whale-watching charters are available during the annual migration of the California gray whale; call: (213) 374-4015 or 372-3566. Seaside Lagoon, located between Basins 2 and 3, is a sandy-bottomed, warm-water lagoon that is open in summer for swimming; call: (213) 376-9905.

Anglers fish within King Harbor from the 200-foot-long Redondo Sportfishing Pier, located north of Basin 3, and from the harbor breakwater; bonita and yellowtail are commonly caught. Grebes, mallards, gulls, occasional black-crowned night herons, and harbor seals frequent the harbor. The harbor can be viewed from Plaza Park, a small, grassy park located east of Basin Three between Harbor Dr. and Catalina Avenue.

Redondo Beach Municipal Pier and Monstad Pier: *Foot of Torrance Blvd., Redondo Beach.*

The horseshoe-shaped municipal pier was first built in 1915 of concrete and steel, and was known as the Endless Pier. Damaged by a storm some years later, the pier was rebuilt of wood in 1929. The 250-foot-long Monstad Pier, which extends straight out from the southern end of the municipal pier, was built in 1927 by W. M.

Monstad as a fishing pier and a dock for sport-fishing boats. A fishing promenade was recently built at the seaward end of Monstad Pier, linking it with the middle of the municipal pier. Numerous shops and restaurants are located on the two piers; the Monstad Pier has a bait and tackle shop. Anglers fish for bonito, yellowtail, California halibut, and surfperch. Offshore of the pier, along the Redondo Canyon, there is deepwater fishing for chilipepper, vermilion rockfish, bocaccio, and canary rockfish.

At the foot of the two piers is a bronze bust of George Freeth, who introduced surfing to California at Redondo Beach in 1907. Just north of the piers, adjacent to Harbor Basin 3, is a commercial area known as the International Boardwalk, featuring shops, fast food restaurants, fish markets, and an amusement arcade.

Redondo State Beach: *W. of Esplanade, Redondo Beach.*

The 85-acre Redondo State Beach is a wide, sandy beach used for swimming, surfing, and fishing; anglers catch barred surfperch, walleye surfperch, and jacksmelt. The beach provides parking, wheelchair-accessible restrooms, and volleyball courts, and is accessible from several stairways and ramps from Harbor Dr. and from Esplanade. A paved walkway and the South Bay Bicycle Trail parallel the length of the state beach. For information, call: (213) 372-2166. On the bluff above the north end of the beach, at the foot of Torrance Blvd., is Veteran's Park, a 6.3-acre park with lawns and palm trees.

City of Torrance: *Along Palos Verdes Blvd., just S. of Redondo Beach.*

Torrance was established in 1911 by Jared S. Torrance, who wished to design an ideal residential and industrial city. Torrance hired landscape architect Frederick Law Olmsted to design the city; architect Irving J. Gill designed many of the first buildings. The residential area along the coast, developed in the 1920s, is called the Hollywood Riviera.

Torrance County Beach is a sandy beach popular for surfing, swimming, surf fishing, and diving. Parking is available above the beach along Paseo de la Playa; restrooms are provided on the beach. The 19-mile-long South Bay Bicycle Trail ends here. For beach information, call: (213) 372-2166. Miramar Park, located above the north end of the beach at Paseo de la Playa and Calle Miramar, is a 1.6-acre grassy park with a garden, benches, and cement walkways. South of Torrance County Beach, the steep bluffs of the Palos Verdes Peninsula begin.

Torrance County Beach

Redondo Beach, ca. 1924

Palos Verdes Peninsula: *Between Torrance and the Port of Los Angeles.*

The peninsula, which is bounded by Santa Monica Bay and San Pedro Bay, emerged as an island as the result of uplift of the sea floor during the early Pleistocene. Continued uplift, combined with sedimentation in the Los Angeles Basin, caused the peninsula to become connected to the mainland in the late Pleistocene. A series of 13 distinct marine terraces rise in succession from sea level to 1,300 feet; the Palos Verdes Hills reach a height of 1,480 feet at San Pedro Hill. Once a rancho of the Sepúlveda family in the 1800s, the peninsula was developed in the 1920s as an elegant subdivision of estates; it now comprises San Pedro, which is part of the city of Los Angeles, and the cities of Palos Verdes Estates, Rancho Palos Verdes, Rolling Hills Estates, and Rolling Hills.

Malaga Cove: *Off Paseo Del Mar, E. of Via Arroyo, Palos Verdes Estates.*

Malaga Cove, also called Rat Beach (for "Right After Torrance"), is popular for swimming, surfing, and diving. A gazebo overlooks the cove from a bluff that is covered with sage scrub vegetation such as Indian paintbrush. A paved path leads down Malaga Canyon to a rocky and sandy beach, and to the Roessler Memorial Swimming Pool, built in 1926 and now open to the public in summer. The cove is also accessible from Torrance County Beach to the north. Offshore rocky reefs and kelp beds provide habitat for gorgonian coral, rock scallops, sea hares, octopuses, sheep crabs, and spiny lobsters as well as garibaldi, kelp bass, horn sharks, and Pacific angel sharks. The Chowigna archaeological site in Malaga Canyon has revealed Gabrielino Indian artifacts, including shell fishhooks, bone harpoon barbs, and soapstone carved figures of canoes and marine mammals. The south end of Malaga Cove,

accessible via a steep trail off Via Chino and Paseo Del Mar, is a surfing and diving spot known as Haggerty's. For beach information, call: (213) 378-0383.

Palos Verdes Estates Shoreline Preserve: *Entire shoreline of Palos Verdes Estates.*

The city of Palos Verdes Estates developed as a residential community in the 1920s and was incorporated in 1939. The community was designed in part by landscape architects Frederick Law Olmsted and John Olmsted, and features a number of Spanish Colonial Revival homes, equestrian and hiking trails, and lush native and exotic vegetation. Peacocks, introduced by an early resident, now roam freely throughout the area. The preserve, which extends along the city's four-and-a-half-mile shoreline, was established in 1969 by combining 130 acres of undeveloped blufftop parkland and a 1963 state tidelands grant that includes the adjacent offshore area. Footpaths that are very steep and hazardous lead from scenic overlooks and blufftop trails down cliffs to the rocky shore. The preserve is used for diving, surfing, hiking, fishing, and scientific research. Call: (213) 378-0383. Sea urchins and crabs are commercially harvested offshore.

A steep trail off the 600 block of Paseo Del Mar leads down to a rocky beach at Flat Rock Point, which marks the north end of Bluff Cove; Flat Rock and Bit Rock are located offshore. The underwater topography is characterized by rocky boulders and reefs that form a series of ridges with sandy areas in between. Extensive kelp beds provide habitat for treefish, bluebanded gobies, señoritas, and nurse sharks. The cove is a resting and overwintering area for shorebirds such as willets, marbled godwits, and plovers. An overlook at the 1300 block of Paseo Del Mar affords views of Bluff Cove, the Channel Islands, and the beach cities to the north.

Lunada Bay, located between Palos Verdes Point (also called Rocky Point) and Resort Point, features a rocky beach, accessible via a steep trail off Paseo Del Mar near Oakley Road. Bivalve shells can be seen embedded in the eroding cliffs. A layer of alluvium deposited by creek runoff covers other rock strata at the mouth of the steep and narrow Agua Amarga Canyon, which cuts through the marine terrace. The remains of the freighter *Dominator* can be seen off Rocky Point, where it ran aground in 1961. Kelp beds provide habitat for crabs, tunicates, ghost shrimp, and blind gobies. Slender green shrimp, blennies, and clingfish inhabit the beds of marine grass along the rocky bottom of the bay. Tidepool life includes brittle stars, peanut worms, and mantis shrimp. Resort Point Cove, also known as Honeymoon Cove, is just south.

A steep trail on the north side of Christmas Tree Cove at the 2800 block of Paseo Del Mar near Via Neve leads down to a small sandy and rocky beach. Snails such as Kellet's whelks and chestnut cowries and fish such as rock wrasses inhabit the offshore kelp beds.

City of Rancho Palos Verdes: *Between Palos Verdes Estates and San Pedro.*

Rancho Palos Verdes, situated along seven and a half miles of coastline, was developed as a residential community in the late 1940s in the area of Abalone Cove and Portuguese Bend; it

garibaldi (*Hypsypops rubicundus*)
to 14 inches long

Malaga Cove

was incorporated in 1973. Flowers, trees, grains, and vegetables are grown at several blufftop locations along the city's shoreline.

The extinct Palos Verdes blue butterfly, which was recognized as a separate species in 1977, inhabited the hills, bluffs, and canyons of the Palos Verdes Peninsula, primarily within the city of Rancho Palos Verdes. The butterfly was dependent on native locoweed as its host plant. Residential development and the clearing of vegetation for fire control management, which resulted in the loss of native perennial plants and the introduction of non-native annuals, led to the extinction of the species in the early 1980s.

Point Vicente Park and Lighthouse: *Palos Verdes Dr. West, Rancho Palos Verdes.*

The park is situated on the blufftop of Point Vicente, high above a rocky shore and overlooking extensive kelp beds. The Point Vicente Interpretive Center is open daily and features displays on the geology, marine life, plants, animals, and history of the Palos Verdes Peninsula, with exhibits on the Gabrielino Indians, whales, and kelp, and a relief map of the peninsula. Picnic areas, a blufftop trail, restrooms, and parking are available. The Point Vicente Lighthouse, near the Coast Guard Station, was built in 1926 and is now open to the public on Tuesday and Thursday afternoons. Guided tours of the lighthouse and interpretive center are available by appointment; call: (213) 377-5370.

Point Vicente Fishing Access: *E. of Point Vicente, off Palos Verdes Dr. South, Rancho Palos Verdes.*

A steep dirt trail leads down to the Point Vicente Fishing Access, a rocky beach between Point Vicente and Long Point. Anglers shore fish for bass, surf perch, and rockfish. Anemones, porcelain crabs, and nudibranchs inhabit offshore kelp beds, which are popular for diving. Restrooms and parking are available. Marineland, which was situated on the bluff of Long Point from 1954 until it closed in 1987, offered shows and attractions featuring marine mammals such as walruses, dolphins, and killer whales. Marineland also operated an extensive marine animal care program.

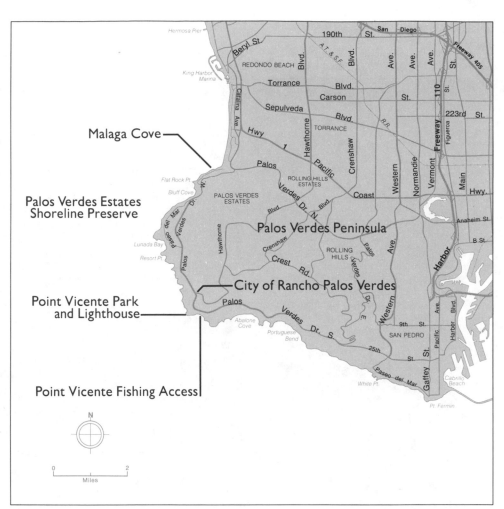

Point Vicente Lighthouse

Wreck of the freighter Dominator *off Lunada Bay*

Abalone Cove Ecological Reserve: *Palos Verdes Dr. South, Rancho Palos Verdes.*

In 1978, Abalone Cove County Beach became the 80-acre Abalone Cove Ecological Reserve, which comprises offshore waters, tidepools, and several beaches backed by 180-foot-high cliffs with blufftop trails. Vegetation along the bluffs includes two species of cactus—the prickly pear and coast cholla. The reserve, which lies at the base of an extensive landslide area, extends from Palos Verdes Dr. South to 300 yards offshore. Upper Beach is a manmade rocky and sandy beach built in Abalone Cove during the 1930s along with a resort hotel, whose ruins include the Old Clubhouse, now used as a lifeguard facility. East Beach, a natural, coarse-grained sandy beach, is at the east end of the cove. Smuggler's Cove, which became famous during Prohibition, is just east of Abalone Cove between Portuguese Point and Inspiration Point; the cove has small, sandy beaches at both ends. The points feature extensive tidepools and offshore surfing spots.

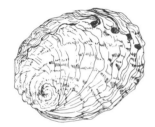

red abalone (*Haliotis rufescens*)
to 11¾ inches long

Offshore kelp beds, popular for snorkeling and scuba diving, provide habitat for marine life such as sea hares, rock scallops, and purple sea urchins; red, green, and black abalones have been planted here to replenish the once-abundant species. No mollusks, crustaceans, or other invertebrates may be taken from the reserve; fishing is permitted for finned fish such as sand bass, perch, and rockfish. Bottle-nosed dolphins pass just outside the surf zone during their spring and fall migration. The reserve is a migratory and overwintering area for shorebirds such as willets, turnstones, and yellowlegs.

Facilities within the reserve include picnic tables, a playground, restrooms, and parking; no dogs or fires are allowed. For information, call: (213) 545-4502 or 832-1130. The Wayfarer's Chapel across Palos Verdes Dr. South was designed in 1946 by Lloyd Wright, son of Frank Lloyd Wright, and made of redwood, stone, and glass, with landscaped gardens.

Portuguese Bend: *Off Palos Verdes Dr. South, Rancho Palos Verdes.*

Portuguese Bend is named for the Portuguese whalers who operated out of the cove in the mid-1800s. Grading of the land in the 1950s for the southwestern extension of Crenshaw Blvd. triggered the Portuguese Bend landslide in 1956, which resulted in extensive damage to many hillside homes in the residential area. The slide, which covers about 270 acres, is an active, slow-moving mass of shale blocks and debris slumping over an underlying layer of seaward-dipping bentonite. Increased levels of ground water contribute to the continued movement of the slide at the rate of a few inches a year. The roadway of Palos Verdes Dr. South in the slide area is constantly under repair due to the ongoing horizontal and vertical displacement of land. Unmarked hillside trails, accessible via Del Cerro Park at the end of Crenshaw Blvd., afford views of some of the 13 marine terraces that make up the Palos Verdes Peninsula.

Royal Palms State Beach: *Western Ave. and Paseo del Mar, San Pedro.*

The Royal Palms Hotel, built here in 1915 at the base of a cliff, was destroyed in the 1930s by storms and an earthquake; ruins of the foundation and walls remain, as well as palm trees and overgrown terraced gardens. The rocky cove is a popular surfing spot. Parking and restrooms are available. Call: (213) 372-2166.

White Point Beach is a rocky cove southeast of the state beach, with extensive tidepools and offshore kelp beds. The ruins of White Point Hot Springs, a Japanese resort hotel and bathhouse built in the early 1900s, can be seen during low tides; the hot springs were fed by underwater vents just offshore. The Japanese harvested abalone here until World War II. Rocky reefs beneath the kelp forest canopy provide habitat for marine life such as moray eels, giant keyhole limpets, sea cucumbers, and California sheephead. A marked, underwater nature trail for divers is located offshore. White Point State Park is currently being developed on former Fort MacArthur land just inland from the rocky coves across Paseo Del Mar. The park, which will have camping facilities, was the site of a Nike missile base between 1954 and 1974. Friendship Park, located northwest of the park site off Western Ave. and Miraleste Dr., offers

Abalone Cove

hillside hiking trails and picnic areas. San Pedro Recreation Center at 1920 Cumbre Dr. features sports facilities and community programs.

Angels Gate Park: *3601 S. Gaffey St. and 35th St., San Pedro.*

The 160-acre park, formerly the Upper Reservation of Fort McArthur, is named after the historic Angels Gate Lighthouse at the end of the San Pedro Breakwater. The park, which overlooks the ocean off Point Fermin as well as the enormous harbor complex in San Pedro Bay, has picnic areas, a play area with basketball courts, and a military museum, open Saturday-Sunday 1-4 PM. The Bell of Friendship, housed in a pavilion off 37th St., is a traditional Korean bell that was given to the U.S. by the Republic of Korea in 1976 to commemorate the U.S. Bicentennial. The Angels Gate Cultural Center at the top of the grassy hillside park offers community programs and classes. Gaffey Pool off 33rd St. is open for swimming during the summer. The Los Angeles International Hostel, also located within the park, offers 60 beds and kitchen and laundry facilities; call: (213) 831-8109.

Point Fermin Park and Lighthouse: *Paseo del Mar and Gaffey St., San Pedro.*

The point was named by British navigator George Vancouver in 1793 for Father Fermín Francisco de Lasuén, who established 9 of the 21 Alta California missions. The 37-acre park, landscaped with Moreton Bay fig trees, is situated on a bluff overlooking the offshore kelp beds of the Point Fermin Marine Life Refuge. Facilities include a playground, picnic tables, restrooms, and parking. Wilder Annex is the western portion of Point Fermin Park at Paseo del Mar and Meyler St.; the grassy blufftop park features a paved path to a rocky beach.

The Point Fermin Lighthouse, built in 1874 with lumber and bricks shipped around Cape Horn, stands near the cliff edge in the park. The lighthouse, now a private residence, operated with an oil lamp, then a vapor incandescent light, and finally an electric light until 1928, when an automated light was installed on the point; the lighthouse was converted to a radar station during World War II. The national headquarters of the American Cetacean Society, located in the Point Fermin Cetacean and Community Center building next to the lighthouse, has information on whales and dolphins; call: (213) 548-6279. The Point Fermin landslide area, composed of sandstone and shale, begins just south of the blufftop park, where sunken remnants of paved streets can be seen.

Point Fermin Marine Life Refuge: *Offshore between Point Fermin and Cabrillo Beach.*

Established in 1969, the Point Fermin Marine Life Refuge consists of a half-mile-long stretch of seashore and the adjacent offshore waters to 600 feet. Tidepool life includes scaly tube snails, piddock clams, rock lice, tidepool sculpins, lined shore crabs, encrusting coralline algae, and feather boa kelp. Offshore beds of giant kelp provide habitat for sea hares, black abalones, and bat stars. All marine life is protected except for spiny lobster and finned fish such as mackerel, sand bass, spotted bass, and corbina. Access to the marine life refuge for tidepooling and diving is via Cabrillo Beach to the south.

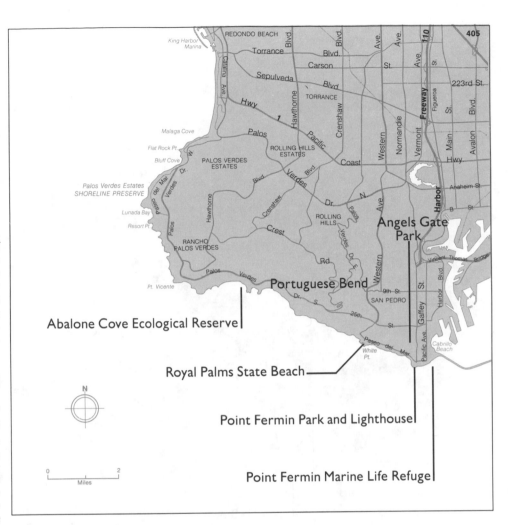

Point Fermin Lighthouse

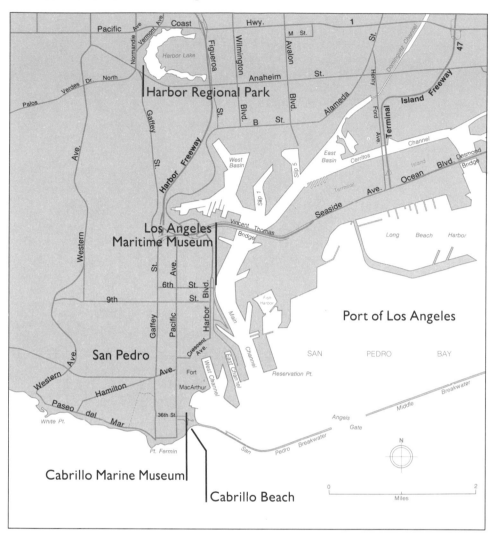

San Pedro, ca. 1900

San Pedro: *E. end of the Palos Verdes Peninsula, off Harbor Fwy., Los Angeles.*

In 1542, Portuguese navigator Juan Cabrillo, sailing for Spain, named the bay here Bahía de los Fumos, "Bay of Smokes," due to the hillside fires of the Gabrielino Indians. Spanish explorer Sebastián Vizcaíno named the bay San Pedro Bay in 1602. In 1784, Juan José Dominguez was granted Rancho San Pedro, which included all of the Palos Verdes Peninsula; it was used for cattle grazing, and later became Rancho de los Palos Verdes under the Sepúlveda family. The eastern edge of Fort MacArthur off Pacific Ave. marks the former location of the adobe Hide House, or Casa de San Pedro, a hide and tallow trading post built in 1823 that was the first known commercial structure on San Pedro Bay; for information on Fort MacArthur tours, call: (213) 643-0667. During the 1850s, construction of the 23-mile-long Los Angeles & San Pedro Railroad, and regular stagecoach and wagon service in the area, led to the development of a major port here. The Southern Pacific Railroad was extended to San Pedro in 1882. San Pedro was an independent city until 1909, when it was absorbed by the city of Los Angeles.

Cabrillo Beach: *End of Stephen M. White Dr., off Pacific Ave., San Pedro.*

Cabrillo Beach comprises two sandy beaches —one on the ocean side and one on San Pedro Bay. The beach was created in 1929 when dredged material was dumped along the base of the western end of the San Pedro Breakwater. The Cabrillo Fishing Pier is adjacent to the breakwater on the bay side; anglers catch bonito, corbina, and perch. Grunion spawn on the beach, and offshore kelp beds provide habitat for marine life such as sea stars, abalones, and kelp surfperch. Beach facilities include picnic tables, parking, wheelchair-accessible restrooms, and a boat ramp; call: (213) 832-1179.

Cabrillo Marine Museum: *3720 Stephen M. White Dr., off Pacific Ave., San Pedro.*

Established in 1934, the museum was moved in 1981 from the historic Bath House building at Cabrillo Beach to a larger facility across the parking lot. The museum features interpretive displays and 34 aquariums that contain marine plants and animals of Southern California. Attractions include a kelp forest tank, sandy beach wave tank, touch tidepool, and bioluminescence exhibit. A small, manmade salt marsh, planted with pickleweed and saltgrass, has been created just north of the museum; it receives tidal action from San Pedro Bay and provides habitat for birds such as godwits, western grebes, and common loons. Open Tuesday-Sunday from 10 AM-5 PM, the museum sponsors numerous programs, including tidepool walks at the nearby Point Fermin Marine Life Refuge west of Cabrillo Beach; call: (213) 548-7562. For information on whale-watching trips, call: (213) 832-4444.

Port of Los Angeles: *W. end of San Pedro Bay off Harbor Fwy., Los Angeles.*

Dredging and filling activities since the 1870s have dramatically transformed this once-extensive estuary from sandbars, mudflats, and salt marshes into the largest artificial harbor complex in the world, containing the ports of Los

Angeles and Long Beach. San Pedro's Main Channel was dredged to ten feet in 1871 and a breakwater was built in 1873 between Rattlesnake Island (now Terminal Island) and Deadman's Island, which no longer exists. The nine-mile-long federal breakwater was built between 1899 and the 1940s to protect San Pedro Bay. In 1909, the city of Los Angeles annexed a 16-mile-long "shoestring" strip of land that connected the city with San Pedro, Wilmington, and Terminal Island. The port's Main Channel was deepened to 45 feet in 1983.

The Port of Los Angeles encompasses 7,400 acres of land and water along 28 miles of waterfront, with 8 shipyards, 22 huge cranes, several marinas, and cargo, container, and passenger ships and terminals. Imports include motor vehicles, bananas, lumber, nails, screws, and bolts; scrap metals, raw cotton, and coal are some of the exports. Enormous petroleum supertankers unload foreign and domestic oil here. Fish Harbor on Terminal Island features the second-largest commercial fishing fleet and fish canning center in the nation. Port facilities include boat hoists, dry dock storage, fuel docks, and marine supplies; call: (213) 519-3400. Endangered California least terns nest on Terminal Island.

Ports O' Call Village between Berths 75-78 features shops, restaurants, charter fishing boats, and harbor cruises; call: (213) 831-0287. For information on whale-watching trips, call: (213) 547-9916 or 775-6111. The Catalina Terminal at Berths 94-95 offers daily ferries to Catalina Island; call: (213) 514-3838.

Los Angeles Maritime Museum: *Foot of 6th St. at Sampson Way, Berth 84, San Pedro.*

The museum is housed in the historic Municipal Ferry Building, which provided service to Terminal Island from 1941 to 1963, when the Vincent Thomas Bridge was completed. Open Tuesday-Sunday from 10 AM-5 PM, the museum contains a history of the Port of Los Angeles, with nautical artifacts, photos, and ship models including an 18-foot-long cutaway model of the R.M.S *Titanic*. Call: (213) 548-7618.

Harbor Regional Park: *Vermont Ave. and Anaheim St., off Harbor Fwy., Harbor City.*

The 231-acre park is vegetated with alders, sycamores, willows, and pines, and surrounds the crescent-shaped Harbor Lake, also called Machado Lake or Bixby Slough. The lake features extensive tule beds and provides habitat for numerous birds such as plovers, coots, green herons, and California least terns. Shore fishing for channel catfish, perch, and carp is popular. Facilities include a youth group campground, baseball field, swimming pool, bike path, boat ramp, picnic areas, and wheelchair-accessible restrooms; call: (213) 548-7515.

The Izaak Walton Wildlife Sanctuary, named after the 19th century English conservationist, is located at the southeast end of the park. Wildlife found here includes Pacific treefrogs, western toads, side-blotched lizards, gopher snakes, western pond turtles, moles, and shrews.

East of Harbor Regional Park is 23-acre Banning Park, site of the Banning Residence Museum at 401 East M St. in Wilmington. The museum building, a State Historical Landmark, is a Greek Revival mansion built in 1864 by General Phineas Banning, known for his work in developing a port for the city of Los Angeles by organizing transportation services in Southern California during the 1850s. For information on museum tours, call: (213) 548-7777.

The Drum Barracks, near Banning Park at 1053 Cary St., is the last remaining building of Camp Drum, the Union Army headquarters for Southern California, Arizona, and New Mexico during the Civil War. The Barracks, now a State Historical Landmark, contains a museum of Civil War memorabilia; call (213) 518-1955.

Cabrillo Marine Museum

Hauling granite for the San Pedro Breakwater, ca. 1908

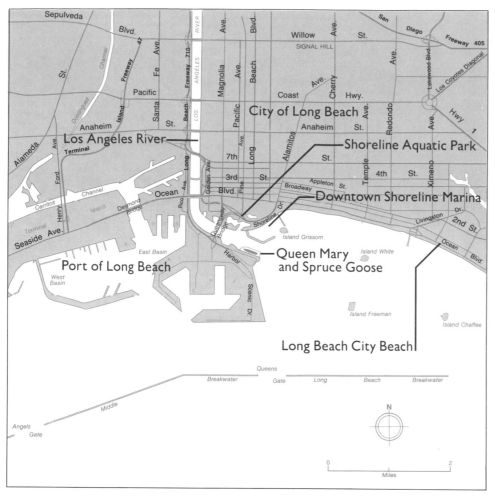

Launching Ramp. The Lario Trail, which begins on the east bank of the river in Long Beach, is an equestrian trail and bike path that extends inland for 20 miles to central Los Angeles.

Queen Mary and Spruce Goose: *Pier J, off Long Beach Fwy. 710, Long Beach Harbor.*

The 81,237-ton *Queen Mary*, which made 1,001 transatlantic voyages between 1934 and 1964, has been docked here as a tourist attraction since 1967. The former British luxury liner now features shops, restaurants, and a hotel. Ship tours include the Engine Room and the Hall of Maritime Heritage. The *Spruce Goose*, the world's largest airplane, is housed nearby the *Queen Mary* in a huge, aluminum geodesic dome. Howard Hughes, who designed and built the 200-ton wooden seaplane out of birch—not spruce—also piloted the aircraft on its one and only flight, above Long Beach Harbor in 1947. Londontown, between the two attractions, is a replica of a 19th century English village, with shops and restaurants. Call: (213) 435-3511.

City of Long Beach: *Off Pacific Coast Hwy., 20 mi. S. E. of downtown Los Angeles.*

The Long Beach area, situated in the Los Angeles Basin, was part of the 1784 Nieto land grant, and, later, the Los Cerritos and Los Alamitos ranchos under the Mexican government. Willmore City, a subdivision established here in 1881, developed into an ocean resort that was incorporated as Long Beach in 1897. The Pine Avenue Pier, built in 1893, was remodeled into the double-decked Long Beach Municipal Pier in 1904. The Pacific Electric Railway was extended to Long Beach in 1906 and brought visitors to the Pike, an amusement park built here on the beach around 1900; attractions included the Walk of a Thousand Lights, a pavilion, a saltwater bathhouse called The Plunge, the Looff Carousel, and the Jackrabbit Racer roller coaster, later the Cyclone Racer. The Rainbow Pier, a recreational pier built in 1932, curved offshore from Linden Ave. to Pine Ave. on what is now landfill.

The discovery of oil at Signal Hill in 1921 triggered a massive building boom around Long Beach. A severe earthquake in 1933 killed 120 people and leveled sections of the city, which were rebuilt after World War II. During the 1950s, over-drilling depleted Long Beach's onshore petroleum reserves and caused the water table under the city to lower, resulting in subsidence, or settling of the land; the power plant at the Port of Long Beach sank 27 feet. Salt water that was injected into the oil-drained cavities to remedy the situation ended up contaminating the city's ground water supply; in 1970 freshwater injection wells alleviated the problem. There are four artificial islands in San Pedro Bay that were built in the 1960s to disguise offshore oil wells; each 10-acre island features palm trees, waterfalls, and fake high-rise buildings that hide the drilling rigs.

Long Beach is today the second largest city in Los Angeles County and the fifth largest in California; it is known for its aerospace industry and for its port. The Long Beach Heritage Foundation sponsors walking tours of the downtown area featuring many distinctive city landmarks, such as the 14-story Villa Riviera apartment building; call: (213) 430-2790. The restored 1844

Port of Long Beach

Port of Long Beach: *E. end of San Pedro Bay, off Ocean Blvd., Long Beach.*

Prior to filling and dredging for the development of an artificial port in 1910, the coast here was composed of sandbars, mudflats, sloughs, and marshes. Today the Port of Long Beach forms an enormous industrial harbor complex with the adjacent Port of Los Angeles. Terminal Island in the middle of the harbor complex is the site of a U.S. naval station. The Port of Long Beach's 67-foot deepwater berths are the deepest in the nation, and the port's extensive container terminals make it the West Coast center for international trade. Exports include citrus fruits, petroleum coke, cement, and coal; salt, bananas, lumber, and automobiles are some of the commodities imported. Queen's Wharf Sportfishing at 555 Pico Ave. offers charter boats, harbor cruises, and whale-watching trips; call: (213) 432-8993.

Los Angeles River: *River mouth is at Ocean Blvd. and Harbor Scenic Dr., Long Beach.*

Flooding in 1815 caused the Los Angeles River to adopt the Ballona Creek course to the north and empty into the ocean at what is now Marina del Rey. In 1825, again due to flooding, the river returned to its earlier discharge point in Wilmington on San Pedro Bay. The river was channelized for flood control in the 1940s; its concrete lining has reduced the amount of sediment that reaches the coast for beach replenishment. Queensway Bay at the river mouth is a boating and water-skiing area, accessible off Ocean Blvd. via the 16-lane Golden Avenue

City of Long Beach

Monterey Style adobe of Rancho Los Cerritos, now a museum and a National Historic Landmark, is located at 6400 Virginia Rd. and is open Wednesday-Sunday, 1-5 PM; call: (213) 424-9423. The Long Beach Convention and Entertainment Center at the foot of Long Beach Blvd. includes exhibit halls, theaters, and a sports arena; for information, call: (213) 436-3636. The Terminal for Long Beach/Catalina Cruises at 330 Golden Shores Blvd. offers harbor cruises and ferries to Catalina Island; call: (213) 547-1162.

Shoreline Aquatic Park: *Shoreline Dr. and Pine Ave., off Ocean Blvd., Long Beach.*

The grassy, landscaped park surrounds an artificial lagoon and offers fishing platforms on Queensway Bay, bicycle and pedestrian paths, and a fully equipped, 70-site R.V. campground at the western end of the park. Park facilities include picnic areas, parking, and wheelchair-accessible restrooms; call: (213) 437-0375.

Downtown Shoreline Marina: *450 E. Shoreline Dr. and Linden Ave., Long Beach.*

The Downtown Shoreline Marina and the much smaller, adjacent Shoreline Harbor Marina are both part of the Long Beach Marina, which also includes Alamitos Bay Marina to the south. Shoreline Village is a tourist attraction near the marinas with shops, restaurants, and the restored 1906 carousel of San Francisco's Playland-at-the-Beach amusement park. Public fishing platforms are located off the western breakwater of the Downtown Shoreline Marina. Parking and wheelchair-accessible restrooms are available. Call: (213) 437-0375.

Long Beach City Beach: *Seaward of Ocean Blvd., between 1st Place and 72nd Place, Long Beach.*

The wide, sandy Long Beach City Beach, also called Long Beach Strand, begins east of the downtown area and extends for several miles past Belmont Pier and along the flat Alamitos Peninsula to the Alamitos Bay Jetty; west of the pier, the beach is backed by a steep bluff. The beach was pounded by surf until the 1940s, when the offshore breakwaters were completed and it was transformed into a protected swimming beach; the beach has since widened considerably. Spiny lobsters are commercially harvested from the breakwaters. The historic Lifeguard Headquarters, built in 1938 at the foot of Linden Ave. and moved to the foot of

Cherry Ave. in 1969, is a clapboard structure that now contains a lifeguard museum. Shorebirds such as godwits, sandpipers, and long-billed curlews rest and feed along the beach. Anglers fish from the beach for surfperch and corbina. Beach facilities include volleyball courts, parking, and wheelchair-accessible restrooms; call: (213) 437-0375.

Bluff Park, along Ocean Blvd. between 20th Place and Redondo Ave., is a grassy blufftop park overlooking San Pedro Bay. The Long Beach Museum of Art at the west end of the park is open Wednesday-Sunday, 12-5 PM; call: (213) 439-2119. Ten-acre Bixby Park just northwest of the museum at Ocean Blvd. and Junipero Ave. has a playground and a picnic area.

Long Beach, ca. 1900

Belmont Pier: *Foot of 39th Place, S. of Ocean Blvd., Long Beach.*

The 1,620-foot-long, T-shaped Belmont Pier was built in 1968 alongside the 1915 Grand Avenue Pier, which was later torn down. Anglers fish from the pier for bonito, mackerel, halibut, perch, and bass. Cormorants, gulls, and endangered California brown pelicans roost on the dock pilings near the end of the pier. Open 5 AM-10 PM, the pier offers skiff rentals and sport fishing boat trips. Facilities include a bait and tackle shop, snack bar, parking, and restrooms; call: (213) 434-6781. For information on whale-watching trips, call: (213) 434-6781 or 434-4434. The section of Long Beach City Beach between the pier and the Alamitos Peninsula to the south is known as Belmont Shore; a sailboat launching ramp is located at the foot of Claremont Place.

Belmont Plaza Olympic Pool is an indoor, T-shaped swimming pool located on the beach just east of the pier. The facility accommodates a variety of recreational and competitive aquatic activities including the annual NCAA Water Polo Championships in November. Adjacent facilities include a grassy picnic area, a playground, beach volleyball courts, and an outdoor pool, open during the summer. For information, call: (213) 438-1141.

Colorado Lagoon: *Appian Way and 4th Street, Long Beach.*

This manmade tidal lagoon, which features a sandy beach and swimming area, was built in conjunction with the Marine Stadium waterway for the 1932 Olympics. The lagoon receives sea water from an inlet that is connected to Marine Stadium on Alamitos Bay. The quahog, an introduced Atlantic coast clam species, inhabits the sandy mud in the low intertidal area of the lagoon; the quahog is found on the West Coast only in Colorado Lagoon and San Francisco and Humboldt bays. Coots, gulls, and sandpipers frequent the lagoon waters and sandy shore. Facilities include picnic areas, playgrounds, parking, and wheelchair-accessible restrooms.

Marine Vista Park, located between Colorado Lagoon and Marine Stadium, is a grassy open area with a baseball field and a soccer field.

Recreation Park, just north of the lagoon, features a picnic area in a eucalyptus grove; call: (213) 434-2868.

Marine Stadium: *Appian Way and 2nd Street, Long Beach.*

Built in the mid-1920s and used for the 1932 Olympic rowing races, Marine Stadium is a narrow, two-mile-long body of sea water that extends past the mouth of the Los Cerritos Channel and into Alamitos Bay to Davies Bridge. The waterway is used for recreational and competitive water-skiing and drag boat racing. Marine Stadium West, located off Nieto Ave. at Appian Way, is a 24-hour boat launching facility with ramps at either end of a small, sandy beach. Marina Park, off 2nd St. and Marina Dr., has a sandy beach called Mothers Beach; Davies Ramp, also called Marine Stadium East, is a 12-lane, 24-hour boat launching ramp. Call: (213) 594-0951.

Naples: *Off Pacific Coast Hwy., along 2nd St., in the middle of Alamitos Bay, Long Beach.*

Named after the city in Italy, Naples is a residential community consisting of three islands in Alamitos Bay that are linked by bridges and separated by the Rivo Alto and Naples canals. Naples was developed by A. M. Parsons between 1903 and 1906 using dredged material as landfill to build up the existing marshland in the center of the bay; the three islands were formed with pilings and retaining walls. In 1907, the development was acquired by Henry Huntington, the creator of the Pacific Electric Railway, an interurban trolley system that extended throughout the Los Angeles Basin. Huntington was at one time the largest single landowner in Southern California.

Waterfront walkways along the canals and perimeter of Naples lead past houses of many architectural styles, numerous boats, and Naples Plaza, a palm-lined park off 2nd Street. Marine Park, just north of Davies Bridge, is a grassy park with a small, sandy beach that forms the southwest bank of Marine Stadium; parking and restrooms are available. Naples is the site of an annual Christmas boat parade.

Rivo Alto Canal, Naples

Marine Stadium

Alamitos Peninsula: *Along Ocean Blvd., between 54th Place and 72nd Place, Long Beach.*

The peninsula, with its rows of duplexes, is reminiscent of Southern California beach towns of the 1920s-1930s such as Newport Beach. The Pacific Electric Railway once ran along the peninsula, and crossed over a bridge to Seal Beach. The Alamitos Bay Jetty, at the end of the peninsula, is a popular fishing spot along the entrance channel to the bay. Bay Shore Walk extends along the northern shore of the peninsula on the bay side; Seaside Walk is a boardwalk along Long Beach City Beach.

Alamitos Bay: *Off Pacific Coast Hwy. and 2nd St., W. of San Gabriel River, Long Beach.*

Alamitos Bay was once an extensive estuary and wetland with sloughs, mudflats, and marshland; it was dredged around the turn of the century for the development of the Naples island community. The bay provides habitat for fish including perch and Pacific tomcod. Within the bay are several marinas including Costa Del Sol, Marina Pacifica, Alamitos Bay Yacht Club, Long Beach Yacht Club, Bahia Marina, and the Alamitos Bay Marina. Facilities include marine supplies, a boat hoist, fuel dock, parking, and wheelchair-accessible restrooms; call: (213) 594-0951. Seaport Village is a tourist attraction with shops and restaurants along the jetty entrance channel. The 1806 adobe of Rancho Los Alamitos at 6400 Bixby Hill Rd. is now a museum; call: (213) 431-2511.

Alamitos Bay Beach, along Bayshore Ave. and north of Ocean Blvd. between 54th Place and 2nd St., offers a stillwater swimming area and summer kayak rentals; the bay waters are also a popular windsurfing spot. Parking and restrooms are available. The Los Cerritos Wetlands, east of Pacific Coast Highway between the Los Cerritos Channel and the San Gabriel River, is the sole remnant of the once-extensive Alamitos Bay marshland. The wetlands consist of a tidal mudflat and marsh area surrounded by oil developments. California killifish, striped mullet, and introduced Mozambique tilapia inhabit the tidal channels. Pickleweed, alkali heath, and cordgrass afford nesting habitat for birds including endangered Belding's savannah sparrows. Shorebirds such as willets, marbled godwits, and turnstones frequent the area. Sims Pond, just north of the wetlands near Highway 1 and Loynes Dr., is a small, seasonal freshwater pond and marsh habitat that is a remnant of what was formerly Upper Alamitos Bay. Endangered California least terns nest here.

San Gabriel River: *River mouth is between Alamitos Bay and Seal Beach.*

The San Gabriel River, which originates in the San Gabriel Mountains, once flowed into the Los Angeles River until flooding in 1867 altered the river's course and caused it to empty into Alamitos Bay. Channelization of the river for flood control in the 1940s involved re-routing the river course so that it bypassed the bay, which had begun to silt up. The warmwater effluent discharged from thermal electric power plants along the river attracts fish such as Pacific barracuda and round stingrays. The San Gabriel River Regional Bikeway off Marina Dr. extends inland for several miles along the river bank past El Dorado Park and Nature Center.

Belmont Pier

Casino at Avalon

Bison near Little Harbor Campground

Santa Catalina Island: *18 nautical mi. S.W. of San Pedro.*

The largest of the Southern Channel Islands, Santa Catalina Island encompasses 75 square miles of land, with 54 miles of coastline. A northwest-southeast trending mountain ridge extends the length of the island for 21 miles. Catalina was formed late in the Miocene Epoch (between 20 and 5 million years ago) by wrenching faults that moved the block on which the island rests 100 miles north from its previous location near what is now the Mexican border. Cliffed shorelines, jagged volcanic peaks, and deep canyons are evidence of Catalina's geologic past.

The earliest records of human habitation on Catalina date back over 4,000 years. The most recent native inhabitants, the Gabrielino, arrived about 500 B.C. There are approximately 2,000 archaeological sites on the island, including remains of villages, steatite quarries, and middens. Juan Rodríguez Cabrillo, who landed here in 1542, named the island San Salvador after his flagship. Sixty years later, Sebastián Vizcaíno anchored at what he thought was an undiscovered island and named it Santa Catalina in honor of that saint's feast day.

In the early 1800s, Russian and Aleut fur hunters came to Santa Catalina waters to hunt the abundant sea otters. The valuable sea otter furs were sold to Chinese merchants in Canton. Catalina Island was also a base for contraband trade, and, until the late 1800s, a layover for smuggled Chinese laborers; it was later used as a transfer point for alcohol and drugs by Prohibition-era smugglers.

Catalina was deeded to Thomas Robbins in 1848 by Governor Pío Pico. The island was the scene of a mining boom in 1863, until the establishment of the still-existing barracks at Two Harbors by Union troops a year later. James Lick, founder of the Lick Observatory, owned Catalina Island from 1867 until 1887, when he sold it to George Shatto; Shatto hoped to develop Avalon as a tourist resort, renting tent spaces to vacationers and leaving remaining areas for cattle and sheep ranching. In 1892, Shatto sold the island to the Banning brothers, who founded the Santa Catalina Island Company for the purpose of developing Catalina into a pleasure resort. William Wrigley, Jr. purchased the island from the Banning brothers in 1919 with the intent of preserving the island's unique natural and cultural resources. This tradition is maintained by the non-profit Santa Catalina Island Conservancy, established in 1972 to preserve Catalina in its natural state. For information, call: (213) 510-1421.

Catalina's summer fog, moderate winter climate, and rugged topography allow for a diversity of plant communities. Maritime desert scrub, characterized by drought-adapted plants including the velvet cactus, prickly pear, and cholla, occurs on exposed headlands on the arid westernmost, or Pacific, side of the island. Uphill from the desert scrub are low-growing, gray-green coastal sage scrub plants. On the Pacific side of the island, black sage and California sagebrush predominate, whereas the endemic St. Catherine's lace, largest of the California buckwheats, grows on the San Pedro Channel side. At higher elevations, expanses of coastal grasslands, restored by revegetation projects, cover lands once stripped by feral goats introduced more than 150 years ago. Chaparral plants, including the California lilac, wild apple, and California mahogany, inhabit the east- and west-facing slopes of stream drainages on the north side of the island. The unusual manicured appearance of the island's chaparral community is the result of grazing by feral goats.

In areas of abundant moisture and rich soil, the woodland community is characterized by island oaks, often hybrids of mainland species; Catalina cherry, one of the island's largest trees; and the endemic Catalina ironwood. Found only on north-facing slopes and rocky ravines and outcroppings, Catalina ironwood trees are remnants of a population that was widespread on the mainland over 20,000 years ago. The highest proportion of endemic plant species on the island occurs on north-facing coastal bluffs, which are little affected by grazing animals.

The most commonly seen animals on Catalina Island are the introduced bison, goats, deer, and pigs that run free in the interior. However, Catalina also supports a wide variety of animals uniquely adapted to the island environment. The Catalina quail, a larger and darker subspecies of its mainland relative, and a subspecies of the Bewick wren are endemic only to Catalina. Populations of endangered bald eagles and peregrine falcons, which became nearly extinct in the 1950s as a result of pesticide use, have been re-established through a program organized by the Institute for Wildlife Studies and the Catalina Conservancy. Reptiles that inhabit the island include a native rattlesnake, aquatic garter snakes, side-blotched lizards, alligator lizards, and skinks. The slender salamander, arboreal salamander, and Pacific treefrog are the only amphibians known to inhabit the island. Catalina's subspecies of the Channel Island fox is the island's largest native land mammal.

Catalina is located in the Southern California Bight, where the cool waters of the California Current meet the warmer waters of the Southern California Countercurrent, resulting in a diversity of marine life in Catalina's nearshore waters. The shallow waters close to shore, excellent for snorkeling and shore fishing, support kelp bass, sheephead, opaleye, and garibaldi. Offshore waters abound with game fish such as marlin, tuna, and sharks. Western gulls, which nest on Bird Rock at Isthmus Harbor, double-crested cormorants, and endangered California brown pelicans are commonly seen. Pilot whales and porpoises can sometimes be seen offshore. Harbor seals and sea lions haul out at Seal Rocks, located at the southeastern tip of the island. Offshore, on the Pacific side of Catalina, is Farnsworth Bank, a rocky outcropping designated as an ecological preserve for the uncommon purple hydrocoral.

The city of Avalon, nestled in the steep hills of Avalon Canyon, is named after a mythical island valley in the Tennyson poem *Idylls of the King*. The small resort town, where most of Catalina's residents live, is known for its pleasant weather, sport fishing, yachting, and scuba diving. (The remainder of the island's population resides at Two Harbors, a small village located between Catalina and Isthmus harbors.) The landmark circular Casino, built in Avalon in 1929, once featured a cinema on the first floor, and a ballroom on the second floor from which Big Band music was broadcast, making Avalon nationally famous. Today, the Casino houses a museum with a collection of Indian artifacts, and a movie theater. The Casino building may be rented for parties and conventions; call the Catalina Island Company: (213) 510-2000. The

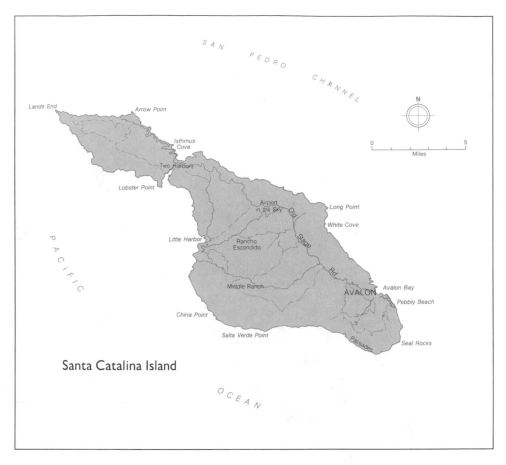

Santa Catalina Island

Wrigley Memorial and Botanical Garden, at 1400 Avalon Canyon Rd., is 1.7 miles from downtown Avalon. The Memorial was built almost entirely with native materials, including blue flagstone rock from Little Harbor; the Botanical Garden below it displays a collection of native plants, cacti, and succulents.

Ferry service to Avalon from San Pedro, Long Beach, and Newport is available; for further information call the Avalon Chamber of Commerce: (213) 510-1520. Helicopters fly daily from San Pedro; call: (213) 548-1314. Airport-in-

the-Sky, where both commercial and private planes land, is 25 minutes from Avalon by bus; call: (213) 510-0143.

Campsites on Catalina are at Black Jack, Little Harbor, Two Harbors, and Parson's Landing. For information on camping at Black Jack or Little Harbor, or for hiking or bicycling permits, call the Los Angeles County Dept. of Parks and Recreation: (213) 510-0688. Two Harbors and Parson's Landing are managed by Catalina Cove and Camp Agency; call: (213) 510-0303.

Little Harbor

Orange County
Selected Species of Interest

Plants: Prickly pear (*Opuntia littoralis*), common cactus on bluffs near ocean; bears edible reddish-purple fruits. **Lemonadeberry** (*Rhus integrifolia*), tall shrub of coastal sage scrub; berries used by Indians to make a beverage.

Trees: California fan palm (*Washingtonia filifera*), tall, slender palm native to California deserts; widely planted throughout county. **Interior live oak** (*Quercus wislizenii*), normally found inland but occurs in hills above South Laguna.

Insects: Southern salt marsh mosquito (*Aedes taeniorhynchus*), breeds in brackish marsh waters. **Kelp muscid** (*Fucellia costalis*), small fly that swarms on kelp washed up on beaches; larva eats kelp, adult preys on amphipods.

Invertebrates: California horn snail (*Cerithidea californica*), small snail with tall, spired shell; abundant on mudflats. **Lined shore crab** (*Pachygrapsus crassipes*), common scavenger of the high intertidal on rocky shores.

Amphibians and Reptiles: Side-blotched lizard (*Uta stansburiana*), abundant on dry terrain. **San Diego gopher snake** (*Pituophis melanoleucus annectens*), large constrictor often mistaken for rattlesnake.

Fish: White croaker (*Genyonemus lineatus*), schools in nearshore waters; uses swim bladder to produce drumming sound. **California corbina** (*Menticirrhus undulatus*), sport fish found in surf along sandy beaches.

Birds: Black-necked stilt (*Himantopus mexicanus*), wading bird with black back and long, spindly legs; inhabits marshes. **Ring-billed gull** (*Larus delawarensis*), winters along coast; adults have black ring encircling bill.

Land Mammals: California mouse (*Peromyscus californicus*), inhabits brushy hillsides; builds nests of grasses and sticks. **Raccoon** (*Procyon lotor*), nocturnal and omnivorous; common in both natural and residential areas.

Marine Mammals: Common dolphin (*Delphinus delphis*), grows to eight feet long, with distinct beak; travels in large schools. **California sea lion** (*Zalophus californianus*), hauls out on offshore rocks near Laguna Beach.

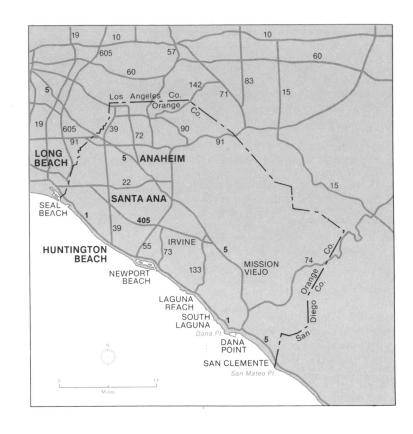

Orange County

ORANGE COUNTY, named for the oranges that were once cultivated in vast orchards, was formed in 1889 from the southeastern portion of Los Angeles County. The county's northern coastal area, from Seal Beach to Newport Beach, is situated on the edge of the Los Angeles Basin, and is characterized by broad, sandy beaches backed by low bluffs and mesas, and lowland areas that once held extensive wetlands. At Corona del Mar the coastal plain ends and the San Joaquin Hills, part of the Peninsular Ranges, begin; from here to Dana Point, steep cliffs rise above picturesque sandy coves bounded by rocky points and tidepools and fringed by offshore rocks. The less dramatic coastline south of Dana Point consists of a high marine terrace above a ribbon of narrow, sandy shoreline.

The original inhabitants of what is now Orange County were two Shoshonean tribes, the Gabrielino and the Juaneño. The Indians fished for shark, mackerel, and surfperch, collected mussels, clams, and limpets, harvested algae, prickly pear, and acorns, and hunted birds and mammals. The Gabrielino are believed to have originated the jimsonweed cult, which spread to the Juaneño and to other Southern California tribes. The cult involved the ceremonial use of jimsonweed, a hallucinogenic plant, in conjunction with initiation rites. Numerous Gabrielino and Juaneño shell middens and other archaeological sites found along the coast attest to several thousand years of Indian presence on the land.

In 1776, seven years after the Portolá Expedition passed through the valley of San Juan Creek, Mission San Juan Capistrano was established there, and the Indians' native way of life came to an end. The Spanish missionaries gathered the Indians into the mission, baptized them, and set them to work farming and tending cattle and sheep. In 1821, when Mexico achieved independence from Spain, the Mexican government legalized trade between the missions and American and British ships. Cattle hides and tallow rendered at the mission were brought to what is now called Dana Cove, one of many anchorages used by ships plying the coastal trade, and exchanged for manufactured goods.

After secularization in 1834, the Mexican government divided up the former mission lands into several land grants, or ranchos, that encompassed nearly all of the Orange County coast. Cattle, which ranged freely over the hillsides, were the mainstay of the rancho economy, and the hide trade flourished. However, a drought in the 1860s ruined the Mexican ranchers, who sold their lands at a loss to Yankee businessmen. One of these was James Irvine, a Scottish-born merchant who merged several land grants into what became the county's largest ranch. Irvine replaced the cattle with sheep; over the next 60 years, the ranch operations were diversified to include the large-scale cultivation of grain, corn, lima beans, walnuts, lemons, and Valencia oranges.

In the 1870s and 1880s, the growth of railroads opened the Southern California coast to development. One of the first large settlements along Orange County's coast was at Newport Beach, where a shipping center was established in 1873. North of Newport Beach, new settlers drained the marshlands for farming; to the south, farmers homesteaded coastal areas from Laguna Beach to Dana Point. Residents of the growing inland towns of Santa Ana and Riverside discovered the recreational possibilities of the coast, and summer resorts appeared at Laguna Beach and South Laguna. By 1906, Henry Huntington had extended his Pacific Electric Railway, an interurban trolley system that served the Los Angeles Basin, into Orange County and down the coast to the Balboa Peninsula. To accommodate vacationers from Los Angeles and inland cities, the resort towns of Seal Beach, Sunset Beach, Huntington Beach, and Balboa were created.

The 1920s saw a surge in development along the coast. In the northern county, growth was stimulated by the discovery of oil at Seal Beach, Bolsa Chica, and Huntington Beach. The completion of Pacific Coast Highway in 1926 opened up the previously isolated coastal area between Crystal Cove and South Laguna. Farther south, developers established the communities of Dana Point, Capistrano Beach, and San Clemente. However, the county remained largely rural until the post-World War II development boom, when suburbs sprang up on former orchard lands. Aerospace, pharmaceutical, and computer industries have largely replaced agriculture in the county's economy. Today, Orange County is California's second most populous county.

Although the landscape has changed drastically, the county retains valuable natural resources. The north coast contains some of the healthiest and largest remaining wetlands in Southern California, including those in Anaheim Bay, Bolsa Chica, and Upper Newport Bay. Several areas of tidepools, reefs, and kelp beds are protected as marine life refuges. However, the county's 40-mile-long coast is better known for its multitude of recreational opportunities, which are enhanced by a benign climate.

Newport Beach, ca. 1905

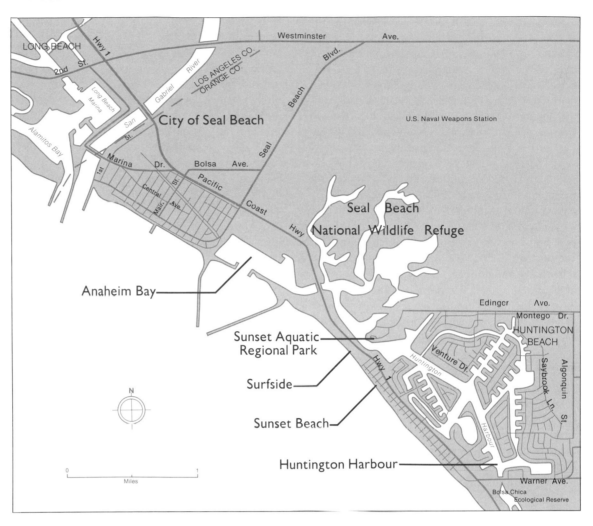

City of Seal Beach: *S.E of San Gabriel River, S.W. of Pacific Coast Hwy.*

Originally called Bay City, Seal Beach was developed in the early 1900s as a resort for inland residents. In 1904 the Pacific Electric Railway, a trolley system that once traversed the Los Angeles Basin, reached Seal Beach, and developers built hotels, bathhouses, and dance halls to accommodate new visitors from the urban north. The 1,865-foot-long Seal Beach Pier, once the longest pier south of San Francisco, was built in 1906, and in 1915, a roller coaster was imported from the world's fair in San Francisco and placed at the beach. Oil was discovered here in 1926, and the oil boom that followed resulted in the development of Seal Beach into a residential community. A marker at Seal Beach Blvd. and Electric Ave. commemorates Anaheim Landing, a shipping port established here in 1864 to serve Anaheim and other towns of the Santa Ana Valley.

The mile-long sandy beach is used for surfing, swimming, and fishing; facilities include restrooms and a wheelchair ramp onto the sand. The Seal Beach Pier, located at the foot of Main St., provides fishing facilities and a restaurant, and is floodlit at night. The pier suffered extensive damage in the storms of 1983, but has since been restored. Anglers fish for California halibut, white croaker, rockfish, and California corbina along the mouth of the San Gabriel River, which marks the northern boundary of Orange County. Adjacent to the river and east of

Pacific Coast Highway are 20 acres of salt marsh and salt flat that support pickleweed, saltgrass, and alkali heath.

Anaheim Bay: *Both sides of Pacific Coast Hwy., Seal Beach.*

Anaheim Bay, once part of an extensive system of coastal marshes, consists of an outer harbor formed by jetties, an inner harbor dredged to accommodate ocean-going ships, and a wetland system of salt marsh, mudflats, and tidal channels. The area's original inhabitants were Gabrielino Indians, who fished the bay and gathered mussels and clams; several shell mounds have been found in the marshland. In 1784, Manuel Nieto, a retired soldier, received a 300,000-acre land grant from the Spanish government that included Anaheim Bay; 50 years later the land was partitioned, and the bay was re-granted in a 28,000-acre parcel called Rancho Los Alamitos. The rancho was purchased in 1842 by Abel Stearns, at one time Southern Califonia's largest landowner, and was used for cattle and sheep grazing. In the late 1880s, farmers began draining the Anaheim Bay marshland for agriculture. The bay is named for the German colony of Anaheim, located inland on the Santa Ana River; in 1864, the colony founded a port on the bay at Seal Beach to ship wine and agricultural products.

In 1944, the U.S. Navy acquired 5,000 acres of the bay for construction of the Naval Weapons Station, which receives, stores, and issues ammunition for the Pacific Fleet. The Navy constructed jetties to form the outer harbor, dredged the inner harbor, and built wharves, docks, and other facilities in part of the marshland. In 1954, oil drilling began in the bay from the manmade "Oil Island," and in 1962, the community of Huntington Harbour was developed in the southeast portion of the bay, known as Sunset Bay. Several hundred acres of productive marshland remain, and are protected as the Seal Beach National Wildlife Refuge.

Seal Beach National Wildlife Refuge: *N.E. of Pacific Coast Hwy., Seal Beach.*

The Seal Beach National Wildlife Refuge preserves 911 acres of salt marsh and upland area in Anaheim Bay. The refuge was established in 1972 in reaction to a proposed freeway through the bay's remaining marshland. The refuge is located within the boundaries of the U.S. Naval Weapons Station, and there is no public access; for information, call: (805) 725-2767.

Although oil drilling continues on Oil Island, the Anaheim Bay marshland is highly productive, and receives ample tidal circulation. The diverse salt marsh community includes pickleweed, cordgrass, saltwort, saltgrass, and alkali heath. The marsh and the adjacent mudflats support worms, snails, clams, and beetles, and provide foraging and resting grounds for migratory shorebirds and waterfowl. Black-crowned night herons, black-necked stilts, long-billed marsh wrens, and endangered Belding's savannah sparrows are permanent residents; the endangered light-footed clapper rail has his-

torically inhabited the marsh, but its numbers are declining.

The upland areas support plants such as tree tobacco, coyote brush, and mustard, and are inhabited by coast horned lizards, side-blotched lizards, western rattlesnakes, San Diego gopher snakes, opossums, harvest mice, long-tailed weasels, and raccoons. Restoration projects in the bay have included the re-establishment of salt marsh in 100 acres of landfill, and the construction of a nesting area for endangered California least terns.

Sunset Aquatic Regional Park: *W. end of Edinger Ave., Huntington Beach.*

In 1962, Orange County acquired 63 acres of Anaheim Bay from the Navy, and filled the site to build a public marina and park. The park provides boat slips, boat ramps, picnic areas, and bicycle paths. Adjacent to the park is the Seal Beach National Wildlife Refuge, where shorebirds, ducks, herons, and California least terns may be seen feeding in the marshlands. For information, call: (714) 834-6106.

Surfside: *Anderson St. and Pacific Coast Hwy., Seal Beach.*

Located on the south spit of Anaheim Bay, Surfside is a locked-gate residential community within the City of Seal Beach. Pedestrian and bicycle access to Surfside Beach, which is popular for surfing and swimming, is through the Anderson Street gate. Ring-billed gulls, western gulls, shorebirds, and Pismo clams can be found on the beach.

Sunset Beach: *S.E. of Surfside, W. of Pacific Coast Hwy., Huntington Beach.*

Established in 1905 as a resort, the oceanfront community of Sunset Beach was developed during the real estate boom that followed the discovery of oil at nearby Seal Beach and Huntington Beach. In 1954, the town's own oil field was discovered. The wide, sandy beach provides restrooms and volleyball nets; access is from street ends between Anderson St. and Warner Avenue.

Huntington Harbour: *E. of Pacific Coast Hwy., Huntington Beach.*

Built in 1962 in the marshland of southeast Anaheim Bay, inland of Sunset Beach, Huntington Harbour is a private waterfront community within the city of Huntington Beach. Although most docks are private, the harbor provides some commercial boat slips and repair facilities. The Warner Avenue Boat Launch is located north of Warner Ave., near Pacific Coast Highway. Small public beaches are at the east end of 11th St., at the intersection of Davenport Dr. and Edgewater Lane, and at Humboldt Dr. and Mandalay Circle. Trinidad Island, a small residential island at the end of Trinidad Ave., has a public fishing dock off Venture Dr., a waterfront park at the corner of Trinidad Ave. and Typhoon Lane, and a bike path and walkway. For information, call the Harbormaster: (714) 846-2873, or in emergencies: (714) 834-3800.

Orange groves and oil fields north of Huntington Beach, ca. 1920s

Bolsa Chica: *E. of Pacific Coast Hwy., S. of Warner Ave., Huntington Beach.*

Originally a 2,300-acre estuary, Bolsa Chica, meaning "little pocket" in Spanish, has undergone major changes since 1890 when much of the marshland was drained for farming. In 1899, sportsmen built a dam across outer Bolsa Bay to restrict tidal flow into the marsh, and constructed ponds and levees to facilitate duck hunting. The outer bay's ocean opening soon silted up, so the hunters dug a channel from the bay into what is now Huntington Harbour. In

1920, oil was found at Bolsa Chica, and roads, drilling pads, and pipelines have since been built throughout the lowland.

In spite of continued oil production, Bolsa Chica still provides essential wildlife habitat. In 1973, the state established the Bolsa Chica Ecological Reserve on 557.5 acres, including outer Bolsa Bay. Tidal flow was restored to 140 acres in 1978, and two nesting islands for endangered California least terns were built. Future development and restoration plans for Bolsa Chica include a marina, a residential community,

regional parks and trails, and a 915-acre restored wetland.

Habitats within Bolsa Chica include open water, intertidal mudflats, and a diverse salt marsh community of cordgrass, pickleweed, saltgrass, jaumea, and marsh heather. Non-tidal portions of the lowland contain solid stands of pickleweed, salt flats, ponds, and grasses. Iceplant, sea rocket, and sand verbena grow on the dunes between the lowland and Pacific Coast Highway. The surrounding mesas support grasses, tree tobacco, prickly pear cactus, and eucalyptus.

Wildlife includes side-blotched lizards, gopher snakes, rattlesnakes, opossums, and skunks; kestrels, hawks, and owls hunt over the mesas, and Monarch butterflies overwinter in the eucalyptus trees. The salt marsh supports water boatmen, brine flies, and endangered Belding's savannah sparrows; shorebirds forage for invertebrates in the mudflats, and waterfowl feed in the open water. Herons, terns, and endangered California brown pelicans fish for killifish, sculpin, and arrow gobies. A parking lot at Warner Ave. and Pacific Coast Highway provides fishing access to the outer bay; a trail with interpretive signs begins at a lot across the highway from the beach entrance.

Above outer Bolsa Bay is a midden known as the Cogged Stone Site, which has yielded over 400 carved, disc-shaped stones dated to around 2500 B.C. Cogged stones, whose purpose is un-

Bolsa Chica Ecological Reserve

known, have been found in only two areas in the Western Hemisphere—coastal Southern California and Central Chile.

Bolsa Chica State Beach: *W. of Pacific Coast Hwy., S. of Warner Ave., Huntington Beach.*

Facilities at the northern half of the six-mile-long sandy beach include restrooms, enroute campsites, and a wheelchair ramp across the sand. The bluff-backed southern portion is accessible from Pacific Coast Highway. A cement path extends the length of the beach, eventually connecting to the Santa Ana River Trail to the southeast. Shorebirds rest and feed on the beach, and Pismo clams can be found in the surf zone. Grunion runs occur between March and August. Call: (714) 846-3460.

City of Huntington Beach: *Off Pacific Coast Hwy., N.W. of the Santa Ana River.*

First inhabited by Native Americans 6,000 years ago, the mesas of Huntington Beach were included in the Nieto land grant of 1784. Cattle were grazed on the mesas until the 1880s, when ranching was replaced by crop farming. In 1901, developers built a resort they hoped would rival Atlantic City; the new resort, first called Pacific City, was given its current name in 1903 to entice Henry Huntington to extend his Pacific Electric Railway to the area. Huntington's trolley cars arrived with vacationers from Los Angeles the following year, but it was not until oil was discovered in 1920 that Huntington Beach began to grow, eventually becoming Orange County's largest coastal city.

Oil production continues today, but Huntington Beach is perhaps best known for the excellent surfing at Huntington City Beach. Huntington Central Park, at Talbert Ave. and Golden West St., features lakes, playgrounds, trails, and an 18-acre nature reserve. The city's oldest building is the Newland House, located at 19820 Beach Blvd. and open Monday-Saturday, 1 PM-4 PM. A Victorian farmhouse built in 1889, the building is a reminder of the city's agricultural origins.

Colonial Inn Hostel: *421 8th St., Huntington Beach.*

The Colonial Inn Hostel occupies a three-story Victorian built as a hotel in 1903. Located four blocks from the beach, the 40-bed hostel is open year-round and provides showers, a kitchen, and a barn for bike storage. Call ahead for information on availability: (714) 536-3315.

Huntington City Beach: *W. of Pacific Coast Hwy., between Main St. and Beach Blvd., Huntington Beach.*

The site of international surfing competitions, the beach provides restrooms and volleyball courts; R.V. camping is available September 15-May 31. Surfing is allowed only in the morning or when the beach is uncrowded. The Huntington Beach Pier, built in 1914, provides snack bars, a cafe, and a tackle shop, and is floodlit at night. At the foot of the pier is a bust of Duke Kahanamoku, the Hawaiian Olympic swimmer who popularized surfing in California in 1911.

Huntington State Beach: *W. of Pacific Coast Hwy., Beach Blvd. to Santa Ana River, Huntington Beach.*

The sandy beach provides restrooms, enroute camping, wheelchair ramps, and a cement path. At the southern end of the beach is a five-acre preserve for the endangered California least tern. Pismo clams may be found on the beach; garibaldi, sand bass, and Pacific barracuda inhabit the offshore waters. Call: (714) 536-1454.

Santa Ana River: *Off Pacific Coast Hwy., 2.2 mi. S. of Beach Blvd., Huntington Beach.*

Named by the Portolá expedition in 1769, the Santa Ana River is the southernmost river of the Los Angeles Basin. The river, which historically changed channels many times, once flowed through a 3,000-acre marshy estuary into Lower Newport Bay, but was rechanneled in 1921 to enter the ocean directly; the lower portion of the river is now completely channelized. However, 114 acres of wetlands persist north of Pacific Coast Highway from Beach Blvd. east to the river channel. Known as the Huntington Beach Wetlands, this productive area supports pickleweed, saltgrass, bulrush, and cattail, and provides important nesting habitat for Belding's savannah sparrows, and feeding grounds for gulls, least terns, shorebirds, and waterfowl. Additional wetlands, vegetated primarily with pickleweed, are found east of the river channel. Victoria Pond, a freshwater pond east of the river channel off Victoria St., supports marsh and riparian vegetation, and is frequented by water birds. The Santa Ana River Trail, used by cyclists, pedestrians, and equestrians, follows the channel from the river mouth inland to Yorba Linda, at the base of the Chino Hills.

The infamous Santa Ana winds are named for the Santa Ana Canyon, but occur throughout the Los Angeles Basin. The winds form in fall and winter when air in the interior deserts piles up against the Transverse Ranges and begins streaming down the mountain passes toward the coast. The air heats as it moves downhill, and may raise temperatures at the coast to over 100 degrees. Because coastal hills are driest in fall, the hot, dry winds pose a serious fire hazard. The winds may reach gale strength—up to 60 miles per hour—and can create dangerous waves offshore.

Huntington Beach

Santa Ana River County Beach: *W. of Seashore Dr., Newport Beach.*

Access to the sandy beach east of the Santa Ana River is from street ends between Summit and 61st streets. Resident western gulls and wintering ring-billed gulls rest and feed on the beach, which is popular for surfing and clamming.

City of Costa Mesa: *S.E. of Santa Ana River, N.E. of Pacific Coast Hwy.*

Once a small farming community known as Harper, Costa Mesa was subdivided in 1915. The city's current name, chosen in a contest, is derived from Spanish to suggest "coastal tableland." A Gabrielino village called Lukup once occupied the bluffs above the Santa Ana River; Indian artifacts and shell mounds have been found here. In 1823, an adobe was built near the Santa Ana River as a way station for priests traveling between Missions San Gabriel and San Juan Capistrano. After the mission lands were partitioned by the Mexican government, the adobe became the property of Diego Sepúlveda. Located at 1900 Adams Ave., the adobe is now a museum; call: (714) 754-5300. The Orange County Fairgrounds, at 88 Fair Dr., is the site of the annual county fair, held in July; call: (714) 751-3247.

City of Newport Beach: *Off Pacific Coast Hwy., S.E. of Huntington Beach.*

In 1873, James and Robert McFadden established a lumber business and shipping center on the large bay at the mouth of the Santa Ana River. The landing, which they called Newport, shipped out local grain, produce, and cattle, and received much of the lumber that built Orange, Riverside, and San Bernardino counties. Because the shallow bay was treacherous for ocean-going ships, the McFaddens eventually moved their business to the ocean side of the Balboa Peninsula and built a wharf near the quiet waters above a submarine canyon. In 1891 the brothers completed a rail line between Santa Ana and the wharf. They bought land on the peninsula and named the town that sprang up around the wharf Newport Beach. When it became apparent that the wharf could not compete with San Pedro Bay in Los Angeles County, the McFaddens sold their business and their townsite to developer William S. Collins. Collins was joined by Henry Huntington, who brought his Pacific Electric Railway south to Newport in 1905. The arrival of Huntington's Red Cars, which connected Newport Beach with Los Angeles to the north, led to the city's incorporation the following year.

Through the 1930s, the city developed as a beach resort comprising the distinct communities of Newport, Balboa, Balboa Island, and Corona del Mar. Hollywood film stars such as John Wayne, James Cagney, and Errol Flynn made their homes here or kept yachts in the bay; tourists rented cottages and pitched tents on the beach, and residents from nearby inland areas

built summer homes here. The post-World War II building boom brought freeways and suburbs to the former agricultural lands around Newport, and while the city's resort atmosphere persists, it has experienced extensive residential and commercial development.

The Natural History Museum of Orange County, at 2627 Vista Del Oro, offers exhibits of local geology, archaeology, and ecology. The museum conducts research on paleontology, and has one of the largest collections of marine fossils in the U.S.; for information, call: (714) 640-7121. The Newport Harbor Art Museum at 850 San Clemente Dr. features contemporary art, emphasizing the work of Southern California artists; call: (714) 759-1122.

Newport Bay: *Pacific Coast Hwy., 3.5 mi. S.E. of the Santa Ana River.*

Newport Bay, with one of the state's largest pleasure harbors, comprises an upper bay carved by river flow during the Pleistocene and a lower bay formed by sediments from the Santa Ana River. The upper bay, a narrow channel between the Newport Mesa and the San Joaquin Hills, originally opened directly to the ocean; in 1825, floodwaters of the Santa Ana River deposited a sand spit extending southeast from the river mouth, thereby creating a wide lagoon below the mouth of the upper bay.

The naturally protected lower bay was first used as a harbor by the McFadden brothers in the late 1800s; however, with its shallow waters and numerous sandbars, the bay proved hazardous for navigation. After the incorporation of the city of Newport Beach, local officials, hoping to

Newport Beach, ca. 1908

develop the bay as a commercial port, lobbied for harbor improvements. Initial work began in 1917, when a jetty was built along the west side of the harbor mouth and the Santa Ana River was diverted from the bay. However, it was not until 1936 that jetty construction and channel dredging were completed and Newport Harbor was officially dedicated as a small boat harbor.

Virtually the entire shoreline of the lower bay is developed for residential and commercial purposes, and the former marshlands have been converted to exclusive island villages featuring posh waterfront homes. The upper bay, however, contains hundreds of acres of productive wetlands, and is protected as the state-owned Upper Newport Bay Ecological Reserve.

Newport Harbor has been a premier yachting center since 1911, when Newport's first yacht club was founded; the harbor is the starting point for the famous Ensenada Race, a 125-mile sailboat race to Baja California held each May. Another annual event is the Christmas Festival of Lights, a nighttime procession of lighted boats. The harbor provides commercial slips, marine supplies, and boat repair facilities. Marina Park, at Balboa Blvd. and 16th St., is a small boat launching area with picnic tables. Newport Dunes Aquatic Park, on Backbay Dr. west of Jamboree Rd., provides swimming and boating access to the bay, and contains day use, boat repair, and camping facilities; call: (714) 644-0510. Harbor cruises depart from the Balboa Pavilion; for information, call: (714) 673-5245. Harbormaster: (714) 834-2654.

Newport Pier: *W. of Ocean Front St., S. of McFadden Place, Newport Beach.*

The oldest pier on the Southern California coast, Newport Pier was built in 1888 as a wharf for trains carrying farm products and passengers from Santa Ana, and soon became the center of a small fishing village. In 1922 the City of Newport Beach bought the wharf and redesigned it as a public fishing pier. Today, anglers fish for white croaker, sculpin, California halibut, and jacksmelt from the pier. The Newport Dory Fishing Fleet, founded in 1891, heads out to sea each morning at dawn and returns to the pier around 9:30 AM to sell its catch, which typically includes crab, lobster, mackerel, rock-

fish, greenling, and seabass. A paved boardwalk along the beach extends from 36th St. to K St. near the tip of the Balboa Peninsula.

The sandy beach north of the pier suffered extensive erosion during the 1960s due to reduced sand supply from local streams. The beach is now stabilized by eight rubblemound groins that trap sand being carried downcoast by longshore currents. Much of the sand is eventually lost in the Newport Submarine Canyon, which begins offshore of the pier, and is thought to have been formed by a series of processes including deflection of littoral drift. Deepwater species such as giant squid, sablefish, and striped marlin are found close to shore here.

Dory Fishing Fleet, Newport Beach

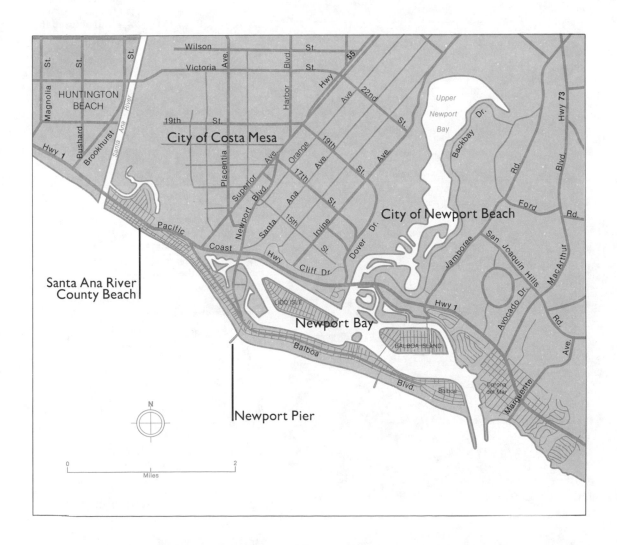

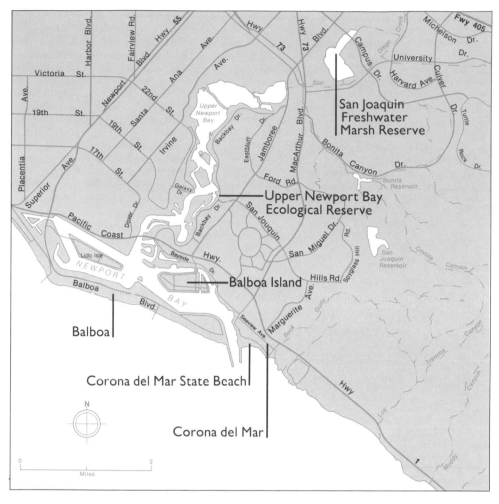

Upper Newport Bay Ecological Reserve

Balboa: *Eastern portion of Balboa Peninsula, New-port Beach.*

The community of Balboa was established as a beach resort in 1905 by a group of local pro-moters who built the Balboa Pier and Pavilion to attract tourism and settlement to the area. Balboa was incorporated in 1906 as part of the City of Newport Beach, yet has retained its own dis-tinct identity. The wide, sandy beach, which draws huge crowds of surfers and sunbathers in the summer, is reached via street ends along Balboa Boulevard. Jetty View Park, at the south end of Channel Rd., is a shaded park adjacent to the West Jetty of Newport Harbor. In the elbow of the jetty is the Wedge, a body surfing area famous for its enormous waves.

The Balboa Pier, at the foot of Main St., provides a restaurant and a tackle shop. A mark-er commemorates the 1912 flight of Glenn L. Martin from the pier to Catalina Island. The flight was the first water-to-water flight, and the longest and fastest overwater flight to that date. Adjacent to the pier is Peninsula Park, with a baseball diamond and picnic tables.

Across the peninsula from the pier, at 400 Main St., is the Balboa Pavilion, a cupola-topped Victorian building facing Newport Bay. The terminus for the Pacific Electric Railway, the pavilion was a dance hall through the 1940s, and became the center of seaside recreation in Newport Beach. Restored in 1962, the pavilion now houses a restaurant and a tackle store. Sightseeing tours of Newport Bay, whale-watch cruises, and passenger service to Catalina Is-land are available; for information, call: (714) 673-5245. Skiff rentals and charter boats are also available; call: (714) 673-1434. Adjacent to the pavilion is the Fun Zone, a small amusement area featuring rides and arcades.

Balboa Island: *S. of Pacific Coast Hwy. on Marine Ave., Newport Beach.*

In 1906, developer William Collins built an island on 90 acres of mudflats in Newport Bay and laid out a residential community. Named for the nearby community of Balboa, the island was annexed by Newport Beach in 1916, and soon became one of the city's principal villages. The island can be reached by a bridge from the mainland, or by an auto ferry from the Balboa Pavilion. A bayfront boardwalk provides access to boat slips and small sandy beaches.

To the north of Balboa Island is Lido Isle, also built on bay tidelands. In 1928, Swiss architect Franz Herding designed a village on the island modeled after the Lido, an Italian island resort; the community features Italian, Spanish, and French street names, and Mediterranean-style homes with red tile roofs.

Upper Newport Bay Ecological Reserve: *W. of Backbay Dr., Newport Beach.*

Established in 1975 and managed by the De-partment of Fish and Game, the ecological re-serve protects 752 acres of productive wetland habitat. Most of the shallow bay is exposed at low tide, and consists of intertidal mudflats and an extensive salt marsh community of cord-grass, pickleweed, saltgrass, jaumea, and the endangered salt marsh bird's beak. Stands of rush, cattail, tule, and willow occur where fresh-water runoff enters the bay, and along portions of the channelized San Diego Creek, the bay's tributary stream. The surrounding bluffs sup-

Balboa Pavilion

port prickly pear cactus, bush sunflower, black sage, and lemonadeberry.

The bay's marsh and mudflats are home to an array of invertebrates, including polychaete worms, California horn snails, littleneck and chione clams, bay mussels, ghost shrimp, crabs, brine flies, and rove beetles. Ocean-dwelling fish such as California halibut, white croaker, and barred sandbass depend on the bay as a spawning and nursery ground; the deepbody anchovy, California killifish, arrow goby, and longjaw mudsucker are year-round residents.

From September through March, thousands of birds, including dowitchers, willets, plovers, sandpipers, pintails, shovelers, and buffleheads, may be seen foraging on exposed mudflats, dabbling in shallow water near the lower marsh, or diving in tidal channels. The marsh vegetation provides nesting habitat for the light-footed clapper rail and Belding's savannah sparrow, both endangered species. The adjacent upland areas are inhabited by reptiles, raptors, owls, songbirds, and small mammals.

Upper Newport Bay is accessible on the west side at North Star Beach, located on North Star Lane off Polaris Dr.; there are also overlooks on Galaxy Drive. Backbay Dr., a one-way road that follows the east shore of the bay, provides parking, overlooks, and access to a small boat launch. Friends of Newport Bay offers guided bird watching tours during fall and winter; for information, call: (714) 646-8009.

San Joaquin Freshwater Marsh Reserve:
Campus Dr. near Jamboree Rd., Irvine.

Part of the University of California Natural Reserve System, the reserve protects 202 acres of disturbed freshwater wetlands above Upper Newport Bay; these wetlands, remnants of an extensive marsh system along the Santa Ana River and San Diego Creek, have been diked, dammed, and partially filled. Thousands of migratory birds use the wetlands each winter.

Dense stands of tules, bulrushes, and willows shelter amphibians, western pond turtles, perching birds, and small mammals. In addition to preserving one of the few significant freshwater wetlands remaining in coastal Southern California, the reserve is used for teaching and research by the University of California at Irvine; access is by permit or with guided tours only. The U.C. Cooperative Outdoor Program offers public tours of the reserve October-May; call: (714) 856-5181. For information on special group tours or obtaining permits, call the Reserve Steward: (714) 856-6031.

Corona del Mar State Beach: *Ocean Blvd. and Iris Ave., Corona Del Mar.*

The sandy beach, a popular surfing and diving spot, provides parking, restrooms, and day use facilities. The adjacent East Jetty of Newport Harbor and the offshore reefs attract fish such as garibaldi, California sheephead, and California halibut, as well as lobster and octopus. The beach affords views of the harbor mouth, where the S.S. *Minnow*'s departure was filmed for the television series "Gilligan's Island." For information, call: (714) 644-3047.

Corona del Mar: *Off Pacific Coast Hwy., S.E. of Newport Harbor, Newport Beach.*

The blufftop community of Corona del Mar, whose name means "Crown of the Sea," was subdivided in 1904 by developer George E. Hart on 700 acres he had purchased from the extensive Irvine Ranch. To assure a reliable water supply, the community voted in 1923 to annex to Newport Beach.

Little Corona del Mar Beach, at Ocean Blvd. and Poppy Ave., is a sandy cove with rocky tidepools and reefs. The intertidal and nearshore areas are part of the Newport Beach Marine Life Refuge, and support numerous species of algae, invertebrates, and fish. Buck Gully, a small stream canyon that opens onto the beach, is lushly vegetated with riparian and sage scrub plants, and is inhabited by frogs, lizards, birds, and small mammals. Other sandy beaches in Corona del Mar include Pirates Cove Beach, adjacent to the Coast Guard Station at 1911 Bayside Dr., and China Cove Beach, between Dahlia and Carnation streets.

Crystal Cove State Park: *W. of Pacific Coast Hwy., S. of Corona del Mar.*

Established in 1979 on land acquired from the Irvine Ranch, the 2,791-acre state park encompasses 3.25 miles of scenic shoreline between Corona del Mar and Laguna Beach, and most of the Moro Canyon watershed in the San Joaquin Hills. Parking and access to sandy, bluff-backed pocket beaches are provided at Pelican Point, Crystal Cove, and Reef Point; a parking area at El Moro provides access to trails into Moro Canyon. Other facilities include wheelchair-accessible restrooms, picnic areas, and a bike path on the bluffs. A campground at El Moro and hike-in and equestrian campsites in Moro Canyon are planned. Call: (714) 494-3539.

The park's long, sandy beach, interrupted by rocky points, is backed by steep sandstone bluffs. Atop the bluffs is a marine terrace that supports introduced grasses and coastal sage

scrub plants such as black sage and bush sunflower; the many-stemmed dudleya and Turkish rugging, both endangered plants, are also found here. Chaparral and riparian woodland occur in Moro Canyon. Park wildlife includes side-blotched lizards, San Diego gopher snakes, red-tailed hawks, California quail, striped skunks, and southern mule deer. The rocky intertidal area supports algae, surfgrass, anemones, California mussels, turban snails, and shore crabs. Rockfish, California sheephead, and kelp bass inhabit the nearshore waters. The shoreline and nearshore waters have been designated as the Irvine Coast Marine Life Refuge.

At the time of the arrival of Spanish missionaries, the park area was within the territory of the Gabrielino Indians, and numerous village sites, shell mounds, and tool remains have been found. The area was later included in the vast grazing lands of Mission San Juan Capistrano, and, following secularization, the shoreline and the hills were granted as Rancho San Joaquín to José Sepúlveda. After the devastating drought of 1864, Sepúlveda sold his property to San Francisco merchant and real estate speculator James Irvine and his partners. Twelve years later Irvine bought out his partners, becoming the county's largest landowner. His son later incorporated to form the Irvine Company, and diversified the ranch pastures into one of the most productive farms in the state. The ranch's main activities were centered in the inland area, and the coastal strip was largely ignored.

In the 1920s a small resort community called Crystal Cove was established on leased land on the marine terrace above the beach; the community, which consists of some 46 wood-frame cot-

tages, has remained virtually unchanged since the 1940s and was recently added to the National Register of Historic Places. The completion of the Coast Highway in 1926 drew Japanese-American truck farmers to the area. Until their relocation during World War II, they grew string beans, tomatoes, and peas inland of the highway, selling their produce at roadside stands. Since then, the coastal area has been used primarily for cattle grazing, and now constitutes the county's longest stretch of undeveloped shoreline.

Heisler Park: *W. of Cliff Dr., Laguna Beach.*

Heisler Park, which consists of a palm tree-lined grassy strip on the bluffs above several small coves, provides picnic tables, restrooms, shuffleboard courts, and a lawn bowling green. A paved walkway that extends to Main Beach affords views of the picturesque Laguna Beach coastline. Below Heisler Park are Picnic Beach and Rock Pile Beach, two sandy coves used for swimming, surfing, and diving. Bottle-nosed dolphins and common dolphins are occasionally seen offshore. Crescent Bay Point Park to the north is a good whale-watching spot, and provides views of Seal Rocks, the coastline, and Catalina and San Clemente islands.

Laguna Beach Marine Life Refuge: *Shoreline and nearshore area from Crescent Bay to Main Beach.*

The marine life refuge comprises the shoreline and nearshore waters from the northern end of Crescent Bay to the northern end of Main Beach. The rocky intertidal area is inhabited by California mussels, limpets, snails, barnacles, shore crabs, and several species of algae. Subtidal reefs support forests of giant kelp, and pro-

Picnic Beach at Heisler Park

vide a habitat for fish such as the kelp rockfish, California sheephead, señorita, and giant kelpfish. Cormorants, endangered California brown pelicans, and California sea lions rest on offshore rocks. Within the refuge is the 30-acre Glenn E. Vedder Ecological Reserve, named for the mayor of Laguna Beach; no fishing is allowed in the reserve, and collecting of tidepool organisms is prohibited throughout the marine life refuge. For information, call: (714) 494-6572.

City of Laguna Beach: *Along Pacific Coast Hwy., 6 mi. S. of Corona del Mar.*

One of the few areas on the Orange County coast not originally included in a Mexican land grant, Laguna Beach was first homesteaded by settlers in the 1870s. Its picturesque sandy coves and backdrop of rugged hills soon made it a favorite vacation spot for inland residents, who traveled rough wagon roads through Laguna and Aliso canyons to set up camp on the beach. Artists began to congregate in the growing resort town, attracted by its beauty and isolation. In 1926 the Coast Highway opened, bringing vacationers from the north and south.

Laguna Beach remains both a popular resort area and an art colony, and numerous shops and galleries feature the work of local artists. The city sponsors three annual art festivals, which run from July through mid-August. The most famous of these is the Festival of Arts and its Pageant of the Masters, in which models pose to create tableaux of famous works of art; call: (714) 494-1145. The Friends of the Sea Lion Marine Mammal Center, located at 20612 Laguna Canyon Rd., rescues, treats, and releases seals and sea lions found stranded on Orange County beaches. The volunteer-staffed center is open to the public, and offers programs for groups; for information or to report an injured animal, call: (714) 494-3050.

Main Beach: *W. end of Broadway, W. of Pacific Coast Hwy., Laguna Beach.*

Located at the mouth of Laguna Canyon, this popular, crescent-shaped sandy beach attracts swimmers, surfers, and anglers. Facilities include volleyball nets, a grassy area with basketball courts, picnic areas, a boardwalk, and restrooms. Numerous small sandy beaches and coves are found north of Main Beach from Circle Way to Jasmine St., and south of the beach to Dumond Drive.

Aliso Beach County Park: *31000 block of Pacific Coast Hwy., South Laguna.*

The sandy beach at the mouth of Aliso Creek is used for body surfing, surf fishing, and scuba diving. Facilities include parking, wheelchair-accessible restrooms, a picnic area, and a bike trail. Aliso Creek, whose name is Spanish for alder, is a 19-mile-long intermittent stream arising in the Santa Ana Mountains; the endangered Laguna Beach dudleya grows in the creek canyon. The Aliso Pier, built in 1972, is a 620-foot-long fishing pier that projects from the shore to a diamond-shaped head. Anglers catch white croaker, California halibut, jacksmelt, mackerel, and surfperch. The southern portion of the beach and offshore waters have been designated as the South Laguna Marine Life Refuge. Offshore of the beach are beds of giant kelp and a commercial fishing area for spiny lobster.

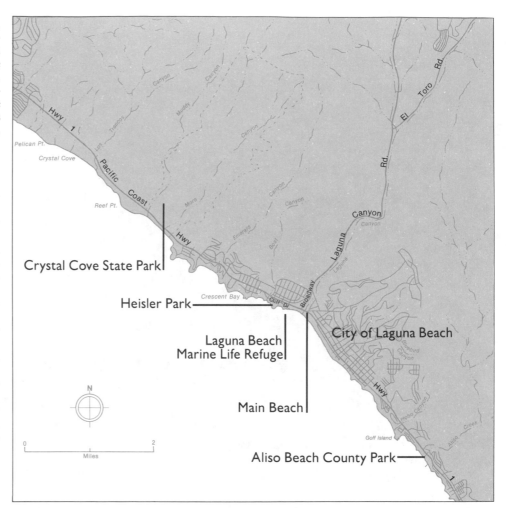

Main Beach, Laguna Beach

Pilgrim *replica, Dana Point Harbor*

South Laguna: *Off Pacific Coast Hwy., S.E. of Laguna Beach.*

South Laguna is built upon steep, high bluffs that rise above cove beaches separated by rocky points. Like Laguna Beach to the north, South Laguna was excluded from lands granted by the Mexican government in the mid-1800s, and was homesteaded by white settlers in the 1870s. The small farming and fishing community that evolved here remained fairly isolated until the opening of the Pacific Coast Highway in 1926, which led to development of the area as a beach resort for Los Angeles residents. In the 1920s and 1930s, the scenic local beaches were used as settings for several Hollywood films, including *Captain Blood* with Errol Flynn, and *The Life of Emile Zola* with Paul Muni. The resort community was at first called Three Arches for a rock formation on the beach, but in 1934 the name was changed to South Laguna, after the city of Laguna Beach to the north.

The sandy Coast Royale Beach can be reached via stairways at the end of West Street. A sandy cove beach is accessible at Thousand Steps, a long stairway located opposite Ninth Ave. off Pacific Coast Highway. Littleneck clams can be found on the beach; the nearshore waters support California corbina, jack mackerel, opaleye, and California sheephead.

Several thousand acres on the undeveloped hills above South Laguna, known as the Aliso Greenbelt, have been designated for recreation and resource protection. The hills are vegetated with coastal sage scrub and chaparral plants; Wood Canyon, which opens into Aliso Creek, supports California sycamore, coast live oak, and interior live oak, which is normally found farther inland. Wildlife includes side-blotched lizards, gopher snakes, acorn woodpeckers, red-tailed hawks, brush rabbits, California mice, coyotes, and southern mule deer. A trail system is planned for the greenbelt; however, most of the area is not yet publicly owned. Nearby is Badlands Park, located on Isla Vista St. off Pacific Island Dr., west of Crown Valley Parkway. The park features unusual sandstone formations that have been eroded by wind and water, and affords a sweeping view of the coast.

Salt Creek Beach Park: *Pacific Coast Hwy. and Whitewater Dr., Laguna Niguel.*

The long, sandy Salt Creek Beach is a popular surfing spot. The southern entrance to the beach is at Laguna Niguel Beach Park, located off Selva Rd.; parking and restrooms are available at both entrances. The intertidal and nearshore areas have been designated the Niguel Marine Life Refuge.

The unincorporated community of Laguna Niguel was developed on the former Rancho Niguel, an 1842 Mexican land grant to Juan Ávila. Niguel is believed to have been the name of a nearby Juaneño Indian village.

Dana Point: *Off Pacific Coast Hwy., 7.5 mi. S.E. of Laguna Beach.*

Dana Point, a steep, massive headland, is named for author Richard Henry Dana, who anchored here in 1835 while a sailor on the brig *Pilgrim.* In the early 1800s the cove below the point was used as an anchorage for New England and British vessels trading with the nearby Mission San Juan Capistrano. Hides and tallow

Ken Sampson Lookout, Dana Point Harbor

obtained from the mission's cattle were brought to the cove and traded for manufactured goods, including shoes and boots made from California cowhides. During the 1830s and 1840s, hides were so important a trade item that they were referred to as "California banknotes." Dana, who described the California hide trade in his book *Two Years Before the Mast*, described the cove as "the only romantic spot on the coast." Dana Cove was also visited in 1818 by privateer Hippolyte de Bouchard, who, after attacking Monterey, landed here and looted the mission.

The Dana Point area was homesteaded in the late 1800s by settlers who farmed the marine terrace above the cove. In 1926 developer Sydney Woodruff subdivided the residential community of Dana Point; his extensive plans called for Mediterranean-style homes, a yacht harbor, a polo field, and different colored street lights for each street. This inspired such street names as Golden Lantern, Violet Lantern, and Silver Lantern. However, construction halted during the Depression, and Woodruff's plans failed to materialize. In the 1960s, residential and commercial development was spurred by construction of the Dana Point Harbor.

Dana Point Harbor and the coastline to the south can be viewed from Ken Sampson Lookout, located at the south end of Blue Lantern St., and from Heritage Park, near the foot of Golden Lantern Street. The headlands area of Dana Point is a good place for watching endangered California gray whales during their annual migration; common dolphins and bottle-nosed dolphins are also occasionally seen offshore. The rocky intertidal areas at the base of the bluffs, which support a variety of algae and invertebrates, and the San Juan Rocks offshore are included in the Dana Point Marine Life Refuge. The nearshore waters support spiny lobster, garibaldi, opaleye, kelp bass, and jack mackerel.

Dana Point Harbor: *Dana Point Harbor Dr. and Island Way, Dana Point.*

Completed in 1971, the Dana Point Harbor provides extensive boating facilities, including guest slips, a launch ramp, maintenance facilities, and marine supplies. Wheelchair-accessible restrooms, grassy areas with picnic tables, a boardwalk with restaurants and shops, a swimming beach, and a small fishing pier are also available. Anglers fish from the harbor breakwaters for barred sand bass, chub mackerel, California halibut, and Pacific bonito. For information on boat charters, sport fishing, and whale-watching cruises, call: (714) 496-5794. The Dana Point Harbor Festival of Whales, held from February 15-March 9, offers entertainment and educational programs pertaining to gray whales.

The Orange County Marine Institute, at 24200 Dana Point Harbor Dr., offers a variety of oceanographic classes and whale-watching tours for children, and contains exhibits on local natural history. The institute also conducts theater productions and children's programs on a replica of the hide ship *Pilgrim*. For information, call: (714) 496-2274.

Doheny State Beach: *Pacific Coast Hwy. and Dana Point Harbor Dr., Dana Point.*

The 62-acre state beach provides wheelchair-accessible restrooms, day use areas, and a campground; an interpretive facility is under construction. The wide, sandy beach is used for surf fishing, swimming, and surfing. A rocky intertidal area is located at the northern end of the beach. Anglers fish for black surfperch, walleye surfperch, and California halibut; divers take crab and lobster. Cormorants roost on Crawfish Rock offshore. The intertidal and nearshore areas constitute the Doheny Marine Life Refuge. For beach information, call: (714) 496-6171.

San Juan Creek, named for the nearby Mission San Juan Capistrano, enters the ocean at Doheny State Beach. In summer a sandbar closes off the mouth of the creek, forming a small lagoon that supports waterfowl, killdeer, avocets, egrets, and gulls. Tules and willows grow along the creek, sheltering songbirds and small mammals; saltgrass and brass buttons occur at the creek mouth. The San Juan Creek Bike Trail, which runs on the west side of the creek, and an equestrian trail that follows the east side begin just north of the beach.

Mission San Juan Capistrano

Mission San Juan Capistrano: *Ortega Hwy. and Camino Capistrano, San Juan Capistrano.*

Named for St. John of Capistrano, a 14th century Italian theologian, Mission San Juan Capistrano is situated near the banks of San Juan Creek, about three miles inland from the coast. The mission was dedicated by Father Junípero Serra in 1776, and a chapel was built the following year. In 1806 a larger church was completed; the most elaborate of the California mission churches, the building, made of carved sandstone, was designed in the shape of a cross, with a 120-foot bell tower and an arched roof with seven domes. However, the church was destroyed by earthquake only six years after it was built. The chapel and some of the outbuildings have been restored, but the large church is still in ruins. The chapel, known as Serra's Chapel, is believed to be the oldest California mission structure still standing. A new church, designed to resemble the ruined church, has been constructed on the mission grounds. The mission, which contains exhibits and a gift shop, is open daily; call: (714) 493-1111.

The Spanish called the native people they found living in the valley of San Juan Creek the Juaneño, after the mission. The Juaneño were inducted into the mission, where they labored in its farming and manufacturing operations. The Indian neophytes grew wheat, barley, corn, and grapes on mission lands, and raised cattle, horses, and sheep. They also produced olive oil, and tanned cattle hides and rendered tallow for trade. The native social and religious customs of the Juaneño were recorded by Gerónimo Boscana, the mission's priest from 1814 to 1826.

Sunday walking tours of the city of San Juan Capistrano begin at the mission; call: (714) 493-8444. In addition to several 19th century adobes, buildings of note include the Amtrak station at Los Rios St. near Verdugo St., built in 1894 in the Mission Revival style. The annual Heritage Festival, held in mid-March, celebrates the return of migratory cliff swallows from their wintering grounds in South America to their nests at the mission; call: (714) 493-4700.

Capistrano Beach: *Off Pacific Coast Hwy., S.E. of Dana Point.*

The residential community of Capistrano Beach is situated on a marine terrace above a stretch of sandy shoreline. The town was originally subdivided as San Juan By-The-Sea in 1887 by the Pacific Land Improvement Company, a subsidiary of the Santa Fe Railroad Company. The development of railroads in Southern California in the 1880s led to a real estate boom, and towns and resorts were laid out along future rail lines in anticipation of the arrival of vacationers and settlers. However, the land boom was short-lived, and San Juan By-The-Sea and other such projects failed. In 1925 developers created a second community, called

Capistrano Beach after the nearby city of San Juan Capistrano. During the Depression the property was taken over by Edward L. Doheny, an oil magnate who drilled the first successful oil well in Los Angeles in 1892. For a time the town was known as Doheny Park, but in 1948 the name was changed back to Capistrano Beach.

Capistrano Beach Park, at Pacific Coast Highway and Palisade Dr., provides access to the sandy beach south of Doheny State Beach; facilities include wheelchair-accessible restrooms, picnic areas, and bike trails. Louise Leyden Park, at the end of Via Verde off Camino Capistrano, affords views of the coastline.

Poche Beach: *Pacific Coast Hwy. and Camino Capistrano, Capistrano Beach.*

The sandy beach is reached by a stairway at the end of Camino Capistrano on the inland side of Pacific Coast Highway. Ring-billed gulls, western gulls, killdeer, and sanderlings rest and feed along the beach.

City of San Clemente: *Off I-5, just S. of Capistrano Beach.*

Named for San Clemente Island offshore, San Clemente was created in 1925 by Ole Hanson, a Wisconsin-born real estate dealer and one-time mayor of Seattle. Hanson's residential community, promoted as "The Spanish Village," featured wide, meandering streets that conformed to the contours of the hills, houses situated to provide an ocean view, and mandatory white stucco exteriors and red tile roofs for every building. San Clemente was incorporated in 1928, and grew rapidly until the Depression, when development halted. The growth rate picked up again during the 1950s, and was later boosted by construction of the San Diego Freeway.

San Clemente Municipal Pier

In 1769, while camped in the San Clemente area, priests accompanying the Portolá Expedition performed the first Catholic baptisms of California Indians. The event is commemorated in the annual La Cristianita ("the little Christian") Pageant, held for several days in July; call: (714) 498-0880. San Clemente is probably better known as the one-time residence of former President Richard Nixon. During Nixon's presidency, his blufftop estate, Casa Pacifica, was known as the "Western White House." Nixon, an Orange County native, sold his estate and left California in 1979.

San Clemente Hostel: *233 Avenida Granada, San Clemente.*

Located in the original San Clemente Public Library, the hostel provides 40 beds and a fully equipped kitchen, and is wheelchair accessible. Reservations are recommended in summer; call: (714) 492-2848.

San Clemente City Beach: *Beach area from Ave. Estacion to San Clemente State Beach, San Clemente.*

San Clemente's sandy shoreline can be reached from several street ends between Dije Court and Plaza a la Playa. The Ole Hanson Beach Club, located at the northern end of the city beach at Avenida Estacion, offers picnic tables, a playground, and a public pool. After its completion in 1928, the beach club was used by the U.S. Olympic swimming team. Linda Lane Park, located on Linda Lane, also provides access to the beach, and has parking, restrooms, and a playground.

San Clemente Municipal Pier: *W. end of Avenida Del Mar, San Clemente.*

Built by Ole Hanson in 1928, the 1,200-foot-long San Clemente Pier provides parking, wheelchair-accessible restrooms, a restaurant, and a tackle shop. The pier was severely damaged in the storms of 1983, but has since been renovated. Anglers fish from the pier for walleye surfperch, rubberlip surfperch, sculpin, and California corbina. The pier is adjacent to the Amtrak station, a popular disembarking point for beachgoers from Los Angeles.

San Clemente State Beach: *Off Avenida Calafia, San Clemente.*

The 100-acre state beach was established in 1931 on a blufftop above a sandy beach. Located near both Los Angeles and San Diego, the beach draws large crowds year-round; its warm waters attract surfers, body surfers, swimmers, and skin divers. The blufftop area, landscaped with palms, acacias, and other exotics, provides wheelchair-accessible restrooms, picnic areas,

and a campground; call : (714) 492-3156. The bluffs support coastal sage scrub plants such as coyote brush, lemonadeberry, goldfields, and prickly pear cactus. Animal life includes meadowlarks, sparrows, and small mammals such as ground squirrels, desert cottontails, and striped skunks. The beach is frequented by gulls and shorebirds. California sea lions haul out on the San Mateo Rocks offshore.

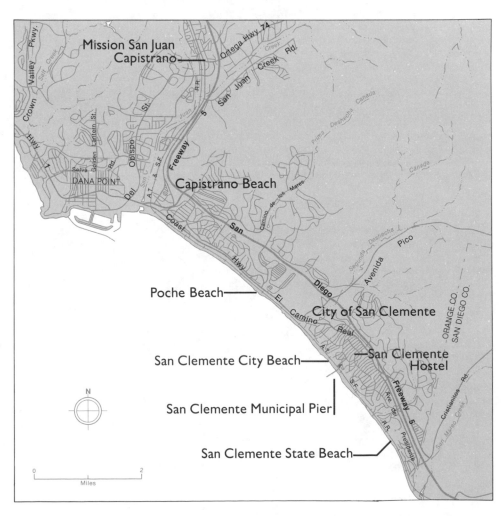

San Diego County
Selected Species of Interest

 Plants: Pickleweed (*Salicornia virginica*), an important food source for the endangered Belding's savannah sparrow. **Salt marsh daisy** (*Lasthenia glabrata*), found on salt flats at San Elijo and Los Peñasquitos lagoons.

 Trees: Torrey pine (*Pinus torreyana*), one of the world's rarest pine trees; found only at Torrey Pines State Reserve and on Santa Rosa Island **Fremont cottonwood** (*Populus fremontii*), a dominant tree at river edges.

 Insects: Salt marsh water boatman (*Trichocorixa reticulata*), lives exclusively in brackish or saltwater marshes. **Globose dune beetle** (*Coelus globosus*), candidate for endangered status; occurs on coastal dunes.

 Invertebrates: Red sea urchin (*Strongylocentrotus franciscanus*), largest California urchin; found in kelp beds. **California mussel** (*Mytilus californianus*), bluish-black bivalve, attaches firmly to surf-swept rocks.

 Amphibians and Reptiles: Pacific treefrog (*Hyla regilla*), small, green frog; can be seen in San Elijo Lagoon. **Western pond turtle** (*Clemmys marmorata*); a resident population lives in San Dieguito Lagoon.

 Fish: Garibaldi (*Hypsypops rubicundus*), distinctive gold-orange color; found in nearshore kelp beds. **California grunion** (*Leuresthes tenuis*), spawns on sandy beaches several nights after the full or new moon.

 Birds: Belding's savannah sparrow (*Passerculus sandwichensis beldingi*), endangered; year-round resident of coastal salt marshes. **California least tern** (*Sterna antillarum browni*), endangered; one of a few birds that nest on sandy beaches.

 Land Mammals: Brush rabbit (*Sylvilagus bachmani*), small, brown rabbit, commonly seen in chaparral. **Coyote** (*Canis latrans*), widespread throughout the county; noted for its distinctive yapping howl.

 Marine Mammals: Bottle-nosed dolphin (*Tursiops truncatus*), commonly seen offshore. **California sea lion** (*Zalophus californianus*), seen off the coast of San Onofre State Beach and the Coast Walk in La Jolla.

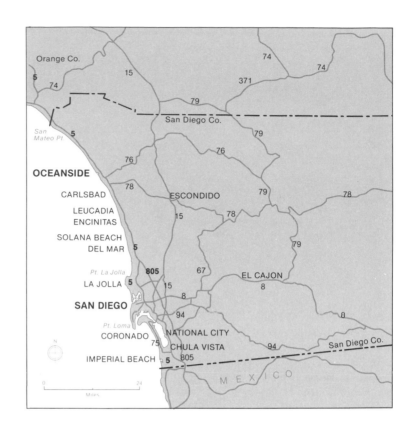

San Diego County

THE SAN DIEGO COAST was first inhabited by semi-nomadic hunter-gatherers who migrated west from the deserts along the Colorado River more than 10,000 years ago. Eight permanent settlements were established at various sites including La Jolla, the northern banks of the San Diego River, the south side of Mission Bay, the bay side of Point Loma, and along the shore of San Diego Bay.

The climate of San Diego was wetter and possibly warmer, and the land more wooded, than it is today. The native people hunted abundant deer, rabbits, and antelope with bows and arrows, and moved as season and food supply dictated. Acorns were their staple food, gathered from the live oak, white oak, and scrub oak. The natives fished both from shore and from a type of canoe made from bundles of tule.

This traditional lifestyle ended with the arrival of the Spanish in the early 1700s. The native people, named Diegueños by the Spanish missionaries from the Misión San Diego de Alcalá, were organized into groups to live at the mission where they were Christianized and taught to eat with spoons and wear clothes.

In 1542, the Portuguese-born explorer Juan Rodríguez Cabrillo, sailing under the flag of Spain, discovered the bay, which he named San Miguel. Sixty years later, Sebastián Vizcaíno entered the bay on the feast day of St. Didacus, known in Spanish as San Diego de Alcalá, and renamed the bay.

In the 1760s, with threats of Russian advancement into California, the expansion of the missions that had begun in Mexico continued northward. In 1769, Misión San Diego de Alcalá, the first of the 21 Alta California missions, was founded by Father Junípero Serra on what later became known as Presidio Hill; on the same spot, the first presidio or fort in California was also established. Agricultural crops including olives, oranges, grapes, plums, corn, and wheat were planted and herds of cattle were raised to supply food for the missionaries and Indians. The village that developed adjacent to the mission, known today as Old Town, became the center for Spanish domain in Alta California and, briefly, the northern terminus of El Camino Real, the King's Highway, which eventually led north to San Francisco.

For more than 50 years San Diego remained under Spanish rule. In 1821, Mexico declared its independence from Spain and gained control over Alta California until 1848. During this period, the missions were secularized and ranchos were granted to friends of the Mexican governors. Many place names and land divisions, including Rancho Santa Margarita y Las Flores, which is now Camp Pendleton, can be traced to these early land grants.

In 1850 California became a state and San Diego became a county and city. In the 1870s, the center of town shifted from Old Town, its plaza once noisy and dusty with bullfights and hangings, to the "new town" on San Diego Bay, which soon became the nucleus of the present city.

San Diego County's population boomed as the first railroads arrived in the late 1800s, and agriculture prospered with the construction of dams and the introduction of irrigation. In the early 1900s, the U.S. Navy built shipyards in the protected natural harbor of San Diego Bay for the construction and maintenance of the nation's largest West Coast fleet. In the 1920s, San Diego was the terminus of the first nonstop cross-continental flight, which originated in New York. Military facilities expanded during World War II, increasing San Diego's population. After the war, the balmy climate and employment opportunities drew a steady stream of newcomers.

Within the downtown area, a modern city of skyscrapers developed in the 1960s and 1970s. Massive urban renewal projects including renovation of the Gaslamp Quarter, with its historic and architecturally significant buildings, and Horton Plaza, a 15-block restoration project, were initiated in the late 1970s.

San Diego County, the "birthplace of California," is rich in history and geographic diversity. Extending south 76 miles from the Orange County line to the Mexican border, the county lures tourists as well as new residents with its temperate, sunny climate, extensive sandy beaches, deserts, mountains, museums, marinas, parks, Sea World, and the world-famous San Diego Zoo. North of La Jolla are raised marine terraces and beach ridges, coastal marshes and lagoons, and canyon-cut mesas. Seaside villages, fields of flowers, rows of citrus and avocado trees, and greenhouses dominate the landscape. South of La Jolla, the coast forms lowlands with estuaries, sandy beaches, tidepools, and coves. Inland valleys, oak woodlands, and deserts spread east, rising to mountain ranges over 6,000 feet high.

San Diego Harbor, ca. 1910

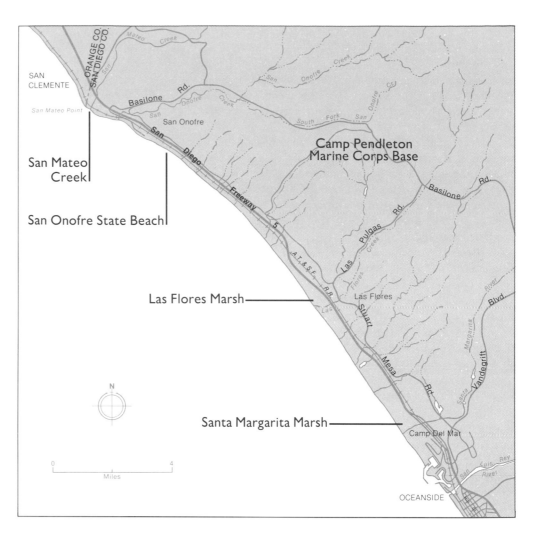

San Mateo Creek

San Mateo Creek: *Off I-5 at Basilone Rd., San Onofre.*

San Mateo Creek is an intermittent stream with a large drainage basin extending throughout Riverside, Orange, and San Diego counties. The mouth of the creek, which empties into the Pacific Ocean just southeast of the San Diego/ Orange County line, supports plant and animal species common to both freshwater and saltwater marshes. Cattail, bulrush, jaumea, saltgrass, and spike rush are the dominant plants found at the creek mouth. Waterfowl commonly seen in the marsh include coots and diving and dabbling ducks. Shorebirds such as sandpipers, and wading birds including herons, rails, and egrets use the vegetation at the mouth of the creek for food and shelter.

The canyon through which the creek flows is bordered by riparian woodland and hillsides of chaparral. Lemonadeberry, toyon, chamise, and laurel sumac are common chaparral species. Riparian vegetation includes such trees as sycamore, white alder, canyon live oak, black willow, and California bay laurel. San Mateo Creek canyon provides habitat for raptors, with nesting populations of black-shouldered kites and red-tailed hawks; these hawks are so named because the adults show red on the upper side of their tails when in flight.

Several species of pelagic fish such as corbina, white seabass, and barracuda inhabit the offshore waters. Surf fishing and clamming are popular on the beaches south of the San Onofre Nuclear Generating Station.

San Onofre State Beach: *S.W. of I-5 at Basilone Rd., San Onofre.*

San Onofre State Beach is a 3.5-mile-long sandy beach below sheer sandstone cliffs, named after the Egyptian Saint Onuphrius. The state beach includes Trestles Beach, a wetland area at the mouth of San Mateo Creek, and the adjacent San Onofre Surf Beach, a popular surfing spot, to the north of the San Onofre Nuclear

Generating Station. These beaches are separated from the undeveloped main beach to the south by a public walkway along the seawall of the nuclear plant. Some restrooms at the main beach are wheelchair accessible.

The San Onofre Nuclear Generating Station began commercial operation from its first unit in January, 1968. The nuclear reactors for Units 2 and 3, south of Unit 1, are contained in the 170-foot-high dome-shaped structures visible from the highway. Small cylindrical pellets of uranium dioxide are used to fuel the reactors. More than six million pellets are sealed into 28,000 high-strength tubes. These tubes are bundled together to form the reactor core, which is ten feet high and nearly ten feet in diameter. When operating at full capacity, the nuclear generating plant will provide electrical power for more than a million people.

Inland from the beaches are coastal terraces vegetated with lemonadeberry, toyon, and chamise. This chaparral community supports brush rabbits, raccoons, skunks, coyotes, deer, opossums, and several species of snakes. Birds such as owls, ospreys, black-shouldered kites, and rufous-sided towhees inhabit the denser interior of the chaparral zone.

Sea lions, harbor seals, common dolphins, and California gray whales can be observed from the blufftops and beaches. Between November and February, gray whales head southward to their calving grounds in Baja California; in spring, they move northward to feed in the Bering and Chukchi seas. Common gulls, sandpipers, and terns feed along the sandy beach. Halibut, bonito, sheephead, and jack mackerel live in the offshore waters. An artificial reef of quarry rock, built in 1980, lies about four miles southwest of the generating station.

A camping area with restrooms and outdoor showers is located on the bluffs above the main beach; primitive campsites are sited on a terrace between the bluffs and the main beach. For information, call: (714) 492-4872 or 492-0802.

Camp Pendleton Marine Corps Base: *North of Oceanside.*

A military base named after Joseph H. Pendleton, a veteran of the "banana wars" in Central America during the 1920s, Camp Pendleton borders 18 miles of ocean front. The base was the former site of Rancho Santa Margarita y Las Flores, once a part of Mission San Luis Rey. In 1823, the outpost of Las Flores was built to serve as a hospice for travelers between Missions San Luis Rey and San Juan Capistrano. The former ranch house of Pío Pico, the last of the Mexican governors, is also located on the base.

Marine terraces extending inland from the ocean are vegetated with scrub oak, laurel sumac, toyon, chamise, and coastal sage scrub. Rattlesnakes, lizards, badgers, and bobcats are commonly seen in this area.

There is restricted public access by lottery to Las Pulgas (Red) Beach. For more information, call: (619) 725-3360.

Las Flores Marsh: *Off I-5 at Las Pulgas Rd., Camp Pendleton.*

Las Flores Marsh is a wetland supplied by freshwater discharge from Las Pulgas River and salt water from tidal influx. Vegetation is composed of freshwater and brackish marsh species with pockets of salt marsh plants. The freshwater marsh supports a community of cattail, California bulrush, and olney bulrush, whereas pickleweed dominates the salt marsh.

Las Flores Marsh supports a variety of bird species including rails, coots, dabbling and diving ducks, herons, and egrets. These birds feed in the open water on small fish and in tidal flats on crabs, clams, and worms that live in the mud. Waterfowl use the marsh during migration as an overwintering area.

Santa Margarita Marsh: *2.7 mi. N. of Oceanside.*

One of the few major rivers in San Diego County with unrestricted flow, the Santa Margarita River forms a beach and salt marsh at its mouth. Salt marsh vegetation is dominated by pickleweed, iodine bush, alkali bulrush, saltgrass, and jaumea.

To protect one of the coast's largest breeding colonies of the endangered California least tern, the U.S. Marine Corps has established a bird sanctuary in the marsh at the river's mouth. The light-footed clapper rail and Belding's savannah sparrow, both endangered species, also use the area as a breeding and resting site. Grebes, herons, and egrets nest in the marshlands.

Fish found in the salt marsh include diamond turbot and striped mullet. Surfperch, halibut, corbina, seabass, and sablefish are common offshore fish.

San Onofre Nuclear Generating Station

Oceanside Harbor

Oceanside: *38 mi. N. of San Diego.*

The City of Oceanside was named by the San Luis Rey missionites and rancho workers who reportedly said "let's go to the ocean side" on warm days. The name "Orella del Mar" (Shore of the Sea) was suggested but was later adapted to become Ocean Side and then contracted into a single word.

The early settlers of Oceanside were mostly English gentry who had established landholdings and introduced agriculture into the San Luis Rey Valley, five miles inland from the ocean. In 1883, the city was officially founded and by 1888, Oceanside had become a thriving commercial and agricultural distribution center. Between 1940 and 1950, the city's population tripled as a result of the development of Camp Pendleton Marine Corps Base to the north.

Misión San Luís Rey de Francia, named in honor of St. Louis, King of France, is located in a secluded valley four miles east of Highway 5 in Oceanside. Founded in June 1798 by Father Fermín Francisco de Lasuén, the mission is one of the most architecturally impressive of all the California missions; built of adobe and faced with brick, it is a composite of Spanish, Mexican, and Moorish styles.

For over thirty years the mission prospered under the direction of Father Antonio Peyrí. By 1801, over 300 Indians had been enrolled in the mission, making it one of the most populous in California. After secularization in the 1830s, the mission grounds were used for bullfights and, later, as a military post by U.S. troops. In 1893, the mission was rededicated as a Franciscan seminary. Today, the "King of Missions" includes a picnic area and museum. The mission is open to the public Monday-Saturday, 9 AM-4 PM. Tours are available to the public. For information, call: (619) 757-3250.

Oceanside Harbor: *Harbor Dr., Oceanside.*

Completed in 1963, Oceanside Harbor was once a beach and dune area. Today, this small craft harbor provides berths, a yacht club, boatel, boat launch, restaurants, and shops. The harbor area also provides picnic facilities, walkways, benches, and fishing piers. Shore fishing for surfperch, halibut, and seabass, and ocean fishing for tuna, barracuda, and marlin are popular in this area. An artificial reef of quarry rock, built offshore in 1964, is located about two miles west of the marina entrance. Whale-watching boat trips are available from January 1-March 31; for information, call: (619) 722-2133.

Harbor Beach: *Corner of Harbor Dr. South and Pacific St., Oceanside.*

The wide, sandy beach is popular for swimming and surf and rock fishing; anglers fish for surfperch, bonito, and sculpin from the jetty. Gulls and shorebirds such as sanderlings and sandpipers rest and feed near shore.

San Luis Rey River: *Harbor Dr. South and Pacific St., Oceanside.*

The San Luis Rey River originates in the foothills of Mount Palomar and flows through several plant communities, including coastal oak woodland, chaparral, coastal sage scrub, and fresh and saltwater marsh, before emptying into the Pacific Ocean.

Mission San Luís Rey de Francia

Willow, western sycamore, and Fremont cottonwood are common riparian species dependent on the high water table or overbank flooding from the river. Herbaceous vegetation and grasses dominate the wet soils area at the river's edge. Passerine birds, raptors, waterfowl, and small mammals use the riparian habitat for food and shelter.

The chaparral community, found on the drier slopes of the stream canyon, includes laurel sumac, black sage, California buckwheat, and mountain mahogany. The coastal sage scrub community is characterized by drought-tolerant plant species such as white and black sages, buckwheat, and box-thorn. This habitat supports passerine birds, small burrowing rodents, and a variety of reptile species.

The wetland area of the river includes both freshwater and saltwater marshlands. Freshwater marshes, which occur along the edges of the river and in small pockets, are dominated by cattails, bulrushes, and tules. The coastal salt marsh, restricted to the San Luis Rey Lagoon, contains saltgrass, pickleweed, and sea lavender. Fish such as bass, sunfish, chub, and mosquito fish inhabit the marsh waters. Aquatic insects, turtles, salamanders, waterfowl, and shorebirds are also found here. The California brown pelican and California least tern, both of which are endangered, and the black-crowned night heron feed and rest near shore and in the lagoon waters.

Oceanside City Beach: *Along The Strand, from the San Luis Rey River to Witherby St., Oceanside.*

Stairways located at some street ends between Ninth St. and Witherby St. provide access to this wide, sandy beach suitable for swimming, surfing, and shore fishing. Parking is available at Ninth St., near the Oceanside Pier, at the end of Third St., and at the end of Wisconsin Street.

Oceanside Pier: *W. end of 3rd St., Oceanside.*

The original 1,700-foot steel pleasure pier was constructed in 1910 at a cost of $100,000. Claimed to be the longest pier on the West Coast, the restored pier was constructed of wood and measured 1,600 feet. However, storms in recent years have reduced the length of the pier by 600 feet in 1978 and by 90 feet in 1982. The remaining 910-foot pier provides fish cleaning facilities and is lighted at night. The pier is closed during storms.

Loma Alta Marsh: *E. of Pacific St. and N. of Morse St., Oceanside.*

A freshwater lagoon and salt marsh, Loma Alta Marsh is closed to tidal influx by a sandbar. The wetland area supports both freshwater and saltwater marsh plants such as cattail, bulrush, saltgrass, and pickleweed. Dabbling ducks, ruddy ducks, coots, herons, and snowy egrets feed and rest in the lagoon.

Buccaneer Park, a small park with a picnic area, basketball courts, and a paved walkway along the lagoon, is located adjacent to the southern boundary of the marsh.

South Oceanside Beach: *W. of Pacific St., between Morse St. and Eaton St., Oceanside.*

A sandy beach accessible by a stairway at the end of Cassidy St. and at the 1600 block of Pacific St., South Oceanside Beach is popular for surfing and surf fishing.

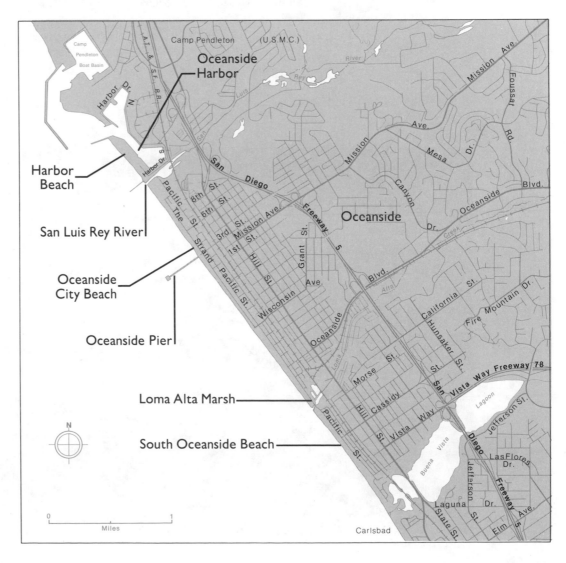

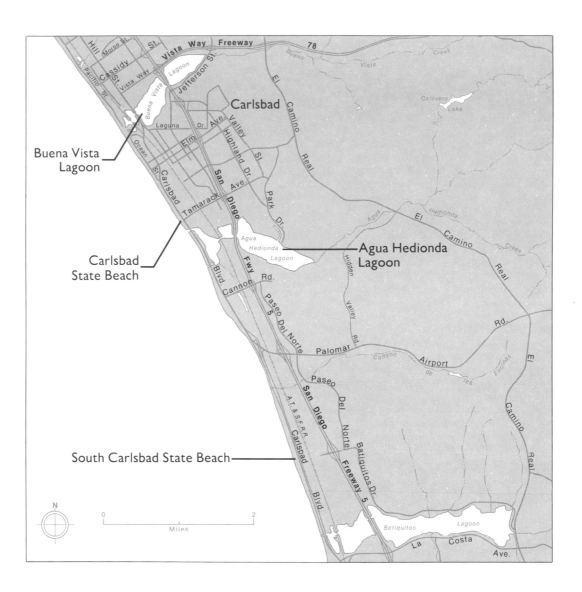

Buena Vista Lagoon

Buena Vista Lagoon: *E. and W. of I-5, 2.5 mi. S. of downtown Oceanside.*

The lagoon comprises a series of four coastal ponds bordered by marsh vegetation. The area between Jefferson St. and the Santa Fe Railroad is part of an ecological reserve. This wetland habitat is an important resting and feeding site for migratory waterfowl on the Pacific Flyway. Ducks, geese, avocets, stilts, snowy egrets, black-crowned night herons, plovers, turnstones, and dowitchers are often seen in the lagoon. The lagoon provides breeding sites for three endangered species: the light-footed clapper rail, California least tern, and Belding's savannah sparrow.

Lagoon vegetation is composed of brackish water marsh plants such as pickleweed, saltgrass, cattail, and alkali bulrush. The upland region is a riparian woodland with arroyo willows and elderberry.

Located on the shore of Buena Vista Lagoon is Maxton Brown Park, with a landscaped picnic area and panoramic views of the lagoon. For information, call: (619) 438-5571.

Carlsbad: *S.E. of Oceanside.*

In 1884 the town was named Frazier's Station after Mr. Frazier, who had drilled a well on the property opposite the Carlsbad Hotel and discovered water rich in minerals. The water was analyzed in 1886-87 and found to be identical to the famous mineral water of Karlsbad, Germany, a village founded in the 14th century by King Karl I.

In the late 1800s, Carlsbad was designated by the local newspaper, the *Daily San Diegan*, as the "pleasure city of the sunset seas" offering "health, wealth, and happiness." Commercial farming of vegetables, grains, flowers, and avocados was introduced into the area in 1914. In 1952, Carlsbad was incorporated as a city.

Carlsbad City Beach, a sandy beach backed by bluffs, is accessible by stairways at the ends of Cedar Ave., Grand Ave., Elm Ave., and Ocean Street. The beach is used for swimming, surfing, skin diving, and fishing.

Carlsbad State Beach: *W. of Carlsbad Blvd. at Tamarack Ave., Carlsbad.*

A long sandy and rocky beach at the base of coastal bluffs, Carlsbad State Beach is a popular area for swimming, surfing, fishing, and picnicking. Facilities include restrooms, parking, and a picnic area. Call: (619) 729-8947.

The shore area supports birds such as gulls, sanderlings, and sandpipers. Few native plant species grow on the blufftop; exotics such as the sea fig have established widespread communities and overtaken the native plants' habitat.

Agua Hedionda Lagoon: *E. and W. of I-5, 1.4 mi. S. of Carlsbad Civic Center, Carlsbad.*

Originally a salt marsh, Agua Hedionda Lagoon was extensively dredged and channelized in the early 1950s to accommodate the Encina Power Plant. The lagoon habitats include mudflats, saltwater and freshwater marshes, and areas of deep water. The lagoon is part of a complex of coastal wetlands that serves as a link in the Pacific Flyway. Over 55 species of water-associated birds including shorebirds, waterfowl, and wading birds use the area for feeding, resting, and nesting. The California

least tern and Belding's savannah sparrow, both of which are endangered, nest in the lagoon area. Wading and diving birds, including western grebes, surf scoters, and ruddy ducks, can be seen in the lagoon waters. Other birds that frequent the lagoon include snowy plovers, killdeer, godwits, sanderlings, western and ring-billed gulls, and Forster's and Caspian terns.

Terrestrial animals such as raccoons, coyotes, and rabbits also inhabit the area. Lagoon vegetation ranges from species of the coastal sage and scrub communities to those found in saltwater marshes and sand flats.

Clamming, fishing, bird watching, and water-skiing are permitted in the lagoon area. A dirt parking lot located above a rocky seawall provides access to the Encina Fishing Area, which is privately owned; permission to pass is revocable by the owner. A paved public walkway provides access to a small sandy beach above the lagoon at Cove Drive. There is also parking and lagoon access near the dirt road at the end of Hoover Street. The Snug Harbor Marina, located on the lagoon at 4215 Harrison St., has a three-lane boat ramp, a guest dock, snack bar, picnic area, and water-ski rentals.

South Carlsbad State Beach: *W. of Carlsbad Blvd. at Ponto Dr., Carlsbad.*

A sandy beach backed by bluffs, South Carlsbad State Beach is a popular area for swimming, surfing, fishing, skin diving, and camping. Developed family campsites, some which are wheelchair accessible, are located on the bluffs overlooking the beach. Stairways provide access from the campgrounds to the beach. Sanderlings, western gulls, sandpipers, and other water-associated birds feed and rest along the shore. Call: (619) 729-8947 or 438-3143.

Belding's savannah sparrow
(*Passerculus sandwichensis beldingi*)
4½ to 5¾ inches long

Agua Hedionda Lagoon

Batiquitos Lagoon

The lagoon is habitat for wintering coots, ducks, and grebes. The Belding's savannah sparrow and California least tern, both endangered species, nest on the islands in the marshlands north and south of the San Marcos Creek mouth. Shorebirds such as snowy plovers, willets, sandpipers, sanderlings, and avocets feed in the lagoon waters. Sandpipers, often called "peeps," feed in small groups in the mudflats on insects such as the brine fly.

The wetland area is used for both scientific research and recreation. Between 1969 and 1971, ornithologists conducted shorebird studies at the lagoon. Other scientific studies of the area included monitoring the water quality of the lagoon and research on modern and prehistoric shellfish. The eastern end of the lagoon is used for model aircraft flying and the adjacent roadways are used as equestrian trails.

Batiquitos Lagoon: *Carlsbad Blvd. at La Costa Ave., Leucadia.*

San Marcos Creek, originating in the Merriam Mountains, drains into Batiquitos Lagoon, forming saltwater marshes, mudflats, and salt flats. Approximately one-third of the lagoon consists of mudflats and saltwater marsh, while the remaining two-thirds contains seasonally shallow water and periodically dry, barren salt flats. In the early 1900s, the California Salt Company utilized 25 acres of salt-evaporation ponds in the eastern lagoon. Today, this area supports brackish and saltwater marsh plant communities dominated by sedges, cattails, rushes, and saltgrass, while the damp open mudflats are vegetated by saltbush, goosefoot, and salt marsh fleabane.

Leucadia: *23 mi. N. of San Diego.*

Leucadia, founded in 1885 by English colonists, is named after one of the Ionian Islands located off the west coast of Greece, where it is said that Sappho, the lyric poet of Lesbos, leaped from the cliffs into the sea. The word "leucadia" is Greek for "sheltered place."

Encinitas Beach County Park and Seaside Gardens County Park, both located in Leucadia, have beaches suitable for swimming, surfing, and shore fishing. Encinitas Beach County Park is accessible by walking south along the shore from Leucadia State Beach or north from Seaside Gardens County Park. A stairway at El Portal St. west of Neptune Ave. provides access

to Seaside Gardens County Park; on-street parking is available along Neptune Avenue.

Leucadia State Beach: *W. of Neptune Ave., between Grandview St. and Leucadia Blvd., Leucadia.*

A sandy beach backed by bluffs, this area is popular for swimming, surfing, fishing, and picnicking. Currently, the only public access is a viewing platform and a stairway and ramp leading to the beach, located at the end of Leucadia Boulevard. The stairway at the end of Grandview St. was destroyed by storms in 1983. For park information, call: (619) 729-8947.

Moonlight State Beach: *4th St. at the W. end of B St., Leucadia.*

Moonlight State Beach is a favorite spot for swimming, picnicking, surfing, and shore fishing. The name originated in the early 1900s, when residents of Leucadia and Encinitas held picnics at night at this beach. Facilities include volleyball and tennis courts, equipment rentals, and a snack bar. A blufftop viewpoint with benches is located at the end of D Street. For information, call: (619) 729-8947.

Wildlife is limited to a few small mammals and land birds associated with Cottonwood Creek, a channelized stream that drains into the Pacific Ocean at Moonlight State Beach. The beach area supports shorebirds including sandpipers, plovers, and avocets, and seabirds such as cormorants.

Encinitas: *21 mi. N. of San Diego.*

The name Encinitas is derived from the Spanish word *encina*, meaning "live oak." The Portolá Expedition discovered the area in 1769, two days after leaving San Diego in search of Monterey Bay; upon entering the valley of small oak trees, Father Juan Crespí named it Cañada de los Encinos. Rancho Las Encinitas, several miles east of what is now the community of Encinitas, served as a station on the San Diego-Los Angeles stage route.

In the early 1920s, the San Dieguito Irrigation District and South Coast Land Company introduced agriculture into the coastal valleys. Avocado, vegetable, and flower crops have been grown in Encinitas since that time. The inland mesas adjacent to Encinitas are a prime area for commercial flower growing, having some of the largest poinsettia fields in the state. In April, spring flower and greenhouse tours are available. For information, call the Encinitas-Leucadia Chamber of Commerce: (619) 753-6041.

Self-Realization Fellowship Ashram Center: *215 K St., Encinitas.*

The Self-Realization Fellowship Ashram Center, sited on a cliff overlooking the Pacific Ocean, includes over 1,000 feet of beach front. Established in 1937, the Center provides a retreat house for members, a refectory, a main hermitage, and a meditation area with panoramic views of the coast. The Self-Realization Fellowship was founded in the U.S. in 1920 by Paramahansa Yogananda to spread the practice of the ancient science of yoga.

The Center is open to the public Tuesday-Saturday, 9 AM-5 PM. Commercial photography and bathing attire are prohibited.

Just south of the Ashram Center is Sea Cliff Roadside Park, a small blufftop park with a grassy picnic area. Stairs lead to "Swami's," a narrow beach noted as an excellent surfing spot and a popular area for surf fishing, skin diving, and swimming.

snowy plover (*Charadrius alexandrinus*)
6 to 7 inches long

Moonlight State Beach

San Elijo State Beach: *Old Hwy. 101, N. of Chesterfield Dr., Cardiff-by-the-Sea.*

A narrow, sandy beach backed by upland bluffs, San Elijo State Beach includes over 1.5 miles of ocean front. Developed campsites are located on the blufftops overlooking the beach; stairs lead from the campground to the beach. Swimming, surfing, fishing, sunbathing, and picnicking are popular beach activities. For campground information, call: (619) 753-5091. For park information, call: (619) 729-8947.

Wildlife within the park is composed primarily of shorebirds and gulls, and a few small mammals and invertebrates.

Cardiff-by-the-Sea: *19 mi. N. of San Diego.*

A coastal community founded in 1911 by J. Frank Cullen, Cardiff-by-the-Sea is named after a seaport in Wales. Formerly called San Elijo after the river and the lagoon, the community was once a part of the Las Encinitas Rancho. Today, the community of Cardiff-by-the-Sea is best known for its beaches and agricultural crops including avocados, vegetables, and flowers. Agriculture is limited mainly to greenhouse operations; much of the agricultural land and open space is being converted to residential and commercial uses.

In 1915, a pier was built at Cardiff-by-the-Sea extending 300 feet into the Pacific Ocean; at the end of the pier, a "perpetual motion machine" was erected to harness the energy of the waves. A year later, both the machine and the pier were washed away in a winter storm.

A kelp bed comprising giant kelp and feather boa kelp extends more than 600 feet offshore from Cardiff-by-the-Sea. Gorgonian corals, bryozoans, and tunicates inhabit the rocky bottom of the kelp forest. Tunicates, commonly called sea squirts, reproduce by budding, or asexual division, to form chains, lobes, or encrusting colonies.

Cardiff State Beach: *Old Hwy. 101, 1 mi. S. of San Elijo State Beach, Cardiff-by-the-Sea.*

Separated from San Elijo Lagoon by a sandbar at the north end and ocean bluffs to the south, Cardiff State Beach is a narrow strip of sandy beach suitable for surfing, swimming, and surf fishing. Shorebirds such as snowy plovers use the beach area for feeding and resting. For information, call: (619) 729-8947.

San Elijo Lagoon: *Old Hwy. 101, E. of Cardiff State Beach, Cardiff-by-the-Sea.*

Prior to 1887, San Elijo Lagoon was a saltwater marsh supplied with fresh water from Escondido Creek. Since then, the ecology of the wetland has been altered by human activity. The construction of a railroad crossing, two dams on Escondido Creek, and two major highways restricted circulation of water in the lagoon, resulting in an increase in salinity.

The lagoon area adjacent to the Pacific Ocean is dominated by salt marsh vegetation including pickleweed, saltgrass, alkali heath, and other highly salt-tolerant species. Farther east, brackish to freshwater species of marsh vegetation predominate. These include mule fat, rye grass, arrowweed, curly dock, and California bulrush. The eastern shore of the lagoon is dominated by brackish marsh vegetation interspersed with salt marsh vegetation. Plant species include alkali bulrush, salt marsh fleabane, and the salt marsh daisy, which occupies the salt flats in the

Cardiff State Beach

transition area between the lagoon and the Escondido Creek floodplain.

The lagoon supports populations of migratory birds, including many species of shorebirds and waterfowl; this diversity can be attributed to the gradient in water salinity and the protective cover provided by the marsh vegetation. Small mammals such as the southern pocket gopher and desert cottontail, and reptiles and amphibians including the western fence lizard and the Pacific treefrog inhabit the lagoon area.

Ten archaeological sites have been found near the lagoon. Five of these have been identified by the San Diego Museum of Man as midden sites of the La Jollan Indian culture. On the north shore east of the Santa Fe Railroad tracks are remains of a kelp factory that operated in 1915.

Tide Beach County Park: *Pacific Ave. at Solana Vista Dr., Solana Beach.*

This sandy beach is popular for surfing, skin diving, swimming, and surf fishing. Beach access is provided by a stairway down the bluffs.

Solana Beach County Park: *Sierra Ave. at Plaza St., Solana Beach.*

From 1908-1922, Solana Beach County Park was the site of a bean field. The sandy beach, known by the local residents as "The Plaza," is a popular area for catching grunion, skin diving, swimming, surfing, and surf fishing. Park facilities include basketball and shuffleboard courts; call: (619) 755-1569. The Community Center Building is located within the park; for information, call: (619) 755-2998.

San Dieguito Lagoon: *E. of Camino Del Mar at the San Dieguito River mouth, Del Mar.*

In the early 1900s, San Dieguito Lagoon was a 600-acre expanse of salt marsh, tidal channels, and freshwater-brackish marsh extending two miles inland. In the last 80 years, the lagoon has been altered considerably by the construction of dams on the San Dieguito River and extensive landfilling. This loss of wetland acreage resulted in a decrease of habitat types, most importantly the freshwater marsh and mudflats used as feeding and nesting areas for the California least tern and Belding's savannah sparrow, both of which are endangered. Recent lagoon improvements include the dredging of tidal channels and the development of bird nesting islands.

Despite degradation, the lagoon still supports a number of plant communities including salt marsh, freshwater-brackish marsh, and coastal sage scrub. Salt marsh species, adapted to the fluctuations in the salt concentration in the water, include saltgrass, pickleweed, and alkali heath. Juncus, cattails, and sedges dominate the freshwater-brackish marsh. A coastal sage scrub community is found in the upland areas and on east-facing slopes. Representative species include lemonadeberry, toyon, and chamise.

Birds, mammals, and reptiles use the lagoon area as a food source and for shelter. Water-associated birds such as grebes, loons, herons, ducks, and coots, and land birds including swallows, quails, and doves are commonly sighted here. Mammals such as skunks, foxes, and brush rabbits also inhabit the area. The lagoon is one of three Southern California coastal wetlands that has a resident population of the western pond turtle.

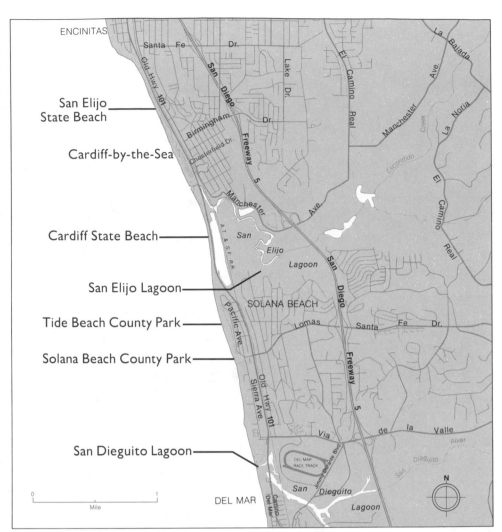

San Elijo Lagoon

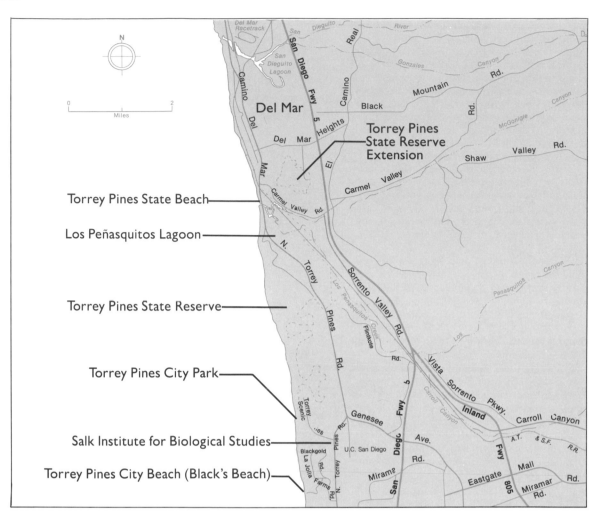

Torrey Pines State Reserve

Del Mar: *15 mi. N. of San Diego.*

Del Mar was built in the 1880s during a land boom promoted by T. M. Loop; his wife suggested the name Del Mar after reading Bayard Taylor's poem "Paso del Mar." According to initial plans, the village of Del Mar was to be a literary and artistic center.

Del Mar Bluffs City Park and Del Mar City Beach are two local beaches noted for swimming, surfing, surf fishing, and grunion. Access to Del Mar City Beach is from the street ends between 29th St. and 18th St.; off-street parking is located adjacent to the Amtrak station.

Claimed to be one of the finest tracks in the state, Del Mar Racetrack was built during the depression with Works Progress Administration (WPA) funds and was opened in 1937. Racing season is July 25-September 12. The Southern California Exposition is held at the fairgrounds annually from June 21-July 4.

Torrey Pines State Beach: *McGonigle Rd., off Carmel Valley Road.*

A wide, sandy beach backed by sandstone bluffs, Torrey Pines State Beach extends 4.5 miles from 6th St. near Del Mar Heights Rd. south to Torrey Pines City Beach. Beach access and the main parking lot are at the North Beach area adjacent to Los Peñasquitos Lagoon.

Shorebirds and other water-associated birds, and rodents, snakes, and lizards inhabit the area. In March through September, grunion swim ashore to deposit their eggs in the sand, usually on the second, third, and fourth nights

following the new or full moon. Dolphins and sea lions may be seen offshore. Carbonaceous beds of the Del Mar Formation are exposed in the cliffs bordering the beach, revealing fossils of shallow water mollusks from the middle Eocene. An assortment of oysters, burrowing clams, petrified wood, and leaf imprints can be seen.

Los Peñasquitos Lagoon: *W. of I-5, just south of Del Mar.*

Los Peñasquitos Lagoon is a 385-acre wetland consisting of coastal salt marsh with deep tidal channels and pocket areas of mudflats and salt flats. The lagoon is separated from the ocean by sand dunes and Torrey Pines State Beach.

Salt marsh vegetation is dominated by pickleweed, saltgrass, and sea lavender. Following winter rains, the salt marsh daisy is common in the salt flats. Cattails, bulrushes, and several species of rushes occur in limited areas of brackish water marsh.

The salt marsh vegetation provides nesting sites for the California least tern, Belding's savannah sparrow, and light-footed clapper rail, all of which are endangered. Thirteen species of waterfowl, including dabbling and diving ducks, feed and rest in the lagoon. Willets, dowitchers, and other migratory shorebirds use the lagoon in the fall and spring.

The lagoon is an important nursery ground for fish, including halibut and staghorn sculpin. These fish breed in the inshore ocean waters and enter the lagoon as fingerlings, usually returning to the ocean as juveniles.

Torrey Pines State Reserve Extension: *W. of I-5, at the end of Del Mar Scenic Parkway.*

The Reserve Extension includes more than 150 acres of chaparral, coastal uplands, and pine-covered cliffs. Numerous trails provide views of Los Peñasquitos Lagoon, Torrey Pines State Reserve, and the Pacific Ocean.

Torrey Pines State Reserve: *W. of N. Torrey Pines Rd., 2 mi. N. of Genessee Avenue.*

In the early 1900s, Ellen B. Scripps purchased 1,000 acres of coastal land which she donated to the public. Park planners and botanists were employed by Ms. Scripps to design an area that would preserve the habitat of one of the world's rarest pine trees, the Torrey pine; the only other habitat for this tree occurs off the coast of Southern California on Santa Rosa Island. The Torrey pine was recognized as a new species in 1850 by Dr. J. Le Conte and Dr. C. C. Parry of Columbia University, who named the tree after their professor, Dr. John Torrey.

Two areas within Torrey Pines State Reserve have been designated as natural preserves: the Ellen B. Scripps Natural Preserve and Los Peñasquitos Lagoon and Marsh. The Ellen B. Scripps Natural Preserve encompasses the North Grove area, which includes some of the finest stands of Torrey pines. The .6-mile self-guided Guy Fleming Trail, extending throughout the North Grove, offers panoramic views of the coast from its two overlooks. At the beginning of the trail is the Whitaker Memorial Native Plant Garden, a collection of California native plants. A .4-mile loop trail runs through Parry Grove, named for the botanist who described and named the Torrey pine. Los Peñasquitos Marsh Natural Preserve is one of the last remaining salt marsh areas and waterfowl refuges in Southern California.

A network of trails begins at the visitor center, leading to several viewpoints and to the beach. Along these trails, plants and animals native to the area can be observed, including California quails, scrub jays, brush rabbits, small rodents, gray foxes, coyotes, mule deer, and reptiles. Trail maps and species lists are available at the visitor center; interpretive displays are located throughout the reserve. In order to protect the area's natural resources, only a limited number of people can be accommodated at the reserve. Visitors may be asked to return at a later time or date if the reserve is full. Call: (619) 755-2063.

Torrey Pines City Park: *W. of N. Torrey Pines Rd., at the end of Torrey Pines Scenic Drive.*

The park is located on the bluffs overlooking the ocean; landslides have closed the steep and hazardous paths at the north and south ends of the park that formerly led to Black's Beach. Strong winds striking the bluffs below the park create updrafts suitable for hang gliding.

Salk Institute for Biological Studies: *10010 N. Torrey Pines Road.*

Considered one of the finest examples of modern architecture in California, the Salk Institute was designed by Philadelphia architect Louis I. Kahn. The independent research center was founded by Dr. Jonas Salk, who discovered the polio vaccine. Over 120 scientists at the institute are involved in a variety of biological research projects including studies of the brain, cancer, and diabetes.

The architectural design of the complex, referred to as "Cut-into Box" style, incorporates two banks of concrete buildings facing a rectangular, travertine-paved central court whose far side provides a view of the ocean. This design has been described as uniting pure form and utility. Tours of the institute are offered weekdays, 11 AM-2 PM. Call: (619) 453-4100.

Torrey Pines City Beach (Black's Beach): *La Jolla Farms Rd. at Blackgold Road.*

In 1974, voters approved the designation of a 900-foot-long strip of sandy beach for swimsuit optional use; in 1977, the ordinance was revoked. This popular beach backed by highly eroded bluffs is noted for good swimming, surf fishing, and surfing. The only safe access is via a very steep road for pedestrians only, located at the south end of Blackgold Road.

Torrey Pines State Reserve and Los Peñasquitos Lagoon

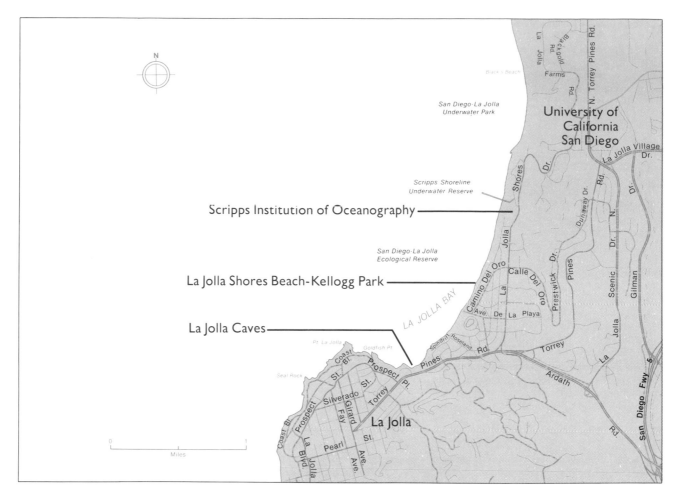

Scripps Beach

University of California, San Diego: *End of N. Torrey Pines Rd., La Jolla.*

The original facilities for the University of California at San Diego were established at the Scripps Marine Biological Research Laboratory in 1912. In 1964, land once belonging to Camp Matthews, a marine corps training camp from 1917-1964, was designated as the site for a new and expanded campus. The new campus, which includes colleges devoted to science, fine arts, social science, engineering, and medicine, occupies 1,200 acres on a eucalyptus-covered mesa overlooking the ocean. Call: (619) 534-2230.

Scripps Institution of Oceanography: *8602 La Jolla Shores Dr., La Jolla.*

One of the world's oldest and foremost centers for oceanographic research, Scripps was founded in 1903 by Dr. W. Ritter, chairman of the Zoology Department at the University of California, Berkeley, and was operated out of the Hotel del Coronado's boathouse until 1905, when it was moved to La Jolla Cove. In 1907 a permanent 170 acre site was donated by Ellen B. Scripps and E. W. Scripps. In 1912, the marine station became a part of the University of California and, in honor of its benefactors, was named Scripps Institution of Biological Research of the University of California, later becoming Scripps Institution of Oceanography. From 1964 to 1986, a major research program at the institution was the Deep Sea Drilling Project, designed to explore the history of the earth through the study of core sediments. The theories of continental drift and sea floor spreading were confirmed with evidence supplied by this drilling project.

Public facilities at the institution include an aquarium and a museum. In the aquarium, tanks simulating local, deep-sea, and tropical marine environments display representative plant and animal species. Models that demonstrate beach formation, wave generation, and tide and current patterns are displayed in the museum. An artificial tidepool located near the aquarium entrance exhibits marine life adapted to tidal action, such as sea stars, urchins, abalones, rock crabs, and limpets. The aquarium and museum are open daily from 9 AM-5 PM. For information, call: (619) 534-4086.

Scripps Beach and tidepools are located north of Scripps Institution and the 1,000-foot Scripps Pier. Research ships such as the FLIP, which can be manipulated vertically to study the ocean floor, are sometimes displayed at the pier.

Underwater Reserves: *From the S. end of the City of Del Mar to Goldfish Pt., La Jolla.*

The underwater reserves, which include the Scripps Shoreline-Underwater Reserve, the San Diego-La Jolla Underwater Park, and the San Diego-La Jolla Ecological Reserve, were established to preserve the shoreline and underwater life of La Jolla Canyon. Extending seaward 1.5 miles, the reserves encompass 5,977 acres of tide and submerged lands.

Offshore, giant kelp forests provide extraordinary areas for skin diving. Kelp crabs, squid, and shrimp use the kelp forest as a nursery for their young. Anchovy and several species of perch use the kelp plants as a shelter from predators, while kelp bass, Pacific barracuda, and sea lions search for prey in the kelp forests.

La Jolla Shores Beach-Kellogg Park: *Camino del Oro at Calle Frescota, La Jolla.*

In the 1900s, La Jolla Shores Beach was known as "Chinese Run" for the Chinese who operated their boats from the area. Also called Long Beach, 15.5-acre La Jolla Shores Beach is heavily used for swimming and surfing. Kellogg Park, donated by Florence Scripps as a memorial to her husband William Kellogg, is a grassy area adjacent to La Jolla Shores Beach and is equipped with picnic facilities.

The sculpin, a darting tidepool fish, and the sting ray, which has a long, whiplike tail, can be seen near shore. La Jolla Shores Beach is also a favorite spawning ground for grunion, slender, silver-colored fish that swim ashore to spawn for several nights following the full or new moon.

La Jolla: *9 mi. N. of San Diego.*

The name La Jolla, derived from the Mexican geographical term referring to a hollow on the coast worn by waves, is exemplified by the caves at the north side of Point La Jolla. Originally part of two Spanish pueblos, the town of La Jolla was developed in 1887 by Botsford and Heald, a pair of boom-time investors. In the 1920s, the town grew to accommodate wealthy retirees looking for an "American Riviera." In the 1960s, La Jolla became known as a luxury shopping area for San Diego and surrounding communities. Institutions constructed in the early 1960s, notably the University of California and the Salk Institute, provided new sources of employment in the fields of education and science.

The La Jolla Women's Club, erected in 1913, and the Bishop's School for Girls, built in 1906-1919, were designed by San Diego architect Irving J. Gill. These structures, using earthquake-resistant poured concrete, are among the most important architectural achievements in California. Gill's works are characterized by artistically abstract yet practical designs. The original Bishop's School for Girls is considered to be Gill's best abstract interpretation of the Mission Style.

La Jolla Caves: *Torrey Pines Rd., at Coast Walk and Coast Blvd., La Jolla.*

The La Jolla Caves are deep caves carved by wind and waves into the sandstone cliffs along the shore. Cormorants, considered sacred birds by Native Americans, use the bluffs as rookeries. Common gulls and the endangered California brown pelican also feed and rest along the bluffs.

Inland from the caves is a blufftop trail, the Coast Walk, that runs east for a half mile past a rocky gorge known as Devil's Slide. The Coast Walk, once named Angel's Walk, provides a panoramic view of the ocean, beach, and caves along the shoreline. The stairs located at the western entrance to the Coast Walk at Goldfish Point, also known as Alligator Head, lead to tidepool areas. The Cave Curio Shop provides access to the sea caves via a constructed tunnel. During prohibition, bootleggers hid liquor in the caves.

La Jolla Women's Club, designed by Irving J. Gill

Goldfish Point, La Jolla, ca. 1905

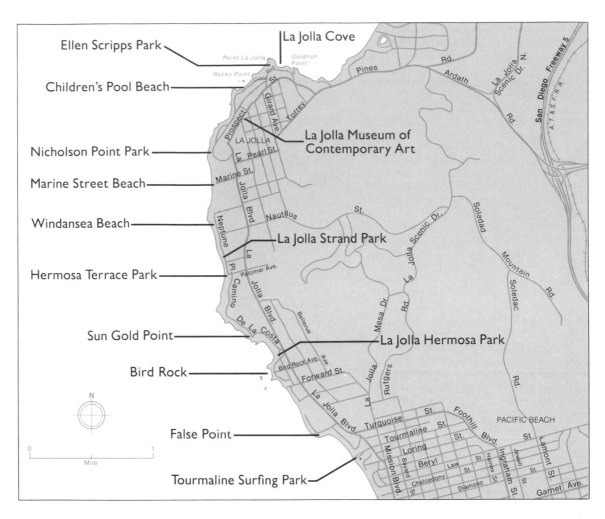

Ellen Scripps Park

La Jolla Cove

Children's Pool Beach

Nicholson Point Park

Marine Street Beach

Windansea Beach

Hermosa Terrace Park

Sun Gold Point

Bird Rock

La Jolla Museum of Contemporary Art

La Jolla Strand Park

La Jolla Hermosa Park

False Point

Tourmaline Surfing Park

California spiny lobster (*Panulirus interruptus*)
to 16 inches long

La Jolla Cove: *Off Coast Blvd., La Jolla.*

Since 1860, the La Jolla Cove has been a favorite beach resort area. A dance pavilion built in 1894 became the social center of the town. During the Gay Nineties, on the Fourth of July, divers were paid $25 by a railroad company for each dive made "flambé"; a springboard was placed on the blufftops over the ocean and the diver would pour oil on his body and set himself afire before leaping. In 1905, a building was erected in the area with hot saltwater baths and a bowling alley.

Monterey cypress and palms grow on the blufftops surrounding the tiny pocket beaches and rocky outcroppings adjoining the La Jolla Cove. The sandy, protected beach at the cove offers calm, clear water ideal for scuba and skin diving. In the rocky crevices offshore, abalone and spiny lobster, also known as rock lobster, can be found.

Ellen Scripps Park: *Coast Blvd. at Girard Ave., La Jolla.*

On the blufftop above La Jolla Cove is a grassy area with picnic sites and shuffleboard courts named for Ellen Browning Scripps, one of the most generous and influential La Jollans. Ms. Scripps, born in London, was the half-sister of Edward Wyllis Scripps, the publisher and founder of the United Press Syndicate.

A path and stairs lead down the bluffs to Boomer Beach, world famous for body surfing, but suitable for experts only. In the summer, Boomer Beach is a coarse sandy beach while in winter, storms wash the sand away and expose underlying boulders.

Children's Pool Beach: *Coast Blvd. at Jenner St., La Jolla.*

Also known as Casa Pool, this beach is partially enclosed by a curving breakwater. Strong rip currents often make this beach more hazardous than its name suggests; however, it is still a popular swimming and surf fishing area. The cove and beach were donated in 1931 by Ellen B. Scripps to provide the children of the area with a safe place to swim and play.

La Jolla Museum of Contemporary Art: *700 Prospect Ave., La Jolla.*

The museum is located at the site of the Scripps House, built in 1915 and considered to be one of Irving J. Gill's masterpieces. The architectural firm of Mosher and Drew modified the original structure of the house in 1948 and 1960 to provide facilities for the art museum.

Exhibits include an eclectic collection of paintings, sculpture, and photographs dating from the mid-1950s, as well as temporary shows of recent works of art. The museum is open Tuesday-Sunday. Weekday tours are available; call: (619) 454-3541. Coast Boulevard Park, a grassy shoreline park with picnic tables and a path that leads down a low bluff to a rocky beach, is located just seaward of the museum.

Nicholson Point Park: *South end of Coast Blvd., La Jolla.*

This hard-to-reach beach is noted for skin diving and rock and surf fishing. The opaleye is a common nearshore fish that uses the kelp beds near the park for food and shelter. Opaleye are named for their blue opalescent eyes.

Marine Street Beach: *W. of La Jolla Blvd., at the end of Marine St., La Jolla.*

Marine Street Beach, also known as Jones Beach or Whispering Beach, is a sandy beach popular for swimming, surfing, skin diving, and surf fishing. Halibut, Pacific bonito, and white croaker are common fish caught offshore.

Windansea Beach: *W. of Neptune Pl., from Vista de la Playa to Bonair St., La Jolla.*

A reef 500 feet offshore forms high, challenging waves, making this beach a popular surfing site. Windansea Beach is also recognized as the area where Tom Wolfe discovered a subculture of surfing youth made famous in his book, *The Pumphouse Gang.* Several blocks east, on La Jolla Blvd., is the site of a popular restaurant known in the late 1950s as the Pour House, where poets such as Allen Ginsberg and Lawrence Ferlinghetti read their work.

La Jolla Strand Park: *W. of Neptune Pl., from Playa del Sur to Palomar Ave., La Jolla*

This seasonally sandy beach is noted for swimming, surfing, skin diving, and rock fishing. Spiny lobster and abalone can be found in sheltered rocky areas offshore.

Hermosa Terrace Park: *W. of Neptune Pl., at Palomar Ave., La Jolla.*

A paved path at the end of Winamar Ave. provides access to this swimming and surfing beach, which is rocky in winter.

Sun Gold Point: *W. of Camino de la Costa, at Sun Gold Pt., La Jolla.*

Sun Gold Point's rocky shoreline provides a good area for rock fishing. Rock cod, kelp bass, and lingcod are common fish found offshore. The lingcod spawn from February until November, depositing their orange-colored eggs in low-growing algae on rocky areas. The males guard the nest until hatching occurs. Lingcod feed on fish, squid, and octopus.

La Jolla Hermosa Park: *Camino de la Costa at Chelsea Ave., La Jolla.*

An unimproved park on the blufftop provides views of the rocky beach below, which is accessible by traversing a steep bluff face. The area is popular for rock fishing and skin diving.

Bird Rock: *W. of La Jolla Blvd., at the end of Bird Rock Ave., La Jolla.*

A large guano-covered rock which extends 120 feet offshore, Bird Rock serves as a resting place for gulls, cormorants, and the endangered California brown pelican. The area was called Bird Rock, not for the rock itself, but after Mr. Bird, who was one of the first developers of the shoreline community. In 1907, this subdivision was known as "Bird Rock, City by the Sea." At the foot of Bird Rock Ave. was the Bird Rock Inn, built from stone taken from the beach; Charles Lindbergh was said to have eaten dinner at the Inn before his historic flight in the *Spirit of St. Louis* to New York and Paris.

To the south, paths at the ends of Chelsea Place, Midway St., and Forward St. lead to a rocky beach and tidepool area where sea stars, anemones, barnacles, and mussels are found.

False Point: *Off Sea Ridge Dr., at the end of Linda Way, La Jolla.*

This rocky shoreline is accessible by paths at the ends of Linda Way and Bandera Street. The area is popular for fishing; common nearshore species include surfperch and rockcod.

Tourmaline Surfing Park: *W. of La Jolla Blvd., at the end of Tourmaline St., La Jolla.*

Large offshore waves at Tourmaline Surfing Park have made the rocky beach popular for surfing and windsurfing; swimming is not permitted. Fishing and skin diving are also popular in the area.

La Jolla Museum of Contemporary Art

Ellen Scripps Park and Boomer Beach

Palisades Park: *W. of Mission Blvd., between Wilbur Ave. and Law St., Pacific Beach.*

Several paths lead from a grassy picnic area to a sandy beach; surfing is not permitted from 11 AM-6 PM when swimmers are present. Park facilities include parking and restrooms. Western gulls and shorebirds such as sanderlings and sandpipers feed and rest on the beach.

Pacific Beach Park: *W. of Ocean Blvd., from Diamond St. to Thomas Ave., Pacific Beach.*

Pacific Beach Park includes a landscaped area with benches, a bike path, restrooms, and a pedestrian walkway on the blufftops overlooking the ocean. Two stairways provide access to the sandy beach, which is popular for swimming and surfing; surfing is prohibited from 11 AM-6 PM when swimmers are present. Offshore, anglers fish for topsmelt and California yellowtail. The yellowtail is a member of the jack family and is a highly prized game fish.

The first major development constructed in the community of Pacific Beach was a racetrack built in 1860; in the late 1890s, the surrounding lands were used to cultivate lemons. In 1887, the San Diego College of Letters, the forerunner of today's San Diego State University, was founded in Pacific Beach. During World War II, Pacific Beach provided housing for defense workers.

Crystal Pier: *End of Garnet St., Pacific Beach.*

The 1,000-foot-long Crystal Pier was opened at Pacific Beach in 1926 to attract land buyers to what was then a rural area. The pier contained an amusement midway lined with shops and arcades. The major attraction was a stucco ballroom claimed to be "the only dance floor in the nation cushioned with cork where couples 70 and 80 years old can dance all night without getting tired." The ballroom was later demolished because of faulty construction.

In 1936, the pier was remodeled and a motel with cottages replaced the amusement midway. Today, Crystal Pier is the only pier on the West Coast which provides lodging over the ocean. The pier is open daily from 7 AM-5 PM for fishing; anglers fish for surfperch and rockfish.

Mission Beach Park: *W. of Strand Way, from Santa Rita Pl. to the Mission Bay entrance channel, Mission Beach.*

In 1916, J.M. Asher built a tent city, a large swimming pool, a bayfront pier, and a bathhouse on the sandbar that stretches from Pacific Beach south to Mission Bay channel. Nine years later, to stimulate real estate sales, John D. Spreckels constructed the Mission Beach Amusement Center on the same site. The Amusement Center included a dance hall, a casino, cafes, a roller-skating rink, and a natatorium, better known as the Plunge, an indoor saltwater swimming pool. Plans for a hotel, a stadium for water sports, an auditorium for conventions and theatrical productions, and an ice-skating rink never materialized.

The Mission Beach Amusement Center, also known as Belmont Amusement Center, is the site of the Giant Dipper, a roller coaster that opened July 4, 1925. The ride closed in 1976 and is currently being restored. The roller coaster was declared a State Historical Landmark in 1975. Today, only the Plunge remains open; for information, call: (619) 488-2087.

A paved boardwalk that extends along the beach is popular for walking, jogging, roller-skating, and bicycling. Public parking is available south of West Mission Bay Dr. and Mission Blvd., and at the south end of Mission Boulevard. A number of shops and stores line the boardwalk south of West Mission Bay Drive. There are basketball courts and a grassy lawn at

Crystal Pier

the south end of the beach. Offshore from Mission Beach Park, anglers fish for halibut, Pacific bonito, and croaker.

Mission Bay Marsh and Preserves: *N.E. corner of Mission Bay City Park, San Diego.*

Mission Bay was once known as "False Bay" because early mariners, including Cabrillo, mistook it for the entrance to San Diego Bay. The bay consisted of marshlands formed by the delta of the San Diego River. In the early 1960s, Mission Bay was dredged from a labyrinth of mudflats, salt marshes, and tidal channels. Before dredging and other modifications, the entire bay was comparatively shallow with few areas deeper than ten feet. The only remaining natural vegetation that survived is the coastal salt marsh community at Campland Marsh, which is part of the Northern Wildlife Reserve, and the adjacent Kendall-Frost Marsh, dominated by pickleweed, cordgrass, and alkali heath.

There are two wildlife preserves within Mission Bay City Park, both in the northeast section. The Northern Wildlife Reserve, an 88-acre salt marsh-mudflat complex, is owned by the city of San Diego, and 21-acre Kendall-Frost Marsh is part of the University of California Natural Reserve System. The 125-acre San Diego River Flood Control Channel Preserve, which is located south of Mission Beach Park and east of Ingraham Dr., was established to protect sensitive marshlands.

Historically, Mission Bay provided feeding and nesting habitat for migratory and resident birds. Despite the dredging and filling of natural areas, several species of birds continue to use the Mission Bay Marsh and Preserves as nesting, feeding, and resting sites. The endangered California least tern breeds at the Crown Point Tern Sanctuary, at South Island, and at Fiesta Island. Other birds seen in the area include grebes, loons, egrets, herons, teals, turnstones, terns, and gulls. Resident populations of the light-footed clapper rail and Belding's savannah sparrow, both of which are endangered, inhabit the Northern Wildlife Preserve.

California clapper rail (*Rallus longirostris obsoletus*)
14 to 16 ½ inches long

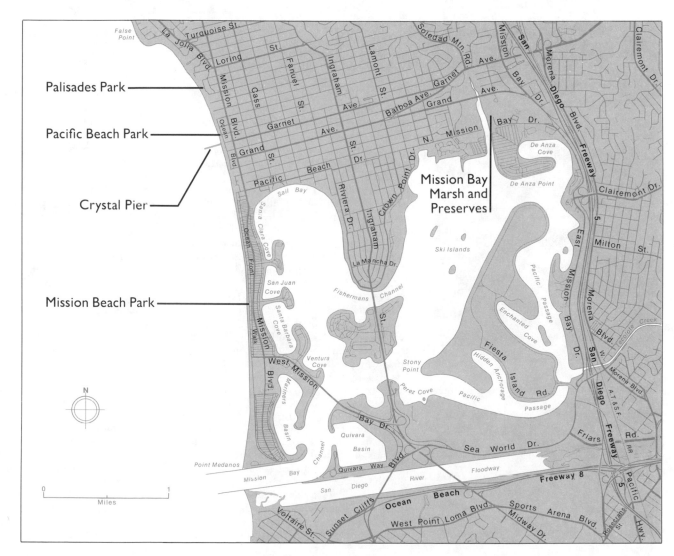

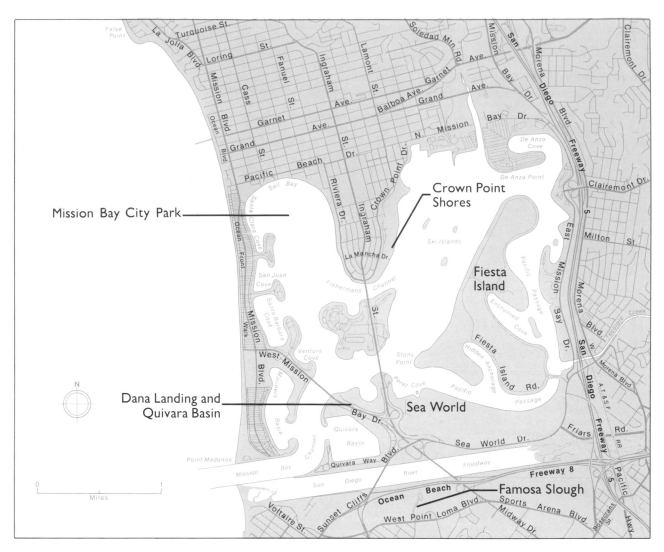

De Anza Cove, Mission Bay

Mission Bay City Park: *Mission Bay shoreline.*

In 1929, the California legislature declared the tidelands and waters of Mission Bay a state park. After World War II, the city of San Diego initiated a long-term project to develop the bay into a 4,600-acre recreational park offering water-skiing, fishing, swimming, sailing, picnicking, camping, boat rentals, and speedboat racing. Twenty-five per cent of the land in Mission Bay City Park is used for commercial activities, while the remainder, including 27 miles of beaches, is reserved for public use.

Mission Bay City Park, the largest aquatic park on the West Coast, includes a number of recreation areas. Sail Bay and Riviera Shores, in the northwest portion of Mission Bay, both have sandy swimming beaches; Riviera Shores also has a water-ski take off and landing area. De Anza Cove, in the northeast corner of the bay, has a sandy beach and swimming area, picnic areas, a concrete boat ramp, and a nearby trailer park and private campground.

The East Shore of Mission Bay is the site of the Visitor's Information Center; additional facilities include landscaped picnic areas, playgrounds, a physical fitness course, swimming and fishing areas, and a hotel. Santa Clara Point and El Carmel Point are in the western part of the bay. Facilities at Santa Clara Point include the city's boathouse, a boat launch, boat slips, a recreation center, a baseball field, and tennis courts. The Mission Bay Yacht Club, a parking

area, and a sandy beach are located on El Carmel Point, about a half-mile south of Santa Clara Point. A public beach is located between the two points in San Juan Cove.

Vacation Isle, in the center of the bay, is bisected by Ingraham St.; the west side contains a hotel and golf course, public swimming area, boat rentals, and a youth camping area. Ski Beach, on the east side of the island, is a noted water-skiing and boating spot, with a water-ski take off and landing area, concrete boat launch, picnic areas, volleyball courts, and a swimming beach. Bonita Cove, north of Mission Bay Channel, is popular for swimming, picnicking, over-the-line softball, and volleyball. Trails and a playground are located along the cove; shops, restaurants, and recreation equipment rentals are within walking distance. The Bayside Walk begins south of Bonita Cove and continues north to Sail Bay. Northeast of Bonita Cove is Ventura Cove, whose calm waters provide a popular swimming spot for children.

Crown Point Shores: *E. shore of Crown Pt. peninsula, Mission Bay.*

Crown Point Shores, one of the few remaining marshland areas in Mission Bay, is a U.S. Fish and Wildlife designated breeding site for the endangered California least tern. A sandy beach, picnic area, nature study area, physical fitness course, water-ski take off and landing areas, and a public loading dock are available south of the wildlife refuge. Special events include an annual sand castle building contest.

Fiesta Island: *Fiesta Island Rd. at E. Mission Bay Dr., Mission Bay.*

The gradually sloping mudflats of Fiesta Island provide habitat for shorebirds such as the ruddy turnstone, willet, and black-bellied plover. The sandy beach of the western shore is a nesting area for the snowy plover. Land birds including the house finch, horned lark, western meadowlark, and mourning dove nest on the island in protected areas vegetated with coastal chaparral. The California least tern has also been sighted on the island.

The western and southern shores are used for jet-skiing and fishing, and there are several swimming beaches; a youth campground is located at the island's eastern end. An over-the-line softball tournament is held here annually.

Dana Landing and Quivara Basin: *Off W. Mission Bay Dr., at Dana Landing Rd. or Quivara Rd., Mission Bay.*

Dana Landing and the Dana Marina provide marine services such as a fuel dock, boat ramp, and boat sales and services. For marina information, call: (619) 222-6440. Sunset Point is a public park with picnic facilities, and is a popular fishing spot for sandy bottom species including surfperch, diamond turbot, sole, and halibut.

Quivara Basin includes a large grassy picnic area with excellent bay views, sportfishing and marina services, and the Mission Bay Marina Aquatic Center. The Mission Bay Marina, open daily, provides a boat hoist; call: (619) 225-9627. A bike path extends from the basin east to Friars Rd., where it connects with another bike path that runs along East Mission Bay Drive.

Sea World: *1720 S. Shores Rd., Mission Bay.*

This 130-acre aquatic park, opened in 1964, contains beautifully landscaped grounds, more than 5,000 species of decorative plants, over 200 bird species, and a variety of marine mammals, including whales, dolphins, and pinnipeds. Thirty educational exhibits, five marine shows, and four aquariums contribute to the popularity of this recreational park. The Hubbs/Sea World Research Institute conducts studies on aquatic animal adaptations, behavior and training, communications, and marine ecology.

The Penguin Encounter, which houses 400 penguins and alcids, simulates the icy world of the Antarctic, with representative species such as emperor, chinstrap, macaroni, and Adélie penguins, as well as puffins and gulls. For park information, call: (619) 226-3901. Facilities for the disabled are available.

Famosa Slough: *Off West Point Loma Blvd. and adjacent to Famosa Blvd., San Diego.*

The 25-acre Famosa Slough is a remnant of the once extensive Mission Bay wetland complex, which was dredged and filled in the early 1960s to develop Mission Bay City Park. Vegetation ranges from saltwater to freshwater marsh species. Pickleweed dominates the salt marsh, bulrush grows in the brackish water areas, and cattail is the predominant freshwater plant.

The slough is a significant feeding and resting site for birds using the Pacific Flyway. Dabbling ducks including mallards, pintails, cinnamon teals, and shovelers rest and feed in the shallow area of the slough in the fall and winter. California killifish and mosquito fish provide food for great blue herons, egrets, green-backed herons, and black-crowned night herons. California least terns and shorebirds including avocets, black-necked stilts, and killdeer forage and nest in sheltered areas of the wetland. The endangered Belding's savannah sparrow feeds on pickleweed in the slough.

Killer whale, Sea World

Crown Point Shores

San Diego River: *S. of Mission Bay.*

In 1792, one of the first dam and water diversion projects in California was constructed on the San Diego River to bring water to Misión San Diego de Alcalá at the east end of Mission Valley. The Mission Dam, begun in 1807 and completed in 1816, brought water to the fertile Mission Valley. The remains of this dam are a registered National Historical Landmark. For centuries, the river alternately emptied into San Diego Bay and Mission Bay. In 1952, the San Diego River, which tended to silt up the marshes and fill in the bay, was channelized by the Army Corps of Engineers to prevent flooding.

The mouth of the river is open to tidal influx at all times. This marshy area provides a nursery for marine fish such as halibut and turbot. Large waterfowl populations, including ducks and coots, feed on the marsh vegetation.

Robb Field and Playground is a large athletic park at the mouth of the river with facilities for baseball, tennis, and basketball. For information, call: (619) 224-7581. A bike path runs along the river's south bank.

Ocean Beach Park: *Between the ends of Niagara Ave. and Voltaire St., Ocean Beach.*

In 1913, the Wonderland Amusement Park was developed on eight acres on the bay side of Voltaire St. from Abbott St. to the ocean. Attractions included a casino, dance hall, rides, a zoo, and a restaurant. The Amusement Park has since been demolished to provide new areas for housing development.

Ocean Beach, a sandy beach with tidepools and a small grassy picnic area, is noted for excellent surfing. Swimming and surf fishing are also popular; anglers catch rockfish, lingcod, kelp bass, and Pacific bonito. The north end of the park, known as "Dog Beach," is the only city beach where dogs are allowed to be unleashed during the day.

Ocean Beach, originally named Mussel Beds for the mussel-covered rocks near the Ocean Beach Pier, began in the early 1900s as a summer cottage and resort community. In the 1920s-1930s, many of the cottages were converted to year-round residences.

Ocean Beach Fishing Pier: *End of Niagara Ave., Ocean Beach.*

Claimed to be the longest pier on the west coast, the 1,971-foot, T-shaped Ocean Beach Fishing Pier opened in 1966 with the financial assistance of the local residents; a section of the pier was constructed with money raised from bake sales and car washes. Facilities include bait and tackle shops and a fish cleaning area.

Rocky areas and tidepools are found near the pier. Surfing is popular between the pier and the jetty; in 1916, during Ocean Beach's "Hawaiian Days," Olympic swimmer Duke Kahanamoku held surfing exhibitions near the jetty.

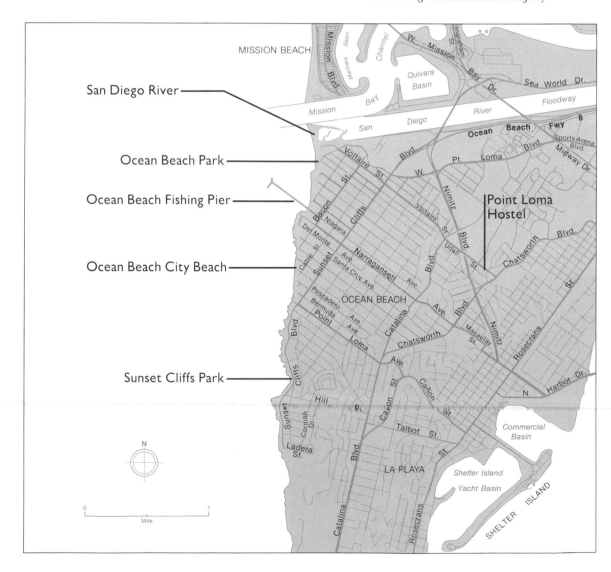

Ocean Beach City Beach: *Between Ocean Beach Pier and the end of Pescadero Ave., Ocean Beach.*

A series of small pocket beaches and tidepools extend along the coast south from Ocean Beach Pier. The beach is accessible by stairways at the ends of Cable St., Del Monte Ave., Santa Cruz Ave., Pescadero Ave., and Bermuda Avenue.

Divers find abalone and spiny lobster in the rocky crevices near shore. The red abalone, in particular, is highly prized. The pinkish-red shell is somewhat rippled, often partially covered with growths of algae, tube worms, and bryozoans. The interior of the shell is lined with beautiful iridescent mother-of-pearl. The spiny lobster is a native of the rocky habitats of Southern California and lacks the pinching claw of the East Coast lobsters. These lobsters are most active at night, scavenging along the ocean floor for a variety of food such as mollusks, sea worms, small fish, and plants.

Sunset Cliffs Park: *Along Sunset Cliffs Blvd., from Pt. Loma Ave. to Ladera St., Ocean Beach.*

A dirt path along the sandstone cliffs provides an excellent view of the coastline. Several steep trails, which are highly eroded and potentially dangerous, lead from the parking lot at the end of Cornish Dr. to sandy coves and rocky beaches used by experienced divers and surfers.

At the southern end of the park, upland hiking trails surrounded by eucalyptus trees provide views of the beaches and tidepools below the cliffs. Western gulls and great blue herons feed and rest in the coves. Rockfish, lingcod, kelp bass, and croakers are caught offshore.

Point Loma Hostel: *3790 Udall St., Ocean Beach.*

Point Loma Hostel is centrally located between Mission Bay and San Diego Bay, about a mile east of Ocean Beach. The hostel accommodates 36 men and 24 women; guests are provided a room for 2 to 14 people. There is a fully equipped community kitchen. The hostel opens at 4:30 PM, with an 11 PM curfew. For information, call: (619) 223-4778.

Sunset Cliffs Park

Ocean Beach City Beach

Fort Rosecrans National Cemetery: *Along Cabrillo Memorial Dr., Point Loma.*

This 71-acre military cemetery, situated on the Point Loma peninsula, was named for General W. S. Rosecrans, a Civil War hero. The cemetery was founded soon after the boundaries of Fort Rosecrans were established in 1852; of the existing 47,147 graves, 19 are dedicated to men awarded the Medal of Honor, the nation's highest military award.

Cabrillo National Monument: *S. end of Cabrillo Memorial Dr., Point Loma.*

One of the most visited national monuments in the U.S., the 81-acre Cabrillo National Monument commemorates explorer Juan Rodríguez Cabrillo's discovery of San Diego Bay in 1542. Monument facilities include a visitor center, exhibit hall, auditorium, gift shop, and a scenic overlook. From late November through April, migrating California gray whales can be viewed from the overlook. A sandstone statue of Cabrillo, designed by Portuguese sculptor Alvaro de Bree, was erected at the site in 1939. The

monument, administered by the National Park Service, is open daily from 9 AM-5:15 PM. Facilities for the disabled are available. For information, call: (619) 293-5450.

The 1.5-mile Bayside Trail provides an hour-long nature walk that winds along the eastern slope of Point Loma through coastal chaparral. Birds frequently sighted along the trail include great horned owls, red-tailed hawks, and, nearer to the ocean, great blue herons and endangered California brown pelicans. The trail also provides views of the San Diego harbor entrance and of the abandoned World War II gunnery emplacements built to protect the harbor.

Along the southwest shore of the monument grounds are tidepools inhabited by such species as the slug-like sea hare, a large snail with an internal shell, the green sea anemone, and the sand castle worm, which builds colonies of tube-shaped sand shelters on the undersides of boulders. Sea lettuce, dead men's fingers, and feather boa kelp are conspicuous intertidal plants.

Old Point Loma Lighthouse: *S. end of Cabrillo Memorial Dr., Point Loma.*

The old Point Loma Lighthouse, built in 1854 with sandstone from Monterey and bricks from Ballast Point and Point Loma, is one of the eight original New England-style lighthouses found along the West Coast. The lighthouse is located 462 feet above the sea on the east side of Point Loma. Heavy fogs that obscured the beacon of the lighthouse made the station inoperable; it was abandoned in 1891 for a more suitable site

closer to the water's edge. The old lighthouse attracts more than two million visitors annually, appearing as it did in the mid-1800s when its oil lamp beacon was first made visible.

Point Loma Lighthouse: *S. end of Cabrillo Rd., Point Loma.*

In 1891, the U.S. Government established a new site for the Point Loma Lighthouse, 88 feet above the sea at the west side of San Diego Bay on Point Loma. At its new location, the lighthouse guides ships far better than did its predecessor; some mariners claim that its beacon can be seen 23 miles out to sea.

Point Loma Ecological Reserve: *Offshore, W. side of Point Loma.*

Along the western shore of Point Loma, 400-foot sandstone cliffs rise from narrow, sandy beaches dotted with rocky outcrops and tidepools. Coastal sage scrub dominates the blufftops. Several endangered plants such as Shaw's agave, Orcutt's spineflower, and coast wallflower grow in this area.

The predominantly rock and cobble shoreline below the cliffs contains an extensive intertidal zone. Marine animals are abundant in the area, including abalones, sea stars, snails, giant keyhole limpets, and hydrocorals. Surfgrass is found on rocky outcrops, whereas eelgrass grows in protected areas. Gulls and shorebirds including black oystercatchers feed and rest along the sandy beach. Offshore, rocky reefs provide habitat for spiny lobster and abalone.

Lover's Leap, Point Loma, ca. 1905

The Point Loma nearshore waters support the largest coastal kelp beds in Southern California. The kelp beds were almost completely decimated between 1947 and the early 1960s, partly due to the effects of sewage effluent discharged into the Pacific Ocean and an increase in sea urchin populations. Now partially recovered, the kelp beds provide habitat for fish including kelp bass, garibaldi, butterfly fish, and black croaker. Underwater artifact sites of the La Jollan culture have been discovered off the Point Loma headlands.

Commercial Basin: *E. of Rosecrans St., N. of Shelter Island Dr., San Diego.*

Home to a large fleet of commercial fishing vessels, Commercial Basin can accommodate more than 600 small craft. Facilities include sportfishing services, a fueling dock, launching ramp, marine railway, repair yards, and marine supplies. The basin can be viewed from a public observation deck located on the west side of Shelter Island, 400 feet north of the traffic circle. For information, call: (619) 291-3900.

Shelter Island: *Along Shelter Island Dr., San Diego.*

Shelter Island was a submerged shoal located off the Point Loma peninsula until the City of San Diego began dredging San Diego Bay in the 1930s and 1940s, dumping the surplus onto the shoal. In 1950, the city added a causeway to connect the island to the mainland. Today, most of Shelter Island is commercially developed, including yacht clubs, hotels, and restaurants. A Coast Guard Station marks the south end of the island.

The island's beach is popular for swimming, fishing, water-skiing, and picnicking. A landscaped pedestrian/bicycle path runs the length of the island, just inland from the sandy beach, providing views of the downtown San Diego skyline; other features include public moorings, launching ramps, picnic areas, and a fishing pier. At the southwest end of the island is a 2.5-ton Bell of Friendship presented to San Diego by its sister city, Yokohama, Japan.

La Playa: *Along San Antonio Ave., between Bessemer and Kellogg Streets, San Diego.*

La Playa is a narrow, sandy beach located on the Point Loma peninsula just west of Shelter Island, with excellent views of the bay and yacht basin. Between 1824 and 1846, La Playa was the site of the most successful hide tanning operation on the Pacific Coast; the area was then known as "Hide Park."

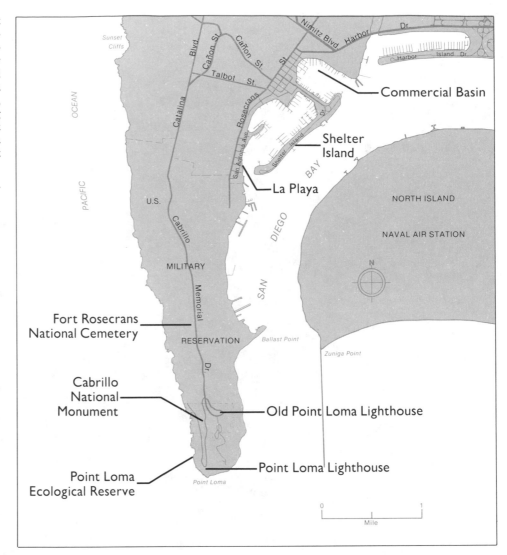

Old Point Loma Lighthouse

Point Loma Lighthouse

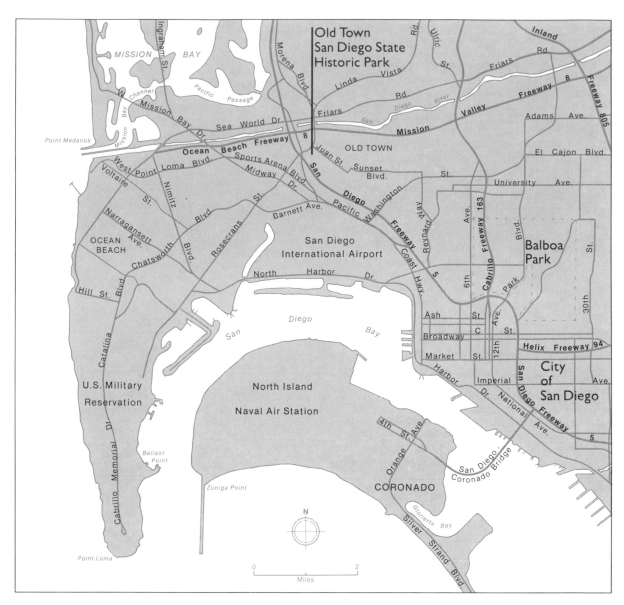

Botanical Building, Balboa Park

Old Town San Diego State Historic Park:
San Diego Ave. and Mason St., San Diego.

In 1769, the first Spanish settlement in San Diego was founded at the foot of Presidio Hill. The settlement grew, and in the early 1820s a plaza was laid out and a small adobe town developed around it. This area was considered the center of town until the early 1870s when Alonzo Horton established a "new town" to the west, closer to the harbor. Old Town today re-creates the lifestyle of California in the Mexican and early American periods from 1821 to 1872. The site consists of historic buildings, shops, and restaurants. In 1968, Old Town became a State Historic Park, and to prepare for San Diego's bicentennial celebration, work was begun to restore its buildings, primarily the remaining original adobes—Casa de Bandini, Casa de Estudillo, and Casa de Machado y Silvas.

Casa de Estudillo, the most famous of Old Town's original adobes, was built in 1827 by José Antonio Estudillo, commander of the San Diego presidio. The house, with its 12 rooms and beamed chapel opening into a spacious inner court, was restored in 1910. Valuable Spanish, Indian, and early American antiquities are displayed in the house. In 1905, John D. Spreckels bought the adobe, had it rebuilt, and inaccurately renamed it "Ramona's Marriage Place" to attract visitors.

Casa de Bandini, originally a one-story adobe, was owned by Juan Bandini, one of the leading citizens of Alta California. The house was Old Town's social and political affairs center for nearly 20 years. Casa de Bandini was sold to A. L. Seeley in the 1860s and was used as a stagecoach station known as the Cosmopolitan Hotel. Over the years, the house has also been used as a store, a pickle factory, and a motel annex. Casa de Machado y Silvas was built by José Nicasio Silvas between 1830 and 1843 for his wife. The house was later used at various times as a saloon, boarding house, art studio, souvenir shop, museum, and church.

The visitor information center is at San Diego Ave. and Twiggs Street. A living history program is offered at the Machado y Stewart adobe on Saturdays; guided walking tours of Old Town are also available. For information, call: (619) 237-6770.

Balboa Park: *Off Hwy. 163 at Laurel St., or Hwy. 5 at Park Blvd., San Diego.*

The largest municipal cultural park in the nation, the 1,400-acre Balboa Park was the site of the Panama-California Exposition in 1915-

1916 and the California-Pacific International Exposition in 1935-1936. Lands for the park had been set aside by the city of San Diego in 1868, remaining undeveloped and covered with chaparral vegetation until 1889 when Kate Sessions began extensive tree planting.

The park was named for Vasco Núñez de Balboa, the Spanish conquistador who discovered the Pacific Ocean. The smaller western portion of the park adjacent to Sixth Ave. is comprised mostly of grassy lawn dotted with shrubs and trees, including Monterey cypress and several varieties of eucalyptus and oak. East of Highway 163, across the Cabrillo Bridge, is the park's central mesa which houses the San Diego Zoo and the area called El Prado-Palisades. East of Park Blvd. across from El Prado-Palisades is Florida Canyon, a protected area of dry mesas and canyons, sage scrub, and chaparral. A hiking trail extends the length of the canyon, winding through wild cucumber, prickly pear cactus, tarweed, and bush monkeyflower. Wildlife sighted in the area includes red-tailed hawks, rabbits, gray foxes, and coyotes. South and east of Florida Canyon are two recreational areas—Golden Hill, a popular golf course, and Morley Field, a sports complex.

Many of the buildings in the El Prado-Palisades area were designed and built for the 1915 exposition to commemorate the opening of the Panama Canal. A Spanish colonial city of fountains, arched colonnades, tiled domes, and elaborate stucco decoration was designed by New York architect Bertram Goodhue.

The main attractions in El Prado-Palisades are the San Diego Museum of Art, San Diego Museum of Man, San Diego Natural History Museum, Reuben H. Fleet Space Theater, Old Globe Theatre, Timken Art Gallery, Botanical Building, and San Diego Art Institute.

Just north of El Prado-Palisades is the San Diego Zoo, with its collection of more than 3,200 animals representing 800 species. Long-billed kiwis from New Zealand, koalas from Australia, and wild Pryzewalski's horses from Mongolia are some of the unique animals that are on display. Elephant and camel rides are available, and there are free animal shows daily. A three-mile guided bus tour is also available. For information, call: (619) 234-3153.

City of San Diego: *119 mi. S. of Los Angeles.*

Founded in 1769 as the first Spanish fort and mission in Alta California, the early settlement of San Diego was a plaza surrounded by adobe structures. In 1867, San Francisco land developer Alonzo Horton bought 960 acres from the city trustees and laid out a "new town" adjacent to the San Diego Harbor; the old settlement founded in Mission Valley became known as "Old Town."

The expansion of the Santa Fe Railroad in 1885 and the lure of a balmy climate sparked a real estate boom drawing middle-class retirees looking for sun. The establishment of Navy bases in 1917 introduced a source of employment for the city's residents. In 1982, new high-rise office buildings were constructed and urban renewal projects located between downtown and the Embarcadero were begun. San Diego is today the second most populous city in California, Los Angeles being the first.

Misión San Diego de Alcalá, named for St. Didacus of Alcalá, is located five miles east of Highway 5 in Mission Valley and was originally sited on Presidio Hill. In 1774, Father Junípero Serra moved the mission to more fertile lands farther away from the influence of Spanish soldiers. The mission was burned in an Indian attack in 1775, destroyed by an earthquake in 1803, and restored and enlarged in 1813. The present building is a restoration of the 1813 church, rebuilt in 1931. The mission is an active parish church open from 9 AM-5 PM daily with tours available.

Misíon San Diego de Alcalá

Casa de Estudillo, Old Town San Diego State Historic Park

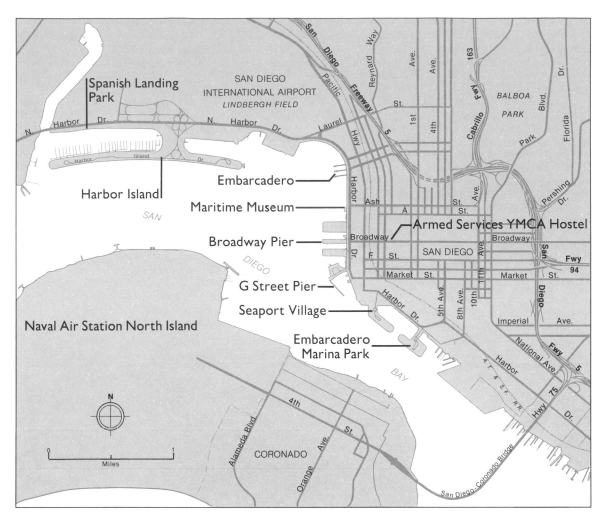

Carved wood figurehead of the Star of India *represents Euterpe, the goddess of lyric poetry.*

Spanish Landing Park: *S. of Lindbergh Field, on N. Harbor Dr., San Diego.*

Spanish Landing Park, located just south of the San Diego International Airport, has a sandy beach popular for swimming, and grassy picnic areas near the shore. A concrete walkway along a seawall, used for fishing and strolling, provides views of the bay. Each year, Sebastián Vizcaíno's historic landing of 1602 is re-enacted at the park.

Harbor Island: *S. of Lindbergh Field, on Harbor Island Dr., San Diego.*

In 1961, the U.S. Navy dredged the harbor channel to create safe passage for supercarriers. The dredged material was sold to the City of San Diego for the development of Harbor Island. In 1969, hotels and restaurants were built on the island for the Republican National Convention scheduled for 1972; however, the convention was not held in San Diego, and Harbor Island now functions primarily as a boating center. Its various marinas can accommodate a total of about 1,000 vessels, and some have guest berths or moorings. Other facilities include picnic areas, shops, and on the western tip of the island, a Spanish-style building which houses a combination restaurant and decorative lighthouse. A walkway, bordered by a grassy lawn with benches, extends along the length of the island.

Embarcadero: *Along Harbor Dr., at the end of Hawthorne St., San Diego.*

The Embarcadero provides restaurants, fish markets, and a walkway with benches along the east side of the bay that offers views of Coronado. Commercial fishermen unload their catches and mend their nets here. Harbor excursion boats depart from the area.

Maritime Museum: *W. of Harbor Dr., at the end of Ash St., San Diego.*

Founded in 1948, the maritime museum consists of three historic ships: the *Star of India*, the *Medea*, and the *Berkeley*, representing both sail and steam power. Exhibits include displays of life at sea, steam engines, naval history, and demonstrations of maritime skills.

The *Star of India*, built on the Isle of Man in 1863, was the full-rigged merchant ship, *Euterpe*, that once hauled general cargo and transported emigrants from London to New Zealand. In 1901, the ship was used in the Alaska salmon industry by the Alaskan Packers Association, who changed her rigging and, in 1906, changed her name to *Star of India*. The *Star of India* was acquired by the City of San Diego in 1926; restoration culminated in her sailing July 4, 1976 in honor of America's Bicentennial. The *Medea*, a steam yacht built in 1904 in Scotland, was owned at various times by an eccentric millionaire and members of Parliament. The *Medea* is one of a few remaining large steam yachts in the world. The *Berkeley*, a ferryboat built in 1898 to carry railroad passengers, commuters, and tourists between Oakland and San Francisco, now houses maritime exhibits, a research library, and a model ship shop. For information, call: (619) 234-9153.

Broadway Pier: *W. end of Broadway, San Diego.*

Panoramic views of San Diego Bay and downtown, and the park-like setting created by wooden decks, landscaped areas, and benches, make Broadway Pier a popular place to visit. Foreign ships dock at the pier, and the U.S. Customs office is located at the pier's end. One or more U.S. Navy ships are available for public tours on most weekends from 1 PM-4 PM. For information, call: (619) 235-3534.

G Street Pier: *W. of North Harbor Dr., at the end of G St., San Diego.*

Fishing for halibut, bonito, turbot, and top-smelt is popular from the pier. The walkway is used for strolling and viewing.

Seaport Village: *849 W. Harbor Dr., San Diego.*

Located on the site of the Old Coronado Ferry Landing, Seaport Village encompasses 22 acres of restaurants, shops, galleries, and parklands. A variety of architectural influences, including Mexican, Western, and Victorian, create a unique atmosphere. The Broadway Flying Horses Carousel, located in the west plaza of the village, is a restored 1880s model that once operated at Coney Island, New York and Salisbury Beach, Massachusetts; it is one of 300 carousels in the world with authentic hand-carved wooden animals. The official symbol for the village is a 45-foot-high lighthouse, recreating the Mukilteo lighthouse built more than 75 years ago to guide sailors safely into the harbor at Everett, Washington.

Embarcadero Marina Park: *Harbor Dr. at the end of Kettner Blvd., San Diego.*

The park's two sections are connected by a walkway along a seawall on the bay. The northern section, popular for fishing and viewing, has a lawn, picnic tables, and path and is accessible from the Seaport Village Center on Harbor Drive. The entrance to the southern section is at the intersection of Harbor Dr. and Harbor St.; facilities include a grassy picnic area, pedestrian paths, a fishing pier, basketball courts, and an athletic course.

Armed Services YMCA Hostel: *500 W. Broadway, San Diego.*

There are 100 private rooms and a dormitory with complete toilet, bath, and clothes washing facilities. The hostel is open year-round. For further information, call: (619) 232-1133.

Naval Air Station North Island: *2 mi. N. of Coronado.*

Prior to 1940, North Island was separated from Coronado by a small inlet called Spanish Bight. Sand and mud dredged from San Diego Harbor were used to fill the inlet and connect the "island" to Coronado. In 1911, the U.S. Navy's first aviator, Lieutenant T. Ellyson, was trained at North Island by Glenn Curtis, the aviation pioneer who designed the world's first airplane engine. Also in 1911, the first seaplane flight and the first parachute jump took place here. In 1917, the U.S. government purchased North Island to be used as a permanent aviation facility for both the Army and Navy. Charles Lindbergh began his famous trans-Atlantic flight to Paris from North Island in 1927.

Today, the island is home to all carrier-based antisubmarine warfare squadrons and is home port to three aircraft carriers, the U.S.S. *Ranger*, U.S.S. *Kittyhawk*, and U.S.S. *Constellation*.

The Star of India

Santa Fe Wharf, ca. 1899

San Diego County
Coronado and San Diego Bay

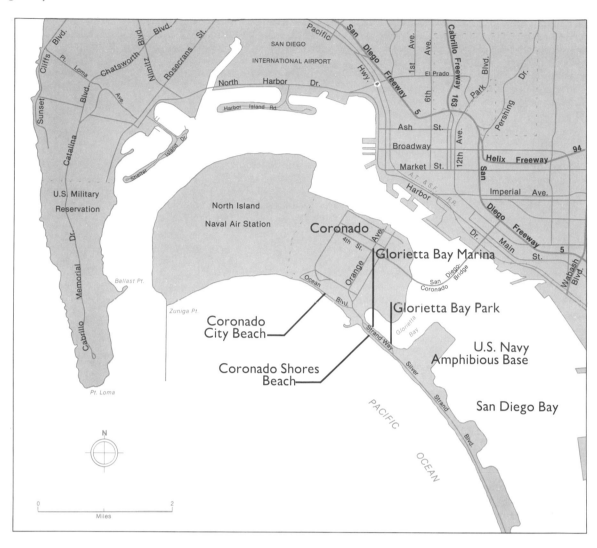

Hotel del Coronado, ca. 1902

Coronado: *4 mi. S.W. of downtown San Diego.*

Coronado was once two islands connected by a swamp; in 1602, Sebastián Vizcaíno named these islands Los Coronados after the four Coronado brothers who were martyred in ancient Rome by Emperor Diocletian. The swamp was later filled with sediment dredged from San Diego Bay by the U.S. Navy.

In 1885, the Coronado peninsula and North Island were purchased by Elisha Babcock and H. Story. The two men formed the Coronado Beach Company, drew up a city plan, held land auctions, and sold lots to finance the building of a dream hotel. In 1887-1888, the Hotel del Coronado was built on a sand spit populated by jack rabbits and coyotes. The "Del" was the first hotel west of the Mississippi to use electric lights and is now the largest wooden Victorian building in California.

In 1904, Thomas Edison came to supervise the lighting of the nation's first outdoor Christmas tree on the hotel lawn. The Hotel del Coronado's dining room, the Crown Room, with crown-shaped crystal chandeliers and a vaulted ceiling made entirely of rubbed sugar pine, was the site of a ball held in 1920 in honor of Edward, Prince of Wales.

In the lower level of the hotel is the Hall of History, which contains a collection of old silverware, menus, building plans, guest lists, tools, and memorabilia. Designed by New York architects, the Reid brothers, the "Del" was named a National Historical Landmark in 1977.

The San Diego-Coronado Bay Bridge, built in 1969 to replace ferry service to Coronado, is a boomerang-shaped bridge rising 246 feet above the bay at the highest point. The concrete abutments that support the bridge on the San Diego side at Chicano Park are painted with murals.

Glorietta Bay Marina: *Strand Way, Coronado.*

Glorietta Bay Marina is a full service facility with moorings and slips, a boat launch ramp, and a dry dock. The Hotel del Coronado's old boathouse, the Eastlake Boathouse on Glorietta Bay, has been converted to a restaurant. Nearby is a pier marked "Del Coronado Boathouse," where sailboat rentals and sportfishing charters

can be arranged. For information, call: (619) 435-5203. Glorietta Bay is also home of the Coronado Yacht Club.

Mollusks living in the mudflats near the marina include bay mussels, burrowing clams, and jackknife clams.

Glorietta Bay Park: *E. of Hwy. 75, at the S. end of Strand Way, Coronado.*

Glorietta Bay Park is a grassy park along the bay with a playground, picnic area, and a boat launch open 24 hours a day year-round. The Coronado Municipal Swimming Pool is located next to the park; call: (619) 435-4179.

Coronado City Beach: *W. of Ocean Blvd., Coronado.*

Coronado City Beach is a sandy beach popular for swimming, surfing, and surf fishing. Fishermen catch shallow sandy bottom fish including surfperch, corbina, butterfish, queenfish, and croaker. Along the beach, bean clams and Pismo clams burrow and live in the wet sand. A large grassy picnic area is located at Sunset Park, at the north end of Ocean Boulevard.

Coronado Shores Beach: *Seaward of Coronado Shores Condominiums on Hwy. 75, Coronado.*

The entrance and public parking area for Coronado Shores Beach are located at the Coronado Shores condominium development. The wide, sandy beach is popular for swimming, surfing, and surf fishing; anglers catch corbina and surfperch from the shore. California barracuda and white seabass spawn near shore.

A concrete promenade runs along the top of a seawall adjacent to the shore. A parking lot and wheelchair ramp are located at the end of Avenida de las Arenas.

U.S. Navy Amphibious Base: *E. of Hwy. 75, at the end of Tulagi Rd., Coronado.*

In 1943, the 11th Naval District and Public Works Department dredged San Diego Bay and filled in an area on the bay side of Silver Strand to create a new, larger amphibious base. The 934-acre site is home of the Underwater Demoli-

tion Teams (U.D.T.s) and Seals, amphibious commandos or "frogmen."

San Diego Bay: *Extends 17 mi. from the harbor entrance to Imperial Beach, San Diego.*

The early inhabitants of what is now San Diego were nomadic Indian tribes that periodically occupied the bay shore, attracted by the abundance of shellfish found there. In 1769, Spanish settlers established a small community, considered to be the birthplace of Alta California, near the mouth of the San Diego River. This was the first area to be colonized in California and the first section of the state to be explored by Europeans.

Claimed to be one of the best natural harbors in the world, San Diego Bay offers a well-protected deepwater port extending 17 miles from the harbor entrance to Imperial Beach. In 1936, tideland areas in the bay were filled to provide additional lands for new wharf and marine facilities. The existing tidal areas are habitat for waterfowl and shorebirds. Eelgrass beds that grow in shallow waters provide food for the black brant, a small goose with a black head, neck, and chest. Migrating shorebirds, such as sandpipers, plovers, dowitchers, willets, curlews, godwits, phalaropes, and avocets, use the mudflats as wintering grounds. The dikes bordering the salt ponds in the southeastern section of the bay support nesting colonies of Caspian terns, Forster's terns, elegant terns, endangered California least terns, black-necked stilts, and snowy plovers.

Recreational fishing for black croaker, halibut, diamond turbot, sand bass, and striped mullet is popular from the piers and shore.

Coronado, ca. 1890

National City: *5 mi. S.E. of San Diego.*

Once known as Rancho del Rey, what is now National City was used as a grazing area for cattle owned by Spanish soldiers at the Presidio. In the 1820s, the name was changed to Rancho de la Nación. In 1868, the Kimball brothers developed the area into a modern city; a wharf was built and the land adjacent to the bay was subdivided. National City is the second oldest city in San Diego County. The city's economy is dependent principally on manufactured goods such as wood products, machine equipment, and marine cables.

A concrete boat ramp, docks, a landscaped picnic area, and a fishing platform are located at the south end of Goesno Place. For information, call: (619) 291-3900.

Sweetwater Paradise Marsh Complex: *Between 24th St., National City, and E St., Chula Vista.*

Prior to dredging and filling operations in San Diego Bay, an extensive salt marsh system existed at the mouth of Paradise Creek. The creek has since been diverted by a dredged channel into the lower Sweetwater River. The small salt marsh now remaining at Paradise Creek mouth is vegetated with pickleweed communities in which California horn snails, olive ear snails, and shore crabs thrive.

At the mouth of Sweetwater River is the largest remaining salt marsh in San Diego Bay. The marsh is covered with pickleweed, cordgrass, and glasswort, and supports the endangered salt marsh bird's beak. The mudflats are heavily populated with clams, bubbleshells, California horn snails, and crabs. Black-necked stilts nest on the saltflats, while the mudflats and salt marsh attract large numbers of shorebirds and wading birds year-round. Nesting pairs of light-footed clapper rails and a thriving population of Belding's savannah sparrows, both endangered species, occur in the Sweetwater Marsh Complex. The saltwater or brackish water marshes are inhabited by brine flies, salt marsh mosquitos, and water boatmen.

Chula Vista: *9 mi. S. of San Diego.*

Known as the "gateway" to Tijuana and Baja, Chula Vista is the second largest city in San Diego County; major growth occurred during the 1960s when agricultural land was converted to residential developments. Chula Vista is Spanish for "beautiful view."

A concrete boat launching ramp, located at the west end of J St., includes docks, picnic areas, a playground, and a jogging and bicycle path. The area is noted for swimming, fishing, and water-skiing; however, swimming and skiing are prohibited within the launch basin. Pedestrian access to the South Bay tidal areas is provided at the end of G Street. For information, call the Port of San Diego: (619) 291-3900.

Silver Strand State Beach: *3500 Hwy. 75, Coronado.*

From 1903-1941, a summer retreat owned by John D. Spreckels was situated on the narrow sand spit extending from the Hotel del Coronado to the south end of San Diego Bay along the Silver Strand. Better known as "Tent City," the retreat featured a boardwalk, library, grocery store, restaurant, bowling alley, shooting gallery, bandstand, and tents furnished with electric lightbulbs, old beds, wooden tables, and folding chairs. In 1941, the state widened Highway 75, expanding into the resort's grounds, and the tent city disappeared.

"Tent City," Coronado, ca. 1910

Silver Strand State Beach, named for the tiny shells that are mixed with the sand, extends for 2.5 miles and includes an ocean beach and bay shore. Along the ocean side, the wide, sandy beach with low dunes is noted for swimming, surfing, clamming, surf fishing, and grunion catching. Perch, corbina, and croakers are commonly caught from the shore. Digging for Pismo clams is popular at the south end of the beach. The bay side offers shaded picnic areas, a boat launch for water-skiers, and a calm-water swimming basin; pedestrian tunnels connect the ocean beach with the bay shore. Interpretive displays of the local plant and animal life are exhibited at the ranger station. Other facilities include first-aid stations and picnic areas with wheelchair-accessible restrooms. For information, call: (619) 435-5184.

Over 140 species of native and exotic plants grow within the Silver Strand area, including such coastal strand plants as saltbush and sand verbena, and coastal salt marsh plants such as pickleweed and glasswort. Two endangered plants that grow in the dunes are the coast wallflower and Nuttall's lotus.

Mammals including cottontails, jackrabbits, California ground squirrels, and pocket gophers are widespread in protected areas of the beach. Kangaroo rats, white-footed mice, and meadow mice have been sighted in some areas.

Snowy plovers and endangered California least terns nest on the sandy beach. Gulls, terns, plovers, sandpipers, godwits, curlews, herons, ducks, grebes, and loons frequent the shallow water adjacent to the dune areas on the ocean side, and the mudflats on the bay side. Flocks of black brant, a species of goose, feed along the bay in spring.

South Bay Marine Biological Study Area: *E. of Hwy. 75, 1 mi. N. of Imperial Beach.*

Encompassing a small salt marsh system, the nature refuge provides an opportunity to observe the plants and animals indigenous to the area. Salt-tolerant plants such as glasswort, pickleweed, saltbush, and Torrey sea-blite provide nesting and feeding areas for migratory waterfowl including pintails, cinnamon teals, and surf scoters, and water birds such as terns. California horn snails, brine flies, and fiddler crabs are abundant in the tidal channels of the area.

Otay River Marsh: *Between 18th St. and Boundary Ave., San Diego.*

The Otay River Marsh is a wetland that comprises a series of salt marsh fragments lining the downstream areas of the river, expanding near the ocean into a broad mudflat system. The lowest levels of the salt marsh are dominated by pickleweed communities, whereas glasswort predominates in higher elevations.

California horn snails and brine flies occur where the salt marsh grades into a brackish water cattail-bulrush community.

Sweetwater Marsh

San Diego County
Imperial Beach and Tijuana River

Tijuana River National Estuarine Research Reserve

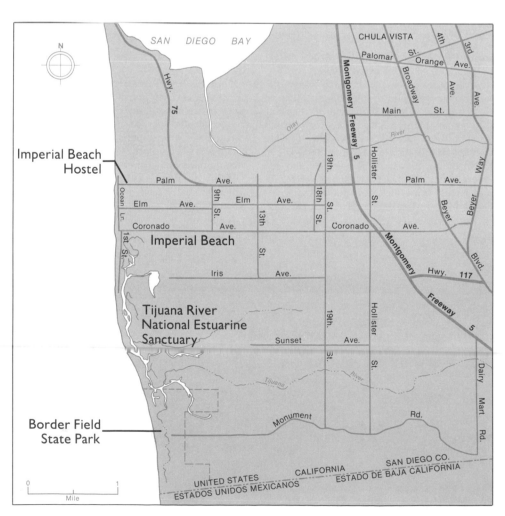

Imperial Beach Hostel: *170 Palm Ave., Imperial Beach.*

Located in a former firehouse one block from the ocean, the hostel accommodates up to 18 men and 12 women. Facilities include bunk beds, a community kitchen, and a common room. The hostel opens daily at 4:30 PM, and there is a curfew at 11 PM. For information and reservations, call: (619) 423-8039.

Imperial Beach: *14 mi. S. of San Diego.*

Imperial Beach was named by the South San Diego Investment Company in order to lure the residents of the Imperial Valley to build summer cottages on the beach, where the balmy weather would "cure rheumatic proclivities, catarrhal trouble, and lesions of the lungs." Imperial Beach was a quiet seaside village until 1906 when ferry and railroad connections with downtown San Diego were completed. In the early 1900s, a popular Sunday pastime was to board a ferry downtown that would sail through a channel dredged in the bay to a landing where an electric train would take you to "beautiful Imperial Beach."

Today, Imperial Beach is a residential community, and is also the site of the Naval Auxiliary Landing Field. The Imperial Beach Municipal Pier, located at the western end of Evergreen Ave., is popular for corbina and surf-perch fishing.

Tijuana River National Estuarine Sanctuary: *Off Hwy. 5 at Coronado Avenue.*

The Tijuana River National Estuarine Sanctuary (since renamed "National Estuarine Research Reserve") encompasses approximately 2,531 acres of tidally-flushed wetland, riparian, and upland habitats, and includes the Tijuana Slough National Wildlife Refuge and Border Field State Park. Tijuana River Estuary, Southern California's largest and most ecologically diverse wetland, extends two and a half miles along the shoreline and approximately one and a half miles inland. The lower estuary and upland areas support a diversity of plants, invertebrates, fish, and birds.

The lowest elevations are dominated by cordgrass, which forms stands along tidal channels, interspersed with pickleweed. Above the cordgrass-dominated community are several succulents, including pickleweed, saltwort, and sea-blite. Farther inland, jaumea and alkali heath predominate.

The invertebrate population in the estuarine sanctuary includes intertidal organisms such as worms, clams, horn snails, and crabs. The small tidal creeks and channels of the estuary support marine fish such as topsmelt, northern anchovy, opaleye, and white croaker. The wandering skipper, which inhabits the salt marsh, and the globose dune beetle, which occurs on coastal dunes, are two insects proposed for listing as endangered species.

Approximately 245 species of birds have been sighted in the estuary, including California least terns, light-footed clapper rails, California brown pelicans, Belding's savannah sparrows, and peregrine falcons, all of which are endangered. Under normal conditions, nearly one-fourth of California's light-footed clapper rail populations nest in the estuary. California least terns nest in the dunes and along the river

mouth, while California brown pelicans rest at the estuary between foraging trips to offshore feeding grounds. Peregrine falcons forage for prey throughout the estuary and river valley. The estuary is located along the Pacific Flyway and is used as a wintering site by a variety of waterfowl and shorebirds. Wintering waterfowl include pintails, cinnamon teals, surf scoters, and ruddy ducks.

Almost 20 species of shorebirds use the mudflats and sandflats of the estuary. Four species—the willet, dowitcher, sandpiper, and marbled godwit—account for most of the shorebird population throughout the year.

The Tijuana River National Estuarine Sanctuary supports diverse educational, scientific, recreational, and agricultural uses. The sanctuary's main purposes include research on salt marsh ecology, educational programs, and nature observation. A visitor center will be located on Caspian Way.

Border Field State Park: *W. end of Monument Rd., Imperial Beach.*

Located in the southwestern corner of the U.S., with Mexico at its southern boundary, Border Field State Park includes the International Boundary Markers that were established as a result of the 1848 Treaty of Guadalupe Hidalgo with Mexico. The park also contains a

mile of sandy beach popular for swimming, fishing, and clamming. Anglers catch perch, corbina, and halibut in the surf or in the estuary. Horseback riding, hiking, and bird watching are popular activities on the beach and in the interior areas of the park. Most of Border Field State Park is within the boundaries of the Tijuana River National Estuarine Sanctuary. For park information, call: (619) 428-3034.

Within the park are 400 acres of salt marsh and upland located on the floodplain and at the mouth of the Tijuana River. Salt marsh vegetation is dominated by pickleweed, saltgrass, and alkali heath; sand verbena and beach primrose grow in the sand dunes. The adjacent hillsides are covered with native coastal sage scrub. Three endangered plants—the green spine cactus, Shaw's agave, and salt marsh bird's beak—occur in the park.

Over 170 bird species have been sighted here. Northern harriers, red-tailed hawks, golden eagles, kestrels, egrets, herons, gulls, shorebirds, and waterfowl are commonly seen. Three endangered birds—the Belding's savannah sparrow, light-footed clapper rail, and California least tern—nest in the lagoon area. Snowy plovers nest on the beach near the dunes.

Commonly sighted mammals in the park include California ground squirrels, jack rabbits, and cottontails; occasionally weasels, opossums, and coyotes are also seen.

Great egret and long-billed dowitcher, Tijuana River Estuary

Coastal Management Agencies

California State Agencies:

California Coastal Commission
631 Howard Street, 4th Floor
San Francisco, CA 94105
(415) 543-8555

California Dept. of Boating and Waterways
1629 S Street
Sacramento, CA 95814
(916) 445-9657

California Dept. of Conservation
Division of Oil and Gas
1416 Ninth Street, Room 1310
Sacramento, CA 95814
(916) 323-1777

California Dept. of Fish and Game
1416 Ninth Street, 12th Floor
Sacramento, CA 95814
(916) 445-3531

California Dept. of Parks and Recreation
P.O. Box 942896
Sacramento, CA 94296-0001
(916) 445-6477

California Dept. of Water Resources
P.O. Box 942836
Sacramento, CA 94236-0001
(916) 445-9248

Resources Agency
1416 Ninth Street, Room 1311
Sacramento, CA 95814
(916) 445-5656

San Francisco Bay Conservation
    and Development Commission (BCDC)
30 Van Ness Avenue, Room 2011
San Francisco, CA 94102
(415) 557-3686

Santa Monica Mountains Conservancy
107 S. Broadway, Suite 7117
Los Angeles, CA 90012
(213) 620-2021

State Coastal Conservancy
1330 Broadway, Suite 1100
Oakland, CA 94612
(415) 464-1015

State Lands Commission
1807 13th Street
Sacramento, CA 95814
(916) 322-7777

State Water Resources Control Board
P.O. Box 100
Sacramento, CA 95801
(916) 322-3132

Wildlife Conservation Board
1416 Ninth Street
Sacramento, CA 95814
(916) 445-8448

Federal Agencies:

Camp Pendleton Marine Corps Base
Director of Natural Resources
Camp Pendleton, CA 92055
(619) 725-3360

Channel Islands National Marine Sanctuary
1901 Spinnaker Drive
Ventura, CA 93001
(805) 644-8464

Channel Islands National Park
1901 Spinnaker Drive
Ventura, CA 93001
(805) 644-8157

Elkhorn Slough National Estuarine Research Reserve
1700 Elkhorn Road
Watsonville, CA 95076
(408) 728-2822

Fort Ord Military Reservation
Attention AFZW-PO
Public Affairs Office
Ford Ord, CA 93941-5660
(408) 242-3133

Golden Gate National Recreation Area
Fort Mason, Building 201
San Francisco, CA 94123
(415) 556-0560

Gulf of the Farallones National Marine Sanctuary
Fort Mason, Building 201
San Francisco, CA 94123
(415) 556-3509

King Range National Conservation Area
Arcata Resource Area—BLM
P. O. Box 1112
Arcata, CA 95521
(707) 822-7648

Los Padres National Forest, U.S. Forest Service
6144 Calle Real
Goleta, CA 93117
(805) 683-6711

Mugu Lagoon, Public Affairs Officer
Pacific Missile Test Center
Point Mugu, CA 93042-5000
(805) 989-8094

National Marine Fisheries Service
Dept. of Commerce, Southwest Region
300 South Ferry Street, Room 2016
Terminal Island, CA 90731
(213) 514-6196

National Oceanic and Atmospheric Administration
Office of Ocean and Coastal Resource Management
1825 Connecticut Avenue N. W., Suite 706
Universal Building South
Washington, D. C. 20235
(202) 673-5111

National Park Service
Western Region Information Office
Fort Mason, Building 201
San Francisco, CA 94123
(415) 556-4122

Point Reyes National Seashore
Bear Valley Road
Point Reyes, CA 94956
(415) 663-1092

Redwood National Park
1111 2nd Street
Crescent City, CA 95531
(707) 464-6101

Santa Monica Mountains National Recreation Area
22900 Ventura Boulevard, Suite 140
Woodland Hills, CA 91364
(818) 888-3770

Tijuana River National Estuarine Research Reserve
3990 Old Town Avenue, Suite 300C
San Diego, CA 92110
(619) 237-6766

U.S. Army Corps of Engineers
211 Main Street
San Francisco, CA 94105   (415) 974-0429

U.S. Army Corps of Engineers
300 N. Los Angeles Street
Los Angeles, CA 90053-2325
(213) 894-5522

U.S. Coast Guard
Commander 11th Coast Guard
400 Ocean Gate
Long Beach, CA 90822-5399
(213) 590-2213

U.S. Fish and Wildlife Service
Office of Public Affairs
500 N. E. Multnomah, Suite 1692
Portland, OR 97232   (503) 231-6121

U. S. Naval Amphibious Base, Coronado
Attention Public Affairs Officer
San Diego, CA 92155-5000
(619) 437-3232

Vandenberg Air Force Base
1 Strategic Areospace Division
Public Affairs
Vandenberg Air Force Base, CA 93437-5000
(805) 866-3891

Private Agencies:

Audubon Canyon Ranch
4900 Shoreline Highway
Stinson Beach, CA 94970   (415) 383-1644

The Big Sur Land Trust
P. O. Box 221864
Carmel, CA 93921   (408) 625-5522

The Nature Conservancy
785 Market Street
San Francisco, CA 94103   (415) 777-0541

Santa Catalina Island Conservancy
P. O. Box 2739
Avalon, CA 90704   (213) 510-1421

The Trust for Public Land
116 New Montgomery
San Francisco, CA 94105   (415) 495-4014

Institutions:

Bodega Marine Reserve
P. O. Box 247
Bodega, CA 94923   (707) 875-2211

Catalina Marine Science Center
University of Southern California
P. O. Box 398
Avalon, CA 90704   (213) 743-6792

Hopkins Marine Station
Pacific Grove, CA 93950   (408) 373-0464

Moss Landing Marine Laboratories
P. O. Box 450
Moss Landing, CA 95039   (408) 633-3304

Scripps Institution of Oceanography
University of California, San Diego
Public Affairs Office, A-033
La Jolla, CA 92093   (619) 534-3626

University of California Natural Reserve System
Agriculture and Natural Resources
2120 University Avenue, 4th Floor
University of California
Berkeley, CA 94720   (415) 644-4211

Acknowledgments

It is impossible to name each of the many individuals at the California Coastal Commission and the staff members of the numerous local, state, and federal agencies and private institutions who helped make this book possible, but we extend our thanks and sincere gratitude to them all.

We would like to thank the following people who aided in the gathering, preparation, and review of material for this book:

California Coastal Commission Staff

Bill Allayaud	John Leslie
Brian E. Baird	Jack Liebster
Gary Berrigan	Linda Locklin
Mark Capelli	Dave Loomis
Joy Chase	Margaret Macleod
Chuck Damm	Richard J. McCarthy
Pamela D. Emerson	Jim McGrath
Bruce Fodge	James J. Muth
Herb Fox	Lee Otter
Liz Fuchs	James R. Raives
Susan Hatfield	Dan Ray
Teresa Henry	Rick Rayburn
Gary L. Holloway	Les Strnad
Lisa Horowitz	Noah Tilghman
Rick Hyman	Mei Mei Wang
Robert F. Joseph	Mark Wheetley
Diane Landry	Wayne Woodroof
Eugenia Laychak	Peter Xander
Deborah Lee	

Review and Consultation

David Ainley, *Point Reyes Bird Observatory*
Dr. Richard A. Arnold, *Entomological Consultant*
Alan Baldridge, *Hopkins Marine Station*
Robert Belous, *Redwood National Park*
Dr. Howell Daly, *U.C. Berkeley, Department of Entomology*
John De Benedictus, *U.C. Berkeley, Department of Entomology*
Dr. John T. Doyen, *U.C. Berkeley, Department of Entomology*
Bruce Elliott, *California Department of Fish and Game*
Phyllis M. Faber, *Wetlands Biologist*
Wayne R. Ferren, Jr., *Curator, U.C. Santa Barbara Herbarium*
Dr. Reinhard E. Flick, *California Department of Boating and Waterways*
John Gallinatti, *Project Geologist, Converse Consultants*
Dr. David L. Garrison, *Institute of Marine Studies, U.C. Santa Cruz*
John Grant, *California Department of Fish and Game*
Dr. H. Gary Greene, *U.S. Geological Survey*
Dr. Harry Greene, *Museum of Vertebrate Zoology, U.C. Berkeley*
Austin Griffiths, Jr., *Botanical Field Consultant*
Ronald F. Hein, *California Department of Fish and Game*
Ronald J. Jameson, *U.S. Fish and Wildlife Service*
Bruce L. Johnson, *California Historical Society*
John Kelly, *Point Reyes Bird Observatory*
Jeff Kennedy, *University of California Natural Reserve System*
Bud Laurent, *California Department of Fish and Game*
Charles Mehlert, *California Department of Parks and Recreation*
Will Murray, *Santa Cruz Island Nature Conservancy*
Chris Nagano, *L.A. Museum of Natural History*
Dr. Robert Orndoff, *U.C. Berkeley, Department of Botany*
Dr. James L. Patton, *Museum of Vertebrate Zoology, U.C. Berkeley*
Susan Peaslee, *Point Reyes Bird Observatory*
Carol Pillsbury, *Channel Islands National Marine Sanctuary*
Dr. Jerry A. Powell, *U.C. Berkeley, Department of Entomology*
Douglas Propst, *Santa Catalina Island Conservancy*
Gar Salzberg, *Pismo State Beach Park Ranger*
Mark Silberstein, *Elkhorn Slough National Estuarine Research Reserve*
Rich Stallcup, *Point Reyes Bird Observatory*
Nancy Stone, *Gulf of the Farallones National Marine Sanctuary*
William Travis, *S.F. Bay Conservation and Development Commission*
Dr. Richard Walker, *U.C. Berkeley, Department of Geography*
Dr. Steve Webster, *Monterey Bay Aquarium*
Fred Wendell, *California Department of Fish and Game*
John West, *U.C. Berkeley, Department of Botany*
Wayne C. Wheeler, *U.S. Coast Guard*
Nick Whelan, *Channel Islands National Marine Sanctuary*
Ken Wilson, *California Department of Fish and Game*
Vernal L. Yadon, *Pacific Grove Museum of Natural History*
Rick York, *California Native Plant Society*
Dan Yparraguirre, *California Department of Fish and Game*
Dr. Joy B. Zedler, *San Diego State University, Department of Biology*

Photo Credits

Photographs Courtesy of:
Ansel Adams Publishing Rights Trust, cover photo
Jim Alinder, dedication page photo
The Bancroft Library, University of California at Berkeley, Hazeltine Collection, p. 66; Redwood Empire Association, pp. 81, 91, 94; George Reed, p. 154; Hills-Hecht Collection, pp. 165, 167; Taber Collection, p. 357
Ed Brady, Aero Photographers, pp. 140, 143, 148, 162
California Historical Society, San Francisco, The Photographic Archives, pp. 78, 84, 184, 252, 255, 257, 331; A.W. Erickson, p. 56; Challiss Gore, pp. 208, 210, 245; Anderson Photo Service, Santa Barbara, p. 250; Frank L. Park and Co., p. 360; Parker, San Diego, p. 361
California Historical Society, Ticor Title Insurance and Trust Collection, Los Angeles, pp. 79, 271, 275, 292, 294, 295, 301, 315, 317, 320, 345, 354
California State Library, p. 168, 309
Del Norte County Historical Society, p. 85
El Moro Publications, p. 231
Harry Mayo and the Santa Cruz Surfing Museum, p. 188
The J. Paul Getty Museum, Julius Shulman, p. 286
National Maritime Museum, San Francisco, pp. 66, 84, 86, 117, 121, 190, 306, 307, 359
National Park Service, Robert Belous, p. 89
Point Reyes Bird Observatory, p. 158; Teya Penniman, p. 159; Burr Heneman, pp. 28, 159
Redwood Empire Association, p. 136
The Society of California Pioneers, pp. 103, 104, 115, 119, 125, 169, 177, 362
David H. Swanlund, p. 109
Tijuana River National Estuarine Research Reserve, Paul Jorgenson, pp. 22, 364, 365
University of California at Santa Cruz Library, Special Collections, p. 183, 187, 189, 195

Special thanks to the following photographers:

Ruth Askevold	Michael L. Fischer	Gianmaria Mussio
Brian Baird	Susan Hansch	Briggs Nisbet
Debbie Benrubi	Eric Hunziker	Mindy Richter
Gina Bentzley	Christopher Kroll	Mark Safran
Michael Buck	Alyse Jacobson	Steve Scholl
Madge Caughman	John Lentz	Dave Scott
Scott Cochran	Jack Liebster	Sabrina Simpson
Kati Corsaut	Eric Metz	Pat Stebbins
Trevor Cralle	Trish Mihalek	Noah Tilghman
Linda Goff Evans	David Miller	Bill Van Beckum

Composition

Grateful acknowledgment is made to Pete Stoelzl of Mackenzie-Harris Corp., San Francisco, for his cheerful and patient assistance in the composition of this book.

Illustrators

Robert A. Bennett: pp. 70, 72, originally prepared for *Historic Preservation Plan, Santa Cruz, California*
Madge Caughman: pp. 32, 33, 72, 73, 75
Pieter Folkens: pp. 53, 54, 55
Judith Feins: pp. 22, 24, 26, 27, 30, 31, 34, 35, 36, 37, 38, 40, 41, 42, 43, 44, 51, 58, 59, 61, 64, 65, 89, 107, 108, 135, 142, 144, 152, 164, 172, 198, 202, 220, 222, 236, 255, 256, 265, 280, 282, 286, 288, 291, 304, 346
Jane Heaphy: pp. 12, 13, 27, 64, 70, 73, 75, 98, 119, 146, 154, 205, 239, 251, 254, 290, 302, 334, 357
Karen Jacobsen: pp. 45, 46, 47, 210
Valerie Kells: pp. 40, 52, 174, 197, 235, 243, 262
Anna V. Kondolf: pp. 74, 75, 99, 124, 180, 303
Kendal Morris: pp. 48, 50, 130, 132, 134, 191, 249, 272, 337
Gianmaria Mussio: pp. 58, 59, 60, 62, 63, 64, 65, 82, 88, 110, 172, 230, 246, 276, 277, 339, 349

page 179: historic print from San Mateo County Historical Museum
page 180: from *South from San Francisco*, Frank M. Stanger
page 205: diagram prepared after drawing by Tau Rho Alpha, United States Department of the Interior, Geological Survey
page 355: from *History of California*, Bandini
pages 58, 358: from *The Islands and Ports of California, A Guide to Coastal California*, Duncan Gleason, New York: Devin-Adair Co., 1958. Permission to reprint granted by Devin-Adair Publishers of Greenwich, CT.

Special thanks to Pieter Folkens, instructor of the Biological Illustration Program at U.C. Santa Cruz for his illustrations and for providing illustrations prepared by his students Karen Jacobsen, Valerie Kells, and Kendal Morris. Copyright © 1987, All rights reserved.

Thanks also to our production staff: Ruth Askevold and Anna Goode

Abbott, Isabella A., and George J. Hollenberg. *Marine Algae of California.* Stanford, Ca.: Stanford Univ. Press, 1976.

Alt, David, and Donald Hyndman. *Roadside Geology of Northern California.* 2d ed. Missoula, Mont.: Mountain Press Publishing Co., 1978.

American Littoral Society. *California Coastal Catalogue.* Sandy Hook, Highlands, N.J., 1980.

Bailey, Harry P. *Weather of Southern California.* Berkeley: Univ. of California Press, 1966.

Bakker, Elna. *An Island Called California.* 2d ed. Berkeley: Univ. of California Press, 1984.

Balls, Edward K. *Early Uses of California Plants.* Berkeley: Univ. of California Press, 1962.

Bancroft, Hubert Howe. *History of California.* San Francisco: The History Co., 1886-1890.

Banham, Reyner. *Los Angeles: The Architecture of Four Ecologies.* Harmondsworth, Middlesex, England: Penguin Books, Ltd., 1971.

Barbour, M.G., and J. Major, eds. *Terrestrial Vegetation of California.* New York: John Wiley and Sons, 1977.

Barbour, Michael G., Robert B. Craig, Frank R. Drysdale, and Michael T. Ghiselin. *Coastal Ecology, Bodega Head.* Berkeley: Univ. of California Press, 1973.

Barry, W. James, and Evert I. Schlinger, eds. *Inglenook Fen, A Study and Plan.* Sacramento, Ca.: California Dept. of Parks and Recreation, 1977.

Bascom, Willard. *Waves and Beaches.* rev. ed. Garden City, N.Y.: Anchor Books, 1980.

Beck, Warren A., and Ynez D. Haase. *Historical Atlas of California.* Norman, Ok.: Univ. of Oklahoma Press, 1974.

Behrens, David W. *Pacific Coast Nudibranchs.* Los Osos, Ca.: Sea Challengers, 1980.

Berry, William D., and Elizabeth Berry. *Mammals of the San Francisco Bay Region.* Berkeley: Univ. of California Press, 1959.

Berssen, Capt. William, ed. *Pacific Boating Almanac.* Ventura, Ca.: Western Marine Enterprises, 1986.

Booth, Ernest Sheldon. *Mammals of Southern California.* Berkeley: Univ. of California Press, 1968.

Bowen, Oliver E., Jr. *Rocks and Minerals of the San Francisco Bay Region.* Berkeley: Univ. of California Press, 1962.

California Coastal Commission. *California Coastal Access Guide.* 3d ed. Berkeley: Univ. of California Press, 1983.

California Native Plant Society. *Inventory of Rare and Endangered Vascular Plants of California.* 3d ed. Special Publication No. 1, Berkeley, 1980.

California Sea Grant College Program. *California's Coastal Wetlands.* Sea Grant Report Series No. 2. La Jolla, Ca.: 1979.

California Dept. of Fish and Game. *Atlas of California Coastal Marine Resources.* Sacramento, Ca., 1980.

California Dept. of Fish and Game and U.S. Fish and Wildlife Service. *Coastal Wetlands Series,* nos. 1-21. Sacramento, Ca., 1970-1977.

California State Dept. of Parks and Recreation. *California Historical Landmarks.* rev. ed. Sacramento, Ca., 1982.

California State Dept. of Parks and Recreation. *Guide to California State Parks,* and map. rev. ed. Sacramento, Ca., 1985.

California State Dept. of Parks and Recreation and California State Dept. of Conservation. *Pygmy Forest Ecological Staircase Feasibility Study.* Sacramento, Ca., 1974.

Carefoot, Thomas. *Pacific Seashores, A Guide to Intertidal Ecology.* Seattle: Univ. of Washington Press, 1977.

Carr, Pat, and Steve Tracy. *Monterey Peninsula Walking Tours.* Carmel, Ca.: The Hampton-Brown Company, Inc., 1984.

Carranco, Lynwood. *Redwood Lumber Industry.* San Marino, Ca.: Golden West Books, 1982.

Cogswell, Howard L. *Water Birds of California.* Berkeley: Univ. of California Press, 1977.

Conradson, Diane R. *Exploring Our Baylands.* Point Reyes, Ca.: Coastal Park Association, 1982.

Cooper, William S. "Coastal Dunes of California." *Geological Society of America Memoir No. 104* (1967).

Coy, Owen C. *The Humboldt Bay Region: 1850-1875.* 1929. Reprint. Eureka, Ca.: Humboldt County Historical Society, 1982.

Crampton, Beecher. *Grasses in California.* Berkeley: Univ. of California Press, 1974.

Crump, Spencer. *Ride the Big Red Cars: The Pacific Electric Story.* Glendale, Ca.: Trans-Anglo Books, 1983.

Dale, Nancy. *Flowering Plants: The Santa Monica Mountains.* Santa Barbara, Ca.: Capra Press, 1986.

Dames and Moore. *Pacific Coast Ecological Inventory: User's Guide and Information Base,* and maps. Washington, D.C.: Biological Services Program, U.S. Fish and Wildlife Service, 1981.

Dana, Richard Henry, Jr. *Two Years Before the Mast.* New York, 1840. Available in various editions.

Daugherty, Anita E. *Marine Mammals of California.* Sacramento, Ca.: California State Dept. of Fish and Game, 1972.

Davis, John, and Alan Baldridge. *The Bird Year—With Special Reference to the Monterey Bay Area.* Pacific Grove, Ca.: The Boxwood Press, 1980.

Dawson, E. Yale, and Michael S. Foster. *Seashore Plants of California.* Berkeley: Univ. of California Press, 1982.

Delahanty, Randolph. *California: A Guidebook.* San Diego: Harcourt Brace Jovanovich, 1984.

Delkin, James Ladd. *Monterey Peninsula.* 2d ed. Northern California Writers' Project, 1946.

Dohl, Thomas P., Michael L. Bonnell, Robert C. Guess, and Kenneth T. Briggs. *Marine Mammal and Seabird Study, Central and Northern California.* POCS Technical Paper No. 82-1. Prepared for the U.S. Bureau of Land Management by the Center for Coastal Marine Studies, Univ. of California at Santa Cruz, 1982.

Doss, Margot Patterson. *The Bay Area at Your Feet.* rev. ed. San Rafael, Ca.: Presidio Press, 1981.

Doss, Margot Patterson. *Paths of Gold, In and Around the Golden Gate National Recreation Area.* San Francisco: Chronicle Books, 1974.

Edwards, Don. *Making the Most of Sonoma.* San Rafael, Ca.: Presidio Press, 1982.

Eschmeyer, William M., Earl S. Herald, and Howard Hammond. *A Field Guide to Pacific Coast Fishes of North America.* The Peterson Field Guide Series. Boston: Houghton Mifflin Company, 1983.

Faber, Phyllis M. *Common Wetland Plants of Coastal California.* Mill Valley, Ca.: Pickleweed Press, 1982.

Fagan, Brian. *Cruising Guide to California's Channel Islands.* rev. ed. Ventura, Ca.: Western Marine Enterprises, Inc., 1983.

Fay, James S., Anne Lipow, and Stephanie W. Fay, eds. *California Almanac.* Novato, Ca.: Presidio Press, 1984.

Federal Writers' Project of the Works Progress Administration, State of California. *The WPA Guide to California.* 1939. Reprint. New York: Pantheon Books, 1984.

Fehrenbacher, D.E., and N.E. Tutorow. *California, An Illustrated History.* New York: D. Van Nostrand Company, Inc., 1968.

Felton, James P., ed. *Newport Beach 75, 1906-1981; A Diamond Jubilee History.* Fullerton, Ca.: Sultana Press, 1981.

Femling, Jean. *Great Piers of California.* Santa Barbara, Ca.: Capra Press, 1984.

Ferris, R.S. *Flowers of Point Reyes National Seashore.* Berkeley: Univ. of California Press, 1970.

Fink, Augusta. *Monterey County: The Dramatic Story of Its Past.* Santa Cruz, Ca.: Western Tanager Press, 1982.

Finson, Bruce, ed. *Discovering California.* San Francisco: California Academy of Sciences, 1983.

Fitch, John E., and Robert J. Lavenberg. *Tidepool and Nearshore Fishes of California.* Berkeley: Univ. of California Press, 1975.

Foster, Lee. *Making the Most of the Peninsula.* San Francisco: Presidio Press, 1983.

Foster, M.S., and D.R. Schiel. *The Ecology of Giant Kelp Forests in California.* Biological Services Program, U.S. Fish and Wildlife Service, Washington, D.C., 1985.

Friis, Leo J. *Orange County Through Four Centuries.* Santa Ana, Ca.: Pioneer Press, 1965.

Futcher, Jane. *Marin, the Place, the People.* New York: Holt, Rinehart and Winston, 1981.

Gebhard, David, Roger Montgomery, Robert Winter, John Woodbridge, and Sally Woodbridge. *A Guide to Architecture in San Francisco and Northern California.* 2d ed. Santa Barbara: Peregrine Smith, Inc., 1976.

Gebhard, David, and Robert Winter. *Architecture in Los Angeles: A Compleat Guide.* Salt Lake City: Peregrine Smith Books, 1985.

Gilliam, Harold. *Between the Devil and the Deep Blue Bay: The Struggle to Save San Francisco Bay.* San Francisco: Chronicle Books, 1969.

Gilliam, Harold. *The Natural World of San Francisco.* New York: Doubleday and Co., Inc., 1967.

Gilliam, Harold. *San Francisco Bay.* New York: Doubleday and Co., 1957.

Gilliam, Harold. *Weather of the San Francisco Bay Region.* Berkeley: Univ. of California Press, 1962.

Glassow, Michael A. *An Archeological Overview of the Northern Channel Islands, California.* Dept. of Anthropology, Univ. of California at Santa Barbara, and U.S. National Park Service.

Gordon, Burton L. *Monterey Bay Area: Natural History and Cultural Imprints.* 2d ed. Pacific Grove, Ca.: The Boxwood Press, 1977.

Gotshall, Daniel W., and Laurence L. Laurent. *Pacific Coast Subtidal Marine Invertebrates.* Los

Osos, Ca.: Sea Challengers, 1979.

Gotshall, Daniel W. *Pacific Coast Inshore Fishes.* Los Osos, Ca.: Sea Challengers, 1981.

Griggs, Gary, and Laret Savoy, eds. *Living with the California Coast.* Durham, N.C.: Duke Univ. Press, 1985.

Grillos, Steve J. *Ferns and Fern Allies of California.* Berkeley: Univ. of California Press, 1966.

Gudde, Erwin B. *California Place Names.* 3d ed. Berkeley: Univ. of California Press, 1969.

Hamilton, Geneva. *Where the Highway Ends— Cambria, San Simeon and the Ranchos.* San Luis Obispo, Ca.: Padre Productions, 1974.

Hansen, Gladys. *San Francisco Almanac.* Novato, Ca.: Presidio Press, 1980.

Hart, James D. *A Companion to California.* New York: Oxford Univ. Press, 1978.

Hayden, Mike. *Exploring the North Coast.* rev. ed. San Francisco: Chronicle Books, 1982.

Hedgpeth, Joel W. *Introduction to Seashore Life of the San Francisco Bay Region and the Coast of Northern California.* Berkeley: Univ. of California Press, 1962.

Heizer, Robert F., and Albert B. Elsasser. *The Natural World of the California Indians.* Berkeley: Univ. of California Press, 1980.

Heizer, R.F., and M.A. Whipple. *The California Indians; A Source Book.* 2d ed. Berkeley: Univ. of California Press, 1971.

Hill, Mary. *California Landscape: Origin and Evolution.* Berkeley: Univ. of California Press, 1984.

Hinton, Sam. *Seashore Life of Southern California.* Berkeley: Univ. of California Press, 1969.

Holland, Robert F., and F. Thomas Griggs. "A Unique Habitat—California's Vernal Pools." *Fremontia* 4 no. 3 (Oct. 1976): 3-6.

Hoopes, Chad L. *Lure of Humboldt Bay Region.* Dubuque, Iowa: Wm. C. Brown Book Co., 1966.

Hoover, Mildred Brooke, Hero Eugene Rensch, and Ethel Grace Rensch. *Historic Spots in California.* Stanford: Stanford Univ. Press, 1966.

Hoover, Robert F. *The Vascular Plants of San Luis Obispo County, California.* Berkeley: Univ. of California Press, 1970.

Hornbeck, David. *California Patterns, A Geographical and Historical Atlas.* Palo Alto, Ca.: Mayfield Publishing Co., 1983.

Horton, Tom, and Karen Horton. *The Dolphin Guide to Los Angeles.* Garden City, N.Y.: Doubleday and Company, Inc., 1984.

Howard, Arthur D. *Geologic History of Middle California.* Berkeley: Univ. of California Press, 1979.

Howitt, Beatrice F. *Wildflowers of the Monterey Area, California.* Salt Lake City: The Wheelwright Press, 1965.

Howorth, Peter. *Foraging Along the California Coast.* Santa Barbara, Ca.: Capra Press, 1977.

Hutchinson, W.H. *California: Two Centuries of Man, Land, and Growth.* Palo Alto, Ca.: American West Publishing Company, 1971.

Hynding, Alan. *From Frontier to Suburb: The Story of the San Mateo Peninsula.* Belmont, Ca.: Star Publishing Company, 1982.

Iacopi, Robert. *Earthquake Country.* Menlo Park, Ca.: Lane Books, 1973.

Inman, D.L., and J.D. Frautschy. "Littoral Processes and the Development of Shorelines." *Proceedings of the Coastal Engineering Specialty Conference.* Santa Barbara, Ca., 1966.

Jackson, Ruth A. *Combing the Coast: Highway One from San Francisco to San Luis Obispo.* San Francisco: Chronicle Books, 1985.

Jaeger, Edmund C., and Arthur C. Smith. *Introduction to the Natural History of Southern California.* Berkeley: Univ. of California Press, 1966.

Jepson, W.L. *A Manual of the Flowering Plants of California.* San Francisco: California School Book Depository, 1923.

Johnson, Paul. *Pictorial History of California.* Garden City, N.Y.: Doubleday and Company, Inc., 1970.

Jones, Kathleen Goddard. "The Nipomo Dunes." *Fremontia* 2 no. 4 (Jan. 1984): 3-10.

Jones and Stokes Associates, Inc. *An Ecological Characterization of the Central and Northern California Coastal Region.* Prepared for the U.S. Bureau of Land Management and U.S. Fish and Wildlife Service, Sacramento, Ca., 1981.

Johnsgard, Paul A. *A Guide to North American Waterfowl.* Bloomington, Ind.: Indiana Univ. Press, 1979.

Josselyn, Michael. *The Ecology of San Francisco Bay Tidal Marshes.* U.S. Fish and Wildlife Service, Division of Biological Services, Washington, D.C., 1983.

Jurmain, Claudia K., and James J. Rawls, eds. *California, A Place, A People, A Dream.* San Francisco: Chronicle Books, 1986.

Kerr, Richard A. "Ophiolites: Windows on Which Ocean Crust?" *Science 219* (March 18 1983): 1307-1309.

Knox, Maxine, and Mary Rodriguez. *Making the Most of the Monterey Peninsula and Big Sur.* San Rafael, Ca.: Presidio Press, 1978.

Knox, Maxine, and Mary Rodriguez. *Steinbeck's Street: Cannery Row.* San Rafael, Ca.: Presidio Press, 1980.

Koch, Margaret. *Santa Cruz County, Parade of the Past.* Fresno, Ca.: Valley Publishers, 1973.

Koch, Margaret. *The Walk Around Santa Cruz Book.* Fresno, Ca.: Valley Publishers, 1978.

Kozloff, Eugene N. *Seashore Life of the Northern Pacific Coast.* rev. ed. Seattle: Univ. of Washington Press, 1983.

Kroeber, A.L. *Handbook of the Indians of California.* New York: Dover Publications, Inc., 1976.

Kuhn, Gerald G., and Francis P. Shepard. *Sea Cliffs, Beaches, and Coastal Valleys of San Diego County.* Berkeley: Univ. of California Press, 1984.

Lane, John. "California's Monarch Butterfly Trees." *Pacific Discovery* 38 no. 1 (January/ March 1985): 13-15.

Leatherwood, Stephen, and Randall R. Reeves. *The Sierra Club Handbook of Whales and Dolphins.* San Francisco: Sierra Club Books, 1983.

Le Boeuf, Burney J. *The Natural History of Año Nuevo.* Pacific Grove, Ca.: The Boxwood Press, 1981.

Lee, Georgia, Vicki Leon, and Lachland MacDonald. *An Uncommon Guide to San Luis Obispo County, California.* San Luis Obispo, Ca.: Padre Productions, 1977.

Lussier, Tomi Kay. *Big Sur: A Complete History and Guide.* Monterey, Ca.: Big Sur Publications, 1979.

Lydon, Sandy. *Chinese Gold: The Chinese in the Monterey Bay Region.* Capitola, Ca.: Capitola Book Company, 1985.

Margolin, Malcolm. *The Ohlone Way: Indian Life in the San Francisco–Monterey Bay Area.* Berkeley: Heyday Books, 1978.

Marinacci, Barbara, and Rudy Marinacci. *California's Spanish Place-Names.* San Rafael, Ca.: Presidio Press, 1980.

Mason, Herbert L. *A Flora of the Marshes of California.* Berkeley: Univ. of California Press, 1957.

Mason, Jack. *Point Reyes: The Solemn Land.* Inverness, Ca.: North Shore Books, 1972.

McAuley, Milt. *Hiking Trails of the Santa Monica Mountains.* 3d ed. Canoga Park, Ca.: Canyon Publishing Co., 1984.

McMinn, Howard E., and Evelyn Maino. *An Illustrated Manual of Pacific Coast Trees.* 2d ed. Berkeley: Univ. of California Press, 1981.

McWilliams, Carey. *Southern California: An Island on the Land.* Salt Lake City: Peregrine Smith Books, 1946.

Metcalf, Woodbridge. *Native Trees of the San Francisco Bay Region.* Berkeley: Univ. of California Press, 1959.

Miller, Crane S. *California: The Geography of Diversity.* Palo Alto, Ca.: Mayfield Publishing Company, 1983.

Milne, Terry. *The Ultimate Bay Book: The Discovery & Delights of San Francisco Bay.* San Francisco: California Living Books, 1979.

Moore, Charles, Peter Becker, and Regula Campbell. *The City Observed: Los Angeles, A Guide to Its Architecture and Landscapes.* New York: Vintage Books, 1984.

Morris, Robert H., Donald P. Abbott, and Eugene C. Haderlie. *Intertidal Invertebrates of California.* Stanford: Stanford Univ. Press, 1980.

Munz, Philip A., and David D. Keck. *A California Flora.* Berkeley: Univ. of California Press, 1959.

Munz, Philip A. *California Mountain Wildflowers.* Berkeley: Univ. of California Press, 1963.

Munz, Philip A. *Shore Wildflowers of California, Oregon and Washington.* Berkeley: Univ. of California Press, 1964.

Murphy, Bill. *A Pictorial History of California.* San Francisco: Fearon Publishers, 1958.

National Geographic Society Field Guide to the Birds of North America. Kingsport, Tenn.: Kingsport Press, 1983.

Nicholson, Loren, and Bernice Loughran. *San Luis Obispo County Pathways.* San Luis Obispo, Ca.: New Paradigm Press, 1981.

Nickerson, Roy. *Sea Otters; A Natural History and Guide.* San Francisco: Chronicle Books, 1984.

Nordhoff, Charles. *California for Travellers and Settlers.* 1873. Reprint. Berkeley: Ten Speed Press, 1973.

Nordhoff, Charles. *Northern California, Oregon, and the Sandwich Islands.* 1874. Reprint. Berkeley: Ten Speed Press, 1974.

Norris, Robert M., and Robert W. Webb. *Geology of California.* New York: John Wiley & Sons, 1976.

Oakeshott, Gordon B. *California's Changing Landscapes; A Guide to the Geology of the State.* San Francisco: McGraw-Hill Book Company, 1971.

Ornduff, Robert. *Introduction to California Plant Life*. Berkeley: Univ. of California Press, 1974.

Orr, Robert T. *Marine Mammals of California*. Berkeley: Univ. of California Press, 1972.

Parks, Annette White. *Qhawala-li "Water Coming Down Place": A History of Gualala, Mendocino County, California*. Ukiah, Ca.: Freshcut Press, 1980.

Perry, John, and Jane Perry. *The Sierra Club Guide to the Natural Areas of California*. San Francisco: Sierra Club Books, 1983.

Peterson, Roger Tory. *A Field Guide to Western Birds*. The Peterson Field Guide Series. 2d ed. Boston: Houghton Mifflin Company, 1961.

Peterson, Victor P. *Native Trees of Southern California*. Berkeley: Univ. of California Press, 1966.

Pierson, Robert John. *The Beach Towns: A Walker's Guide to L.A.'s Beach Communities*. San Francisco: Chronicle Books, 1985.

Pourade, Richard F. *The History of San Diego: The Explorers*. San Diego: Union-Tribune Publishing Company, 1960.

Powell, Jerry A., and Charles L. Hogue. *California Insects*. Berkeley: Univ. of California Press, 1979.

Power, Dennis M., ed. *The California Islands: Proceedings of a Multidisciplinary Symposium*. Santa Barbara, Ca.: Santa Barbara Museum of Natural History, 1980.

Powers, Stephen. *Tribes of California*. Berkeley: Univ. of California Press, 1976.

Pryde, Philip R, ed. *San Diego: An Introduction to the Region*. 2d ed. Dubuque, Iowa: Kendall/Hunt Publishing Company, 1984.

Rand McNally. *Guide to California*. Chicago, 1982.

Rapoport, Roger, and Margot Lind. *The California Catalogue*. New York: E.P. Dutton & Co., Inc., 1977.

Raven, Peter H. *Native Shrubs of Southern California*. Berkeley: Univ. of California Press, 1966.

Reisner, Marc. *Cadillac Desert*. New York: Viking Press, 1987.

Reiter, Martin. *The Palos Verdes Peninsula: A Geologic Guide and More*. Dubuque, Iowa: Kendall/Hunt Publishing Company, 1984.

Ricketts, Edward F., Jack Calvin, and Joel W. Hedgpeth, rev. by David W. Phillips. *Between Pacific Tides*. 5th ed. Stanford: Stanford Univ. Press, 1985.

Robbins, Chandler S., Bertel Bruun, and Herbert S. Zim. *A Guide to Field Identification: Birds of North America*. The Golden Field Guides Series. rev. ed. New York: Golden Press, 1983.

Roberson, Don. *Monterey Birds*. Carmel, Ca.: Monterey Peninsula Audubon Society, 1985.

San Luis Obispo County Heritage Series, *Captain Portolá in San Luis Obispo County in 1769*. Morro Bay, Ca.: Tabula Rasa Press, 1984.

Shanks, Ralph C., Jr., and Janetta Thompson Shanks. *Lighthouses and Lifeboats on the Redwood Coast*. San Anselmo, Ca.: Costano Books, 1978.

Shapiro and Associates, Inc. *Humboldt Bay Wetlands Review and Baylands Analysis*. Prepared for U.S. Army Corps of Engineers. Seattle, 1980.

Sharsmith, Helen K. *Spring Wildflowers of the San Francisco Bay Region*. Berkeley: Univ. of California Press, 1965.

Shepard, Francis P. *Geological Oceanography: Evolution of Coasts, Continental Margins, and the Deep Sea Floor*. New York: Crane, Russak and Company, Inc., 1977.

Shepard, Francis P., and Harold R. Wanless. *Our Changing Coastlines*. New York: McGraw-Hill, Inc., 1971.

Silka, Henry P. *San Pedro, a Pictorial History*. San Pedro, Ca.: San Pedro Bay Historical Society, 1984.

Smith, Arthur C. *Introduction to the Natural History of the San Francisco Bay Region*. Berkeley: Univ. of California Press, 1960.

Smith, Clifton F. *A Flora of the Santa Barbara Region, California*. Santa Barbara, Ca.: Santa Barbara Museum of Natural History, 1976.

Sowls, Arthur L., Anthony R. DeGange, Jay W. Nelson, and Gary S. Lester. *Catalog of California Seabird Colonies*. Washington, D.C.: Office of Biological Services, U.S. Fish and Wildlife Service, 1980.

Squire, James L., Jr., and Susan E. Smith. *Anglers' Guide to the United States Pacific Coast*. Seattle: U. S. Department of Commerce, National Oceanic and Atmospheric Administration, 1977.

Stanger, Frank M. *South from San Francisco: San Mateo County, California; Its History and Heritage*. San Mateo, Ca.: San Mateo County Historical Association, 1963.

State of California. *The California Water Atlas*. Los Altos, Ca.: William Kaufman, Inc., 1979.

Stebbins, Robert C. *California Amphibians and Reptiles*. Berkeley: Univ. of California Press, 1972.

Stebbins, Robert C. *A Field Guide to Western Reptiles and Amphibians*. The Peterson Field Guide Series. 2d ed. Boston: Houghton Mifflin Company, 1985.

Sumich, James L. *An Introduction to the Biology of Marine Life*. 3d ed. Dubuque, Iowa: Wm. C. Brown Publishers, 1984.

Taber, Tom. *The Expanded Santa Cruz Mountains Trail Book*. 3d ed. San Mateo, Ca.: Oak Valley Press, 1982.

Taber, Tom. *Where to See Wildlife in California*. San Mateo, Ca.: Oak Valley Press, 1983.

Teather, Louise. *Discovering Marin*. Fairfax, Ca.: A. Philpott, The Tamal Land Press, 1974.

Thompson, Frances. *Point Lobos; An Illustrated Walker's Handbook*. Carmel, Ca.: Inkstone Books, 1984.

Thompson, Robert A. *Historical and Descriptive Sketch of Sonoma County, California*. Philadelphia: L.H. Everts and Company, 1877.

Tompkins, Walter A. *Santa Barbara Past and Present, An Illustrated History*. Santa Barbara, Ca.: Tecolote Books, 1975.

U.S. Army Corps of Engineers. *Explore: California Coastline Explore Series*, nos. 1-13. 1980.

Wagner, Jack R. *The Last Whistle (Ocean Shore Railroad)*. Berkeley: Howell-North Books, 1974.

Wahrhaftig, Clyde. *A Streetcar to Subduction and Other Plate Tectonic Trips by Public Transport in San Francisco*. Washington, D.C.: American Geophysical Union, 1984.

Warrick, Sheridan F., ed. *The Natural History of the UC Santa Cruz Campus*. Publication No. 11. Environmental Field Program, Univ. of California at Santa Cruz, 1982.

Washburn, Viola. *Birds of Monterey Bay and Central California Coastal Regions*. Santa Cruz, Ca.: Handy Books, 1980.

Watkins, T.H. *California, An Illustrated History*. Palo Alto, Ca.: America West Publishing Company, 1973.

Wertheim, Anne. *The Intertidal Wilderness*. San Francisco: Sierra Club Books, 1984.

Whitaker, John O., Jr. *The Audubon Society Field Guide to North American Mammals*. New York: Alfred A. Knopf, Inc., 1980.

Wieman, Harold. *The Living Estuary*. Natural History Association of the San Luis Obispo Coast, 1980.

Wieman, Harold. *Morro Bay Meanderings*. San Luis Obispo, Ca.: Padre Productions, 1984.

Wieman, Harold. *Nature Walks on the San Luis Coast*. San Luis Obispo, Ca.: Padre Productions, 1980.

Wollenberg, Charles. *Golden Gate Metropolis*. Institute of Governmental Studies, Univ. of California, Berkeley, 1985.

Woolfenden, John. *Big Sur; A Battle for the Wilderness 1869-1981* . . . Pacific Grove, Ca.: The Boxwood Press, 1981.

Wright, Bank. *Surfing California*. Mountain and Sea Publishing Co., 1973.

Wurman, Richard Saul. *LA Access*. rev. ed. Los Angeles: Access Press, Ltd., 1984.

Wurman, Richard Saul. *San Francisco Access*. Los Angeles: Access Press, Ltd., 1982.

Zedler, J. B. *The Ecology of Southern California Coastal Salt Marshes*. Washington, D.C.: U.S. Fish & Wildlife Service, Biological Services Program, 1982.

adobe: Spanish for sun-baked brick of clay and straw; structure built with adobe bricks.

alluvial: having stream deposits and sediments formed by the action of running water.

anadromous: migrating from salt water to fresh water in order to reproduce.

annual: a plant that germinates, flowers, sets seed, and dies within one year or less.

archaeological site: any area where evidence of historic or prehistoric human activity or residence is visible or detectable, and containing artifacts or modified land features that provide contextual information about the people who occupied the site; defined as a special resource by the California Coastal Act.

arroyo: Spanish for dry creek or gulch; an intermittent stream.

arthropods: a group of invertebrates characterized by jointed limbs, segmented bodies, and chitinous exoskeletons; e.g., spiders, insects, and crustaceans.

artifact: in archaeology, implements or ornamental objects of human manufacture, usually of bone, stone, or shell.

baleen: in some whales, the comblike, fibrous plates in rows on each side of the upper jaw.

barrier beach: a long, narrow beach created by wave action and separated from the mainland by a lagoon, bay, or river mouth.

basalt: an igneous rock of volcanic origin; hardened magma, commonly found on the sea floor and along rocky coasts.

bay: a partially enclosed inlet of the ocean.

benthic: pertaining to the ocean bottom, and the organisms that inhabit the bottom.

bioluminescence: the production of visible light by biochemical reaction in living organisms, such as phytoplankton.

biomass: the total amount of living matter in a given area.

biota: the collective plant and animal life, or flora and fauna, of a region.

bivalves: mollusks such as clams and oysters that have two-piece, hinged shells.

bluff: a steep headland or cliff.

bottom fish: fish species that feed on the sea floor, such as rockfish and flounder; commercial fish harvested with trolling nets.

brackish: water that contains some salt, but less than sea water.

bryozoans: a group of sessile, aquatic invertebrates that reproduce by budding to form erect or encrusting colonies.

bunchgrass: California native perennial grass forming tufted clumps; includes needlegrass, bentgrass, reedgrass, and hairgrass.

calcareous: composed of or containing calcium carbonate; e.g., the shells of mollusks.

California Current: a cold-water ocean current in the North Pacific that flows southward along the west coast of North America.

cetaceans: a group of aquatic mammals including whales, dolphins, and porpoises.

chaparral: characteristic plant community in semi-arid areas that includes shrubs such as ceanothus, chamise, and numerous species of sage and manzanita; Spanish word meaning "where the scrub oak grows."

chert: a siliceous sedimentary rock, often found in limestone; a source of flint used by California Indians to make spear and arrow blades.

chitin: an organic substance that forms the hard exoskeletons of arthropods.

class: a taxonomic classification ranking below a phylum and above an order.

closed-cone: refers to coniferous trees having cones that remain closed for several or many years after maturing; e.g., Monterey cypress, Monterey pine, and Bishop pine.

coastal plain: emerged continental shelf forming a flat belt along the coast.

coastal sage scrub: a plant association typical of Southern California coastal bluffs and canyons, characterized by drought-adapted shrubs; also referred to as soft-chaparral.

coastal scrub: a plant association characterized by low, woody shrubs; includes coastal sage scrub and northern coastal scrub.

coastal strand: a plant association endemic to bluffs, dunes, and sandy beaches, and adapted to saline conditions; includes sea rocket and sand verbena.

coastal terrace: see *marine terrace*.

conifer: a cone-bearing tree of the pine family, usually evergreen.

continental shelf: the shallow, gradually sloping area of the sea floor adjacent to the shoreline, terminating seaward at the continental slope.

coralline algae: a family of red algae characterized by firm tissue with calcareous deposits in the cell walls; some species are erect, some encrusting.

crustaceans: a group of mostly marine arthropods; e.g., barnacles, shrimp, and crabs.

current: local or large-scale water movements that result in the horizontal transport of water masses.

dabbling ducks: ducks that feed by skimming the water surface with their bills.

Davidson Current: a northward flowing, warm-water current that flows inshore of the California Current along the coast in late fall and winter.

deciduous plant: tree or shrub that sheds its leaves seasonally.

delta: a fan-shaped alluvial deposit at the mouth of a river.

detritus: fine particles of organic and inorganic matter formed by excrement and by plant and animal remains; may be suspended in water or accumulated on the bottom of a water body.

diatomaceous earth: a siliceous deposit formed by the cell walls of diatoms.

diatoms: microscopic, single-celled algae having two-part, siliceous cell walls; can be planktonic or benthic.

diving ducks: ducks that dive for food.

doghole port: coves of the Northern California coast just big enough for "a dog to turn around in," used by ships in the 19th century lumber trade.

dominant: most abundant species within a plant community or habitat.

drowned valley: a stream or river valley that has been inundated by the sea, such as San Francisco Bay or Bolinas Bay.

dune: a mound, ridge, or hill of wind-blown sand, either bare or covered with vegetation.

ecology: the study of the relationships between living organisms, and between organisms and their environment.

ecosystem: an ecological unit, or system, comprising the plant and animal communities and the environment in a particular region or habitat.

ectothermic: having a body temperature dependent upon, and that varies with, ambient temperature; incorrectly called "cold-blooded."

El Niño: an anomalous warming of the ocean surface, associated with a vast fluctuation in atmospheric pressure, that triggers abnormal northward migration of southern species of seabirds and marine life, and results in global changes in weather patterns that have been linked to droughts, severe storms, flooding, and landslides. Named for the Christ child because of its periodic appearance around Christmas off the coast of Peru.

endangered: plants and animals classified as endangered by the California Dept. of Fish and Game or the U.S. Fish and Wildlife Service, and also those plants classified by the California Native Plant Society as endangered throughout their range or in part of their range; species that are experiencing radical decreases in population.

endemic: a plant or animal species occurring naturally in a restricted locale; may consist of a single population.

endothermic: having the ability to internally regulate the body temperature; incorrectly called "warm-blooded."

en route campsites: portions of existing day-use parking areas in state park units that have been officially designated for one-night-only overnight camping in self-contained recreational vehicles.

environmental campsites: isolated, primitive campsites within state parks where cars are not allowed, and supplies must be carried in.

erosion: the gradual breakdown of landforms by weathering, solution, corrasion, and transportation caused by action of the wind, water, or ice; often accelerated by human activities.

estero: Spanish for estuary, inlet, or marsh.

estuary: a semi-enclosed body of water having a free connection with the open sea, and within which sea water mixes with fresh water derived from land drainage.

exotic: any species, especially a plant, not native to the area where it occurs; introduced.

family: a taxonomic term meaning a group of related genera.

fault: a fracture or fracture zone along which visible displacement of the earth occurs resulting from seismic activity.

fault block: an elevated or depressed body of rock bounded by one or more faults.

fishery: pertaining to both a population of a particular fish, mollusk, or other marine species, and to the economic activity related to its harvest or exploitation.

floodplain: level lowlands alongside a river that are periodically flooded.

flora and fauna: the collective plant life (flora) and animal life (fauna) of a region; the biota.

food chain: the succession of levels through which energy flows in an ecosystem; formed of many different organisms, each of which becomes the food for organisms at a higher level in the chain.

food web: the combined food chains of a community or ecosystem.

foredune: unvegetated dune closest to the seashore that is unstable or susceptible to wind or wave action.

Franciscan Formation: sedimentary and volcanic rocks consisting predominantly of shale and chert, with limestone, serpentine, and schist, formed from the Late Jurassic to early Tertiary periods.

Fresnel lens: handmade crystal lens used in lighthouses, invented by Augustin Jean Fresnel.

genus: a taxonomic term meaning a group of closely related species whose scientific names begin with the same word, the generic name. (pl., genera.)

granite: igneous rock consisting mainly of quartz and feldspar, and having a speckled appearance.

groin: wall or embankment, constructed at right angles to the shoreline, that projects out into the water; a shoreline protective device.

ground water: water beneath the earth's surface, occupying saturated soil and rock, that supplies wells and springs.

guano: a substance composed of bird or bat dung that collects at nesting sites on rocks and islands, or in bat caves; used as fertilizer.

gyre: a circular or spiral motion of ocean currents; an eddy.

habitat: the sum total of all the living and non-living factors that surround and potentially influence an organism; a particular organism's environment.

halophyte: a plant that is adapted to grow in salty soils.

hardpan: a hard, impervious layer of soil, composed chiefly of clay.

haul-out: a place where pinnipeds emerge from the water onto land to rest or breed.

headland: a point of land, usually high and with a sheer drop, extending out into a body of water, especially the sea; a promontory.

herbaceous: pertaining to or characteristic of an herb, as distinguished from a woody plant; green and leaflike in appearance or texture.

holdfast: the basal attachment structure of a kelp or other alga.

hybrid: the offspring of plants or animals of different genera, species, or subspecies.

hydroids: colonial marine invertebrates that typically form branched, upright stalks.

Ice Ages: refers to the four episodes of massive glaciation occurring within the Pleistocene geologic epoch.

igneous: rock derived from once-molten or nearly molten magma; e.g., granite and basalt.

indigenous: occurring or living naturally in an area; not introduced; native.

intermittent stream: stream or creek that is dry for much of the year.

intertidal: the shoreline area between the highest high tide mark and the lowest low tide mark.

introduced: non-native plant or animal intentionally or accidentally established in an area as a result of human activity; exotic.

intruded or intrusive: geologic term for igneous rock that has invaded an older rock formation.

invertebrate: an animal with no backbone or spinal column; invertebrates include 95 per cent of the animal kingdom.

jetty: a structure built of rock, cement, or steel, projecting into a body of water; a coastal protective device.

kelp: any of a number of large brown algae.

kelp forest: a marine plant community composed of dense stands of large kelp with an understory of other species of algae.

krill: shrimplike, planktonic crustaceans occurring in huge numbers in the open seas and in areas of upwelling; eaten by whales, seabirds, and other marine animals.

lagoon: a shallow body of water separated from a larger bay or from the open ocean by a landform such as a sand spit or reef.

land grant: tract of land given by the government to individuals; particularly refers to the Mexican land grants of California in the early to mid-1800s.

larva: post-hatching, juvenile animal that differs in appearance from an adult and that must undergo metamorphosis before assuming adult form.

littoral drift: combined transport of sediment by the longshore current and wave-induced deposit of sediment on the beach.

longshore current: a stream of water flowing parallel to and near shore that is the result of waves hitting the beach at an oblique angle.

longshore transport: transport of sediments by a longshore current.

magma: high-temperature molten rock beneath the solid crust of the earth that solidifies to form igneous rock; flowing magma on the surface of the earth is called lava.

mariculture: cultivation of marine organisms such as oysters or abalone.

marine terrace: a flat plain edging the ocean; uplifted sea floor that was cut and eroded by wave action. Also called coastal terrace or wave-cut bench.

marsh: general term for a semi-aquatic area with relatively still, shallow water, such as the shore of a pond, lake, or protected bay or estuary, and characterized by mineral soils that support herbaceous vegetation.

Mediterranean climate: characterized by a dry summer and a mild, rainy winter, as occurs in areas bordering the Mediterranean Sea, and in parts of Chile, Australia, South Africa, and California.

mesa: Spanish for table; a level, elevated terrain bounded on at least one side by a steep bluff.

metamorphic: rocks that have been altered in composition, structure, or texture as a result of temperature change, pressure, or chemical environment; e.g., blueschist or marble.

microhabitat: a small, often highly specialized habitat.

midden: a deposit of discarded shells, bones, or artifacts near a former human habitation; a prehistoric refuse dump.

migratory: refers to any species that moves seasonally from one region to another.

mollusks: soft-bodied, generally shelled invertebrates; for example, chitons, snails, limpets, bivalves, and squid.

morphology: the form and structure of living organisms or of earth features.

mudflat: a broad expanse of muddy substrate commonly occurring in estuaries and bays; may be intertidal or subtidal.

native: general term for a naturally occurring plant or animal inhabitant of a place or region; not introduced by humans; indigenous.

nearshore: the relatively shallow ocean area close to shore; often refers to the area over the continental shelf.

neophyte: a baptised convert to Christianity, especially Christianized Indians of the Franciscan missions.

nudibranch: a group of snail-like mollusks lacking shells and having exposed respiratory appendages; also known as sea slugs.

nursery: a site where animals breed or mature.

order: a taxonomic classification that ranks below a class and consists of a group of related families.

overwinter: to reside at a particular location during winter.

Pacific Flyway: one of the four longitudinal routes across North America used by migratory birds: specifically, the Pacific West Coast migration route.

Pacific Plate: a segment of the earth's crust lying beneath the Pacific Ocean that is subject to movement and deformation.

parabolic dune: a U-shaped sand dune in which the concave side points into the prevailing wind.

passerine birds: a group of birds that includes perching birds and songbirds, such as jays, warblers, and sparrows; comprises over half of all known bird species.

pelagic: living in the open ocean rather than in inland waters or waters adjacent to land.

peninsula: a projection of land into a body of water.

perennial: a plant that lives longer than a year.

photic zone: the upper portion of the ocean waters where light intensity is sufficient to sustain growth.

photosynthesis: the process by which plants use light energy to synthesize organic matter from carbon dioxide and water; oxygen is released in the reaction.

phytoplankton: microscopic, free-floating plants that drift in the water.

pinnipeds: marine mammals that have finlike flippers, including seals, sea lions, and walruses.

plant community: a distinctive assemblage of individual plants typically inhabiting a particular terrain; species of plants forming a characteristic association, e.g., the coastal strand plant community.

plant succession: the gradual replacement of one plant community by another over very long periods of time.

plate tectonics: the geologic theory explaining structural deformation of the earth's crust that results in formation of land masses and mountain building owing to the movement and deformation of massive plates, or segments of the earth's crust.

Pleistocene: geologic epoch of worldwide glaciation, also called the Ice Ages, beginning about 2 million years ago and lasting until about 10,000 years ago.

pocket beach: a small, crescent-shaped beach inside a cove or between rocky headlands, often inundated at high tide.

population: a group of individuals of the same species inhabiting a specific geographic area within which interbreeding can occur.

predator: an animal that eats other animals; a carnivore.

presidio: Spanish word for military garrison or barracks; Spanish colonial forts established along the California coast.

prey: an animal that is eaten by other animals.

productivity: biologically, the amount of organic matter produced by plants via photosynthesis in an ecosystem.

promontory: a coastal landform that juts into the ocean; a headland or rocky point.

rancheria: Spanish for small farm settlements that were located near the missions and inhabited by Indian neophytes; also, modern-day Indian reservations within California.

rancho: Spanish for cattle farm; farms of the Spanish and Mexican colonists in California.

range: the geographical area or areas inhabited by a species.

raptors: birds of prey, such as falcons, eagles, and owls.

rare plant: specifically, native plants that the California Native Plant Society classifies as "rare"; a plant having a limited occurrence.

reef: an assemblage of rocks or a ridge below the surface of the water.

relict: in ecology, a genus or species from a previous era that has survived radical environmental changes resulting from climatic shifts.

resident: an animal species such as a fish or a bird that remains in one place all year; non-migratory.

revetment: a structure built along the coast to prevent erosion and other damage by wave action; similar to a sea wall.

rift zone: the strip of land bounded by parallel rifts or faults.

rip current: a narrow, seaward-flowing current that results from breaking of waves and subsequent accumulation or build-up of water in the nearshore zone.

riparian: pertaining to the habitat along the bank of a stream, river, pond, or lake.

riprap: boulders or rubble used to construct a jetty or revetment.

rookery: a breeding site, such as an island, for seabirds or marine mammals.

salinity: the total amount of dissolved salts in water.

salt marsh: a community of vegetation rooted in saline soils that is alternately inundated and exposed by tides; occurs on the shores of bays and estuaries.

salt pan: a flat terrain with a layer of encrusting salt minerals.

sandbar: submerged offshore deposit of sand or sediment created by littoral drift or wave action; also occurs at a river mouth.

sand spit: narrow, finger-like embankment of sand deposited by littoral drift into the open water of a bay; seasonal or permanent sand or sediment deposit at the mouth of a river.

sea stack: a small, steep-sided rocky projection above sea level near a cliffed shore.

sediment: fine-grained mineral and organic material in suspension, in transit, or deposited by air, water, or ice on the earth's surface.

sedimentary: rock formed of sediments, either from other rocks on the earth's surface, by precipitation, or by deposit of organic remains, such as gypsum or limestone.

seismic sea wave: a long-period wave generated by an underwater earthquake, landslide, or volcanic eruption; a tsunami; erroneously called a tidal wave.

serpentine: a green or black magnesium silicate mineral or rock; a nutrient-poor soil of serpentine origin supporting a unique association of endemic plants.

sessile: pertaining to an organism, such as a barnacle or a tunicate, that is permanently attached to a substrate.

shale: laminated sediment, predominantly clay and silt.

shell mound: see *midden*.

shorebirds: water birds of beaches, tidal mudflats, marshes, and rocky intertidal areas that forage by standing on the ground or in shallow water.

siliceous: containing or consisting of silica.

slip face: the steep face of an active sand dune, created by deposit of wind-blown sand across the dune crest that slides continuously down the face.

slough: a small marshland or tidal waterway that usually connects with other tidal areas.

soapstone: see *steatite*.

spawn: to release eggs and sperm into the water.

spawning ground: a specific site, such as a sandy beach or a stream, where fish lay their eggs.

species: a taxonomic classification ranking below a genus, and consisting of a group of closely related organisms that are capable of interbreeding and producing similar offspring.

stabilized dune: a permanent dune protected from wind dispersal by a cover of vegetation.

steatite: a talc-rich rock occurring in massive formations, common on Santa Catalina Island; soapstone. Chumash and Gabrielino Indians carved bowls and utensils from steatite.

submarine canyon: a steep, underwater, V-shaped valley cut into the continental shelf and slope.

subspecies: a subdivision of a species, usually a geographical population that is slightly different from other populations of that species; also called a race, or variety.

substrate: the surface on which an organism grows or is attached.

surf zone: the area affected by wave action, extending from the shoreline high-water mark seaward to where the waves start to break.

surge channel: a narrow gap in rocky intertidal areas through which waves surge; habitat for species of barnacles, mussels, and algae.

threatened: refers specifically to those animals designated by the California Dept. of Fish and Game or the U.S. Fish and Wildlife Service as "threatened."

tide: the periodic rising and falling of sea level generated by the gravitational forces of the moon and sun.

tidepool: habitat in the rocky intertidal zone that retains some water at low tide.

tombolo: a bar of gravel or sand connecting an island or rock with the mainland or with another island.

trawling: a method of ocean fishing using boats with nets on rollers that cover the seafloor, entrapping bottom fish such as flounder.

tribelet: a cultural group belonging to a larger tribe, or language family, but differentiated by location, customs, and dialect.

trolling: a method of ocean fishing, in particular for salmon and other large fish, using a long line with multiple hooks that is dragged from the stern of the boat.

tsunami: see *seismic sea wave*.

tunicates: a group of sessile, filter-feeding marine invertebrates; may occur as stalked, saclike individuals or as encrusting colonies.

understory: a layer or level of vegetation occurring under a vegetative canopy, such as the herbaceous plants growing under the taller trees of a riparian woodland.

uplifted: pertaining to a segment of the earth's surface that has been elevated relative to the surrounding surface, especially as a result of tectonic activity.

upwelling: a process by which surface waters that have been driven offshore by winds are replaced near shore by deeper, colder, nutrient-rich water; generally results in high biologic productivity.

vascular plants: plants with special tissue for the transport of water or nutrients; include ferns, conifers, and flowering plants.

vernal pool: a small depression with a dense claypan or hardpan soil that fills with water during the rainy season and dries out in the spring; supports an endemic vegetation.

waterfowl: ducks, geese, and swans.

watershed: the land area drained by a river or stream system or other body of water.

wetland: general term referring to land that is tidally or seasonally inundated, including marshes, mudflats, lagoons, sloughs, bogs, swamps, and fens.

zonation: the arrangement of organisms in horizontal bands on the shore.

zooplankton: free-floating animals that drift in the water; range from microscopic organisms to larger animals such as jellyfish.

The information in this guide is current as of Spring 1987. If you have any corrections or suggestions, please write:

California Coastal Commission
California Coastal Resource Guide
631 Howard Street, 4th Floor
San Francisco, California 94105